AF718468

FISCAL REGIMES AND THE POLITICAL ECONOMY OF PREMODERN STATES

Inspired by the New Fiscal History, this book represents the first global survey of taxation in the premodern world. What emerges is a rich variety of institutions, including experiments with sophisticated instruments such as sovereign debt and fiduciary money, challenging the notion of a typical premodern stage of fiscal development. The studies also reveal patterns and correlations across widely dispersed societies that shed light on the basic factors driving the intensification, abatement, and innovation of fiscal regimes. Twenty scholars have contributed perspectives from a wide range of fields besides history, including anthropology, economics, political science, and sociology. The volume's coverage extends beyond Europe, the Mediterranean, and the Near East to East Asia and the Americas, thereby transcending the Eurocentric approach of most scholarship on fiscal history.

ANDREW MONSON is Associate Professor of Classics at New York University. While co-editing this volume, he has held the Alexander von Humboldt Fellowship for Experienced Researchers at the University of Heidelberg as well as the Charles A. Ryskamp Fellowship of the American Council of Learned Societies. He is the author of *From the Ptolemies to the Romans: Political and Economic Change in Egypt* (2012) and *Agriculture and Taxation in Early Ptolemaic Egypt: Demotic Land Surveys and Accounts* (2012).

WALTER SCHEIDEL is the Dickason Professor in the Humanities, Professor of Classics and History, and Kennedy–Grossman Fellow in Human Biology at Stanford University. He is the author or editor of fifteen books on the ancient world, including *The Cambridge Companion to the Roman Economy* (2012). His work, which has focused on ancient social and economic history, historical demography, and the history of empire, has been widely recognized for its innovative quantitative and comparative modelling, cross-cultural scope, and transdisciplinary breadth across the social sciences and life sciences.

FISCAL REGIMES AND THE POLITICAL ECONOMY OF PREMODERN STATES

EDITED BY

ANDREW MONSON AND WALTER SCHEIDEL

CAMBRIDGE
UNIVERSITY PRESS

CAMBRIDGE
UNIVERSITY PRESS

University Printing House, Cambridge CB2 8BS, United Kingdom

Cambridge University Press is part of the University of Cambridge.

It furthers the University's mission by disseminating knowledge in the pursuit of education, learning and research at the highest international levels of excellence.

www.cambridge.org
Information on this title: www.cambridge.org/9781107089204

© Cambridge University Press 2015

This publication is in copyright. Subject to statutory exception and to the provisions of relevant collective licensing agreements, no reproduction of any part may take place without the written permission of Cambridge University Press.

First published 2015

Printed in the United States of America by Sheridan Books, Inc.

A catalogue record for this publication is available from the British Library

ISBN 978-1-107-08920-4 Hardback

Cambridge University Press has no responsibility for the persistence or accuracy of URLs for external or third-party internet websites referred to in this publication, and does not guarantee that any content on such websites is, or will remain, accurate or appropriate.

Contents

Figures

Tables

Notes on contributors

Peter F. Bang is Associate Professor of History at the Saxo Institute, University of Copenhagen. He is a Roman historian interested in comparative and world history. From 2005 to 2009 he was Chair of the European research network "Tributary Empires Compared," and he has been a visiting professor at the universities of Tübingen and Heidelberg. Among his publications are *The Roman Bazaar: A Comparative Study of Trade and Markets in a Tributary Empire* (2008) and the co-edited volumes *Tributary Empires in Global History* (with Chris Bayly, 2011), *Universal Empire: A Comparative Approach to Imperial Culture and Representation in Eurasian History* (with Dariusz Kolodziejczyk, 2012), and *The Oxford Handbook of the State in the Ancient Near East and Mediterranean* (with Walter Scheidel, 2013).

Gilles Bransbourg, an economist and former banker, is a Research Associate at New York University's Institute for the Study of the Ancient World and an Adjunct Curator at the American Numismatic Society, where he runs the "Online Coins of the Roman Empire" project. His work deals with economic and monetary aspects of the Greco-Roman Mediterranean world, with an aim at comparative economic history up to the contemporary period. In addition to several papers on this topic he has co-authored *La politique monétaire de l'euro* (2009) and curated the exhibition "Signs of Inflation" at the Federal Reserve Bank of New York (2012).

Philip C. Brown is Professor of Japanese and East Asian History at the Ohio State University. His early work focused on changing patterns of samurai control over rural populations and extraction of obligations from them in the late sixteenth and early seventeenth centuries (*Central Authority and Local Autonomy in the Formation of Early Modern Japan: The Case of Kaga Domain*, 1993). This work constitutes part of a current project on the evolution of fiscal regimes over the seventeenth to mid-nineteenth centuries. His other current project explores transformations in Japan's efforts to ameliorate the impacts of floods and landslides in the nineteenth and twentieth centuries. A third thrust of his research analyzes joint ownership customs and the sharing of environmental risks in early modern Japan (*Cultivating Commons: Joint Ownership of Arable Land in Early Modern Japan*, 2011).

Metin M. Coşgel is Professor and Head, Department of Economics, at the University of Connecticut. He works on the economic history of the Ottoman Empire, including the system of taxation, the transmission and inequality of wealth, the resolution of disputes in courts, and the organization of law enforcement. He is also interested in the political economy of religion, more specifically the ability of religious authorities to legitimize rulers. He is exploring the implications of this relationship for state control of religion, the rise of theocracy, political conflict, the adoption of new technology, and economic growth.

Terence N. D'Altroy is the Loubat Professor of American Archaeology in the Department of Anthropology and founding Director of the Center for Archaeology at Columbia University. His research interests concern the organizational and intellectual formations of ancient empires, most particularly the Inkas. He has conducted more than forty years of research in Peru, Argentina, the United States, and Mexico. His publications include *Provincial Power in the Inka Empire* (1992), *Empires: Perspectives from Archaeology and History* (co-editor, 2001), *Empire and Domestic Economy* (first author, 2001), *The Incas: Inside an American Empire* (2004), and *The Incas* (second edition, 2014).

Kent Gang Deng, an economic historian of China, is Reader in Economic History at the London School of Economics. He is also a Fellow of the Royal Historical Society. His research covers both premodern and modern times over the very long run. He has published six monographs and a number of articles, ranging from knowledge formation, technological diffusion, and maritime development to demography, commerce, the peasantry, and the state.

John Haldon is Shelby Cullom Davis '30 Professor of European History and Professor of Byzantine History and Hellenic Studies at Princeton University. His research focuses on the history of the early and middle

Byzantine Empire, in particular in the period from the seventh to the eleventh centuries; on state systems and structures across the European and Islamic worlds from late ancient to early modern times; and on the production, distribution, and consumption of resources in the late ancient and medieval world, especially in the context of warfare.

Michael Jursa is Professor of Assyriology at Vienna University. He specializes in the study of the socio-economic history of Babylonia in the Iron Age. Recent books include *Aspects of the Economic History of Babylonia in the First Millennium BC* (2010) and *Neo-Babylonian Letters and Contracts from the Eanna Archive* (with Eckart Frahm, 2011).

Hugh Kennedy is Professor of Arabic at the School of Oriental and African Studies, University of London. He taught in the Department of Mediaeval History in the University of St Andrews for thirty-five years before moving to London in 2007. He has written numerous books and articles on the history of the Middle East in the early Islamic period (600–1050 CE), including *The Prophet and the Age of the Caliphates* (2004) and *The Great Arab Conquests* (2007). He is currently working on a book on the economic history of the early Islamic world.

Edgar Kiser is Professor of Sociology at the University of Washington. He has published articles in sociology, political science, history, and economics journals on topics including the determinants of war, the development and decline of voting institutions, the evolution of systems of taxation, and the methodology of historical research.

Margaret Levi is Director of the Center for Advanced Study in the Behavioral Sciences and Professor of Political Science, Stanford University, and Jere L. Bacharach Professor Emerita of International Studies, Department of Political Science, University of Washington. She authored *Of Rule and Revenue* (1988) and is the co-author (with John Ahlquist) of *In the Interests of Others* (2013). She is a former President of the American Political Science Association, the former general editor of Cambridge Studies in Comparative Politics, and the co-general editor of *Annual Review of Political Science.*

Mark E. Lewis is Kwoh-Ting Li Professor in Chinese Culture at Stanford University. He specializes in the history of ancient China and is the author of *Sanctioned Violence in Early China* (1989), *Writing and*

Authority in Early China (1999), *The Construction of Space in Early China* (2006), and *The Flood Myths of Early China* (2006). He has completed a series of three books on the history of early Chinese empires: *The Early Chinese Empires: Qin and Han* (2007), *China between Empires: The Northern and Southern Dynasties* (2009), and *China's Cosmopolitan Empire: The Tang Dynasty* (2012). He is currently completing a volume entitled *Emotional Communities in Early China.*

Emily Mackil is Associate Professor in the Department of History at the University of California, Berkeley. She is the author of *Creating a Common Polity: Religion, Economy, and Politics in the Making of the Greek Koinon* (2013) and numerous articles in the fields of Greek history and epigraphy.

Andrew Monson is Associate Professor of Classics at New York University. While co-editing this volume, he has held the Alexander von Humboldt Fellowship for Experienced Researchers at the University of Heidelberg as well as the Charles A. Ryskamp Fellowship of the American Council of Learned Societies. He is the author of *From the Ptolemies to the Romans: Political and Economic Change in Egypt* (2012) and *Agriculture and Taxation in Early Ptolemaic Egypt: Demotic Land Surveys and Accounts* (2012).

Juan Carlos Moreno García is a CNRS senior researcher at the University of Paris IV – Sorbonne. He has published extensively on pharaonic administration, socio-economic history, and landscape organization, usually in a comparative perspective with other civilizations of the ancient world, and has organized several conferences on these topics. Recent publications include *Ancient Egyptian Administration* (2013), *Élites et pouvoir en Égypte ancienne* (2010), *L'agriculture institutionnelle en Égypte ancienne* (2006), and *Egipto en el Imperio Antiguo* (2004).

Josiah Ober, Mitsotakis Professor of Political Science and Classics at Stanford University, works on historical institutionalism and political theory, focusing on the political thought and practice of the ancient Greek world. His 2008 book *Democracy and Knowledge: Innovation and Learning in Classical Athens* analyzes ancient Greek democracy as a system for the aggregation, alignment, and codification of useful knowledge. He is currently completing a book on the economic and political development of the classical Greek world, seeking to explain both the surprising strength and duration of the classical efflorescence and the capture of the city-state ecology by imperial Macedon.

Walter Scheidel is the Dickason Professor in the Humanities, Professor of Classics and History, and Kennedy–Grossman Fellow in Human Biology at Stanford University. He has worked on ancient social and economic history, premodern demography, state formation, and comparative and transdisciplinary approaches to the study of the past. He is the author or (co-)editor of fifteen books.

David Stasavage is Professor and Chair of the Wilf Family Department of Politics at New York University. He works on the political economy of state finance in both historical and current contexts. He is the author of *States of Credit: Size, Power, and the Development of European Polities* (2011) as well as *Public Debt and the Birth of the Democratic State: France and Great Britain, 1688–1789* (2003).

Michael E. Smith is Professor of Anthropology at Arizona State University. He is an archaeologist who has directed fieldwork projects at numerous sites in the provinces of the Aztec Empire in central Mexico. His fieldwork focuses on the excavation of houses and the study of daily life. He has published six books and numerous scholarly articles on the Aztecs; his books include *Aztec City-State Capitals* (2008) and *Aztec Imperial Strategies* (with Frances Berdan and others, 1996). He has also published widely on the organization of the Aztec Empire, on archaeological methods for studying ancient states and empires, and on comparative urbanism.

James Tan studied at the University of Sydney and at Columbia University. He is Assistant Professor of History and Classics at Hofstra University, specializing in the political and economic history of the Roman Republic.

Acknowledgements

The editors wish to express their gratitude to the Classics Department of Stanford University as well as the Alexander Hamilton Center for Political Economy at New York University (NYU). The funding that they provided for the conference at Stanford University in 2010 planted the seeds of this volume. We would like to thank Bruce Bueno de Mesquita in particular for his interest in the project and for making possible the support from NYU. Several participants at the conference made significant contributions, which ought to be recognized here. Elio Lo Cascio and Dingxin Zhao presented papers on ancient Rome and China, respectively, that stimulated our discussions. Stephen Haber and John A. Hall served as respondents, offering keen insights on the presentations. We are also grateful to Michael Sharp of Cambridge University Press for his interest in our project.

Introduction

CHAPTER I

Studying fiscal regimes

Andrew Monson and Walter Scheidel

Entering the second decade of the twenty-first century and driven in part by current affairs, historians have put taxation and public spending back on the scholarly agenda. The New Fiscal History has begun to investigate intensively the origins and variations of modern fiscal regimes. In his seminal essay "The crisis of the tax state," Joseph Schumpeter reminds us that the term "tax state" may be a pleonastic one, because no state can be identified as such without the authority to collect tax revenue. He was well aware that it was not an exclusively modern phenomenon.[1] The chapters in this volume, which emerged from a symposium at Stanford University in May 2010, reveal that certain characteristics of the tax state recur almost universally in state-level societies as far-flung and as independent as Aztecan Mexico, early China, and the Fertile Crescent.

The New Fiscal History has furnished a valuable set of concepts and questions but so far its scope has been limited to post-classical Europe, tracing the path to modernity.[2] For example, Bonney's collaborative work, which culminated in several important volumes, represents one of the most pioneering attempts to integrate economic, political, and sociological perspectives on the history of European taxation.[3] A recent volume edited by Yun-Casalilla and O'Brien adds an essential global perspective to the rise of the fiscal state since 1500 CE that is likely to stimulate further research.[4] The chronological depth of our volume promises to complement and enrich this endeavor. While the question of how the dominant forms of public finance arose is an important one, a broader historical scope is needed to understand the basic factors shaping public finance as well as its effects on the economy and society.

[1] Schumpeter (1918).

[2] Bonney (1995a; 1999); Hoffman and Norberg (1994); Ormrod, Bonney, and Bonney (1999); Cavaciocchi (2008).

[3] Bonney 1995b). [4] Yun-Casalilla and O'Brien (2012).

It is common in these and other works to portray the rise of the tax state in Europe as a triumphal narrative. Amid pressure for states to modernize themselves, those with less intensive tributary and labor-extractive regimes often fell prey to conquering rivals that possessed more sophisticated and stable systems of public finance. Hence it is tempting to dismiss them altogether as dead ends along an evolutionary path. This narrative is closely tied to the vigorous debate about the West's ascent to military and economic superiority over the rest of the world.[5] The events of the past decades have shifted attention to East Asia, however, and raised doubts about the future of Western dominance. Meanwhile, exorbitant national debts and looming fiscal crises in the European Union and the United States have created apprehension in some quarters about the merits of the tax state. Bonney and Ormrod note a shift in attitudes in the late twentieth century that has only grown more acute in the past few years.[6] Just as the fiscal crisis in Austria after the First World War prompted Schumpeter to analyze its origins, the time is now ripe for an even more comprehensive evaluation of state revenue in world history.

Our volume is about premodern states, for which we take the significant cut-off to be the widespread appearance of sovereign borrowing. Bureaucratization and territorial sovereignty are other elements of modernity but these are also relevant to varying degrees for studying premodern states. Public debt was an innovation that allowed modern states to carry deficits and thereby temporally defer the fiscal burden of their spending. It enabled them to raise large amounts of money by non-coercive means in order to meet challenges that might have devastated premodern states. Admittedly, the ability of rulers to borrow money constitutes a fluid boundary, the significance of which varied by time and place. The phenomenon is not even unique to Western modernity. Short-lived experiments in public credit among the Greek city states make for illuminating comparisons with its development much later among small European polities. Several contributors, especially Stasavage, Deng, and Brown, do explore the more recent spread of public debt, but tracing the origins of institutions that characterize the modern tax state is not the primary purpose of this volume. The impossibility of excluding public debt from a volume on premodern fiscal regimes goes to show how tentative this criterion actually is. The chapters invite further discussion about whether states' dependence on it marks a significant turning point.

[5] See, for example, Diamond (1997), Landes (1999), Pomeranz (2000), and Morris (2011).
[6] Bonney and Ormrod (1999: 20–1).

A deeper and wider historical perspective reveals a larger range of repertoires and trajectories in the development of fiscal regimes than the post-1500 European experience suggests. The goal of this volume is to facilitate the study and comparison of the formation of fiscal regimes, the methods states used to implement them, and the effects they had on political and economic history. The comparative study of fiscal regimes can potentially reveal structural factors that explain similarities as well as differences across a number of independent cases. By making these cases accessible and by engaging with social scientific research, historians can improve the empirical basis for testing the explanatory power of competing theories.

Historical studies of taxes and other revenue tend to get buried in obscure publications, especially in the fragmented academic disciplines that deal with ancient and non-European societies.[7] Scholars working in these areas have tended to be somewhat impervious to interdisciplinary trends and have not developed the kind of collaborative research agenda analogous to the New Fiscal History and sociology for Europe and the modern world. Many remain implicitly grounded in the concepts of redistribution and reciprocity that Polanyi introduced to ancient studies in the 1950s. We hope to remedy the situation to some extent with this volume, which brings together chapters by specialists in geographically and chronologically diverse societies. Two disclaimers are in order, however, before we set out the conceptual framework that has guided the preparation of the volume.

First, the editors have not aimed for comprehensive coverage of all periods and regions of the world, much less of all premodern states. We did solicit a few additional chapters but it was preferable to rely mainly on those who revised their contributions based on discussions at the symposium, which inevitably included only a sampling of relevant cases. For some periods there is simply not enough evidence, and for others there are few scholars with the relevant expertise. Some who accepted our invitation had to take it upon themselves to provide the first synthesis of the topic. Thus it is premature to expect a comprehensive survey of every important facet of premodern fiscal history.

Second, the chapters represent a variety of styles and methods of writing about fiscal regimes. Several authors have chosen to present a detailed historical survey, describing basic institutions, their development over time, and the sources for studying them. Others have adopted a more

[7] The volume by Klinkott, Kubisch, and Müller-Wollerman (2007) is one of the rare exceptions.

analytical approach, presenting an abstract model and using historical evidence from their particular period to evaluate it. An earlier version of this introduction was circulated before the symposium, and to contributors who joined the project afterwards, as a bibliographical essay to encourage comparisons. All the authors have touched upon these theoretical questions in one way or another in their chapters, but the editors have considered it a virtue to let them adhere to their own methodology and to address whatever issues arise from their sources. This defers the inevitably controversial task of testing grand theories across multiple cases to the reader. The editors can do no more than provide some preliminary observations about the patterns that emerge.

Concepts and definitions

The methodological diversity of the chapters extends to the definition and application of key concepts, for which no universally agreed set has been adopted. Defining the state itself is notoriously tricky. For the purpose of delimiting our scope, it may be sufficient to define the state by what it is not.[8] We deliberately exclude chiefdoms and similar forms of social organization with less complexity than states even though they may involve some redistribution.[9] Deng (Chapter 10) characterizes the state by the exclusivity of its authority to maintain social order within its territory, to protect it from external interference, and to monopolize violence and information. This is broadly in keeping with Weber's succinct and judicious definition, implicit in many of the chapters of this book: that a state is a continuous and compulsory political organization whose "administrative staff successfully upholds the claim to the monopoly of the legitimate use of physical force in the enforcement of its order." A political organization, he adds, is an organization that protects by force its own "existence and order. . .within a territorial area."[10] Thus states must be distinguished from rival coercion-wielding organizations that have state-like properties, such as criminal organizations. Bandit theories of the states are popular in the social sciences (see below) but Weber's definition reminds us that legitimacy is also essential for a state's recognition.

The concept of fiscal regimes appears throughout this volume in a very broad sense. The Latin word *fiscus*, literally "a basket" (for holding money), was used figuratively to refer to various funds available to the Roman

[8] See Tilly (1992: 1–3). See most recently Scheidel (2013) for the scope of premodern states.

[9] See Earle (1997; 2002) for the political economy of chiefdoms.

[10] Weber (1978: 54).

emperor or subordinate officials for expenditure, and by extension to the financial administration of the empire as a whole.[11] It therefore included virtually every type of state revenue, including rents on imperial estates and direct and indirect taxes, as well as fines and confiscations. Hence it is well suited for abstract generalization. The notion of a fiscal *regime* evokes a systematic order or institutional structure. For understanding fiscal regimes it is not enough to give an account of the assortment of taxes, rents, tolls, etc. that generated state income. One should regard them ultimately as a related set of measures that both arises from and profoundly affects the state's political, economic, military, and social development. Thus there is close correspondence to what Bonney, following Brennan and Buchanan, labels the "fiscal constitution."[12]

The important role of compulsory services in some early states stretches this definition but ultimately enriches our understanding of fiscal regimes. These include forced labor, conscription for military duty, and various other public liturgies. States that rely heavily on them in lieu of taxes or other payments may seem deficient in their fiscal capacity. The case of Egypt and early Mesopotamia, however, discussed by Moreno García and Jursa in Chapter 4, shows an accounting system by which state officials could convert any sort of revenue into its equivalent value in one of the three media – labor time, grain, and money – as well as these into one another in order to determine total revenue and collect amounts due. Thus labor time was conceived as revenue and integrated into a sophisticated system of state finance. The same was evidently true of the Inka and Aztec regimes.

A starting point for the New Fiscal History is Schumpeter's analysis of the transition of European feudal domains before 1500 into the so-called "tax states" that gradually emerged thereafter. As alluded to above, he is reticent to call feudally organized principalities *states* because the rulers hardly differed from feudal lords or other landowners except in the practical disparities of power. For revenue they had to rely on their own patrimony, just like the others. Only as European rulers – under the pressure of military competition – asserted sovereign rights and penetrated the private resources of their subjects by virtue of their public authority could one justly speak of the state.[13]

Some contributors to this volume have found it useful to engage with the typology and the models of fiscal development inspired by

[11] Jones (1950: 25). [12] Bonney (1995b: 6–7); compare Brennan and Buchanan (1980).
[13] Schumpeter (1991: 102–4, 108–11).

Schumpeter's approach. Bonney and Ormrod have supplemented the domain and tax states with two further types: tribute states and fiscal states. The main criterion is the percentage of state revenue that came from the payments of conquered subjects (tribute states), from the ruler's personal property and perquisites (domain states), and from demands on the property of others by the ruler's authority (tax states). The fourth (fiscal states) are defined as states that experience "self-sustaining growth" by using fiscal policy, especially public credit, to stimulate the economy and thereby generate higher revenue. Although they admit that most states possess attributes of several types and have the potential to develop from one into any of the others, they identify one dominant type for each state, and they seem to regard tribute–domain–tax–fiscal to be the overall sequence in European history.[14]

The notion of the "fiscal state" in Bonney and Ormrod's typology is not easily applicable to premodern states, since it implies an important role for public credit. England at the time of the Napoleonic Wars is commonly regarded as the first state to have reached this level. Yet some scholars use the term more generally, sometimes synonymously with Schumpeter's "tax state."[15] Others have introduced the term "fiscal-military state" to highlight a key characteristic of states in competitive military environments that had to drastically increase revenue.[16] Only Deng in this volume (Chapter 10) adopts the term "fiscal state," but he does so merely to designate a state whose rulers strive to maximize its revenue.

Revenue maximization is, of course, an economic concept akin to profit maximization that is derived from rational choice theory. Assuming that rulers wish to maximize revenue can help explain the behavior of rulers under some circumstances. Rational choice theory is a powerful analytical tool when one can establish the agents' preferences or when it deals with fungible commodities that can be converted easily to satisfy a wide range of preferences.[17] Increasing revenue indefinitely may have undesirable consequences that outweigh the benefits, however. Some economists favor the term "satisficing" over "maximizing" because, due to cognitive and practical constraints, people's appetite for what they putatively want has a limit, after which other preferences gain priority.[18] The advantages of higher revenue for rulers may seem boundless but their preferences could also be influenced by ideological or political factors, such as maintaining

[14] Bonney and Ormrod (1999). [15] Yun-Casalilla (2012: 2–3 n. 4).
[16] Daunton (2001: 32–57); Glete (2002); compare Moore (2004: 299–301).
[17] Kiser and Hechter (1998). [18] Simon (2008).

stability or promoting economic growth. Nevertheless, there may be certain historical circumstances in which rulers are more prone to maximize revenue than in others, such as when expenditure is rising out of control or when short-term exigencies push aside other considerations.[19]

The term "political economy" in our title recalls the traditional designation for the study of economics, which in the course of the twentieth century became increasingly divorced from political science. The New Institutional Economics contributed to a reversal of that trend in the last generation, spawning many applications of economic methods in political science and sociology. It furnishes us with an array of additional concepts for studying fiscal regimes that recur throughout the chapters of this volume. Institutions are the formal or informal rules that align individuals' expectations about the consequences of any social behavior.[20] Given some basic human needs, it is possible for similar institutions to evolve independently, but generally they constitute a historically specific environment in which agents form their preferences and pursue their goals. The institutional approach reminds us to be cautious about assuming that states behave as rational actors or that rulers raise or lower revenue at will to match resources and expenditures without regard to political constraints. Schumpeter himself regarded fiscal regimes as symptomatic of the social relations and mentalities that prevail within states.[21]

Historians will inevitably find fault with concepts at this level of generality, but they raise a number of issues that ought to be central to the historical analysis of fiscal regimes. One may also quarrel over definitions of what one means by "high" versus "low" taxes. Those specializing in different areas will sometimes use the terms with implicit assumptions that are not valid when one attempts to make comparisons across states or periods. It may be impossible to agree on a historical benchmark for the "normal" rate of taxation in premodern history, for example, as a percentage of harvests or subsistence income, but more effort could be made to ensure that there are explicit points of reference.[22] The following sections of this introduction highlight several approaches that provide a thematic overview of the chapters in this volume: the effect of institutions on fiscal regimes; the role of bargaining and collective action; the influence of war-making on tax structures; and, finally, the effects of collection methods themselves on state revenue.

19 See Monson, Chapter 5 in this volume, and Kiser and Levi, Chapter 19.

20 This definition combines North (1990) and Greif (2006).

21 Schumpeter (1918).

22 Monson, Chapter 5, defines tax rates on land exceeding 10 percent of the yield as high; compare Wickham (2005: 64–5).

Transcending the European model

One of the priorities that our volume sets for the New Fiscal History is to move beyond the "rise of the tax state" framework that has guided previous research. The unit of analysis in this literature tends to be the nation state, while premodern states exhibit various imperial or hegemonic structures as well as republican or tribal forms of social organization. There is no telling how states will develop in the future but it is unlikely that European nation states have rendered such alternatives obsolete. Rather than seeing fiscal history as advancing in stages, as in the model of Bonney and Ormrod described above, new models of fiscal evolution are needed that recognize the "modern" features of ancient and non-European states.[23] The European trajectory does not necessarily apply to the development of systems elsewhere. By including premodern regimes in the study of fiscal history we deploy a wider range of cases and types of evidence for testing the implications and predications of competing social scientific theories, some of which are outlined in the next section below.

Bonney and Ormrod briefly attempted to apply their concepts to the Roman Empire, concluding that it combined aspects of a tax and domain state but could ultimately be classified as a "tribute state," because Roman citizens in Italy were exempt from direct taxes until Late Antiquity. Yet this puts the Roman Empire into the same category as the post-classical Germanic kingdoms that succeeded them, despite the enormous differences in their fiscal structures highlighted by Haldon (Chapter 11).[24] Bonney and Ormrod also suggest, rather vaguely, that ancient Near Eastern states such as the "Egyptian and Persian Empires" were predominantly tribute states.[25] Jursa and Moreno García (Chapter 4), however, find much more resemblance to "domain" and "tax states." Thus, to the extent that the contributors have found such ideal types useful for studying premodern states, it was chiefly to highlight the hybrid nature of all fiscal regimes.[26]

Hudson has offered a sketch of ancient fiscal evolution, emphasizing the role of revenue from public assets and labor services, which reduced demand for market transactions and the taxation of crops and goods. In his view, the principal characteristics of ancient fiscal regimes were military conscription, reliance on temple and palace lands, tribute-taking, civic

[23] France (2007) provides an exemplary study of Roman fiscal evolution; see also Corbier (2007).

[24] See Wickham (2005) for the rupture in fiscal systems between late Roman and early medieval Europe.

[25] Bonney and Ormrod (1999: 11–12).

[26] Especially Smith, Chapter 3, and Brown, Chapter 14.

contributions and liturgies, a lack of consolidated budgets, the absence of public debt, strong tax–rent competition, and successful tax evasion by elites.[27] Several contributors to this volume have questioned the factual basis of Hudson's depiction, however, especially for the early extraction regimes of the Inka, Aztecs, and the ancient Near East. In these cases, compulsory labor played a major role, but still maintained highly complex states that are not necessarily comparable with feudal European ones.

This raises questions about the differences between early states that shared these features and others that developed more regular forms of taxation, such as early China or the late Roman Empire. Using European fiscal history as a model for the development of these premodern and non-European tax states invites skepticism. The prolonged fragmentation of Europe after the fall of the Roman Empire differs from the experience in most other parts of the world, especially from eastern Eurasia.[28] Elsewhere, secure states (such as Tokugawa Japan) or cyclical phases of imperial order and disintegration (as in India, China, and the Middle East) were the norm.

On the other hand, comparison with Europe can be helpful precisely because it exposes such contrasts and because some states did exhibit similarities to the European experience. For example, several chapters in this volume examine periods of political fragmentation and competition. Often these accompanied the expansion of fiscal innovations to capture revenue from a wider tax base beyond traditional domains, just as in Europe. The profound non-linearity of long-term fiscal development, even in Europe, is underlined by the fact that the tribute and domain states of medieval Europe arose as a result of the erosion of the Roman tax state.[29]

The growing importance of public debt occupies a prominent position in the study of medieval and modern European fiscal practice. From a Eurocentric perspective, its eventual emergence tends to be taken as a given, as a corollary of political or economic development; in Bonney's words, "[A]s a broad generalization, we may suggest that in the Middle Ages the revenue base of the European monarchies. . .was neither sufficiently secure nor sufficiently large to permit large-scale permanent debts to be established."[30] While this may be true of medieval states, however, a number of ancient and non-European states did not face

[27] Hudson (2000). [28] Morris (2011). See Scheidel (2011) for divergent fiscal developments.
[29] Wickham (2005).
[30] Bonney (1995b: 15). Public debt first appeared in Italian city states in the twelfth century; see Stasavage, Chapter 17.

comparable constraints on state power and nonetheless never developed public debt on a grand scale – or, indeed, at all.[31] This warrants further investigation in order to determine whether similar variables can account for both the modern European experience and those rare cases when public debt may have emerged independently, as in ancient Greece.[32]

Theories of the formation of fiscal regimes

One way to investigate institutional effects on fiscal institutions is to look at how the constitutional and organizational forms of states correspond to the characteristics of their revenue systems. Montesquieu, in *The Spirit of the Laws*, claimed that the type of constitution determined the nature of taxation. He maintained that the burden of taxation was higher relative to the degree of liberty that the population enjoyed as well as to the rising military expenses. Thus he perceived the Ottoman and Chinese Empires to have a lighter fiscal regime than most European states because despotic rulers had to compensate their subjects' lack of freedom with low taxes, while European ruler could expect free citizens to acquiesce to higher taxes for the maintenance of the state.[33] This observation would seem to be consistent with the hypothesis that political rights lead to higher revenues in the long run.

Neo-institutional theories of the state tend to conceive of paying taxes as a market-like transaction by which the subjects provide their rulers with the means and incentive to protect their property rights.[34] Levi points out that winning the "quasi-voluntary compliance" of taxpayers by providing them with services helps to raise net revenue.[35] Obviously, states are not markets, as there is no impartial judge to enforce agreements, so for it to exist this mutually beneficial relationship has to be "self-enforcing," which means that both sides have an incentive to fulfill their obligations.[36] Extending political franchise to citizens allowed them to assert control over state expenditure, which arguably accounts for the parallel development of representative government and the tax state in modern

[31] For example, public debt was unknown in the Roman Empire, though local (city) governments took out loans: Andreau (2006). The most recent survey of government borrowing in non-European states is that by Andreau, Béaur, and Grenier (2006).

[32] Greek cities took out loans, as the texts analyzed by Migeotte (1984) illustrate, but nonrefundable emergency contributions were more common: Migeotte (1992); see also Mackil, Chapter 15.

[33] Montesquieu (1989: 220–5 [part II, chs. 12–18]).

[34] See, for example, Levi (1981), Bates, Greif, and Singh (2002), and North, Wallis, and Weingast (2009).

[35] Levi (1988). [36] Greif (2006).

Europe. Those states that failed to achieve the fiscal and economic growth potential of this arrangement did so because their rulers were not in a position to credibly commit to the lawful recognition of their subjects' property.

Historical research has the potential to enrich our understanding of how different political regimes shape fiscal institutions. One can begin by refining the abstract topology introduced by Olson, who distinguishes between roving bandits, stationary bandits, and democratic governments. Roving bandits plunder thoroughly and arbitrarily, while stationary bandits prefer to develop the tax base to capture long-term revenue. Yet stationary bandits are free riders on the productivity of others, while democratic regimes must calibrate the needs of state expenditure with the demands of their constituents.[37] In the view of North, Wallace, and Weingast, the logic of bandits represents the "natural state," which has characterized virtually all of human history, in contrast to the "open-access" states that emerged in modern Europe. An open-access regime is one based on a market-like principle in which revenue extraction and public spending are held in check by competitive pressures between politicians.[38] Many historians would, understandably, object to this blanket generalization because it ignores the variability and particularity among premodern states. Yet the burden is on those with the relevant expertise to show how these diverse forms of governance, including hybrid regimes that incorporated elements of open access, correspond to divergent fiscal and economic institutions.

An invitation for comparing the fiscal dynamics of political regimes on the basis of historical cases comes from the "selectorate theory" of Bueno de Mesquita and his collaborators. Departing from the typical economist's assumption that rulers aim to maximize their own wealth, they posit the notion of "political survival" as the overriding concern of all political actors. In other words, the imperatives of satisfying the coalition that could potentially install or oust them from power guide rulers' behavior more than narrowly economic incentives. Though both are rational choice approaches, the shift of emphasis is significant because it means that the size and shape of the coalition are the main determinants of taxation and expenditure, including what groups bear the heavier fiscal burden and whether the state spends its revenue on public goods for the population at large or on special beneficiaries. The authors illustrate their case with examples as diverse as ancient Sparta, the Roman Republic, and Mamluk

[37] Olson (1993; 2000). [38] North, Wallis, and Weingast (2009).

Egypt. Intensive collaboration between political scientists and historians could help to determine the reliability of the theory as a predictive tool.[39]

Fiscal sociology has developed more diverse theoretical perspectives to contextualize fiscal regimes within political, economic, and cultural factors.[40] Here there is stronger line of continuity from Goldscheid's and Schumpeter's programmatic essays analyzing taxation in terms of group conflicts involving economic or class interests.[41] One of the most promising new approaches adds demography to the core elements of fiscal sociology. The structural-demographic theory analyzes the relationship between population pressure, elite competition, and fiscal crises. It builds on the classic Malthusian idea of population cycles: high wages and low land rents stimulate population growth until its pressure lowers wages and raises rents, causing economic hardship. The theory adds to this another layer of elite dynamics: low wages and high land rents may hurt the population and, eventually, the state, but they create a golden age for elites, whose numbers grow accordingly. The analog to overpopulation among the commoners, which benefited elites, is what Turchin and Nefedov call "elite overproduction," and it has largely negative consequences for them. As rents fall, imperiled elites turn increasingly to the state for fiscal privilege and redistribution to compensate for now declining private revenue and to stave off downward mobility. This leads to fiscal crisis and, ultimately, revolutionary conflict, which purges elite numbers. For Goldstone the key point is that peasant rebellions are likely to become successful revolutions only when elites are no longer united in support of the government and its fiscal policy.[42]

What has been called the "fiscal (social) contract" proposition suggests a link between the emergence of the tax state and accountable government. This raises the question of whether the phenomenon is observable in premodern systems or whether it was specific to western Europe.[43] Political deficiencies in developing countries have been traced to their reliance on natural resource rents (from mineral resources) and strategic rents (such as foreign aid). This is thought to increase state autonomy from society and to be associated with coups, the absence of incentives for civic

[39] Bueno de Mesquita *et al.* (2003); Bueno de Mesquita and Smith (2009).

[40] The literature review by Campbell (1993) is still useful, but the collections of essays by Backhaus (2005) and Martin, Mehrotra and Prasad (2009) illustrate the rapidly growing interest in this field.

[41] Goldscheid (1958); Goldscheid and Schumpeter (1976); compare Musgrave (1980; 1992); Swedberg (2003: 174–6).

[42] Goldstone (1991); Turchin (2003: 118–49); Turchin and Nefedov (2009).

[43] Moore (2004: 299–304); he emphasizes the mobility of capital and naval development as specific preconditions for this process.

politics, and vulnerability to subversion. In early states, functionally analogous revenue could be derived from imperialism, creating "rentier states" that depended on unearned income.[44] Did this have comparable consequences?

This question ties in with broader issues of collective action. In medieval and modern European history, we observe a strengthening link between taxation, representation, and sustained collective action. This nexus has only just begun to be systematically analyzed for premodern states. Blanton and Fargher distinguish between "external" and "internal" revenues, the former derived from a small base or few collection points (such as trade taxes) and the latter from a broad base (such as farmers), with discrete consequences for state–society bargaining and resultant state policies. States usually rely on a combination of both revenue types, and their respective contributions are often difficult to measure. Even so, in a survey of thirty premodern states around the world, Blanton and Fargher find a "revenue emphasis" on "external" sources in about a half of all cases and on "internal" sources in about a quarter, with the remaining ones too mixed to be assigned to either category. They observe strong statistical correlations between "internal" revenue sources, the provision of public goods, bureaucratization, and principal control, and conclude that stable polities arise only when the state provides public goods, controls the agency of its officials, and relinquishes some aspects of its power in exchange for taxpayer compliance. This represents a more general version of the "fiscal (social) contract" model developed for western Europe, which may be of use for historians of premodern fiscal regimes.[45]

Since this model attributes great significance to revenue sources, it raises the question of how these sources were determined.[46] In principle, rulers ought to favor "external" revenues in order to increase their autonomy, but in practice this option was frequently not chosen (or available?). A related question is whether there was competition between different fiscal systems outside modern Europe, where the tax state and then the fiscal state outcompeted others. Or was a particular mode of revenue collection – coercive taxation in agrarian societies without taxpayer representation and with high corruption and low efficiency – so common that there were no real alternatives? The case of ancient Greek city states with high participation ratios speaks against this generalization.[47]

[44] Ibid.: 304–8. [45] Blanton and Fargher (2008). [46] Ibid.: 254–6.

[47] Classical Athens is an extreme example of popular representation and public goods provision; for economic studies of its state revenue, see Lyttkens (1994; 1997), Kaiser (2007), and Carmichael (2009).

Another basic issue is the relationship between fiscal regimes and expenditures, especially on warfare.[48] Ardant and Tilly represent one of the most systematic attempts to explain the historical evolution of fiscal regimes in relation to competitive military pressures.[49] A simplified statement of Tilly's formulation of the theory is that warfare constitutes a selection mechanism, which in European history drove out the more extreme capital-intensive and coercion-intensive states, favoring the development of hybrid fiscal systems in which rulers could mobilize resources but still sustain economic productivity. Similarly, the "ratchet effect" – according to which tax hikes due to wartime crises become permanent because the acceptance of the new rates and methods lingers on – has been postulated as an explanation for the apparent long-term rise in state expenditure as a share of the economy in Europe after *c.* 1660, but the phenomenon is not universal.[50]

Taxonomies of revenue collection

The collective action problem highlights the importance of the specifics of different forms of taxation. There is no single taxonomy of taxation, as taxes may be classified in several overlapping ways. The most familiar distinction is between direct and indirect taxes. We may also distinguish between personal taxes (levied on people or households, such as the poll tax), trade taxes (levied on marketed goods and services), and production taxes (levied on farming and manufacturing). Production taxes consist of input and output taxes, the former levied on assets such as land or trees, the latter on harvest or craft production. Another distinction is between fixed and variable taxes: the former include input taxes (based on property), personal taxes (such as poll taxes), and lump-sum enterprise taxes, while the latter comprise all output taxes and trade taxes. Variable taxes are defined as "risky" because yield is less predictable. In addition, we must take account of other sources of revenue, such as tribute, plunder, revenue from state-owned assets (domains), or income from fees (such as the sale of offices) and fines (including politically motivated expropriations). "Internal" and "external" revenues are spread across the entire spectrum of these various sources of state income.

48 Brewer (1988) and Glete (2002) illustrate the link between fiscal reform and military success in early modern Europe.

49 Ardant (1971–2); Tilly (1992).

50 Bonney (1995b: 8–9), discussing Peacock and Wiseman (1967: 26–7).

Different types of taxes pose different challenges. For instance, trade and output taxes are more costly to administer and collect than personal or input taxes; output taxes allow risk-sharing between the state and taxpayers. A number of recent studies have sought to link specific types of taxes to particular collection techniques. Several theoretical approaches converge in predicting a link between indirect taxes and tax-farming in Europe, with agency theory (focusing on the significance of control) providing the most comprehensive explanation.[51] The size of the tax base and the degree of ruler autonomy tend to be positively correlated with the incidence of tax-farming, but exceptions occurred. Contract duration has also been shown to be important, as long-term arrangements facilitated the farming of direct taxes. Measurement costs matter: low measurement costs favor output taxes; more elevated ones favor input taxes; and, if costs are very high, lump-sum payments may work best.[52] Coşgel and Miceli find that, in the Ottoman case, transaction costs played a greater role than risk in determining tax collection arrangements.[53] Regarding all these linkages, the inclusion of ancient and non-European data will help test predictions and put frequently Eurocentric models on a more solid footing.

Coşgel and Miceli have developed a comprehensive explanatory model of variation in contractual forms of revenue collection, such as share contracts, fixed-rent contracts (that is, tax-farming, awarded through auction or direct bargaining), and fixed-wage contracts (the employment of salaried tax collectors), the latter two being the historically dominant forms.[54] In rent contracts the agent has a greater interest in performance, whereas in wage contracts the principal bears the risk and must monitor collection to ensure satisfactory results.[55] Share contracts are expected to be chosen if the cost of measuring tax revenue after collection is lower than the cost of measuring the tax base or the collector's effort; rent contracts should be chosen if the cost of measuring the tax base is low and the cost of measuring tax revenue and effort are high; and wage contracts should be chosen if the cost of measuring the tax base or revenue are high and variance in the tax base and the cost of measuring effort are low. There is a connection between the strength of bureaucracies and reliance on wage contracts, accounting for its spread over time. In this context, early instances such as ancient China and the later Roman Empire are of particular interest. Comparative historical analysis of the kind that this

[51] Kiser (1994); Kiser and Kane (2007). [52] Coşgel (2005). [53] Ibid.; Coşgel and Miceli (2005).
[54] Coşgel and Miceli (2009). [55] Kiser (1994).

volume promotes will enable us to relate observed choices to framing conditions in order to determine if this model applies more generally.

This emphasis on what are ultimately economic interpretations of observed taxation practices is justified by the observation that purely historical explanations are insufficient to account for either changes or continuities in fiscal regimes and for the correspondence of particular collection practices to particular revenue sources. At the same time, this does not mean that institutions of revenue collection should always be regarded as efficient.[56] In practice, considerations of efficiency and historical path dependence interacted in shaping actual institutions.[57] Given the usual tendency for historians to privilege contingent cultural explanations, however, it is particularly important to give due weight to the question of the efficiency of fiscal institutions. It is highly desirable to marshal a wide variety of empirical data to test the relevance of putatively general models that focus on transaction costs and agency problems.

The coexistence of different kinds of taxes, which is normally observed in most systems, can be explained only with reference to factors that varied among activities: these can be economic (in the sense that a particular mode of tax collection is the most efficient for a certain type of activity) or historical (in the sense that a given mode of tax collection is particularly entrenched for a certain type of activity). Attention must be paid to the ways in which different types of revenue were assessed and collected, and in the configuration of different sources of state revenue and their relative significance. In a tributary state – to use the typology of Bonney and Ormrod discussed above – the bulk of state revenue may come from tribute and plunder; in a domain state, from income generated by state-owned assets; in a tax state, from output tax (on land) or from trade taxes (in the form of dues). These differences can be expected to correlate with differences in overall state structure.

As Kiser has pointed out, different taxation systems also correspond to different types of corruption, such as overtaxation through surcharges in the case of share and fixed-rent contracts, and bribes for the underassessment of assets and embezzlement in the case of wage contracts.[58] Fiscal performance is also of interest, but often it is difficult to measure. Evidence from early modern Europe points to very substantial collection costs (variously amounting to 20, 60, and 70–80 percent of gross revenue in early modern England and France).[59] Even in poorly documented early

[56] See Ogilvie (2007). [57] Coşgel (2005).
[58] Kiser (1994: 291); Kiser and Schneider (1994: 190–8). [59] Kiser (1994: 302–3).

states it may sometimes be feasible to estimate the gap between nominal gross demands (derived from tax rates and output estimates) and actual net revenue (derived from state spending). Wherever this is possible it might allow us to judge the comparative efficiency of different fiscal regimes.

Big questions, testable claims, and global patterns

The exceptional breadth of this volume allows us to pose ambitious questions. Are certain kinds of fiscal regimes linked to particular circumstances or levels of development (for example, the taxation of labor versus the taxation of goods, with and without monetization)? Is it possible to identify factors that were crucial in shaping fiscal regimes regardless of the properties of the underlying societies (such as the intensity of interstate competition)? Did particular configurations of variables produce comparable outcomes across a wide range of different societies? A generalized working hypothesis for the significance of competition entails the following series of claims.

(1) In all state-level societies the state and elites compete for the surplus.
(2) This competition may be direct – as between tax paid to the state and rent paid to landlords – and indirect, in cases in which the state relies on elites to assess and collect taxes on behalf of the state and elites seek to privatize tax revenue.
(3) The share of the surplus claimed by the state via taxation is expected to increase as state demands for revenue are raised by interstate competition (that is, war-making in all its forms, including preparation for and prevention of war).
(4) Conversely, the relaxation of interstate competition reduces the state's incentives for maximizing net tax collection, a process that facilitates increased (direct or indirect) rent-taking by elites.
(5) The extent to which the level of tax extraction correlates with the intensity of interstate competition is mediated by the relative importance of taxation for war-making.
(6) The relative importance of taxation for war-making depends on the military demand for taxed resources.
(7) In societies that rely on conscription, conscription should be regarded as a form of tax on labor and, accordingly, reveal the same type of correlations.
(8) While the taxation of military labor and the taxation of products for the purpose of sustaining war-making may translate to different systems of extraction, it is necessary to consider both of them together in order to assess the overall strength of the relationship between levels of extraction and the intensity of interstate competition.

The existing case studies provide ample support for this general hypothesis. Intense interstate competition tended to coincide with high levels of tax extraction in the form of the taxation of goods or of the taxation of (military) labor, or both. Examples include the Neo-Assyrian Empire, the Chinese Warring States (labor and goods), some Greek *poleis* (labor), the Roman Republic (labor), the Hellenistic kingdoms (goods), the Han Empire under Wu, the later Roman Empire, Sui and early Tang China, Song and late Qing China, the Aztecs (?), and early modern Europe (goods, later goods and labor). Periods of relative relaxation due to the formation of world empires or other reasons for state security tended to result in reduced gross and/or net tax-taking by the state (where "gross" refers to nominal tax demands and "net" to the share actually received by the central state). Examples include the Achaemenid Empire (gross), the Roman Principate (gross and net), the post-Roman Germanic successor states (gross), the Umayyads (net), the Inka (net), Ming China (gross), and Tokugawa Japan (gross). If correct, this suggests that monopolistic states preferred satisficing solutions to the maximization of monopoly rents.

Another question is that of the degree and the causes of the relative efficiency of fiscal regimes, a concept that may be defined either as the ratio of gross to net revenue or as the degree of deviation from the mode that would have been the most efficient in a given environment. Net revenue would have been determined, among other things, by transaction costs such as information and enforcement costs as well as agency costs (competition between rulers and agents), and the degree of tax–rent competition between the state and elites. The distance between optimal and actual fiscal regimes was determined by constraints arising from power relations and the negotiations they engendered and that engendered them (such as administrative capacity and state penetration, state–society bargaining [voice], non-compliance, exit options, habit) and by path dependence, among other factors.

The taxation of labor (civilian and/or military) may be linked to particular physical ecologies (Egypt, Mesopotamia, Andes) or political ecologies (Greece, Roman Italy, post-Roman Europe). In other words, differences in fiscal regimes may be caused by differences in the natural environment and by the degree to which states/rulers are constrained in their actions. The "range" of tax revenue (spatial, temporal, and contextual) merits consideration.

All this raises a number of questions that can fruitfully be addressed with the help of data derived from highly diverse cases. What was the nature of tax – on inputs or outputs, on civilian or military labor – and which factors determined this nature? Where did revenue come from – "internal" versus "external" sources, domain rents, booty, tribute, taxes, corvée, credit? Who collected taxes, why was it they, and did it matter? How were fiscal responsibilities enforced to deter free-riding? What were taxes used for? Were taxation levels related to war-making? Under which circumstances were tax revenues primarily devoted to non-military purposes? How efficient were fiscal regimes (in the sense discussed above) and what factors constrained efficiency? How did fiscal regimes change and what were the reasons for change (for example, interstate competition, regime change, internal pressures, and exogenous non-anthropogenic factors). Is it helpful to interpret the properties of particular premodern fiscal regimes in terms of a "fiscal contract" (predicated on credible commitments to deliver public goods and enforce compliance) or are premodern fiscal regimes primarily determined by the outcomes of bargaining between specific constituencies without much regard for equity and the provision of public goods beyond "protection"? How did different kinds of societies (such as Greek polis versus tributary empires) differ in this respect?

We conceive of all these questions, and others that have emerged in the previous sections, as means of structuring the empirical study of fiscal regimes and their relationship to political economies in ways that are conducive to cross-cultural comparison, the testing of generalizing claims, and model-building. Given the inevitable constraints of (historical) evidence and (contemporary) word counts, no single case study will be able to engage with all of these issues. Each case study engages with some of them, however, and the emphasis on chosen issues is determined not merely by data quality but also by their broader illustrative value.

The structure of this book

This volume analyzes the logic of fiscal development and its relationship to the political economy in major premodern states. As noted above, we define as "premodern" any fiscal systems in state-level polities that preceded the great expansion of public debt in early modern Europe and the rise of the modern "tax state." This is a developmental rather than a chronological demarcation: coverage extends to later non-European systems that had not yet experienced comparable developments, such as China and Japan, but excludes the growing colonial possessions of the European powers as well as less complex polities such as chiefdoms.[60] The

[60] Richards (2012) deals with Mughal India, which obviates the need for coverage in the present volume.

individual case studies, instead of being schematically arranged in chronological or geographical order, are grouped in ways that reflect analytically significant analogies among particular systems.

The first section brings together information from societies that are usually treated in isolation but share a number of putatively significant features. The Inka and Aztec polities (Chapters 2 and 3) can be compared with ancient Egypt and Mesopotamia (Chapter 4), enabling us to identify core characteristics of fiscal regimes that arise independently. The most striking of these are the reliance of early states on labor service, as well as their growing capacity to organize and mobilize their populations with the aid of sophisticated accounting techniques. The authors also remind us of the powerful ecological constraints acting on each of these states, so that at least some of the institutional differences could be traceable to their unique geographies. Yet similar factors, such as warfare, state expansion, and economic development, can be discerned behind the formation of fiscal regimes that went beyond labor extraction to the capture of fungible commodities.

Rich evidence for long-term cycles of fiscal intensification and abatement is gathered in the second section. It pairs the empires of the ancient Mediterranean from the Hellenistic to the late Roman imperial period (Chapters 5 to 8) with Chinese imperial history from the Qin and Han to the Qing Dynasties (Chapters 9 and 10). This comparative approach makes it easier to identify driving forces behind the development of regimes that operated in different environments. Taken together, the chapters shed considerable light on the inverse effects of political fragmentation and imperial unification on fiscal institutions. Another common thread is the emphasis on competition between central authorities and local elites for the economic surplus in the form of taxes versus rents.

The third section focuses on polities that experienced comparatively low external pressures and investigates the fiscal practices that arose under these circumstances. The dynamics of intensification and abatement are evident in these cases as well but the chapters align most in describing the heterogeneity of fiscal institutions. In the case of the Byzantine Empire (Chapter 11), the continuation of the late Roman tax system contrasts sharply with the erosion of the fiscal capacity in western Europe, illustrating the primacy of political stability in the maintenance of institutions. The early Islamic and Ottoman studies (Chapters 12 and 13) furnish cases in which the institutionalized practices of conquered territories were adapted to the needs of expansionist states. Tokugawa Japan is something of an outlier in the study of fiscal regimes, because the monarchy was relatively insulated from interstate competition until modern times but then took rapid strides to introduce Western fiscal institutions.

The Greek *poleis* represent one of the most fragmented and highly competitive political ecologies of the premodern world for which there is good evidence. Here we find intriguing similarities to late medieval and early modern Europe that merit a separate section, focusing on institutional innovation. The Greek polis and the federal state or *koinon* (Chapter 15) were distinct from ancient empires but their fiscal systems were not as unusual as sometimes imagined, often relying on both direct and indirect taxes. Amid diverse forms of tyranny, oligarchy, and democracy, Greek states tended to have a comparatively high degree of political participation – illustrated most clearly in the case of Classical Athens (Chapter 16). The comparison with Europe (Chapter 17) suggests that their small size facilitated the formation of governments that could credibly commit to repay loans, and thereby explains the emergence of public debt, which has become the standard of fiscal modernity.

The final section is devoted to comparative assessments. Bang (Chapter 18) paints with broad brushstrokes the predatory character of premodern states, which finds expression in their fiscal institutions. Kiser and Levi (Chapter 19) deliver a final verdict on some ideas presented in the previous chapters and point toward further avenues of research. This chapter serves as a fitting conclusion, as the two scholars, a sociologist and political scientist respectively, are cited numerous times in the volume for path-breaking work that has guided the study of fiscal institutions and created new lines of communication between history and social science.

References

Andreau, J. (2006) "Existait-il une dette publique dans l'antiquité romaine?," in Andreau, Béaur, and Grenier (2006): 101–14.

Andreau, J., Béaur, G., and Grenier, J.-Y. (eds.) (2006) *La dette publique dans l'histoire*. Paris.

Ardant, G. (1971–2) *L'histoire de l'impôt*, 2 vols. Paris.

Backhaus, J. G. (ed.) (2005) *Essays on Fiscal Sociology*. Frankfurt.

Bates, R. H., Greif, A., and Singh, S. (2002) "Organizing violence," *Journal of Conflict Resolution* 46: 599–628.

Blanton, R., and Fargher, L. (2008) *Collective Action in the Formation of Pre-Modern States*. New York.

Bonney, R. (ed.) (1995a) *Economic Systems and State Finance*. Oxford.

(1995b) "Introduction," in Bonney (1995a): 1–18.

(ed.) (1999) *The Rise of the Fiscal State in Europe* c. *1200–1815*. Oxford.

Bonney, R., and Ormrod, W. M. (1999) "Introduction: crises, revolutions and self-sustained growth: towards a conceptual model of change in fiscal history," in Ormrod, Bonney, and Bonney (1999): 1–21.

Brennan, G., and Buchanan, J. M. (1980) *The Power to Tax: Analytical Foundations of a Fiscal Constitution*. Indianapolis.

Brewer, J. (1988) *The Sinews of Power: War, Money, and the English State, 1688–1783*. Cambridge, MA.

Bueno de Mesquita, B., and Smith, A. (2009) "Political survival and endogenous institutional change," *Comparative Political Studies* 42: 167–97.

Bueno de Mesquita, B., Smith, A., Siverson, R. M., and Morrow, J. D. (2003) *The Logic of Political Survival*. Cambridge, MA.

Campbell, J. L. (1993) "The state and fiscal sociology," *Annual Review of Sociology* 19: 163–85.

Carmichael, C. M. (2009) "Managing munificence: the reform of naval finance in classical Athens," *Historical Methods* 42: 83–96.

Cavaciocchi, S. (ed.) (2008) *Fiscal Systems in the European Economy from the Thirteenth to the Eighteenth Centuries*, 2 vols. Florence.

Corbier, M. (2007) "De la razzia au butin. Du tribute à l'impôt. Aux origins de la fiscalité: prélèvements tributaries et naissance de l'état," in *Rome et l'état moderne européen*, ed. J.-P. Genet. Rome: 95–107.

Coşgel, M. M. (2005) "Efficiency and continuity in public finance: the Ottoman system of taxation," *International Journal of Middle East Studies* 37: 567–86.

Coşgel, M. M., and Miceli, T. J. (2005) "Risk, transaction costs, and tax assignment: government finance in the Ottoman Empire," *Journal of Economic History* 65: 806–21.

——— (2009) "Tax collection in history," *Public Finance Review* 37: 399–420.

Daunton, M. (2001) *Trusting Leviathan: The Politics of Taxation in Britain 1799–1914*. Cambridge.

Diamond, J. (1997) *Guns, Germs and Steel: The Fates of Human Societies*. New York.

Earle, T. (1997) *How Chiefs Came to Power: The Political Economy in Prehistory*. Stanford, CA.

——— (ed.) (2002) *Bronze Age Economics: The Beginnings of Political Economies*. Cambridge, MA.

France, J. (2007) "Fiscalité et société politique romaine," in *Rome et l'état moderne européen*, ed. J.-P. Genet. Rome: 365–80.

Glete, J. (2002) *War and the State in Early Modern Europe: Spain, the Dutch Republic and Sweden as Fiscal-Military States, 1500–1660*. London.

Goldscheid, R. (1958) "A sociological approach to problems in public finance," in *Classics in the Theory of Public Finance*, ed. R. A. Musgrave and A. T. Peacock. London: 202–13.

Goldscheid, R., and Schumpeter, J. A. (1976) *Die Finanzkrise des Steuerstaats: Beiträge zur politischen Ökonomie der Staatsfinanzen*, ed. R. Hickel. Frankfurt.

Goldstone, J. A. (1991) *Revolution and Rebellion in the Early Modern World.* Berkeley, CA.

Greif, A. (2006) *Institutions and the Path to the Modern Economy: Lessons from Medieval Trade.* Cambridge.

Hoffman, P. T., and Norberg, K. (eds.) (1994) *Fiscal Crises, Liberty, and Representative Government, 1450–1789.* Stanford, CA.

Hudson, M. (2000) "Mesopotamia and classical antiquity," in *Land-Value Taxation around the World*, 3rd edn, ed. R. V. Andelson. Malden, MA: 3–25.

Jones, A. H. M. (1950) "The *aerarium* and the *fiscus*," *Journal of Roman Studies* 40: 22–9.

Kaiser, B. A. (2007) "The Athenian trierarchy: mechanism designed for the private provision of public goods," *Journal of Economic History* 67: 445–80.

Kiser, E. (1994) "Markets and hierarchies in early modern tax systems: a principal–agent analysis," *Politics and Society* 22: 284–315.

Kiser, E., and Hechter, M. (1998) "The debate on historical sociology: rational choice theory and its critics," *American Journal of Sociology* 104: 785–816.

Kiser, E., and Kane, D. (2007) "The perils of privatization: how the characteristics of principals affected tax farming in the Roman Republic and Empire," *Social Science History* 31: 191–212.

Kiser, E., and Schneider, J. (1994) "Bureaucracy and efficiency: an analysis of taxation in early modern Prussia," *American Sociological Review* 59: 187–204.

Klinkott, H., Kubisch, S., and Müller-Wollermann, R. (eds.) (2007) *Geschenke und Steuern, Zölle und Tribute: antike Abgabenformen in Anspruch und Wirklichkeit.* Leiden.

Landes, D. (1999) *The Wealth and Poverty of Nations: Why Some Are Rich and Some Are Poor.* New York.

Levi, M. (1981) "The predatory theory of rule," *Politics and Society* 10: 431–65.

(1988) *Of Rule and Revenue.* Berkeley, CA.

Lyttkens, C. H. (1994) "A predatory democracy? An essay on taxation in classical Athens," *Explorations in Economic History* 31: 62–90.

(1997) "A rational-actor perspective on the origins of liturgies in ancient Greece," *Journal of Institutional and Theoretical Economics* 153: 462–84.

Martin, I. W., Mehrotra, A. K., and Prasad, M. (eds.) (2009) *The New Fiscal Sociology: Taxation in Comparative and Historical Perspective.* New York.

Migeotte, L. (1984) *L'emprunt public dans les cités grecques: receuil des documents et analyse critique.* Quebec.

(1992) *Les souscriptions publiques dans les cités grecques.* Geneva.

Moore, M. (2004) "Revenues, state formation, and the quality of governance in developing countries," *International Political Science Review* 25: 297–319.

Montesquieu, Charles de Secondat, baron de (1989) *The Spirit of the Laws*, trans. and ed. A. M. Cohler, B. C. Miller, and H. S. Stone. Cambridge.

Morris, I. (2011) *Why the West Rules – For Now.* New York.

Musgrave, R. A. (1980) "Theories of fiscal crisis: an essay in fiscal sociology," in *The Economics of Taxation*, ed. H. J. Aaron and M. J. Boskin. Washington, DC: 361–90.

(1992) "Schumpeter's crisis of the tax state: an essay in fiscal sociology," *Journal of Evolutionary Economics* 2: 89–113.

North, D. C. (1990) *Institutions, Institutional Change, and Economic Performance*. Cambridge.

North, D. C., Wallis, J. J., and Weingast, B. R. (2009) *Violence and Social Orders: A Conceptual Framework for Interpreting Recorded Human History*. New York.

Ogilvie, S. (2007) "'Whatever is, is right'? Economic institutions in pre-industrial Europe," *Economic History Review* 60: 649–84.

Olson, M. (1993) "Dictatorship, democracy, and development," *American Political Science Review* 83: 567–76.

(2000) *Power and Prosperity: Outgrowing Communist and Capitalist Dictatorships*. New York.

Ormrod, W. M., Bonney, M., and Bonney, R. (eds.) (1999) *Crises, Revolutions and Self-Sustained Growth: Essays in European Fiscal History, 1130–1830*. Stamford, UK.

Peacock, A., and Wiseman, J. (1967) *The Growth of Public Expenditure in the United Kingdom, 1890–1955*. London.

Pomeranz, K. (2000) *The Great Divergence: China, Europe, and the Making of the Modern World Economy*. Princeton, NJ.

Richards, J. F. (2012) "Fiscal states in Mughal and British India," in Yun-Casalilla and O'Brien (2012): 410–41.

Scheidel, W. (2011) "Fiscal regimes and the 'first great divergence' between eastern and western Eurasia," in *Tributary Empires in Global History*, ed. P. F. Bang and C. A. Bayly. Basingstoke, UK: 193–204.

(2013) "Studying the state," in *The Oxford Handbook of the State in the Ancient Near East and Mediterranean*, ed. P. F. Bang and W. Scheidel. New York: 5–57.

Schumpeter, J. A. (1918) Die Krise des Steuerstaats. Graz [repr. in Goldscheid and Schumpeter (1976): 329–79; English trans. in Schumpeter (1991): 99–140].

(1991) *The Economics and Sociology of Capitalism*, trans. H. Norden *et al.*, ed. R. Swedberg. Princeton, NJ.

Simon, H. A. (2008) "Satisficing," in *The New Palgrave Dictionary of Economics*, 2nd edn, ed. S. N. Durlauf and L. E. Blume. New York; online version www.dictionaryofeconomics.com/article?id=pde2008_S000013 doi:10.1057/9780230226203.1471 (accessed June 3, 2012).

Swedberg, R. (2003) *Principles of Economic Sociology*. Princeton, NJ.

Tilly, C. (1992) *Coercion, Capital, and European States: AD 990–1992*, rev. edn. Malden, MA.

Turchin, P. (2003) *Historical Dynamics: Why States Rise and Fall*. Princeton, NJ.

Turchin, P., and Nefedov, S. A. (2009) *Secular Cycles*. Princeton, NJ.
Weber, M. (1978) *Economy and Society: An Outline of Interpretive Sociology*, trans. E. Fischoff *et al.*, ed. G. Roth and C. Wittich. Berkeley, CA.
Wickham, C. (2005) *Framing the Early Middle Ages: Europe and the Mediterranean, 400–800*. Oxford.
Yun-Casalilla, B. (2012) "Introduction: the rise of the fiscal state in Eurasia from a global, comparative and transnational perspective," in Yun-Casalilla and O'Brien (2012): 1–38.
Yun-Casalilla, B., and O'Brien, P. K., with Comín Comín, F. (2012) *The Rise of Fiscal States: A Global History, 1500–1914*. Cambridge.

PART I

Diversity and Commonalities in Early Extraction Regimes

CHAPTER 2

The Inka Empire

Terence N. D'Altroy

The Inka Empire is often seen as an outlier in comparative studies of premodern economics, as scholars can run down a checklist of missing features that collectively mark it as an anomaly in the grand scheme of human history. The scope of the negatives is daunting: a general lack of money, markets, and commerce, or even a tax in kind that could effectively sustain state activities. The Inkas had no notions of capital, investment, return, or profit. They had no writing system (that we can decipher today), and no effective waterborne or wheeled transport, nor any draft animals that could be mounted or harnessed to pull vehicles. Two-thirds of the populace lived above 3,000 meters, where they faced extraordinary environmental challenges with only a Bronze Age technology at hand.

And yet the Inka realm is also renowned for its organization and accomplishments, many of them in the arena we treat as economics today. During its century-long run of power, Tawantinsuyu ("The Four Parts Together") was the largest polity ever seen in the indigenous Americas (see Figure 2.1). It counted 10 to 12 million inhabitants in a territory that encompassed about 1 million square kilometers. To impose order on the empire, the Inkas created a complex administrative system, which kept systematic censuses and precise tabs on a vast array of resources and products. They extracted labor duties from some 2 million taxpayers, which provided the foundation for state and aristocratic institutions and activities. Their road system linked some 2,000 state installations, traversing mountain peaks, desert, and jungle, along about 40,000 km of routes from modern Colombia to central Chile. The rulers undertook massive land modification programs, most notably by terracing mountain hillsides and harnessing the water flowing off the highest glaciers of the western hemisphere. And they could field armies in excess of 100,000 effectives, apparently without exhausting the land.

The present chapter is intended to describe the Inkas' state economy in a comparative conceptual framework, while explaining how their own view

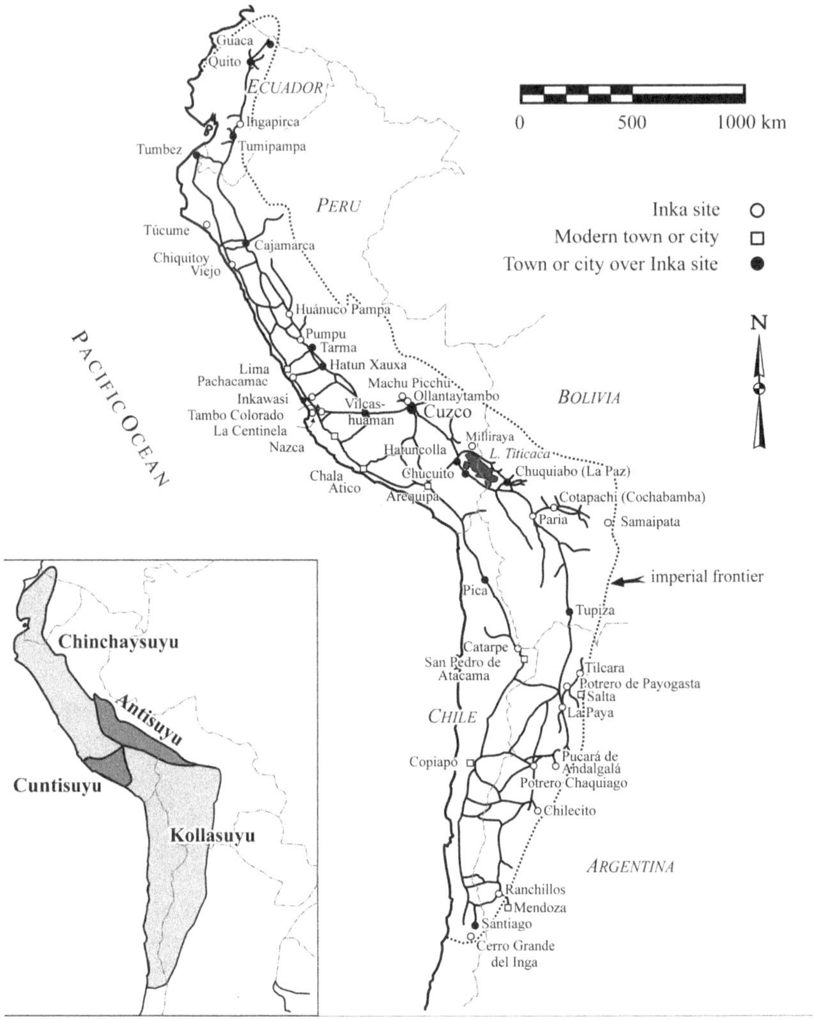

Figure 2.1 Map of the Inka Empire as it existed in 1532, showing the main Inka installations and the road system that linked them; the four parts of the realm are shown in the inset (after Hyslop 1984: frontispiece)

of things directed the economy's trajectory. Although other authors have made similar efforts, most prominently from Marxist perspectives,[1]

[1] See, for example, Godelier (1974), Espinoza Soriano (1978), Patterson (1991), and Trigger (2003); see also see Mann (1986).

investigators working in the Andes generally work with terminology that is distinctly Andean in content and grounded in economic anthropology (see below). Most of this chapter is devoted to describing the state economy, but it will be useful at the inception to ask how applicable the Eurocentric frameworks described in this volume's introduction are to the premodern American cases. The analytical vocabularies employed for European fiscal history, such as "fiscal state," "domain state," or "fiscal regime," are seldom if ever applied. This situation does not necessarily imply that such concepts are not translatable to the Inka Empire, but it does require that we assess the utility of their application.

My reading is that the models that trace out the economic histories that have resulted in industrial capitalism (especially that of Bonney and Ormrod)[2] posit a logical linkage among systems of governance, forms of economic organization, the character of fiscal regimes, and rationales for taxation. The arguments seem to rely on an implicit assumption that a single kind of economic rationality governed the economic policies of premodern states, even if the particular revenue-generating practices varied from plunder to feudalism to monetary levies. Issues of efficiency, costs versus benefits, and control of a revenue stream seem to be taken as the overriding concerns of the dominant authorities. Given the wide array of non-Western economic formations and histories, however, it may be suggested that those posited linkages may be collectively based more on a particular historical trajectory than on a necessary integration. Additional elements that raise concern for early non-European states include the following: (1) an evolutionary, progressive, or directional bias to some of the arguments; (2) an assumption that efficiency and the fungibility of revenues were increasingly important goals of the state economies as they developed; and (3) an overall assumption that military concerns organized state fiscal practice. As a consequence, a state economy such as the Inkas' may be classed as primitive, weak, or underdeveloped, because it was based on the control of raw resources, labor extraction, and the control of services and a particular range of goods.[3]

The problems arising from some of the assumptions inherent in these, or any other, cross-cultural models are vexing, if we are to bring the Inkas into comparative discussion. Such issues recall the well-known debate between formalists and substantivists in economic anthropology.[4] Two core issues

[2] Bonney and Ormrod (1999). [3] See, for example, Yun-Casalilla (2012).

[4] Fostered by Polanyi's (1957) work, along with that of his colleagues Dalton and Bohannon (see Wilk and Cliggett 2007).

are at stake: (1) what constitutes economics, and (2) whether the economy is subordinate to social conventions and political formations or is an independent field of order and action. In essence, the substantivists argue, economics is a coherent field of study whose main issues concern how society's material needs are satisfied, and how exchange systems are organized. They generally take a culturalist view, in which the economy is shaped by individual societies' beliefs, not by generally applicable cross-cultural rationalities.[5] In the Andes, Murra has been the chief proponent of such a view.[6] The formalists, led by Burling,[7] Cook,[8] and Schneider,[9] argue that economics is an aspect of all behavior, concerned with choices made among competing ends, given limited means. Economics is not a separate domain subject to self-contained analysis, but is a dimension of all behavior and decision-making.

Without explicitly taking a position on this debate, the Eurocentric models appear to come down squarely on the side of the argument that presumes that a discrete set of arrangements, practices, and policies that we consider to constitute *the economy* or *economics* would have made sense to the actors in pretty much any early complex society. While we may acknowledge that the modern concept of economics owes its genesis to Smith and Ricardo, it still seems to be accepted that the production, distribution, and consumption of goods and services would have generally been seen as a coherent field of action, even among non-Western and premodern societies. As we will see for the Inkas, however, disentangling these concepts from other aspects of life is problematic, and almost surely would have made no sense to them.

How, then, did the Inkas approach the problem of sustaining institutional and aristocratic activities? What were their economic goals and how did they think they could accomplish them? What forces did they think were operational in the world that were relevant to such pursuits? What did the Inkas consider to be the opportunities in and constraints on their economic order? In short, what was the logic of the Inka state system and how did they put it into operation? In earlier works, I have been interested in studying decision-making rationalities, cost–benefit analyses, energetic efficiencies, and transport costs as driving forces in Inka economics.[10] As we will see, however, the Inkas worked within a framework of integrated social/political/economic relationships that structured the state economic organization. We should not overlook the fact that the Inkas incorporated

[5] Sahlins (1972; 1976). [6] Especially Murra (1980 [1956]). [7] Burling (1962).
[8] Cook (1966). [9] Schneider (1974). [10] See, for example, D'Altroy (1992; 1994; 2000).

societies with money and market systems into their domain but did not adopt those features into their own state economy, even if they were willing to exploit them to their own ends. To complicate matters further, the Spaniards, who were beginning a transition from a feudal society with money, markets, and an incipient banking system to a proto-capitalist economy, still marveled at the sophistication and efficiency of some aspects of Inka economic statecraft. The character of the Inka economy therefore merits closer examination.

A brief outline of Inka history

To set the stage, it will be useful to outline the Inkas' rise to power. In the early fifteenth century life in the Andes was transformed by the creation of the empire, the largest and most complex of all the native American polities.[11] It was centered on Cuzco, whose immediate environs took in about 100,000 people in Peru's southern highlands. The Inkas are the only Andean society for which both extensive documentary and archaeological records exist, but their path to dominance remains a matter of debate. The Inkas remembered their past through oral narratives and genealogies, recalled by court savants and mnemonic specialists. No formal writing existed, in the sense that linguistic expression was represented graphically. Instead, a set of semasiographic tools served to record information, most prominently the *khipu* knot registers, which were maintained by functionaries and complemented by oral accounts. Modern historians draw from Spanish eyewitness accounts, chronicles, inquiries, and administrative records, supplemented by works by mestizo authors such as Garcilaso de la Vega[12] and Guaman Poma de Ayala,[13] who completed their writings soon after 1600 CE – more than seventy-five years after the Spanish invasion. While some researchers infer that the narratives contain a reasonably accurate core account,[14] others feel that they inseparably merge myth and history.[15]

The Inka narrative that settled out as the standard account (of the more than fifty that were recorded) recalled that there had been only thirteen kings, beginning with the deified founding ancestor Manqo Qhapaq. The imperial era encompassed three reigns, from Pachakuti through his son Thupa Inka Yupanki and grandson Wayna Qhapaq. In the last five years before the Spanish invasion of 1532 CE the half-brothers Waskhar and

[11] D'Altroy (2002). [12] Garcilaso de la Vega (1966 [1609]).
[13] Guaman Poma de Ayala (1980 [1613]). [14] Such as Rowe (1946). [15] Such as Zuidema (1982).

Atawallpa waged a dynastic war that split the empire. Atawallpa's side prevailed just as the Spaniards arrived, so that his men were holding Waskhar near Cuzco when Atawallpa himself was captured by Francisco Pizarro in Cajamarca (north-central Peru). Each of the rival brothers was subsequently executed by his captors. Miguel Cabello Valboa's widely used chronology estimated that Pachakuti ascended to power about 1438 CE, before which time the Inka polity had been a small, town-based affair.[16] He quickly set the imperial expansion in motion, and successions occurred in 1471, 1493, and 1526 CE, but scholars recognize that these dates are not truly reliable.

In contrast to the historical narrative that remembered the Inka polity as covering no more than a mountain valley several decades into the fifteenth century, archaeological evidence suggests that the Inkas had forged a regional state focused on Cuzco by the middle of the fourteenth century, by allying with some neighbors and subjecting others.[17] The major expansionist phase began early in the fifteenth century, a time frame that is more generous that the narratives' more condensed story.[18] In either case, it is accepted that the Inkas began a rapid campaign of expansion that ultimately lasted about a century and incorporated virtually the entirety of the civilized world as they knew it.

The Inka expansion was achieved through a combination of inducement, diplomacy, coercion, and military conquest. The most widely told account said that Pachakuti began to expand his domain soon after usurping Cuzco's throne from his father, Wiraqocha Inka.[19] His early campaigns focused on the Bolivian altiplano and Peruvian highlands. Thupa Inka Yupanki assumed leadership of the armies while his father still ruled, annexing most of the rest of the empire, first as general and later as emperor. Wayna Qhapaq's reign was largely devoted to administrative reorganization and campaigning in the north. He founded a second royal capital at Tumipampa, Ecuador, where he died of a smallpox epidemic that foreshadowed the Spanish arrival.

[16] Cabello Valboa (1951 [1586]). [17] Bauer (2004); Covey 2006b).

[18] The chronology of the Inka Empire is a matter of constant attention and debate among specialists. Without going into too much detail, two points are worth making about the histories: (1) the royal Inka kin groups themselves told multiple versions of their own histories, each one of which tended to favor their own ancestors' exploits; and (2) the dates provided for reigns and lengths of life are patently unbelievable, as they extend to hundreds of years (see Covey 2006a). Efforts to resolve the question of time frames through chronometric dating are hotly contested.

[19] See Diez de Betanzos (1996) and Sarmiento de Gamboa (2007).

Archaeologically, the Inka accomplishments are visible primarily in Cuzco, the nearby royal estates in the Vilcanota Valley, the infrastructure of provincial centers and way stations along the road network, and agricultural and storage facilities.[20] Cuzco itself was a small capital of thatched-roof stone buildings. Within about 60 km of Cuzco lie many of the empire's most impressive archaeological sites, now recognized as royal estates. Among them are the spectacular Machu Picchu, Pisaq, and Ollantaytambo, all of which were reportedly Pachakuti's country manors. Within a 15 km radius around Cuzco are also found over 400 shrines (*wak'a*), situated on forty-one or forty-two imaginary lines called *zeq'e* that radiated out from the city center. Those shrines, including sites such as Q'enqo and Tambomachay, were the locations for many of the important ceremonies in an annual cycle of rituals.

The Inkas' approach to statecraft in the provinces applied a standardized set of policies, developed over time, to an enormously varied subject populace. Their organizational challenge and the mark of their success was the assimilation of a wide variety of societies, ranging from autonomous villages to the Chimu Empire, into a single polity. To this end, they used local social and economic relations as an ideological model for the state and assigned many local elites to positions in the administrative apparatus. Provincial activities were administered through ethnic Inka governors, assisted by a coterie of aides, notably the *khipu kamayuq*, or masters of the mnemonic knot records. Officials below the governor were typically local elites confirmed in their positions by state representatives, or replaced if they were resistant. In much of the empire, households were grouped in a decimal hierarchy for administrative purposes (Figure 2.2). The governors resided in provincial centers distributed throughout the empire.

The provincial impacts of Inka domination varied. Overall, it is estimated that about 3 to 5 million people were resettled under Inka dominion. Some regions were largely vacated and claimed for state use, such as Cochabamba, Bolivia; Ayaviri, Peru; and Tumipampa, Ecuador. Some societies that were thought exceptionally useful or that resisted Inka rule were set to special duties, such as military service, or dispersed throughout the empire, such as Chachapoyas, Peru; and Kañari, Ecuador. In contrast, the populous north coast of Peru, home to the Chimu Empire, contains very few Inka installations, and the major impact seems to have been the dismantling of the top echelon of the Chimu

[20] Hyslop (1984); (1990).

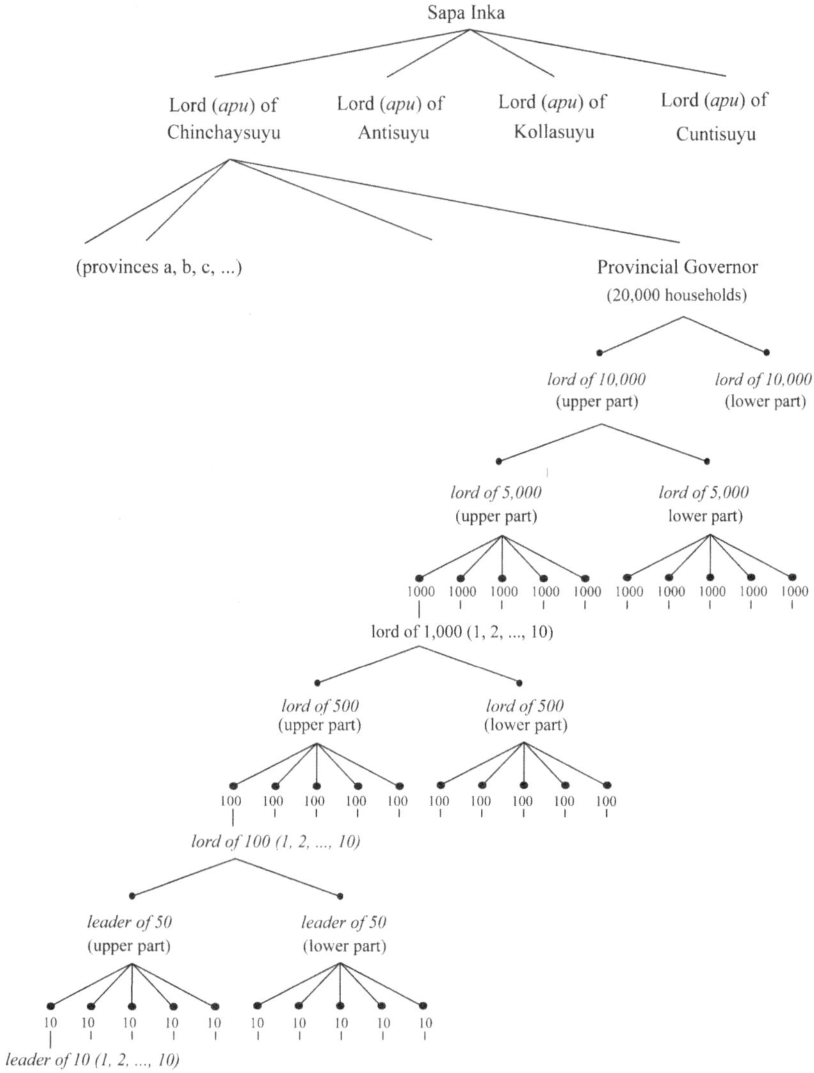

Figure 2.2 The Inka decimal administrative hierarchy, which ordered taxpaying household units

government. The regions most tightly assimilated into the empire occupied the highlands between the southern altiplano and southern Ecuador. Even there, the impacts of Inka rule within local societies were often focused on particular kinds of relationships, such as labor extraction, ceremony, and politics.[21] In daily life, subjects were generally left to their own devices.

The Inka Empire fell to the Spanish invasion from a combination of factors. Many subject peoples rapidly allied themselves with the Spaniards, whom they saw as potential saviors from either Atawallpa's reprisals or Cuzco's domination. In battle, the Spaniards' horses and armaments made them almost invulnerable in early encounters. Once Francisco Pizarro had captured and executed Atawallpa, after extracting an enormous ransom, resistance to Spanish rule was undercut by the failure of the Andean peoples to rally behind a recognized leader. The fragility of Inka control is illustrated by the rapid disappearance of the administrative structure and religion of the Sun, and the abandonment of most provincial facilities, in the first few years after 1532.

Two analytical vocabularies for the Inka state economy

A comparative framework

We may now turn to the fiscal regime that the Inkas implemented to sustain their activities. In a paper on the Inka state economy published some years ago,[22] Timothy Earle and I partitioned systems of non-monetary finance in archaic states into two general types, called "staple finance" and "wealth finance," on the basis of the form in which the material support was mobilized. Drawing initially from the work of the economic historian Karl Polanyi (whose work I largely disagree with), we conceived of a heuristic continuum of options for funding centrally run activities. At the time we recognized that the division between staple and wealth finance is partly one of conceptual convenience, and that the financial base of complex premodern societies typically involves a contextual mixture.

At one pole lies *staple finance*,[23] which includes systems that have been called "redistribution",[24] "mobilization",[25] and "tax in kind." It often involves obligatory payments in kind to the state of subsistence goods such as grains, livestock, and clothing. The staples form accounting units (a bushel of wheat or a head of sheep) that have established values. Staples are collected by the state as a share of commoner produce, as a specified levy, or

[21] See, for example, Costin and Earle (1989) and D'Altroy and Hastorf (2002).
[22] D'Altroy and Earle (1985). [23] Polanyi (1968: 321); Earle and D'Altroy (1982: 266).
[24] Polanyi (1957); Dalton (1961). [25] Smelser (1959); Earle (1977).

as produce from land worked with corvée. Such revenue is then used to support personnel attached to the state and others working for the state on a part-time basis. The obvious advantages of such a finance system are its simplicity and directness in collecting generally available products needed by the households that are involved in state activities rather than solely in subsistence production. The main disadvantages are the costs involved in transportation, storage, spoilage, and the lack of fungibility. Such goods are typically heavy in relation to their value, and it is inefficient to move them over long distances. Staple goods as tax revenues therefore have a highly restricted range. For this reason, a taxation system based on staple finance is most appropriate for relatively small agrarian states and for larger polities with dispersed or replicated activities that can be supported by regional mobilizations.

Wealth finance involves the manufacture and procurement of valuables and special-purpose moneys[26] that are used to underwrite centrally financed activities. We conceived of this form of mobilization as something of an intermediate state (not stage) between corvée or tax in kind, and a fully monetized system. Widely described in the anthropological literature, wealth items often have established values with respect to other goods of a similar nature but vary in their convertibility into staples or in their ability to cross over from one context of use to another.[27] Wealth may include consumable currencies, such as salt, spices, cacao, coca leaf, tobacco, sugar, liquor, opium, or cloth. Such materials may be accrued as taxes from a subject populace, or may be produced by artisans or farmers working for the central authorities. In some cases, raw materials rendered to the state or other authority are used in the manufacturing process, and craftsmen may work as part of a labor obligation owed by subject communities. Such wealth may be used to remunerate officials and other personnel who work for the state.

The obvious advantages of such financial units are their relative durability and transportability – features that allow a more centralized control over finance than is possible with bulky staples. They are distinguished from fully developed money because they typically lack at least one of money's essential features: repository of value, standard of value, standard of accounting, or medium of exchange. Even so, wealth finance may be an effective means of taxation for territorially extensive states in which the goods used in finance are moved over long distances. The main disadvantages of wealth items are that they may be consumed and often

[26] See Dalton (1977). [27] Bohannan (1955); Earle (1982).

have restricted intrinsic use value. As a result, they must often be converted into subsistence or utilitarian goods for them to be used to support nonagricultural personnel. As has been shown for the Aztec case,[28] conversion on a large scale may require a market system in which the tribute goods used as state payment can be exchanged for subsistence or utilitarian goods.

My point in reviewing this argument is that it may prove useful in disentangling the complexities of fiscal regimes in largely non-monetized early states and empires. At the risk of radical oversimplification, it can be argued that, in a fully monetized fiscal system, that which is rendered by the taxpayers, received by the state, and disbursed by the state is essentially a single thing: money. Favors, status, power, and honors are also surely involved, but they are largely mediated through the circulation of money. In an essentially non-monetized fiscal regime, the consonance of payment, receipt, and disbursement is not so clear. Specifically in the Inka case, taxpayers rendered labor and expertise; the state received services and goods; and the central institutions disbursed supplies, sustenance, commensal hospitality, favors, and power. I recognize that the concepts of "tribute state" and "domain state" were intended to encompass the kinds of fiscal regimes to which I am referring here, but it seems that the commonly cited modes of mobilizing resources (such as plunder and tribute) and the core goals of the fiscal regime (especially sustaining militarism) are insufficient to account for the nature of the non-monetized fiscal regimes with which I am familiar.

An Andean framework

Let us shift the direction of the discussion for a moment to consider how the Inkas understood the world to work. This, in turn, will help explain how they thought relationships were constituted among matters we call economic – property, labor, exchange, natural resources, and products, for example. I ask the reader to bear with me if some issues raised here may seem a bit far afield at the outset, but they are essential to explaining the Inka fiscal regime. If we do not have a sense of the Inkas' notions of being in the world (ontology), causality, and knowledge (epistemology), we cannot understand how they made choices about fiscal practices and policies.[29]

[28] Brumfiel (1980); Hassig (1985); Smith, Chapter 3 in this volume. [29] D'Altroy (2014: ch. 5).

An essential point is that the Inkas maintained social and interactive relationships with the cosmos. Elements of the land that Western thought would treat as natural resources or the environment were, for the Inkas, living entities with whom they shared a social space.[30] Many features of the Earth were powerful beings (*tirakuna*) as fully alive as humans (*runakuna*).[31] Mountain peaks (*apu*), springs, meadows, rock outcrops, and other such things were sentient, gendered actors, with kin relationships, will, agency, rights of ownership, sentiments, and histories. In this light, the Earth itself was a living female (*Pachamama*), rather than being a physical thing nurtured or inhabited by a goddess. The mountain peaks were among the most powerful beings of the landscape: creators of the weather and owners of the flocks, surpassed only by the celestial beings Sun (*Inti*) and Moon (*Mama-quilla*), along with the Mother Sea (*Mamacocha*) and Earth Shaker (*Pachacamac*). The water that flowed from the glaciated peaks to irrigate the soil and bring forth its fertility was understood to be the mountains' semen. Together, the *tirakuna* formed a social world that paralleled humanity's, and were fully integrated with it in some contexts (see below on the *ayllu*). As a corollary, no separation existed between the spiritual and physical, as everything found in the cosmos lay in the same integrated reality.

A second principle turns on Inka notions of space-time and causality within it. Without going into too much detail, we may note that the Inkas treated space-time as a single thing (*pacha*). Past and present were conceived of as a unified entity, visible before us, while the future was separate, hidden behind us. There were no long-term calendars, nor any fixed models of space, such as maps on a coordinate system. Instead, both space and time were generally understood in context, oriented with respect to a person, other being, or an event, not to some external framework.[32] Anything that had existed in the past was still present in some form to be interacted with. So the ancestors of living society were still present as vital beings, albeit as mummies or in a purified hard state as skeletons. Their beneficence was essential for a successful life. The relationship was reciprocal, as the living people took care of the ancestors with offerings and received their blessings in return.

A closely related idea was that everything animate in the world received a perpetual infusion of vitality (*camaquen*) from paradigmatic

[30] Van de Guchte (1999). [31] Allen (2002).

[32] In Aymara, which was probably the Inkas' main language before the imperial era, time is envisioned as passing through a person, rather than individuals living out their lives in a space-time framework that encompassed peoples and history.

beings.[33] For humans, those were the ancestors, while, for llamas, they were dark-cloud constellations in the Milky Way. Metal ores that we would call natural resources were the sweat of the Sun (gold) or tears of the Moon (silver) – gifts of their celestial prototypes. Just as places on the landscape could be vital and conscious, so too could certain objects contain vitality.[34] Brother images of the rulers and some manufactured icons of deities stand out in this regard. But it is also the case that the Inkas thought that they could affect the behavior of things through sympathetic magic. A model of something, when properly manipulated or propitiated, could move the original toward some desired end.

A further principle was that rights to farmland, pastures, water, and other productive features of the world arose from membership in a social group. The *ayllu,* often understood to be a corporate kin group, formed the basic resource-holding unit in Peru and northern Bolivia, while analogous social units were found elsewhere. With populations that could attain several thousand individuals, *ayllus* allocated member households access to resources through usufruct. Pastures or agricultural lands could not be bought or sold; nor could labor. The *ayllu* resources were often worked by the collective, though the elite members of society enjoyed access to more and a greater variety of productive spaces than did lower-echelon families. The origin point for an *ayllu* lay in a particular place within their space – a peak, a cave, a spring – to which the dead returned after the end of their fleshly life. The relationship between the people and the land was so intimate that the ethnographer Marisol de la Cadena argues that the people, the land, and its *tirakuna* together constituted the *ayllu* – that is, the people, resources, and the landscape were an inseparable social entity.[35] To remove a person from the place was to make him or her a diminished being.

If we take these ideas and extrapolate them to an imperial scale, we may begin to see how the foundations of the Inka fiscal regime were conceived by the people involved. Since there was little sense of progress in time, the Inkas lived in a constant today that was perpetually regenerated through social relationships with the ancestors and the many beings of the land and heavens. Economic planning often meant establishing conditions for the production and circulation of products that were repeatable across a thousand-year sequence of annual cycles.[36] Economic ends and means were not cleanly separable, since the overarching Inka imperial goal was to control the order of the world as a social whole – human and otherwise.

[33] Salomon (1991). [34] Bray (2009). [35] De la Cadena (2010).
[36] The Inkas viewed themselves as living in the fifth world of a thousand years.

To this end, they essayed to control the productivity of non-human beings, as both the means and the consequence of applying imperial order. Consequently, Wilkinson argues, much of the state's economic efforts were directed toward disciplining both human (*runakuna*) and non-human (*tirakuna*) imperial subjects through unified policies.[37] Western thought may classify terracing, irrigation, and agriculture as forms of land intensification, but the Inkas viewed them as interactive negotiations with living co-inhabitants of social space. Because labor was an integral part of mutual efforts to ensure the continued existence of all the inhabitants of the world, it could not be commodified. To be sure, the Inkas innovated and transformed economic activities, but they were working within a framework in which property and its products were theoretically inalienable, resources were at least partially animate entities, labor was a social relationship, and no specie or markets existed. With these thoughts in mind, we may now turn to the way the system functioned.

The foundations of the Inka fiscal regime

Tawantinsuyu, in addition to the logic just described, was unusual in many other respects. The Inkas did not have a large urban population to support in their capital of Cuzco, nor could they move bulk goods across great distances as part of a regular subsistence system. Even so, the conquests put the labor of millions of workers, expanses of farmlands and pastures, and the Andes' mineral wealth at their disposal. How best to take advantage of the situation was the challenge. When the Inka expansion began, economic activities in the highlands were organized community by community, or at most by a regional polity; no significant institutions, such as a temple, existed that would allow easy diversion of their productivity to Cuzco's ends. People living on the north Peruvian coast, on the other hand, had economies that were more specialized, interdependent, and contextually monetized, which the Inkas were ill-equipped to supervise directly. In the far south and to east of the mountains, the societies were generally smaller and less complex than their highland counterparts.

The core dilemma for the Inkas was, therefore, that their fiscal regime was attempting to make effective use of societies with economic systems that ranged from much simpler to more complex than their own. Beginning with his classic doctoral thesis,[38] John Murra has shown how the Inkas used the language of kin-based production and exchange seen

[37] Wilkinson (2013). [38] Murra (1980 [1956]).

among highland peoples such as themselves to represent their economy as if it were just an extension of familiar obligations. They intensified the mountain economies they knew best and left the more integrated coastal systems largely alone, once the subject political superstructure had been dismantled. Simpler societies were situationally exploited for resources to which they had access, often through a local individual recognized or appointed by the Inkas. Groups that were situated at the geographic interface between Inka-controlled lands and places beyond that had beguiling resources, such as gold, forest hardwoods, *Spondylus princeps* (thorny oyster) shell, and brilliant feathers, were induced to trade for those resources. The materials could then be obtained as tribute. Over time they shifted from a system that relied on a corvée tax to produce their agro-pastoral and craft products to an increasingly independent state economy that owned its own resources and had a dedicated corps of workers.

The astute magistrate of Cuzco, Juan Polo Ondegardo,[39] took pains to explain how things differed from coeval Europe. Polo and his compatriots described how the Inkas claimed farmlands, pastures, and flocks, and all the wild and mineral resources of the land, for themselves. The peasants paid their taxes in labor on a rotating basis, while the products of their own fields and flocks were untouched. In return, the state owed largess, security, and leadership in all its forms. To make the system work, the Inkas periodically counted the empire's heads of household and organized many of them into a pyramid of taxpaying units that encompassed from ten to 10,000 households. Over time, state officials also resettled entire communities of farmers and artisans, who were set to work for particular needs. Although they annexed lands with markets, money, and specialized communities, the Inkas created an independent set of state resources and institutions that provided for their needs.

The highland taxpayer economy

The Peruvian sierra economies present at the time of the Inka expansion were generalized in subsistence production and only modestly specialized in craft production. As noted above, the *ayllu,* a corporate kin group, formed the basic resource-holding unit in Peru and northern Bolivia, while analogous social units were found elsewhere. With populations

[39] Polo Ondegardo (1916 [1571]), See also Falcón (1946 [1567]), Garcilaso (1966 [1609]), and Cobo (1979 [1653]).

that could attain several thousand individuals, *ayllus* allocated member households access to resources through usufruct. *Ayllus* and communities often attempted to distribute their members across a range of complementary ecological zones, so that the products obtained could be pooled and economic independence maintained.[40] Apart from household service, specialization in services was apparently rare, but the data on this subject are scant. Among many Andean societies, the Inkas included, property rights passed through both male and female lines.[41] Elites had rights to have their lands worked, herds tended, and some craft products manufactured, in return for their leadership.[42] It may be noted, however, that numerous oral histories taken down by the Spaniards described the immediate pre-Inka period as one in which the military elites augmented their personal wealth and status through conflict and forcible appropriation.[43]

In the Andes, household and corporate decision-making centered around the manipulation of customary relationships within stable social structures. Reciprocity and redistribution were the key means by which traditional societies organized exchange. Reciprocity assumed two forms: balanced and asymmetrical. The classic form of balanced reciprocity is *waje waje*, in which households of equal status exchange services in expectation of a return of equivalent value. Asymmetrical reciprocity (*minka*) takes various forms, such as the services provided to in-laws or contributions of agricultural labor to upper-status by lower-status households who expect to share in the produce. In *minka* exchange, inequality between the parties is the key to defining the nature of the exchange.

Andean redistribution consisted of two central elements. The first was the elite's provisioning of certain kinds of material goods and edibles, especially cloth and *chicha* (maize beer), to the subject populace as part of the elite's obligations to his group.[44] The second consisted of the allocation of particular specialized resources, controlled by the elites, to the general populace. Coca and capsicum peppers were among the key goods provided in this manner. In each case, the goods were often produced by specialists working as part of the elite's household and were distributed in contexts of political feasting. Such largess did not substitute for subsistence production or market exchange. Instead, it bonded societies together, reinforced inequality, and provided access to goods that might

[40] Murra (1972). [41] Rostworowski de Diez Canseco (1999). [42] Murra (1980 [1956]).
[43] See, for example, Toledo (1940 [1570]), D'Altroy (2002), and D'Altroy and Hastorf (2002).
[44] For example, Rostworowski de Diez Canseco (1999).

otherwise be difficult to obtain. In the volatile pre-Inka era, the commensal hospitality may well have also attracted followers to the powerful elites, or groups, fostering political reorganization.

The Inka fiscal regime in practice

The Inka state economy built upon these existing features, using the ideology of local obligations to legitimize their rule and to dampen the appearance of exploitation. They appropriated rights to all resources in newly annexed territories, allocating them to the state (personified by the divine ruler), the state religion (of the Sun), and the subject communities. The available evidence suggests that the state commanded substantially more resources than the religion. A parallel system of landed estates existed throughout the empire, but was focused on the Sacred Valley region (Vilcanota/Urubamba drainage) just north of Cuzco. The living and dead rulers, their descendant kin, and provincial aristocrats all developed manors, sustained by thousands of dedicated personnel. Subject communities retained a substantial portion of their original resources, if they were not overly resistant to state demands. In return, they were required to provide rotating corvée (*mit'a*). The Inkas also claimed all wild and mineral resources as their own, but the purported monopoly on metals may not have been achieved, as the provincial elites were required to provide annual gifts of gold and silver to the ruler from their production.[45]

Households within the local communities were tapped for a welter of duties. The most detailed reports available come from the Chupaychu ethnic group of Huánuco region, in north-central Peru. In 1549 and 1562 they reported to Spanish inspectors that they had fulfilled thirty-one distinct duties.[46] Each assignment was allocated according to the population of the region, as assessed by a periodic census. While they were carrying out state directives, the laborers were entitled to be supported with food and *chicha* in return for their efforts. More generally, soldiers on duty were supposed to receive a set of clothing and sandals annually. State goods were stored in enormous warehouse complexes at Cuzco, provincial centers, and *tampu* (way stations). The supplies kept near Cuzco were for use by royalty and their retainers, while those stored in the provinces were intended for use primarily by the armies and workers discharging their duties.[47] Personnel housed at state settlements for extended periods and itinerant state travelers also drew from the stocks. A sense of the scale

[45] Berthelot (1986). [46] Helmer (1955); Ortiz de Zúñiga (1967; 1972). [47] LeVine (1992).

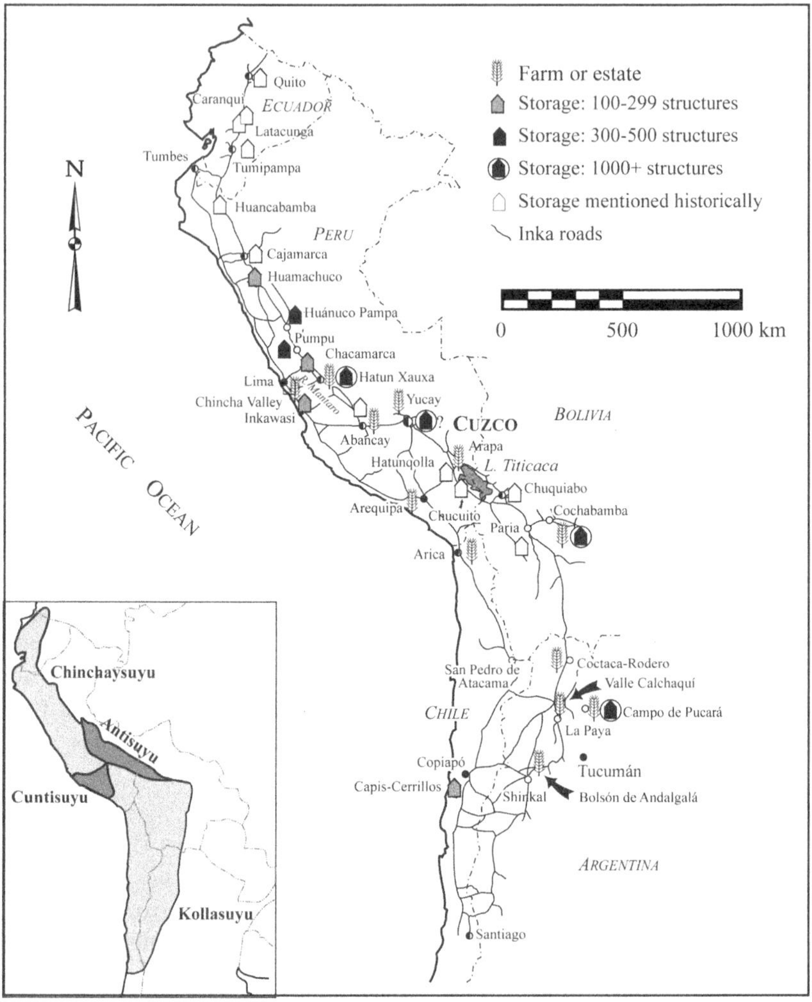

Figure 2.3 Distribution of principal known state farms and storage facilities throughout the Inka realm

involved can be obtained by observing that one of the largest of these storage facilities, in the Upper Mantaro Valley, could have supported an army of 35,000 for about a year on the food potentially stockpiled in the 3,000 storehouses (*qollqa*) (Figure 2.3).[48]

[48] D'Altroy (1992).

Over time, the Inkas instituted changes in the relations of production between themselves and their subjects. Initially dependent upon the capacities of the general populace, the state was moving its production from corvée toward attached specialization in the latter decades of its rule.[49] The Inkas created several specialized labor statuses, most importantly the *mitmaqkuna, yanakuna,* and *aqllakuna.* The first category were colonists resettled to meet military, political, economic, and ideological goals (see section entitled "Specialized assignments for state colonists" below). In addition to staffing garrisons and religious facilities, colonists tended crops, such as maize, coca, and peppers, and made craft items, such as cloth and pottery. By the end of the imperial era some 3 to 5 million people had been resettled, upwards of a third of the entire populace. The *yanakuna* were individuals detached from their kin group and assigned permanent duties, including farming and household service for the elites. Although often viewed as slaves by later commentators, *yanakuna* could attain positions of high status within the administration. The last category – the *aqllakuna* – were adolescent girls separated from their families and assigned to live in segregated precincts within state installations. There they wove cloth and brewed *chicha*, until awarded in marriage to men honored by the state.[50]

Not all Andean regions conformed to this sketch. The central and northern Peruvian coast and the Ecuadorian Andes, especially, differed in important ways from the Inka heartland. On the north coast, entire communities or local socio-political groups specialized as potters, weavers, farmers, fishers, traders, and sandal-makers, exchanging their products for those made by others.[51] The region differed also in the scale of irrigated agricultural systems, as the most expansive canal networks in the Americas lay in the Lambayeque/La Leche region. The leadership of the Chimu state, which governed the coast and was the last major power to fall to the Inkas, favored enormous investments of its public labor in agricultural projects rather than in monumental architecture.[52] The small-scale chiefdom societies of Ecuador were markedly less complex socio-politically than the Chimu, but used monetary goods in regional marketing systems.[53] The Inkas took advantage of their extra-imperial trade relationships to requisition key goods, such as gold, cinnamon, specialized woods, and feathers from the forests, and thorny oyster from the Ecuadorian coast. Even in the Bolivian altiplano, where the mixed herding/farming

[49] Murra (1980 [1956]: 183–6). [50] See Morris (1974).
[51] See, for example, Rostworowski de Diez Canseco (1977) and Netherly (1978).
[52] Moseley and Cordy-Collins (1990). [53] Hosler, Lechtman, and Holm (1990).

economy was roughly comparable to that of the Inkas, the balance much more heavily favored the pastoral sector.

Calculating labor taxes: generalized, rotating assessments

Although the Inkas mobilized much of their income through rotating labor taxes, even in the last years of the empire, the creation of specialist cadres suggests that they found this system inadequate.[54] It will therefore be useful to consider how each of those forms of fiscal support functioned in practice. Because most taxes were assessed as labor, it is easy to lose sight of the fact that these taxes were not constant. Instead, the exactions balanced administrators' estimates of needs for products and services against the available personnel. The chronicler Bernabé Cobo explained things as follows:

> One thing that should be pointed out with respect to the amount of tribute that they brought to the king. . .is that there was no other rate or limit, either of the people that the provinces gave for the *mita* labor service or in the other requirements, except the will of the Inka. The people were never asked to make a fixed contribution of anything, but all of the people needed were called for the aforementioned jobs, sometimes in larger numbers, other times in lesser numbers, according to the Inka's desire, and the result of those labors was the royal tribute and income; and in this way the people extracted all the gold and silver that the Inkas and the *guacas* [shrines] had.[55]

In Chucuito, witnesses in the Spanish inspection of 1567 said that the Inkas annually specified the area to be farmed, or the amount of seed to be sown, and the amount of wool to be woven by local communities.[56] The notion of periodic reassignments may also be found in other documents.[57] Regardless of the periodicity of reassessments, we may infer that labor taxes resulted from administrators' appraisal of the state's needs and informed estimates of the outcome of labor investments in both services and materiel. Some clues to the proportions assigned to each kind of service may be gained by looking at known labor categories and the numbers of individuals assigned to each category in areas for which we have data. The chroniclers Francisco Falcón,[58] Martín de Murúa,[59] and Felipe Guaman Poma[60] recorded the kinds of labor service that due the state (see Table 2.1). Falcón specified thirty-two coastal and thirty-seven highland categories, in addition to the two most demanding taxes – agricultural and military duties. Among the coastal categories were specialists responsible for human sacrifice; miners; people who worked with stones, colored earth,

[54] Murra (1980 [1956]). [55] Cobo (1979 [1653]: 234).
[56] Diez de San Miguel (1964 [1567]: 9, 31, 39).
[57] See, for example, Falcón (1946 [1567]: 137–40) and Murúa (1986 [1605]: 402–4).
[58] Falcón (1946 [1567]). [59] Murúa (1986 [1605]). [60] Guaman Poma (1980 [1613]: 183).

Table 2.1 *Labor service owed the Inkas*

Murúa	Falcón: coast	Falcón: highlands
Miners: gold, silver, pigments	Human sacrifice administrators	Human sacrifice administrators
Smiths: gold, silver	Gold miners	Guardians of the Sun?
Feathered-cloth weavers: fine, ordinary	Lapidary workers	Servants of dead Inkas
Weavers: fine, ordinary	Pigment workers	Gold specialists
Dyers	Guardians of sacred objects or locations	Silver specialists
Sandal-makers	Feathered-cloth weavers: fine, ordinary	Copper (?) specialists
Sacrificial llama keepers	Weavers: fine, ordinary	Pigment (?) specialists
Gardeners	Dyers	Guardians of sacred objects/ locations
Field workers	Sandal-makers: fine, ordinary	Feathered-cloth weavers: fine, ordinary
Coca farmers	Guards: Women of the Sun and services	Weavers: four classes
Salt miners	Llama keepers	Sandal-makers: fine, ordinary
Aji farmers	Storehouse guardians	Hunting noose specialists
Maize sprout workers	Coca farmers	Guards for Women of the Sun
Orchard workers	Ash/lime loaf-makers	*Oclla* farmers
Granary guards and their supervisors	*Aji* farmers	Potato farmers
Guards: landmarks, rivers, fords,	Salt miners	Coca farmers
Bridges, basket bridges	Fishers	Llama keepers: two kinds
Town accountants for state resources	Potters	Ash/lime loaf-makers
Gatekeepers: palaces, houses of retreat of the Inka [the ruler] and Daughters of the Sun	Carpenters	*Aji* specialists
Record-keepers	Masons: three kinds	Salt specialists
Mitmaq: guards for forts, farmers	Shell messengers	Maize sprout specialists
Masons	Feather specialists	Early maize specialists: two kinds
Fishers	Porters	Potters: fine, ordinary
Hunters: guanaco, vicuña, deer	Colonists	Orchard keepers
Hunters: *cuyes*, viscachas, small animals	General farmers, porters	River (?) specialists
Hunters: birds and fowl	Other public workers	Bridge keepers
Carpenters: fine, ordinary		Masons
Potters: fine, ordinary		Messengers
Spies		Earspool makers
Anti-insurgency specialists		Lead cord makers (bolas?)
		Colonists
		Agricultural workers for Inka
		Agricultural workers for lords
		Laborers on other public works: temples, roads, bad passes, bridges, houses, corrals, buildings
		Porters

Note: According to Murúa (1987 [1605]: 402–4) and Falcón (1946 [1567]: 137–40).

and salt; artisans, including weavers, sandal-makers, potters, woodworkers, and masons; guards for Women of the Sun, priestesses, llamas, and storehouses; coca farmers; and fishers. Additional highland specialists included individuals to serve the bodies of the deceased Inkas, and artisans who made earspools and cords of lead with which the emperors played. Murúa's list generally corresponds well with Falcón's, and both chroniclers often distinguished between artisans producing high-quality and more ordinary goods.

The best evidence on how the categories were locally assigned comes from Spanish inspections, called *visitas*, recorded in the first few decades after the Inka demise. The 1549 and 1567 inspections in the province of León de Huánuco, in north-central Peru,[61] and the 1562 inspection in Chucuito, south Peru,[62] are especially rich in detail. Analyses by Julien[63] and LeVine[64] show that the labor exactions were systematically based on regional census counts, which were both recorded on knot registers.[65] Julien notes that some populations were reordered into administratively convenient units either by dividing large groups or merging smaller groups that had previously been under fragmented leadership. Similar policies were followed with the most populous of the highland Peruvian societies, the Xauxas and Wankas, which were organized into three provincial subdivisions, each under its own native paramount.[66] Elsewhere, the administration accommodated its units to the scale of the indigenous population, such as among the seven Lupaqa sub-polities of the Titicaca basin.[67] Julien argues that the standardization of administrative units eased the application of labor exactions and facilitated comparisons in productivity among subject groups. In turn, the needs for administrative personnel could have been minimized and competition stimulated among productive units. Finally, notions of fairness could have been met by assigning comparable tasks across census units.

Labor requirements were assessed according to the census counts of these administrative units. For example, according to the Huánuco *visita* of 1549, the Chupachus and Yachas together constituted 4,108 households. This total was divided into four *waranqas* (units of 1,000 households) and forty *pachacas* (units of 100 households). Many labor requirements were assessed as forty households or a multiple thereof, perhaps indicating that the assessments were spread evenly across all *pachacas* (Table 2.2).[68] For

[61] Helmer (1955); Ortiz de Zuñiga (1964 [1567]: 1972 [1562]).
[62] Diez de San Miguel (1967 [1562]). [63] Julien (1982; 1988). [64] LeVine (1987).
[65] See also Cobo (1979 [1653]: 233–4). [66] LeVine (1987); D'Altroy (1992).
[67] Julien (1988: 268). [68] Ibid.: 264–6.

Table 2.2 *Labor service provided to the Inkas by the Chupachu of central Peru, as reported in 1549 and 1562*

	1549						1562
Assignment	Total households	Extraction	Manufacture	Agriculture	Building/ maintenance	Service	
Gold miners: 120 men, 120 women	120	120					+
Silver miners: 60 men, 60 women	60	60					+
Construction (Cuzco area)	400				400		+
Agriculture (Cuzco area)	400			400			
Retainers of Wayna Qhapaq (Cuzco)	150					150	+
Guards for body of Thupa Inka Yupanki (Cuzco)	150					150	
Guards for weapons of Thupa Inka Yupanki (Cuzco)	10					10	
Garrison in Chachapoyas	200					200	
Garrison in Quito	200					200	
Guards for body of the Inka [the ruler] (Cuzco)	20					20	
Feather workers	120	120					+
Honey gatherers	60	60					+
Weavers of tapestry cloth	400		400				+
Dye makers	40		40				
Herders of the Inka's [the ruler's] flocks	240					240	+
Guards for maize fields	40					40	+
Pepper cultivators	40			40			
Salt miners (varied: 40, 50, 60)	50	50					+
Coca cultivators	60			60			+
Hunters for royal deer hunt	40	40					
Sandal makers (Cuzco, Huánuco)	40		40				+
Wood workers, products to Cuzco	40		40				+
Potters, products to Huánuco	40		40				+
Guards for Huánuco Pampa	58					68	
Porters carrying loads to Huánuco	30					80	

Table 2.2 *(cont.)*

Assignment	1549						1562
	Total households	Extraction	Manufacture	Agriculture	Building/ maintenance	Service	
Guards for women of the Inka	40					40	
Soldiers and litter bearers	500					500	
Cultivators of Inka lands	500			500			
Makers of weapons and litters (Cuzco)							
Processors of dried, salted fish							+
Snare-makers for the hunt							+
Women in service to the Inka							+
Subtotals	4,108	450	560	1,000	400	1,698	
Percentage shares		11.0	13.6	24.3	9.7	41.3	
Total	4,108					4,108	

Note: The figures for miners are ambiguous, since the inspection lists 120 and 60 individuals of each for gold and silver mining, respectively, whereas other figures appear to cite men only. Because this table represents households, I follow Julien (1988) in citing 120 and 60 households rather than 240 and 120 invididuals.

Sources: Helmer (1955); Ortiz de Zúñiga (1967 [1562]); modified from LeVine (1987: 23); Julien (1988: 265); D'Altroy (1994: 184–5; 2002).

those few cases in which the assessments were not evenly divisible by forty, Julien argues plausibly that some specialized personnel, such as silver miners, coca cultivators, or salt miners, might have been drawn from certain *pachacas*, thus bringing the accounting into balance. LeVine's study shows that labor exactions resulting in material products were assessed evenly by units of 100 households, whereas services were assigned evenly by units of 1,000.[69] This policy suggests that decisions about the production of goods were tailored to environmental variations, while decisions about services did not need to take into account such local detail.

The 4,108 Chupachu taxpayers can be summed analytically as follows: 15.0 percent (640) to extract natural materials, 13.1 percent (560) to manufacture material goods, 22.9 percent (980) to cultivate state fields, 9.4 percent (400) to build or maintain the physical infrastructure, and 39.7 percent (1,698) to provide services that did not yield a material product (such as guard duty). Although it is unwise to generalize from a single data source, the balance among these categories is intriguing. For example, less than 10 percent of the labor was assigned to construction or maintenance of the physical infrastructure, and all those workers were sent to toil in Cuzco. This assessment was put into practice even though the Chupachu inhabited the province administered from Huánuco Pampa, architecturally the greatest of all preserved provincial centers.[70] That anomaly may possibly be attributed to the completion of the center by the time that the reported apportionment of duties was assigned; earlier assessments may have included more construction workers.

Although we often think of labor specialists in terms of craft production, only about one in eight of the Chupachu specialists was an artisan. Forty (1.0 percent) were potters, whereas 400 (10 percent) made tapestry cloth and 200 worked with feathers. The same ratio (1:10) of potters to weavers is found in the colonist settlement of Cupi, Bolivia, suggesting that the Inkas linked the two kinds of production.[71] It may have been that textiles were far more labor-intensive than ceramics and therefore required greater investment than for any other product, but it is also true that cloth was the most highly valued product in the realm.

The allocation of almost 40 percent of labor to services that would not have directly produced material objects highlights several issues. Many such individuals were either military guards or security personnel for high-status individuals, perhaps reflecting Inka views about the distinction

[69] LeVine (1987). [70] Morris, Covey, and Stein (2011).
[71] See Murra (1978) and D'Altroy, Williams, and Lorandi (2007).

or safety of their positions. This situation was surely at variance with pre-imperial circumstances, when most permanent service was limited to household servants for the elites. Conversely, only 440 individuals labored at tasks that yielded the two principal kinds of remains that archaeologists employ to study the Inka economy in the sierra: physical infrastructure and ceramics. The relative imbalance of labor assignments and material remains should encourage us to think carefully about how to model economic sectors for which we do not have written records. The archaeological assessment of such important service sectors of the imperial economy, which leave scant trace in the material record, presents a special challenge.

A related issue concerns how the individuals or households were chosen for labor service. Some societies were favored for particular kinds of duty because they were thought to have exceptional abilities. The Rucanas were employed as litter bearers, the Qollqa as stonemasons, the Chumbivilcas as dancers, and the Chachapoyas, Kañari, Chuyes, and Charcas as warriors.[72] About a third of the populace – the entire coastal population – was considered unfit for military duty because of their untrustworthiness. Among these central sierra provinces, labor duty ostensibly rotated among households, but the elites' discretion in assigning odious or easy service gave them enormous local power.[73] It seems safe to infer that political favor or kin ties were influential in making labor assignments and that equal assignments were construed in a variety of ways in practice.

The creation of state resources and resistance to tax service

Generally speaking, state resources were established by (1) setting off lands for state production, on which the local populace was required to render labor service, (2) requisitioning flocks that were set aside to be tended for state needs, and (3) claiming all the natural mineral and biotic resources as state property. Farmlands seem often to have been located around state administrative centers, but could also be established in particularly favorable agricultural locations, such as the fertile valleys of Abancay and Cochabamba (Figure 2.4).[74] The standard sources often emphasize two points concerning the use of state lands and the labor allocated to their cultivation. First, state and state religion lands were cultivated by the subject populace before they were allowed to turn to their own lands.[75]

[72] Rowe (1946). [73] Moore (1958). [74] Wachtel (1982); La Lone and La Lone (1987).
[75] See, for example, Polo (1916 [1571]: 58–60).

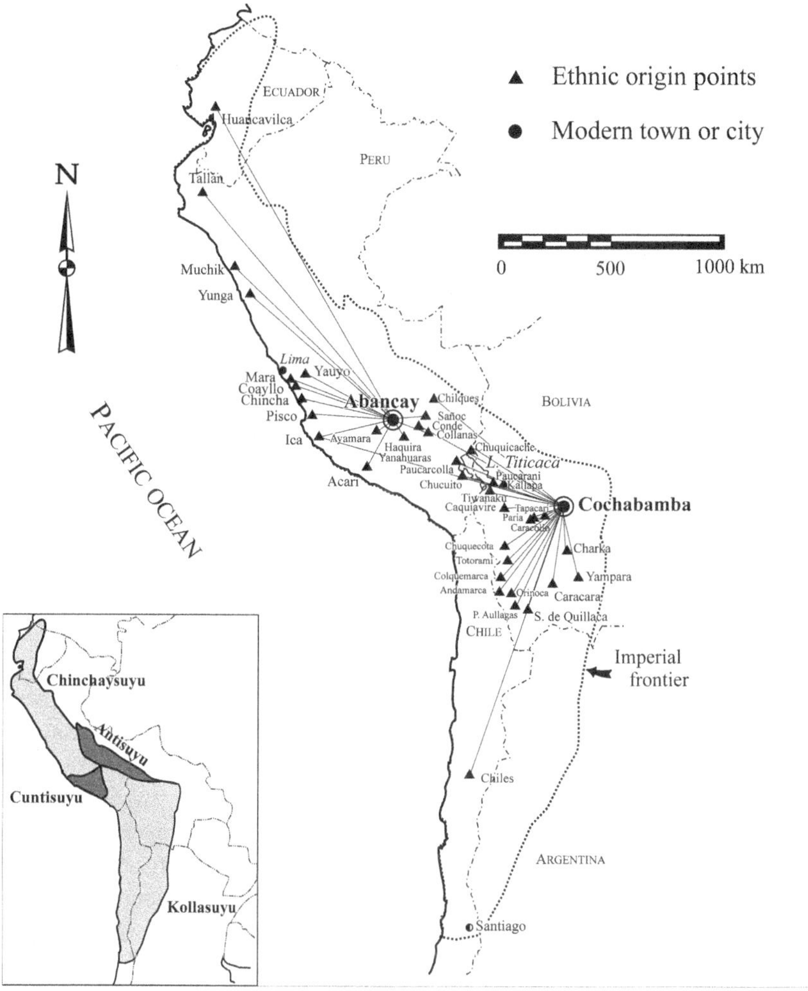

Figure 2.4 Ethnic staffing of major Inka state farms at Abancay and Cochabamba

Second, the state emphasized the production of maize on its lands to feed state personnel, and especially to provide *chicha* to soldiers.[76] Both points put a gloss on reality.

Agricultural and military service almost surely posed labor-scheduling dilemmas for the participating households, since crops can be planted and

[76] See, for example, Wachtel (1982).

harvested only during short windows of opportunity. Other strains arose from the periodic, and unpredictable, reassessments of state needs.[77] For instance, the burdensome call to military duty, which could last for years at a stretch, could be applied with scant notice. Aside from resistance to service, we may expect several possible consequences of such bottlenecks. One solution would have been for farmers to alternate labor devoted to state and personal tasks according to the sequential demands of the complex agricultural cycles, or they might have divided tasks among household members.[78] Another possibility is that the subject households manipulated their composition by having large families and delaying marriage, to reduce their per capita obligations. Finally, the households may have altered their labor exchanges to ensure that their lands were tended. The state's reliance on corvée for much of its production thus shifted the parameters of decision-making among its subjects. As a result, the Inkas had much to gained by creating specialized production enclaves, in which workers were more directly under the control of state administrators.[79] Scheduling conflicts could have been reduced and compliance more easily enforced.

Specialized assignments for state colonists

State farms

One of the tenets of Inka rule was that the resources that sustained the state and temple economies were separate from those of their subjects.[80] In order to ensure a steady supply of food, beer (*chicha*), cloth, and other supplies, officials set aside lands for state farms and pastures in every province where it was feasible. Most farms were located near provincial centers, but some also lay in favorable locales for particular crops, especially maize and coca leaf, and even trees.[81] The lands dedicated to supporting state and Sun (religion) activities often lay near one another, but their products were stored and administered separately. The farms were cultivated both by corvée workers as part of their rotating labor duties and by multitudes of colonists.

The farms at Cochabamba, Bolivia, were among the most extensive in the empire. During a tour of the realm early in his reign, Wayna Qhapaq ordered the western part of the warm eastern valley vacated. Some 14,000 workers were set to work, mostly from the adjacent altiplano: Quillacas,

[77] Cobo (1979 [1653]: 234). [78] Mitchell (1980). [79] Murra (1980 [1956]).
[80] This section reprises material expounded by D'Altroy (2005).
[81] Chepstow-Lusty and Winfield (2000).

Chilques, Chiles, Collas from Azángaro, Uros and Soras from Paria, and Caracaras, Chichas, Charkas, and Yamparaes from the southern altiplano. Other documents mention the Condes from Condesuyo and Icas from the Peruvian south coast.[82] Permanent colonists and seasonal laborers were both present, but the proportions of each type are unclear. The farms were divided into seventy-seven narrow strips that transected the valley's eco-zones. Workers were assigned specific strips the margins of which they cultivated for their own use, supplementing the produce of separate plots. The magistrate Polo was told that the farms were used to grow maize – more likely a full crop complex – for the Inka's armies. Archaeological evidence for an intensive Inka occupation is found throughout the valley, in more than 100 Inka-era sites.[83] They also built 2,400 storehouses at Cotapachi, where the produce was stored before being shipped to Paria, Cuzco, and elsewhere. The colonists were responsible for maintaining the storehouses on top of their agricultural duties.

Farms elsewhere were dedicated to military uses, including some at Arica,[84] Arequipa,[85] and Abancay.[86] The farms in the warm western Abancay Valley were also founded by Wayna Qhapaq to support his wars in the north. They were dedicated to coca, cotton, pepper, and fruits. Members of at least thirteen different ethnic groups were brought in to staff the Abancay farms permanently. If a family died out, another was brought in to keep the number of households at a total of 1,000.[87] Extensive Inka farms have also been identified archaeologically in the Upper Mantaro Valley, Peru, and in northwest Argentina. In the Upper Mantaro, the prime farmlands were within about 5 km of the provincial center at Hatun Xauxa, and, within 15 km down the valley, were virtually bereft of villages. The Inka-era sites that are present contain many farming tools but little evidence of other kinds of production, in sharp contrast to communities farther afield. On the hillslopes above the farmlands, the Inkas built thirty-three storage facilities with more than 3,000 individual storehouses – the largest known concentration in the empire. Several colonist groups were brought into the general region, such as the Yauyos, Tarama, Huamachucos, Chachapoyas, and Collaguas.

The fact that the Inka project was still a work in progress may be seen at Coctaca-Rodero, Argentina. There, a massive, unfinished terraced field system covers about 6 square km on the piedmont (3,700 m) just below the

[82] Wachtel (1982). [83] Gyarmati and Varga (1999).
[84] Jiménez de la Espada (1965 [1557–1586]: vol. I, 338). [85] La Lone and La Lone (1987).
[86] Espinoza (1973). [87] Ibid.

altiplano.[88] Large tracts may have also been farmed at the Campo de Pucará, in the Lerma Valley of the eastern piedmont.[89] The positioning of the Lerma farms parallels that of Cochabamba, since they lie well below the imperial fortifications in the mountains. Their location suggests that the lower valleys were considered to be peaceful enough that they could be farmed with little danger from the mobile bands who lived on the eastern plains. In each case, there is substantial evidence for an intensive imperial investment of labor in land improvements, provincial installations, or storage facilities.

Artisans

To meet their demands for textile, metal, ceramic, stone, and other craft goods, the Inkas set entire communities of artisans to work (Figure 2.5). Many artisans were chosen because their societies had reputations for particular skills: metal smiths from the coast, wood-workers from the eastern slopes, and weavers and masons from the altiplano. Recognizing the skills of the coastal smiths, honed over two millennia, the Inkas transferred artisans en masse to Cuzco to fashion sumptuary items for aristocrats and temples. Regrettably, most of those objects met their fate in the Spanish forges in 1532 and 1533 as part of Atawallpa's ransom or during the sack of Cuzco. The documentary sources indicate that the smiths were given lands upon which to support themselves; their raw materials came from state supplies. That the smiths had been coastal craftsmen and not highland farmers apparently had no effect on state policy; the Inkas provided resources, not sustenance, to their colonists.[90]

Some weaving and potting settlements contained as many as 1,000 households. Both state facilities and royal estates benefited in this manner. Wayna Qhapaq's estate at Lamay, in the Sacred Valley, reportedly had 500 weavers in residence, for example.[91] Similarly, 400 of the 4,108 enumerated Chupachu households had been assigned to work as tapestry cloth weavers. The altiplano was especially favored for weaving colonies because of the region's textile traditions and great herds.[92] The Milliraya enclave contained two neighboring settlements, one with either 100 or 300 potters and the other with 1,000 tapestry cloth weavers.[93] By founding the enclave along the border between two political divisions while taking lands from only one, the Inkas nourished local tensions with an eye to stifling an

[88] Albeck and Scattolin (1991); Albeck (1992). [89] González (1983). [90] Espinoza (1983).

[91] Toledo (1940 [1570]: 71).

[92] Acosta (1962 [1590]: 210, 211); Diez de San Miguel (1964 [1567]: 106); Julien (1988; 1993); Spurling (1992: 234–6).

[93] Murra (1978).

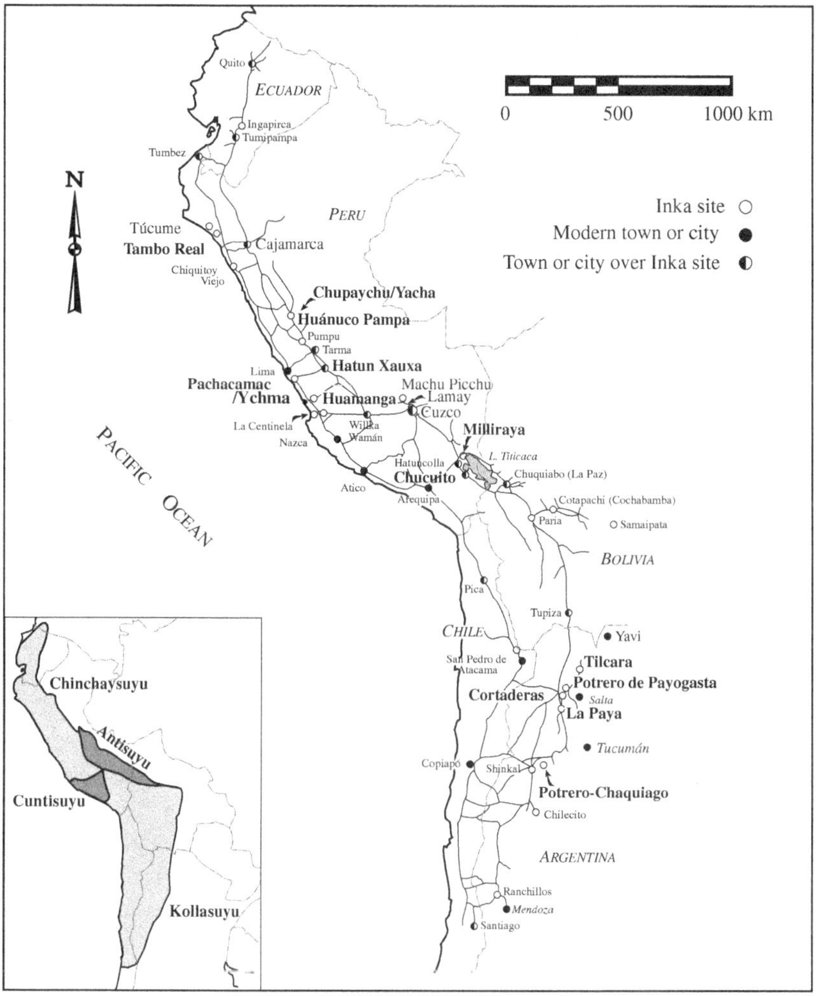

Figure 2.5 Locations of major artisan communities named in early colonial-era documents

alliance that had threatened their rule a few decades earlier.[94] Each town received irrigated fields, pastures, lakeshore lands, and lowland maize fields to support itself. The weavers were installed to help outfit Wayna Qhapaq's northern campaigns, but the potters said they distributed their products around the north end of the lake. Many other cases of craft production in

[94] Spurling (1992).

state colonies can be cited, but the essential point here is that the artisans were expected to sustain themselves while producing for the state. The products that they manufactured were of high quality and labor-intensive, in a distinctive style that provided the ideological imprint of Inka power.

The imposition of Spanish rule: mutual accommodations

What happened when the Spanish ideas about economic practice ran headlong into Andean economic formations in 1532? An initial point is that the Spaniards who invaded the Inka domain were soldier-entrepreneurs.[95] Shut out of access to land or other forms of wealth in their homeland, they had designs on establishing their prosperity in the newly discovered land of *Pirú*. The economic framework of their enterprise can be seen both in the terms of the grants awarded to the expedition's leaders, Francisco Pizarro and his partner Diego de Almagro, and in the apportioning of rewards based on the investments made by the participants. A soldier with a horse, for example, received twice the booty of a foot soldier and Pizarro took seven times that of the *caballero*. Their initial haul was astonishing. The horsemen each received the equivalent of about US$2.5 million (at current values) in gold and silver from Atawallpa's ransom, a figure that was markedly enhanced when they plundered Cuzco and its riches.[96]

As the invasion gave way to occupation, the Spaniards needed to set up more permanent means of ensuring the flow of the wealth they coveted. Many soldiers simply packed up their riches and went back home to a life of relative opulence in Iberia. Those who stayed in the Andes tried to create a hybrid system that exploited Andean forms of productivity for Spanish ends. In essence, numerous conquistadores set themselves up as landed nobility, presiding over Inka estates. Other invaders focused on mining silver and gold, or extracting other commercially viable products. The details of the transformation provide a fascinating, complicated narrative in and of themselves, but here I would simply like to highlight a very few implications for Andean economic practice.

The first Spanish policy was to award a set of resources and a resident population to a grantee. As the indigenous populace was devastated by a combination of war, disease, and overwork, the level of per capita exploitation expanded to unsustainable levels. Within fifty years the native population was about half that of 1532, and in some valleys the population

[95] Lockhart (1972). [96] MacQuarrie (2007).

ultimately fell to no more than 5 percent of its pre-conquest level.[97] Two consequences from the Spanish side were repeated changes in the level of taxation – relief being imposed by the Crown and resisted by the estate holders – and a shift in the nature of the tax base from people to territory. On the Andean side, the levies were so onerous that upwards of a half of the surviving populace simply moved.[98] Two classes of indigenous peoples were created: the people who stayed (*originarios*) and those who fled (*forasteros*). The disruption entailed in moving to a new home is hard to exaggerate for Andean people. The essence of the social fabric was ripped apart – their very identity, their access to the beneficence of the ancestors, their ability to enjoy a peaceful afterlife, and their relationships to the beings of the land. In those areas where the populace largely stayed put, despite the Spanish resettlement (*reducciones*) implemented by Viceroy Toledo, large swaths of productive, intensified lands went begging for people.[99] Fully one-half of the terraced lands of the central Andes were still unused in the middle of the twentieth century[100] – a pattern that persists at high elevations today.

One of the most intriguing aspects of post-conquest economic formations was the development of parallel economies: one based on Spanish principles of money, markets, and the commodification of resources and goods, and an internal Andean one, based on traditional notions of an integrated socio-economy. In some early colonial areas the Spanish exactions included items such as cloth, which were then commodified and sold in newly established markets. Andean peoples participated in this system while continuing to employ prehispanic principles for within-community economics. The fact that members of Andean societies could wear two economic hats simultaneously should not be a surprise, since some areas already had monetary devices in the prehispanic era, and the Inkas themselves were perfectly willing to take advantage of the exchange relationships mediated through these media to obtain extra-territorial goods. The point is not that the Inkas did not understand how money and markets might work, but that their vision of how resource extraction, production, exchange, and the provisioning of services were properly deployed did not employ those features.

Two situations exemplify how the dual economic concepts still persist. In high-elevation, traditional communities, socio-economic relations are still based on collective ownership and obligation. Any activity is accompanied by gifts to (especially coca) or negotiations with the *tirakuna*. The obligations of members to the community are meticulously accounted

97 Cook (1981). 98 Lockhart (1984). 99 Wernke (2012). 100 Denevan (1986)

for and verified in public gatherings.[101] The social formation and its relationship to the social existence and memory of the land is regularly reconstituted through rituals performed along long-trodden pathways and pilgrimages to the peaks and other locations of power.[102] As the members of the traditional communities near Cuzco move away from their home villages to the city, they are lamented not just for their absence, but because they have been severed from the real people (*runakuna*) of the land.

The second example is the persistence of dual accounting systems for differing kinds of arithmetic or financial transactions. Urton has shown that, among the traditional populace, women who participate in market economics use Spanish for their monetary transactions.[103] In Peru, for instance, they buy and sell in *soles*. When it comes to within-community transactions in Quechua, however, the social order of numbers comes into play. No transaction is complete unless it ends in an even number, since dual balance is an essential part of reality, ontologically preceding both human and quantitative existence or action. Such examples could be multiplied, but the point is that, even today, resources, labor, and transactions are still imbued fundamentally with social relations. Those economic behaviors that do not conform to such ideas are literally treated as a separate culture and mediated through a different language.

Conclusions

This chapter has been intended to address two key issues for this volume. The first, more obvious, subject is the nature of the Inka fiscal regime. As can be seen, the Inkas operated with a few key principles that were in part systematically and in part opportunistically applied to the peoples and lands that they dominated. The systematic principles included (1) assessing taxes largely through command of the labor capacities of their subjects, (2) the requisitioning of productive resources for state and state church uses, and (3) the massive resettlement of subject peoples to places where their positioning made it possible to defuse resistance and exploit natural resources. The opportunistic principles focused on the exploitation of particular, localized resources, and on the use of the perceived skills of particular subject groups. This was all cast in terms of mutual obligation that had existed prior to the rise of Inka power. Overall, the trend in the imperial period, which lasted about a century,

101 See, for example, Isbell (1978), Allen (2002), and Salomon (2004).

102 See, for example, Abercrombie (1998).

103 Urton (1997).

was to shift from generalized assessments to specialized production. Even though there were limited markets and monetary devices in the northern part of their domain, the Inkas appear to have preferred to use these regional features to obtain extra-territorial materials that would otherwise have been difficult to procure. The marketing systems were allowed to function below the mantle of state oversight, but were never directly incorporated into state economics.

The second goal of this chapter has been to assess the degree to which the questions and models posed in the introductory chapter could effectively address the Inka situation. It appears that many of the questions raised and models proposed – while certainly of considerable interest – are focused on economies that assume a degree of monetization that was not present among the Inkas. That does not necessarily render the Inka system weaker, but it certainly does make its character more particular to the socio-economic fabric of the Andean case. And, while supporting the Inka military was an essential and perhaps the primary expenditure of state resources, this was surely not the only important expenditure, and it became increasingly less significant as the Inkas reached the frontiers of the world that they deemed worth civilizing or that could threaten their hegemony. Instead, the two principal fiscal goals of the Inka state economy were to sustain the elites in the style that they aspired to become accustomed to and to underwrite the ceremony and public feasting that encouraged the subject populace to discipline itself. The immediacy of the collapse of the Inka fiscal regime upon Spanish invasion is just indication of the degree to which it was seen as a burdensome, extractive economy, and not an integral part of life in the Andes among the subject populace.

References

Abercrombie, T. A. (1998) *Pathways of Memory and Power: Ethnography and History among an Andean People*. Madison, WI.

Acosta, J. de (1962 [1590]) *Historia natural y moral de las Indias*, ed. E. O'Gorman. Mexico City.

Albeck, M. E. (1992) "Areas agrícolas y densidad de ocupación prehispánica en la Quebrada de Humahuaca," *Avances en Arqueología* 2: 56–77.

Albeck, M. E., and Scattolin, M. C. (1991) "Cálculo fotogramétrico de superficies de cultivo en Coctaca y Rodero, Quebrada de Humahuaca," *Avances en Arqueología* 1: 43–58.

Allen, C. (2002) *The Hold Life Has*, 2nd edn. Washington, DC.

Bauer, B. S. (2004) *Ancient Cuzco*. Austin, TX.

Berthelot, J. (1986) "The extraction of precious metals at the time of the Inka," in *Anthropological History of Andean Polities*, ed. J. V. Murra, N. Wachtel, and J. Revel. Cambridge: 69–88.

Bohannan, P. (1955) "Some principles of exchange and investment among the Tiv," *American Anthropologist* 57: 60–70.

Bonney, R., and Ormrod, W. M. (1999) "Introduction: crises, revolutions and self-sustained growth: towards a conceptual model of change in fiscal history," in *Crises, Revolutions and Self-Sustained Growth: Essays in European Fiscal History, 1130–1830*, ed. W. M. Ormrod, M. Bonney, and R. Bonney. Stamford, UK: 1–21.

Bray, T. (2009) "An archaeological perspective on the Andean concept of *camaquen*: thinking through late pre-Columbian *ofrendas* and *huacas*," *Cambridge Archaeological Journal* 19: 357–66.

Brumfiel, E. (1980) "Specialization, market exchange, and the Aztec state: a view from Huexotla," *Current Anthropology* 21: 459–78.

Burling, R. (1962) "Maximization theories and the study of economic anthropology," *American Anthropologist* 64: 802–21.

Cabello Valboa, M. (1951 [1586]) *Miscelánea antártica: una historia del Perú antiguo*. Lima.

Chepstow-Lusty, A., and Winfield, M. (2000) "Agroforestry by the Inca: lessons from the past," *Ambio* 29: 322–8.

Cobo, B. (1979 [1653]) *History of the Inca Empire*, trans. R. Hamilton. Austin, TX.

Cook, N. D. (1981) *Demographic Collapse: Indian Peru, 1520–1620*. Cambridge.

Cook, S. (1966) "The obsolete 'anti-market' mentality: a critique of the substantive approach to economic anthropology," *American Anthropologist* 68: 323–45.

Costin, C. L., and Earle, T. K. (1989) "Status distinction and legitimation of power as reflected in changing patterns of consumption in late prehispanic Peru," *American Antiquity* 54: 691–714.

Covey, R. A. (2006a) "Chronology, succession, and sovereignty: the politics of Inka historiography and its modern interpretation," *Comparative Studies in Society and History* 48: 166–99.

(2006b) *How the Incas Built Their Heartland*. Ann Arbor, MI.

Dalton, G. (1961) "Economic theory and primitive society," *American Anthropologist* 63: 1–25.

(1977) "Aboriginal economies in stateless societies," in *Exchange Systems in Prehistory*, ed. T. K. Earle and J. E. Ericson. New York: 191–212.

D'Altroy, T. N. (1992) *Provincial Power in the Inka Empire*. Washington, DC.

(1994) "Public and private economy in the Inka empire," in *The Economic Anthropology of the State*, ed. E. Brumfiel. Lanham, MD: 171–222.

(2000) "Andean land use at the cusp of history," in *Imperfect Balance: Landscape Transformations in the Precolumbian Americas*, ed. D. Lentz. New York: 357–89.

(2002) *The Incas*. Malden, MA.

(2005) "Remaking the social landscape: colonization in the Inka empire," in *The Archaeology of Colonial Encounters*, ed. G. Stein. Albuquerque, NM: 263–95.

(2014) *The Incas*, 2nd edn. New York.
D'Altroy, T. N., and Earle, T. K. (1985) "Staple finance, wealth finance, and storage in the Inka political economy (with comment and reply)," *Current Anthropology* 25: 187–206.
D'Altroy, T. N., and Hastorf, C. A. (2002) *Empire and Domestic Economy*. New York.
D'Altroy, T. N., Williams, V. I., and Lorandi, A. M. (2007) "The Inkas in the Southlands," in *Variations in the Expression of Inka Power*, ed. R. Burger, C. Morris, and R. Matos Mendieta. Washington, DC: 88–135.
De la Cadena, M. (2010) "Indigenous cosmopolitics in the Andes: conceptual reflections beyond 'politics,'" *Cultural Anthropology* 25: 334–70.
Denevan, W. (1986) *The Cultural Ecology, Archaeology, and History of Terracing and Terrace Abandonment in the Colca Valley of Southern Peru*. Madison, WI.
Diez de Betanzos, J. (1996) *Narrative of the Incas*, trans. and ed. R. Hamilton and D. Buchanan. Austin, TX.
Diez de San Miguel, G. (1964 [1567]) *Visita hecha a la provincia de Chucuito por Garci Diez de San Miguel en el año 1567*, ed. W. Espinoza Soriano. Lima.
Earle, T. K. (1977) "A reappraisal of redistribution: complex Hawaiian chiefdoms," in *Exchange Systems in Prehistory*, ed. T. K. Earle and J. E. Ericson. New York: 213–29.
(1982) "The ecology and politics of primitive valuables," in *Cultural Ecology: Eclectic Perspectives*, ed. J. Kennedy and R. Edgerton. Washington, DC: 65–83.
Earle, T. K., and D'Altroy, T. N. (1982) "Storage facilities and state finance in the Upper Mantaro Valley, Peru," in *Contexts for Prehistoric Exchange*, ed. J. E. Ericson and T. K. Earle. New York: 265–90.
Espinoza Soriano, W.(1973) "Las colonias de mitmas múltiples en Abancay, siglos XV y XVI," *Revista del Museo Nacional* 39: 225–99.
(1978) *Los modos de producción en el imperio de los Incas*. Lima.
(1983) "Los mitmas plateros de Ishma en le país de los Ayamarca, siglos XV–XIX," *Boletín de Lima* 30: 38–52.
Falcón, F. (1946 [1567]) "Representación hecha por el Licenciado Falcón en concilio provincial sobre los daños y molestias que se hacen a los indios," in *Los pequeños grandes libros de historia Americana*, vol. X, ed. F. A. Loayza. Lima: 121–64.
Garcilaso de la Vega, I. (1966 [1609]) *Royal Commentaries of the Incas and General History of Peru*, trans. H. V. Livermore. Austin, TX.
Godelier, M. (1974) "On the definition of a social formation: the example of the Incas," *Critique of Anthropology* 1: 63–73.
González, A. R. (1983) "Inca settlement patterns in a marginal province of the empire: sociocultural implications," in *Prehistoric Settlement Patterns: Essays in Honor of Gordon R. Willey*, ed. E. Z. Vogt and R. M. Leventhal. Cambridge, MA: 337–60.
Guaman Poma de Ayala, F. (1980 [1613]) *El primer nueva corónica y buen gobierno*, ed. J. V. Murra, R. Adorno, and J. Urioste. Mexico City.

Gyarmati, J., and Varga, A. (1999) *The Chacaras of War: An Inka State in the Cochabamba Valley, Bolivia*. Budapest.

Hassig, R. (1985) *Trade, Tribute, and Transportation: The Sixteenth-Century Political Economy of the Valley of Mexico*. Norman, OK.

Helmer, M. (1955) "'La visitación de los Yndios Chupachos': Inka et encomendero 1549," *Travaux de L'Institut Français d'Etudes Andines* 5: 3–50.

Hosler, D., Lechtman, H., and Holm, O. (1990) *Axe-Monies and Their Relatives*. Washington, DC.

Hyslop, J. (1984) *The Inka Road System*. New York.

(1990) *Inka Settlement Planning*. Austin, TX.

Isbell, B. J. (1978) *To Defend Ourselves: Ecology and Ritual in an Andean Village*. Austin, TX.

Jiménez de la Espada, M. (ed.) (1965 [1557–1586]) *Relaciones geográficas de Indias: Perú*, 3 vols. Madrid.

Julien, C. J. (1982) "Inca decimal administration in the Lake Titicaca region," in *The Inca and Aztec States 1400–1800: Anthropology and History*, ed. G. A. Collier, R. I. Rosaldo, and J. D. Wirth. New York: 119–51.

(1988) "How Inca decimal administration worked," *Ethnohistory* 35: 257–79.

(1993) "Finding a fit: archaeology and ethnohistory of the Incas," in *Provincial Inca: Archaeological and Ethnohistorical Assessment of the Impact of the Inca State*, ed. M. Malpass. Iowa City: 177–233.

La Lone, M. B., and La Lone, D. E. (1987) "The Inka state in the southern highlands: state administrative and production enclaves," *Ethnohistory* 34: 47–62.

LeVine, T. Y. (1987) "Inka labor service at the regional level: the functional reality," *Ethnohistory* 34: 14–46.

(ed.) (1992) *Inka Storage Systems*. Norman, OK.

Lockhart, J. (1972) *The Men of Cajamarca*. Austin, TX.

(1984) *Spanish Peru, 1532–1560: A Social History*. Madison, WI.

MacQuarrie, K. (2007) *The Last Days of the Incas*. New York.

Mann, M. (1986) *The Sources of Social Power*, vol. I. Cambridge.

Mitchell, W. (1980) "Local ecology and the state: implications of contemporary Quechua land use for the Inca sequence of agricultural work," in *Beyond the Myths of Culture: Essays in Cultural Materialism*, ed. E. B. Ross. New York: 139–54.

Moore, S. F. (1958) *Power and Property in Inca Peru*. Westport, CT.

Morris, C. (1974) "Reconstructing patterns of nonagricultural production in the Inca economy: archaeology and documents in instituted analysis," in *Reconstructing Complex Societies*, ed. C. Moore. Chicago: 49–68.

Morris, C., Covey, R. A., and Stein, P. (2011) *The Huánuco Pampa Archaeological Project*, vol. I, *The Plaza and Palace Complex*. New York.

Moseley, M. E., and Cordy-Collins, A. (eds.) (1990) *The Northern Dynasties: Kingship and Statecraft in Chimor*. Washington, DC.

Murra, J. V. (1972) "El 'control vertical' de un máximo de pisos ecológicos en la economía de las sociedades andinas," in *Visita de la Provincia de León de*

Huánuco en 1562, Iñigo Ortiz de Zúñiga, visitador, vol. II, *Visita de los Yacha y Mitmaqkuna Cuzqueños encomendados en Juan Sanchez Falcón,* ed. J. V. Murra. Huánuco, Peru: 427–76.

(1978) "Los olleros del Inka: hacia una historia y arqueología del Qollasuyu," in *Historia, problema, y promesa: homenaje a Jorge Basadre,* ed. F. Miro Quesada, F. Pease García Yrigoyen, and D. Sobrevilla. Lima: 415–23.

(1980 [1956]) *The Economic Organization of the Inka State.* Greenwich, CT.

Murúa, M. de (1986 [1605]) *Historia general del Perú,* ed. M. Ballesteros. Madrid.

Netherly, P. J. (1978) "Local level lords on the north coast of Peru," PhD dissertation. Cornell University, Ann Arbor, MI.

Ortiz de Zúñiga, I. (1967 [1562]) *Visita de la Provincia de León de Huánuco en 1562, Iñigo Ortiz de Zúñiga, visitador,* vol. I, *Visita de las cuatro Waranqa de los Chupachu,* ed. J. V. Murra. Huánuco, Peru.

(1972 [1562]) *Visita de la Provincia de León de Huánuco en 1562, Iñigo Ortiz de Zúñiga, visitador,* vol. II, *Visita de los Yacha y Mitmaqkuna Cuzqueños encomendados en Juan Sanchez Falcón,* ed. J. V. Murra. Huánuco, Peru.

Patterson, T. C. (1991) *Inca Empire: The Formation and Disintegration of a Pre-Capitalist State.* New York.

Polanyi, K. (1957) "The economy as instituted process," in *Trade and Market in the Early Empires,* ed. K. Polanyi, C. Arensberg, and H. Pearson. Glencoe, IL: 243–69.

(1968) *Primitive, Archaic, and Modern Economies: Essays of Karl Polanyi,* ed. G. Dalton. Garden City, NY.

Polo Ondegardo, J. (1916 [1571]) "Relación de los fundamentos acerca del notable daño que resulta de no guardar a los indios sus fueros," in *Colección de libros y documentos referentes a la historia del Perú,* vol. III, ed. H. H. Urteaga. Lima: 45–188.

Rostworowski de Diez Canseco, M. (1977) *Etnía y sociedad costa Peruana prehispánica.* Lima.

(1999) *History of the Inca Realm.* trans. H. B. Iceland. Cambridge.

Rowe, J. H. (1946) "Inca culture at the time of the Spanish conquest," in *Handbook of South American Indians,* vol. II, *The Andean Civilizations,* ed. J. Steward. Washington, DC: 183–330.

Sahlins, M. (1972) *Stone Age Economics.* Chicago.

(1976) *Culture and Practical Reason.* Chicago.

Salomon, F. L. (1991) "Introductory essay: the Huarochirí Manuscript," in *The Huarochirí Manuscript: A Testament of Ancient and Colonial Andean Religion,* trans. and ed. F. L. Salomon and J. Urioste. Austin, TX: 1–38.

(2004) *The Cord-Keepers.* Durham, NC.

Sarmiento de Gamboa, P. (2007) *The History of the Incas,* trans. and ed. B. S. Bauer and V. Smith. Austin, TX.

Schneider, H. (1974) *Economic Man.* New York.

Smelser, N. (1959) "A comparative view of exchange systems," *Economic Development* 7: 173–82.

Spurling, G. E. (1992) "The organization of craft production in the Inka state: the potters and weavers of Milliraya," unpublished PhD dissertation. Cornell University, Ann Arbor, MI.

Toledo, F. de (1940 [1570]) Información hecha por orden de Don Francisco de Toledo en su visita de las Provincias del Perú, en la que declaran indios ancianos sobre el derecho de los cicaciques y sobre el gobierno que tenían aquellos pueblos antes que los Incas los conquistasen, in *Don Francisco de Toledo, supremo organizador del Perú: su vida, su obra (1515–1582)*, ed. R. Levillier. Buenos Aires: 14–37.

Trigger, B. G. (2003) *Understanding Early Civilizations: A Comparative Study*. Cambridge.

Urton, G. (1997) *The Social Life of Numbers*. Austin, TX.

Van de Guchte, M. (1999) "The Inca cognition of landscape: archaeology, ethnohistory, and the aesthetic of alterity." in *Archaeologies of Landscape: Contemporary Perspectives*, ed. W. Ashmore and A. B. Knapp. Malden, MA: 149–68.

Wachtel, N. (1982) "The Mitimas of the Cochabamba Valley: the colonization policy of Huayna Capac," in *The Inca and Aztec States 1400–1800: Anthropology and History*, ed. G. A. Collier, R. I. Rosaldo, and J. D. Wirth. New York: 199–235.

Wernke, S. (2012) *Negotiated Settlements: Andean Communities and Landscapes under Inka and Spanish Colonialism*. Gainesville, FL.

Wilk, R. R., and Cliggett, L. (2007) *Economies and Cultures: Foundations of Economic Anthropology*, 2nd edn. Boulder, CO.

Wilkinson, D. A. (2013) "Politics, infrastructure, and non-human subjects: the Inka occupation of the Amaybamba cloud forests," PhD dissertation. Columbia University, New York.

Yun-Casalilla, B. (2012) "Introduction: the rise of the fiscal state in Eurasia from a global, comparative and transnational perspective," in *The Rise of Fiscal States: A Global History, 1500–1914*, ed. B. Yun-Casalilla and P. K. O'Brien, with F. Comín Comín. Cambridge: 1–36.

Zuidema, R. T. (1982.) "Myth and history in ancient Peru," in *The Logic of Culture*, ed. I. Rossi. South Hadley, MA: 150–75.

CHAPTER 3

The Aztec Empire

Michael E. Smith

Aztec fiscal organization does not conform well to existing historical or comparative models. In terms of evolutionary development, technology, and societal scale, Aztec society can be lined up with early Mesopotamian society,[1] yet Aztec fiscal organization was nothing like that described by Michael Hudson for the ancient Near East.[2] There were few important non-state institutions like Mesopotamian temples, and state taxation was far more regular and routinized, including payments in money. Similarly, when we compare the Aztec case to models of fiscal development in Europe,[3] it does not easily fit into the developmental sequence of tributary state – domain state – tax state – fiscal state (see Chapter 1). In overall economic and political complexity the Aztecs ought to line up most closely with domain states, but their system of taxation in many ways was more typical of the tax state. Yet the political scale and military organization were nothing like polities in the latter category. Briefly, the Aztecs had a true system of taxation, following standard definitions: "In contrast to tributes, taxes are normally recurrent, predictable, routinized, and based on statutory obligations."[4] Yet the overall scale and dynamics of the Aztec state are quite a bit smaller than most of the cases considered in this volume.

In this chapter I summarize the Aztec economic and political system, review what is known about taxation and state revenue, and address a few

I thank Walter Scheidel and Andrew Monson for their invitation to participate in the "Fiscal regimes and the political economy of early states" conference in 2010. I benefited greatly from discussion with the other participants, particularly Metin Coşgel, Edgar Kiser, and Margaret Levi. Frances Berdan and Jerome Offner responded kindly to my requests for information on Aztec taxation, and this chapter has benefited from comments on earlier drafts by Juan José Batalla Rosado, Frances Berdan, Metin Coşgel, Gerardo Gutiérrez, Frederic Hicks, Kenneth Hirth, Jerome Offner, José Luis de Rojas, Maëlle Sergheraert, and Jay Silverstein. I especially think Gerardo Gutiérrez and Viola König for sending me a copy of their new edition of the Tlapa tax roll (Gutiérrez, König, and Brito 2009) at just the right time. Figures 3, 5A, and 7 were drawn by Jacqueline Fox.

[1] Adams (1966); Trigger (2003). [2] Hudson (2000).

[3] See, for example, Bonney (1995) and Bonney and Ormrod (1999). [4] Tarschys (1988: 7).

of the questions motivating the present book. Although some topics in Aztec political economy have been subjected to comparative interrogation (such as city states, empires, markets, and long-distance trade), students of the Aztec state have so far resisted comparative perspectives on taxation and the fiscal aspects of warfare. More than this, Aztec specialists have yet to produce a thorough and systematic analysis of taxation and fiscal organization. This chapter is a step in that direction.

Introduction to the Aztecs

Historical context

Aztec society flourished between the twelfth century AD and the arrival of Hernando Cortés in 1519.[5] As heirs to over a millennium of state-level urban society in Mesoamerica, the Aztecs shared many social and cultural traits with their predecessors, including the Classic Maya of the tropical lowlands and Teotihuacan in highland central Mexico. In the realm of political and economic institutions, though, the Aztecs made many innovations. Their growth was driven by the largest population surge of the pre-Columbian New World, and demographic expansion fueled territorial expansion as well as social innovation.

Aztec culture had its origin in the aftermath of the collapse of the city of Tula, capital of the Toltec state. Waves of immigrants moved into central Mexico from northern Mexico and established new towns. Nobles claiming descent from the Toltec kings set themselves up as petty kings of *altepetl,* or city states.[6] Demographic increase led to the expansion of settlement across the landscape. As kings warred with one another, some polities conquered their neighbors, leading to the formation of the Triple Alliance Empire in 1428. One member of the triumvirate – Tenochtitlan – continued to grow in size power at the expense of its co-capitals. By the time the Spaniards arrived, in 1519, Tenochtitlan was a city of some 200,000 inhabitants and capital of an empire that included several million subjects.

The institutions and processes of Aztec political economy are studied through three types of evidence: native historical and political narratives; early Spanish-period documents; and archaeology. The Aztecs had a phonetic, pictorial writing system, but only a few texts have survived from the pre-Columbian period. One of these, however, is a tax register, the *Matrícula de*

[5] This section is based on material expounded by Smith (2012). [6] Smith (2000).

Tributos;[7] this material is also available in an early Spanish-period copy of the list known as the *Codex Mendoza*.[8] Other native accounts were recorded in European script in the decades following 1519, and these preserve much useful information on political and economic topics. Administrative documents from the early colonial period – in both Spanish and Nahuatl (the Aztec language) – and the descriptions of Spanish chroniclers are important sources of information. Finally, archaeology provides much information on cities, agriculture, commerce, and craft production; unfortunately, few if any fiscal details survive in the archaeological record.

Aztec political economy

The Aztec political system consisted of several hundred city states integrated through what Hansen calls a "city-state culture."[9] These small polities had their origins in the twelfth century, and they continued to function under the Triple Alliance Empire. Indeed, they even retained significance in the regulation of local affairs after the Spanish conquest. City states were ruled by a king (*tlatoani*), aided by a governing council of important nobles. The council met upon the death of a king to select his successor from among the royal lineage. Aztec society consisted of two social classes: a hereditary noble class (*c.* 5 percent of the population) that ran city-state government and controlled all the farmland; and commoners. Both classes had internal gradations in wealth, power, and social attributes.[10]

City states expanded their domains, occasionally forming small empires or conquest states by conquering their peers. Kings led their troops into battle, and military ability was an important factor in the selection of new kings by governing councils. Military service was a duty of all young men, and battlefield success (as measured by taking captives for rituals of human sacrifice) was rewarded with advancement in the ranks and the granting of visible status symbols to the soldier and his family. Most battles took place during the dry season, when there were few agricultural tasks to attend to; soldiers returned home to farm during the rainy season. Food and arms were supplied for each expedition by the general population of the city state (see city-state tax number 7, below), but apart from this activity it is difficult to find linkages between taxation and warfare for the Aztecs.

Compared to city states, the Triple Alliance Empire (also called the Aztec Empire or the Mexica Empire) is far more extensively documented.

[7] Berdan and de Durant-Forest (1980); [8] Berdan and Anawalt (1992). [9] Hansen (2000).
[10] Hicks (1996); Smith (1986).

As a result, most scholarly analyses of Aztec political economy focus on the empire, with little concern for patterns at the city-state level. I have long argued, however, that city states were more important polities in the lives of the Aztec people than was the empire, and that attention should be directed at this level to redress the imbalance in the scholarly literature.[11]

The Triple Alliance Empire was established by three city states (Tenochtitlan, Texcoco, and Tlacopan) upon the defeat of the earlier Tepanec Empire (based in Azcapotzalco) in 1428. The imperial armies quickly began a program of expansion out of the Basin of Mexico, and by the time Cortés arrived in 1519 the empire covered some 170,000 square km, with several million subjects. The empire ruled through indirect methods for the most part, using what scholars refer to as "hegemonic control."[12] Most local rulers were left in power so long as they made regular payments to Tenochtitlan. These payments are called "tribute" by Aztec scholars, but it seems clear that they in fact conform to standard definitions of "tax."

The Aztec period (*c.* 1100 to 1519) saw a tremendous population surge throughout central Mexico, accompanied by agricultural intensification in the form of canal irrigation, hillside terracing, and raised fields (a highly productive system of swamp cultivation). By 1519 the regional population density was on the order of 100 to 150 persons per square km.[13] Land was controlled by nobles, who granted access to commoner farmers through a variety of mechanisms. In Morelos, an area with particularly detailed documentation (census enumerations from shortly after the Spanish conquest), the system combined elements of sharecropping and rent. Commoner households provided a portion of their harvest to the landowner, as well as labor service (see discussion below).[14]

On the basis of both written and archaeological data, two categories of craft producers have been identified. Luxury goods were produced by full-time specialists who worked for royal and noble patrons, often in royal palaces. Utilitarian goods, on the other hand, were produced by independent part-time artisans in their homes (typically farmers, working during the dry season), who sold their wares in periodic markets. The Aztec economy was highly commercialized, with several forms of money (principally cotton textiles and cacao beans), at least two types of professional merchant, and a system of periodic marketplaces. The central market of

[11] Smith (2000; 2008; 2012).
[12] Berdan *et al.* (1996); Hassig (1985; 1988), following Luttwak (1976).
[13] Sanders (1976); Smith (1994). [14] Carrasco (1972).

Tenochtitlan (located in Tlatelolco, the northern sector of the island capital) greatly impressed Cortés and the other conquerors with its size and complexity (tens of thousands of participants daily), and several extensive first-hand descriptions survive.[15]

Fiscal scholarship on the Aztecs

Prior scholarship on Aztec taxation and its fiscal context is quite limited and inadequate. Understanding has been held back by the adherence of many writers to unproductive theoretical frameworks, such as the Asiatic mode of production,[16] and Polanyi's distorted view of ancient economies.[17] These perspectives, which long dominated Aztec studies, portrayed Aztec political and economic organization as much less complex, with stronger state domination, than most current models suggest. Echoes of this primitivist bias are still heard, however, in the continuing use of the term "tribute" for what were clearly taxes. The origins of this usage are understandable; native terms for various types of tax were described in early Spanish sources as "tribute" (*tributo*). Although on one level it matters little what term we use for a particular historical practice or institution, on another level the avoidance of the term "tax" by scholars has contributed to limiting the range of theoretical and comparative frameworks that have been applied to the Aztecs.

A number of scholars have made important contributions to the study of particular aspects of the Aztec tax system, but these scholars have failed to step back and view the fiscal system as an integrated whole. The major prior studies include Teresa Rojas Rabiela's research on corvée and other labor taxes;[18] studies of imperial taxation by Frances Berdan,[19] José Luis de Rojas,[20] and others; and analyses of individual aspects of the tax system in the polity of the imperial co-capital, Texcoco.[21] In this chapter I build on this work to produce the first comprehensive description of Aztec taxation at the city-state and imperial levels. I organize the data into eleven categories (Table 3.1): three types of imperial tax, and eight types of city-state tax. This is a provisional scheme, pending further research and insights from Aztec specialists and comparative fiscal specialists alike.

[15] Rojas (1986). [16] For discussion, see Offner (1981). [17] For discussion, see Smith (2004).
[18] Rojas Rabiela (1979; 1984; 1986). [19] Berdan (1976; 1992a). [20] Rojas (1986).
[21] Hicks (1978; 1984; 2012); Offner (1981; 1983).

Table 3.1 *Types of taxes in Aztec central Mexico*

Imperial taxes		City-state taxes	
I-1	Triple Alliance tax system	C-1	Land tax
I-2	Triple Alliance gift tribute system	C-2	Rent on royal estates
I-3	Conquest-state tax system	C-3	Rotational labor
		C-4	Public works corvée
		C-5	Military corvée
		C-6	Market tax
		C-7	Military supply tax
		C-8	Labor by youths in the telpochcalli

Imperial taxes

Research on Aztec taxation has been dominated by an overwhelming focus on imperial taxes as described in the surviving written tribute records (what I call tax I-1). The *Matrícula de Tributos*[22] is a pre-Spanish pictorial list of taxes paid by the provinces of the Triple Alliance Empire. Two decades after the Spanish conquest this information was copied into the composite document known as the *Codex Mendoza*,[23] intended for the king of Spain. The painted pages in this document were annotated with Spanish-language glosses and a brief explanatory text. The relationship between these two documents and a parallel textual version of imperial taxes[24] is a topic of considerable scholarship.[25] Here I rely on the *Codex Mendoza* as the most informative primary source on imperial taxation, acknowledging the fact that research on comparisons with the other documents still holds promise. I do not review all the relevant literature; well-studied topics, such as the geographic origins of tax goods, or the food supply of Tenochtitlan, are of less relevance for present purposes. In addition to imperial tax 1, I also review briefly the Triple Alliance gift tribute system (tax I-2), and a related but poorly understood type of tax that existed simultaneously with the first two (tax I-3).

Tax I-1: Triple Alliance tax system

After an area was conquered by the Triple Alliance armies, imperial agents negotiated with local rulers to establish the tax that would be imposed. Provincial areas were organized into provinces with a head city, and tax was

[22] Anders, Jansen, and Reyes García (1997). [23] Berdan and Anawalt (1992).
[24] Scholes and Adams (1957).
[25] Batalla Rosado (2007); Berdan (1992a); Mohar Betancourt (1978).

Figure 3.1 Tax for the province of Huaxtepec, as listed in the *Codex Mendoza* (reproduced with permission from Berdan and Anawalt 1992: vol. IV, 54–5, ff. 24v, 25r); the rows of signs on the left and bottom are the constituent towns

assessed by province. The *Codex Mendoza* contains one or more pages listing the tax for each province. Figure 3.1 shows the tax list for the province of Huaxtepec, located in the modern Mexican state of Morelos.[26] The towns included in the province are indicated by toponyms along the left and bottom sides of the page; the top sign is the capital, Huaxtepec. The remaining signs portray the items provided; the goods and quantities are listed in Table 3.2. At the top left are ten depictions of cotton textiles (five different types), each with a feather indicating 400 items. These were paid semi-annually, resulting in an annual total of 8,000 textiles, which served as money in the Aztec economy. Also shown are forty-six warrior costumes with feather-decorated shields, paid annually (the rectangular flags indicate twenty items). At lower right are two large bins of grain that stand for four bins, paid annually. Finally 2,000 gourd bowls and 8,000 pieces of bark paper were paid semi-annually. The annual

[26] Berdan and Anawalt (1992: vol. IV, 54–5).

Table 3.2 *Annual imperial tax receipts for the province of Huaxtepec*

Item	Quantity	Item	Quantity
Staple foodstuffs, bins		**Textiles**	
Maize	1	Loincloths	800
Amaranth	1	Women's tunics and skirts	800
Beans	1	Large white mantas	4,800
Chia	1	White mantas with multicolored borders	800
Utilitarian goods		Diagonally divided mantas	800
Red and yellow varnished gourd bowls	4,000	**Warriors' costumes**	
Sheets (or reams) of native paper	16,000	Red warrior costumes with shields, type 1	20
		Red warrior costumes with shields, type 2	20
		Other warrior costumes with shields	6

Source: Berdan and Anawalt (1992: vol. IV, 54–5, f. 25r).

income from all provinces (Table 3.3) added up to a substantial quantity of goods, including 128,000 textiles.[27]

Officials called *calpixque* were in charge of collecting, transporting, and receiving the tribute from each province. *Calpixque* was a generic term for "tax collector," and in this chapter I identify five types: three at the imperial level, and two at the city-state level. There is a frustrating lack of systematic information on the imperial *calpixque* and the organization of imperial tax collection.[28] Some sources mention two senior *calpixque* for each province: one stationed in the provincial capital and one in Tenochtitlan. The Spanish text in the *Codex Mendoza* contains contradictory information, in some cases suggesting that a *calpixque* was stationed in each of the constituent towns (that is, in all twenty-six towns in Figure 3.1), and in other cases mentioning only an official in the

[27] Berdan (1992a). I am relying here on Berdan's analysis of the *Codex Mendoza*, but other interpretations produce different quantifications that could change the amounts dramatically. José Luis de Rojas (personal communication), for example, argues – with some justification – that the payments were made quarterly instead of semi-annually; and Juan José Batalla Rosado (personal communication) favors the interpretation that the textiles depicted should be counted as bundles of twenty items, not individual items. These two changes could increase the annual textile quota of Huaxtepec from 8,000 items to 320,000 items – a significant alteration.

[28] As discussed by Berdan (1996: 122–4).

Table 3.3 *Annual tax receipts of the Aztec Empire*

Item	Quantity	Item	Quantity
Staple foodstuffs, bins:		***Items for ritual***	
Maize	28	Copper bells	80
Beans	21	Rubber, balls	16,000
Chia	21	Copal, unrefined balls	64,000
Amaranth	18	Copal, baskets of white incense	3,200
Textiles:		Yellow, ocher, pans	40
(15 distinct types listed)	128,000	***Other plant and animal products:***	
Other food items:		Seashells	1,600
Chile, loads	1,600	Live eagles	2 or more
Pots or jars maguey honey	1,600	Jaguar skins	40
Pots or jars bees' honey	2,200	Deerskin	3,200
Salt, "loaves"	4,000	Liquidambar, jars	100
Pinolli, baskets	160	Liquidambar, cakes	1,000
Cacao, loads	680	***Jewelry and precious stones:***	
Cacao, ground, in baskets	160	Lip plugs	82
Utilitarian goods:		Amber	2
Cotton, loads	4,400	Turquoise	15
Lime, loads	16,800	Jade beads, strung	19
Cochineal, bags	63	Jade stones	3
Wood beams and planks	14,400	Gold dust, in bowls	60
Carrying frames	800	Gold bars and disks	70
Firewood, loads	4,800	Other gold items	5
Reed mats and seats	16,000	***Feathers and feather objects:***	
Paper, loads	32,000	"Bunches" of rich-colored feathers	4
Canes for spears	32,000	Feathered headpieces	2
Smoking canes	32,000	Back device of yellow feathers	1
Other canes	16,000	Feather down, bags	20
Gourd bowls (*xicalli*)	17,600	Bird skins	160
Pottery bowls (*tecomatl*)	2,400	***Other:***	
Copper axes	560	Enemy warriors	unspecified

Source: Berdan (1992b).

head town of the province. In a few cases, local rulers were deposed and an official called a *tlacochcaltectli* was sent to govern a province and to collect the imperial taxes.[29] In most cases, however, local rulers were left in power. It seems logical to assume that local kings – in both the provincial head town and in the individual city states that made up a province – organized much of the tax collection efforts.[30]

The payments recorded in the *Codex Mendoza* fit most definitions of taxation. For example:

[29] Ramírez de Fuenleal (1870). [30] Smith (1994).

> When compared to tributes and tariffs, taxes stand out as steady and regular disbursements. Their payment is based on the calendar, not on particular events or on the arrival of certain commodities. In contrast to tributes, taxes are normally recurrent, predictable, routinized, and based on statutory obligations.[31]

Aztec payments conform to this definitional in all aspects, except perhaps that of "statutory obligations." The Aztec legal system lacked written codes, but one can assume that the requirement to pay imperial taxes was equivalent to a statutory obligation in Western legal systems. Failure to pay was considered a rebellion on the part of a province, and led to punitive military actions. Offner discusses the Aztec legal system.[32] The collection schedule and details about the *calpixque* are discussed below.

Tax I-2: Triple Alliance gift tribute system

A second system of imperial administration was implemented in the distant areas of the empire, particularly along enemy frontiers. The provincial areas administered in this system were initially called "strategic provinces" by the group that first identified this system;[33] this term was used as an alternative to the "tributary provinces" that paid tax I-1 described above. Nevertheless, a better term for these frontier polities is client states, based on their similarity to the client states in the eastern Roman Empire.[34] These were independent city states that were not organized into "provinces." Their relationship to the Triple Alliance was less formal than the polities included in the *Codex Mendoza*.

Aztec client states typically provided military support for imperial armies, sometimes by staffing border fortresses. They were not included in the tax lists, and in some sources it is stated explicitly that they did not pay tax (*tributo*) but, rather, gave gifts to the emperor.[35] Table 3.4 lists the available data on the types of items given by the client states. There is no surviving register of these payments; these (very incomplete) data were assembled from local documentary sources, particularly the *Relaciones*

[31] Tarschys (1988: 7). [32] Offner (1983). [33] Berdan *et al.* (1996).

[34] Among the traits shared with Roman client states were the provision of gifts to the emperor; the lack of regular taxes; a general lack of imperial interference in local affairs; and military roles related to their position along enemy frontiers, such as the provision of troops and supplies: Braund (1984: 55–6); Sands (1908).

[35] Smith (1996: 147).

Table 3.4 *Types of tribute goods from the client states*

Item	No. states	Item	No. states
Military supplies and support:		Foodstuffs:	
Soldiers	6	Maize	2
Weapons	3	Salt	1
Supplies for garrisons	9	Turkeys and deer	6
Transport and other services[a]	6	Other goods:	
Luxury goods:		Textiles	11
Gold dust	7	Captives for sacrifice	5
Gold jewelry	3	Liquidambar	2
Precious stones	6	Wood	2
Feathers	5	Other rare goods[b]	5
Unspecified luxury goods	1	Unspecified goods	10

Notes:
[a] This category includes unspecified personal service.
[b] Goods that were each provided by one town: cochineal dye; wax and salt; flowers; pelts; lime powder.
Source: Smith (1996: 148).

Geográficas de Indias.[36] These payments emphasized military service and goods, luxuries, and textiles. The biggest differences from the tax levies in the *Codex Mendoza* are the smaller emphasis on textiles and the greater relative emphasis on luxury goods and military service. The payments by client kings, phrased in the sources as "gifts," fit Tarschys's definition of tribute: "variable levies extracted at irregular intervals."[37]

Tax I-3: conquest-state tax system

This tax system describes payments made by subordinate kings to more powerful kings. The Triple Alliance tax systems (taxes I-1 and I-2) almost certainly developed out of this system, which remains very poorly documented. There were several small empires ruled by Aztec kings prior to the formation of the Triple Alliance in 1428, including polities ruled from Azcapotzalco and Texcoco in the Basin of Mexico Cuauhnahuac in Morelos and Calixtlahuaca/Matlatzinco in the Toluca Valley; I use the term "conquest state" here to distinguish between these smaller empires and the Triple Alliance Empire. As the Triple Alliance was formed and grew, each of the three co-capitals maintained a conquest state of its own,

[36] Acuña (1984–88). [37] Tarschys (1988).

separate from the provincial organization of the Triple Alliance. These four separate systems overlapped in territory and in organization, and their disentanglement has presented major obstacles for scholars, particularly because early Spanish writers often confused the systems. Two major analyses of Aztec imperialism illustrate differing approaches to this problem. The authors of *Aztec Imperial Strategies*[38] deliberately ignore the smaller structures in order to come to an understanding of the Triple Alliance and its broader economic and social context, whereas Pedro Carrasco devotes an entire book[39] to disentangling the four systems on the level of specific towns and payments.

Although Carrasco largely succeeded in establishing the existence of the three conquest states under the Triple Alliance, it is still not possible to document the principles of their fiscal organization in any detail. It appears that in most ways they were organized like the Triple Alliance in terms of the kinds of goods that were paid and the presence of *calpixque* as tax collectors. In the state of Morelos, I have documented six conquest states at the time of the Spanish conquest.

Each of the Morelos conquest states was converted into an *encomienda* by Hernando Cortés. I have used descriptions of early colonial *encomienda* payments[40] to infer the types and quantities of cotton textiles paid in taxes to these polities.[41] Table 3.5 shows my quantitative reconstruction of this system (this is model 2 from that source); readers can consult the original paper for the gory details. The conquest-state tax income is assumed to include two components: tax for the local king (line E.i) and the Triple Alliance taxes as recorded in the *Codex Mendoza* (lines D and E.ii). The "tax rate" is the ratio of tax paid out to the Triple Alliance to the total tax collected. The city-state taxes here are calculated as portions of the total taxes collected in each conquest state, and the assumption of an average tax rate of 0.40 allows the calculation of average tax income of the city states (line I) and total tax collected (city-state and conquest-state levels) within each conquest state.[42]

City-state taxes

Because Aztec city states pre-dated the formation of the conquest states and the Triple Alliance, it is likely that the imperial taxes described above developed out of preexisting systems of taxation at the city-state level. Data on

[38] Berdan *et al.* (1996). [39] Carrasco (1999b). [40] Riley (1973: appendix). [41] Smith (1994).

[42] The calculated tax rates for conquest states (Table 3.2) range from 0.234 to 0.391. I assume that city-state kings were able to hold on to a larger portion of their local tax receipts in comparison with the rulers of conquest states, and thus I used an estimated tax rate of 0.40 for the city-state level.

Table 3.5 *Quantitative reconstruction of conquest-state taxes in Morelos*

	Huaxtapec province				
Category	Cuauhnahuac	Tepoztlan	Yauhtepec	Huaxtepec	Yacapixtlan
Attributes of conquest states					
A. Total population	230,300	39,000	69,300	79,900	106,400
B. Total commoner households	30,500	5,160	9,180	10,580	14,090
C. No. of subject city states	27	0	5	10	10
Conquest-state tax income					
D. Tax to the Triple Alliance	16,000	3,200	3,200	3,200	3,200
E. Total tax collected:	41,353	11,050	11,050	13,702	8,186
i. For the conquest state	25,353	7,850	7,850	10,502	4,986
ii. For theTriple alliance	16,000	3,200	3,200	3,200	3,200
F. Tax rate (D/E)	0.387	0.290	0.290	0.234	0.391
City-state tax income					
G. Average tax to the conquest state (E/C)	1,532	11,050	2,210	1,370	819
H. Tax rate (estimated)	0.40	0.40	0.40	0.40	0.40
I. Average tax collected (G/H)	3,830	27,625	5,525	3,425	2,048
J. Total tax collected (E/H)	103,383	27,625	27,625	34,255	20,465
Household tax burden					
K. Average annual burden (J/B)	3.4	5.4	3.0	3.2	1.5

Source: Smith (1994: model 2).

these taxes are much more scattered in the sources, and have been the target of far less scholarly attention, than the imperial taxation system. Taxation was deeply engrained in many aspects of Aztec society. In 1532 a Spanish administrator, Sebastian Ramírez de Fuenleal (1870: 256–7), commented of the natives that "the activity of paying taxes is so well understood, that I expect they will be paying taxes in gold and silver in no time" [author's translation]. I have identified eight types of taxes at the city-state level (Table 3.1). It is possible that several of these are alternative descriptions of a single kind of tax and might be combined or organized differently as new data appear.

Tax C-1: land tax

The most fundamental and widespread form of payment in Aztec central Mexico was rent on agricultural land. As noted above, land was controlled by nobles, who allowed commoners to use their land in exchange for rent in goods and service.[43] A portion of these goods was passed on to the city-state as tax. City-state officials recorded these payments in terms of the *calpolli*, a group of commoners who lived near one another, were subject to the same noble, and organized a number of local activities in common.[44] In rural areas a *calpolli* was a village or town, and in urban settings a *calpolli* was a neighborhood or district. There were two hierarchical levels of *calpolli* in the Morelos census documents: small *calpolli* had some twenty to thirty households, and large *calpolli* were composed of several small *calpolli* and had some 150 households.[45] Membership in a *calpolli* provided a household with access to farmland. The census documents describe payments from individual households to their controlling noble, who then evidently turned a portion over to the Spanish authorities; it can be inferred that this latter payment went to the city-state king prior to 1519.

[43] In this and subsequent sections I depend heavily on documents from the Mexican state of Morelos. Some of the most detailed documentation on local economic and social phenomena anywhere in central Mexico is found in a series of house-by-house census enumerations, recorded in Nahuatl shortly after the Spanish conquest. These documents and their scholarly potential are discussed by Carrasco (1964b; 1976b) and Smith (1993). Although scholars have identified regional variation in social structure (Lockhart 1992) and in the degree of collective government institutions (Fargher, Heredia Expinoza, and Blanton 2011), there is far less information on land and taxes from other areas. In the absence of such documentation, I use the Morelos data as the standard for describing taxes C-1 and C-2.

[44] The nature and significance of the *calpolli* have been the subject of an extensive literature, much of it polemic and based on limited information. We now know that there was regional variation and that some of the key Spanish sources were seriously misinformed about the *calpolli*. The history of debate is summarized by Offner (1983: 163–75). My information is based primarily on Carrasco's analyses of the Morelos census data, on Lockhart's analysis of regional patterns, and on information from Sahagún, Durán, and other standard colonial sources (Smith and Novic 2012: 1–26).

[45] Friedman (2009); Smith (1993).

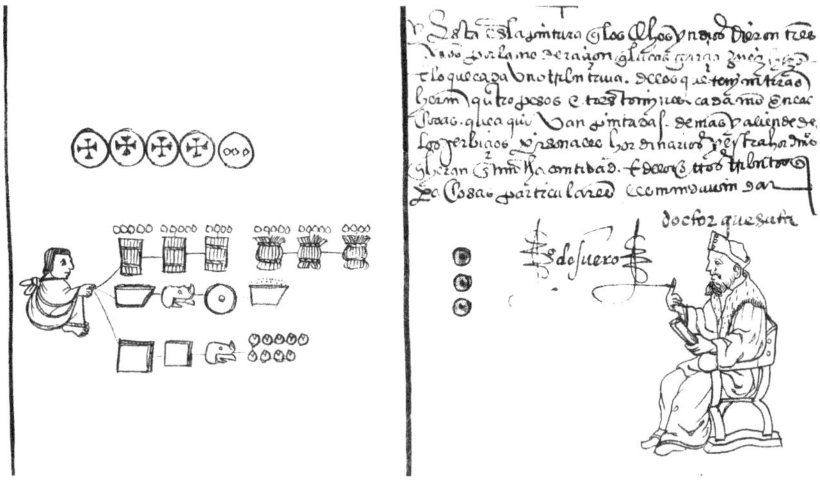

Figure 3.2 Goods paid by a *calpolli* to a Spaniard ("Doctor Quezada") in the sixteenth century (reproduced with permission from the *Tributos de Coyoacán* [Batalla Rosado 2002]); this payment was a continuation of the basic Aztec land tax (tax C-1)

City-state fiscal records, on the other hand, consist of tax receipts from individual *calpolli*. Some *calpolli*, along with some commoner households that did not belong to a *calpolli*, were subject directly to the king; their payments are separated out here as tax C-2: rent on royal estates.

A variety of goods were paid for the land tax. Figure 3.2, a colonial-period record of payments by a *calpolli* in Coyoacán to a Spaniard, illustrates these goods. The circles at the top represent Spanish coins (four pesos and three *tomines*). The next row shows fifteen loads of firewood and fifteen loads of silage. Row three has a bowl or basket of uncertain contents; a turkey; a coin; and a basket of salt. The lowest row shows two cotton textiles, a turkey, and nine batches of twenty cacao beans each.[46] These same goods are depicted and described repeatedly in early colonial documents, along with foodstuffs and a variety of utilitarian items (ceramic vessels, pine pitch, etc.). I interpret these payments to Spaniards as representing Spanish-period transformations of Aztec tax payments originally made to the city state, as organized by the *calpolli* and its dominant noble. Instead of coins, there would have been a larger number of textiles; forage (for horses) was another Spanish innovation. The items

[46] For discussion, see Batalla Rosado (2002) and León-Portilla (1971).

paid in local land taxes emphasized subsistence and utilitarian goods to a greater extent than the imperial tax goods (Tables 3.3 and 3.4). Nevertheless, the presence of cotton and cacao, along with Spanish coins, shows that a portion of local taxes was paid in money (see the discussion of the noble Molotecatl below).

These payments were assessed by household head, based on the amount of land worked by the household. Commoners without land (2 to 5 percent of the population in Morelos)[47] did not make these payments, though they probably participated in various labor exactions (see below). Numerous sources are in agreement that tax amounts were based on land, including the Morelos census documents,[48] various documents cited by Lockhart[49] and Gibson,[50] and statements by Spanish chroniclers. For example, Fray Juan de Torquemada noted, "[I]n that district they paid tribute in accordance with the amount of land owned" [author's translation].[51] The tax rate is difficult to reconstruct. In one place Carrasco[52] claims that peasants paid one-third of their harvest, presumably basing this on his earlier analyses of the Morelos documents. To my knowledge, however, no one has analyzed these documents to determine the rates for individual households.

Some information on the organization of payments is provided by the case of Molotecatl, a noble whose estate in the town of Yautepec is described in one of the census documents. The document is translated by Carrasco,[53] who provides a bilingual text (Nahuatl and Spanish) and a brief analysis and discussion. Molotecatl was in charge of a small *calpolli* with ten dependent households, to which he distributed 228 of his 600 *brazas* of land (the *braza* was a unit of measure 2.5 meters in length). The remaining 372 *brazas* were probably worked by his landless dependent laborers who did not belong to the *calpolli* (this latter category resembles medieval European serfs). Molotecatl's payments to the Yautepec *encomienda* can be interpreted as a continuation of pre-Spanish payments to the local city state.[54] Molotecatl paid ninety-four cotton textiles, 1800 cacao beans, thirteen turkeys, and several other food items, in addition to labor service (provided by his dependants). These goods must have constituted either the tax obligations of his ten dependent households, or perhaps the combined obligations of Molotecatl himself and his dependent households.

[47] See Carrasco (1976b: 109). [48] Carrasco (1976a). [49] Lockhart (1992).
[50] Gibson (1964: 198, 518). [51] Torquemada (1975–83: vol. IV, 333). [52] Carrasco (1999b: 225).
[53] Carrasco (1972). [54] Smith (1994: 336–7).

Molotecatl's tenants paid him seven textiles, plus food and labor services. This can be considered the non-tax rent on their lands. The ninety-four textiles that Molotecatl paid out to higher authorities were almost certainly produced by his dependent commoner women. The census documents (and other sources) indicate that commoner women went to the house of their noble patrons to provide two types of labor service: kitchen labor and textile production.[55]

Although many of the details remain obscure, the example of Molotecatl and his *calpolli* illustrates several points about the organization of the land tax:

- commoners made payments in exchange for use of the land, which they received from their local noble;
- landless laborers did not pay taxes;
- all, or a portion, of the goods paid ended up as taxes to the local king; and
- nobles who controlled the *calpolli* land were involved somehow in organizing the collection and payment of taxes from their commoner subjects.

The role of nobles in organizing tax payments from their dependent *calpolli* members should be kept separate from their own tax obligations. A major source of confusion in the literature has been the erroneous notion that Aztec nobles did not pay taxes. Several of the Spanish chroniclers express this error, which is repeated in textbooks and other secondary sources. Lockhart's research[56] is definitive, however, in showing that nobles did indeed pay taxes (termed "tribute" in most works); the faulty statements originated when colonial-period Aztec nobles tried to fool the Spaniards by calling on fabricated "ancient traditions" in order to lighten their burdens under Spanish rule. "Even if they did not use the calpolli mechanism, the lords were delivering tribute assessed on their lands in the same manner as calpolli members."[57]

One aspect of tax collection at the *calpolli* level that is not clear from the case of Molotecatl is the role of *calpixque* (tax collectors). The census documents identify some individual *calpolli* members as having low-level administrative duties, including helping with tax collection, but specific titles are not specified. There are few details on the specific duties of these officials. In Spanish sources, they are called heads of *calpolli* and labeled *calpixque*.[58] In my discussion of *calpixque* below, these would be *calpixque* type E (see below).

[55] Ibid.: 337. [56] Lockhart (1992: 106). [57] Ibid.: 106–7.
[58] Durán (1967: vol. I, 116; vol. II, 182); Ramírez de Fuenleal (1870: 255).

Tax C-2: rent on royal estates

This tax is identical to the payments described above, except for the fact that the land involved is owned by the king and not by lower nobles such as Molotecatl. Thus payments on this land can be considered state revenue. These royal lands are similar in function to the royal demesne of medieval Europe.[59] There is little direct information on this kind of tax, although one of the Morelos census documents provides some context. In the city state of Tepoztlan, the king's 201 subject households constituted 9.1 percent of the total population of the polity (and 35.5 percent of the population of the large *calpolli* centered on the capital). With roughly 10 percent of the total population subject directly to the king, this was a significant source of revenue for the king.

Tax C-3: rotational labor

The category of rotational labor was closely linked to the land tax discussed above. It is treated as a separate category here because, on the one hand, its administration and significance were somewhat distinct from the land tax and, on the other hand, it seems to differ from corvée labor (tax C-4, below). Spanish sources seem to confuse rotational labor with corvée, making them difficult to disentangle; I follow Frederic Hicks (1984) in separating them. There were two types of rotational labor: payments to nobles and payments to the king. Rotational labor refers to the process whereby individual social groups (households or *calpolli*) contributed labor to a given task or setting consecutively, or in rotation.

C-3A: rotational labor for nobles

I use this category to describe the labor portion of the basic household tax levy described above. It is not a "land tax" because it was paid by all households, both those that had land and those that were landless. Most descriptions of early colonial *encomienda* payments (described above) include labor in addition to goods. As noted above, women's labor for kitchen tasks and textile production was a crucial part of this system. Two of the Morelos census communities (Huitzillilan and Quauhchichinola)[60] mention labor tasks specifically required of newly arrived people who did not yet have land: "helping to feed people in Cuernavaca" (the *encomienda* seat, some 20 km distant) and "looking for cotton." As discussed by Cline,[61] the meanings of these tasks remains obscure.

[59] Ormrod and Barta (1995). [60] See Cline (1993). [61] Ibid.

C-3B: rotational labor for kings

This tax consisted of personal service performed at the royal palace. A study of rotational labor at Texcoco by Hicks[62] is the most extensive analysis of this tax. Individual *calpolli* alternated in providing workers who supplied firewood, charcoal, and mats to the palace; they also swept, carried water, and did whatever errands were needed.[63] Much of this labor was supplied by households that resided on land owned by the king, and this was their primary tax burden. In the words of Torquemada, "There were many peoples who did not work and who had no other thing to do but serve the palace and government" [author's translation].[64] In another passage, the chronicler notes that such rotational labor was provided by both men and women.[65] The workers were supervised by *calpixque* (probably type E). Unfortunately, there is little information about the level of labor required in this tax (person-days per household per year), which Hicks is careful to distinguish from corvée.[66]

Tax C-4: public works corvée

After the Spanish conquest, the colonial authorities quickly adapted the Aztec system of corvée to their needs, and this was the major labor source for building Mexico City and other Spanish cities. For this reason, Spanish documentation of the system is relatively abundant, and there is scholarly debate about the extent to which the details of the Spanish system apply to the Aztec period. The major scholarly studies that use colonial data to reconstruct Aztec practices are the works of Rojas Rabiela[67] and Pérez Rocha;[68] in addition, there is a large scholarly literature on colonial labor organization that I have not consulted.

The public works corvée (called *coatequitl*) was a universal obligation of all commoner households, regardless of whether they belonged to a *calpolli* or not. Workers were organized into teams or gangs based on their *calpolli* or their place origin,[69] but according to Rojas Rabiela[70] individual teams did not map directly onto local social groups. Figure 3.3 illustrates the labor obligations of three *calpolli* in the city state of Tepetlaoztoc.

Numerous primary sources, including those describing both colonial-period and Aztec practices, attest to the existence of a system of organization based on teams of twenty and 100 workers. A *centecpantli* was a team of

[62] Hicks (1984). [63] Ibid.; Lockhart (1992: 17). [64] Torquemada (1975–83: vol. II, 232).
[65] Ibid.: vol. IV, 333. [66] Hicks (1984: 148). [67] Rojas Rabiela (1979; 1984; 1986).
[68] Pérez Rocha (1978; 2008). [69] Gibson (1964: 222). [70] Rojas Rabiela (1979: 45).

Figure 3.3 Tax levies for public works corvée for three *calpolli* in the city state of Tepetlaoztoc (redrawn by Jacqueline Fox from the Codez Kingsborough [Valle 1995: f. 5, lám. A]); the upper registers contain the name glyphs for the communities; the kneeling figure with a horizontal digging stick is the glyph for public works corvée, with the number of laborers indicated by the symbols above their heads (the quantities are twenty-one, fifteen, and fifteen)

twenty workers, supervised by an official called a *centecpanpixqui*; the larger teams of 100 workers were called *macuiltecpantli* (and their supervising official was a *macuiltecpanpixqui*). The chronicler Diego Durán described the chain of command, in which officials at the royal palace (high-level city-state *calpixque*, type D) notified successively lower-ranking officials (probably the labor bosses mentioned above), who then mobilized their workers for the task at hand.[71] These lower-level labor bosses were similar to, or perhaps examples of, lower-ranking city-state *calpixque* (type E).

The system of teams of twenty and 100 workers is described in numerous sources on Mexico City/Tenochtitlan and the Puebla-Tlaxcala region.[72] Pérez Rocha cites documents from Coyoacán and Tacuba (towns now part of Mexico City) that provide actual counts of workers in corvée labor teams from early in the Spanish colonial period.[73] These figures vary considerably, with little correspondence to groups of twenty workers. For example, the work teams from seven *calpolli* in Coyoacán ranged from fourteen to seventy-seven workers, with a mean of 34.0 and a standard deviation of 22.5, while those from Tacubaya ranged from seven to seventeen workers,

[71] Diego Durán (1967: vol. I, 116). [72] Rojas Rabiela (1979). [73] Pérez Rocha (2008).

with a mean of 12.3 and a standard deviation of 3.6.[74] Pérez Rocha concludes that the idea of twenty-person work teams was a Spanish innovation that had yet to be applied in these towns, and not an Aztec practice. Given the extensive documentation of this practice, however, it seems more likely to me that the Coyoacán data reflect the typical distinction between ideal and real in human affairs, with the implication that the twenty-worker groups (whether or not they actually had twenty laborers) were indeed an Aztec institution.

The official Alonso de Zorita contrasted corvée labor in the Spanish colonial era (as grim and difficult work to be avoided if possible) with the institution in pre-conquest times. Workers were well treated, he claims, and "worked together with much merriment." People "went about their work, cheerfully and harmoniously."[75] It is difficult today to determine the extent to which Zorita may have been exaggerating. The Aztec situation was probably better than that described for corvée under the Achaeminid king Cyrus, when workers had to be locked up because they constantly fled and had to be hunted down by the authorities.[76] Aztec government was more collective or representative than Achaemenid rule,[77] but whether the Aztecs had merry work parties may perhaps be doubted.

Tax C-5: military corvée

The Aztec polities did not have standing armies. Troops were raised for individual campaigns of conquest or defense. All young males were obligated to serve in the army, whether of their local city state or the imperial army. Little is known of the details of recruitment and service, however. This was a significant corvée burden, but we have little information on the rules or periods of service involved.

Tax C-6: market tax

The conqueror Hernando Cortés was the first Spaniard to describe Aztec market taxes:

> At all the gateways to the city and at the places where these canoes are unloaded, which is where the greater part of the provisions enter the city, there are guards in huts who receive a *certum quid* of all that enters. I have not yet discovered whether this goes to the chief or to the city, but I think to

[74] Ibid.: 59. [75] Zorita (1963: 203). [76] MacGinnis (2003). [77] Blanton and Fargher (2008).

> the chief, because in other markets in other parts I have seen this tax paid to the ruler of the place.[78]

Durán stated that the market tax was divided between the king and the community.[79] Each market had two judges, who both heard suits about transactions and collected the market tax.[80]

Hicks infers that larger markets yielded more tax revenue than smaller markets.[81] Although this is a reasonable assumption, there are no direct data on tax revenues of different markets. Market tax records from Coyoacán shortly after the Spanish conquest give an idea of the nature of the market taxes, which were assessed in Spanish *tomines*.[82] Amounts ranged from ½ *tomin* (paid by the small bell makers and the warping frame makers) to 4 *tomines* (the pine torch splitters). Most merchants paid 1 *tomin* (for example, the tobacco sellers, obsidian blade sellers, and fish sellers) or 2 *tomines* (garment makers, broom sellers, and the Mexica boat people). The periods of payment are not indicated in this document.

Tax C-7: military supply tax

The fiscal aspects of Aztec warfare remain almost completely unexplored by Aztec scholars. One feature that is mentioned in several sources, however, is the provision of food and supplies for the army, and I treat this here as a separate tax. Some weapons were supplied by the state (from imperial armories in Tenochtitlan) and some were provided by each *calpolli* at the time of a campaign.[83] Food was accumulated from a variety of sources. Kings had some lands set aside for food for soldiers (for example: "large fields with which they sustained their households and maintained military personnel" [author's translation]).[84] Each *calpolli* was required to prepare food and equipment, and market vendors were singled out to contribute food. Finally, some food was obtained from towns along the travel routes of the troops.[85] This information is just about the sum of available documentation for the military supply tax.

Tax C-8: labor by youths in the telpochcalli

The *telpochcalli* is one of two types of schools in Aztec society; the other is the *calmecac*.[86] Each urban neighborhood (large *calpolli*) had a *telpochcalli*,

[78] Cortés (1986: 108). [79] Durán (1967: vol. I, 180). [80] Ramírez de Fuenleal (1870: 255).
[81] Hicks (1987). [82] Anderson, Berdan, and Lockhart (1976: 138–49). [83] Hassig (1988: 61).
[84] Torquemada (1975–83: vol. IV, 335). [85] Hassig (1988: 61–2). [86] Calnek (1988).

where young men learned a variety of practical and religious knowledge. As part of their training these youths reported to the palace for various labor tasks. At the palace, this labor was organized by a poorly understood institution known as a *cuicacalli* ("house of song"). In the words of the chronicler Bernardino de Sahagún: "Cuicacalli: there were the masters of the youths and the rulers of the youths, there established in order to oversee what was by way of work."[87]

Rojas Rabiela interprets the labor obligations of the *telpochcalli* students as a kind of training for some of the specialized tasks of the public works corvée,[88] and it might make sense to merge this category of tax with that category.

Organizational principles

Periods of tax collection

In the *Codex Mendoza*, the best-known Aztec tax record, some of the goods were paid annually and others were paid semi-annually;[89] the other imperial tax records, on the other hand, point to quarterly payments for tax I-1.[90] Other sources suggest that many taxes were paid quarterly. Figure 3.4 shows a segment of a pre-conquest tax register from the city state of Tlappa for seven quarters that include the year 1516. The Aztec year was divided into eighteen months of twenty days each (plus five additional days). The glyphs in the fourth column of the tax document are signs for four of the months, spread out through the year: "*Tlaloc* head" (*Etzalcualiztli*), "Brushes" (*Ochpaniztli*), "Banner" (*Panquetzaliztli*), and "*Xipe* head" (*Tlacaxipehualiztli*). Thus payments were made four times per year at intervals of eighty, 100, eighty, and 105 days. Each quarterly payment (columns 1 to 3) consisted of ten square gold bars, four rectangular gold bars, five triangular gold bars, five bowls of gold dust, and three cotton textiles.[91]

Barlow discusses this system of quarterly tax payment and gives several other examples of pictorial records that incorporate the four monthly glyphs to indicate payment dates.[92] For semi-annual payments, taxes would have been paid in *Ochpaniztli* and *Tlacaxipehualiztli*. Unfortunately, most descriptions of taxes do not indicate the periods of collection, perhaps

[87] Sahagún (1950–82: vol. VIII, 43). [88] Rojas Rabiela (1979: 51). [89] Berdan (1992b);
[90] José Luis de Rojas, personal communication.
[91] Tlapa was an area of gold mining and production. It is not completely clear which tax is recorded in this document. Gutiérrez, König, and Brito (2009) argue that this is a record of imperial taxes kept by provincial calpixque. See also Seler (1904: 144–8) and Vega Sosa (1991; 1994).
[92] Barlow (1943).

Figure 3.4 Portion of a tax record from the city state of Tlappa known as the Humboldt Fragment no. 1. This segment of a register over 4 meters long shows seven quarterly payments of gold and textiles (leftmost three columns), the month of payment (column 4), and the year and important historical events (rightmost column)

because this was well understood and did not need specification. But scattered references suggest that the four months shown in the Tlapa document were considered standard tax collection times.[93] Information from other parts of Mesoamerica suggests a similar schedule. For example, taxes in the Pokomam Maya area of highland Guatemala at the time of Spanish conquest were collected every eighty days.[94]

*Tax collectors (*calpixque*)*

A wide variety of administrative officials were called *calpixque*, and the written sources rarely distinguish them. There are no detailed descriptions of *calpixque* in the documentary sources, and the available information is fragmentary and scattered.[95] I have identified five types of *calpixque*, three at the imperial level and two at the city-state level (Table 3.6). This is a provisional scheme intended to clarify some of the confusion in the sources.

Imperial calpixque

Imperial *calpixque*, type A, were high-level government officials who operated in the imperial capital. There was one official in charge of receipts from each of the imperial provinces. These *calpixque* must have used the *Matrícula de Tributos* or similar pictorial records to check the payments that arrived in the capital two or four times a year. These officials were in charge of the storage and distribution of the tax goods. Carrasco and Hicks argue that these *calpixque* were nobles.[96]

Table 3.6 *Types of* calpixque *(tax collectors)*

Type	Duties	Class
Imperial level		
A	Receive and organize goods in Tenochtitlan	Noble
B	Ship goods from provincial capital	Noble
C	Collect goods in provincial city states	Commoner
City-state level		
D	Receive and organize goods at the royal palace	Commoner
E	Collect tax and carry out other official tasks in the *calpolli*	Commoner

[93] Ibid. [94] Miles (1957: 772).

[95] For general discussion, see Berdan (1996: 122–4) and Hicks (1978).

[96] Carrasco (1999b: 226); Hicks (2005).

Figure 3.5 Imperial *calpixque* (type B):
A – *calpixque* in Tlapa, Guerrero, depicted at the start of the lengthy register of taxes excerpted in Figure 3.4 (redrawn by Jacqueline Fox from the Azoyu/Humboldt Codex: Gutiérrez, König, and Brito 2009)
B – Mexica imperial official who might be a *calpixque* (reproduced with permission from Berdan and Anawalt 1992: vol. IV, 137)

Imperial *calpixque*, type B, were high-level government officials, probably nobles, who operated in the provincial head towns. There is little specific information about this category. Each province had one head tax collector (of type B) who worked with his counterpart stationed in the imperial capital (type A). Figure 3.5A shows a *calpixque* whose image was painted in a long fold-out tax register, receiving his first payment in the province of Tlapa in February 1487 (folio 1, position A2). This individual, dressed in rich clothing, is probably a noble *calpixque* of type B.

Imperial *calpixque*, type C, were lower-level government officials, probably commoners, who were stationed in individual provincial city states to organize the production, collection, and shipment of taxes. Carrasco notes: "Local sources indicate the existence of a hierarchy of tribute collectors in the tributary provinces" (he seems to be referring here to imperial *calpixque*, not city-state *calpixque*).[97] One difficulty in studying these officials derives from an inconsistency in the Spanish glosses of the *Codex Mendoza*. Descriptions of some provinces state that a *calpixque* was based in each of the towns of the province (for example, in each of the towns listed on the left and bottom of Figure 3.1), whereas this statement is omitted from the descriptions of most provinces. Given that

[97] Carrasco (1999b: 224).

the document was prepared in great haste, it would not be surprising if the scribe stopped adding this "boilerplate" text to the page for every province.

Carrasco believes that there was indeed an imperial *calpixque* in each of the several hundred towns in the *Codex Mendoza*,[98] basing this interpretation at least in part on a statement by Torquemada: "In every town there was a lord or official, who was a *regidor* and carried in his left hand a staff and in his right hand a fan, which were the signs that he was a royal official" [author's translation].[99] Torquemada used the term *tecuhtli* for these officials, which Carrasco translates as "steward or *tecuhtli*" in his paraphrase of Torquemada.[100] Rojas shows for the Tepeaca region of Puebla that *calpixque* were installed in a number of towns after the Mexica conquest, and that they had additional administrative and governing duties beyond imperial tax collection.[101]

Continuing with his English-language paraphrase of Torquemada, Carrasco notes that these lower-level town-based *calpixques* "reported to the accountants and stewards of the king [type B *calpixque*] on what they had collected and the people they had registered in the towns under their care. If they gave an inexact or falsified account, they suffered the death penalty, and even the people of their lineage were punished as relatives of traitors."[102] The type C *calpixque* were most likely commoners, not nobles,[103] and they were evidently not natives of the areas in which they worked.[104]

Figure 3.5B, from the *Codex Mendoza*,[105] shows an imperial official of Tenochtitlan who might be a *calpixque*. He is participating in a mission in a provincial area and is not labeled specifically as a *calpixque* (the Spanish gloss says "Officer and ambassador of the lord of Mexico"). He carries the wood staff and feather fan that are general insignias of imperial officials. The hands in which he carries them are the reverse of his three companions, and they match the hands specified in Torquemada's description of type C *calpixque*.[106] Although this is probably insufficient evidence to identify this official confidently as a *calpixque*,[107] it seems to be one of the best candidates for a pictorial representation of a Mexica or Triple Alliance *calpixque*.

There is another type of imperial official in provincial areas sometimes described as collecting tribute. These were governors, however, and should not be confused with *calpixque*. Various titles are noted for these officials, including *tlacochcaltectli*. Ramírez de Fuenleal lists three duties for these

[98] Ibid.: 75–6. [99] Torquemada (1975–83: vol. IV, 334–5). [100] Carrasco (1999b: 223).
[101] Rojas (1994). [102] Carrasco (1999b: 224), paraphrasing Torquemada (1975–83: vol. IV, 334).
[103] Carrasco (1999b: 226). [104] Ibid.; Sergheraert (2009: 366).
[105] Berdan and Anawalt (1992: vol. IV, 137, f. 66r). [106] Torquemada (1975–83: vol. IV, 334).
[107] Frances Berdan, personal communication, December 2009.

officials: (1) governing the polity for the emperor, (2) collecting taxes, and (3) organizing lower-level officials.[108] To confuse matters, the realms governed by these officials were sometimes called *calpixcazgo*. Carrasco discusses many examples of *calpixcazgo*, particularly those pertaining to the imperial co-capital Texcoco.[109] In several places, Hicks discusses these governors and argues that they should not be considered *calpixque*.[110] Sergheraert identifies several provinces listed as containing both an imperial governor and an imperial *calpixque*.[111]

City-state calpixque

A quote from the chronicler Durán shows the existence of multiple levels of *calpixque* at the city-state level:

> These orders came from the [royal] council and were carried to the chambers of the *calpixque* [type D], who immediately sent them to the officials of a village [type E], and from that village they were transmitted to another [type E], and from another to another.[112]

It is not difficult to isolate the highest level of city-state *calpixque* (type D), but below these a variety of officials were involved in tax collection, and these are more poorly documented. Here I categorize the lower-level city-state *calpixque* as type E, with the caveat that this may be a heterogeneous category that oversimplifies a complex situation.

City-state *calpixque*, type D, were appointed by, and worked for, the king and/or the royal council of the city state. Lockhart (1992: 43) calls them "middle-level officials."[113] Durán's description emphasizes their role in organizing corvée labor (and probably the rotational labor as well):

> These were like judges or heads of the wards in charge of the distribution of jobs and public works, such as building roads, cleaning the streets or canals, obtaining the necessary provisions for the community. These *calpixque* resided in these apartments, where usually they were to be found. They gathered to hear the decisions and commands of the royal council. To them were sent edicts, the laws, to be enforced.[114]

If these officials were indeed the heads of *calpolli* ("wards"), as stated by Durán, they must have headed the large *calpolli*. As analyzed by Lockhart, there was a limited number of large *calpolli* in each city state, and their commoner heads (not to be confused with the nobles who owned or

[108] Ramírez de Fuenleal (1870: 154). [109] Carrasco (1999b: 146–54). [110] Hicks (1992; 1994).
[111] Sergheraert (2009: 390–1). [112] Durán (1971: 201); original in Durán (1967: vol. I, 116).
[113] Lockhart (1992: 43). [114] Durán (1971: 201); original in Durán (1967: vol. I, 116).

Figure 3.6 City-state *calpixque* (probably type D) with 800 corvée laborers; the individual at right, in front of a palace, is the *calpixque*; the speech scroll is a symbol of royal authority; the head with a feather represents 400 workers, and each smaller head with a flag represents twenty workers; at top left is a temple, and the toponym for Tenochtitlan is at bottom left (reproduced with permission from the Codex San Andres [Galarza 1963: 74])

controlled their land) could easily have been the high-level *calpixque* within the city states.[115] The Spanish official Juan Pomar noted that "these stewards, who were called *calpixque*, were the ones in each town who administered the rents and tributes, turning them over to the king."[116] In the census from Tepoztlan, the first household head in each large *calpolli* served this role; his title is given as *onca tlapachoua*."[117] Figure 3.6 shows one of these officials. He is located in front of a palace with a speech scroll, addressing 800 laborers. (The use of written records by *calpixque* is discussed under type E.)

[115] Lockhart (1992: 15–20). [116] Pomar (1975: 7–8). [117] Carrasco (1964a: 187).

Hicks analyzes an early colonial lawsuit that provides insights into the pre-Spanish organization of type D *calpixque* in Texcoco (it is possible that these officials correspond to type B above, but it seems to me that they fit better in my type D).[118] These officials were commoners, and the office was passed from father to son. They collected taxes and brought them to the king. Part of their duties included making sure that specified commoners planted specified fields, whose yields went to the king. Other duties involved guarding community storehouses and war booty.[119]

City-state *calpixque*, type E, were minor functionaries within the *calpolli* (probably the small level of *calpolli*). In the words of Ramírez de Fuenleal: "They also had a type of official, which we call headmen [*principales*], of which there are two in each barrio [small *calpolli*]. These officials gathered together the barrio members to assign tribute obligations or to comply with whatever was ordered by the governor or other officials" [author's translation].[120] In the census from Tepoztlan, the first household head listed for each small *calpolli* was the official who collected taxes, although the term *calpixque* is not used.[121]

These lowest-level *calpixque* are probably the officials who maintained the pictorial records of the inhabitants of each small *calpolli*. Durán noted: "As soon as a child is born, he is registered with the heads of the barrios and with the captains."[122] There are also accounts that people were "registered" at the time of marriage, particularly males who were liable for public works corvée, tax C-4.[123] For an early colonial Spanish judicial hearing in Yecapixtla, Morelos, native officials of the town were instructed to bring their pictorial records containing population counts. The town officials assembled the *calpolli* officials (*calpules e tequitos de los barrios*), who brought their records of the people in their *calpolli*. The lawsuit states that twenty-seven such records were presented to the court.[124] These documents (Figure 3.7) contained information on household size and composition, land holdings, and tax obligations. The Morelos census documents are written versions (in Nahuatl) of this kind of pre-Spanish pictorial record.[125]

A Spanish official reported that type E *calpixque* were residents of the *calpolli* in which they served.[126] Lockhart calls them "ward officers," and suggests that they "are perhaps better imagined as citizens with some special duties than as functionaries. It appears that in preconquest times

118 Hicks (1978). 119 See also Hicks (2009). 120 Ramírez de Fuenleal (1870: 255).
121 Carrasco (1964a: 187). 122 Durán (1994: 309); original in Durán (1967: vol. II, 313).
123 Hicks (2009). 124 Visita (1946: 253).
125 For discussion, see Williams and Harvey (1997) and Harvey and Williams (1980).
126 Solórzano (1958: 127).

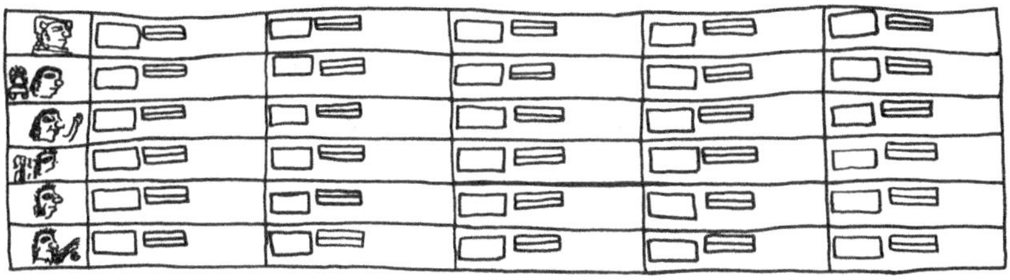

Figure 3.7 Fragment from a local census record showing household lands from Tlaquiltenango, Morelos; household heads are indicated in the left column, and different categories of land are shown in each of the four other columns; the rectangles, which probably signify plots of land, are filled with different colors in each column (redrawn by Jacqueline Fox, based on Vaillant 1933: plate XVII, fragment 63)

they were commonly named after the size of the unit with which they were charged."[127]

Recruitment and compensation

The scholarly consensus seems to be that the highest levels of *calpixque* (types A and B) were nobles, but all other types were commoners. It is not clear whether lower-level *calpixque* (type E) were selected by *calpolli* members or by city-state officials. Torquemada suggests that the higher-level city-state *calpixque* (type D) may have selected the lower-level officials,[128] but in the absence of additional documentation it seems equally likely that the type E *calpixque* were selected by their own *calpolli* members.

Next to nothing is known about the compensation of the *calpixque*. Hicks suggests that they (probably high-ranking city-state *calpixque*, type D) may have been given land and other goods by the king for their subsistence.[129] He bases this interpretation on a passage in Pomar, but the source is not at all clear on the matter.[130] Hicks also notes an emphasis in the document on the importance of loyalty by the *calpixque*.[131] Although the documentation does not permit us to specify the nature of compensation, much of the documentation does suggest that the imperial *calpixque* worked directly for the empire rather than as independent contractors, or tax farmers (see comments below).

[127] Lockhart (1992: 43). [128] Torquemada (1975–83: vol. IV, 332). [129] Hicks (1978: 146).
[130] Pomar (1975: 7–8). [131] Hicks (1978: 145).

Comparative discussion

In this section I provide some informal remarks relating the Aztec case to some of the key themes in the literature on comparative fiscal regimes;[132] see also Chapter 1.

Hudson's model

As noted in my introduction, the Aztec fiscal system seems to diverge considerably from those of the ancient economies of the Old World. Hudson provides the broadest study of ancient fiscal systems of the Old World, ranging from early Mesopotamia through Classical antiquity.[133] The Aztec case corresponds poorly to Hudson's nine-point scheme.

(1) ***Warfare was the largest absorber of economic surplus.*** Although we lack quantification for the Aztecs, it appears that war consumed only a modest portion of total production (see discussion below).

(2) ***Temple and palace activities were financed through ownership of their own resources, not through taxation in money or crops.*** The Aztecs did not have temple-based institutions as in the ancient Near East, and palaces raised funds through normal kinds of taxation activities.

(3) ***The first taxes were levied as tribute or forced gifts by conquering rulers.*** No evidence.

(4) ***Special levies were imposed in time of war.*** This was indeed the case for the Aztecs.

(5) ***Major civic spending programs fell on the richest members of society.*** There is no evidence for this in Aztec Mexico.

(6) ***State activities were organized through fiscal compartmentalization*** (that is, the lack of a comprehensive budget led to separate levies for individual activities). This probably fits the Aztec state, although we lack detail.

(7) ***An absence of public debt.*** Again, this probably applies to the Aztecs.

(8) ***Private debt was a significant problem, dealt with by "clean slate" programs.*** This does not seem to have been a major problem. Colonial-period sources mention cases of individual indebtedness (often with moral disapproval expressed by the Spanish friars), but there is no indication that it was a widespread or serious problem.

[132] See, for example, Bonney (1999), Coşgel and Miceli (2009), Kiser and Baer (2005), Kiser and Kane (2007), Ormrod and Barta (1995), Swedberg (2003), and Tarschys (1988).

[133] Hudson (2000).

(9) ***The wealthiest families were able to break free of fiscal obligations, leaving the tax burden on the poorer households.*** This does not fit the Aztec state, where nobles paid taxes alongside commoners.

Bonney and Ormrod's typology

The typology presented by Bonney and Ormrod is very Eurocentric.[134] Here is a quick evaluation of where I think the Aztec fiscal system would fit with respect to their four types.

(1) ***Closest to a tribute state*** (two features):
- credit structure; causes of instability.

(2) ***Closest to a domain state*** (seven features):
- central administration; local administration; method of financing; role in the economy; economic policy; public enterprises; social consequences.

(3) ***Intermediate between, or relating to both, a domain state and a tax state*** (five features):
- form of government; office holders; state responsibilities; revenues; accounting.

(4) ***Closest to a tax state*** (one feature):
- public finance.

(5) ***Features whose categories are difficult to relate to the Aztec case*** (two features):
- expenditure; political participation.

(6) ***No data*** (one feature):
- financial theory.

If forced by a roving bandit to place the Aztec case into Bonney and Ormrod's scheme, I would call it a domain state with an unusually advanced system of taxation. But the results of this informal exercise suggest that the basic typology is inadequate to account for the Aztec case; indeed, it is probably not very effective for other premodern and non-European cases. This is another way of saying that the early modern European trajectory should not be generalized or extended to other domains without modification – a very unremarkable suggestion to an anthropologist.

[134] Bonney and Ormrod (1999).

The finances of warfare

Scholarship on Aztec warfare has concentrated overwhelmingly on its religious and symbolic dimensions,[135] with some attention to military strategy and logistics.[136] Scholars have yet to think much about the fiscal aspects of warfare; indeed, when I polled a group of colleagues only one (Jay Silverstein) had any kind of answer to the question "How was Aztec warfare financed?" Warfare was organized and financed within the structures of the city state and the empire. Armies were raised from among the pool of subjects of the king; there were no mercenary forces. Military technology was simple. Some weapons were provided by individual soldiers and others were provided by their *calpolli*. Military supplies were raised within the normal channels of taxation.

The main source of battlefield advantage was the size of the army, but since soldiers could be recruited only from within the polity there was no way to use fiscal measures to increase the size of the army. Taxation could be used to increase the amount of food and materiel, but these were not the limiting factors in military success. Larger, more populous states obviously had an advantage, and I have argued that regional demography provides a large part of the explanation for the success of the Triple Alliance: the Basin of Mexico had a significant demographic advantage over adjacent areas in the Late Aztec period.[137] But kings could not use taxes to increase the size of their army.

Variation in tax burdens

The variation in tax burdens throughout the empire is amenable to study, but no one has done the work yet. Tax rates are known from the *Codex Mendoza*, and the locations and extents of the provinces are relatively well documented.[138] What has not been done is a systematic study of the demography of the empire. We considered gathering population data during our 1996 mapping project,[139] but the information was widely scattered, not standardized, and required too much analysis for the scope of that project.

Some idea of variation can be inferred from my reconstruction of taxes in the state of Morelos (Table 3.5). The overall burdens per household are quite low but show regional variation; they range from 1.5 to 5.4 pieces of

135 See, for example, Bueno Bravo (2007) and Carrasco (1999a). 136 Hassig (1988); Isaac (1983).
137 Smith (1986). 138 Berdan *et al.* (1996); Sergheraert (2009). 139 Berdan *et al.* (1996).

cloth in the different conquest states. If the quantitative adjustment suggested by codex scholar Juan José Batalla Rosado were carried out, however (counting textile images as bundles of twenty items instead of individual items), this would increase the figures by a factor of 20. It is likely that tax burdens varied by greater amounts throughout different areas of the empire, but this cannot yet be determined. The regional demography of the empire is another topic that urgently needs attention by scholars.

Calpixque*: wage or rent contracts?*

Were *calpixque* state employees or independent tax farmers? Fiscal theory suggests that the former are found when the costs of monitoring tax collectors are low, whereas high costs of monitoring favor tax-farming.[140] Most scholars assume wage contracts for the imperial *calpixque* (and that is my impression of the data), but hard facts are scarce. Accounts that the empire imposed *calpixque* on conquered provinces may favor the wage interpretation, but these accounts are not definitive. For example, in Atitlalaquia, "a Mexica collector was imposed to collect taxes and bring them to the Mexica kings" [author's translation].[141]

Several features of imperial *calpixque* organization are in line with Max Weber's model of agent selection for wage contracts.[142] First, the fact that the highest-level *calpixque* were probably nobles increases the shared interests between agents and principals. Second, the use of two high-ranking *calpixque* per province (types A and B), one in the capital and the other in the province, is a form a "collegiate organization" that may have reduced monitoring problems. Third, the use of a hierarchical scheme (subject city states within tax provinces) also reduced monitoring problems. Even so, there is much that we do not know about how the imperial *calpixque* operated. Although the possibility that they were tax farmers is not contradicted by the existing sources, my feeling is that the data favor a wage contracts model.

As discussed above, the scanty information available for the city-state *calpixque* (types D and E) also favors a wage contract interpretation of their livelihood. The type D *calpixque* seem to have lived in special residences, and Lockhart suggests that they were appointed by the king.[143] *Calixque* of types D and E performed a variety of duties in addition to collecting taxes;

140 Coşgel and Miceli (2009); Kiser and Kane (2007). 141 Acuña (1984–88: vol. VI, 62).
142 As discussed by Kiser (1999: 158–9). 143 Lockhart (1992: 43).

they maintained lists of people in each neighborhood, they organized corvée labor activities, and they performed a variety of minor tasks when ordered by the king of royal council. Monitoring the activities of tax collectors was much easier at the city-state level because of the smaller size of the polity, both in terms of distance and population. All in all, the evidence favors a wage contract model for the city-state *calpixque*.

Collective action

The Aztecs are included in Blanton and Fargher's studies of collective action and political dynamics in thirty premodern states.[144] They use rigorous comparison and ordinal scale data to place these states along a continuum from collective or democratic rule (such as Classical Greece and Republican Rome) to despotic or autocratic rule (African chiefdoms). Although the dominant trend in Aztec studies has been to emphasize despotic rulership and a strongly centralized state, the Aztec state actually falls closer to the collective end of Blanton and Fargher's scale. In the imperial capital Tenochtitlan (the focus of Blanton and Fargher), the power of kings was checked by a high council, and public goods were provided at a relatively high level.[145] There is much less information for the other Aztec city states, but it does appear that these features of rulership, bureaucratization, and public goods provision were at least broadly similar.[146]

Roving and stationary bandits?

I close with a few remarks on Mancur Olson's model of roving and stationary bandits.[147] Although I have found Levi's theory of predatory rule[148] helpful in understanding Aztec city states, kings, and cities,[149] Olson's bandit model has *not* been helpful. Olson's model describes the emergence of states out of conditions of chaos and anarchy – such as the Viking era[150] or among the failed states in modern times[151] – but it does not apply to the origin of the earliest states in antiquity.

[144] Blanton and Fargher (2008; 2009); Fargher and Blanton (2007).

[145] I disagree with Blanton and Fargher's (2008; 2009) classification of Aztec revenue. They include imperial taxes from the *Codex Mendoza* as internal revenue, which seems incorrect to me. These taxes were mostly paid by foreigners, yet the public goods were provided only in the imperial capital. Within city states, nearly all taxes were local in origin, but Blanton and Fargher concentrate on Tenochtitlan for their discussion of rulership and public goods.

[146] Smith (2008). [147] Olson (1993). [148] Levi (1981; 1988). [149] Smith (2008: ch. 8).

[150] Kurrild-Klitgaard and Tsvendsen (2003). [151] Levi (2006).

States developed out of tribal societies and chiefdoms. Contrary to the views of Thomas Hobbes and his modern followers, such as North, Wallis, and Weingast,[152] however, social life before elites and states was not chaotic and paralyzed by violence; it was not "a world of endemic violence."[153] Ethnographers have documented numerous mechanisms for resolving disputes and keeping order in pre-state societies, and these practices do not involve elites or kings.[154] Indeed, one could argue that a major finding of a century of ethnography among non-Western groups is that non-state societies can get along just fine without elites or private property. And, although some have argued for continual war and violence in the ancient past,[155] considerable evidence and the dominant view in anthropology go against this interpretation.[156]

Olson's roving bandits are products of the state, not its initial creators. They exist in periods when state authority has broken down. Before states came along rulers of chiefdoms may have been predatory in Levi's sense, but their realms were not filled with violence and conflict such that economic and social life could not proceed efficiently and successfully. And, in most regions, they did not even have horses! So how did those early chiefs collect their revenue? This is a poorly researched topic that requires consideration of the (minimal) archaeological and ethnographic literature on chiefdom revenue.[157] The Aztec and Inka states may represent the most exotic and "primitive" states in this volume, but they are far removed from the evolutionary origins of fiscal organization.

References

Acuña, R. (1984–88) *Relaciones geográficas del siglo XVI*, 10 vols. Mexico City.

Adams, R. M. (1966), *The Evolution of Urban Society: Early Mesopotamia and Prehispanic Mexico*. Chicago.

Anders, F., Jansen, M. E. R. G. N., and Reyes García, L. (1997), *Matrícula de Tributos o Códice de Moctezuma*. Graz.

Anderson, A. J. O., Berdan, F. F., and Lockhart, J. (eds.) (1976) *Beyond the Codices: The Nahua View of Colonial Mexico*. Berkeley, CA.

Barlow, R. H. (1943) "The periods of tribute collection in Moctezuma's empire," *Notes on Middle American Archaeology and Ethnology* 23: 152–5.

Batalla Rosado, J. J. (ed.) (2002) *Códice Tributos de Coyoacán*. Madrid.

152 North, Wallis, and Weingast (2009b; 2009a).
153 North, Wallis, and Weingast (2009a: 59).
154 Harris (1989); Roberts (1979; 2003); Sillitoe and Kuwimb (2010).
155 Keeley (1996); LeBlanc and Register (2004).
156 Ferguson (1995; 2006); Ferguson and Whitehead (1999); Kelly (2000; 2005).
157 See, for example, Jungerberg (1990), Peterson and Drennan (2012), and Wright (2000).

(2007) "The scribes who painted the *Matrícula de Tributos* and the *Codex Mendoza*," *Ancient Mesoamerica* 18: 31–52.
Berdan, F. F. (1976) "La organización del tributo en el imperio azteca," *Estudios de Cultura Náhuatl* 12: 185–95.
(1992a) "The imperial tribute roll of the *Codex Mendoza*," in Berdan and Anawalt (1992): vol. I, 55–79.
(1992b) "Appendix B: annual tribute in the *Codex Mendoza*," in Berdan and Anawalt (1992): vol. I, 154–7.
(1996) "The tributary provinces," in Berdan, Blanton, Boone, Hodge, Smith, and Umberger (1996): 115–35.
Berdan, F. F., and Anawalt, P. R. (eds.) (1992) *The Codex Mendoza*, 4 vols. Berkeley, CA.
Berdan, F. F., Blanton, R. E., Boone, E. H., Hodge, M. G., Smith, M. E., and Umberger, E. (1996) *Aztec Imperial Strategies*. Washington, DC.
Berdan, F. F., and de Durand-Forest, J. (eds.) (1980) *Matrícula de Tributos (Códice de Moctezuma)*. Graz.
Blanton, R. E., and Fargher, L. F. (2008) *Collective Action in the Formation of Pre-Modern States*. New York.
(2009) "Collective action in the evolution of pre-modern states," *Social Evolution and History* 8: 133–66.
Bonney, R. (1995) "Revenues," in *Economic Systems and State Finance*, ed. R. Bonney. Oxford: 423–505.
(ed.) (1999) *The Rise of the Fiscal State in Europe* c. *1200–1815*. Oxford.
Bonney, R., and Ormrod, W. M. (1999) "Introduction: crises, revolutions and self-sustained growth: towards a conceptual model of change in fiscal history," in *Crises, Revolutions and Self-Sustained Growth: Essays in European Fiscal History, 1130–1830*, ed. W. M. Ormrod, M. Bonney, and R. Bonney. Stamford, UK: 1–21.
Braund, D. (1984) *Rome and the Friendly King: The Character of the Client Kingship*. New York.
Bueno Bravo, I. (2007) *La guerra en el imperio azteca: expansión, ideología y arte* Madrid.
Calnek, E. E. (1988) "The *calmecac* and *telpochcalli* in pre-conquest Tenochtitlan," in *The Work of Bernardino de Sahagún: Pioneer Ethnographer of Sixteenth-Century Aztec Mexico*, ed. J. Klor de Alva, H. B. Nicholson, and E. Quiñones Keber. Albany, NY: 169–77.
Carrasco, D. (1999a) *City of Sacrifice: The Aztec Empire and the Role of Violence in Civilization*. Boston.
Carrasco, P. (1964a) "Family structure of sixteenth-century Tepoztlan," in *Process and Pattern in Culture: Essays in Honor of Julian H. Steward*, ed. R. A. Manners. Chicago: 185–210.
(1964b) "Tres libros de tributos del Museo Nacional de México y su importancia para los estudios demográficos," in *XXXV Congreso internacional de Americanistas, México, 1962: actas y memorias*. Mexico City: 373–8.

(1972) "La casa y hacienda de un señor *tlahuica*," *Estudios de Cultura Náhuatl* 10: 235–44.
(1976a) "The joint family in ancient Mexico: the case of Molotla," in *Essays on Mexican Kinship*, ed. H. Nutini, P. Carrasco, and J. M. Taggert. Pittsburgh: 45–64.
(1976b) "Estratificación social indígena en Morelos durante el siglo XVI," in *Estratifiación social en la Mesoamérica Prehispánica*, ed. P. Carrasco and J. Broda. Mexico City: 102–17.
(1999b) *The Tenochca Empire of Ancient Mexico: The Triple Alliance of Tenochtitlan, Tetzcoco, and Tlacopan*. Norman, OK.
Cline, S. L. (1993) *The Book of Tributes: Early Sixteenth-Century Nahuatl Censuses from Morelos*. Los Angeles.
Cortés, H. (1986) *Letters from Mexico*, trans. and ed. A. Pagden. New Haven, CT.
Coşgel, M. M., and Miceli, T. J. (2009) "Tax collection in history," *Public Finance Review* 37: 399–420.
Durán, D. (1967) *Historia de las Indias de Nueva España*, trans. and ed. A. M. Garibay Kintana, 2 vols. Mexico City.
(1971) *Book of the Gods and Rites and the Ancient Calendar*, trans. and ed. F. Horcasitas and D. Heyden. Norman, OK.
(1994) *The History of the Indies of New Spain*, trans. D. Heyden. Norman, OK.
Fargher, L. F., and Blanton, R. E. (2007) "Revenue, voice, and public goods in three pre-modern states," *Comparative Studies in Society and History* 49: 848–82.
Fargher, L. F., Heredia Expinoza, V. Y., and Blanton, R. E. (2011) "Alternative pathways to power in late postclassic highland Mesoamerica," *Journal of Anthropological Archaeology* 30: 306–26.
Ferguson, R. B. (1995) *Yanomami Warfare: A Political History*. Santa Fe, NM.
(2006) "Archaeology, cultural anthropology, and the origins and intensification of war," in *The Archaeology of Warfare: Prehistories of Raiding and Conquest*, ed. E. N. Arkush and M. W. Allen. Gainesville, FL: 469–523.
Ferguson, R. B., and Whitehead, N. L. (eds.) (1999) *War in the Tribal Zone: Expanding States and Indigenous Warfare*, rev. edn. Santa Fe, NM.
Friedman, M. (2009) "Urban neighborhoods in ancient Mesoamerica," senior honors thesis. Arizona State University, Phoenix.
Galarza, J. (1963) "Codex San Andrés (juridiction de Cuautitlan): manuscrit pictographique du Musée de l'Homme de Paris (II)," *Journal de la Société des Amréicanistes* 52: 61–90.
Gibson, C. (1964) *The Aztecs under Spanish Rule: A History of the Indians of the Valley of Mexico, 1519–1810*. Stanford, CA.
Gutiérrez, G., König, V., and Brito, B. (2009) *Códice Humboldt Fragmento 1, Ms. amer. 2, y Códice Azoyú 2, Reverso: nómina de tributos de Tlapa y su provincia al Imperial Mexicano*, bilingual edn. Mexico City.
Hansen, M. H. (2000) "Introduction: the concepts of city-state and city-state culture," in *A Comparative Study of Thirty City-State Cultures*, ed. M. H. Hansen. Copenhagen: 11–34.

Harris, M. (1989) "Life without chiefs," *New Age Journal* Nov/Dec: 42–5, 205–9.
Harvey, H. R., and Williams, B. J. (1980) "Aztec arithmetic: positional notation and area calculation," *Science* 210: 499–505.
Hassig, R. (1985) *Trade, Tribute, and Transportation: The Sixteenth-Century Political Economy of the Valley of Mexico*. Norman, OK.
(1988) *Aztec Warfare: Imperial Expansion and Political Control*. Norman, OK.
Hicks, F. (1978) "Los *calpixque* de Nezahualcoyotl," *Estudios de Cultura Náhuatl* 13: 129–52.
(1984) "Rotational labor and urban development in prehispanic Tetzcoco," in *Explorations in Ethnohistory: Indians of Central Mexico in the Sixteenth Century*, ed. H. R. Harvey and H. J. Prem. Albuquerque, NM: 147–74.
(1987) "First steps toward a market-integrated economy in Aztec Mexico," in *Early State Dynamics*, ed. H. J. M. Claessen and P. van de Velde. Leiden: 91–107.
(1992) "Subject states and tributary provinces: the Aztec Empire in the Northern Valley of Mexico," *Ancient Mesoamerica* 3: 1–10.
(1994) "Xaltocan under Mexica domination, 1435–1520," in *Caciques and Their People: A Volume in Honor of Ronald Spores*, ed. J. Marcus and J. F. Zeitlin. Ann Arbor, MI: 67–86.
(1996) "Class and state in Aztec official ideology," in *Ideology and the Formation of Early States*, ed. H. J. M. Claessen and J. G. Oosten. Leiden: 256–77.
(2005) "The lesser nobility of the Basin of Mexico in late prehispanic times," paper presented at annual meeting of American Society for Ethnohistory, Santa Fe, NM, November 17.
(2012) "Governing smaller communities in Aztec Mexico," *Ancient Mesoamerica* 23: 47–56.
Hudson, M. (2000) "Mesopotamia and classical antiquity," in *Land-Value Taxation around the World*, 3rd edn, ed. R. V. Andelson. Malden, MA: 3–25.
Isaac, B. L. (1983) "Aztec warfare: goals and battlefield comportment," *Ethnology* 22: 121–31.
Jungerberg, R. A. (1990) "The contributions of women to taxation effort in chiefdoms and states," *Research in Economic Anthropology* 12: 347–91.
Keeley, L. H. (1996) *War before Civilization: The Myth of the Peaceful Savage*. New York.
Kelly, R. C. (2000) *Warless Societies and the Origin of War*. Ann Arbor, MI.
(2005) "The evolution of lethal intergroup violence," *Proceedings of the National Academy of Sciences* 102: 15294–8.
Kiser, E. (1999) "Comparing varieties of agency theory in economics, political science, and sociology: an illustration from state policy implementation," *Sociological Theory* 17: 146–70.
Kiser, E., and Baer, J. (2005) "The bureaucratization of states: toward an analytical Weberianism," in *Remaking Modernity: Politics, History, and Sociology*, ed. J. Adams, E. S. Clemens, and A. S. Orloff. Durham, NC: 225–48.

Kiser, E., and Kane, D. (2007) "The perils of privatization: how the characteristics of principals affected tax farming in the Roman Republic and Empire," *Social Science History* 31: 191–212.

Kurrild-Klitgaard, P., and Tsvendsen, G. T. (2003) "Rational bandits: plunder, public goods, and the Vikings," *Public Choice* 117: 255–72.

LeBlanc, S. A., and Register, K. E. (2004) *Constant Battles: Why We Fight*. New York.

León-Portilla, M. (1971) "Códice de Coyoacan: nómina de tributos, siglo XVI," *Estudios de Cultura Náhuatl* 9: 57–74.

Levi, M. (1981) "The predatory theory of rule," *Politics and Society* 10: 431–66.

(1988) *Of Rule and Revenue*. Berkeley, CA.

(2006) "Why we need a new theory of government," *Perspectives on Politics* 4: 5–19.

Lockhart, J. (1992) *The Nahuas after the Conquest: A Social and Cultural History of the Indians of Central Mexico, Sixteenth through Eighteenth Centuries*. Stanford, CA.

Luttwak, E. N. (1976) *The Grand Strategy of the Roman Empire: From the First Century AD to the Third*. Baltimore.

MacGinnis, J. (2003) "A corvée gang from the time of Cyrus," *Zeitschrift für Assyrologie* 93: 88–115.

Miles, S. W. (1957) "The sixteenth-century Pokom-Maya: a documentary analysis of social structure and archaeological setting," *Transactions of the American Philosophical Society* 47: 731–81.

Mohar Betancourt, L. M. (1978) *El tributo mexica en el siglo XVI: análisis de dos fuentes pictográficas*. Mexico City.

North, D. C., Wallis, J. J., and Weingast, B. R. (2009a) "Violence, natural states, and open access orders," *Journal of Democracy* 20: 55–68.

(2009b) *Violence and Social Orders: A Conceptual Framework for Interpreting Recorded Human History*. New York.

Offner, J. A. (1981) "On the inapplicability of 'oriental despotism' and the 'Asiatic mode of production' to the Aztecs of Texcoco," *American Antiquity* 46: 43–61.

(1983) *Law and Politics in Aztec Texcoco*. New York.

Olson, M. (1993) "Dictatorship, democracy, and development," *American Political Science Review* 87: 567–76.

Ormrod, W. M., and Barta, J. (1995) "The feudal structure and the beginnings of state finance," in *Economic Systems and State Finance*, ed. R. Bonney. Oxford: 53–80.

Pérez Rocha, E. (1978) *Servicio personal y tributo en Coyoacán: 1551–1553*. Mexico City.

(2008) *El tributo en Coyoacán en el siglo XVI*. Mexico City.

Peterson, C. E., and Drennan, R. D. (2012) "Patterned variation in regional trajectories of community growth," in *The Comparative Archaeology of Complex Societies*, ed. M. E. Smith. New York: 88–137.

Pomar, J. B. (1975) *Relación de Tezcoco (siglo XVI)*, facsimile 1891 edn. Mexico City.

Ramírez de Fuenleal, S. (1870) "Carta a su magestad del obispo de Santo Domingo. . .tratando de varias cosas pertenecientes al gobierno y real hacienda de aquel reino (3 de Noviembre de 1532)," in *Colección de documentos inéditos. . .de Indias*, vol. XIII. Madrid: 250–61.

Riley, G. M. (1973) *Fernando Cortés and the Marquesado in Morelos, 1522–1547*. Albuquerque, NM.

Roberts, S. (1979) *Order and Dispute: An Introduction to Legal Anthropology*. New York.

(2003) "The study of dispute: anthropological perspectives," in *Disputes and Settlements: Law and Human Relations in the West*, ed. J. Bossy. New York: 1–24.

Rojas, J. L. d. (1986) *México Tenochtitlan: economía y sociedad en el siglo XVI*. Mexico City.

(1994) "After the conquest: Quauhtinchan and the Mexica province of Tepeacac," in *Economies and Polities in the Aztec Realm*, ed. M. G. Hodge and M. E. Smith. Albany, NY: 405–32.

Rojas Rabiela, T. (1979) "La organización del trabajo para las obras públicas: el coatequitl y las cuadrillas de trabajadores," in *El trabajo y los trabajadores en la historia de México*, ed. E. C. Frost, M. C. Meyer, and J. Z. Vázquez. Mexico City: 41–66.

(1984) "El tributo en trabajo en la construcción de las obras públicas de México Tenochtitlan," in *El modo de producción tributario en Mesoamérica*, ed. A. Barrera Rubio. Merida, Mexico: 51–76.

(1986) "El sistema de organización en cuadrillas," in *Origen y formación del estado en Mesoamérica*, ed. A. Medina, A. López Austin, and M. C. Serra. Mexico City: 135–50.

Sahagún, F. B. de (1950–82) *Florentine Codex: General History of the Things of New Spain*, trans. and ed. A. J. O. Anderson and C. E. Dibble, 12 vols. Santa Fe, NM.

Sanders, W. T. (1976) "The population of the Teotihuacan Valley, the Basin of Mexico, and the Central Mexican Symbiotic Region in the 16th century," in *The Native Population of the Americas in 1492*, ed. W. M. Denevan. Madison, WI: 85–150.

Sands, P. C. (1908) *The Client Princes of the Roman Empire under the Republic*. Cambridge.

Scholes, F. V., and Adams, E. B. (1957), *Información sobre los Tributos que los Indios Pagaban a Moctezuma, año de 1554*. Mexico City.

Seler, E. (1904) "Alexander von Humboldt's picture manuscripts in the Royal Library at Berlin," in *Mexican and Central American Antiquities, Calendar Systems, and History*, ed. C. P. Bowditch. Washington, DC: 123–229.

Sergheraert, M. (2009), "L'expansion mexica (1430–1520 après J-C): la question du contrôle impérial dans les provinces extérieures de l'Empire," PhD dissertation. University of Paris 1, Panthéon-Sorbonne.

Sillitoe, P., and Kuwimb, M. J. (2010) "Rebutting Jared Diamond's savage portrait: what tribal societies can tell us about justice and liberty," *iMediaEthics*; www.mediaethics.org/News/170/Rebutting_jared_diamonds_savage_portrait__.php.

Smith, M. E. (1986) "The role of social stratification in the Aztec Empire: a view from the provinces," *American Anthropologist* 88: 70–91.

(1993) "Houses and the settlement hierarchy in late postclassic Morelos: a comparison of archaeology and ethnohistory," in *Prehispanic Domestic Units in Western Mesoamerica: Studies of the Household, Compound, and Residence*, ed. R. S. Santley and K. G. Hirth. Boca Raton, FL: 191–206.

(1994) "Economies and polities in Aztec-period Morelos: ethnohistoric introduction," in *Economies and Polities in the Aztec Realm*, ed. M. G. Hodge and M. E. Smith. Albany, NY: 313–48.

(1996) "The strategic provinces," in Berdan, Blanton, Boone, Hodge, Smith, and Umberger (1996): 137–50.

(2000) "Aztec city-states," in *A Comparative Study of Thirty City-State Cultures*, ed. M. H. Hansen. Copenhagen: 581–95.

(2004) "The archaeology of ancient state economies," *Annual Review of Anthropology* 33: 73–102.

(2008) *Aztec City-State Capitals*. Gainesville, FL.

(2012) *The Aztecs*, 3rd edn. Oxford.

Smith, M. E., and Novic, J. (2012) "Neighborhoods and districts in ancient Mesoamerica," in *The Neighborhood as a Social and Spatial Unit in Mesoamerican Cities*, ed. M. C. Arnauld, L. Manzanilla, and M. E. Smith. Tucson, AZ: 1–26.

Solórzano, A. de (1958) "Visita de Tlalmanalco, 1564," in *Sobre el modo de tributar los indios de Nueva España a Su Magestad, 1561–1564*, ed. F. V. Scholes and E. B. Adams. Mexico City: 126–9.

Swedberg, R. (2003) *Principles of Economic Sociology*. Princeton, NJ.

Tarschys, D. (1988) "Tributes, tariffs, taxes and trade: the changing sources of government revenue," *British Journal of Political Science* 19: 1–20.

Torquemada, J. de (1975–83) *Monarquía indiana*, ed. M. León-Portilla, 7 vols. Mexico City.

Trigger, B. G. (2003), *Understanding Early Civilizations: A Comparative Study*. New York.

Vaillant, G. C. (1933) "Native Mexican manuscripts from Tlaquiltenango, Morelos: photographs from folio original, with typewritten notes by George C. Vaillant." New York.

Valle, P. (ed.) (1995) *Códice de Tepetlaoztoc (Códice Kingsborough), Estado de México: edición facsimilar*. 2 vols. Toluca.

Vega Sosa, C. (1991) "Relaciones intercalendáricas de los códices Azoyú, Humboldt fragmento 1, y Azoyú 2," *Estudios de Cultura Náhuatl* 21: 99–107.

(1994) "Tributación en la provincia de Tlapa: códices Azoyú 2 y Humboldt fragmento 1," in *Códices y documentos sobre México: primer simposio*, ed. C. Vega Sosa. Mexico City: 161–72.

Visita (1946) "Visita, tasación y cuenta de la Villa de Yecapixtla, Morelos, a petición de Don Martín Cortés, Marques del Valle, año de 1561," in *Nuevos Documentos Relativos a los Bienes de Hernan Cortés, 1547–1947*. Mexico City: 169–265.

Williams, B. J., and Harvey, H. R. (1997) *The Códice de Santa María Asunción: Facsimile and Commentary: Households and Lands in Sixteenth-Century Tepetlaoztoc*. Salt Lake City, UT.

Wright, H. T. (2000) "Modeling tributary economies and hierarchical polities: a prologue," in *Cultural Evolution: Contemporary Viewpoints*, ed. G. M. Feinman and L. Manzanilla. New York: 197–214.

Zorita, A. de (1963) *Life and Labor in Ancient Mexico: The Brief and Summary Relation of the Lords of New Spain*, trans. B. Keen. New Brunswick, NJ.

CHAPTER 4

The ancient Near East and Egypt

Michael Jursa and Juan Carlos Moreno García

The ancient Near East

Introduction

Ancient Near Eastern sources cover some 3,000 years of history from the invention of writing until the final disappearance of the cuneiform writing system and the culture and traditions that were inextricably linked to it, in the first centuries AD. The textual documentation can usefully be divided into three categories: monumental, canonical, and archival.[1]

The first category comprises royal inscriptions and similar texts: documents intended for public display, or at least for wider dissemination, that carried an ideological and/or religious message. These texts are mostly uninformative regarding the practical minutiae of government, but they are essential for understanding the Mesopotamian concept of kingship. Their principal purpose was to establish the legitimacy of the ruler as a successful leader of his realm on the basis of his performance with respect to two core values: protecting the peace and prosperity of the country, and maintaining "good relations" with the divine sphere by providing the necessary framework for the upkeep of the official cult, in particular the regular offerings intended to feed (literally) the gods residing in the temples. Other sources of legitimacy, in particular success in war with outside enemies and descent from a royal line, are of comparatively minor importance.[2] Divine approval could be assumed to have been withdrawn,

The first section of this chapter, by Jursa, deals with taxation in the ancient Near East. Pharaonic Egypt is discussed in the second section, by Moreno García. Section 3, written jointly by the two authors, presents the conclusions of the Mesopotamian data and their evaluation in the light of the preceding section on ancient Egypt.

[1] See van de Mieroop (1999) for an introduction to the cuneiform record as source material for the historian, where documentation for what follows can be found. See also, for example, Sallaberger (1999), for the records of the Ur III period (late third millennium BC); Charpin (2004), for the documentation of the Old Babylonian period; and Jursa (2005), for the evidence from first-millennium Babylonia.

[2] Diachronically, these aspects of royal legitimacy are of shifting importance. Generally, legitimate descent is given more weight in the second and first millennia BC than in the third millennium.

and legitimacy of rule lost, when a king failed to keep his principal duties. The power of a Mesopotamian monarch was always contingent upon his success as provider for the gods and guarantor for internal stability and prosperity. Only in the case of the Neo-Assyrian Empire in the ninth, eighth, and seventh centuries does the duty aggressively to enlarge the realm (then conceived as the domain of the chief god, Assur) form part of the fundamental tasks of a Mesopotamian king.

Canonical texts, namely works of literature and religious compositions, as well as scholarly material such as magical, medical, or divinatory texts, were transmitted in a (more or less) stable form in the realm of professional scribes, priests, diviners, exorcists, and the like, as well as in the context of scribal training. Such material is of minor importance for the present context.

Archival or "practical" texts belonged in the sphere of daily life: this category includes contracts, letters, administrative notes, settlements of accounts, and the like. Eighty percent or more of the Mesopotamian written record belong here:[3] for the purpose of this chapter, they constitute by far the most important source of information. A reconstruction of fiscal practices that is based on such material has to try and deduce general principles from a wide range of detailed but frequently unconnected information. It is for this reason that the range of the available information varies greatly from period to period, and even synchronically; some aspects of an administrative system may be known in considerable detail while others remain entirely in the dark.

Given the unequal distribution of the sources and the great deal of diachronic development of governmental and fiscal structures from the third to the first millennium BC, it is necessary to focus on selected historical phases that are documented by a comparatively wide range of sources and that can be considered representative for longer periods of time.

For the third millennium BC we treat the period in which Mesopotamia was ruled by the Third Dynasty of Ur, the "Ur III" period in Assyriological jargon. From only about sixty years of the twenty-first century, over 120,000 cuneiform tablets of administrative content have been preserved, of which about 87,000 are published or available in one form or another. No other period of Mesopotamian history is equally well documented.[4]

[3] Since a meaningful archaeological context is very frequently lacking for tablets housed in Western museums.

[4] Molina (2008).

For the second millennium BC our focus lies on the Old Babylonian period, a phase of about 400 years from 1950 BC onwards, and in particular on the kingdom of Babylon, which under its first dynasty controlled much of Mesopotamia for more than a century. Some 25,000 tablets dating to this period have been published.[5] In contrast to the Ur III period, a majority of the archival texts of the Old Babylonian period originates not from institutional archives (archives of temples, palaces, or other institutions of government) but from private archives, typically the archives of urban landowning families.

For the first millennium BC we discuss first the evidence for the Neo-Assyrian Empire. This first stable Near Eastern empire ruled for several centuries over large parts of Mesopotamia, Syria, and the Levant, as well as, for a short period, Egypt. The governmental structures and the royal ideology of this period are both exceptionally well known, through a wide range of sources. We have numerous royal inscriptions as well as several thousand documents of palace administrations, as well as an archive of royal correspondence numbering around 10,000 letters and spanning about a century.[6]

The Neo-Babylonian kingdom succeeded the Neo-Assyrian Empire as dominant power in the Near East for about seventy years, only to fall to the emerging Persian Empire in 539 BC. From the core area of Babylonia we have over 25,000 texts that are available to research (as well as over 30,000 texts that are not yet published).[7] In contrast to the Neo-Assyrian period, no state archives are preserved, but the information on institutionally unaffiliated, private urban households is much richer. This has a bearing on the aspects of the fiscal system that can be reconstructed in some detail. In part we also address evidence from the Achaemenid period, inasmuch as it concerns the case of Babylonia (a full treatment of the different forms of taxation found in all parts of the Persian Empire is beyond the scope of this chapter). The Neo-Babylonian evidence is discussed here in greater detail than the less well known earlier taxation systems, for which we will only outline the basic pattern of the management of state resources, with an eye toward structural and comparative analysis. The Neo-Babylonian case, on the other hand, allows the reconstruction of numerous details of the make-up and functioning of a Mesopotamian taxation system that may be useful for in-depth comparative purposes.

[5] See Charpin (2004) and Stol (2004) for surveys of the data.

[6] For surveys of the sources, see Radner (1997) and Fales (2001).

[7] Jursa (2005).

The economic background: agriculture

A large part of the resources a state can extract from a premodern economy are bound to be based directly or indirectly on agricultural production. The peculiarities of the Mesopotamian agrarian regime, in particular in the south of the country (Babylonia), are decisive for the forms of government and, generally, social organization that developed in the area. A brief introduction follows.[8] Arable agriculture was the mainstay of the country's economic life. Vast grain fields lay along the river banks and canals and were extended down the river levees toward marginal (either potentially waterlogged or saline) land. The nature of arable farming in Mesopotamia was determined by the fact that throughout Mesopotamian history there was practically no shortage of land.[9] The main constraints on agriculture were access to water, on the one hand, and a shortage of the means of production – that is, men (especially during harvest time), plough animals, and seed – on the other.

The main field crop was barley. The fields, which were typically very elongated with access to water on their short side, were cultivated with the seeder plough. This ingenious device enabled the Mesopotamian farmers to achieve high returns on seed: harvests of about twenty-four times the seed were quite normal, but the amount of seed used per unit of field was low in comparison to modern practices. Cultivation by the seeder plough economized on the scarce means of production – manpower, seed grain, and water – whereas land was used generously. In such an extensive low-input farming system, even a slight shift of the quantitative parameters can produce significant change in terms of output.[10]

Agriculture in southern Mesopotamia is based on the cultivation of two leading crops, barley and dates, rather than just on cereals. Date palms are typically found in the most easily irrigated zones (that is, on the levees of the canals), but there are few environmental limits for horticulture in Iraq: usually, the belt of date palms can be extended some distance down the levees. In practice, the chief restriction to date culture is the availability of water, labor, and time: young date palms need several years before they

[8] For general surveys of Mesopotamian agricultural practice, see Postgate (1994: 155ff.), Potts (1997: 56ff.), and Liverani (1998: 45ff.). Many specialist studies can be found in issues 4 to 6 of the *Bulletin on Sumerian Agriculture* (Cambridge). Charles (1988; 1990), van Driel (1988; 1990), Halstead (1990), and Maekawa (1990) are essential.

[9] Only toward the end of the Sasanian period, after nearly 1,000 years of more or less continuous agrarian expansion, might land have become scarce in some regions.

[10] See, for example, Jursa (2010: 48ff.) for the intensification and increased productivity of arable farming in first millennium BC Babylonia.

bear fruit. Date gardening is a far more intensive form of agriculture than arable farming; the yields per surface area are much higher. Its decisive characteristic, however, from an economic viewpoint, lies in the fact that it is not only more labor-intensive in absolute terms than arable farming but also more productive in terms of output per capita.[11] A comparison of the output (in calories of food) of date growing and arable farming (in antiquity) shows that the labor productivity of date gardening exceeded that of arable farming by a margin of at least 10, and potentially more than 100 percent, depending on which combination of parameters is used.[12]

Since it was potentially dependent on two very different leading crops rather than just on cereal farming, Mesopotamian agriculture was fundamentally different from contemporaneous agrarian regimes in the Mediterranean area: the potential for structural change within an essentially stable technical, climatic, and socio-economic framework was much greater. Given advantageous background conditions – especially a favorable, sufficiently humid climate, stable political conditions, and a willingness on the part of the authorities to invest in the agrarian infrastructure by extending the canal network – the focus of agricultural production could always be shifted to horticulture. When such a shift occurred on a sufficiently large scale, it changed the overall nature of the agrarian economy, and thus of the economy in general: aggregate as well as per capita production increased.

The agrarian regime described above had a significant impact on the social and political structure of Mesopotamian political entities.[13] The introduction of the seeder plough and the highly efficient form of agrarian production that depended on it late in the fourth millennium BC allowed southern Mesopotamian communities to produce a surplus, which led to a rapid increase of social stratification. The high initial cost of the principal means of production, the plough and the plough animals, and the need to use these means as efficiently as possible strongly favored large-scale land ownership of arable land over individual smallholding. Historically, an important part of the arable land was always owned by institutions: temples and/or "palaces" (that is, the rulers' extended households). Surplus grain was produced probably nearly exclusively by such institutional households. To function efficiently, these households did not necessarily need (or want) a large number of permanent dependants on

[11] Ibid.: 50ff.. [12] Date yields can fluctuate widely from year to year; hence the wide margin.

[13] The following depends largely on Liverani (1998), who provides the best structural description of the nexus between ecology, economy, and social structures that characterized the nature of Mesopotamian urbanism.

their books (although such dependants were always present); access to a pool of temporary labor in time of particular need was more important. Cultivation did not require much manpower, but harvesting the vast institutional fields under permanent threat of flooding did (high water coincides with the harvest period in southern Mesopotamia). Furthermore, the network of irrigation installations needed a regular input of labor; maintaining it was overall the most important task of governmental institutions on the local, regional, and even interregional level.

In the third and second millennium BC irrigation networks in southern Mesopotamia were not closely interconnected; planning and management were apparently done mostly on a local level, though they always involved representatives of the central government, the Crown. Only from the sixth century BC onward does one find a qualitative shift: genuinely interconnected regional and interregional irrigation networks begin to appear. This development eventually led to the unparalleled degree of centralization and integration of the irrigation network in the late Sasanian period.[14] In the Iron Age and thereafter, the input of labor and resources in the irrigation system was therefore higher than in earlier periods. This must reflect different governmental structures (and mentalities), as well as a larger surplus that could be extracted from society for this purpose.[15]

The basic structure of the agrarian economy largely determined the way the states harnessed society's resources; as we will see throughout this section, labor service was the single most important contribution that was exacted from the Mesopotamian population by its rulers. While obviously present and indispensable, payments in kind or money were, in comparison, overall of lesser importance.

"Fiscal structures" from the end of the third millennium to the fourth century: the evidence

Generalities

The principal purposes for which the Mesopotamian states and their elites drew on the resources of society at large fell into two basic categories: public works and military expense, on the one hand; and the upkeep of the ruling elites and the religious system, on the other.[16]

[14] Adams (1981).

[15] A case for a higher prosperity of Iron Age Babylonia in comparison to earlier periods of Mesopotamian history is made by Jursa (2010: esp. 99, 804ff.).

[16] We do not make here the traditional distinction between temples (religious institutions) and palaces (or, generally, institutions of central government) within the institutional sphere. This supposed

The first category includes: maintenance of the irrigation system; military expenses; the construction of "prestige buildings" (palaces and temples); the construction of defense systems (against floods as well as against human enemies); and seasonal work on institutional estates (Crown or temple).

The second category includes, foremost, the day-to-day costs of the official cult and religion, and the costs of government and of the requirements of the elites (court life, conspicuous consumption, etc.).

Public works, whether on the irrigation system or devoted to large-scale urban construction, required by far the largest input of resources. Owing to the ubiquity and cheapness of the principal construction materials (mud bricks, reed, bitumen), the main resource that was consumed by these public works was labor. On the level of individuals with service obligations there was frequently the possibility to commute a labor obligation into a payment for a substitute worker. Such a commutation could also happen on a lower or higher level of the administrative structure extracting the labor service, thereby in practice turning the payment for the substitute into a tax payment. Mesopotamian taxation cannot be studied independently of labor and military service obligations.

Mesopotamian sources from the second millennium onward offer much evidence for tax-farming, both for direct and (especially) indirect taxes. The importance of the phenomenon (which cannot be discussed in any detail here) increased radically in Babylonia in the sixth century concomitantly with the broadening of the tax base. Collection costs were high, and efficiency a permanent problem. This was one of the main incentives for tax-farming, in fact: the state wished to pass on the risk related to tax collection to the tax farmer. Contracts were of the fixed-rent type, which helped keeping transaction costs low. Tax estimates in Mesopotamia were typically made on the basis of rules of thumb ("Every hundred ewes will produce sixty-six lambs every year, and ten ewes of 100 will die"), which owed as much to Mesopotamian arithmetic and metrology as to practical experience. Such estimates frequently produced unrealistic expectations, but they had the advantage of being very easily applicable. Tax farmers were frequently hard-put to meet the goals set them by the state.[17]

dichotomy has played an important role in the discussion of early Mesopotamian states, but more recent research has shown that temples, the specificity of their social, religious, and economic function notwithstanding, were in the final count controlled at least indirectly by the Crown; they were institutions of the state at least at one remove and did not have an independent political function. See, for example, Kleber (2008).

[17] These matters are discussed by Jursa (2002).

Anecdotal evidence suggests that in all periods maximizing the efficiency of revenue collection (or, rather, minimizing inefficiency in this respect) and securing the necessary cooperation of the agents of revenue extractions (usually members of local elites that had been co-opted by the state in different ways) was a huge problem.[18]

The role of credit in Mesopotamian taxation is in need of additional study. There was no public debt, but credit was indispensable for the functioning of the system, on the level of the individuals who were subject to tax and service demands made by the state. The role of merchant creditors in this respect is portrayed as negative in Mesopotamian literature as well as in partly propagandistic royal debt remission documents,[19] but in fact the merchants' access to liquid funds was essential for bridging gaps between state demands for money payments and the limited means of taxpaying agricultural producers.

The Ur III period (end of the third millennium BC)

In this period Mesopotamian society was dominated by large institutional households that were controlled by the elites of society. In fact, the majority of the population (if not its entirety, according to some scholars) was subject to the authority of one of these households. These households included temples under the control of a small number of priestly families holding the highest offices in the temple administrations, the extended households of provincial governors, and of course also the extended household of the king and his family.[20]

The richness of the documentary record dating to this period reflects the desire to achieve centralized control of the economy and society's resources of manpower on the part of the ruling elites, in particular the king and his family.[21] This was done by extending the control exercised by the

[18] These matters have not yet been discussed in print comprehensively; a detailed study would be a desideratum. Such a discussion would have to be framed from a theoretical and methodological viewpoint in terms of North's New Institutional Economy; for similar thoughts on the basis of the Ptolemaic evidence, see Manning (2003: 10–11, 136).

[19] See also, for example, Hudson (2000: 13–16).

[20] The following is based foremost on Garfinkle (2008). Other important studies for our purpose include those by Sharlach (2004) and, in particular, Steinkeller (1991). A general introduction to the period is provided by Sallaberger (1999). A new approach to the history of the period is now provided by Michalowski (2011).

[21] This is in particular true for the second king of the dynasty, Šulgi, in whose reign a series of administrative reforms were introduced that clearly aimed at strengthening the authority of the king and his administrative apparatus, thereby diminishing the importance of divergent local traditions. Among these reforms one should note in particular the creation of a standing army, the reorganization of temple households, and the introduction of a uniform taxation system (see below) and an administrative apparatus (and the scribal schools necessary for the training of the scribes) that was

administrative apparatus of the kings' extended household over the other institutional households, or at least by attempting to do so. These households were intended to be bound together by a closely interlocking network of obligations monitored by the kings' administrators. Ur III administration was predominantly concerned with the control of such obligations through an (in theory) unbroken chain of records monitoring the transactions undertaken by one administrative entity with another. These primary records were consolidated into interlocking yearly settlements of accounts, with surpluses or debits carried over to the next accounting year. For this reason the Ur III state is frequently considered to have been a "bureaucratic" state, but this label does not do justice to the fact that the control over individual institutional households was monopolized by elite families whose power was based on local social networks and who were motivated by status concerns, not by "objective" principles of a rational bureaucracy in a Weberian sense.[22] The principal political tensions within the Ur III state resulted from the interaction of the kings' authority with the local power structures. The central government never achieved the full control over local institutions it strove for.

The regions dominated by the Ur III state have to be divided into a core area, essentially central and southern Mesopotamia, and a periphery, the flat land east of the river Tigris extending from the delta in the south into northern Mesopotamia. A third zone is formed by the Zagros Mountains in the north and in the (western) Iranian highlands; there, a number of vassal states of the Ur III kingdom were located.[23]

The core area was divided into about twenty provinces, the seat of provincial government being formerly the capital of an earlier independent city state that had been integrated into the Ur III state. The governors (*énsi*) were in theory royal appointees, but in practice the office was hereditary: local elite families dominated the various provinces; they were presumably descendants of the ruling houses of the earlier independent city states. These governors were the focus of particularistic, even secessionist tendencies throughout the history of the Ur III kingdom. Their power was in part counterbalanced by the provincial "generals" (*šagina*), royal appointees who also resided in the provincial capitals and who seemed to have enjoyed full independence from the provincial governors, being answerable

designed to meet the particular needs of the king's government. See, for example, Steinkeller (1991: 16ff.).

[22] See, for example, Michalowski (2011: 9–12), with further references.

[23] The following is based on material expounded by Steinkeller (1991: 19ff.) and Sharlach (2004). See also the brief summary provided by Paoletti and Schrakamp (2011: 163–4).

only to the king and his chief minister (the *sukkal-maḫ*). The generals did not originate from the province in which they were stationed; some of them were related to the royal house. Others were of foreign ethnic origin (that is, they were not Sumerians, but bore Semitic, Elamite, or Hurrian names); these men formed a new upper class that owed its position directly to the king. The governors seem to have controlled in particular the temples, their estates, and their dependants, while the generals were responsible for Crown land and the soldier-colonists who were settled on these royal estates. The sector of the population that was entirely independent of these two large sectors of the institutional sphere of the economy and society was at best small, if not non-existent in some provinces.[24]

The contributions of the country to the needs of the central government, which obviously included the "conspicuous consumption" of the elites, were structured by the provincial system. Within this system, there was a distinction between the three sectors of society and economy listed above: the temples and generally the part of society dependent on the provincial governors owed different services and taxes from the royal domain controlled by the generals, and the small institutionally unattached part of the population was taxed in yet another form (about which we know very little).

The royal domain provided the military and labor service of its inhabitants according to the demands and needs of the central government; the fruits of the labor of the royal dependants, agricultural and industrial products, particularly the mass-produced textiles, were likewise the generals' and – in the final count – the kings' to dispose of, without an intervening mechanism that might have limited or structured the grip of the central government on this sector of the economy.

The taxation of the domains of the provincial governors was achieved through what was called a "rotation" (*bala*) system. Provinces – or, rather, the temples located in the different provinces – were supposed to deliver to the government up to about 50 percent of their supply of certain key commodities.[25] The requirements made by the central government took note of certain economic specializations. Some provinces produced

[24] Merchants engaged in long-distance trade, some craftsmen, and men with professions requiring much mobility and independence (shepherds and fishermen, in particular) seem often to have been free of ties to sectors of the institutional economy.

[25] This is at least known for the province of Umma, which was supposed to deliver about 1,500 tonnes of barley – 48 percent of its total production, according to one summary record (Sharlach 2004: 160). Usually it is impossible to establish the relation between the *bala* requirements and the total production of a province.

predominantly barley, others livestock and wool or finished goods, especially garments. These goods were to be delivered to a small number of collection centers run by the central government.[26] Provinces also had to field a stated quantity of laborers for public works (canal building and the like) for a stated period of time. The aspect of "rotation" that was inherent in the name of this type of taxation is best visible in the provision that, normally for one month, individual provinces were responsible for providing the animals for the sacrifices in the most important shrines of the country. Additionally, some other expenses that benefited the king and his entourage, as well as certain households under the direct control of the Crown, were supposed to be met by the province in question.[27] Moreover, the cost of transporting the taxed goods (the cost of boats and barges, packing, loading the goods, and hauling the boats upstream or downstream) were added to the tax load during the taxation (or *bala*) period.

The provinces' obligations were monitored by the royal administration. A sophisticated accounting system was in use that allowed the conversion of the value of every imaginable commodity into either silver, grain, or labor time, and these three could also be converted into each other. In the final accounts for a taxation period, the total value of a province's contribution was computed and compared to expectations (thus, a shortfall concerning, for instance, grain could be balanced by an excess of labor time worked for the king by the province's labor force). Overall credits or debits were carried over to the following accounting period.

The *bala* taxation system was, in essence, a complex redistribution system. Provinces not only contributed substantial parts of their surplus, they also received, through the decentralized spending of the royal administration (via the collection centers), parts of the *bala* contributions of other provinces. In this way it was possible that some provinces, such as the province of Umma, were taxed for nearly half their production of essential goods such as grain; in good years southern Mesopotamian agriculture could achieve a surplus of 100 percent – that is, it could produce enough grain to pay for the costs of production (seed, fodder, transport) and feed the entire workforce and as many people again for an entire year.[28] This

[26] Tens of thousands of tablets originated from the administration of one of these collection centres (for livestock), Puzriš-Dagān.

[27] This is documented by the *šag*$_4$ *bala* texts.

[28] At least, this is what one can deduce from the accounting for institutional agriculture. The same is true, by the way, for northern Mesopotamian irrigation agriculture: Wiggermann (2000).

would not have been the case always, however, and redistribution throughout the state must have been essential to make the system viable.[29]

Other forms of taxation of the production of the core of the Ur III state include a cattle tax, paid to the king and his household either in beasts or in silver by the provincial governors and the chief priests.[30] These payments were made around the New Year's festival (in spring, after the lambing season), and may have (also) been intended to finance the extensive spring festival in the capital city, Ur. There was also a "generic" tax called *gún* ("impost"), which is not yet well understood. In some cases at least, this word seems to refer in fact to the *bala* contribution, which in any case was undoubtedly the principal form of provincial taxation.

Moving from the core to the "periphery" of the Ur III state, an entirely different taxation system is encountered. There has not yet been a thorough study of the matter, and details remain opaque. The main contribution made by the periphery, the sheep- and cattle-breeding zones east of the Tigris, consisted in livestock, but was usually accounted for in silver. The tax in question was called *gún ma-da*, "impost of the land/provinces."[31] According to the way this tax was accounted for, it was paid *by* military personnel garrisoned in over ninety locations in the peripheral areas, according to a fixed rate: for a "general" (*šagina*), the annual contribution was ten oxen and 100 sheep, or 1.66 kilograms of silver according to the standard conversion rate; for a senior 'captain' (*nu-banda*), two oxen and twenty sheep (332 grams of silver); for a common soldier, 1/300th of an oxen and one-thirtieth of a sheep (0.55 g of silver).[32] In actual fact, the tax must of course have been paid by the sheep- and cattle-breeding population of the periphery, and the taxation rates quoted have to be understood as a goal set for the occupying military force that it was supposed to achieve through (more or less forcible) extraction. The garrisons were maintained (that is, fed) to a large extent through redistribution of the *bala* contributions of the core of the Ur III state: large quantities of grain were shipped to the periphery from the core. The rational, but entirely schematic, manner in which Ur III accountants established a system for estimating the benefits and costs of the military occupation of foreign territory as a direct function

[29] It has been suggested that an agricultural crisis contributed substantially to the fall of the Ur III dynasty at the end of the third millennium BC, but the evidence is far from clear: Michalowski (2011: 173–6).

[30] The *máš-da-ri-a* tax: Paoletti in Paoletti and Schrakamp (2011: 164).

[31] Steinkeller (1991: 25ff.); Paoletti in Paoletti and Schrakamp (2011: 153).

[32] Steinkeller (1991: 30).

of the size of the occupying force is entirely typical of the bureaucratic[33] mentality of this administration.

Tribute and booty, as well as gifts, obtained from vassal states and other political entities beyond the peripheral sphere of the Ur III state contributed substantially to the income of the state, but there is no reason to believe that they were indispensable for the survival of the system.

The resulting image is that of a fairly coherent and centralized system of resource extraction that tapped most, if not all, areas of economic production, withdrawing, according to a very rough estimate, on average perhaps about one-third of the output.[34] It is important to note that, impressive as the evidence for the Ur III government's interest in administrative standardization and effective bureaucratic control over the state is, this interest was directed exclusively toward the maximization of resource accumulation (which included, most importantly, the mobilization of manpower) for the benefit of the ruling family and the local elites.[35]

The Old Babylonian period (c. first half of the second millennium BC)

Only a few hundred years after the Ur III period one encounters an entirely different economic and social system in the very same region. After the political domination of Sumerian elites during the Ur III period, the Old Babylonian city states, and the unified state created by the first dynasty of Babylon, especially by Hammurapi, were dominated by Semites – that is, by Akkadians (Babylonians) and Amorrites. The language of accounting was Akkadian and no longer Sumerian (which continued to be taught in the schools, however, and was the established language of learning).

In the early Old Babylonian period the southern Babylonian city states financed themselves mostly through the production of the royal domain, which was under direct management and was worked by dependent laborers.[36] Later in the period the nature of public finance changed. Particularly in the north of the country, the large institutional households underwent a transformation: temples still farmed a part of their domain with dependent personnel, but much land was rented to free tenants. Overall, one notes an "individualization" of agricultural production. Royal land was in large part not under the direct management of the royal administration anymore. It was mostly in the hand of numerous (soldier-)tenants, who owed the state service and rents in return for the

33 The word is used in a non-technical sense here.

34 Paoletti in Paoletti and Schrakamp (2011: 163).

35 Garfinkle (2008: 60).

36 Documentation for the following and further references can be found in the surveys of the evidence offered by Renger (2011) and Stol (2004: esp. 747–76).

usufruct of the land granted to them.[37] The terminology for the various types of soldiers and their respective obligations is not yet well understood. The basic principle, however (the granting of land to individuals and groups in exchange for service obligations and rent), is characteristic of Mesopotamian state organization from this period onward.

Temple estates were indirectly subject to the demands of the royal administration too. Temple households had to deliver a part of their agricultural production and had to make available their labor force when required.

Evaluating the role of private ownership of arable land is the principal difficulty encountered in this period.[38] In southern Babylonia, most of the arable land seems to have been Crown land; therefore, the southern city states (and later the first dynasty of Babylon during the time it controlled the south of Babylonia) could draw on the revenues of these estates (whether they were under direct management or granted to soldier-tenants) and on the labor of the part of the population that farmed them. In the north of Babylonia, however, a large part of the arable land was in private ownership. Structurally, one would expect that private landownership was taxed to compensate for the corresponding lack of income from royal estates, but that seems not to have been the case; there was also no head tax or a similar obligation. The most important demand made by the state consisted in periodical collective labor and service obligations imposed on communities (cities and villages); these were intended for military purposes and the upkeep of the irrigation system.

The (probable) minor importance of the direct taxation of the income of private agricultural production was compensated for (at least in part) by the introduction, for the first time in Mesopotamian history on a larger scale, of indirect taxation. We hear in particular of taxes that were levied on transported goods (*miksu*). Certain professionals had to pay a regular due related to their activities; these include bakers and tavern keepers (who were mostly women; the due was called *nēmettu*: "impost"). A certain category of women, the *kezrētu*, characterized by a distinctive hairstyle, had to pay a money tax that was denoted by a word etymologically related to the word designating this hairstyle: *kezēru*. They may have been prostitutes.

[37] In the secondary literature these payments are sometimes designated as "taxes," but as they are owed as payment for the use of royal land they should be considered "rents."

[38] Renger (1995).

The business of collecting rents owed to the state (*ekallu*: "palace," in Babylonian terminology) as well as (indirect) taxes and labor services was to a large extent in private hands; merchants in particular served frequently as tax farmers. For the state, they had the additional important function of converting perishable agricultural goods into hoardable silver: merchants/tax farmers traded with state rents and taxes and paid the state silver in return. Soldier-tenants frequently had to rely on credit extended by such merchants to be able to pay their rents, especially when their military duties kept them away from their fields. Widespread systemic indebtedness resulted. The Babylonian kings tried to address this problem by the promulgation of periodic debt remissions, but the long-term effect of these measures seems to have been limited.

Old Babylonian city states and the unified state of the first dynasty of Babylon were frequently engaged in military conflict with their neighbors. Booty and tribute were therefore an important source of income, but their importance for the overall financing of these states cannot be gauged.

The Neo-Assyrian Empire

The Assyrian kingdom had its roots in the second half of the second millennium: its territorial expansion began in the fourteenth century BC under Aššur-uballiṭ. After various phases of extension and contraction it ended up dominating the entire Near East in the eighth and seventh centuries BC. The vicissitudes of these seven centuries notwithstanding, Assyria was at its core an astonishingly stable state: it was ruled for all this time by the same family. Nevertheless, the Assyrian state experienced several phases of administrative restructuring and reform; the empire of the seventh century was very different from the struggling city state to which Assyria had been reduced around the turn of the millennium. Assyria's last two centuries are the period of its history that is known best, and the following remarks mostly refer to this phase, in which the Assyrian Empire had reached a scale far beyond that of any of the Mesopotamian states of the third and second millennia BC.[39]

Direct taxes and service obligations were based on landownership, or at least land use. Land taxes were payable not to a central institution but either to provincial governments (the most frequent option) or to temples

[39] The best extant survey of the Neo-Assyrian system of taxes and tribute is that by Radner (2007), which we are following here; references for observations made here can generally be traced to this article. See also Postgate (2011), with further references. Fales (2001) provides the best synthesis on the Neo-Assyrian Empire as a whole.

that were entitled to the revenues from a certain region (without being necessarily landowners in their own right). The term for the most basic obligation tied to landownership is *ilku*, which meant originally "service." It was in fact a service obligation, in the old Mesopotamian tradition: it referred to periodical corvée work for the benefit of the state, in particular with respect to the irrigation system. It also included military service in a kind of militia; in this respect the word is contrasted with *dikût māti,* the "general levy of the land," which referred not to the periodic service of selected men but to a full mobilization of all forces. *Ilku* could occasionally be discharged through a compensatory payment. In the second millennium BC the use of this term would suggest that land thus encumbered had been granted to its tenants by the king; in the first millennium, at least in Babylonia, it was a term for a general service and tax obligation, which does not necessarily imply that the land in question formed part of the land-for-service sector of the economy. For Assyria, the situation is not entirely clear. It seems likely, however, that the word referred to a general obligation resulting from any type of landownership (in fact, we hear most often of exemptions from *ilku* duties that were granted as a royal favor).

Actual direct taxes levied by the state – or, rather, its representatives, mostly the provincial governors – included an agricultural tax, *nusāḫu*, which amounted to 10 percent of all yields, and *šibšu*, the "straw tax," which required the payment of a quarter of the straw harvested. There was also a tax on livestock, *ṣibtu*, which was levied on cattle, sheep, and goats. It cannot be quantified. The straw tax was an innovation of the first millennium BC; it was essential for military purposes: the straw was intended for the army's horses, chariots and cavalry forming the backbone of Assyria's military power.

The Assyrian state also extracted some indirect taxes on the movement of goods. Tolls were levied on goods entering and leaving the empire; there were also customs dues owed for the use of river ports and crossings, perhaps also for the passing of city gates. Quantification is difficult; in one case it is known that the import tax payable for a horse amounted to about a quarter of the animal's value.[40]

In addition to regular taxes and service obligations, the Assyrian Empire gained very substantial funds from outside its realm in the form of gifts from its friends and allies, in the form of regular tribute from its vassals,

[40] Radner (2007: 226).

and in the form of booty from its enemies. It has been suggested that the substantial military apparatus of the Neo-Assyrian Empire as well as the conspicuous spending of its royal house and its elites[41] could not have been maintained had it not been for the constant influx of financial resources from outside the empire.[42] This is hard to substantiate, but there can be no doubt that during periods of great military success, such as during the eighth and early seventh centuries, the economic structure of the empire as a whole was heavily influenced by the huge quantities of tribute and booty that were brought to Assyria.[43]

The Neo-Babylonian Empire and Achaemenid Babylonia

Of all the periods discussed here, this is the phase with the richest pertinent documentation.[44] As in the Neo-Assyrian period, taxation has to be considered the principal source of state revenue; the yield of royal domain land would seem to have been of less importance. Taxation in Babylonia developed continuously during the time of the Neo-Babylonian Empire (612 to 539 BC) and after the Persian conquest of Babylonia in 539 BC. There is no fundamental break between the two periods/systems; we will therefore discuss Neo-Babylonian and Persian evidence together.

Direct taxation of (agrarian) income, as well as the extraction of labor and military service, is attested in three forms, with respect to three distinct social agents: we hear of taxation and service obligations (1) in the realm of the temples; (2) with respect to agricultural land that had been granted by the Crown to individuals or groups who in return owed the king taxes and/or labor and military service; and (3) with respect to private urban households.

We will not engage with the details of tax collection and levies of personnel. The sources refer to various officials engaged with these duties: military commanders and recruiting officers (*rab hanšê, rab ešerti, dēkû*). Indirect taxes could be collected by tax farmers. Since credit was often extended by businessmen to taxpayers for tax purposes, such entrepreneurs

[41] Suffice it to recall the ambitious building activities of kings such as Sargon II, who had a new capital city built within a period of just a few years.

[42] As a corollary of this assumption, it would follow that the empire had to expand continuously, and that an ending of military expansion necessarily had to result in the empire's collapse. This model is certainly too deterministic.

[43] The change from copper and lead to silver as the principal metal means of payment as a result of Sargon's conquests is the clearest case in point; see Radner (1999). For the quantities of silver brought as booty from the Aramean cities of Syria, see Fuchs (2008).

[44] Van Driel (2002); Jursa (2010: 645ff.; 2011a; 2011b).

also came to play an important structural role in the process of the collection of taxes and dues.[45]

Taxes levied on the income of temple lands As in all other periods of Mesopotamian history, temple households were important landowners. From the middle of the sixth century onward state taxes on temple income were collected by an official attached to the Esangila temple in Babylon, the "governor of Esangila," *bēl pīhāt Esangila*;[46] the Esangila, the principal temple of Babylon, therefore served as a collection point for this type of agricultural income. This tax on temple lands is in fact attested even earlier, around 600 BC, when it was collected by another royal official. Around 530 BC the tax amounted to a moderate 3.33 percent of the temples' harvest; for earlier and later periods a quantification is impossible. On occasion the royal administration also accepted, or perhaps indeed encouraged, payments in silver money rather than in kind.

The royal administration could, and did, draw on temple resources over and above the regular taxation of the temples' agricultural income by requesting manpower for royal building projects and victuals for the provisioning of royal palaces. These royal demands were met by the temples in part with their own funds and by drawing on the reservoir of dependent labor at their disposal, while part of the obligation was passed on to free members of the temple community, such as priests (and generally to the heads of private urban households?) in the form of service obligations or obligations to pay for substitute labor. Royal pressure was always high, but quantification is out of reach. Demands increased under the Persians, perhaps even to a level that was barely sustainable; the political upheavals that engulfed Babylonia after the death of Darius I[47] probably had as one of their reasons Darius's increase of direct and indirect taxation.

The land-for-service sector and "military colonists" The basic outlines of this system of land tenure are well known and have parallels in the Neo-Assyrian period.[48] Numerous individuals and groups of individuals, often of non-Babylonian origin, were assigned land by the Crown; in return, they owed service as soldiers and/or corvée workers, as well as taxes paid in kind and (increasingly) in money. The estates in question were often situated on recently reclaimed or even marginal land; sometimes they seem to have

[45] Jursa (2011a: 174f.).
[46] Here and in the following paragaphs, the basic documentation is provided by Jursa (2011b). Additional references will be kept to a minimum.
[47] See, for example, Waerzeggers (2003). [48] Van Driel (2002: 226ff.).

consisted of such temple land as could not be farmed by the temples themselves. In this way, the land-for-service system served both to integrate foreign groups into the society and the fabric of the state and to extend the range of state-controlled agriculture into otherwise under-exploited areas. Individual holdings were usually designated as "bow property," *bīt qašti* or *qaqqar qašti*, the "fief" of an archer, or common soldier, and less frequently as *bīt narkabti*, "chariot property," the "fief" of a chariot soldier, and *bīt sīsê*, "horse property," the "fief" of a cavalryman. There were further distinctions between lands held by "active" soldiers in contrast to those of the "reserve," as well as to those who owed only partial service.[49]

This phenomenon has, as we have seen, a very long history in Mesopotamia.[50] From early on there was a tendency to dissociate the actual service and the exploitation of the land connected with the service. Inheritance procedures, heavy service obligations (such as military service away from home), and the fact that some soldier-tenants held more than one grant all caused outsiders to be brought in to do the actual agricultural work.[51] There was also always a role for entrepreneurs (traders, mostly) with access to money in this system: they could extend credit (for tax purposes) to the holders of the grants and eventually achieve control over their land. The land grants of indebted soldiers could be pledged to businessmen to be exploited by their agents or to be sublet by them, frequently to the original holders of the land. Furthermore, collectives of soldiers with a common tax load would have an interest in having as much of the land within their remit as possible cultivated. Therefore, there was an incentive to make use of outsiders whenever the numbers of grant-holders were insufficient for the land available.

The land-for-service system as found in the Persian period sources, in particular in the well-studied Murašû archive of the fifth century,[52] had its roots in earlier Neo-Babylonian practice (which in turn may or may not have been influenced by Assyrian institutions). The Persian administration may have extended this system by reclaiming and settling additional marginal land, but it did so on the basis of pre-extant institutions and customs. The reign of Darius I did not constitute a caesura in this respect, as has sometimes been assumed.

The taxation of urban households For the urban population of Babylonia, the modes of taxation remained structurally unchanged throughout the

[49] See Joannès (2006: 54) on terminology. [50] Stol (2004: 732ff.). [51] Van Driel (2002: 219f.).
[52] Stolper (1985).

late sixth and early fifth centuries, from the late reign of Nebuchadnezzar to the end of the reign of Darius I. Neither the Achaemenid conquest nor the reign of Darius brought qualitative change in the system. This fact is masked by variants in terminology over time and an overall increase of the taxation rate, especially under Darius. While there was an increase of taxes under Darius, however, the Babylonian evidence does not confirm, and in part clearly contradicts, the thesis that there was a general shift to money taxes under Darius accompanied by large-scale hoarding of this money.[53]

The majority of the pertinent sources are receipts of silver payments made by men owing tax or service obligations. The principal purpose of the entire system was not to bring cash into the coffers of the state, however, but to pay for corvée laborers or soldiers. Payments made by individuals for *ilku* ("tax/service (obligation)"), *qaštu* ("bow tax"), and the like were used for hiring substitutes who undertook to do the actual service in lieu of those who paid for them. Such substitute laborers were hired either by the taxpayers themselves, in an entirely decentralized manner, or by officials on the next level of the administrative hierarchy (that is, by the heads of tax units and low-ranking military commanders). These money payments were therefore fed into the local economy again.

Taxpayers – heads of households – were grouped together in tax and service units most often called *ešertu*, "decury," in which (ten) men sharing a similar social and economic background were united. Members of these *ešertus* had the (theoretical) choice between serving in person, according to a rota system, or hiring men to do service for them. One text listing the members of such a tax unit and their financial contributions concludes with the statement that "one mina [0.5 kg] of silver. . ., the wage of one hireling for six months, is at the disposal of" the head of the tax unit;[54] money had been pooled by the members of the tax unit to pay for half a year of service by an outsider. This grouping together of several households spread the weight of the tax and service demands and allowed an inclusion of less affluent households into the system as well. Overall, however, the system targeted urban households that were comparatively well off and

[53] Herodotus III 89–97 relates that Darius reformed the Achaemenid Empire's tribute and taxation system by imposing regular money taxes when previously only irregular ("voluntary") tribute had been extracted from the empire's subject populations. The tax load imposed on Babylonia and Assyria, for instance, consisted of 1,000 talents of silver (as well as 500 eunuch boys). The cash was collected centrally and hoarded, Herodotus tells us. For a critique of reconstructions based on this evidence, see Jursa (2011b).

[54] Jursa (1999: 219f.).

disposed at least of some surpluses in kind, money, or manpower that could be claimed by the state. We cannot prove that the free population in general was subjected directly to such demands, especially poor families that did not own rural or urban land. There was no general head tax or the like or a generalized service obligation, as far as we can tell. Poorer members of society could probably be called upon by their communities in some circumstances; villages, for instance, demonstrably could be forced to contribute as collectives to state-controlled building activities,[55] and the same was probably true also for larger cities, but in general the workforce of non-propertied and institutionally unattached Babylonians was harnessed by the state only indirectly: it was they who were hired by well-to-do city dwellers to do service in their stead. And, of course, the population at large paid indirect taxes (see below).

The taxation of city dwellers was based on the possession of certain types of agricultural land or urban real estate or on the affiliation to a certain social or professional group. The most frequently attested basis for service and tax obligations was landownership. Many well-to-do city dwellers (frequently priests and other member of the urban elite) owned gardens in the hinterland of their cities that were located in regular field systems (*ḫanšûs*, literally "fifties"[56]). These "fifties" were as a rule situated on land that had been reclaimed late in the seventh century or early in the sixth through state intervention (or at least on royal instigation). The possession of (alienable!) land in such areas brought certain tax and service obligations.

This system was taken over by the Persian administration, which partly changed the terminology of the field systems, but not their structure; the terminology related to the bow properties of the land-for-service sector (which, it should be recorded, had an entirely different social and economic/legal background) was adopted. From the reign of Cambyses onward, one hears of bow taxes (*qaštu*) being owed for *ḫanšû* property. Under Darius, bow properties (*bīt qašti*) are frequently encountered in an urban context, and even more so the *qaštu* obligation. This does not mean that all the prosperous urban families owing such payments had been granted *bīt qašti* land by the

[55] See, for example, Jursa (2010: 57 n. 253).

[56] The name of these field complexes refers to the standardized size of the plots, which was defined by their frontage on the main canal (50 cubits [25 meters] or multiples thereof). According to one text, TCL 12, 11, a "fifty" plot was divided into five parts representing the allotment of individual taxation units of ten men/households (*ešertu*). In this case at least, a single household was allotted 2 *kurru* of land (2.5 hectares).

Persian administration; rather, the old land grants of the *ḫanšû* type had entirely been integrated into the *qaštu* system.

Taxation levied on the basis of urban residence was likewise dependent on the creation of tax units (of ten or fifty men/households) sharing service and tax obligations.[57] The city ward (*bābtu*) seems to have been a unit of reference: one hears of "levies of the city ward," *dīku ša bābti*. Additionally in this case, *ešertu* units were formed that normally paid for substitute laborers doing the actual work.

Finally, an affiliation to certain professional groups, or to an institution, could also form the basis of service obligations. Tax units formed by professional colleagues, such as priests, are known from Achaemenid Borsippa.[58] The distinction between such tax units formed on the basis of social/economic criteria and the tax units based on residence patterns mentioned above is probably to some extent artificial.

The terminology for the various service obligations that were incumbent on individuals and groups (tax units) is used inconsistently in the sources, in that one and the same obligation can be referred to by different terms.[59] The most frequent terms include *ilku*, "service obligation (or corresponding payment)," *qaštu* "(payment for) archer (service),"[60] and *urāšu*, "corvée, corvée worker."

In particular, the blanket term *ilku* frequently subsumed other obligations, such as *qaštu* and *urāšu*. In the fifth century *ilku* payments consisted of several components (such as "king's soldier," *ṣāb šarri*, "flour of the king," and others) that were normally paid in silver.[61] *Qaštu* was the most common obligation under Darius, when it was usually tied to membership in a tax unit. The full cost of equipping an archer for a year was up to one mina (0.5 kg) of silver. In this period the term interchanged with *urāšu*, which was the obligation that was most frequently imposed on private households before the end of the sixth century: it referred to a corvée obligation that did not (necessarily) have the connotation of *qaštu*. Other terms are even less specific terminological variants: *dullu*, "labor," and *kutallūtu*, "substitute service," are the most important.

57 See Stolper (2000), for the later Achaemenid period; van Driel (2002: 294f.), for some evidence from the sixth century; and Jursa and Waerzeggers (2009: 251f.).

58 Jursa and Waerzeggers (2009: 252f.); Waerzeggers (2010a: 345ff.).

59 The most detailed treatment of this subject is that by van Driel (2002: 237ff.). Additional discussion and references are provided by Jursa (2011a; 2011b) and Jursa and Waerzeggers (2009: 254ff.) (a catalogue of taxes attested in the Borsippean documentation).

60 Perhaps the term should be better understood as referring to military service in general.

61 Van Driel (2002: 255); Joannès (2006: 53).

Payments in kind played a minor role in the context of the taxation of city dwellers. In general, the agricultural income of private urban households does not seem to have been taxed by the Crown. In the Achaemenid period at least, however, the Crown taxed the income (in kind and in cash) that priests received from their offices; this amounted essentially to an income tax for this important stratum of society.[62] A flour tax, intended to benefit the local palace institutions, is mentioned frequently in documents from the sixth and fifth centuries alike. In the final count this was a labor obligation, however: the grain that was to be milled could be furnished by royal officials from the royal stores. This obligation belonged in the wider context of the manifold obligations borne by the subject populations of the Achaemenid Empire to contribute to the supplying of the Persian court. The *upiyātu* foodstuffs that were destined for Iran and had to be transported there (and probably furnished), for instance, by the Borsippean priests refer to the same general kind of obligation. Sipparean priests occasionally had to contribute to the provisioning of palace personnel in Babylon. Finally, individual urban households could be made responsible for the provisioning of royal dependants who were quartered with them; this phenomenon, which is so far attested only for the Teispids and the early years of Darius, is known from Borsippa and Babylon, where Egypto-Carian and Jewish mercenaries were stationed,[63] and from Uruk, where at least one Iranian boy was placed in a household of temple dependants by an Iranian noble.

The ubiquitous silver payments attested in a taxation-related context refer to labor obligations and are intended in most cases for the hiring of substitutes; the silver that was paid in these contexts therefore continued to circulate mostly within Babylonia and among Babylonians. Even though on the level of the individual taxpayer these arrangements could be mistaken for straightforward money taxes in those cases in which the money was collected either by the commanders of military/corvée units or by tax farmers and was subsequently passed on to higher authorities or was used locally to hire the necessary men, in fact the original link to service obligations, and consequently the intention to finance actual work/service with the tax money, was always maintained. The "taxation system" was geared primarily toward the mobilization of manpower. Silver payments demonstrably intended for the Persian court and therefore potentially for

62 Waerzeggers (2010a: 345ff.). If there was a tax that was likely to have been resented by the Babylonian upper class that may have contributed particularly to the revolts against Persian rule early in the reign of Xerxes, it is this tax.

63 Waerzeggers (2006).

hoarding (as predicted by the Herodotean model) were restricted to those rare cases in which Babylonians transported tax silver to Susa.[64]

Indirect taxation in Babylonia under Persian rule until the end of the reign of Darius I Indirect taxation and fees collected by the government, or by tax farmers on behalf of the government, are richly documented. The taxation of real estate sales began at the latest during the reign of Nabonidus – that is, already under Chaldean rule.[65] Under Darius (at the latest) the authorities kept a land register for monitoring and taxing such transactions.[66] In the same period slave sales were also taxed. This system was maintained and developed continuously until the Hellenistic period.[67] There was probably also a tax on the sale of priestly offices, and priests had to pay a fee to the state upon their initiation into office.[68]

The second principal type of indirect tax was levied on the transport of goods. At the latest since the reign of Nebuchadnezzar, numerous fees were levied for the use of harbors, bridges, and gates. In addition, there was a continuous development from Chaldean times throughout the Achaemenid period until the third century and Macedonian rule.[69] Transporting grain by boat from southern to central Babylonia, which required about ten days of travel upstream, could cost about 12 percent of the value of the cargo. Of these twelve percentage points, nine were spent on transport costs (boat rental costs and labor), three on bridge and harbor taxes.[70]

Payment for water rights was owed to landowners, apparently – that is, not necessarily, but frequently, also to the Crown.[71] Whether there was a general tax on water rights is uncertain.

Tribute The sources do not allow quantification of the importance of tribute (that is, of royal income extracted from the imperial periphery) in comparison to that of "internal" revenue. As the principal heir of the Neo-Assyrian Empire, the core area of the Neo-Babylonian Empire experienced an influx of vast quantities of silver and precious metals brought to Babylonia as booty from Assyria and Syria, or paid over the years as tribute

[64] For example, VS 6, 155. See the comprehensive study of this matter by Waerzeggers (2010b).
[65] Van Driel (2002: 185). [66] Baker (2004: 59ff.). [67] Stolper (1989); Jursa (2008: 608f.).
[68] Waerzeggers (2010a: 348); Jursa (2008: 609f.).
[69] Van Driel (2002: 274ff.); Joannès (2002: 509ff.); Weszeli (2009: 165).
[70] Weszeli (2010: 140ff.).
[71] Most payments for water rights that are attested in the sixth century were payments to temples.

by the vassal states of the Levant.[72] Much of this wealth was spent in Babylonia on public building projects: Nebuchadnezzar in particular transformed the principal Babylonian cities with his ambitious temple and palace building schemes and with the massive fortifications he had his architects construct.[73] The labor required for these projects was predominantly free hired labor, which was unusual in a Mesopotamian context; the laborers were paid silver wages. In this way, much of the tribute and booty silver came into local circulation. The (relative) prosperity of Babylonia in the sixth century was owed to this incoming wealth at least to a certain degree, as were the changes in the monetary system: we see an increase of monetization and clear inflationary tendencies toward the end of the Neo-Babylonian period, and in particular during the first decades of Persian rule.[74]

Fiscal regimes in ancient Egypt

Problems and limits of the sources

The study of fiscal regimes in Pharaonic Egypt, before the Macedonian conquest (332 BCE), faces problems related to methodology and the documentary record that make it difficult to achieve a comprehensive overall analysis of the system. Sources are scarce and selective. Although traditionally considered *the* quintessential model of a bureaucratic state,[75] in reality Pharaonic Egypt provides a very limited amount of administrative and governmental documents that deal with direct and indirect taxation. In many cases, the texts correspond to specific institutions, such as Old and Middle Kingdom (2686–1650 BCE) royal mortuary temples, or New Kingdom (1550–1069 BCE) temples. In other instances, monumental inscriptions recording royal decrees, donations, and specific governmental measures provide some data, but these usually reflect an ideological framework that stresses good governance and general prosperity. It is therefore indispensable to treat these sources carefully and to check their contents against documents of administrative practice. In fact, the conceptualization and the actual implementation of fiscal measures could differ greatly.

[72] The royal inscriptions of this period make reference to this; see, for example, Da Riva (2008: 12, 97) for pertinent examples.

[73] Da Riva (2008: 109ff.). [74] Jursa (2010).

[75] The literature is overwhelming. Useful approaches are given by Guksch (1999) and Rathbone (2000).

A second problem is the scarcity of absolute and relative data about the capacity of the state at any given period to collect taxes. It is therefore impossible to evaluate either the wealth produced by Pharaonic Egypt or the percentage thereof that was extracted by the central government and by other "public" entities (temples, high dignitaries) – that is, the revenue that was actually available to the state for its use. Nor can we say much about the general evolution of taxation and tax collection capacities depending on normal and exceptional demands (wars, famine, new building programs, etc.). Only sources from, roughly, 500 BCE to 650 CE cast some light on the tribute exacted by foreign rulers from Egypt, as well as on the annual revenue of the rulers of Egypt; according to Herodotus, Achaemenid kings perceived 700 Babylonian talents plus another 230 (365, according to Diodorus) from fisheries of Lake Moeris plus 120,000 *artabas* of grain paid to the Persian garrison – a sum to which the contribution to the table of the king should be added.[76] The annual income of the state under the Ptolemaic kings has been evaluated as being around 10,000 to 15,000 talents.[77] Finally, Byzantine Egypt paid annually 8 million *artabas* of grain, plus 3.67 millions of *artabas* as *annona* and about 452,000 *solidi*, thus making a total of around 1,600,000 *solidi*, while the first Arab governor of Egypt obtained around 2 millions of gold *solidi*. Estimating the total revenue of the state in the Pharaonic period on the basis of the available data gives therefore rather partial, impressionistic figures at best.

A further problem is that the fiscal vocabulary used in Egyptian sources is far from thoroughly understood.[78] A plethora of terms designate general taxes (*bak, inw*) or specific forms of state income (*heter, shayt, shemu*); a single term may occasionally express both a general tax and a specific levy depending on the context. In other cases, the meaning of terms is rendered opaque by ideological connotations. Thus *inw*, which designates irregular revenue (from diplomatic gifts to occasional deliveries), has the underlying meaning of "tribute" and, consequently, expresses submission to the recipient, a point of view not necessarily shared by the donor of an *inw*. Finally, there are instances when a single term appears to have contradictory meanings. Despite the many attempts to clarify the meaning of the fiscal vocabulary and the differences and nuances carried by the terms employed, the scarcity of sources issued from current fiscal practices still represents a major obstacle for the comprehension of the taxes collected, the relations between them, the rates involved, and the modalities of collection.

[76] Rathbone (1989). [77] Préaux (1939: 159). [78] Warburton (1997).

Chronology is another element to be considered in any analysis of the fiscal structure of ancient Egypt, owing to the transformations over time that the country experienced. No single fiscal regime was operative and reproduced once and again over three millennia, but considerable changes were introduced over the centuries. Thus, for instance, in the third millennium BCE a network of agricultural and work centers of the Crown called *hwt* aimed to organize agricultural work for the state and to stock and deliver supplies to the agents of the king. Such centers were in fact one of the most conspicuous elements of the Egyptian landscape at the time, being distributed over most of the country. Nevertheless, they were replaced by another category of work center (*kheneret*) at the beginning of the second millennium. Subsequently, after the middle of the second millennium, *hwt* and *kheneret* disappeared from the documentary record (except in stereotypical formulae) and temples appeared instead as important managerial institutions, frequently at the service of the Crown, paying taxes to the treasury and cultivating royal land. Later on the gradual introduction of money during the first millennium[79] made it possible to collect taxes both in kind and in money, and probably promoted market transactions that allowed taxpayers to obtain cash. Further chronological considerations involve political changes over time, when fiscal regimes were to be reconstructed after periods of central authority collapse, not to mention occasional fiscal reforms and exceptional fiscal measures aiming to cope with special needs (such as the extraordinary levies on temple wealth in order to finance the wars of Saite pharaohs, from 664 to 525 BCE).

A final problem concerns the structure of the socio-economic relations that formed the framework within which fiscal regimes were implemented, modified, and dismantled over time. Taxation involves the exercise of sovereignty within specific frontiers as well as a specific economic relation with producers. Competition between different authorities (the state, local potentates, autonomous institutions) with respect to the capability (and legitimacy) to tax resources and people could lead to the appearance of autonomous spheres of power able to accumulate considerable income and defy the supremacy of the state. Nonetheless, the apparent political stability of the country throughout long periods of its history (the Old, Middle, and New Kingdoms) reveals an astonishing capacity on the part of the Egyptian state to prevent the emergence and consolidation of any durable alternative power. It also reveals that the state was largely able to preserve a

[79] Müller-Wollermann (2011).

direct and exclusive fiscal link over producers, with no serious rival in view. Of course, corruption and other "distortions" occurred, but it is noteworthy that nothing like a feudal system emerged in periods of state collapse but, rather, the reproduction of the state on a smaller, local scale, from which it re-emerged to begin a new cycle of fiscal centralization. The social and political implications of this transcend the scope of this chapter, but it should be noted that the fiscal regimes operative in ancient Egypt were able to collect resources without any noticeable interference. This made elites dependent on state revenue for most of Egyptian history and precluded the emergence of rivals to the state who were able to usurp the state's fiscal power for their own purposes. In fact, the allocation of state resources to the elites (ranging from rewards to gifts and donations, including symbolic ones) helped preserve the dependence of the elites and their collaboration with the state, perhaps at the cost of a certain prize to be paid in terms of priorities in "public" spending and investments. "Public expenditure" also provided subsistence in exchange for work for many Egyptians (in architectural projects, expeditions to the quarries, the army, seasonal labor service, "wage-earners", etc.), thus supporting the official ideology, which focused on a paternal pharaoh who provided for his people.

Building a fiscal regime

The evaluation of the resources of the kingdom figures prominently in the royal annals of the Old Kingdom (2686 to 2125 BCE) as one of the most important activities of the pharaoh, to the point that the biennial census of cattle became the standard event by which years were dated in the Old Kingdom ("the year of the Xth occasion of the count of the cattle"). It should also be noticed that the counting of gold was occasionally celebrated in the annals of the archaic kings ("fourth year: first time for counting gold"), sometimes together with the assessment of fields (or the countryside) and also on a biennial basis ("year thirteen: seventh time for counting gold and fields/countryside" and "year fifteen: eighth time for counting gold and fields/countryside").[80] The existence of departments and officials engaged in the evaluation of the resources of the kingdom (land, cattle, manpower) is well attested at all periods, as well as bombastic assertions regarding the fiscal skills of some officials, expressed by the *topos*

80 Wilkinson (2000: 133, 134, 248). Later on, the annals of Thutmose III also record gold and cattle as tribute brought from Nubia.

of having assessed much more than was originally expected: "I acted for him [= the king] as an overseer of Upper Egypt satisfactorily. [. . .] I undertook every task, counting everything due to the (royal) residence in this Upper Egypt twice, every corvée due to the (royal) residence in this Upper Egypt twice;"[81] "Great was my excess of the harvest-taxes and dues (by) tenfold over my assessment of the harvest-taxes and dues."[82] Such assertions reveal perhaps quite vividly the limits of Egyptian bureaucracy, as general evaluations of wealth were probably approximate at best and left broad margin for corruption, further taxation by zealous officials, or extra income when needed. In other cases, assessments were contested as considered abusive or based on erroneous data: "You shall go with the standard-bearer Ptahemmaini and report to the vizier concerning the excessive silver that the retainer Iay tells me to give, for it is not my due tax at all."[83]

The make-up of the fiscal system is best perceived when state structures were under reconstruction, after a period of internal division and political turmoil. The end of the third millennium is a good example, thanks to the abundant references that throw light on the reorganization of the nucleus of the southern Theban kingdom and the subsequent restoration of the fiscal system in the entire country, after the incorporation of the northern Heracleopolitan territory and the oasis. First, officials and governors of agricultural and administrative centers (*hwt*) were appointed in the south, thus laying the foundations for the fiscal reorganization of this area, as stated by Redikhnum.[84] Another official, the great steward Henenu, proclaimed that "I taxed for him [= the pharaoh] Thinis of the Thinite province and the Lower Aphroditopolite province," before evoking his activities as treasurer of the produce of the (western) oasis and supplier of the provinces of Upper Egypt with oxen, goats, asses, and other goods.[85] Similar claims figure in General Djemi's inscriptions, when he said that "I taxed the people of Nubia for any chief who appeared in this province in bringing taxes (also) from the Thinite province." Other officials mention the census of cattle belonging to the house of the king and the control over a treasury filled with the choicest from the kingdom.[86]

Finally, the slightly later literary text *The Teaching for Merikare* provides invaluable evidence about the fiscal reorganization of a given area: "Look, the [land] which they had destroyed is made into provinces and every great town [is refounded], officials are appointed and provided

[81] Strudwick (2005: 355–6). [82] Davies (1997: 341). [83] Caminos (1954: 19).
[84] Lichtheim (1988: 43). [85] Hayes (1949). [86] Lichtheim (1988: 46–8).

with labor-services, with knowledge of every tax. Pure priests are provided with taxable fields;" "[T]he labor-services of the Delta belong to you;" "[T]he region of Djedsut totals ten thousand men, commoners and pure priests who are without labor-service. Officials have been in it since the time of the (royal) residence; the borders are confirmed, its strongholds are mighty; many northerners irrigate it as far as the Delta, taxed in grain in charge of the pure priests;" and "[B]uild (agricultural and administrative) *hwt* (centers) in the Delta!"[87] A key term, *neheb* ("provide, supply"), conveys the specific sense of endowing goods (fields, cattle) with the obligation to return a certain amount as taxes: "I spent the years as ruler of the Oryx province with all contributions for the king's house being in my charge. I gave gang-overseers to the domains of the herdsmen of the Oryx province and 3,000 oxen as their allocation. I was praised for it in the king's house in every year of the cattle tax. I delivered all their dues to the king's house, and there was no shortage against me in any bureau of his, for the entire Oryx province labored for me in steady stride." Also "[T]he man who fixes (literally: provides) the contributions in proportion to the barley is [a just] man in God's eyes."[88] Chiefs of the treasury and great stewards were the main protagonists in charge of rebuilding the fiscal system of the kingdom at the beginning of the second millennium.

Leaving aside such general fiscal reorganizations of the kingdom,[89] specific reforms aimed at providing a new institution with fresh income, such as new taxes or the redirection of finances in their interest. New cults and the mortuary temples of the reigning pharaoh were the main beneficiaries of these measures.[90] In other cases, reforms simply aimed at eradicating abuse, confirming previous endowments, and proclaiming the restoration of order and good governance. Not surprisingly, they were usually issued at the beginning of a new reign as a powerful ideological tool of legitimization.[91] Raising additional income under exceptional pressure (wars), especially from the temples, also included the abolition of previous fiscal exemptions and privileges.

Taxes and agriculture

Egypt being a pre-industrial society, agriculture played an essential role in pharaonic economy and taxation. In fact, some of the most extensive and

[87] Parkinson (1997: 223–4). [88] Ibid.: 241.
[89] For a late example, undertaken by King Psamtek I (664–610 BCE), see now Chauveau (2011).
[90] Spalinger (1990); Grandet (1994); Traunecker (2005).
[91] Davies (1997: 277–308); Murnane (1995: 212–14, 235–40).

precise administrative records preserved deal with land tenure and taxation. Two different spheres must be distinguished: on the one hand, institutional agriculture (that is to say, the exploitation of fields belonging to temples, the Crown, high dignitaries, and other institutions, such as the royal harem); on the other, domestic agriculture, referring to private fields exploited by non-institutional cultivators on an individual or collective basis (such as a family group).

Institutional agriculture was taxed according to several modalities, which changed over time. First of all, sources evoke the *jhwtj* system (especially in the second millennium). Under this system, cultivators (*jhwtj*) working for institutions, the Crown, and high dignitaries exploited standard fields of 20 *arouras* (*c.* 5.5 hectares) and delivered standard grain quota of 200 sacks (1 sack = 76.88 liters). The quantity of grain depended on the quality of the soil labored, and thus "high" fields delivered 5 sacks per *aroura*, "tired" fields 7.5 sacks per *aroura*, and "fresh" fields 10 sacks per *aroura*. Each cultivator had, in fact, responsibility for a yoke provided by the institution.[92] The *jhwtj* system was employed only on part of the fields of an institution, however, the bulk being cultivated by means of corvée work, whose modalities are evoked in the decree of Seti I (1294–1279 BCE) at Nauri: "[B]y requisition, (by transfer) from district to district, by *beret*-work, as forced labor for plowing and as forced labor for reaping."[93] Another part of institutional land was bestowed on individuals as smallholdings, perhaps as reward and remuneration for their services; they were assessed on the basis of a tax calculated on only a very small portion of the plots in their hands, at a fixed rate of 1.5 sacks per aroura. Finally, texts from around 1500 to 500 BCE mention a special kind of institutional field granted as privileged reward ("granted [*sah*] fields", "free [*nemeh*] fields"); their holders could subsequently sell, lease, or transfer their rights over these plots, but these operations were liable to a tax of about 10 percent of the harvest.[94] Late second-millennium papyri nevertheless show differences in the tax assessment of these "free" tenures. The differences were related to the social status of the landholders. Thus members of the priesthood benefited from a higher tax reduction that other landholders, with the exception of scribes.[95]

Other modalities of agricultural taxation concerned the activities of mayors. The documentary evidence reveals that they were constrained to cultivate the fields of temples and the Crown (*khato* fields), even fields

[92] Moreno García (2008; 2010b). [93] Davies (1997: 293). [94] Moreno García (2011).
[95] Katary (2011: 13).

ascribed to quays and intended to support officials and workers passing through in the course of their missions for the state. The royal decrees of the Old Kingdom reveal that mayors were part of the administrative counsel in charge of the exploitation of the domains of the temples, while a Middle Kingdom statue mentions the contributions (*baku*) expected from mayors for a temple at Elephantine. Later on, an early New Kingdom (about 1500 BCE) passage from the *Duties of the Vizier* states that it was the vizier "who dispatches the mayors and the governors of the *hwt*- (Crown) centers in order to cultivate and take care of the harvest/harvest tax." The complexity of the fiscal procedure involved is illustrated by a late second-millennium letter. The document shows that some Crown land at Kom Ombo was administrated by the domain of a priestess and supposed to be actually exploited by a mayor liable to hand over 100 sacks of barley.[96]

A controversial fiscal term related to agriculture is the harvest tax (*shemu*). A papyrus dating of the eighteenth dynasty (more precisely, about 1451 to 1444 BCE) reveals that several localities paid important amounts of grain as harvest tax.[97] In other cases the harvest tax was assessed on smallholders and institutions such as temples, and it was also collected from foreign territories subject to Egyptian control. A similar situation is attested in the Turin Taxation Papyrus, concerning the collection of grain from the crown fields (*khato*) in several localities and including also the harvest tax. The amount of the tax has been estimated to have been equivalent to about 10 percent of the entire yield.[98] Other grain taxes were assessed and collected according to the statements of the overseers of the royal granaries. Thus, during the eighteenth dynasty, Sennefri proclaimed that "I was placed as overseer of the Double Granary and I received. . .their contributions (*baku*), consisting of the assigned duties of their cities as the tax of every year," while Iamnedjeh was "counter of cattle and fowl, overseer of granaries who counts the taxes of Upper and Lower Egypt."

The transport of agricultural tax revenues is the subject of numerous New Kingdom papyri, such as the Turin Taxation Papyrus (dealing with the collection of grain revenues payable to the state by various institutions and individuals), Papyrus Amiens and Papyrus Baldwin, and others. They also testify to the closely interwoven network of bureaucrats and agencies engaged in revenue collection, transportation, and distribution.[99]

[96] Wente (1990: 131). [97] Megally (1977: 220–5). [98] Donker van Heel (1995: 91).
[99] Katary (2012); Gardiner (1941).

As for the taxation of privately held agricultural land, outside the institutional sphere, the evidence is scarce. A passage of an Old Kingdom royal decree reveals that trees and hydraulic installations such as wells and ponds were liable to census, and thus, quite probably, to some kind of tax. In fact, later sources enumerate the trees (even by their type) and cisterns present in agricultural plots. Artificial irrigation made it possible to cultivate small gardens and plantations where profitable crops were cultivated, especially by the elite. The papyrus Louvre E 3226 reveals that the Royal Granary delivered grain in exchange from dates to particulars, which might be interpreted as compulsory deliveries of specific foodstuff produced by particulars in their gardens. In fact, fleets belonging to the state or to temples traveled across the Nile and collected from particulars not just dates but also honey and vegetables. According to the New Kingdom Wilbour Papyrus, smallholders of a wide variety of occupations and titles, who were "private-possessors" or "virtual owners" of their plots located on institutional land, paid dues on their harvest on only a tiny portion of their plot at a fixed rate of 1½ sacks per *aroura*. These plots were usually 3 or 5 *arouras* in size (1 *aroura* equals 0.27 hectares or 0.66 acres).[100]

Taxing trade and private property

The traditional belief that the pharaonic economy was almost entirely state-administered has caused a lack of interest in private and/or non-institutional economic activities in current Egyptological literature. Markets and private trade have thus particularly suffered from such a distorted view and have been considered as of little significance in an otherwise overwhelmingly redistributive system. The significant amounts of taxes and gold collected from settlements, temples, and individuals mean that precious metals circulated widely in Egyptian society, however, and were subject to fiscal assessment. This would explain why the huge amounts of precious metals stolen from temples and royal tombs toward the end of the New Kingdom were easily exchanged by the robbers for fields, slaves, and cattle. Not surprisingly, the overseer of gold and silver Tutu, who lived in the times of Pharaoh Akhenaten (1352–1336 BCE), stated: "Pharaoh – life, prosperity, health! –, his good lord, ordains that all the officials and the chief men of the entire land be obliged to give him silver, gold, [cattle], clothing and copper vessels, they being imposed upon you like taxes (*heter*)."[101]

[100] Katary (2012). [101] Murnane (1995: 193).

In addition, fishermen, for instance, appear frequently in Egyptian sources as liable to payments in silver: a Ramesside ostracon states that fishermen in the Nile Delta paid 273 g each in silver annually,[102] while King Taharqa endowed a temple in Memphis with fields, offerings, and precious items, as well as with 2.7 kg of silver as the contribution of the fishermen of Memphis. Gold too was delivered by officials, such as a keeper of natron in the locality of Ramuna who paid 91 kg in gold as his annual contribution (around 1250 BCE),[103] while a late second-millennium letter states that independent cultivators exploiting some land of the Crown at Kom Ombo paid gold directly into the pharaoh's treasury on a regular basis.[104] Trade appears, then, as an important economic activity that made it possible to accumulate wealth (as well as social prestige; Prince Simentu, son of Ramesses II, for example, married the daughter of a Syrian ship owner) and that was liable to taxation. Unfortunately, little is known about customs in pharaonic times. The Naukratis stela of King Nektanebo I (379 BCE) granted a temple in Sais one-tenth of the revenue derived from seaborne imports that were subject to a customs tax, but the rate at which the tax was levied remains unspecified.[105] Other late sources, from the Saite period (664 to 525 BCE), reveal the existence of customs at Elephantine (in southernmost Egypt) as well as in the eastern delta and in the Canopic branch of the Nile in the central delta.[106]

Private wealth was equally subject to requisitions and payments, and these give a glimpse into the kinds of goods sought by the state. The decree of Pharaoh Horemheb enumerates some of them, such as the boat service (boats taxable for service obligations), carrying wood, the requisition of slaves belonging to individuals, collecting hides, fodder, linen, and plants. There is even mention of the use of false units of measure when assessing the grain to be delivered as taxes.[107] The palace accounts of Seti I contain a census of timber and parts of boats, probably to be imminently requisitioned by the authorities, from about seventy houses of individuals, several chapels of deities, and royal properties, within and across a number of city districts or wards.[108] Several papyri of the New Kingdom evoke the goods collected from particulars by fleets belonging to temples or specialized royal departments, especially cloth, honey, meat, wine, bread, vegetables, charcoal, and sesame oil, among others.[109] Finally, at least in some cases officials, high dignitaries, local chiefs, or simply patrons provided services

[102] Warburton (1997: 145). [103] Ibid.: 160. [104] Wente (1990: 131).
[105] Lichtheim (1980: 86–9). [106] Briant and Descat (1998). [107] Murnane (1995: 235–40).
[108] Kitchen (1993: 219–22, 225–30, 231). [109] Janssen (1961); Condon (1984).

or accomplished missions for the state from their own resources, as providers of manpower under their direct control, which could be interpreted as evidence for a kind of indirect tax system that burdened them.[110]

Collecting taxes from towns and villages

Setting aside regular deliveries of agricultural produce, pharaonic sources contain abundant evidence for the fiscal revenue collected from cities and villages. A famous scene in the tomb of vizier Rekhmire (*c.* 1450–1400 BCE) shows the taxes levied in eighty localities of Upper Egypt. They include gold (ranging from 0.1 to 3.6 kg), silver, cattle, garments, and honey.[111] Slightly later inscriptions from the reign of Akhenaten confirm this pattern, as each mayor mentioned in the texts paid taxes consisting in gold, silver, bronze, garments, oil, wine, and honey.[112] In this context, the statement of the overseer of the double silver and gold houses Djehuty becomes clear: "I counted with regard to the mayors; I accepted all their taxes (*baku*)." Once more, the deliveries of gold reveal that precious metals circulated widely in Egyptian society, were stocked, and were partially returned to the treasury as fiscal revenue for the state. Other fiscal obligations included the provision of quays and the cultivation of fields ascribed to them, in order to supply royal expeditions.[113] Cattle were also exacted from villages as annual levies in order to supply temples in particular months,[114] and a Middle Kingdom contract from Siut reveals that the first fruits from the fields of commoners were customarily delivered to the local temple.[115] New Kingdom sources state that the deliveries due by mayors were controlled by the vizier, thus confirming the procedure shown in the tomb of Rekhmire.[116]

Granting villages to dignitaries as reward or remuneration was a particular form of fiscal contribution, as the tax revenue from these localities was thus directly transferred to the beneficiary of the endowment. Such measures, which are attested as early as the third millennium, occurred overall quite rarely, however.[117] The papyri of Gebelein, for instance, deal with some villages that formed one of these grants, bestowed on an unknown official in the late fourth dynasty (about 2500 BCE); they also

[110] Arnold (1990: 26); Andrássy (2007; 2009). See also the statements by Sabni of Aswan about the missions accomplished by the troops and dependents of his personal endowment: Strudwick (2005: 336).

[111] Davies (1943: plates 29–35). [112] Traunecker (2005). [113] Murnane (1995: 237–8).

[114] Ritner (2009: 180–6). [115] Montet (1936: 56–7). [116] Van den Boorn (1988: 287).

[117] Strudwick (2005: 191, 267, 364).

reveal that the obligations of the villagers included many contributions to the royal administration, such as working on architectural projects and delivering cereals and cloth.[118] In fact, the main fiscal contribution of villages was manpower. Old Kingdom sources evoke many distinct administrative bureaus, each of them able to request workers from Upper Egypt, and each of which kept lists of men liable to be conscripted. The Gebelein papyri are a good example of such lists, while the royal decrees from Coptos suggest that villagers were recruited to work for an agricultural domain just endowed to the temple of Min.[119] The stone marks in the mastaba of Khentika at Balat also show a system whereby people from different localities successively carried the blocks to be employed in the construction of the monument,[120] while Middle Kingdom sources such as the Reisner and Lahun papyri, the stone marks in the pyramids of the kings, and the Wadi Hammamat inscriptions describe in detail the local organization of teams of workers, their conscription, and the role played by the governors of the villages in their recruitment.[121]

Temples as taxpayers

The once common assumption that temples were independent institutions, even rivals and potential threats to the state, is no longer tenable.[122] Certainly, their domains were quite substantial, in particular in the period of the New Kingdom, when they appear as true management "agencies," in charge not only of their own property but also of fields belonging to the Crown. They also benefited from occasional privileges and exemptions of taxes, but such awards were revocable, while endowments were also subject to reestablishment when their "finances" had been redirected by previous kings, especially in the case of the mortuary temples. Such exemptions thus prove that taxes were normally collected from temples. An early example is the royal decree Coptos C:

> [D]ecrees had been sealed for this Upper Egypt, to the effect of the carrying out of required works for the king, (whether it be) in the form of every transport or every digging work which is ordered to be done in this Upper Egypt; in the control of (?) the overseer of Upper Egypt: gold, copper, decorative items (?); for the requirements of the House of Life: the annual requirements of rations and animal feed, offerings, ropes and bindings, animal skins; for the 19⅝ *arouras* of land and the rights of plowing; for all

[118] Posener-Kriéger and Demichelis (2004). [119] Strudwick (2005: 112–15).
[120] Castel, Pantalacci, and Cherpion (2001: 147–9).
[121] See Moreno García (2006: 113–19), with references. [122] Janssen (1979).

taxes and all works which are due on water and on land, (all this) is what is ordered to be done in this Upper Egypt.[123]

The fiscal demands on temples included not only the provision of workers and selected items, as well as the execution of specific tasks, but also the delivery of precious metals, thus revealing once again their widespread circulation outside the economic circuits controlled by the state, and that they could be stocked and subsequently taxed.

Later sources confirm this fiscal pattern. New Kingdom papyri reveal that temples were assessed and taxes collected from them,[124] while surviving epigraphic evidence from Akhenaten's reign show that thirty-one sanctuaries in Lower Egypt, twenty-eight in Middle Egypt, and twenty-eight in Upper Egypt paid annual impositions to the newly found cult of Aten, each one contributing with a fixed amount of silver (91 g), incense, wine, and garments.[125] Nevertheless, fiscal revenue assessed on individuals and royal domains was also redirected to temples, and the amounts transferred were on some occasions enormous.[126] Later on, Saite sources also provide some evidence regarding fiscal assessment on temples, especially the collection of the harvest tax,[127] as well as about extraordinary contributions intended to finance the military activities of the kings. Finally, abuses entailing the forced requisitions of temple property are evoked in the epigraphic record.[128]

The impact of labor services on the Egyptian population

The impact of the pharaonic fiscal regime on the Egyptian population can be ascertained only in a very approximate way. Members of the elite were obliged to contribute cattle and gold, for instance for the upkeep of specific cults, as fiscal contribution to the state, or as delivery to the funerary temple of the pharaoh.[129] They were also the main beneficiaries of the fiscal regime, however, as recipients of endowments, awards, rewards, gifts, and positions in the administration and the court. In fact, it seems that the revenue received from the state represented quite a significant part of their wealth, thus preventing the development of feudal tendencies when the state collapsed.[130] High officials such as Hapidjefa distinguished carefully between his own, family-held household (*pr jt*: "the house of the father") and the domain granted as a reward for his position of governor

[123] Strudwick (2005: 111). [124] Janssen (1991). [125] Traunecker (2005). [126] Grandet (1994).
[127] Černy (1932). [128] Vernus (1980: 216–18); Agut-Labordère and Chauveau (2011: 162).
[129] Janssen (1991); Luft (2006: 35–41); Ritner (2009: 180–6). [130] Moreno García (2010a: 32–8).

(*pr haty-a*: "the house of the governor");[131] domains of this kind usually included not only provisions but also serfs, fields, specialized workers and a suitable residence.[132] A priest of Amun, Nakhtefmut, stated that his property included goods inherited from his father and mother, possessions acquired by his own initiative, and rewards granted by the king.[133] Similar claims were made by Ibi of Der el-Gebrawi at the end of the third millennium.[134]

For the most part, the case of the Egyptian population is different. The contributions in work, services, and deliveries undermined the autonomy in the organization of subsistence production on a family basis, because work had to be diverted for the state and specific items had to be produced, which led to a withdrawal of part of the economic output of domestic production. The rations delivered by the state to the workers during their compulsory labor service can hardly be considered as a proof of a "social policy" or equitable redistribution, even to compensate for the disturbance of the productive cycle of peasants. Rather, they helped to increase the dependence of the working population on the state for its subsistence. Literary texts evoke in vivid terms the penury endured by peasants because of the fiscal demands of the agents of the Crown, to the point that fleeing was an option open to them. Papyri confirm this pattern. A Middle Kingdom papyrus from the great work camp of Thebes, for instance, evokes different kinds of compulsory work that Egyptians performed for the state (tilling the fields, keeping irrigation channels, harvesting crops, and clearing bushy areas); it also shows that, in the event that they fled the compulsory labor, they became fugitives and were punished by permanent compulsory work on the fields of the state.[135] In other cases, people were recruited and assigned to specific tasks by the administration.[136]

Bombastic expressions express what normal conditions of work were: "I gave a gift to this town without the use of corvée labor from Upper Egypt or draft labor from Lower Egypt"; "I installed a gate. . .a thing of lasting use, in a single construction, without dispossessing a household."[137] Not surprisingly, funerary figurines representing the servants of the deceased evoke the heavy workload for the Crown that they were supposed to accomplish for their master in the other life in his stead, which included terracing riverbanks, working on dykes, preparing fields, and irrigating land.[138] "Irregular taxes" included abuses such as requisitions by armies on

131 Montet (1936). 132 Lacau (1933: 11). 133 Jansen-Winkeln (2007: 143).
134 Strudwick (2005: 364–5). See also Moreno García (1999: 210–22). 135 Hayes (1955).
136 Moreno García (2006: 114–15). 137 Lichtheim 1988: 28).
138 Schneider (1977: 50–3, 57–60).

the march, as Commander Weni recorded in his inscriptions: "[S]o that no one took bread or sandals from the traveler, so that no one took cloth from any town, so that no one took a goat from any man;"[139] in other cases, fraud in the measures used: "Do not move the scales nor alter the weights, nor diminish the fractions of the measure, do not desire a measure of the fields, nor neglect those of the treasury."[140] That illegal requisitions or tax demands were quite common is proved by the fact that royal edicts tried to prevent and punish them.[141] Moreover, literary texts promoted compassion and flexibility in order to keep the system running: "Do not make a cultivator wretched with taxes, let him be well off and he will still be there for you the next year. . . [T]he man who fixes the taxes in proportion to the barley is [a just] man in God's eyes."[142] Nevertheless, frauds, abuses and requisitions were not the only calamities afflicting Egyptians; service in the army and in the expeditions to the quarries also took a heavy toll: up to 10 percent of the total contingent in the times of Ramesses IV, even 50 percent in other texts.[143]

Fiscal regime and empire

Egyptian conquests abroad opened a flow of revenue into Egypt. Prisoners of war, deportees, slaves, tribute, exotic goods, and deliveries filled the treasuries of the state, and significant amounts of these were reverted to the temples. In fact, expressions such as "filling the storerooms of the temples" with produce and serfs became a *topos* in New Kingdom royal ideology. The quantities thus obtained could be quite significant. Old Kingdom campaigns against Nubians and Libyans were followed by the capture of prisoners (1,100 Libyans and 7,000 – even 17,000 – Nubians in the campaigns of Sneferu)[144] and flocks amounting to hundreds of thousands of animals. This tendency is especially visible during the New Kingdom, when a durable empire was created in Nubia and the Levant, and tribute was imposed over these territories. It consisted of taxes (slaves, cattle, horses, cereals, wine, oil, metals, timber; in the case of Nubia, gold, ivory, precious skins of exotic animals, ebony) and prestige deliveries (incense, gold, silver, precious stones, and specialized prized workmanship: chariots, wooden objects, prized textiles, stone vessels, and gold and silver items). Other services involved the supply of harbors and stock centers in

[139] Strudwick (2005: 354). [140] Lichtheim (1976: 156); Murnane (1995: 238).
[141] Murnane (1995: 235–40); Davies (1997: 277–308); Strudwick (2005: 103 5, 107–13).
[142] Parkinson (1997: 241). [143] Peden (1994: 97). [144] See Strudwick (2005: 66–7, 150).

order to provision armies, messengers, diplomats, and Egyptian officials in transit. This usually meant that the resources of a given area were evaluated and taxes imposed, as in the case of the agricultural domains founded in the Jezreel Valley, which produced 207,300 sacks of wheat.[145] And, as it happened in Egypt, mayors were assigned with specific fiscal tasks and obligations towards Egyptian officials.

The impact of this flow of wealth within Egypt fueled specific economic activities. The arrival of prisoners and slaves who subsequently settled on temple estates contributed to the expansion of the *jhwtj* system in institutional agriculture, and there is some evidence that grain was exported in exchange for silver.[146] The Nile Delta appears to have been a particularly favored area, as it experienced true economic expansion founded on fishing, wine and olive oil production, agriculture, and cattle-rearing,[147] partly thanks to the settlement of prisoners such as Libyan herders, partly because of the foundation of a new capital at Pi-Ramesses in the eastern delta, together with a harbor and military facilities. Other sectors closely related to the needs of the army (specialized craftsmanship, merchants, mining) and of an expanding urban population (orchards and plantations) also flourished, and the resources devoted to massive building programs at Thebes, Pi-Ramesses, and other cities doubtless were a source of employment and revenue not only for artisans but for many Egyptians. Extraordinary fiscal revenues from foreign lands were thus reinvested in Egypt and partly treasured in temples and tombs, and it probably explains why precious metals appear to have circulated more widely than previously supposed in Egyptian society. Of course, military personnel, diplomats, garrisons, and administrators sent abroad expanded in New Kingdom times and opened new paths of promotion and employment for Egyptians. But the expenditures related to these activities, as well as the reinvestment of resources in conquered areas in order to gain the collaboration of local elites (such as New Kingdom temples and decorated tombs in Nubia), were the inevitable cost of imperial expansion, and diverted part of the state revenue.

Fiscal regimes in Egypt: conclusions

The fiscal regime built by the pharaohs experienced multiple changes in the course of three millennia, in order to cope with recurrent periods of state

[145] Na'aman (1988); Redford (1990: 40–63); Liverani (1990: 205–82); Smith (1995).
[146] Liverani (1990: 235–6). [147] Grandet (1994); Warburton (1997: 143–5).

collapse (and the subsequent rebuilding of the apparatus of government), reforms introduced by specific kings, and periods of imperial expansion and war in foreign territories. In spite of the lack of detailed fiscal records, the main outlines of the system can be ascertained, and, not surprisingly, taxes on agricultural production represented the bulk of the state's revenue. Temples appear to have been specialized management agencies at the service of the Crown, particularly when exploiting Crown fields and sustaining the army. Consequently, the previously held common assumption that temples and their privileges deprived the state of most of its resources should definitely be abandoned. The workforce was another fundamental asset assessed by the state, and in this respect mayors and rural potentates played an important role as intermediaries when recruiting people for the central administration. As for trade, the sources are scant, but increasing evidence shows that precious metals circulated outside the institutional sphere and the official rewards granted by the king, so that the treasury could collect them in various manners. The obvious conclusion is that markets made it possible to convert agricultural and craft production into silver and gold, as late second-millennium evidence for the "recycling" of stolen metals into land, flocks, and slaves through the intervention of merchants shows. Unfortunately, there is virtually no information on customs and private long-distance trade, but this subject seems to have been largely neglected in traditional interpretations of the pharaonic economy and tax system. In any case, what emerges is that the tax system fueled institutional mechanisms of redistribution of wealth within Egyptian society, both directly (when rations were exchanged for compelled labor) and indirectly (when state demand financed huge building programs and substantial craft production and thus employed manpower outside the labor service system). It also appears to have ensured the collaboration of the elite, as most of its revenue came from the state, thus enabling the stability of the kingdom in the *longue durée*. In any event, the literary record considers the tax system as inseparable from the state: "What is a treasury for, without its taxes? For the heart of a king is happy only when true tribute comes to him."[148]

Some concluding observations

The bird-eye's view of the development of Mesopotamian fiscal systems that results from the foregoing survey of the best-attested systems reveals

[148] Parkinson (1997: 174).

structural similarities with the case of ancient Egypt. All Mesopotamian states (not just those discussed here) mobilized and redistributed resources on a large scale. This is true independently of their political structure: it is as true for the highly integrated patrimonial state of the Ur III period as for the much more inhomogeneous Neo-Babylonian Empire.[149] This follows from the ecological and economic setting of agrarian societies that are dependent on irrigation agriculture, and is therefore also true for Egypt. Such societies could achieve a considerable agrarian surplus that supported social hierarchization and elite formation in a general sense, but this required a society-wide effort in order to establish and maintain the necessary infrastructure.[150] It is for this reason that both in Mesopotamia and in Egypt the extraction of labor has to be considered together with all issues of taxation; structurally, at least in Mesopotamia it is in fact the most important form in which the state drew on society's resources. It was also essential for the functioning of society at large: without communal labor, neither the Mesopotamian nor the Egyptian economy could not have functioned. Large-scale spending by the state for prestige buildings and for investment in the agrarian infrastructure and the like not only absorbed huge resources through the labor service system, it also stimulated the economy because of the resultant demand for hired labor, skilled and unskilled, which is in evidence in Egypt and (especially first-millennium) Mesopotamia alike. Overall, the modes of resource mobilization adopted by the ancient Mesopotamian and Egyptian states were a decisive factor for the shaping of the economy and society.

The survey of fiscal systems offered here shows the need for making diachronic distinctions. Michael Hudson's survey of ancient (and in particular Mesopotamian) fiscal evolution is useful as a point of departure.[151] He posits "nine principles of ancient fiscal evolution," of which the most important are the following: the paramount importance of military conscription among the various demands made by the state on its population, its

[149] The political structure of this empire was characterized by a division of power between Aramean and Chaldean sedentary and nomadic tribes, the Old Babylonian cities of the heartland, and the central monarchy, which was always contested between tribes and cities (as well as among the tribes themselves).

[150] It should be emphasized that this is not tantamount to claiming that the requirements of irrigation agriculture favored the formation of large, highly centralized states, in the vein of Wittfogel's thesis of hydraulic civilizations. While such states developed in Mesopotamia, the irrigation systems were usually not highly integrated and could be maintained on a local level. Before the first millennium BC there was little central planning and interregional coordination between irrigation works. Building projects, while very numerous, were of limited scale and followed largely the patterns determined by the natural development of the river network: Adams (1981).

[151] Hudson (2000).

cost being covered not by direct taxation but by drawing on the resources of landholders in proportion to their holdings; the widespread reliance on temple and palace dominions for the support of these institutions; tribute-taking as a form of society-wide tax, typically imposed on subjected population groups (that is, on "others"); an absence of public debt and of comprehensive budgeting; and successful tax evasion by elites. In Hudson's view, the overall strong reliance on revenue from public assets and on labor services reduced the need for market transactions and the taxation of crops and goods.

All these points are valid at least for some periods and to some extent, but in the light of the evidence presented one should add some qualifications. First, the importance of labor services[152] is undeniable. It should be noted, however, that from the second millennium onward the conversion of labor services into substitute payments, more often in cash than in kind, was extremely common in Mesopotamia: the distinction between taxation and the extraction of labor was always blurred. Access to manpower continued to be the primary interest of the state, but this demand was channeled through a labor market; substitutes had to be hired and paid competitive wages. This is particularly clear in first-millennium Babylonia, where landowners had to market their produce aggressively because they had to raise cash to pay for the substitute laborers who fulfilled the service obligations incumbent on their land; market exchange of various forms, monetization, and taxation are inextricably linked in this period. The scarce evidence from Egypt, with its institutional bias, does not allow similar conclusions. Local potentates and village chiefs appear as indispensable intermediaries in order to enlist their fellow citizens for state work, and corvées are evoked in sources from all periods. The role of a market/wage system remains obscure, however, not only because of the absence of evidence but also, quite probably, because of the use of a kinship terminology that considered employees as members of the employer's household. Thus, for instance, early second-millennium private letters and literary texts already mention land leasing and lessees, thus implying that some workforce was available and hired, at least in the agricultural sector, at such an early date.[153] Early first-millennium inscriptions also give the price for several agricultural workers, but only some of them were "slaves." It is,

[152] Conceptually, for Mesopotamian states, and also for Egypt, military conscription was just a special case of forced labour service. The terminology that was used was often the same for soldiers and workers (the common collective terms *érin* (Sumerian) and *ṣābu* (Akkadian) both mean "workers" and "troops").

[153] Allen (2002); Parkinson (1997: 240–1).

then, possible that such prices correspond, in fact, to wages.[154] In any event, the very existence of a labor market in other economic sectors is unattested until the late first millennium BCE.

Second, one should question the assumption of the ubiquitous reliance of Mesopotamian states on revenue from temple and palace lands, which is tantamount to assuming that these states were (largely) domain states in the sense of the "Bonney–Ormrod model."[155] This is undoubtedly true for the Ur III state, at least in the sense that it was conceptualized by its ruling elites: here we do have a pyramidical structure of interlocking households with mutual obligations, all of which are in the end subject to the direct or indirect demands of the king.[156] Additionally, the early Old Babylonian city states of the south fit this assumption. It is not true for the large empires of the first millennium; of course, domain revenue continued to play an important role, but we do see strong tendencies toward the development of a tax state in the sense of the Bonney–Ormrod model: the kings/states increasingly demand contributions that are based not on the ownership of land or other resources (which makes the revenue a rent rather than a tax) but on the ruler's authority as such. The Neo-Assyrian Empire developed a fairly uniform and effective taxation model with its grain, straw, and cattle taxes. In the Neo-Babylonian and Achaemenid period we have clear evidence for the broadening of the tax base by a considerable expansion of indirect taxation and the corresponding extension of accounting and information-gathering procedures.[157] Other elements of the tax state according to the Bonney–Ormrod model that are present in first-millennium Mesopotamia, but less so in earlier periods, include: a professional class of bureaucrats that worked side by side with members of the traditional (patrimonial) social stratum of elite families;[158] state responsibilities seeming to expand; a general tendency toward money payments in the taxation sphere, especially in Babylonia in the sixth and fifth century, but not so much earlier in Assyria; and taxation becoming increasingly regular and predictable. Unfortunately, the Egyptian sources are much less detailed, but some changes over time suggest that the focus

[154] Ritner (2009: 170–1). [155] Bonney and Ormrod (1999).

[156] In actual practice, local particularism and resistance on the part of local elites undermined the uniform monolithic structure of the Ur III state.

[157] The introduction of land registers is a case in point, as is the centralized monitoring of various sale transactions.

[158] This is particularly clear in the case of the Neo-Assyrian and Neo-Babylonian "courtiers," *ša rēši*. These men, perhaps eunuchs, owed special allegiance to the king as the head of their household (as they were by definition devoid of family ties). They formed the backbone of the higher administrative ranks and were clearly specially trained for the purpose in palace (scribal) schools.

on direct agricultural production on temple and Crown land was being replaced by a more decentralized system for which indirect taxation became increasingly important. This is why the third-millennium *hwt* system (based on royal agricultural domains) and the early second-millennium *kheneret* system (based on work camps) were replaced in the second half of the second millennium by an indirect form of resource extraction. Temples appeared then to have been managerial agencies in charge of the cultivation not only of their vast domains but also of Crown land, and they handled huge quantities of silver and gold in their economic activities and transactions, also involving merchants in their service.[159] Moreover, town and cities appear as taxpayers furnishing agricultural goods, textiles, and important amounts of gold and silver, thus pointing to the wide circulation of precious metals and, consequently, to the existence of markets in which agricultural produce and artisanal goods were exchanged and converted into gold and silver. First-millennium sources are scanty, but private documents and literary texts reveal that the use of silver in everyday transactions was expanding,[160] especially during the Saite period, when huge numbers of mercenaries were recruited for the pharaonic armies and paid in silver.

Third, there is not a single Mesopotamian state, not even the Neo-Assyrian Empire, for which tribute and war booty were the mainstay of public finance, nor can this be claimed for any phase of Egyptian history. Tribute, gifts, and booty were more important for some states than for others, but we have no structural reason to assume that the importance of such income exceeded that of internal revenue. In certain instances, however, a "windfall" of tribute and booty demonstrably could change the structure of an economy.[161]

In conclusion, within the framework of the Bonney–Ormrod model, one might say that, while elements of the domain state and the tax state always coexisted in Mesopotamia, the overall trend certainly favored the latter over the former in the first millennium BC, contrary to the view expressed, for example, by Hudson.[162] Elements of the tribute state were likewise present at all times, but they never dominated. A similar trend is also discernible in ancient Egypt, as the gradual integration of the country

[159] Peet (1934); Grandet (1994: 237–8).

[160] Lichtheim (1980: 172, 206); Donker van Heel (1995: 125–33; 229–35); Agut-Labordère and Chauveau (2011: 151).

[161] As was the case in Assyria under Sargon II, when the monetary system changed owing to the influx of large quantities of precious metal.

[162] Hudson (2000) – a view that reflects earlier Assyriological orthodoxy.

into the international exchange networks of the first millennium, as well as the use of huge contingents of mercenaries in the army, fueled the use of silver in ordinary transactions. Nevertheless, a significant difference from the case of Mesopotamia was the strategic role played by exports of grain, which helped preserve a huge cereal-based economy in the institutional sector (the Crown and temple domains) and a tax system for which deliveries of grain continued to play an important role for centuries, thus slowing down the use and diffusion of "money."

References

Adams, R. McC. (1981) *Heartland of Cities: Surveys of Ancient Settlement and Land Use on the Central Floodplain on the Euphrates*. Chicago.

Agut-Labordère, D., and Chauveau, M. (2011) *Héros, magiciens et sages oubliés de l'Égypte ancienne*. Paris.

Allen, J. P. (2002) *The Heqanakhte Papyri*. New York.

Andrássy, P. (2007) "Builders' graffiti and administrative aspects of pyramid and temple building in ancient Egypt", in *Ägyptologische Tempeltagung: Structuring Religion*, ed. R. Preys. Wiesbaden: 1–16.

(2009) "Symbols in the Reisner Papyri", in *Non-Textual Marking Systems: Writing and Pseudo Script from Prehistory to Modern Times*, ed. P. Andrássy, J. Budka, and F. Kammerzell. Göttingen: 113–22.

Arnold, F. (1990) *The South Cemeteries of Lisht*, vol. II, *The Control Notes and Team Marks*: New York.

Baker, H. D. (2004) *The Archive of the Nappāḫu Family. Vienna.*

Bonney, R., and Ormrod, W. M. (1999) "Introduction: crises, revolutions and self-sustained growth: towards a conceptual model of change in fiscal history," in *Crises, Revolutions and Self-Sustained Growth: Essays in European Fiscal History, 1130–1830*, ed. W. M. Ormrod, M. Bonney, and R. Bonney. Stamford, UK: 1–21.

Briant, P., and Descat, R. (1998) "Un registre douanier de la satrapie d'Égypte à l'époque achéménide," in *Le commerce en Égypte ancienne*, ed. B. Menu. Cairo: 59–104.

Caminos, R. A. (1954) *Late-Egyptian Miscellanies*. London.

Castel, G., Pantalacci, L., and Cherpion, N. (2001) *Balat V: le mastaba de Khentika: tombeau d'un gouverneur de l'Oasis à la fin de l'Ancien Empire*. Cairo.

Černy, J. (1932) "The abnormal-hieratic tablet Leiden I 431," in *Studies Presented to F. Ll. Griffith*, ed. S. R. K. Glanville and N. Macdonald Griffith. London: 46–56.

Charles, M. P. (1988) "Irrigation in lowland Mesopotamia," *Bulletin on Sumerian Agriculture* 4: 1–39.

(1990) "Traditional crop husbandry in southern Iraq 1900–1960 AD," *Bulletin on Sumerian Agriculture* 5: 47–64.

Charpin, D. (2004) "Histoire politique du Proche-Orient amorrite (2000–1595)," in *Mesopotamien: die altbabylonische Zeit*, ed. D. Charpin, D. O. Edzard, and M. Stol. Fribourg: 23–480.

Chauveau, M. (2011) "Le saut dans le temps d'un document historique: des Ptolémées aux Saïtes", in *La XXVIe dynastie, continuités et ruptures: promenade saïte avec Jean Yoyotte*, ed. D. Devauchelle. Paris: 39–45.

Condon, V. (1984) "Two account papyri of the late eighteenth dynasty (Brooklyn 35.1453A and B)," *Revue d'Égyptologie* 35: 57–82.

Da Riva, R. (2008) *The Neo-Babylonian Royal Inscriptions: An Introduction.* Münster.

Davies, N. de G. (1943) *The Tomb of Rekh-mi-Re at Thebes.* New York.

Davies, B. G. (1997) *Egyptian Historical Inscriptions of the Nineteenth Dynasty.* Jonsered, Sweden.

Donker van Heel, K. 1995 *Abnormal Hieratic and Early Demotic Texts Collected by the Theban Choachytes in the Reign of Amasis: Papyri from the Louvre Eisenlohr Lot.* Leiden.

Fales, F. M. 2001 *L'impero assiro: storia e amministrazione (IX–VII secolo AC).* Rome.

Fuchs, A. (2008) "Über den Wert von Befestigungsanlagen," *Zeitschrift für Assyriologie* 98: 45–99.

Gardiner, A. H. (1941) "Ramesside texts relating to the taxation and transport of corn", *Journal of Egyptian Archaeology* 27: 19–73.

Garfinkle, S. J. (2008) "Was the Ur III state bureaucratic? Patrimonialism and bureaucracy in the Ur III period," in *The Growth of an Early State in Mesopotamia: Studies in Ur III Administration*, ed. S. J. Garfinkle and J. Cale Johnson. Madrid: 55–61.

Grandet, P. (1994) *Le papyrus Harris I (BM 9999).* Cairo.

Guksch, C. E. (1999) "Anthropology and Egyptology", in *Encyclopedia of the Archaeology of Ancient Egypt*, ed. K. A. Bard. London: 153–7.

Halstead, P. (1990) "Quantifying Sumerian agriculture: some seeds of doubt and hope," *Bulletin on Sumerian Agriculture* 5: 187–95.

Hayes, W. C. (1949) "Career of the great steward Henenu under Nebhepetreʿ Mentuhotpe," *Journal of Egyptian Archaeology* 35: 43–9.

(1955) *A Papyrus of the Late Middle Kingdom in the Brooklyn Museum (Papyrus Brooklyn 35.1446).* New York.

Hudson, M. (2000) "Mesopotamia and classical antiquity," in *Land-Value Taxation around the World*, 3rd edn, ed. R. V. Andelson. Malden, MA: 3–25.

Jansen-Winkeln, K. (2007) *Inschriften der Spätzeit*, vol. II, *Die 22. – 24. Dynastie.* Wiesbaden.

Janssen, J. J. (1961) *Two Ancient Egyptian Ship's Logs: Papyrus Leiden I 350 verso and Papyrus Turin 2008 + 2016.* Leiden.

(1979) "The role of the temple in the Egyptian economy during the New Kingdom," in *State and Temple Economy in the Ancient Near East*, vol. II, ed. E. Lipiński. Leuven: 505–15.

(1991) "Requisitions from Upper Egyptian temples (P. BM 10401)," *Journal of Egyptian Archaeology* 77: 79–94.

Joannès, F. (2006) "La fiscalité de la Babylonie achéménide," in *Fiscality in Mycenaean and Near Eastern Archives: Proceedings of the Conference Held at Soprintendenza Archivistica per la Campania, Naples, 21–23 October 2004*, ed. M. Perna. Winona Lake, IN: 49–57.

Jursa, M. (1999) *Das Archiv des Bēl-rēmanni*. Istanbul.

(2002) *Prywatyzacja i zysk? Przedsiębiorcy a gospodarka instytucjonalna w Mezopotamii od 3 do 1 tysiąclecia przed Chr [Privatisation and Profit? Entrepreneurs and Institutional Households in Mesopotamia from the Third to the First Millennium BC]*. Poznań.

(2005) *Neo-Babylonian Legal and Administrative Documents: Typology, Contents and Archives*. Münster.

(2008) "Economic change and legal innovation in Babylonia", in *I diritti del mondo cuneiforme: Mesopotamia e regioni adiacenti,* ca. *2500–500 aC*, ed. M. Liverani and C. Mora. Pavia: 601–28.

(2010) (contrib. J. Hackl, B. Janković, K. Kleber, E. E. Payne, C. Waerzeggers, and M. Weszeli) *Aspects of the Economic History of Babylonia in the First Millennium BC: Economic Geography, Economic Mentalities, Agriculture, the Use of Money and the Problem of Economic Growth*. Münster.

(2011a) "Steuer. D. Spätbabylonisch," *Reallexikon der Assyriologie* 13: 168–75.

(2011b) "Taxation and service obligations in Babylonia from Nebuchadnezzar to Darius and the evidence for Darius' tax reform", in *Herodot und das Persische Weltreich*, ed. R. Rollinger, B. Truschnegg, and R. Bichler. Wiesbaden: 431–48.

Jursa, M., and Waerzeggers, C. (2009) "On aspects of taxation in Achaemenid Babylonia: new evidence from Borsippa," in *Organisation des pouvoirs et contacts culturels dans les pays de l'empire achéménide*, ed. P. Briant and M. Chaeuveau. Paris: 237–69.

Katary, S. L. D. (2011) "Land tenure (to the end of the Ptolemaic period)", in *UCLA Encyclopedia of Egyptology*, ed. W. Wendrich. Los Angeles. Online version accessed (https://escholarship.org/uc/nelc_uee).

(2012) "Taxation to the end of the Third Intermediate Period", *UCLA Encyclopedia of Egyptology*, ed. W. Wendrich. Los Angeles. Online version accessed (https://escholarship.org/uc/nelc_uee).

Kitchen, K. A. (1993) *Ramesside Inscriptions, Translated and Annotated: Translations,* vol. I, *Ramesses, Sethos I and Contemporaries*. Oxford.

Kleber, K. (2008) *Tempel und Palast: die Beziehungen zwischen dem König und dem Eanna-Tempel im spätbabylonischen Uruk*. Münster.

Lacau, P. (1933) *Une stèle juridique de Karnak*. Cairo.

Lichtheim, M. (1976) *Ancient Egyptian Literature,* vol. II, *The New Kingdom*. Berkeley, CA.

(1980) *Ancient Egyptian Literature,* vol. III, *The Late Period*. Berkeley, CA.

(1988) *Ancient Egyptian Autobiographies Chiefly of the Middle Kingdom: A Study and an Anthology*. Fribourg.

Liverani, M. (1990) *Prestige and Interest: International Relations in the Near East* ca. *1600–1100 BC*. Padua.
(1998) *Uruk, la prima città*. Rome.
Luft, U. (2006) *Urkunden zur Chronologie der späten 12. Dynastie: Briefe aus Illahun*. Vienna.
Maekawa, K. (1990) "Cultivation methods in the Ur III period," *Bulletin on Sumerian Agriculture* 5: 115–45.
Manning, J. G. (2003) *Land and Power in Ptolemaic Egypt: The Structure of Land Tenure*. Cambridge.
Megally, M. 1977 *Recherches sur l'économie, l'administration et la comptabilité égyptiennes à la XVIIIe dynastie d'après le papyrus E. 3226 du Louvre*. Cairo.
Michalowski, P. (2011) *The Correspondence of the Kings of Ur: An Epistolary History of an Ancient Mesopotamian Kingdom*. Winona Lake, IN.
Molina, M. (2008) "The corpus of Neo-Sumerian tablets: an overview," in *The Growth of an Early State in Mesopotamia: Studies in Ur III Administration*, ed. S. J. Garfinkle and J. Cale Johnson. Madrid: 19–53.
Montet, P. (1936) "Les tombeaux de Siout et de Deir Rifeh (troisième article)," *Kêmi* 6: 131–63.
Moreno García, J. C. (1999) *Hwt et le milieu rural égyptien du IIIe millénaire: économie, administration et organization territoriale*. Paris.
(2006) "Les temples provinciaux et leur rôle dans l'agriculture institutionnelle de l'Ancien et du Moyen Empire," in *L'agriculture institutionnelle en Égypte ancienne: état de la question et perspectives interdisciplinaires*, ed. J. C. Moreno García. Villeneuve d'Ascq, France: 93–124.
(2008) "La dependance rurale en Égypte ancienne," *Journal of the Economic and Social History of the Orient* 51: 99–150.
(2010a) "Introduction: élites et états tributaires: le cas de l'Égypte pharaonique," in *Élites et pouvoir en Égypte ancienne*, ed. J. C. Moreno García. Villeneuve d'Ascq, France: 11–50.
(2010b) "Les *jhwtjw* et leur rôle socio-économique au IIIe et IIe millénaires avant J-C," in *Élites et pouvoir en Égypte ancienne*, ed. J. C. Moreno García. Villeneuve d'Ascq, France: 321–51.
(2011) "Les *mnhw*: société et transformations agraires en Égypte entre la fin du IIe et le début du Ier millénaire", *Revue d'Égyptologie* 62: 105–14.
Müller-Wollermann, R. (2011) "The impact of the Greco-Persian conflict on the Egyptian economy," in *Intercultural Contacts in the Ancient Mediterranean*, ed. K. Duistermaat and I. Regulski. Leuven: 589–97.
Murnane, W. J. (1995) *Texts from the Amarna Period in Egypt*. Atlanta.
Na'aman, N. (1988) "Pharaonic lands in the Jezreel Valley in the Late Bronze Age," in *Society and Economy in the Eastern Mediterranean (c. 1500–1000 BC)*, ed. M. Heltzer and E. Lipiński. Leuven: 177–85.
Parkinson, R. B. (1997) *The Tale of Sinuhe and Other Ancient Egyptian Poems 1940–1640 BC*. Oxford.
Paoletti, P., and Schrakamp, I. (2011) "Steuer. A. Babylonien im 3. jahrtausend," *Reallexikon der Assyriologie* 13: 161–4.

Peden, A. J. (1994) *Egyptian Historical Inscriptions of the Twentieth Dynasty.* Jonsered, Sweden.

Peet, T. E (1934) "The unit of value *shati*," in *Mélanges Maspero*, vol. I, *Orient ancien*. Cairo: 184–99.

Posener-Kriéger, P., and Demichelis, S. (2004) *I papiri di Gebelein: Scavi G. Farina 1935*. Turin.

Postgate, J. N. (1994) *Early Mesopotamia: Society and Economy at the Dawn of History*, 2nd edn. London.

(2011) "Steuer. C. Mittel- und neuassyrisch," *Reallexikon der Assyriologie* 13: 168.

Potts, D. (1997) *Mesopotamian Civilization: The Material Foundations*. London.

Préaux, C. (1939) *L'économie royale des Lagides*. Brussels.

Radner, K. 1997 *Die neuassyrischen Privatrechtsurkunden als Quelle für Mensch und Umwelt* (SAAS 6). Helsinki.

(1999) "Money in the Neo-Assyrian Empire," in Dercksen (1999): 127–57.

(2007) "Abgaben an den assyrischen König aus dem In- und Ausland," in *Geschenke und Steuern, Zölle, und Tribute: antike Abgabenformen in Anspruch und Wirklichkeit*, ed. H. Klinkott, S. Kubisch, and R. Müller-Wollermann. Leiden: 213–30.

Rathbone, D. W. (1989) "The ancient economy and Graeco-Roman Egypt," in *Egitto e storia antica dall'ellenismo all'età araba: bilancio di un confronto*, ed. L. Criscuolo and G. Geraci. Bologna: 159–76.

(2000) "Ptolemaic to Roman Egypt: the death of the *dirigiste* state?," in *Production and Public Powers in Classical Antiquity*, ed. E. Lo Cascio and D. W. Rathbone. Cambridge: 44–54.

Redford, D. B. (1990) *Egypt and Canaan in the New Kingdom*. Beersheba.

Renger, J. (1995) "Institutional, communal, and individual ownership or possession of arable land in ancient Mesopotamia from the end of the fourth to the end of the first millennium BC," *Chicago Kent Law Review* 71: 269–319.

(2011) "Steuer. B. Altbabylonisch," *Reallexikon der Assyriologie* 13: 165–8.

Ritner, R. K. (2009) *The Libyan Anarchy: Inscriptions from Egypt's Third Intermediate Period*. Atlanta.

Sallaberger, W. (1999) "Ur III-Zeit," in *Mesopotamien: Akkade-Zeit und Ur III-Zeit*, ed. W. Sallaberger and A. Westenholz. Fribourg: 121–392.

Schneider, H. D. (1977) *Shabtis: An Introduction to the History of Ancient Egyptian Funerary Statuettes*, vol. I. Leiden.

Sharlach, T. (2004) *Provincial Taxation and the Ur III State*. Leiden.

Smith, S. T. (1995) *Askut in Nubia: The Economics and Ideology of Egyptian Imperialism in the Second Millennium BC*. London.

Spalinger, A. 1990 "Some revisions of temple endowments in the New Kingdom", *Journal of the American Research Center in Egypt* 28: 21–39.

Steinkeller, P. (1991) "The administrative and economic organization of the Ur III state: the core and the periphery," in *The Organization of Power: Aspects of Bureaucracy in the Ancient Near East*, ed. McG. Gibson and R. D. Biggs. Chicago: 15–33.

Stol, M. (2004) "Wirtschaft und Gesellschaft in altbabylonischer Zeit," in *Mesopotamien: die altbabylonische Zeit*, ed. D. Charpin, D. O. Edzard and M. Stol. Fribourg: 641–975.

Stolper, M. W. (1985) *Entrepreneurs and Empire: The Murašû Archive, the Murašû Firm, and Persian Rule in Babylonia*. Istanbul.

(1989) "Registration and taxation of slave sales in Achaemenid Babylonia," *Zeitschrift für Assyriologie* 79: 80–101.

(2000) "Buildings on bow land and encumbrances on buildings," in *Variatio Delectat: Iran und der Westen: Gedenkschrift für Peter Calmeyer*, ed. R. Dittmann, B. Hrouda, U. Löw, P. Matthiae, R. Mayer-Opificius, and S. Thürwächter. Münster: 667–80.

Strudwick, N. (2005) *Texts from the Pyramid Age*. Atlanta.

Traunecker, C. (2005) "Amenhotep IV, precepteur royal du Disque," in *Akhénaton et l'époque amarnienne*, ed. T.-L. Bergerot. Paris: 145–82.

Van de Mieroop, M. (1999) *Cuneiform Texts and the Writing of History*. London.

Van den Boorn, G. P. F. (1988) *The Duties of the Vizier: Civil Administration in the Early New Kingdom*. London.

Van Driel, G. (1988) "Neo-Babylonian agriculture," *Bulletin on Sumerian Agriculture* 4: 121–59.

(1990) "Neo-Babylonian agriculture, part III: cultivation," *Bulletin on Sumerian Agriculture* 5: 219–66.

(2002) *Elusive Silver: In Search of a Role for a Market in an Agrarian Environment: Aspects of Mesopotamia's Society*. Istanbul.

Vernus, P. (1980) "Inscriptions de la Troisième Période Intermédiaire (IV)," *Cahiers de Karnak* 6: 215–33.

Waerzeggers, C. (2003) "The Babylonian revolts against Xerxes and the 'end of archives,'" *Archiv für Orientforschung* 50: 150–73.

(2006) "The Carians of Borsippa," *Iraq* 68: 1–22.

(2010a) *The Ezida Temple of Borsippa: Priesthood, Cult, Archives*. Leiden.

(2010b) "Babylonians in Susa: the travels of Babylonian businessmen to Susa reconsidered," in *Der Achämenidenhof*, ed. B. Jacobs and R. Rollinger. Wiesbaden: 777–813.

Warburton, D. A. (1997) *State and Economy in Ancient Egypt: Fiscal Vocabulary of the New Kingdom*. Fribourg.

Wente, E. (1990) *Letters from Ancient Egypt*. Atlanta.

Weszeli, M. (2009) "Schiff und Boot. B. in mesopotamischen Quellen des 2. und 1. Jahrtausends," *Reallexikon der Assyriologie* 12: 160–71.

(2010) "Appendix: the costs of transporting goods," in Jursa (2010): 140–52.

Wiggermann, F. (2000) "Agriculture in the northern Balikh Valley: the case of Middle Assyrian Tell Sabi Abyad," in *Rainfall and Agriculture in Northern Mesopotamia: Proceedings of the Third MOS Symposium (Leiden 1999)*, ed. R. Jas. Leiden: 171–231.

Wilkinson, T. A. H. (2000) *Royal Annals of Ancient Egypt: The Palermo Stone and Its Associated Fragments*. London.

PART II

Determinants of Intensification and Abatement

CHAPTER 5

Hellenistic empires

Andrew Monson

When Alexander the Great died in 323 BCE, there was no clear heir to his position as king of Macedonia and of the Achaemenid Persian Empire that he had conquered. In the ensuing wars, Macedonian generals carved up the empire into a handful of personal kingdoms. Most Greek city states either fell under the influence of one or other Macedonian king, while some (particularly in central Greece, the Peloponnesus, and the Aegean islands) joined multi-city federations to resist interference in their local politics. Egypt, the last of these Macedonian kingdoms, was annexed to the Roman Empire in 30 BCE, ending the so-called "Hellenistic period" (*c.* 323–30 BCE). It was a period characterized by costly interstate warfare, intra-dynastic conflicts, and local rebellions.

The Hellenistic states occupy an interlude between two periods of world empire, when one state overwhelmingly dominated its periphery: the Achaemenid Persian Empire (*c.* 530–330 BCE) and the early Roman monarchy (*c.* 30 BCE–200 CE). The political geography was complex, with a number of minor kingdoms, independent city states, and frequent territorial changes. The focus in this chapter is on the two major imperial Hellenistic states that succeeded the boundaries of Achaemenid Persia: Ptolemaic Egypt and Seleucid Asia. The third most powerful kingdom, Antigonid Macedonia, is treated briefly but the evidence for fiscal institutions there is sparse. Rome too must figure in this discussion, because from 215 BCE onward it was increasingly a factor in Hellenistic interstate relations and because its annexation of the Hellenistic states accompanied fiscal reforms that help us understand the institutions that came beforehand. In other words, the chapter examines only the largest and most successful competitors for Mediterranean hegemony, omitting even those that experienced fleeting phases of regional dominance, such as Pergamon and Rhodes.

The aim of this chapter is not to provide a survey of fiscal institutions but to pose a general question and to frame the discussion around it. Were the revenue demands of Hellenistic empires qualitatively and quantitatively different from those of the preceding Persian and the subsequent Roman Empire? If so, what factors can account for those differences? The working hypothesis is that fragmented warring states would be under pressure to adopt intrusive fiscal measures in the face of immediate external threats and that such measures would exacerbate local resistance as well. Conversely, the formation of a single hegemonic power or world empire could alleviate fiscal pressure, giving taxpayers a peace dividend. One way to test this hypothesis is by looking at the effects of instability of the external and internal political environment on the fiscal institutions for these states. The correlation is not going to be a simple one but is worth establishing nevertheless. The nature of taxation depends on the cooperation mechanisms that govern it, including political institutions, agency costs, intra-elite competition, and collective bargaining. These may work either for or against the adoption of intrusive fiscal measures in war and their alleviation in times of peace.

The Hellenistic kingdoms confronted a cooperation dilemma inherent in their very foundation as spear-won territories.[1] First, the rulers depended for their security on professional soldiers, especially on Macedonian and Greek forces specialized in phalanx-infantry and cavalry techniques. These soldiers required payments and land that had to be redistributed from subject communities. Ptolemaic Egypt and Seleucid Asia raised high levels of tax (significantly greater than 10 percent of annual harvests) from their mostly non-Greek agrarian communities.[2] Competing for the same surplus was an intermediate group of local elites, especially temple personnel and other managers of large estates. In times of plenty the ruling dynasty rewarded elites who showed loyalty with fiscal privileges. This would lower agency costs for the state and encourage voluntary cooperation. More often during the Hellenistic period, however, there were setbacks in war and dynastic conflicts that created fiscal crises and, given the competition for local surplus, rebellions. The resulting pressure for higher levels of taxation entailed more intrusive fiscal control at the expense of local elites, raising agency costs for the state, decreasing cooperation, and thus making rulers more reliant on coercion. A comparison at the end of

[1] The designation of rulers' territory as "spear-won land" (*doriktetos chôra*), which appears in the historiographical sources for this period, illustrates the essential role of the coercive military power in the stability of the regimes; for its ideological and diplomatic connotations, see Billows (1995: 25–8) and Mehl (1980).

[2] The figure of 10 percent of the annual harvest serves here as a baseline, as rates above this, such as a quarter or a third, must surely be counted as high-tax regimes; see Wickham (2005: 64–5).

this chapter between the Hellenistic and Roman Empires will illustrate what factors might have brought about different outcomes.

The question posed here cannot be answered by looking strictly at the Hellenistic period. A comparative approach is necessary in order to determine the causal relationships between interstate conflict, fiscal exploitation, internal unrest, and economic development. Thus one has to pose the question in general terms and seek solutions that are logically consistent and potentially falsifiable. To this end, I focus on distinctive features of the Hellenistic "warring states" vis-à-vis the Persian and Roman Empires, which could explain the structure of the Hellenistic fiscal regimes and the economic performance associated with them. It is useful to consider comparable case studies, such as China's Warring States period in relation to the consolidated Han Chinese Empire, and Japan's Sengoku period vis-à-vis the Tokagawa Shogunate.[3] At the core of the argument are these contrasting dynamics of political and military competition versus the order established by hegemonic or imperial states.

Fiscal dynamics

The relationship between war and taxation has rightly been the focus of attention in fiscal history. As Tilly argues, warfare drives the process of state formation by forcing states to balance capital-intensive and coercion-intensive strategies to stay competitive and avoid extinction. Capital-intensive forms are the protection, property rights, and infrastructure that promote economic productivity, raising revenues in the long run.[4] Coercive-intensive forms are the hierarchical command-and-control mechanisms that enable states to mobilize resources to meet their demands in the short run. During the initial scramble for power after the death of Alexander the Great, the warring dynasts depended largely on plunder to pay their armies. This was especially true of Polyperchon, Cassander, Lysimachus, Eumenes, and Antigonus.[5] Those dynasts who eventually secured their hold on some territory – the Ptolemies in Egypt, the Seleucids in Asia, and the Antigonids in Macedonia – set about creating fiscal institutions that were less arbitrary and more conducive to capital accumulation. Yet even then the choice between capital and coercion depended, arguably, on how much rulers discounted the importance of future revenue. The Hellenistic period as a whole differs markedly from the previous Persian and subsequent Roman imperial regimes.

[3] Kiser and Cai (2003); Brown (1988). [4] Tilly (1992). [5] Serrati (2007: 466–70).

In an earlier paper, the author adopted an approach used by Levi to explain changes in taxation that followed the establishment of the Roman imperial monarchy by Augustus around 27 BCE.[6] She was concerned with the abolition of Rome's tax-farming system for the collection of direct taxes, a system that had become predatory in the late Republic through the collusion of Roman officials. According to her theory, rulers (here the senatorial elite) are not uniformly interested in protecting the productive capacity from profiteering agents. Rather, their interest depends on how much they discount the value of future revenue in relation to the value of immediate revenue. As Rome's political instability intensified, culminating in the civil wars, it was economically rational for Rome's rulers to ignore or partake in the exploitation of its provinces for immediate gain. The Ptolemaic rulers and their agents, especially during the revolts and dynastic conflicts of the second and first centuries BCE, arguably had similar incentives. With the new stability of the imperial monarchy, the rulers had a longer-term perspective as they reined in corruption and reduced the fiscal burden on the provinces (abolishing in Egypt the Ptolemaic harvest taxes), which encouraged investment in land productivity.

In an article that appeared in the same year as my own, Kiser and Kane suggest an alternative model based on agency theory in order to explain the institutional changes. They argue that Republican Rome was an outlier among premodern states for its extension of tax-farming even to direct taxes, which is to be explained by its constitution with rotating magistracies. They persuasively insist that its abolition should be seen as a consequence of the establishment of monarchical rule, not the creation of stability.[7] Kiser and Kane stress the "revolving door" of rotating magistracies, creating disincentives for senatorial families to regulate or curb the private firms or prosecute magistrates, which led to overtaxation. Weber similarly argues that republican governments are more exploitative than monarchies because their short-term magistrates are more prone to corruption.[8]

Kiser and Kane seem to predict that overexploitation would be a constant factor as long as the revolving door remained in place. Therefore, their theory has difficulty explaining why tax-farming apparently became worse in the late Republic.[9] They are skeptical about whether the establishment of the imperial monarchy lowered the discount rate of the rulers, noting the periodic violence over succession.[10] An index of Roman

[6] Monson (2007); Levi (1988). [7] Kiser and Kane (2007: 207–8). [8] Weber (1988 [1909]: 63).
[9] Kiser and Kane (2007: 201–2). [10] Kiser and Kane (2007: 198–9).

instability over time shows low levels during the first two centuries CE, however, between the end of the Republic and the crisis of the third century CE (see Chart 5.6). The third century CE is notably when fiscal pressure became acute. Finally, Ptolemaic Egypt had a monarchical government with bureaucratic collection of direct taxes, but Augustan reforms still marked a major reduction in the fiscal burden compared with the previous regime. As this chapter attempts to show, there is no reason to think that monarchies taxed their subjects any less than the Roman Republic; aside from during Rome's civil wars, the Hellenistic empires probably taxed them more. Thus there seem to be two separate issues at stake: Kiser and Kane's theory may explain the privatization and deregulation of tax collection but not the level of fiscal exploitation, which depended on the discount rates of rulers and tax collectors, making it sensitive to political instability.

According to Goldstone's structural demographic theory, recently elaborated by Turchin and Nefedov, instability is not due primarily to the geopolitical environment but is, rather, endogenous to the interaction of population pressure, elite competition, and fiscal crises. Social cohesiveness can determine the stability of the state because, as long as elites are able to cooperate, peasant uprisings or rebellions are unlikely to be successful.[11] In the following sections, I chart levels of instability within territorial states in order to relate them to fiscal policies, much as Turchin and Nefedov have done for Rome.[12] Each state is scored by decade in four categories, yielding a total on the scale of one to twelve, with twelve being the highest

Table 5.1 *Scoring system for instability indices*

Dynastic/citizen unrest	Subject unrest
0 = None 1 = Ruler change/political killings 2 = Dynastic/civil war 3 = Both 1 and 2	0 = None 1 = Minor revolt/rioting 2 = Major revolt 3 = Multiple revolts
External war	**Military success**
0 = None 1 = Asymmetric war with weaker foe 2 = Symmetric war with strong foe 3 = Multiple wars	0 = Overall victory 1 = No change 2 = Overall defeat 3 = 2 and territory loss

[11] Goldstone (1991); Turchin and Nefedov (2009). [12] Turchin and Nefedov (2009: 177, 223).

level of instability. Gaps in our knowledge, especially concerning the eastern areas of the Persian and Seleucid Empires, limit the usefulness of these charts, but they have the advantage of translating the history insofar as the current scholarship understands it into quantitative terms that are easier to compare.

In this chapter, both external threats to rulers' survival and internal weaknesses caused by elite competition are considered together under the rubric of instability. Increasing taxation to meet these threats could lead to a vicious cycle of revenue loss from overtaxing producers, the siphoning of state revenue by elites, and full-scale revolts. Interstate war and, above all, Roman imperialism has to be seen as a quasi-exogenous dimension interacting with other local factors to explain fiscal crises and the balance between coercive- and capital-intensive approaches to state-building. After examining the Hellenistic states, applying the same logic to Roman fiscal institutions in the newly conquered territories of the east will reveal similar dynamics. One should expect the stable hegemonic or imperial order to create opportunities for capital-intensive reforms promoting economic development and swelling elite numbers. In the long run, the growth of the aristocracy could generate intra-elite competition, causing state breakdown and restarting the cycle at the point of instability. Such instability could invite threats from external competitors (or these threats could be exogenous), heightening instability and instigating further coercive measures until, once again, one party reestablishes a hegemonic or imperial order.

Successors of the Persian Empire

Ideally, the Persian and the Roman Empires could be used as analytical bookends with which to distinguish the characteristic political and fiscal structures of the Hellenistic period. The internal organization and even the basic political history of the Achaemenid dynasty remain obscure due to the emphasis in our (mostly Greek) sources on the northwestern frontier.[13] Historians of the eastern Hellenistic kingdoms, especially of the Seleucids, often argue that they inherited and retained Persian institutions of provincial governance and taxation, so it is important to make reference to them here.[14] Without denying some continuity in local practices, I would hypothesize that the Persian Empire offered fiscal privileges during this

[13] Kuhrt (2007: 6–15).
[14] Hornblower (1982: 161–2); Aphergis (2004: 88); contrast Manning (2010: 28).

usually peaceful and stable period that differed from those of the Hellenistic successor states. If one can believe the classical sources, Persian rulers exacted relatively low fixed tribute (by Hellenistic standards) and granted estates and fiscal privileges to the Persian aristocracy as well as to local elites and temples. In periods of stability the Hellenistic kings would offer similar grants and privileges, but, as we shall see, such periods for them were few and far between, causing local aristocracies to be weakened by the Hellenistic kings and their bureaucracies.

Cyrus, ruler of the peripheral kingdom of Anshan in Persia, overthrew the Median king, subordinating the Iranian tribes and territory further east, and rapidly conquered the major Near Eastern kingdoms from 550 to 530 BCE. His successor, Cambyses, added Egypt in 525. After a dynastic crisis in 522 a Persian usurper, Darius, consolidated the empire, expanded its frontiers, and established the administrative and fiscal structure based on satrapies (provinces) that remained intact even after Alexander the Great's conquest in 332. There were periodic revolts, especially in Egypt, which temporarily broke away from the empire from 401 to 343. The last decades of the Achaemenid dynasty were unstable, leading to the succession crisis that brought Darius III to the throne.[15] While a revisionist trend in recent scholarship doubts that the Achaemenid Empire was in terminal decline when Alexander arrived, it was at least temporarily in a vulnerable situation of intra-elite conflict, which explains Alexander's conscious attempt to win disaffected elites over to his claim for Darius's crown.[16] Figure 5.1 illustrates the effects of political history on levels of instability.

According to the Greek historian Herodotus, writing in the fifth century BCE, each satrapy owed a fixed annual amount of tribute, assessed in silver, and in some cases extra-tributary gifts. If we accept these figures, we can compare them with tax burdens in the corresponding regions during the Hellenistic period.[17] To this point I will return in the next sections on Seleucid Asia and Ptolemaic Egypt, but it is worth anticipating the conclusions here. The figure given for Egypt and Cyrene together is 700 Babylonian talents of silver plus 240 talents from the fisheries of Lake

[15] Kuhrt (2007: 880). [16] Kuhrt (2005: 647–701); Briant (2002).

[17] Herodotus 3.89–95; accepted by Briant (2002: 391) and Aphergis (2004: 51–4); the most compelling doubts about Herodotus's reliability come from Jursa (2009; 2011) (see also Jursa and Moreno García, Chapter 4 in this volume), who notes the discrepancy between a system of fixed tribute in silver and the complexity of Babylonian fiscal obligations. It is conceivable that Herodotus describes only transfers from satraps to the king, not the internal fiscal structures that the satraps utilized, which need not have been disrupted by Persian rule; see Tuplin (2011).

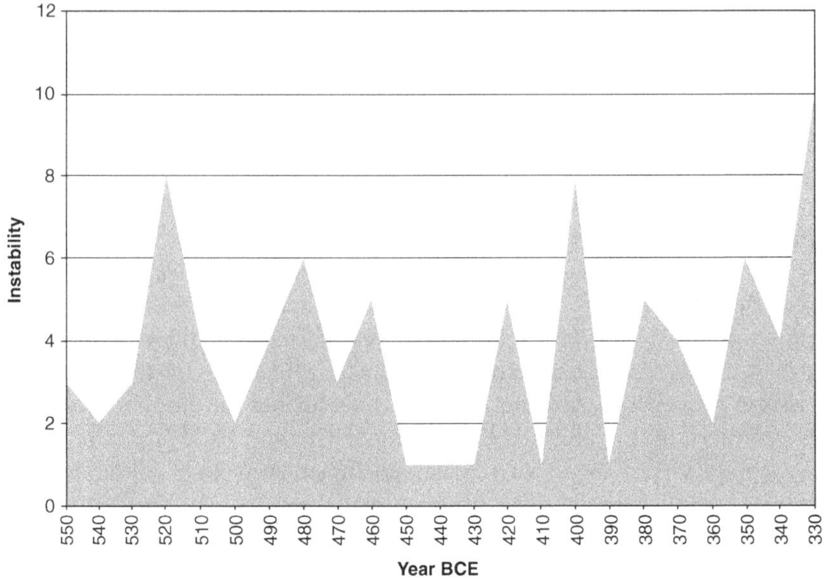

Figure 5.1 Achaemenid instability index, 550–330 BCE

Moeris – that is, less than 1,000 Babylonian talents (= 30,000 kg of silver or 1,150 Attic talents), which despite an additional 120,000 *artabas* of grain paid to the Persian garrison was a pitiful amount compared to Ptolemaic revenue. That amount of fraiu could not add more than ten talents of silver to the total tribute. Similarly, northern Syria and Koile Syria were assessed at a mere 350 talents (or less if Cyprus was included here), which the Seleucids were able to extract almost from Judea alone. Later Greek authors give an anecdote about Darius setting the tributes, then summoning the local elites of each satrapy to ask if they were too burdensome; when they replied that they were not, he anyway reduced them by half again.[18] The most likely explanation is that the Persian Empire lacked the impulse to develop the local coercive capacities to raise revenues as high as the Hellenistic kings would later need.

How these fixed tribute payments corresponded with the taxation regimes within the Persian satrapies likely depended on each satrap and on local institutions. Our Greek sources tell us that the tribute in Ionia remained at the same fixed rate after its revolt; the satrap Artaphernes

[18] Plutarch, *Moralia* 172; Polyaenus 7.11.3; see also Briant (2002: 393–4).

conducted a land survey in 493–2 BCE to determine how it would be distributed by district and by city according to their ability to pay.[19] In addition to tribute-bearing land subject to royal taxation, there were also the kings' own royal estates, gift estates granted to elites, and temple estates, which generally fell outside the tributary system as quasi-private domains.[20] Gift estates were also granted in Egypt.[21] Moreover, Egyptian temples retained their traditional landed domains, and there is no evidence for their direct taxation. A decree of Cambyses is usually interpreted as limiting their revenue. Even if this is true, there is no suggestion that he was confiscating it for royal use, so it may have actually benefited the cultivators and producers who had been forced to make payments to the temples.[22]

In Babylonia, the estates of the king and Persian nobility, as well as temples' estates, were separated off from other tribute-bearing land. We also know that these estates were leased out to entrepreneurial families who managed them for some share of the revenue. The business archive of the Murashu family in Babylon shows them acting as middlemen and profiting from the management of royal and temple estates.[23] These practices continued into the Hellenistic period but there is also evidence for more coercive measures for the state to exact revenue, particularly from temple economies.[24] This brief glimpse at taxation in the Persian Empire suggests that the Achaemenid dynasty did to some extent foster institutions for private capital accumulation by leaving revenues to local elites rather than having the court coercively monopolize the surplus within its territory.

Before turning to the major Hellenistic kingdoms, it is worth mentioning a treatise on political economy, most likely written around 323–300 BCE by a scholar of the Aristotelean school. It divides fiscal governance into four categories: royal, satrapal, city, and private. As other scholars have pointed out, this satrapal domain corresponds well to its position within the Persian imperial structure, but it mainly served as a model for would-be Hellenistic kings and was tailored to contemporary, late fourth-century realities.[25] According to the text, the responsibilities of the royal administration were regulating the currency, managing the inflow and outflow of

19 Herodotus 6.42; Diodorus 10.25.4.

20 Stolper (1985: 36–9); van der Spek (1995: 195–7); Briant (2002: 415–21); Aperghis (2004: 88).

21 Briant (2002: 413–14).

22 P.Bibl.Nat. inv. 215, verso col. 6 = Spiegelberg (1914). Agut-Labordère (2005) argues, somewhat differently, that cutting off these payments to the temples forced them to intensify their own production, and thus that the decree was aimed at stimulating economic activity.

23 Stolper (1985).

24 Jursa (2006); for more coercive measures, see below, section entitled "Antagonid Macedonia."

25 Briant (2002: 389–90); Rostovtzeff (1941: 441); see also Aperghis (2004: 117–35).

resources from the satrapies, and paying expenses in money or in kind. Thus royal administration was one level removed from the satrapal administration, which handled taxation:

> The second kind of administration, that of the satrapy, is concerned with six different classes of revenue; those, namely, arising from agriculture, from the special products of the country, from markets, from taxes, from cattle, and from other sources. Taking these in turn, the first and most important of them is revenue from agriculture, which some call the tithe [*dekate*] and some the harvest tax [*ekphorion*]. The second is that from special products; in one place gold, in another silver, in another copper, and so on. Third in importance is revenue from markets, and fourth that which arises from taxes on land and on sales. In the fifth place we have revenue from cattle, called tithe [*dekate*] or first-fruits; and in the sixth, revenue from other sources, which we term poll-tax, or tax on industry.[26]

This passage describes, albeit in general terms, the fiscal regime within the satrapy. In the Persian Empire, the satrap would have used similar measures to raise the fixed tribute and any additional gifts or military levies for the central government. The Hellenistic kings, on the other hand, would exploit these and other sources of revenue directly wherever possible, so satrapal administration became hardly distinguishable from the royal administration, unlike in the Persian Empire, which served as the basis for this model. In Ptolemaic Egypt this is obvious, because the core of the kingdom was already a Persian satrapy. Even in the Seleucid kingdom, however, which inherited multiple satrapies, military and fiscal crises forced the rulers to adopt more direct oversight through military governors and more interference in local taxation issues, at least in Asia Minor, Syria-Palestine, and Babylonia, if not in the remote eastern provinces, which may have resembled Persian satrapies only because central control over them was inherently weak.[27] Macedonia in some ways stands apart from these former Persian areas, and Antigonid fiscal reform remains obscure.

Ptolemaic Egypt

Ptolemy acquired Egypt in the dispensation of satrapies in Alexander's empire in 323 BCE. The empire was to persist nominally with Perdiccas as guardian for Alexander's half-brother Philip and the yet unborn Alexander IV. Foreign invasion and civil war in Cyrene gave Ptolemy an opportunity to extend his power westward over this fertile part of north

[26] Pseudo-Aristotle, *Oikonomika* 2.4. [27] Ma (1999: 123–30, esp. 129–30).

Africa. In the ensuing wars of the successors, our Greek sources tell us that Ptolemy attracted many of the leading Macedonians and Greeks into his retinue thanks to his generosity, fairness, and wealth.[28] He even welcomed Seleucus after he was driven out of his satrapy of Babylonia and helped him regain power there in 311 BCE. He proclaimed himself king in 304 BCE. Antigonos's defeat at Ipsos in 301 BCE allowed Ptolemy to obtain Koile Syria, Cyprus, and southern Asia Minor. Even among the Egyptians, Ptolemy I cultivated good relations with local elites, especially the temples and their priests. He popularized a new Greco-Egyptian religious cult of Serapis and confirmed temples' rights to their estates and traditional revenue, in some cases even expanding them with new gifts.[29] Some Egyptian elites took high positions at court and in the administration.[30]

The first four generations of the Ptolemaic dynasty, down to the reign of Ptolemy IV (reigned 221–204), were generally marked by stability at home and influence abroad. The beginning of the dynasty, Ptolemy I through Ptolemy III, was evidently a period of demographic and economic expansion to judge by the massive reclamation project in the Fayyum. Ptolemy II instituted wide-ranging judicial and economic reforms, systematizing the Egyptian and Greek legal traditions and creating a system of royal monopolies and tax-farming contracts for specific commodities and money taxes. It would be plausible to postulate population growth in this period, which would likely put downward pressure on wages and upward pressure on rents. According to the structural demographic theory above, these would have improved the living standards of elites while creating greater inequality and impoverishing peasants. Ptolemy III probably brought back copious booty from his campaign against the Seleucids in 245 BCE, but there are the first reports of an Egyptian revolt during his reign.[31]

It is, admittedly, old-fashioned to blame the subsequent decline of Egypt on Ptolemy IV Philopator. The literary portrait is, after all, biased, depicting him as a profligate king, more interested in banquets than in government. On the other hand, there is strong evidence that Philopater indeed experienced a fiscal crisis that had far-reaching economic and political consequences.[32] The evidence is insufficient to identify its causes but the Syrian War and the ensuing unrest allegedly among Egyptian veterans could have contributed. Another hypothesis is the phenomenon that Turchin and Nefedov label "elite overproduction." Increasing prosperity and population growth in Egypt down to Ptolemy IV's reign, for

[28] For example, Diodorus 18.33. [29] Manning (2003: 76–7). [30] Lloyd (2002: 120–31).
[31] McGing (1997: 274–7). [32] Maresch (1996: 7–8); Armoni (2012: 214–15).

which there is unfortunately no direct evidence, could have reached a tipping point. Turchin and Nefedov argue that the conditions that prevail in periods of growth create a certain overcrowding at the upper echelons of society, which precipitates intra-elite competition, especially over tax privileges and state expenditure, leading to fiscal crises and, ultimately, civil war.[33] Elites in Alexandria at any rate had probably grown accustomed to lavish patronage from the royal court. While the king may well have seen such expenses as vital to maintaining loyalty and prestige, outside observers were understandably critical in hindsight. From this perspective, the Greek historians' account of Philopater's reign does not have to be jettisoned completely.

There was probably a connection between the fiscal crisis under Philopator and the series of revolts, including the Great Theban Revolt that broke out at the end of his reign and continued until 185 BCE. Economic explanations are accordingly more persuasive than those of religious nationalism that have occasionally been advanced. The rebels in the south successfully managed to secede and to claim political independence with an Egyptian pharaoh in Thebes (207–185). Meanwhile, there were separate outbreaks in the Nile Delta. The young Ptolemy V's rivals, the Seleucids and Antigonids, used his weakness to seize most of his external empire, including Koile Syria. The second century was plagued by incessant dynastic wars and Egyptian uprisings. Roman interventions could not create lasting stability, and only entangled Egypt in Rome's civil wars until it was finally annexed when Cleopatra VII's plans with Mark Antony failed. Figure 5.2 gauges instability based on Ptolemaic political history.

Compared to the other Hellenistic kingdoms, the fiscal institutions of Egypt are well attested and enable us to track better the effects of instability. During the third century BCE the Ptolemies greatly expanded their fiscal capacity to raise revenue for expensive external wars. Ptolemy II is credited with most of the reforms. The so-called salt tax was a kind of poll tax in money charged on both males and females, free and slave. There is abundant documentation from the third century BCE in the form of tax receipts from Upper Egypt and extensive accounts, as well as house-by-house census lists that were used to calculate this and probably other capitation taxes. The rate of the salt tax was adjusted several times from about 263 to 217 BCE, ranging from 1 drachma 3 obols to as low as 4 obols for men and from 1 drachma to 1½ obols for women, which is low relative

[33] Turchin and Nefedov (2009: 313).

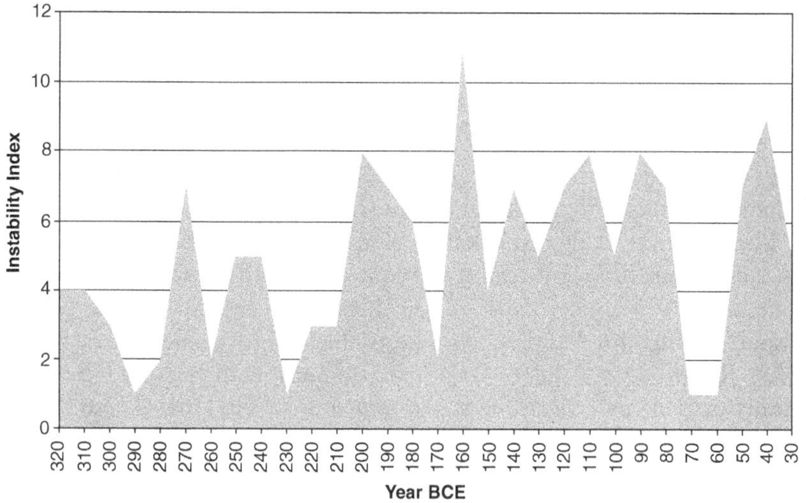

Figure 5.2 Ptolemaic instability index, 320–30 BCE

to the 2-drachma poll tax attested in late Achaemenid and early Hellenistic Koile Syria, which presumably continued under Ptolemaic rule.[34] It is also low by comparison with the Roman poll tax in Egypt, but after the third century BCE our evidence for the salt tax drops off precipitously, so it may have been combined as part of a larger capitation tax known as the *syntaxis*.[35] According to texts of the first century BCE, this tax was charged on adult males on the basis of a census (*laographia*) at a rate possibly as high as or higher than in the Roman period.[36] Accordingly, it is doubtful that the Romans imposed a heavy new fiscal burden with the poll tax on the Egyptians.

In the densely settled and traditionally powerful provinces of the Nile Valley, by contrast, temples retained most of their independence, which would have encouraged loyalty and cooperation even though the Greco-Macedonian and Egyptian social spheres were relatively distinct compared to the later Ptolemaic period. Ptolemy II confirmed the temples' rights to the tax (*apomoira*) on vineyards and orchards of one-sixth of the harvest

34 P.Count = Clarysse and Thompson (2006: esp. 36–89) for the rates; see Lemaire (2004: 139–40; 2007: 58–60) for the Idumaea ostraka.

35 Rathbone (1993: 90–1); Clarysse and Thompson (2006: 88).

36 P.Tebt. I 103, 121, 189; Hoogendijk (2010) reads unpublished columns in P.Tebt. I 189, which seem to confirm that the tax was paid monthly; *O.Mich.* I-IV provide further evidence for *syntaxis* as the precursor of the Roman poll tax.

coupled with a fixed tax charged per *aroura*. The *apomoira* was charged on all land, including cleruchic land and gift estates, but theoretically the state was to use the income to finance a new cult for his sister-wife and queen, Arsinoe II. To the extent that this cult was created within the temples, it need not have damaged their income.[37] On the other hand, these ostensibly benign measures gave the Ptolemies administrative oversight over an important source of agricultural revenue that could be diverted if necessary.

Most revenue in the Ptolemaic period was collected from harvest taxes on land under the royal administration. Such land could be leased from state officials in concert with village elders, who helped mediate peasant disputes, or acquired as private property through royal auctions or private sales. Regardless of the type of tenure, most land acquired by these means carried the obligation to pay *ekphoria* to the king. These "rents" were levied regardless of the possessor's legal rights, so it is sometimes more appropriate to translate them as "harvest taxes," as in the Ps.-Aristotle *Oikonomika*, where *ekphorion* is cited as one common name for land revenue in the satrapal economy. The designation "harvest taxes" is slightly misleading because they were not a share of the harvest but were determined according to an annual survey carried out during the growing season, which established which of several possible rates would apply depending on the land's quality or the flood conditions.[38] The most common rates were 4 to 7 *artabas* per *aroura*, far higher than the 1 *artaba* charged on private land in the Roman period. Some sources suggest a wheat yield of about 12 *artabas* per *aroura*, which would imply a rate of 30 to 60 percent.[39] In Upper Egyptian tax receipts, the harvest tax was typically called *epigraphê*, but it seems to have been the same as *ekphorion*.[40]

Temple land was managed by priestly officials and enjoyed a special fiscal status. Each temple had a high priest (*lesonis*), who bid for the right to manage the temple's estate for one year in exchange for fixed payments to the priests and to the state. Around 235 to 225 BCE the high priest of the temple of Edfu was in arrears, so a special royal controller was appointed to sort out the finances.[41] The high priest had used third-party guarantors to secure his payment, and ultimately his whole property had to be confiscated to repay his debts (but the controller too was later accused of corruption and had to escape). The documents from this incident tell us that the Edfu temple's harvest tax was set at the rate of 25 percent of its

[37] Clarysse and Vandorpe (1998). [38] Monson (2012a: 19–20). [39] Monson (2013: 130–2).
[40] Monson (2012b: 165–71); on *epigraphe*, see Vandorpe (2000).
[41] The texts of the Milon archive are listed and analyzed by Clarysse (2003); see also Monson (2012b: 212–18).

grain harvest.[42] Here the payments were presumably still made to the temple granary. Starting in the reign of Ptolemy IV Philopater, however, royal granary receipts show that the holders of temple land in some areas in Upper Egypt were made to pay harvest taxes (*ekphoria*) directly to the state. They may have been entitled to this revenue as a subsidy from the state but the change clearly represents an expansion of the state's capacity to extract resources from the countryside, which may have contributed to the outbreak of the Great Theban Revolt of 207 to 185 BCE.[43]

Temple land had also been subjected to a fixed land tax at the rate of 1 *artaba* per *aroura* (*artabieia*) sometime before 197 BCE. In that year Ptolemy V agreed to abolish it as part of a package of concessions to Egyptian temples that were still loyal to him after the Delta uprisings had been crushed and after some gains against the southern rebels.[44] This tax – sometimes paid together with the *ekphoria* on temple land – was apparently reintroduced during the subsequent dynastic wars, however.[45] During moments of dynastic unity the Ptolemies took pains to confirm or increase the endangered revenues and fiscal privileges of the temples.[46]

Though privileged, not even soldiers' cleruchic land was free from royal taxation. During the third century BCE some cleruchs in the Fayyum evidently paid *ekphoria* just like royal cultivators.[47] There were substantial reforms in the second century BCE. The main evidence is from a petition dating to about 137 BCE, in which the privileged group designated as "settlers" (*katoikoi*) claim about the implementation of a decree in the year 158/157 BCE, which required a lump sum be paid by their members throughout Egypt, except the Thebaid. It was distributed among them either in the form of a fixed 2-*artaba* tax or as harvest taxes (*epigraphai*) whose rate presumably varied like *ekphoria* according to the quality of the land.[48] By the late second century BCE the special demands had apparently been rescinded, and holders of cleruchic land apparently paid only a low land tax of about 1 *artaba* per *aroura*.[49] Emergency levies were employed periodically during the first century BCE, presumably in response to fiscal

[42] P. Bürgsch. 14 (225 BCE). [43] Vandorpe (2006: 168–9).
[44] SB I 8299 = OGIS 90 (English trans. Austin 2006: text 283).
[45] Boswinkel and Pestman (1978: 115–19).
[46] P. Tebt. 6; P. Tebt. 5, ll. 57–16 (English trans. Austin 2006: text 290).
[47] P.Lille I 39–50 with P.Sorb.inv. 223+229+272+1404 recto, 1418 recto, etc., whose edition I am preparing.
[48] P.Lips. II 124 and P.Tebt. I 99 (both *c.* 137 BCE); for their abolition, see P.Tebt. I 124 = C.Ord.Ptol. 54 (118 BCE); see also Monson (2012b: 176–84).
[49] Capponi (2005: 100–1 n. 27); Monson (2012b: 178).

crises and the political instability of the period.[50] A decree of Cleopatra VII in 41 BCE exempted Alexandrian landowners in the countryside from these "contributions to Crown taxes (*stephanoi*) and harvest taxes (*epigraphai*) that are levied occasionally (*kata kairon*) in nomes according to circumstances."[51]

Because the rents or harvest taxes on royal and temple land were relatively high, much of the surplus of primary producers was captured and redistributed. There was thus no landowning elite, as in the Roman period. Those who did derive their wealth from land did so largely by performing services to the king or the temples that entitled them to the use of land on privileged terms.[52] The large gift estates attested mainly in the third-century Fayyum were non-hereditary and subject to some taxes (such as the *apomoira*) and regulations, though the recipients were able to claim the cultivators' rents.[53] Such landholders are the exceptions that prove the rule. Rather than owning land, holding royal offices was arguably the surest means of obtaining wealth and power in Egypt. As Bingen has shown, Ptolemaic institutions forced would-be elites into state and temple service for access to redistributive flows of revenue or tax privileges.[54]

The Revenue Laws Papyrus of Ptolemy II is an extraordinary text that sheds light on the sale of royal monopolies and the role of the state in the economy.[55] Once seen as evidence for central planning, it has been interpreted as a system derived from Greece that provided incentives to capital-rich investors to secure a stable source of revenue for the government.[56] To be sure, the finance minster (*dioiketes*) took a major interest in keeping detailed records of agricultural production. A sowing schedule, drawn up by local officials, gave the administration an idea of what crops to expect and helped to manage the crops sown by cultivators of royal land.[57] Such records were used to sell royal monopolies, illustrating a close partnership between the buyers and officials, which could serve to limit the discrepancy between the state's revenue and the investor's profits or losses for the security of both parties.

Tax farmers guaranteed an amount of revenue but for certain taxes they did not actually collect the sum themselves. Instead, the royal bureaucracy

[50] BGU VIII 1760 (51/50 BCE), with Monson (2012b: 181–2).
[51] C.Ord.Ptol. 75–6, with Bingen (2007: 143–4). [52] Rowlandson (2007).
[53] Rostovtzeff (1922: 44–5, 50–3, 83–4).
[54] Bingen (2007: 189–205); see also Monson (2012b: 210–11).
[55] P.Rev.Laws = W.Chr. 229 = *SB Beiheft* 1952 (partial English trans. Austin 2006: 524–31).
[56] See the important contribution by (Bingen 2007: 157–88), which also reviews the previous literature.
[57] Vidal-Naquet (1967); Cuvigny (1985).

collected the taxes and balanced accounts with the tax farmers, paying them the surplus if it exceeded their bid or demanding the remainder if it did not.[58] Without tax farmers, the royal officials could reap gains from overtaxation and be held liable by their superiors if taxes were lower than expected, giving them an incentive to under-report income. Tax-farming thus reduced their superiors' monitoring costs by privatizing only the *risk*, so as to guarantee income. Yet the sources for this historically anomalous tax-farming system come exclusively from the third century BCE. It seems to have coexisted with the use of tax farmers to collect certain taxes.[59]

The depredations by local officials can best be explained as one of the effects of instability on state finance. For this the second-century amnesty decrees and other official correspondence are the prime evidence. In one notorious case, a village headman had devised an extortion racket compelling cultivators to pay him surcharges on royal taxes, until one of his henchmen fell foul and reported it in 151 BCE to the finance minister.[60] The amnesty decree of 118 BCE, after a major dynastic civil war, and similar documents from the troubled second century BCE suggest that the central government lost control of its officials during periods of instability, enabling them to raise unlawful taxes or divert royal revenue and exacerbate fiscal crises.[61] Armoni has challenged the characterization of endemic corruption in the Ptolemaic bureaucracy. She emphasizes the multiplicity of officials involved in state business for the purpose of mutual oversight and central control within the fiscal administration, but her evidence is mostly early Ptolemaic.[62] While such corruption was not necessarily intrinsic to the Ptolemaic state as such, one cannot fail to notice its relationship to the dynastic wars and instability of the second century BCE.

To focus too much on the differences within the Ptolemaic period misses the larger point of this chapter. Even the first three Ptolemies adopted strenuous measures to meet the costs of competing in the warring-states environment of the third century BCE. Ptolemy I had to resist a major invasion of Egypt in 321 and an impending one in 312 BCE, while financing an expensive fleet to gain territory and influence in the Aegean and Asia Minor.[63] Relative to what is known about Persian administration in Egypt, Ptolemy II's fiscal reforms represent much deeper

[58] Weber (1988 [1909]: 234); Préaux (1939: 450–9); von Reden (2007: 106–7).

[59] P.BerlinDem. II 13535+23677 (236 BCE; English trans. Martin 1996: 363–5) shows tax farmers involved in the collection of capitation taxes.

[60] SB XX 14708 (151 BCE; English trans. Bagnall and Derow 2004: 158–60).

[61] P.Tebt. I 5 = C.Ord.Ptol. 53 (118 BCE; English trans. Austin 2006: text 290); Veïsse (2004: 110).

[62] Armoni (2012: 4–8). [63] Fischer-Bovet (2008: 137–45).

penetration into local Egyptian power networks to raise revenue. The contemporary historian Hieronymus of Caria claimed that Ptolemy II's annual revenue from Egypt was 14,800 talents and 1 or 2 million *artabas* of wheat.[64] Another ancient author gives Ptolemy XII's total revenue in silver as 12,500 talents in the first century BCE.[65] Modern historians have suggested higher wheat revenues, 6 to 8 million *artabas*, because Rome allegedly took in 6 million from Egypt under Augustus, and Byzantium 8 million under Justinian.[66] At 2 drachmas per *artaba*, 7 million *artabas* adds only about 600 talents, for total Ptolemaic royal revenue on the order of 13,000 to 16,000 silver talents per year. A lower figure of 6,000 talents per year for Ptolemy XII is given by Diodorus Siculus, however.[67] Wilcken argued that the latter was only the revenue from the Alexandrians and that they produced almost half the royal revenue, but this seems somewhat implausible.[68]

If our sources merit credibility, at least with respect to orders of magnitude, Ptolemaic revenue from Egypt was six to twelve times higher than Persian royal tribute from Egypt and probably also higher than Roman tribute during the first and second centuries CE. Admittedly, Herodotus's report about Persian revenue is particularly suspect. He claims that Egypt's tribute to Persia was just 940 Babylonian talents (= 1,085 Attic talents) plus 120,000 *artabas* of wheat (= 10 Attic talents), for a total of about 1,100 talents.[69] Assuming that this is only what was passed on to the Persian king, the revenue of the satrap would have been higher than this, but it is unlikely that he raised revenues as high as Ptolemaic kings given that he had fewer expenses and less personal control over the economy. That leaves a wider pyramid of beneficiaries, including temples, recipients of gift estates, and other landowners.

Historians estimate the total revenue of the Roman Empire during the first and second centuries CE at around 37,500 talents.[70] Unless the overall tax burden on Egypt declined under Roman rule, it would have supplied an unrealistic proportion (between 15 and 40 percent) of imperial revenue. Ptolemaic Egypt had to raise higher revenues because it was locked in a competitive interstate struggle and its rulers discounted future revenue on account of their precarious situation at home. As Goldstein as well as Turchin and Nefedov argue, however, instability and fiscal depredation could both depend on the underlying ability of elites to cooperate.[71] The

[64] Jerome, *Daniel* 11.5; see also Wilcken (1899: 412–13). [65] Strabo 18.1.13.
[66] Fischer-Bovet (2008: 146–7). [67] Diodorus Siculus 17.52.6. [68] Wilcken (1899: 415–16).
[69] Martin (2007: 776–7). [70] Duncan-Jones (1994: 46); Hopkins (2009: 183).
[71] Goldstone (1991); Turchin and Nefedov (2009).

Ptolemies were foreign conquerors initially reliant on mercenary outsiders. In pauses of tranquility, they tried to compensate local elites and co-opt them with fiscal incentives, but these phases were short-lived. The expansion of royal taxation from the late third century BCE onward may reflect intra-elite conflict over potential revenues – especially between the Alexandrian court and the temples – at a time when the available resources were dwindling because of external wars and revolts. The comparison with Rome will show that it had more favorable starting conditions and more success in its interstate relations, which may explain both its stability and its low fiscal burden relative to the Ptolemies and its other rivals.

Seleucid Asia

Seleucus I became satrap of Babylonia in 321 BCE but was driven out before being restored again in 311 BCE with Ptolemy's help. From there he successfully challenged Antigonid power in Asia, gained control of the eastern satrapies, and even made a treaty with Chandragupta Maurya of India, which limited any further expansion. By helping to bring down Antigonus I in 301 and then defeating his rival Lysimachus in 281, Seleucus I gained control of western Asia Minor, so that his son and heir to his royal title, Antiochos I, inherited an empire stretching from the Aegean to Central Asia. The early Seleucids continued a policy of Alexander the Great, founding new cities with colonies of soldiers and civilians across Asia. During the third century BCE the Seleucid kings waged repeated unsuccessful wars against the Ptolemies for control of the Syria-Palestine area. They also faced a number of revolts from local governors and military commanders. The most debilitating conflicts were within the royal family itself. The Laodikean War (246–1 BCE) between rival claimants precipitated Ptolemaic intervention, nearly led to Egypt's annexation of the Seleucid kingdom, and ended with the sack and plunder of the Seleucid capital Antioch and the rich Mesopotamian cities. The "War of the Brothers" (*c.* 240 BCE) divided the kingdom and allowed the rulers of Pergamon to carve away western Asia Minor from Seleucid control, while the eastern governors grew more independent.

Besides the contrast between the Seleucid Empire and its Persian predecessor and Roman successor, the brief period of internal order and stability under Antiochus III lends support to the theoretical model described above. Antiochus III embarked on a massive campaign to consolidate his kingdom, traveling to its eastern extremities to reestablish control and boost his reputation as an heir to Alexander – "Antiochus

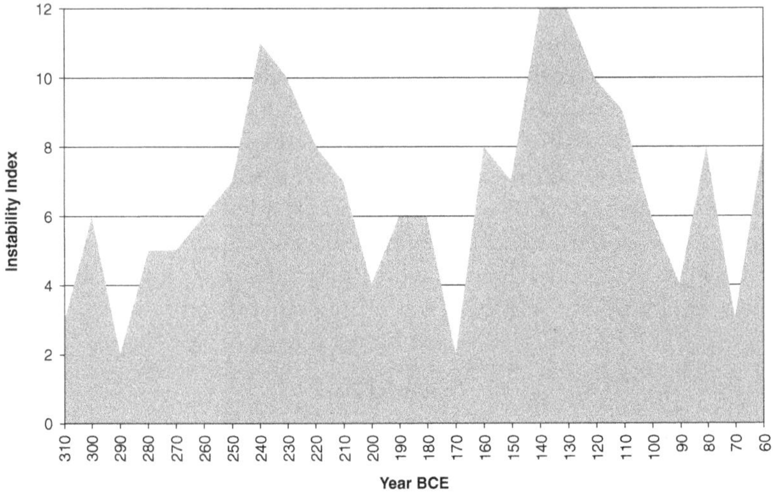

Figure 5.3 Seleucid instability index, 310–60 BCE

the Great". In the final decade of the third century BCE Egypt was in crisis, allowing Antiochus finally to conquer Koile Syria as well as most of Asia Minor. His other potential rival, Antigonid Macedonia, was defeated by Rome in 197 BCE, giving Antiochus the chance to project his power into Europe. Had Rome not intervened in 189 BCE or had Antiochus been victorious, it is not hard to imagine a Seleucid imperial order resembling the earlier Persian Empire. As it happened, the Seleucids suffered a fiscal crisis, as Rome imposed indemnity payments for the war and gave most of Asia Minor to the Attalid kingdom of Pergamon. Antiochus IV tightened fiscal control over his core territory and managed to conquer Egypt in 169 BCE, briefly being regarded as its king before withdrawing under the threat of Roman intervention. The last century of Seleucid history is a story of spectacular intra-elite violence, civil war, and territorial loss, including Judea to the Hasmonean dynasty and Mesopotamia to the Parthians in the 140s BCE, until its annexation first by the king of Armenia in 84 BCE then by Rome two decades later. The quantification of Seleucid political history in Figure 5.3 underscores its extraordinary level of instability.

We know much less about fiscal institutions in the Seleucid kingdom than in Ptolemaic Egypt. The Seleucids did build up fiscal institutions for regular taxation within their territory. The extreme levels of instability in the kingdom, however, also ensured that coercive-intensive measures were used to a much greater extent than in Ptolemaic Egypt. The Seleucids depended largely on plundering their subject communities to maintain their armies during crises.[72]

Some aspects of Seleucid taxation were inherited from the Persian Empire and from the other Macedonian dynasts, who held the territory that would become Seleucid. Alexander the Great, for example, freed many Greek cities in Asia Minor of the royal tribute they paid to Persia but acknowledged his right to collect tribute from the "royal land" outside their territory.[73] In 303 BCE, when Antigonus controlled that area, he was reluctant to allow Teos to set up a subsidy fund for famines because, he argued, there was "tribute-bearing land" nearby, from which the king could divert resources if there was ever a famine.[74] The Seleucid kings, like their Persian and Macedonian predecessors, made grants from these royal tribute-bearing domains to individuals, giving them the privilege to attach the land to a city of their choosing. This evidently allowed city governments to tax the land to meet its fiscal obligations to the king in exchange for recognizing the individual's civic status and property rights, but whether private rights also existed within the royal domain is unclear.[75]

How the "tribute" (*phoros*) on its tribute-bearing land was assessed remains obscure as well. In his model of the "satrapal administration," the political economy treatise quoted above claims about the revenue from land: "[S]ome call it the tithe (*dekate*) and others call it the harvest tax (*ekphorion*)."[76] It seems reasonable to assume that peasant communities on Seleucid royal or tribute-bearing land paid some kind of proportional harvest tax (*ekphorion*) just like the one attested in Ptolemaic Egypt at rates of 20 to 60 percent, which was comparable to the typical rent in private tenancy agreements.[77] On the Seleucid kings' royal estates, the land was cultivated by "royal peasants" (*basilikoi laoi*), who were organized as communities collectively liable for taxes.[78] Again, there is an apparent analogy to the royal cultivators (*basilikoi georgoi*) on Ptolemaic estates. It is usually assumed that such estates generated the largest share of regular Seleucid revenue.[79] Almost nothing is known about their actual fiscal burden but it cannot have been much lower than the going rate of private rent. Otherwise, one would expect that they often leased their plots, but

[72] Serrati (2007: 476–7). [73] Sherwin-White (1985: 84–6); Aperghis (2004: 87–8).
[74] Syll.³ 344 = RC 3/4 (Welles 1934: 15–32) = SEG IV 618; see also Gabrielsen (2011: 239–41).
[75] Aperghis (2004: 99–107); Thorneman (2009: 375). [76] Ps.-Aristotle, *Oikonomica* 2.4.
[77] Welles (1934: 174). [78] Mileta (2008: 111–26 with appendix 2).
[79] Hahn (1978); Musti (1984: 193–4); Callataÿ (2004); Mileta (2008: 215–18).

their designation as *basilikoi georgoi* seems to imply that they normally cultivated the land themselves.

Many historians assume that the tithe (*dekate*) was the regular tax on grain-producing land in the Seleucid kingdom because, in addition to the vague "tribute" (*phoros*), this term appears in a few sources.[80] On the other hand, the term "tithe" (*dekate*) implies a low rate of 10 percent. In those cases in which the term does refer to grain-producing land, it was arguably land with privileged fiscal status. The city of Jerusalem was charged a tithe but it is unclear whether this was an agricultural tax, because Judea and Samaria were charged 33 percent of the grain harvest and 50 percent of the orchards.[81] The tithe is also found in the Greek cities of Aigai, on temple land in Tralles, and on the cleruchic land of soldiers.[82] Especially for the soldiers, taxes must have been lower than rents, otherwise it would have been unfeasible for them ever to lease the land to private tenants. The peasants' taxes on the king's tribute-bearing land, by contrast, were presumably higher than 10 percent and closer to the level of private rents. For comparison, the Romans taxed virtually all land in Sicily via a *dekate*, whose owners still had enough surplus to lease their land to private tenants.[83]

Descat has argued that tribute (*phoros*) was one-twelfth of the land's value and was charged in addition to the tithe (*dekate*). He builds his argument on a single inscription reporting that a certain Mnesimachos, who owned a royal gift estate (or its usufruct), put up the land as security for a loan of 1,325 gold staters, which Descat assumes to be the value of the land.[84] We do not know how large the estate was but he paid an annual tribute (*phoros*) of 110¼ gold staters, which is approximately one-twelfth of the loan. There is no mention of the tithe (*dekate*) but he assumes the cultivators would have paid it as well, in this case to the owner rather than to the king because it was a gift estate.[85] The trouble is that we have no idea how this "value of land" was assessed. Descat and Aperghis suggest that

[80] Capdetrey (2007: 396–422, esp. 413); Mileta (2008: 208–18).

[81] Josephus, *Antiquities* 13.49–51; *1 Maccabees* 10.30; Goldstein (1976: 405–8); Aperghis (2004: 169–71).

[82] Aigai: Malay (1983); Tralles: I.Tralles 17 = RC 41 = SEG XXXVIII 1170; see also Aperghis (2004: 150), who follows Welles (1934: 172–5) in attributing the letter and the decision to exempt the temple from the *dekate* to Antiochus III without reference to the reedition by Piejko (1988), who adduces strong arguments in favor of Eumenes II after 188 BCE. Cleruchic land: OGIS 229 = I.Magnesia am Sipylos, line 101; see a letter of an Attalid king to military cleruchs, I.Perg. 158 = RC 51 = SEG XXVIII 959 (second century BCE), mentioning a one-tenth tax (*dekate*) on arable land and a one-twentieth tax on vineyards.

[83] Pritchard (1970); see below, "Conclusions" section.

[84] I.Sardis 1; Descat (1985).

[85] Descat (1985: 108–9).

during the Persian period assessing the value of each plot of land was the purpose of the satrap Artaphernes' inspections, but this is very doubtful.[86] It is unclear how the bundle of rights would have affected such values since Mnesimachos could mortgage the usufruct to a temple but evidently not sell the land.[87] Thus Aperghis's attempt to link the "tribute" and the presumed rents that Mnesimachos received from the cultivators to the terms harvest tax (*ekphorion*) and tithe (*dekate*) of Ps.-Aristotle's treatise is unpersuasive.[88] Without corroborating evidence, the ratio of his tribute in gold to the value of his loan is of doubtful significance.

There is some evidence for poll taxes in the Seleucid realm as well. The 2 drachma-tax attested in the late Achaemenid and early Hellenistic ostraka from southern Palestine may have survived down to the Roman period. A poll tax is even mentioned in Antiochos III's letter to the Jews reported in Josephus, in which it is distinguished from an additional salt tax.[89] A salt tax is also attested in Seleucid Babylonia, and the parallel with the Ptolemaic capitation tax of that name suggests that it was a regular feature of these two Hellenistic kingdoms.[90] In 181 BCE the inhabitants of the Lykian village of Kardakon in Asia Minor paid a poll tax (*syntaxis*) equivalent to about 3 Attic drachmas per adult, which presumably goes back to the Seleucid period before the village had become Attalid territory in the Roman settlement after Antiochus III's defeat in 189 BCE.[91] It was perhaps comparable to the late Ptolemaic poll tax described above.

Babylonia was where Seleucus I received his satrapy and was his seat of power until he moved his court to Antioch in Syria in the early third century BCE. Even afterwards Mesopotamian cities retained their political, economic, and ideological importance for the dynasty.[92] Babylonia was wealthy, prompting the Seleucids to penetrate local networks of power to obtain resources for their frequent wars and revolts. The Babylonian temples were allowed to continue collecting the traditional one-tenth (Greek *dekate*) of the harvests but were also subject to direct royal taxation and periodic confiscations in emergencies.[93] One text has been interpreted as evidence that Seleucus impoved annual payments of 50 percent of the harvests on the temple of Shamash in Sippar during his war with Antigonus

[86] Descat (1985) and Aperghis (2004: 139–42); see above, section on Ptolemaic Egypt.
[87] Thorneman (2009: 385–90). [88] Aperghis (2004: 137–47, 152).
[89] Josephus, *Antiquities*, 12.138–44; for continuity of the Achaemenid poll tax, see Lemaire (2007).
[90] Apherghis (2004: 154–5).
[91] Maier (1959: 248–50 text 76); Mileta (2008: 212); see also Walbank (1979: 165–6) on Polybius 21.46.2–3.
[92] Sherwin-White and Kuhrt (1994: 38–9); see also Austin (2006: text 166).
[93] Van der Spek (1995); (2007: 412); Jursa (1998).

I in 309 BCE but this reading is untenable.[94] Nevertheless, it certainly illustrates royal taxation of the temple's estate.

Once rulers have established a stable hegemonic or imperial order, one expects them to relax coercive measures and adopt more capital-intensive strategies that increase voluntary cooperation. The only ruler of the Seleucid dynasty and perhaps the only ruler of any Hellenistic kingdom to come close to achieving this was Antiochus III. His dealings with the cities of western Asia Minor are unusually well attested because he issued numerous decrees and letters conferring political and fiscal privileges, which likewise reinforced the power structure.[95] Well-known examples are the benefactions to the Greek city of Teos, *c.* 204/203 BCE, soon after his triumphal return from the east, including exemption from the tribute the city had paid to King Attalus of Pergamon and a similar exemption to Herakleia-Latmos.[96] After defeating the Ptolemaic kingdom in 200 BCE to obtain Syria-Palestine, he issued the city of Jerusalem a generous tax exemption for three years followed by reduction of one-third.[97] At the same time Antiochus III fostered a royal cult to unite his subjects and promoted a discourse of cooperation among imperial elites.[98] Almost three decades of successful (though violent and difficult) expansion make Antiochus III's ultimate defeat to Rome in 189 BCE seem more like an exogenous shock that cut short his imperial project than a symptom of decline.

The resulting loss of western Asia Minor and the eastern provinces as well as the gradual Parthian incursions into Mesopotamia made the Seleucid dynasty increasingly dependent on the revenues of Syria-Palestine. Seleucus IV's reign (187–175 BCE) is not well attested but the fiscal strain of Rome's indemnity makes plausible the biblical account that he sent a minister to confiscate wealth from the Jewish temple in Jerusalem for the royal treasury.[99] In Judea the high priest of the Jewish temple paid the Seleucids an annual tribute giving him the right to distribute the burden and collect the taxes as well as to profit from any surplus (similar to Ptolemaic tax-farming on Egyptian temple estates by the high priests). During the reign of Seleucus IV its annual tribute was 300 talents. In 172 BCE Antiochus IV (175–164 BCE) agreed to make Jason, a Hellenized

[94] Van der Spek (1995: 194; 2007: 412); Jursa (2006: 148).

[95] Ma (1999: 194–201); Aperghis (2004: 150).

[96] Teos: SEG XLI 1003, Ma (1999: 172–3, 371–21, text 19); (Austin 2006: text 191); Herakleia-Latmos: Wörrle (1988); compare Aperghis (2004: 150) and Schuler (2005: 401–2).

[97] Josephus, *Antiquities* 12.138–58; Aperghis (2004: 167).

[98] Ma (1999: 228–35).

[99] *2 Maccabees* 3.1–13; see also Kreissig (1978: 112).

Jew, high priest instead of his more orthodox brother Onias for a higher bid of 440 talents. Then, in 169 BCE, as Antiochus IV went to invade Egypt, he accepted the bid of Menelaos, another Hellenizer, for 740 talents.[100] Antiochus IV conquered Egypt but Rome forced him to withdraw. Menelaos could not raise his total without confiscating temple treasure, which provoked the priestly elite and more orthodox Jews to revolt. Antiochus IV inflamed it with a decree forcing the rebellious Jews to adopt Greek dress and religious practices.[101]

During the prolonged dynastic civil wars after Antiochus IV rival claimants sought to win support from Jerusalem and the surrounding area with promises of relief that reveal the heavy burden of taxation in those areas. Ousted from Syria by the usurper Alexander Balas in 153 BCE, the Seleucid king Demetrius I offered to free Judea and Samaria from the tax of 33 percent on grain produce and 50 percent of orchards and Jerusalem from its tithe (*dekate*) and taxes (*telea*) in order to gain support.[102] The high priest rejected these promises, and Demetrius I was defeated, but his son Demetrius II later made a similar offer, ceding his fiscal rights to the grain and orchards in Samaria to Jerusalem.[103]

Despite the geographical overlap with the earlier Persian Empire, the Seleucid kingdom seems to have abandoned its administrative system based on satrapies that paid an annual fixed tribute, which the satrap was responsible for raising.[104] In Asia Minor, first Antigonus and then Lysimachus began the process of penetrating local power networks by replacing satraps with military governors (*strategoi*), who were more directly subordinate to the central state and had less independent control of their province.[105] Likewise, the instability of Seleucid rule in Asia Minor made the concept of a satrapy increasingly irrelevant.[106] The large Syria-Palestine satrapy of the Persian Empire, which bore an annual tribute of 350 Babylonian silver talents according to Herodotus, was split up into a number of smaller subdivisions with fluid boundaries and administrative organization. This was partly a legacy of its partition with the Ptolemies until 200 BCE but must also reflect the fact that Syria became the seat of the central government.[107] Babylonia was the second seat of the government, traditionally ruled by the heir apparent. Less may have changed in the areas further east,

100 Aperghis (2004: 168–9). 101 *1 Maccabees* 41–56.
102 Josephus, *Antiquities* 13.49–51; *1 Maccabees* 10.30; Goldstein (1976: 405–8).
103 *1 Maccabees* 11.28; Aperghis (2004: 171).
104 Ma (1999: 130–7, 150–74); Aperghis (2004: 289–90). 105 Capdetrey (2007: 236).
106 Ibid.: 243–4. 107 Ibid.: 244–50.

where the distance probably made it difficult to establish more bureaucratic control.[108]

At least within its core territory, the Seleucids must have raised much higher revenue than the Persian Empire had done in the corresponding provinces. As shown above, Judea alone could generate 300 to 740 silver talents per year, in contrast the 350 that the Persians received from all of Syria-Palestine. The total Persian tribute, including Egypt, according to Herodotus was about 9,000 talents. In 316 BCE, while Antigonus was briefly in control over an area from Asia Minor to Central Asia but not Egypt, he reportedly received an annual revenue of 11,000 talents.[109] All the revenue figures from literary sources, including those for the Ptolemaic kingdom cited in the previous section, raise doubts about their accuracy, and the basis for them is unknown. Aperghis estimates that total Seleucid royal revenue peaked during the reigns of Seleucus I and Antiochus III at about 14,000 to 20,000 talents per year.[110] His extrapolation from local tax-to-population ratios depends on the accuracy of his population estimates, however, which have been rightly criticized.[111] On the other hand, it would require them to be off by more than one order of magnitude to contradict the basic point that the Hellenistic kings, whether by plunder or taxation, placed a heavier burden on their territory than the Persian central government, to judge by Herodotus's tribute list.

Antigonid Macedonia

Of the three largest Hellenistic kingdoms, we can know by far the least about Macedonia. In contrast to the Ptolemaic and Seleucid kingdoms, Macedonia experienced its highest levels of instability in the early Hellenistic period, from 323 to 260 BCE. During this time the invasion by the Gauls, together with dynastic struggles and violence among rival members of the Macedonian aristocracy, caused devastation and emigration.[112] This was followed by a period of relative stability and hegemony over much of Greece, between 260 and 200 BCE. Nevertheless, Macedonia did not have the resources to maintain an expensive fleet and to challenge Seleucid and Ptolemaic interests in the east.[113] The preceding instability may have purged many of the elites on whose consent Macedonian kingship traditionally depended, but these still would have been major obstacles to

108 Sherwin-White and Kuhrt (1994) argue for tighter integration of the eastern satrapies, however.

109 Diodorus Siculus 19.56.5.

110 Aperghis (2004: 248–51).

111 Ma (2007); Wiesehöfer (2009).

112 Billows (1995: 206–12).

113 Serrati (2007: 477).

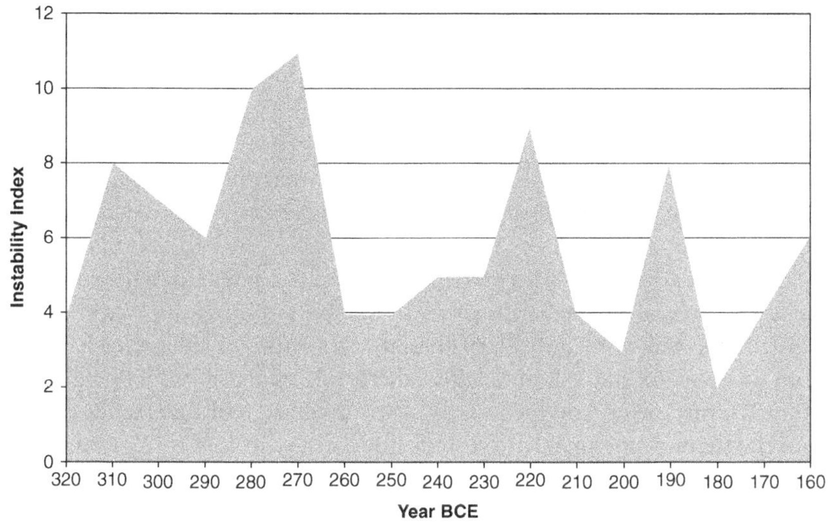

Figure 5.4 Macedonian instability index, 320–160 BCE

bureaucratization and revenue collection, which the Antigonids only gradually overcame.[114] Philip V's defeat to the Romans in 197 BCE drastically cut back Macedonian influence in Greece but the crisis may have also allowed Philip to reorganize the state, creating perhaps at that time the four administrative divisions that became republics in 167 BE. This revival allowed Philip's successor Perseus to challenge Rome in that year, but with disastrous results. Figure 5.4 illustrates the implications of Macedonian political history for instability.

The Roman policies in Macedonia after these wars provide the best clues to Macedonia's fiscal situation. In the year following the Romans' victory at Cynocephalai in 197 BCE Flamininus proclaimed the freedom of the Greek states formerly under Macedonian rule from tribute. Just as in Attalid, Seleucid, and Ptolemaic territory (especially in Asia Minor), Greek cities were often assessed tribute by foreign kings, so Macedonia must have suffered a loss of revenue after the liberation of its Greek possessions as well as its cities and territory in Thrace and Thessaly by the Romans in the settlement ending the Second Macedonian War.

More interesting is the information that ancient authors provide about the provisions after the Romans' victory over Perseus at Pydna in 167 BCE,

[114] Walbank (1984: 225–7).

not only because they relate to Macedonia itself but also because they enable us to compare the Antigonid and the Roman Republican approaches to taxation. The Romans abolished the Macedonian monarchy in 167 BCE and created in its place four independent republics. These four republics may correspond to preexisting administrative districts that each paid annual tribute. According to our sources, the tribute that these Macedonian districts paid under Philip V and Perseus was henceforth paid to the Roman people but was reduced by one-half, from 200 talents to 100 talents per year.[115] Even 200 talents is an extremely low figure compared to the revenues raised in the east by the Seleucids and Ptolemies, though this was after the Antigonids had lost control of Thessaly and most of their Greek cities. Certain scholars have doubted that there was any real reduction by the Romans, but for no good reason.[116] The confiscation of royal land, mines, and the treasury are cited as hardships but there is no reason to assume that this personal patrimony of the king could have been used to offset the four districts' annual tribute. The Romans also conspicuously reduced tribute payments now owed from the neighboring Illyrians to half their pre-Roman levels.

The admittedly pro-Roman account that comes down to us is unambiguous that the halving of royal tribute was felt to be a blessing. Polybius writes: "For the Macedonians had met with signal favors from Rome; the country as a whole had been delivered from the arbitrary rule and taxation of autocrats and, as all confessed, now enjoyed freedom in the place of servitude and the several cities had, owing to the beneficient actions of Rome, been freed from serious civil discord and internecine massacres."[117] Bang cites the reorganization of Macedonia in 167 BCE as an example of the Romans' strategy to obtain an "empire on the cheap." In other words, they sought to reduce the costs of the administration by providing tax incentives to local elites to take over the burden of government.[118] After the complete annexation of Macedonia in 146 BCE, and through the late Republic and early imperial monarchy, the impact of Roman rule is best seen in the emergence of landowning elites responsible for the administration of their cities, which replaced the more bureaucratic system of governance by overseers (*epistatai*) appointed by the Macedonian kings.[119]

[115] Livy 45.18.7, 45.26.13–14, 45.29.11, Diodorus 31.8.3–9, Plutarch *Aem. Paull.* 28.3; see also Polybius 36.17.13 and Gruen (1984: 427–8).

[116] Larsen (1938: 298–9); Hatzopoulos (1996: 221–2). [117] Polybius 36.17.13.

[118] Bang (2009: 106, 108–9). [119] Bartels (2008: 98–100).

The rise of the Roman Empire

Rome's participatory republican institutions, supported by an army of citizens and allies, meant that it did not share the inherent cooperation dilemma of the Hellenistic kingdoms.[120] Thus it responded differently to fiscal crises. For example, while Hannibal was ravaging Italy during the Second Punic War (218–201 BCE), the senate was able to take voluntary loans from its own wealthiest citizens to order to pay its soldiers.[121] The direct taxation of private land was light and was borne mainly by the rich until 167 BCE, when it was abolished for citizens in Italy altogether. As Rome expanded into the Hellenistic world, it too became a potential competitor with local elites for the surplus of agrarian communities, and the same dynamic prevailed. Because of its success it could afford to reward those who showed loyalty with fiscal privileges, which kept agency costs low by encouraging cooperation from provincial elites. Rising economic inequality in the late Republic caused Rome's cooperative institutions to break down, however. Soldiers had to be recruited from men below the army's property qualification, who became dependent on their commanders for payments and land redistributed from subject communities. The increasing instability and civil wars led to extortionate taxes in the east until Augustus consolidated control and established the Roman monarchy. He reinstituted low taxation and high cooperation with provincial elites, which lasted until the crisis of the third century CE triggered by the rise of Sassanid Persia. Instability in the period from 300 BCE to 200 CE is represented in Figure 5.5.

Kiser and Kane argue that the privatization of tax-farming led to fiscal exploitation during the Republic but it is doubtful that the Romans taxed their subjects as much as the Hellenistic kings did, except in extraordinary circumstances.[122] The *lex Hieronica*, a taxation law introduced by the Greek tyrant of Syracuse, Hiero II, subjected landowners to a 10 percent tax in kind on their harvests. When the Romans incorporated Sicily as a province, they extended this system to virtually the entire island and regarded it as a generous fiscal regime that favored local landowners.[123] As noted above in the previous section, the halving of the annual tribute in Illyria and Macedonia, when the latter was broken up into republics in 167 BCE, was likewise perceived by contemporaries as a great benefaction.

[120] See Tan, Chapter 6, and Scheidel, Chapter 7, for more detailed studies that accord with the general picture sketched here.

[121] Gruen (1984: 300); Bringmann (2002: 174–6). [122] Kiser and Kane (2007).

[123] Cicero, *Verrines* 2.3.6.15, 2.3.8.20; Lintott (1993: 71); Pritchard (1970: 353–4).

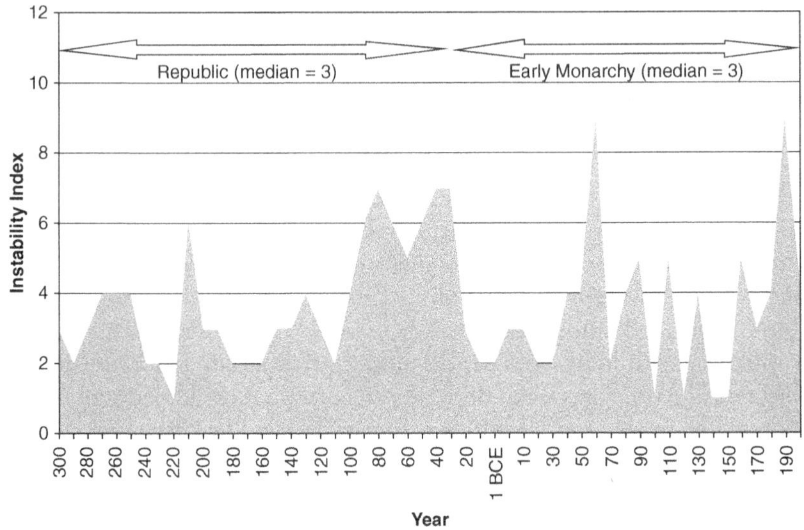

Figure 5.5 Roman instability index, 300 BCE – AD 190

According to a speech of Mark Antony at Ephesus found in Appian, when the kingdom of Pergamon, which had acquired most Seleucid territory in Asia Minor after 188 BCE, became a Roman province in 133 BCE the Romans initially abolished the tribute (*phoros*).[124] Afterwards, Roman "popular agitators" made it necessary, but even then they replaced the tribute (*phoros*) with a proportional tax – most likely the 10 percent tax as in Sicily – which Antony depicts as a fiscal regime that was quite favorable to them.

Tax farmers in collaboration with Roman officials raised these revenues from the provinces. It was only during the period of instability after 100 BCE, however, that fiscal predation and corruption, including the worst abuses of the tax-farming corporations, became critical. Roman mobs, restless Italian allies, slave revolts, electoral fraud, elite conspiracies, and peripheral rogue states in the east (Parthia and Mithradates of Pontus) all contributed to an age of uncertainty that weakened regulation and suppressed inhibitions about overtaxation. The civil wars between rival Roman warlords – Marius versus Sulla, Caesar versus Pompey, Caesarians versus Republicans, Octavian versus Antony – put the most severe strains

[124] Appian, *Civil Wars* 5.4.

on the finances of the eastern provinces. In his speech at Ephesus, Antony added that the tax farmers went out of control (during the unstable middle of the first century BCE) until Caesar put an end to their abusive practices and gave back one-third of what had been paid.[125] Caesar could probably afford to do so in 48 BCE because he had just defeated his rival, Pompey, and established mastery over the Roman world. After his assassination, in 44 BCE, that world was again in turmoil and the Republicans allegedly raised ten years of taxes in the east in a single year to amass an army against the Caesarians. Subsequently, Mark Antony raised another nine years of taxes in Asia, while Octavian reintroduced taxes on citizen property in Italy when the two went to war with each other.[126]

Octavian's victory, ending the civil wars, coincided with the annexation of the last major Hellenistic kingdom (Ptolemaic Egypt) in 30 BCE and established a new age of imperial stability, punctuated only by sporadic succession crises and minor revolts until the third century CE.[127] The early Roman imperial monarchy exhibited surprising similarity to the Persian Empire that preceded the Hellenistic period. Much like Persia's satrapal system of fixed tribute, the Roman Empire established a tribute that was based on a periodic census.[128] It was up to the provincial government and its governor to align the tax burden internally with the demands of the central state.[129] In Egypt, the pervasive Ptolemaic harvest taxes of 20 to 60 percent were abolished on most land. The exception was the public land cultivated by peasant leaseholders, which was, however, greatly reduced by auctions to private owners. Instead of these high variable rates, private landowners paid a low fixed land tax (1 *artaba* per *aroura*). If average harvests were 12 *arouras* or higher, then the burden was less than 10 percent. One sees a similar drop in the rates and a switch from variable to fixed assessments in the case of vineyards and orchards.[130] These low taxes created a new landowning elite that took over responsibility for local governance. It probably also contributed to urbanization and economic development.[131]

Like the Persian Empire, the total Roman imperial revenue was low compared to the total economic potential of their provinces, which ideally served to generate loyalty among provincial elites and to pass on to them

[125] Appian, *Civil Wars* 5.4; Plutarch, *Caesar* 48. [126] Neesen (1980: 1–16).

[127] After King Herod's death in 4 BCE, Augustus appointed an *ethnarch* of Judea, Samaria, and Idumea and reduced the tribute paid to him by one-fourth (Josephus, *Antiquities* 17.11.4). Ten years later these areas were fully annexed to Rome, but how this affected taxation is unclear.

[128] Brunt (1981); Christol (2006). [129] Jördens (2009: 102). [130] Monson (2012b: 190–1).

[131] Ibid.: 275–82.

the responsibility for their own local governance. Hopkins explains why the Roman Empire kept taxes low as the result of its minimal level of bureaucracy and the correspondingly high rents and incomes of the landowners, which made them loyal supporters.[132] He estimates total revenue in the mid-first century CE to have been about 800 HS (= 33,333 talents). Similarly, Duncan-Jones estimates 900 HS (= 37,500 talents) in the second century CE.[133] This would be only two to three times more than the 14,500 talents of revenue attributed to Ptolemaic Egypt under Ptolemy XII despite a population (about 60 million) that was at least ten times greater than Egypt's. If one takes Diodorus's low figure of 6,000 talents for Ptolemaic royal revenue, then it would still be 15 to 20 percent of the imperial revenue. These figures, despite their uncertainty, lend some support for the conclusion based on the documentary sources from Egypt that taxes decreased under Roman rule.

Conclusions

The takeaway point from this chapter is a counter-intuitive proposition: when rulers' hold on power is secure and their states enjoy unmatched supremacy, they lower taxes rather than raise them. Aperghis, while casting unfounded doubts on Antiochus III's fiscal privileges for Jerusalem, argues: "In the position of strength in which he found himself in about 200 BC, the Seleukid king had no particular need to make concessions, nor did he probably have any desire to reduce his revenues more than was absolutely necessary. Indeed he would have preferred to increase them, if he could, which seems to have been the policy of the Seleukid kings all along."[134] This statement echoes the thesis of his book that the Seleucids (and the Ptolemies) were revenue maximizers, which he takes as support for a "modernist" approach to the ancient economy.[135] Following Levi, I have argued in this chapter that rulers' attitudes vary depending on how much they discount future revenue.[136] This in turn depends on the precariousness of their hold on power, which I have gauged with an instability index that incorporates both internal and external threats (Table 5.2).

The Hellenistic states provide a good natural experiment for testing this proposition. They are situated chronologically between two world empires, Achaemenid Persia and the Roman imperial monarchy, which present a stark contrast to this "warring-states" environment. Their own history also

[132] Hopkins (2009: 183–4). [133] Duncan-Jones (1994: 46). [134] Aperghis (2004: 168).
[135] Ibid.: 3. [136] See also Levi (1988).

Table 5.2 *Summary of instability indices*

State	Period	Fiscal pressure	Instability
Persian Empire	550–330 BCE	Low?	4.0
Ptolemaic Egypt	323–30 BCE	High	5.0
Seleucid Asia	311–64 BCE	High	6.5
Macedonia	323–167 BCE	High?	5.0
Republican Rome	300–27 BCE	Low	3.0
Roman Empire	27 BCE–200 CE	Low	3.0

reveals variation over time in fiscal institutions and levels of stability. On one extreme (for example, immediately after Alexander's death), instability for some of the dynasts was so great that they relied on absolute coercion – plundering cities, temples, and the countryside – to pay for their expensive armies. Those who managed to establish relatively stable control over some territory (such as Ptolemy in Egypt) went about creating fiscal institutions that would allow economic activity to continue, so that there would be more revenue in future years. On the other extreme is the stable imperial order (such as the Persian and Roman Empires), which decentralized power with low taxes or strong property rights that favored the development of landowning aristocracies. The Hellenistic states vacillated along this continuum, sometimes giving privileges and incentives and sometimes increasing their level of extraction up to the point of fiscal predation or plundering.

To penetrate local power networks and capture free-floating resources the Hellenistic states developed royal bureaucracies. In doing so, however, they incurred higher administrative and enforcement costs, which I have also called agency costs, at the expense of voluntary cooperation. Higher taxation ought to have diminishing returns, especially as economic activity suffers, so rulers use it only when the immediate revenue (due to impending threats) is much more valuable than future revenue. Republican Rome was similar to the Hellenistic states but enjoyed more favorable starting conditions in terms of social cohesion. The Hellenistic states in the east, if not Macedonia, were based initially on leadership and military specialists from outside, requiring high levels of redistribution from their subjects, and they only gradually integrated non-Greeks into the army and administration.

As long as Rome's political institutions maintained cooperation and stability at home and as long as its armies were successful abroad, it could invest more in capital-intensive state-building with lower administrative and enforcement costs than the Hellenistic states had to bear. When that stability broke down in the late Republic, its leaders were bent on coercive fiscal measures that would secure their immediate interests at the expense of the longer-term economic development of its territory. By that time the Hellenistic states were too weak to take advantage. Had Rome not entered the scene, it is fully conceivable that one of the Hellenistic states would have finally defeated its rivals (as Ptolemy III, Antiochus III, and Antiochus IV almost did) and created an imperial order that would have had much in common with Achaemenid Persia or the Roman imperial monarchy.

References

Agut-Labordère, D. (2005) "Le sens du Décret de Cambyse," *Transeuphratène* 29: 9–16.

Aperghis, G. G. (2004) *The Seleukid Royal Economy: The Finances and Financial Administration of the Seleukid Empire*. Cambridge.

Armoni, C. (2012) *Studien zur Verwaltung des ptolemäischen Ägypten: das Amt des Basilikos Grammateus*. Paderborn.

Austin, M. M. (2006) *The Hellenistic World from Alexander to the Roman Conquest: A Selection of Ancient Sources in Translation*, 2nd edn. Cambridge.

Bagnall, R. S., and Derow, P. (2004) *The Hellenistic Period: Historical Sources in Translation*. Oxford.

Bang, P. F. (2009) "Commanding and consuming the world: empire, tribute, and trade in Roman and Chinese history," in *Rome and China: Comparative Perspectives on Ancient World Empires*, ed. W. Scheidel. Oxford: 100–20.

Bartels, J. (2008) *Städtische Eliten im römischen Makedonien*. Berlin.

Billows, R. A. (1995) *Kings and Colonists: Aspects of Macedonian Imperialism*. Leiden.

Bingen, J. (2007) *Hellenistic Egypt: Monarchy, Society, Economy, Culture*. Berkeley, CA.

Boswinkel, E., and Pestman, P. W. (1978) *Textes grecs, démotiques et bilingues*. Leiden.

Briant, P. (2002) *From Cyrus to Alexander: A History of the Persian Empire*. Winona Lake, IN.

Bringmann, K. (2002) *Geschichte der römischen Republik: von den Anfängen bis Augustus*. Munich.

Brown, P. C. (1988) "Practical constraints on early Tokugawa land taxation: annual versus fixed assessments in Kaga domain," *Journal of Japanese Studies* 14: 369–401.

Brunt, P. A. (1981) "The revenues of Rome," *Journal of Roman Studies* 71: 161–72.

Callataÿ, F. de (2004) "La richesse des rois séleucides et le problème de la taxation en nature," in *Le roi et l'économie: autonomies locales et structures royales dans l'économie de l'empire séleucide*, ed. V. Chankowski and F. Duyrat. Paris: 23–47.

Capdetrey, L. (2007) *Le pouvoir séleucide: territoire, administration, finances d'un royaume hellénistique (312–129 avant J-C)*. Rennes.

Capponi, L. (2005) *Augustan Egypt: The Creation of a Roman Province*. Oxford.

Christol, M. (2006) "Les outils de la fiscalité: l'arrière-plan Romain," in *De l'estime au cadastre en Europe: le Moyen Âge*, ed. A. Rigaudière. Paris: 25–58.

Clarysse, W. (2003) "The archive of the praktor Milon," in *Edfu, an Egyptian Provincial Capital in the Ptolemaic Period*, ed. W. Clarysse and K. Vandorpe. Brussels: 17–27.

Clarysse, W., and Thompson, D. J. (2006) *Counting the People in Hellenistic Egypt*. Cambridge.

Clarysse, W., and Vandorpe, K. (1998) "The Ptolemaic apomoira," in *Le culte du souverain dans l'Égypte ptolémaïque au IIIe siècle avant notre ère*, ed. H. Melaerts. Leuven: 5–42.Cuvigny, H. (1985) *L'arpentage par espèces dans l'Égypte ptolémaïque d'après les papyrus grecs*. Brussels.

Descat, R. (1985) "Mnésimachos, Hérodote et le système tributaire achéménide," *Revue des études anciennes* 87: 97–112.

Duncan-Jones, R. (1994) *Money and Government in the Roman Empire*. Cambridge.

Fischer-Bovet, C. (2008) "Army and society in Ptolemaic Egypt," PhD dissertation. Stanford University, CA.

Gabrielsen, V. (2011) "Profitable partnerships: monopolies, traders, kings, and cities," in *The Economies of Hellenistic Societies: Third to First Centuries BC*, ed. Z. H. Archibald, J. K. Davies, and V. Gabrielsen. Oxford: 216–50.

Goldstein, J. A. (1976) *I Maccabees: A New Translation with Introduction and Commentary*. Garden City, NY.

Goldstone, J. A. (1991) *Revolution and Rebellion in the Early Modern World*. Berkeley, CA.

Gruen, E. (1984) *The Hellenistic World and the Coming of Rome*. Berkeley, CA.

Hahn, I. (1978) "Königsland und königliche Besteuerung im hellenistischen Osten," *Klio* 60: 11–34.

Hatzopoulos, M. B. (1996) *Macedonian Institutions under the Kings: A Historical and Epigraphic Study*. Athens.

Hoogendijk, F. A. J. (2010) "The practice of taxation in three late Ptolemaic papyri," in *Proceedings of the Twenty-Fifth International Congress of Papyrology*, ed. T. Gagos. Ann Arbor, MI: 313–22.

Hopkins, K. (2009) "The political economy of the Roman Empire," in *The Dynamics of Ancient Empires: State Power from Assyria to Byzantium*, ed. I. Morris and W. Scheidel. Oxford: 178–204.

Hornblower, S. (1982) *Mausolus*. Oxford.

Jördens, A. (2009) *Statthalterliche Verwaltung in der römischen Kaiserzeit: Studien zum praefectus Aegypti*. Stuttgart.

Jursa, M. (1998) *Der Tempelzehnt in Babylonien vom siebentem bis zum dritten Jahrhundert v. Chr*. Münster.

(2006) "Agricultural management, tax farming and banking: aspects of entrepreneurial activity in Babylonia in the late Achaemenid and Hellenistic period," in *La transition entre l'empire achéménide et les royaumes hellénistiques (vers 350–300 av. J-C)*, ed. P. Briant and F. Joannès. Paris: 137–222.

(2009) "On aspects of taxation in Achaemenid Babylonia: new evidence from Borsippa," in *Organisation des pouvoirs et contacts culturels dans les pays de l'empire achéménide*, ed. P. Briant and M. Chauveau. Paris: 237–69.

(2011) "Taxation and service obligations in Babylonia from Nebuchadnezzer to Darius and the evidence for Darius' tax reform," in *Herodot und das Persische Weltreich*, ed. R. Rollinger, B. Truschnegg, and R. Bichler. Wiesbaden: 431–48.

Kiser, E., and Cai, Y. (2003) "War and bureaucratization in Qin China: exploring an anomalous case," *American Sociological Review* 68: 511–39.

Kiser, E., and Kane, D. (2007) "The perils of privatization: how the characteristics of principals affected tax farming in the Roman Republic and Empire," *Social Science History* 31: 191–212.

Kreissig, H. (1978) *Wirtschaft und Gesellschaft im Seleukidenreich: die Eigentums- und die Abhängigkeitsverhältnisse*. Berlin.

Kuhrt, A. (2005) *The Ancient Near East, c. 3000–330 BC*. New York.

(2007) *The Persian Empire: A Corpus of Sources from the Achaemenid Period*. New York.

Larsen, J. A. O. (1938) "Roman Greece," in *An Economic Survey of Ancient Rome*, vol. I, ed. T. Frank. Paterson, NJ: 259–498.

Lemaire, A. (2004) "Taxes et impôts dans le sud de la Palestine," *Transeuphratène* 28: 133–42.

(2007) "Administration in fourth-century BCE Judah in light of epigraphy and numismatics," *in Judah and the Judeans in the Fourth Century BCE*, ed. O. Lipschits, G. N. Knoppers, and R. Albertz. Winona Lake, IN: 53–74.

Levi, M. (1988) *Of Rule and Revenue*. Berkeley, CA.

Lintott, A. W. (1993) *Imperium Romanum: Politics and Administration*. London.

Lloyd, A. B. (2002) "The Egyptian elite in the early Ptolemaic period: some hieroglyphic evidence," in *The Hellenistic World: New Perspectives*, ed. D. Ogden. London: 117–36.

Ma, J. (1999) *Antiochos III and the Cities of Western Asia Minor*. Oxford.

(2007) "Review of G. G. Aperghis, The Seleucid Royal Economy: The Finances and Financial Administration of the Seleukid Empire," *Hermathena* 187: 182–8.

McGing, B. C. (1997) "Revolt Egyptian style: internal opposition to Ptolemaic rule," *Archiv für Papyrusforschung* 43: 273–314.

Maier, F. G. (1959) *Griechische Mauerbauinschriften*, vol. I. Heidelberg.

Malay, H. (1983) "A royal document from Aigai in Aiolis," *Greek, Roman, and Byzantine Studies* 24: 349–53.

Manning, J. G. (2003) *Land and Power in Ptolemaic Egypt: The Structure of Land Tenure*. Cambridge.

(2010) *The Last Pharaohs: Egypt under the Ptolemies, 305–30 BC*. Princeton, NJ.

Maresch, K. (1996) *Bronze und Silber: papyrologische Beiträge zur Geschichte der Währung im ptolemäischen und römischen Ägypten biz zum 2. Jahrhundert n. Chr.* Opladen, Germany.

Martin, C. (1996) "Demotic texts," in *The Elephantine Papyri in English: Three Millennia of Cross-Cultural Continuity and Change*, ed. B. Porten. Leiden: 277–385.

Martin, T. R. (2007) "Ancient Greek units of currency, weight, and distance," in *The Landmark Herodotus*, ed. R. B. Strassler. New York: 773–9.

Mehl, A. (1980) "*Doriktetos Chora*: kritische Bemerkungen zum 'Speererwerb' im Politik und Völkerrecht der hellenistischen Epoche," *Ancient Society* 11/12: 173–212.

Mileta, C. (2008) *Der König und sein Land: Untersuchungen zur Herrschaft der hellenistischen Monarchen über das königliche Gebiet Kleinasiens und seine Bevölkerung.* Berlin.

Monson, A. (2007) "Rule and revenue in Egypt and Rome: political stability and fiscal institutions," *Historical Social Research* 32: 252–74.

(2012a) *Agriculture and Taxation in Early Ptolemaic Egypt: Demotic Land Surveys and Accounts (P. Agri.).* Bonn.

(2012b) *From the Ptolemies to the Romans: Political and Economic Change in Egypt.* Cambridge.

(2013) "Salinization and agricultural productivity in the Fayyum," in *Das Fayum in Hellenismus und Kaiserzeit: Fallstudien zu multikulturellem Leben in der Antike*, ed. C. Arlt and M. A. Stadler. Wiesbaden: 123–40.

Musti, D. (1984) "Syria and the East," in *The Cambridge Ancient History,* vol. VII, part 1, *The Hellenistic World*, 2nd edn, ed. F. W. Walbank, A. E. Austin, M. W. Frederiksen, and R. M Oglivie. Cambridge: 175–220.

Neesen, L. (1980) *Untersuchungen zu den direkten Staatsabgaben der römischen Kaiserzeit: 27 v. Chr – 284 n. Chr.* Bonn.

Piejko, F. (1988) "Letter of Eumenes II to Tralles concerning the inviolability and tax exemption for a temple: after 188 BC," *Chiron* 18: 55–69.

Pritchard, R. T. (1970) "Cicero and the *lex Hieronica*," *Historia* 19: 352–68.

Préaux, C. (1939) *L'économie royale des lagides.* Brussels.

Rathbone, D. W. (1993) "Egypt, Augustus and Roman taxation," *Cahiers du Centre Gustave Glotz* 4: 81–112.

Rostovtzeff, M. I. (1922) *A Large Estate in Egypt in the Third Century BC.* Madison, WI.

(1941) *The Social and Economic History of the Hellenistic World.* Oxford.

Rowlandson, J. (2007) "The character of Ptolemaic aristocracy: problems of definition and evidence," in *Jewish Perspectives on Hellenistic Rulers*, ed. T. Rajak, S. Pearce, J. Aitken, and J. Dines. Berkeley, CA: 20–49.

Schuler, C. (2005) "Die διοίκησις τῆς πόλεως im öffentlichen Finanzwesen der hellenistischen Poleis," *Chiron* 35: 385–403.

Serrati, J. (2007) "Warfare and the state," in *The Cambridge History of Greek and Roman Warfare,* vol. I, *Greece, the Hellenistic World and the Rise of Rome*, ed. P. Sabin, H. van Wees, and M. Whitby. Cambridge: 461–97.

Sherwin-White, S. (1985) "Ancient archives: the edict of Alexander to Priene, a reappraisal," *Journal of Hellenic Studies* 105: 69–89.

Sherwin-White, S., and Kuhrt, A. (1994) *From Samarkhand to Sardis: A New Approach to the Seleucid Empire*. Berkeley, CA.

Spiegelberg, W. (1914) *Die sogennante demotische Chronik*. Leipzig.

Stolper, M. W. (1985) *Entrepreneurs and Empire: The Murašu Firm and Persian Rule in Babylonia*. Leiden.

Tilly, C. (1992) *Coercion, Capital, and European States: AD 990–1992*, rev. edn. Malden, MA.

Thornemann, P. (2009) "Estates and the land in early Hellenistic Asia Minor: the estate of Krateuas," *Chiron* 39: 363–93.

Tuplin, C. (2011) "Managing the world: Herodotus on Achaemenid imperial organisation," in *Herodot und das Persische Weltreich*, ed. R. Rollinger, B. Truschnegg, and R. Bichler. Wiesbaden: 39–64.

Turchin, P., and Nefedov, S. A. (2009) *Secular Cycles*. Princeton, NJ.

Van der Spek, R. J. (1995) "Land ownership in Babylonian cuneiform documents," in *Legal Documents of the Hellenistic World*, ed. M. J. Geller, H. Maehler, and A. D. E. Lewis. London: 173–245.

(2007) "The Hellenistic Near East," in *The Cambridge Economic History of the Greco-Roman World*, ed. W. Scheidel, I. Morris, and R. Saller. Cambridge: 409–33.

Vandorpe, K. (2000) "The Ptolemaic *epigraphe* or harvest tax (*shemu*)," *Archiv für Papyrusforschung* 46: 169–232.

(2006) "Agriculture, temples and tax law in Ptolemaic Egypt," in *L'agriculture institutionnelle en Égypte ancienne: état de la question et perspectives interdisciplinaires*, ed. J. C. Moreno García. Villeneuve d'Ascq, France: 165–71.

Veïsse, A.-E. (2004) "Surveiller ou punir? Le contrôle des fonctionnaires dans l'Egypte ptolémaïque," in *Contrôler les agents du pouvoir*, ed. L. Feller. Limoges: 103–11.

Vidal-Naquet, P. (1967) *Le Bordereau d'ensemencement dans l'Égypte ptolémaïque*. Brussels.

Von Reden, S. (2007) *Money in Ptolemaic Egypt: From the Macedonian Conquest to the End of the Third Century BC*. Cambridge.

Walbank, F. W. (1979) *A Historical Commentary on Polybius*, vol. III. Oxford.

(1984) "Macedonia and Greece," in *The Cambridge Ancient History*, vol. VII, part 1, *The Hellenistic World*, 2nd edn, ed. F. W. Walbank, A. E. Austin, M. W. Frederiksen, and R. M Oglivie. Cambridge: 221–56.

Weber, M. (1988 [1909]) *The Agrarian Sociology of Ancient Civilizations*, trans. R. I. Frank. New York.

Welles, C. B. (1934) *Royal Correspondence in the Hellenistic Period: A Study in Greek Epigraphy*. New Haven, CT.

Wickham, C. (2005) *Framing the Early Middle Ages: Europe and the Mediterranean, 400–800*. Oxford.

Wiesehöfer, J. (2009) "The Achaemenid Empire," in *The Dynamics of Ancient Empires: State Power from Assyria to Byzantium*, ed. I. Morris and W. Scheidel. New York: 66–98.
Wilcken, U. (1899) *Griechische Ostraka aus Aegypten und Nubien: ein Beitrag zur antiken Wirtschaftsgeschichte*. Munich.
Wörrle, M. (1988) "Inschriften von Herakleia am Latmos I: Antiochos III, Zeuxis und Herakleia," *Chiron* 18: 421–76.

CHAPTER 6

The Roman Republic

James Tan

Introduction

The laboratory of history contains some fascinating specimens, and the Roman Republic is as interesting as any. Rome in the last two or three centuries BCE had the constitution of a city state yet was an empire on three continents, was an electoral republic, yet was ruled by an almost hereditary aristocracy. It is simultaneously familiar and foreign. The same applies to its fiscal system. After the creation of a tributary empire, Roman citizens enjoyed a rare political privilege, more familiar from modern oil states than from militaristic premodern examples: freedom from taxation. But to what extent could the population actually rejoice in this fiscal freedom? Tax, we have been told, is a blessing, because it empowers its payers and increases their bargaining power. Without it, rulers would have no interest in the onerous business of improving our lives through schools, roads, democratization, etc. The state's reliance on our resources ensures that we are not abandoned by its leaders.[1] In light of these insights, how do we approach the fiscal sociology of Republican Rome? What happens to a tax system when a city state becomes an empire? What happens to society when the tax base is transformed from a local to a continental scale?

To bring out the relationship between fiscal and social developments, we need to address two sets of change. The first traces developments in the tax system and asks why the Romans adopted the particular practices found in the evidence. Rome's decentralized system of power-sharing prevented any leader from freely spending public funds, and my hypothesis is that this discouraged more intensive taxation. The second examines the effect that this tax system had on Roman society. Fiscal sociologists have given us a set of lenses through which to view this problem, and the image revealed pairs an untaxed population of minimal bargaining power with a super-wealthy

[1] Most notably Tilly (1992), and now Blanton and Fargher (2008) and Martin, Mehrotra, and Prasad (2009). See Moore (2003) for the intellectual origins of this school of thought.

elite able to dominate both economy and society. This determinedly oligarchic aristocracy is central to the story. Devoted to a diffuse system of patron–client relationships, the aristocrats saw nothing but danger in the rise of a centralized, powerful state; they would, likewise, run any risk to prevent an individual or faction from gaining control of the treasury and its resources. As a result, the usual incentives toward maximizing public revenues were absent. The elite privatized as much of the empire's profits as possible, which increased inequality in society and ensured that it, and not the state, controlled the distribution of wealth at Rome. Before I can begin to elucidate this portrait, however, it will be worthwhile reexamining the historical context of the Roman Republic.

The Roman Republic

The history of the early Roman Republic is conventionally divided into the internal and the external.[2] At home, the Romans faced the challenges of a split community, with plebeians challenging patricians for political rights. Abroad, Rome was a leading member of a confederacy of Latin cities, but faced regular clashes with neighbors. The internal and external collided, however, when Rome went to war; the patrician elite required the military and economic resources of the plebeian population to face the challenges of hostile neighbors, and conscription and taxation frequently appear in Livy's history as occasioning conflict.[3] If we pick up the story in the year 338 BCE, however, we see the Romans beginning to set out on a new trajectory. They had defeated their fellow Latins to cement their position as hegemon, they had implemented a new set of compromises to allow leading plebeians to share political power with patricians, and they had extended the reach of their legions to the rich plains of Campania in the South. By 295, having defeated the Samnites and Etruscans, they were alone in their dominance of central Italy, and by 264 they had conquered most of the peninsula and were prepared to clash with the Carthaginians in Sicily. It is at this point that the fiscal history of Rome is transformed. Terrestrial by nature, the Romans took on the expensive business of naval warfare. Costs rose as fleets sank. But their eventual victory – after the total

[2] Accounts are provided by Crawford (1978), Bringmann (2007), and Cornell (1995), who expresses the conventional divide perfectly in his chapter divisions.

[3] For example, Livy 2.54.10; 3.10.9–11.2; 5.10.3; 5.12.3; 5.20.5–10; 10.46.6. Many of these instances are, admittedly, anachronistic or simply implausible. They are perhaps a reflection of later difficulties with the levy, especially in 151 and 138, when consuls were imprisoned for their harsh conscription; Broughton (1951) provides the references.

loss of some 700 warships – allowed them to pass the losses onto the Carthaginians: the commander on the spot ordered the vanquished to pay 2,200 talents over twenty years, but, after revisions, the eventual treaty demanded 3,200 talents over just ten years.[4] As a result of this First Punic War, Sicily, Sardinia, and Corsica all came under Roman control.

So began the overseas expansion. Between 218 and 201 the Romans managed to survive the onslaught of Hannibal, to demand a fifty-year indemnity after defeating him on his own African soil, and to convert much of eastern and southern Spain into provinces to boot. They then turned east. After victories over Antigonid Macedonia in 197 and Seleucid Anatolia in 190, they levied further indemnities, but withdrew all troops. Another Macedonian campaign, from 171 to 167, saw the Romans overthrow the king and set up tributary republics. This experiment failed, and in the 140s – after further wars in Greece and a siege of Carthage – Macedonia, Achaea, and Africa all became in some sense subject to Rome. Western Anatolia soon followed after its erstwhile ruler named the Roman people as his heir, followed by southern France and more of the African coastline. After the great campaigns of Pompey (67–62), Egypt remained the only part of the eastern Mediterranean independent of Roman control, and, in the west, Caesar would famously conquer Gaul up to the Rhine.

The city state had become an empire, but its growing pains could not be ignored. The Romans retained most of their old institutions. Magistracies remained collegial, involving short annual terms, and intervals were enforced between the holding of any two offices.[5] The frequent rotation of officials necessarily endowed the Senate – comprising all former magistrates – with great influence, since only here was there a degree of permanence and constancy.[6] This meant that executive power was weak and fleeting, with individuals – except on the battlefield – rarely able to control an agenda or execute autonomous control over policy. Rome also nurtured a timocratic ideal. The army had traditionally relied on landowning soldiers, and this placed a premium on a broad population of peasants capable of military service; the elite was interested in investing its share of imperial profits into Italian land, however, increasing competition for this most valuable of capital and driving the small peasant landowner out of the market for Italian land. Over time fewer small landholders remained, and as their military burden became more and more onerous the amount of

[4] Polyb. 1.63.3. [5] Guides are provided by Lintott (1999) and Astin (1989).
[6] Hölkeskamp (2010: 26–30).

property required for service had to be lowered.[7] Proposed solutions to these and other social problems were sometimes implemented, sometimes ignored, and sometimes opposed in the most violent fashion, yet conflict continued to grow irrespective. The new poorer class of soldiers saw their best hopes of remedy in the powerful leaders of armies, who themselves became more and more desperate for lucrative commands. First Sulla, then Marius, and then Pompey and Caesar all led willing soldiers against other Romans, and, as the last of these magnates became supreme, the Roman Republic began its metamorphosis into the Roman Empire.

Revenues

If we are to understand the relationship between the fiscal and the political, however, we need a more focused description, one that characterizes the tax system itself. Prior to the extraordinary conquest of the Mediterranean, Rome's treasury was perched atop a tripod of taxes.[8] The first leg was made up of *tributum*, a levy on property that was defined by three important features: it was formulated as a kind of loan and could be repaid to the payer in part or as a whole; it applied specifically to the funding of wars and was not demanded in years of peace; and it was probably paid up-front by a distinguished order of citizens known as the *tribuni aerarii*, who then collected it themselves from individual payers. It was in essence a financial contribution by those who, though wealthy enough for military service, had not been called up (whether by chance or because of age, infirmity, etc), and was hence the fiscal equivalent of conscription.[9] In the absence of war, the treasury could lean on the second leg, which comprised various indirect taxes. Rome's location – dominating water traffic up and down the river Tiber as well as road traffic across it – probably ensured an important role for *portorium*, or the range of fees concerning customs and tolls. Tax farmers bid for contracts to collect these revenues, and, as Rome took over new ports across the Mediterranean, these tax farmers took up position astride more and more routes. In addition to *portorium*, however, the state flexed its muscles in areas such as the salt trade (in which it imposed taxes

[7] Brunt (1971; 1988), Hopkins (1978).

[8] For a recent summary of Roman taxation, see Wolters (2007).

[9] On the equation of *tributum* and military service, see especially Livy 5.10.5–11.10, where people complain that war was ruining one-half of the *plebs* through conscription and one-half through *tributum*. For the details of *tributum*, see Nicolet (1976), summarized very briefly in French by Nicolet (2000: 73–5), and at greater length in English by Nicolet (1980: 153–69). On direct taxes in both the Republican and imperial periods, see Neesen (1980).

and reserving a monopoly position for itself) and the manumission of slaves, for which it charged a 5 percent tax.[10] As a third leg, the state also owned large tracts of land, the use of which incurred rents or fees. These ranged from agricultural plots and pasture to forests and fisheries.[11] Though not ubiquitous, contractors had an important role to play, collecting pasture fees, for example, or exploiting forests for timber and pitch.

This tripod was one for a city state, however, and not an empire. In the course of its two centuries, as it expanded ever outward, the Republic saw its tax system completely overhauled in two contrasting directions. The initial trend was toward greater intensification. The Romans had to generate greater and greater revenues during the first two Punic wars (264–241, 218–201), centralizing more and more of society's resources in order to beat down their Carthaginians foes. Warships were particularly expensive, and according to Polybius' count the Romans lost around 700 quinqueremes in the First Punic War.[12] So burdensome were the taxes during this conflict, in fact, that the citizens approved legislation to ban publicly funded fleets in 253 and again in 249; the navy that won the war in 241 had to be funded by voluntary loans from the elite.[13] In the Second Punic War, the Roman fiscal system essentially broke. In 215, after the disastrous battles of Trebia, Trasimene, and Cannae, the state demanded double *tributum*, with half paid up-front and another delayed into the year.[14] Marchetti estimated that the treasury received less than half the war's cost in 214, and Frank more or less agreed.[15] In that same year the state demanded that citizens provide slaves with six months' pay and rations to serve in the navy, simply bypassing the need to extract more revenue to provide more pay.[16] Most extraordinary of all was the treasury's resort to public credit. In 215 the army contractors agreed to supply the Spanish war on credit, and in that

[10] The fundamental work on *portorium* is the book by de Laet (1949); on the semantic range of the term, see Purcell (2005: 205–6). The salt monopoly and tax are recorded by Livy 2.9.6 and 29.37.6. Badian (1972: 24) denies the importance (and even perhaps the existence) of *portoria* in early Rome, though to my mind without great cause.

[11] For a full treatment of public land, see Roselaar (2010, esp. 91–2) on the use – or lack thereof – of contractors to collect rents.

[12] Tusa and Royal (2012) analyze several prows raised from the sea floor and argue that Polybius has overestimated the ratio of large quinqueremes to smaller triremes. In any case, the cost would still have been immense.

[13] 253: Polyb. 1.39.7; Zon. 8.14, 8.15 and 8.16; Bleckmann (2002: 178–9). 249: Polyb. 1.55.2; Zon. 8.16. See also Bleckmann (2002: 192–3). Zonaras dates the ban to 247, but it is very tempting to move it to 248, which was known for a fiery college of tribunes. 241: Polyb. 1.59.6–7.

[14] Livy 23.31.2. [15] Frank (1933: 79), Marchetti (1978: ch. 2.2).

[16] Livy 24.11.7–8, 26.35.2–10, noting that this was the first time a fleet had been manned at private expense. See Rosenstein (2008: 24–6) on the number of slaves involved.

year and the subsequent one Ti. Sempronius Gracchus led an army of slaves purchased on credit by the treasury.[17]

By 210 state finances had stalled. Over the course of the war so far the main bronze coin had collapsed from half a pound to one-twelfth, and when the state demanded another double tax in 210 the people refused, lamenting that they had nothing more to give. In the face of a tax revolt, the elite stepped in and donated privately owned metals to be melted down and minted.[18] Together with the booty from Syracuse in 212, Capua in 211, and New Carthage in 209, these metals facilitated an overhaul of the coinage system and the introduction of the incredibly long-lasting denarius currency. It is clear from this how tightly the fates of the war and treasury were bound together. By the end of the Second Punic War, Rome's finances were restored. The long conflict with Carthage had demanded feats of centralization and a series of fiscal innovations, but within a few decades the Romans would undo this centralizing trend and create a very different tax system, one that shifted the tax burden from citizens to provinces. Far from reviving the double taxes of the Second Punic War, the Romans indefinitely suspended *tributum* in 167, effectively ending direct taxation of citizens in Italy. The critical change in the second century was therefore the rapid swing away from the high taxes of the Punic wars and toward external revenues that allowed the state to fund itself without bargaining with the citizenry. This was the result of two critical transformations brought about by military success.

The first was that Rome instituted more and more indirect taxes. In 204, for example, new contracts were let for the sale of salt under a public monopoly, and this was described by Livy as a revenue source (*vectigal*).[19] It was perhaps a response to increased trade and monetisation. Some new revenues were the direct result of military expansion, however, and chief among these were the *portoria* of different cities. As more and more communities came under their control, the Romans assumed the right to collect tolls and dues on goods being conveyed through them. The landlocked Campanian city of Capua, for example, lost the rights to its own *portorium* when the Romans let the contract for the tax farm in 199.[20] Censors in 179 increased the range of *portoria* and other revenues, and Gaius Gracchus would increase their number again in 123 and 122.[21]

[17] Although enrolled in 216, Gracchus's slave army was freed only once it had proved its worth in battle two years later. The prior owners then declined payment until after the war. See Livy 22.57.11–2, 23.32.2, 24.14–6, 24.18.12. On the Spanish contractors, Livy 23.48.9–49.4.

[18] Livy 26.36.1–12, with Ñaco del Hoyo (2011: 380). They were later repaid.

[19] Livy 29.37.3–5.

[20] Alongside those of the great port at Puteoli: Livy 32.7.3.

[21] Livy 40.51.9. Vell. Pat. II.6.

In some sense, therefore, the end of *tributum* can be seen as the replacement of domestic direct taxation by indirect taxation both at home and abroad.[22]

The second transformation is more obvious, and is directly apparent in the context of 167. In that year the Romans conquered Macedonia, seized an enormous quantity of treasure, and established a permanent tax.[23] Around ten years earlier they had regularized tribute in Spain, codifying in treaties a set of annual payments from local communities.[24] These new provincial revenues – combined with the increased indirect taxes – also played a major role in ending *tributum*. Why bother taxing citizens when external revenues were covering expenses? Further conquests would bring more *portorium*, more tribute, and more taxation, and would further relieve Roman citizens of any part in funding the state's activities; in 60 all *portoria* in Italy were abolished, with new revenues from the east rendering them unnecessary.[25] Over the course of the second and first centuries BCE, therefore, the tax burden was shifted from the citizenry to provincial subjects, and the Romans themselves became a virtually untaxed people.

The provincial tax structure that grew up around them was a mishmash of different systems. Allied cities in every province, if they had earned favor through service in war or peace, were exempted from taxes, but even beyond these exceptions there was no uniformity across the Mediterranean. In some provinces the Romans simply extended the reparations, indemnities, or requisitions demanded after wars: in Spain, for example, it seems that the local communities had been supporting legionaries through pay and victuals, and this arrangement was preserved *ad infinitum*; in Macedonia, the same tribute that had been demanded of the king after the first war was indefinitely imposed on the land's later incarnations, first as independent republics and then as a Roman province. Cicero says that the same approach (the continuation of a war settlement) was taken in Africa.[26] In other provinces the Romans employed contractors. Sicily, the first province, already had an excellent system of tax-farming for agricultural tithes, and the Romans simply continued it. Sicilian contractors would run small tax farms, regulated both by the local city and the Roman governor, and it appears to have worked well.[27]

22 Badian (1972: 62–3). 23 Pliny *N.H.* 33.56. 24 Richardson (1986: 72, 160–1, esp. 115–16).

25 Cic. *Att.* 2.26.1. Dio 37.51.3–4.

26 Spain: Richardson (1986). Macedonia: Polyb. 18.44.7; Plut. *Aem.* 28.4, Livy 45.18.7, with Illyria at 45.26.14. Africa: Cic. II *Verr.* III.12.

27 The system is outlined by Scramuzza (1937: 237–40) and Badian (1972: 79–80). An older but more in-depth study is provided by Carcopino (1919).

A different approach to contracting was adopted in the province of Asia, located in western Anatolia. In this case, a single large contract was let in Rome for the collection of tithes throughout the entire province, and the Italian tax farmers who took on the task quickly became hated.[28] Eventually the system was adjusted so that local cities would collect all the contributions of their constituents, before handing over a lump sum on behalf of all to the tax farmers. This removed publicans from the invasive task of collecting every farmer's individual obligation. Further east, the same system appears more or less to have been adopted, with additional poll, land, or agricultural taxes applying to specific regions.[29]

The total intake from these taxes is unclear, and it is worth separating net taxation (the amount received by the state) from gross taxation (the amount handed over by the payers). The former does not appear to have been all that lavish. Within Italy, Rome's "allies" were required to provide (and fund) military units, but paid nothing in monetary taxes.[30] Livy tells us that the Macedonians paid to the Romans only half what they had paid to their old king, and, while they probably had to assume extra costs in the absence of the monarchy, there can at least be no doubt that the Romans could have demanded greater tribute had they wished.[31] Appian claims to reflect the words of Mark Antony when he writes that the Romans originally lowered the preexisting rate of taxation in Asia.[32] In Sicily the Romans taxed only 10 percent of wheat production, and when they needed more grain they paid for it.[33] Moreover, the indemnity imposed on the Carthaginians after the defeat of Hannibal did not prevent them from accumulating significant wealth.[34] Other situations could be complicated. Because the amounts paid by Asian cities were negotiated by publicans and local leaders, the total very much depended on the intentions of the arbitrating governor; if one party or the other earned his favor, he could

[28] Broughton (1937: 535–6).

[29] The details and evidence for each province can generally be found in the relevant volumes of Frank's *Economic Survey of Ancient Rome*, and for the sake of the non-specialist's convenience I will refer to these when possible throughout this chapter. On whether the same contracting system was imposed by Pompey in the most eastern provinces, see Badian (1972: 99 n. 85); contrast with Lintott (1993: 79).

[30] Polyb. 6.21.5. The cost borne by allies in funding their own units is stressed by Nicolet (2000: ch. 6), Brunt (1988: 70), and (Gabba 1989: 223–4).

[31] Livy 45.18.7. The costly business of defense, for example, had earlier been borne by the throne, and would for a period have to be taken up by the successor republics. It is worth noting, however, that the Romans took over the business of defense when they created a Macedonian province in 146, but they do not appear to have increased the tribute demanded. A tradition presenting the Roman settlement as benevolent is preserved at Diod. Sic. 31.8.3–4 and Plut. *Aem. Paul.* 28.3.

[32] App. *B.C.*. 5.4. [33] Cic. 2 *Verr.* 3.163. See Scramuzza (1937: 255–6, 263).

[34] Plut. *Cat. Mai.* 26.2.

push for a higher or lower sum.[35] In the absence of figures, it is very difficult to prove that official rates of taxation were light, but indications do suggest as much. Certainly, revolts against the Romans were not particularly common, and there is little evidence that they were caused by outrageous taxation.[36]

This ability of the state to pay its way on relatively low levels of taxation meant that it could avoid the build-up of bureaucratic and coercive capacity, since existing practices seem to have sufficed. Old alliances and the settlements of each new province were demonstrably capable of sustaining Rome's war machine, and this removed incentives to intensify extractions from citizens, or even foreign subjects. Fueled by tithes, mines, indirect taxes, and relatively low tribute in the provinces, the state could continue its conquest of the Mediterranean without any major reforms. Far from needing new wars or new coercive means to squeeze more taxes from citizens and subjects, therefore, the treasury could drop direct taxes at home and limit net taxes in the provinces.[37]

By no means is this to say, however, that the Romans did not bleed the provinces, for gross taxation could be significantly higher.[38] Cicero's speeches against C. Verres comprise an unrelenting account of how a governor could force extra payments for his own profit, and, although Verres' deeds are portrayed as the epitome of avarice and villainy, they were not all that far beyond the norm.[39] Even the associates of governors expected to make a profit from time spent in the provinces.[40] Tax farmers would also, by definition, drain the tax revenues for their own profits. Probably the most lucrative business, however, involved credit and finance.[41] Ambassadors to Rome would take out loans to bribe senators, and would then be subject to the horrors of debt collection. It was in the

[35] Cicero, arriving in his province, expressed great relief that this process of negotiation was concluded by his predecessor (Cic. *Att.* 5.13.1; 5.14.1). The agreement was called a *pactio*, and, on the potentially problematic role of the governor in mediating it, see Badian (1972: 79–8).

[36] For a convenient presentation, see again Broughton (1937: 535–6).

[37] For different view on the matter, in which Rome required new wars and conquests in order to justify taxation and raise much-needed revenues, see Eich and Eich (2005).

[38] There is no way to put a number on this, unfortunately, or even to form a clear contrast between Rome's gross extraction and that of other states; on the nature of this question, see Kiser and Levi, Chapter 19 in this volume. One possibility is that the decentralized profiteering of governors was less systematic or evenly spread, so that a few unlucky cities would suffer disproportionate losses in any given year. This remains pure hypothesis, however. On the ability of merchants to make the most of the empire's possibilities, see Eich and Eich (2005: esp. 27).

[39] For the Verrines and Cicero's artful rhetoric, see Steel (2007).

[40] See the very candid hopes of C. Trebatius, visiting Caesar in Gaul, in Cic. *Fam.* 7.9.2; 17.1; 16.3; 8.13.1; 18.1.

[41] Badian (1968: 73–4); Bernhardt (1985: 190–4); Schulz (1997: 193–9).

aftermath of wars, however, that opportunities for creditors were at their ripest. The Roman commander could order the payment of astronomical sums, far in excess of what could be raised on the spot, and defeated parties would be forced to borrow from Italian bankers at usurious rates of interest. Sulla demanded 120 million denarii (20,000 talents) from the cities of Asia after his war against Mithridates, and the debt had apparently ballooned to 720 million a little over a decade later.[42] The prince of Armenia was kept in Rome as security on loans after Pompey had, with ceremonial magnanimity, confirmed his father on the throne of Armenia for a fee of 6,000 talents.[43] All these practices ensured that there would be a significant gap between gross and net tax.

In many respects, this gap defined Rome's particular form of imperial exploitation. Tax-farming companies, moneylenders, and corrupt officials squeezed increasing profits from the provinces, but, because the treasury received fixed tributes from some provinces and predetermined contract prices from publicans, its share of imperial profits could not increase along with the increasing level of extraction. In other words, the provincials were tapped for more and more, paying extra fees, extra taxes, and immense rates of interest, while the treasury was allotted no more than the same old revenues. An empire won through public sacrifice yielded profits privatized for the elite. It is worth examining two dynamics related to this phenomenon. First, how and why did the tax system facilitate this kind of decentralization of revenues? Second, what effect did decentralization have on the state and on society?

A fiscal system for an aristocracy

Every state that has employed tax farmers has done so for different reasons, and the Roman case is no exception to this.[44] Levi argues that the contracting system allowed the Romans to maximize public revenue given three fundamental factors: discount rates (how much money leaders were willing to sacrifice in order to receive their share sooner); transaction costs (how much a system cost to operate); and the state's relative bargaining power (whether the state had the power to impose its chosen system on

[42] Broughton (1937: 516–19) provides all the evidence, with further discussion by Merola (2001: 53–5).

[43] App. *Mith.* 104; Plut. *Pomp.* 33.4; Strabo 11.14.10; Tac. *Ann.* 11.14.10. Dio 36.53.5 adds that Pompey received more than the promised 6,000 talents. The son tried to flee his captivity (Asc. 47C, Cic. *Mil.* 18).

[44] See Copland and Godley (1993: 45), Reid (1993), and Barkey (2008: 229) for references to various case studies.

others).[45] The model is intelligent, coherent, and insightful, but each of her three factors is problematic when applied to the historical particulars of the Roman Republic. The first two can be dealt with quite quickly. Our meagre evidence suggests that tax-farming did not actually provide revenues any sooner, since payments for contracts appear not to have been due up-front. According to the *Monumentum Ephesenum* (an inscription found in 1976 that preserves the regulations for a *portorium* tax farm at Ephesus), contractors did not have to pay for their bids until October, which was after most of the taxes would have been collected.[46] In other words, the state was receiving its due at the same time as – or even later than – it would have under a directly administered system. Regarding transaction costs, there is great room for speculation as to whether one system would have been more efficient than another, but one of Caesar's reforms seems to reveal the horrifying inefficiencies of contracting. When he abolished tax-farming in Asia Minor, he was able to cut taxes by a third; moreover, by simply delegating to local cities the task of collecting and transporting tax payments, he avoided the costs of establishing a replacement bureaucracy.[47] This reliance on local leaders – who were, after all, eager to manage their own affairs – was familiar from other provinces, where fixed tribute was handed over to the governor each year, and, as Caesar showed, it could easily have replaced the rent-seeking of tax farmers at any moment for an overall reduction in costs. There is every reason to believe, therefore, that economic and political costs could have been reduced through the abolition of at least some tax farms.

With respect to bargaining power, Levi's argument is twofold. On the one hand, she posits a relationship in which senators, desperate to fund their ever-increasing political expenses, came to rely on the credit of the wealthy tax farmers. Literally indebted to contractors, Rome's policy-makers could not implement reforms that would have undermined the profits of tax-farming, and so the old system persisted. The problem with this thesis is that the most powerful senators were wealthier than any private entrepreneur. Pompey the Great and M. Crassus, for example, were great benefactors of businessmen; the former offered huge numbers of lucrative contracts in the east; the latter championed the tax farmers' request to have the price of their largest contract lowered after an overbid. These two were also the wealthiest men in Rome, however, and needed

[45] Levi (1988: ch. 4). [46] Corbier (2008: 219–20); Lintott (1993: 90).

[47] Broughton (1937: 538). See Kiser and Levi, Chapter 19, for the importance of "non-linear" developments, in which a teleology culminating in the modern bureaucratic state is to be avoided.

financial help from no one.[48] Hopkins has even shown recently that commerce was reliant on the capital of senators, which would turn Levi's formulation on its head.[49] There is no doubt that businessmen had increasing power in the late Republic, but we cannot explain this sway simply through the financial hold they had on wealthier senators.

On the other hand, Levi has also argued that senators came to own shares in tax-farming companies, which gave them a direct financial interest in maximizing their profits. This is also central to the argument of Kiser and Kane, who add that senators were unwilling to monitor tax farmers because they could make personal profits by colluding with them.[50] One problem with this thesis is that policy-makers persisted with quite tight regulation of tax farmers: contractors were forbidden from physically coercing; they were bound by a system of appeals structured in favour of the taxpayer; they were forced to provide enormous security; they had to compete at auction for contracts; and they were required to pay interest on all revenues prior to the payment of their contract, because it was well known that they could lend their earliest revenues at interest to make extra profits. Some of these regulations could be loosened in practice by governors, but some could not, and it is difficult to reconcile this pattern of regulation with some corrupt senatorial preference for increasing the profits of tax farmers. The Romans could easily have abandoned regulation, or even have set up some kind of Roman East India Company, armed and monopolistic, generating greater profits. They never did, however, and it is hard to reconcile Roman policy with Levi's model here.

She is not alone, however, in concentrating on the relationship between state and contractors in the Roman Republic. Kiser and Kane argue that incentives for private profits clashed with (and defeated) incentives for public profit.[51] They depict a situation in which the senate had incentives to minimize rent-seeking, while individual magistrates in the provinces were interested in lax regulation and a bounty of corrupt profits. The Senate is the principal in this arrangement, while governors and other officials are the agents; the problem was that individuals would be senators one year and governors the next. This "revolving door" between office and Senate undermined the Senate's drive to maximize its revenues, because its members had no interest in voting for stricter rules on governorships they themselves could occupy. Hopes of personal gain won out over regulation

[48] On Pompey's contracts, see Badian (1972: 99–100) and Lintott (1993: 79). For Crassus's role in the *publicani* appeal, see Cic. *Att.* 1.17.9. For the scale of Pompey's and Crassus's wealth, see Badian (1968: 82) and Shatzman (1975: 375–8, 389–93).

[49] Hopkins (2009: 189–90). [50] Kiser and Kane (2007: 202–4). [51] Ibid.: esp. 199.

for collective benefits. The most powerful senators, however, were those who had already served at each rung of the ladder and did not expect to hold office – or profit from it – again. They therefore had no incentives to help the next crop of magistrates to bleed the provinces. A sound understanding of the Roman tax system requires an explanation as to why even these men supported the contracting system.

Of critical importance here is the question of whether the elites in the Senate actually wanted to maximize public revenue. Was there, as Levi and Kiser and Kane have posited, a sense among senators – even if ultimately trumped by personal greed – that public wealth ought to be increased? Or were they disinterested in the level of public resources? Hopkins has presented a very persuasive thesis, which argues that the Roman elite was ultimately against the centralization of wealth, because the constitution was designed to prevent any individual member from ever enjoying autonomous control over the resources of the whole community.[52] Fear of tyranny led to short terms of office, enforced intervals between them, and senatorial oversight of all expenditure, meaning that even the most powerful had few opportunities to spend public funds freely. Competitive elections even meant that future offices could not be guaranteed. Funds that found their way to the treasury, therefore, were in some sense out of reach, reserved for use in the brief periods in which an individual was in office; and even then its use required approval by senatorial peers and rivals. Only rarely would it serve any given individual's ambitions. Hopkins shows that this incentivized the accumulation of private property, over which owners enjoyed control indefinitely and regardless of electoral success. *Pace* Kiser and Kane, therefore, he demonstrates that Romans would treat governorships as personal moneymaking exercises, as ways to convert a year's political success into long-term economic power.

The same incentives can be read into the tax system. Fixed tribute and tax-farming each provided guaranteed, predictable revenue. This cut two ways. On the one hand, it is true, these systems ensured that the state would enjoy the level of funding it needed to fulfill its existing obligations (and by no means were Roman leaders interested in bankrupting the treasury); but, on the other hand, they also ensured that the state's revenues could not exceed their predetermined levels. Even if governors or others increased the exactions demanded from provincials, the tax system ensured that the state would see none of this growth, because it was only ever entitled to the contract price set in advance at auction or the fixed tribute

[52] Hopkins (1978: ch. 1).

agreed upon in treaties. This was perfectly suited to the conversion of imperial profits into private property. Predetermined revenues not only capped the state's income, they capped its *entitlement* to income. So long as the state received its due, its defenders could not complain if others went and earned further profits, demanding ever more from the provincials. This freed profiteering from the potentially dangerous charge of stealing from the Roman people, and the elite, thus unencumbered, did indeed find ways to tap the provinces for ever-increasing yields. As the level of gross taxation rose, the level of net taxation stagnated, since its entitlement could not grow. The state did not become poorer in the sense that it took in less revenue, but it did lag behind the elite in terms of relative wealth.

Two factors lay behind this. As we have seen, Rome's political leadership was unusually disinterested in accumulating public wealth; those statesmen who might have been expected to advocate the claims of the state more or less shunned its agenda in favour of policies more suited to the accumulation of private wealth. At the same time, however, Rome's incredible military success transformed the politics of enrichment by seizure. Very obviously, if aristocrats had been confined to siphoning the wealth of Rome's domestic population, they would have faced grave problems of resistance and legitimisation; likewise, if they had been limited to raids on neighbors in central Italy, they could never have achieved the scale of profits allowed by their pan-Mediterranean empire. Conquest, however, brought populations new in both scale and type. The vast number of subjects increased the scale of available riches, while their position as conquered subjects made exploitation less problematic. As the elite grew richer, neither provincials nor the majority of the Roman population could stop them: the provincials were militarily overawed; the citizens – untaxed and entitled only to the fixed provincial revenues discussed earlier – had almost been cut out of the equation altogether. Rome's leaders found themselves in the advantageous position of not needing resources from those who could resist, and being free to levy more from those who could not. These were the perfect conditions for exploitation, and – notwithstanding the exceptions of some notably virtuous governors – they defined Rome's management of the provinces.

The rich and the powerful

The increasing gap between gross and net taxation obviously made itself felt within Roman society. The elite had always preserved its dominance by controlling much of the economic surplus. Inequality was an inescapable part of the social fabric. L. Aemilius Paullus, for example, was famed for his virtuous "poverty," yet his estate could still yield around 130 to 140 times the pay of the average legionary.[53] By the end of the Republic, M. Crassus could famously remark that no man was wealthy unless he could support a legion on his own annual income;[54] during his first consulship, in 70, he supplied grain to the people for three months, and as part of a sacrifice to Hercules he feasted them on 10,000 tables.[55] These sorts of riches obviously had their own, purely economic appeal, but, despite the sources' obsession with luxury and decadence, wealth was not ultimately valued for the furniture or new estates it could provide. The push for greater and greater private resources was not simply the instinct of *homo economicus*. The all-pervading hierarchies of Roman society ensured that inequalities in wealth would become part of identity, part of hierarchical relationships, and part of the social fabric.[56] Riches, in other words, were valued because their possessors gained social power.

Vertical ties ran throughout Roman life, and they were inseparable from wealth. The ancient world offered only a meagre surplus, and the immense estates of elite Romans allowed them to claim an enormous proportion of it for themselves. As a result, those who wished to access it had to ingratiate themselves with the wealthy, and there were standard mechanisms for doing that. Elite and non-elite citizens, for example, were joined by patron–client ties (*clientela*), and much of the urban population consisted of freedmen who still fell within the orbits of their former owners.[57] Superiors could offer their dependents economic support in the form of work or capital, or could provide food or other handouts. From a narrow class of wealthy families, the surplus reached the rest of the population partly through the bottleneck of these distributions. Poorer Romans had to ingratiate themselves with the rich in order to receive any of it. Control of the domestic economic surplus had underpinned the social power of the elite, and so long as this was unchanged the nature of Rome's social hierarchies would be preserved. The flood of resources pouring in from the provinces represented an entirely new kind of surplus, however, independent of the Italian economy and unprecedented in scale. By adding a new surplus to the mix, therefore, imperial success threatened to loosen the elite's hold on the economy: if poorer Romans could access this separate pool of resources, then their dependence on the elite would be broken.

[53] Brunt (1988: 28–9). [54] Pliny *N.H.* 33.134.

[55] Plut. *Cras.* 12.3. "10,000" is a general term in Greek for "lots and lots," and hence should not be taken literally.

[56] On inequalities at Rome, see Hölkeskamp (2010: 33–8). [57] See now Mouritsen (2011: ch. 3).

It was therefore imperative that aristocrats control as much of this transplanted wealth as possible. The greatest threat to their monopoly was the state. If taxation were to become the main pipeline for the riches seized in the provinces, then the state would become the faucet, controlling where resources went, who received them, and the forms in which they would be distributed. Government expenditure would replace the donations of patronage as the main vehicle for distributing the surplus, creating a kind of universal patron, and most Romans would become beholden to its favours instead of the social elite's.

Wealth, therefore, was a means to social power. It was not simply that it could buy more or better goods; it allowed beneficence, which in turn created dependents and hierarchies. To maintain that power, however, the elite had to close off other potential sources of beneficence, hoarding the attention and loyalties of less wealthy Romans. This encouraged the suppression of the state, whose potential to accumulate and distribute resources could draw Roman citizens away from patronage networks. The state, receiving revenues only up to the auction price of the tax farmers' contracts or the fixed tribute of certain cities, could afford its basic expenses, but could not grow its footprint or enter into new areas of (potentially expensive) activity. It is noticeable, for example, that when reformers instituted grain distributions they almost invariably had to raise new funds to afford them.[58] Policy-makers could have radically increased the resources of the treasury, but on the whole they decided not to.

The key factor is the aristocrats' tenuous hold on the state. As we saw above, elite individuals had very little autonomous control over public institutions, and, because no one could be sure that he would be at the helm, there were very few incentives for enhancing the capacities of the state. The result was a system that ensured that the treasury could fund wars and meet its basic obligations, but could not increase its means beyond that level. In the face of tremendous opportunities, public revenues were fixed. The profits made by individuals could grow with new endeavors, however, and, as the exploitation of the empire increased, it was private wealth and not public that benefited.

Untaxed citizens

This would have been an unlikely result, had Roman citizens still been paying taxes and bankrolling expansion. In terms of funding, empire

[58] Badian (1968: 36, 47–9, 76); Nicolet (1980: 204); Garnsey (1988: 215–16).

allowed the state and its rulers to exist independent of the population. As the tax burden was shifted to the provinces, Roman citizens lost the ability to protest at the collection of taxes or to claim some ownership over public funds; this gave the elite much greater freedom in deciding how to exploit the empire for economic advancement. Much of the aristocrats' new wealth came from manipulating taxes and exactions in the provinces, demanding money for new buildings, supplies, or statues, which would then be converted to cash.[59] They demanded resources in the name of the state, but pocketed the riches themselves. The elite, in other words, profited at the loss of the provincials, who lacked the political gravity to resist effectively. Had the victims been Roman citizens, however, the stakes would have been much higher, and profiteering magistrates would have been playing a much more dangerous game. Citizens had appeal to tribunes and patrons, and troops would no doubt have been more reluctant to mistreat their own neighbours. The creation of a foreign tax base, however, made the exploitation of tax revenues a far safer prospect. Governors found themselves ruling over a population that had only limited access to Roman law, and whose resistance could be cowed by a show of force. Abuse of power became more and more feasible.

For members of the aristocracy, a perfect situation had arisen. They preyed upon a peripheral population that lacked the political relevance or military means to resist. At the same time, they needed very little from the Roman population, whose victimization would have been much harder to ignore. The disappearance of taxation was no doubt celebrated by all those citizens who had hitherto paid it, but over time it weakened their bargaining power. The state owed these people very little. They could make no claim that the state's resources were theirs, somehow "lent" to the state as *tributum* had been, and they could not withhold or resist collection to open a process of bargaining. For leaders, there was very little reason to organize for the delivery of public goods, because the citizens, untaxed and unneeded, could do little to threaten the elite or the state. Rome came to resemble – even if it did not meet the exact definition of – a rentier state like Kuwait or Saudi Arabia. In these cases, the sale of oil allows the ruling elite to escape any dependence on the broader population, and as a result few people have a strong bargaining position vis-à-vis their rulers or enjoy a high degree of political freedom.[60] In the Roman Republic, the lack of

[59] Cicero's speeches against Verres provide an array of techniques allegedly used by a governor in Sicily.

[60] For rentier states in the guise of oil states, see Luciani (1990). Rentier states will offer state services if these are seen to be in the rulers' interests: see the case of Saudi Arabia provided by Al-Rasheed (2002: esp. 125–7).

taxation led to a similarly emasculated citizenry. Members of the elite had no economic need to appease the population, because they found all necessary funding elsewhere. Most Roman men had nothing with which to bargain except their military service, and, as more and more had resort to this one valued commodity, the Republic became embroiled in an increasingly dangerous kind of politics.

Conclusions

Imperial expansion had a series of effects on Roman society. Italy as a whole grew richer, but the elite ensured that it benefited from this economic bounty disproportionately. By reserving the lion's share of profits for themselves, Rome's rulers limited the state to its old functions, and (with some exceptions) prevented it from patronizing any new segments of the population through public expenditure. Despite an enormous increase in available wealth, therefore, there was very little in the way of state creation. The old ties of patronage continued to dominate society.

The fiscal sociology of the Roman Republic is dominated by the power of an oligarchy. There was no problem with incredible inequalities between classes, but the same could not be allowed within the aristocracy itself. Collectively, they were strong enough to hoard money and power within their privileged ranks, but, if one family or faction were to pull too far ahead of the other aristocrats, then the universal cry of "Tyranny" would be heard. The greatest threat of all was, naturally, that someone would gain control of the state, and as a result of this paranoia the occasions on which an individual could spend the state's resource were severely limited. Without the opportunity to utilize state resources, however, there were few incentives to centralize wealth, and so the Roman Republic emerged as a rare example of a state whose rulers were not interested in maximizing tax revenues. Models of Rome's fiscal sociology therefore cannot assume public profit maximization as a motive for rational behavior among the policy-making elite.

It is also worth pointing out that this conclusion accords with Tilly's model for the rise of later European states.[61] According to Tilly, the relentless wars of the early modern period increased the bargaining power of non-elite taxpayers because militaries would grind to a halt without the revenues needed to sustain them. In exchange for taxes, rulers promised the delivery of greater public services and increased the footprints

[61] Tilly (1992).

of states.New conquests, however, led to the end of most taxes on Roman citizens. Free of any role in funding critical state activities, Roman plebeians made none of the demands that French, British, and other European citizens would later make, and the Roman state therefore experienced little of the growth that was seen in states of the eighteenth and nineteenth centuries. Instead, decentralization persisted, and the population remained as bound as ever to the old networks of aristocratic patronage.

References

Al-Rasheed, M. (2002) *A History of Saudi Arabia*. Cambridge.

Astin, A. E. (1989) "Roman government and politics, 200–134 BC," in *The Cambridge Ancient History, vol. VIII, Rome and the Mediterranean to 133 BC*, ed. A. E. Astin, F. W. Walbank, M. W. Frederiksen, and R. M. Oglivie. Cambridge: 163–96.

Badian, E. (1968) *Roman Imperialism in the Late Republic*, 2nd edn. Oxford.

(1972) *Publicans and Sinners: Private Enterprise in the Service of the Roman Republic*. Oxford.

Barkey, K. (2008) *Empire of Difference: The Ottomans in Comparative Perspective*. Cambridge.

Bernhardt, R. (1985) *Polis und römische Herrschaft in der späteren Republik (149–31 v. Chr)*. Berlin.

Blanton, R., and Fargher, L. (2008) *Collective Action in the Formation of Pre-Modern States*. New York.

Bleckmann, B. (2002) *Die römische Nobilität im Ersten Punischen Krieg: Untersuchungen zur aristokratischen Konkurrenz in der Republik*. Berlin.

Bringmann, K. (2007) *A History of the Roman Republic*. Cambridge.

Broughton, T. R. S. (1937) "Roman Asia Minor," in *An Economic Survey of Ancient Rome*, vol. III, *Roman Britain, Roman Spain, Roman Sicily, La Gaule Romaine*, ed. T. Frank. Baltimore: 499–916.

(1951) *The Magistrates of the Roman Republic*, vol. I, *509 BC – 100 BC*. Atlanta.

Brunt, P. A. (1971) *Italian Manpower 225 BC – AD 14*. Oxford.

(1988) *The Fall of the Roman Republic and Related Essays*. Oxford.

Carcopino, J. (1919) *La Loi de Hieron et les Romains*. Paris.

Copland, I., and Godley, M. R. (1993) "Revenue farming in comparative perspective: reflections on taxation, social structure and development in the early-modern period," in *The Rise and Fall of Revenue Farming: Business Elites and the Emergence of the State in Southeast Asia*, ed. J. G. D. Butcher and H. W. Dick. London: 45–68.

Corbier, M. (2008) "The *Lex Portorii Asiae* and financial administration," in *The Customs Law of Asia*, ed. M. Cottier, M. H. Crawford, C. V. Crowther, J.-L. Ferrary, B. M. Levick, O. Salomies, and M. Wörrle. Oxford: 202–35.

Cornell, T. J. (1995) *The Beginnings of Rome: Italy and Rome from the Bronze Age to the Punic Wars (c. 1000–264 BC)*. London.

Crawford, M. (1978) *The Roman Republic*. Cambridge, MA.

De Laet, S. J. (1949) *Portorium: étude sur l'organisation douanière chez les Romains, surtout à l'époque du Haut-Empire*. Bruges.

Eich, A., and Eich, P. (2005) "War and state-building in the Roman Republic," *Scripta Classica Israelica* 24: 1–33.

Frank, T. (1933) *Rome and Italy of the Republic. An Economic Survey of Ancient Rome*, vol. I. Baltimore.

Gabba, E. (1989) "Rome and Italy in the second century βC," in *The Cambridge Ancient History*, vol. VIII, *Rome and the Mediterranean to 133 BC*, ed. A. E. Astin, F. W. Walbank, M. W. Frederiksen, and R. M. Oglivie. Cambridge: 197–243.

Garnsey, P. (1988) *Famine and Food Supply in the Graeco-Roman World: Responses to Risk and Crisis*. Cambridge.

Hölkeskamp, K.-J. (2010) *Reconstructing the Roman Republic: An Ancient Political Culture and Modern Research*. Princeton, NJ.

Hopkins, K. (1978) *Conquerors and Slaves*. Cambridge.

(2009) "The political economy of the Roman Empire," in *The Dynamics of Ancient Empires: State Power from Assyria to Byzantium*, ed. I. Morris and W. Scheidel. Oxford: 178–204.

Kiser, E., and Kane, D. (2007) "The perils of privatization: how the characteristics of principals affected tax farming in the Roman Republic and Empire," *Social Science History* 31: 191–212.

Levi, M. (1988) *Of Rule and Revenue*. Berkeley, CA.

Lintott, A. W. (1993) *Imperium Romanum: Politics and Administration*. London.

(1999) *The Constitution of the Roman Republic*. Oxford.

Luciani, G. (ed.) (1990) *The Arab State*. Berkeley, CA.

Marchetti, P. (1978) *Histoire économique et monétaire de la deuxième guerre punique*. Brussels.

Martin, I. W., Mehrotra, A. K., and Prasad, M. (eds.) (2009) *The New Fiscal Sociology: Taxation in Comparative and Historical Perspective*. New York.

Merola, G. D. (2001) *Autonomia locale, governo imperiale: fiscalità e amministrazione nelle province asiane*. Bari.

Moore, M. (2003) "The new fiscal sociology in developing countries," paper presented at annual meeting of American Political Science Association, Philadelphia, August 28; available at www.allacademic.com/meta/p64000_index.html.

Mouritsen, H. (2011) *The Freedman in the Roman World*. Cambridge.

Ñaco del Hoyo, T. (2011) "Roman economy, finance, and politics in the Second Punic War," in *A Companion to the Punic Wars*, ed. D. Hoyos. Oxford: 376–92.

Neesen, L. (1980) *Untersuchungen zu den direkten Staatsabgaben der römischen Kaiserzeit: 27 v. Chr – 284 n. Chr*. Bonn.

Nicolet, C. (1976) *Tributum: recherches sur la fiscalité directe sous la Republique Romaine*. Bonn.

(1980) *The World of the Citizen in Republican Rome*. Berkeley, CA.

(2000) *Censeurs et publicains: économie et fiscalité dans le Rome antique*. Paris.

Purcell, N. (2005) "The ancient Mediterranean: the view from the customs house," in *Rethinking the Mediterranean*, ed. W. V. Harris. Oxford: 200–32.

Reid, A. (1993) "The origins of revenue farming in southeast Asia," in *The Rise and Fall of Revenue Farming: Business Elites and the Emergence of the State in Southeast Asia*, ed. J. G. D. Butcher and H. W. Dick. London: 69–79.

Richardson, J. S. (1986) *Hispaniae: Spain and the Development of Roman Imperialism*. Cambridge.

Roselaar, S. T. (2010) *Public Land in the Roman Republic: A Social and Economic History of Ager Publicus in Italy, 396–89 BC*. Oxford.

Rosenstein, N. (2008) "Aristocrats and agriculture in the middle and late Republic," *Journal of Roman Studies* 98: 1–26.

Schulz, R. (1997) *Herrschaft und Regierung: Roms Regiment in den Provinzen in der Zeit der Republik*. Paderborn.

Scramuzza, V. M. (1937) "Roman Sicily," in *An Economic Survey of Ancient Rome*, vol. III, *Roman Britain, Roman Spain, Roman Sicily, La Gaule Romaine*, ed. T. Frank. Baltimore: 226–46.

Shatzman, I. (1975) *Senatorial Wealth and Roman Politics*. Brussels.

Steel, C. (2007) "The rhetoric of the de Frumento," in *Sicilia Nutrix Plebis Romanae: Rhetoric, Law, and Taxation in Cicero's Verrines*, ed. J. Prag. London: 37–48.

Tilly, C. (1992) *Capital, Coercion, and European States: AD 990–1992*, rev edn. Malden, MA.

Tusa, S., and Royal, J. (2012) "The landscape of the naval battle at the Egadi Islands (241 BC)," *Journal of Roman Archaeology* 25: 7–48.

Wolters, R. (2007) "Vectigal, tributum and stipendium: Abgabenformen in römischer Republik und Kaiserzeit," in *Geschenke und Steuern, Zölle und Tribute: antike Abgabenformen in Anspruch und Wirklichkeit*, ed. H. Klinkott, S. Kubisch, and R. Müller-Wollermann. Leiden: 407–30.

CHAPTER 7

The early Roman monarchy

Walter Scheidel

General conditions

The oligarchic regime described by Tan, in Chapter 6, failed in a series of increasingly costly civil wars in the 40s and 30s BCE until unitary autocracy was established starting in 30 BCE. At that point the empire as a whole entered a period of unusual stability, which lasted almost two centuries (until the 160s CE), and it did not encounter any potentially fatal challenges for about 280 years. Imperial rule took the form of a military dictatorship that was supported by a large standing army managed by a professionalized officer corps but masked by the formal continuation of certain Republican institutions. Rulers drew on the services of a very small but gradually expanding patrimonial proto-bureaucracy and the cooperation of select members of the wealth elite. Some 2,000 autonomous local communities provided governance for an imperial population of perhaps 60 to 70 million that spread across 4 million square kilometers. The creation of an effectively monarchic regime triggered a final round of frantic expansion that began with the annexation of Egypt in 30 BCE. Ambitious campaigning in continental Europe resulted in the successful capture of the entire southern part of the Danube basin and failed attempts to reach toward the Elbe and the western Carpathians (from 12 BCE to 9 CE). Subsequent conquests were limited to Britain, Dacia, and other peripheral regions but stalled along the border with the Parthian Empire, which maintained control of much of Mesopotamia and Iran.

In fiscal terms, these developments had several important consequences. The political arrangement of ostensible power-sharing between emperors and the senatorial aristocracy produced multiple treasuries even though actual control over all state finances rested with the rulers and their patrimonial agents. The basic compact between rulers and elite associates preserved considerable opportunities for continuing elite enrichment through state office and provincial governance. Rulers who were for the most part based in the city of Rome were committed to strong spending on civil amenities in the capital. The scale and scope of the initial expansion into more remote and less developed regions permanently increased the cost of empire by requiring larger standing forces.

At the same time, with few exceptions, the entire period from 30 BCE to 160 CE was characterized by (largely geographically peripheral) wars of choice. Given the absence of serious external pressures or any sustained internal challenges, rulers lacked a strong incentive to maximize (net) revenue or rationalize revenue assessment and collection. This period consequently serves as an example of the phenomenon of relaxation of fiscal demands in the absence of intense interstate competition.[1] This chapter seeks to substantiate this ideal-typical premise by considering changes in revenue intake and expenditure relative to the previous period (in the second section), the organization of fiscal administration and problems of agency (third section), the scale and structure of state spending (fourth section), the sources of state revenue (fifth section), and the implications of these estimates for our understanding of the social benefits and costs of this system and its resultant performance limitations (sixth and seventh sections).

Change in extraction and spending levels

Any discussion of overall trends in extraction levels – of the fiscal "size" of the Roman state – depends on our choice of reference points. Three stages lend themselves to comparative evaluation: conditions prior to the first triumviral alliance of 60 BCE that precipitated the slide into autocracy, here represented by the mid-60s BCE; the civil war years of the 40s and 30s BCE; and the period of unified monarchy that de facto commenced in 30 BCE. Definitions are likewise critical: I distinguish between nominal revenue (that is, what taxpayers were supposed to pay, for instance a tithe on the harvest), gross revenue (the total of resources exacted from taxpayers and other revenue sources, comprised of nominal revenue plus over-collection minus shortfalls), and net revenue (state income that was actually put at the disposal of the central authorities).

Nominal and presumably also net revenues suddenly rose in the late 60s BCE, thanks to the reorganization and expansion of Roman tributary possessions in the economically developed eastern Mediterranean. While the precise scale of this increase is contested, it probably amounted to

[1] See Monson and Scheidel, Chapter 1, and also the other chapters in this part of the volume.

around 70 percent of the previous level.[2] This was the first perturbation of the traditional strategy of containing state revenues discussed in Chapter 6, and marked the onset of a transitional process that was to put state finances on a new footing. Thus, while the conquest of Gaul in the 50s BCE added relatively little revenue at the time (maybe around one-tenth), the annexation of Egypt in 30 BCE is likely to have resulted in another large revenue increase, even if its actual scale is difficult to estimate.[3] I conjecture total net revenue of at least 600 million sesterces in the early years of the monarchy and somewhat more in the first century CE – an estimate that is broadly consistent with conservative assumptions about the volume of regular state expenditure.[4]

These developments imply a trebling or more of state income in the course of little more than a generation. By contrast, revenue and spending need not have grown by much more than a half, and very likely failed to double over the following two centuries.[5] On the revenue side of the equation, the large initial increases were sustained in the first instance by the appropriation of eastern Mediterranean surpluses, augmented by other conquests and the imposition of new taxes on the otherwise privileged Roman citizenry. Expenditure kept pace with revenue because of massive permanent increases in both regular military and civilian spending. The former is illustrated by the fact that the number of legions rose from fifteen in 61/59 BCE to twenty-eight (plus new and large metropolitan forces) in the opening years of the first century CE, the (unsustainable) high watermark of expansion into Germany.[6] The latter was driven in no small part by the introduction of free grain distributions in the city of Rome in the 50s

2 Plutarch, Pompey 45, the most plausible reading of which implies an increase from 200 million to 340 million sesterces per year.

3 Gaul: Suetonius, Caesar 25 (40 million per year for the Tres Galliae). Gaul's contribution went up over time; see below, n. 85. Egypt: for reportedly very high revenues under the Ptolemies, see Monson, Chapter 5. Duncan-Jones (1994: 47–53) estimates a total revenue of 260 million sesterces for Roman Egypt, but this number includes import tolls and his estimate of grain production is too high (see Scheidel 2001: 233 n. 227). Revenue net of tolls may have been closer to 150 million, or perhaps to 200 million overall if toll revenue did indeed grow as rapidly as implied by Strabo 2.5.12, 17.1.13. See also below, note 55. The notion that, under Augustus, Egypt brought in less revenue than the Tres Galliae (Velleius 2.39) cannot possibly be reconciled with anything we know about Egyptian taxes or tolls.

4 Estimated based on Duncan-Jones (1994: 34, 41, 45), and below, the section entitled "The scale and distribution of state expenditure," allowing some 450 to 500 million sesterces for the military, less than 10 million sesterces for handouts, and 150 to 250 million sesterces for agent salaries, the grain dole, construction, and all other items.

5 Based on the estimates below, in the section "The scale and distribution of state expenditure," for total revenue of over 1 billion sesterces in the second century CE.

6 Brunt (1987: 449 tab. 14).

BCE, which benefited anywhere from 150,000 to 320,000 recipients in the following decades alone.[7] To this we must add the cost of new salaried state offices and the imperial court, as well as infrastructural spending on an unprecedented scale. The subsequent fiscal expansion was comparatively modest, as the number of legions peaked at thirty-three in 197 CE, metropolitan welfare spending was stable, and other outlays need not have gone up in excess of the underlying population and gross domestic product (GDP) growth. By way of a simple thought experiment, if we allow for a one-third increase in population and a mean annual rate of 0.1 percent per capita economic growth, a 50 percent increase in overall state expenditure during the first 150 years CE could have been achieved without any increase in effective tax rates. Moreover, increased revenue from import tolls and mineral deposits might arguably even have made it possible for the effective tax share to decline while aggregate net revenue rose.[8] Very broadly speaking, we observe massive fiscal growth for a few decades from the 60s BCE onward and comparatively modest expansion afterward.

At the same time, short-term variation and the complex relationship between nominal, gross, and net revenue also need to be taken into account. Consideration of these factors suggests a more complex picture. Revenue and spending both rose enormously in the 40s and 30s BCE; the increasingly costly civil wars of the 40s and 30s BCE that saw rival leaders engaged in bidding wars for military support prompted a temporary surge in extraction fueled by massive predation, partly in Italy but above all in the subject territories.[9] Net receipts after 30 BCE would have been considerably lower than during this crisis.[10] With respect to aggregate nominal fiscal demands and net revenue, conditions in the early monarchy represented both a big increase relative to the pre-60s BCE period and a strong retrenchment relative to the 40s and 30 BCE.

[7] Rickman (1980: 156–97).

[8] For a matrix of estimates based on different values for population size, tax rates, inflation, and economic real growth, see Scheidel (2009: 60–2). For the arguably great importance of tolls and mines, see below, the section entitled "The sources of state revenue." There is no tangible evidence for overall nominal increases in tax rates, as pertinent references are few and flimsy: Neesen (1980: 68).

[9] See, for example, Millar (2002: 215–37); and especially Scheidel (2007: 330–3), for numbers. Military bonuses alone amounted to some 4 billion sesterces between 49 and 29 BCE (or about ten times regular annual state revenues c. 50 BCE), in addition to salaries for up to seventy legions and the cost of maintaining large navies: Brunt (1987: 498–508). Extraction methods ranged from heavy surtaxes and confiscations of elite assets to the expropriation, enslavement, or destruction of entire cities within Roman territory.

[10] This takes also account of Roman access to Egyptian revenues already in the 30s BCE.

Changes in the ratios of gross revenue to either nominal or net revenue are more difficult to ascertain. How did the share of total collected revenue that reached the central authorities in the pre-50s BCE differ from that in the post-30s BCE? Our answer depends on whether we think that rent-seeking predation by governors and other elite agents was more constrained than in the later stages of the Republic, and whether the shift away from tax-farming that had begun in the intervening years (below, next section) reduced over-collection. There is no solid evidence to address either one of these issues. Continuing accounts of predation in the provinces by senatorial officials and the fact that the power to try them for extortion was transferred to their own peers in the Senate dispel any illusions that monarchical rule put an end to aristocratic self-enrichment. Even so, the logic of monarchical rule conflicted with the antecedent practice of the extreme decentralization of revenue flows identified in Chapter 6: regime change had created a unitary principal with an incentive to curtail predation that might lower his own income in favor of that of his elite associates.[11]

As far as changes in collection practices are concerned, much weight has been given to reports that Caesar in 47 BCE remitted one-third of collected revenue to the cities of the province of Asia in order to compensate them for over-collection by tax farmers, removed the latter, and charged the local city governments with the collection of taxes that were due to the Roman state.[12] Unfortunately, it is not at all clear whether this allows us to assume that their taxes were thus permanently lowered or that the state was able to obtain the same net income as before by cutting out intermediaries. At the very least, however, this suggests that over-collection had been a vexing issue and was curbed by this change, the implications of which are discussed in the next section. We are on much firmer ground in Egypt: as Monson has argued, nominal tax rates for privately owned arable land were reduced by perhaps as much as 80 percent

[11] We must distinguish between the privatization of state revenue by Republican leaders and the enrichment of the emperors' favorites under the monarchy insofar as the latter, in addition to capturing revenue outright, received gifts from the rulers that, technically, count as expenditure out of net revenue. A possibly very sizeable portion of crony enrichment under the monarchy would have been mediated by rulers rather than directly effected by individual beneficiaries.

[12] Thus Appian, Civil Wars 5.4. While Plutarch, Caesar 48, mentions only the remission, Dio 42.6 has Caesar hand collection over to the cities but also levy money ad hoc, and does not mention a remission. Monson, Chapter 5, interprets the remission as a response to a (temporary) relaxation of competitive pressures.

in the wake of the Roman conquest, and taxes on arboricultural land, and possibly even some poll taxes, may have been lowered as well.[13]

These observations, even if they are essentially confined to the unusually well documented case of Egypt, are consistent with the prediction of overall fiscal relaxation in per capita terms – to some extent as far as regular nominal demands and probably also gross exaction levels are concerned, and much more dramatically concerning irregular demands, which abated from wartime heights to the conventional default mode of occasional requisitions of goods and services by the military and state agents and comparable petty exactions. This scenario, at least as far as we can tell, appears to have applied well into the second century CE.

Fiscal organization and agency problems

The principal taxes of the early monarchy were land taxes (*tributum soli*) and poll taxes (*tributum capitis*), which were due from imperial subjects outside Italy with the exception of privileged communities and individuals.[14] In addition to these regular annual taxes, which varied from province to province, Rome imposed taxes on the flow of goods and transactions – tolls on internal and external trade, on legacies, and on the sale and manumission of slaves – augmented by ad hoc exactions (such as *aurum coronarium*, "gifts" in gold gathered to mark special occasions) and requisitions and liturgies (*munera*, unpaid services on behalf of the state).[15] The state likewise obtained revenue from claims on mineral deposits and from imperial estates, legacies to rulers, confiscations, and wartime plunder.[16]

Variation among provincial tax regimes was one legacy of Republican practices; organizational complexity was another, as evolving new layers of

[13] See Monson, Chapter 5, based on Monson (2012: 159–208, 249–74); and see now also Monson (2013). (See also Duncan-Jones 1994: 49, logically implying a 70 percent reduction in the grain tax.) Applying my estimates in note 3, the higher grain tax rate for the Ptolemaic period is consistent with total revenues equivalent to 300 million sesterces or more, in keeping with existing tallies of 300 or over 350 million reported for that earlier period (Duncan-Jones 1994: 254).

[14] For discussion of these types of taxes, see Neesen (1980), with Brunt (1990: 324–46, 531–40). Wallace (1938) still provides the most comprehensive survey of Roman taxation in Egypt. For tax exemptions, see Bernhardt (1980; 1982). For the nature of payments (cash or kind), see below, the section entitled "Cui bono, or the 'skeleton of empire.'"

[15] For the organization of some these taxes, see most recently Günther (2008). I concur with Eck (2000b: 282 n. 66) that many of them do not in a technical sense qualify as "indirect" taxes but are best defined as contingent or temporally irregular impositions.

[16] For an attempt to quantify revenues from different sources, see below, the section "The sources of state revenue," based on Scheidel (2015).

administration were grafted onto existing institutions. Revenue collection was organized in ways that are sometimes only poorly understood.[17] At the center, the monarchical regime accommodated multiple treasuries: the Republican *aerarium Saturni* was maintained while the emperors' *fiscus* developed into the dominant higher-order control agency. In the provinces, local *fisci* handled income and expenditure at the regional level. The extent to which rulers' notionally personal assets and revenues (their *patrimonium*) were kept separate is contested, although we later witness the institutionalization of their management as *res privata.* In the final analysis, given that the ruler ultimately controlled every element of this system, none of these complexities mattered in terms of overall outcomes.

As noted throughout this volume, agency relations are of critical importance for our understanding of fiscal regimes. The two main developments were the expansion of salaried state offices and a partial shift from tax-farming to greater reliance on self-taxing local elites. Key functions were at least nominally supervised by officials drawn from the Senate, a body of about 600 of the wealthiest and best-connected members of the Roman elite. All of them soon came to be directly appointed by the emperor; at Rome we find multiple senatorial *praefecti* of the *aerarium Saturni* and the *aerarium militare*, and others overseeing grain distributions. Actual control lay with a staff of imperial slaves and freedmen, later supplemented by officials recruited from among the equestrian order, a broader tier of the imperial wealth elite. An equestrian *praefectus annonae* was responsible for the metropolitan grain supply, and others were in charge of processing legacies to the emperor and inheritance and manumission taxes. An official known as *a rationibus* headed the fiscal hierarchy, later flanked by other top administrators. In the provinces, although senatorial oversight of financial affairs survived in places (maintained by quaestors – junior senatorial officials), equestrian or manumitted *procuratores* took care of provincial *fisci* and/or the ruler's *patrimonium*, including imperial estates as well as mines, quarries, and manufacturing establishments. Clerks were usually imperial slaves and freedmen, concentrated in Rome and thinly spread out across the empire. Much of the actual tasks were performed by the remaining tax farmers and by local city officials.

The number of fiscal offices kept growing throughout the period under review, in line with an analogous expansion of senior administrative appointments in general.[18] This process mostly took the form of a division

[17] For surveys, see Alpers (1995), Rathbone (1996), Eck (2000b), and Lo Cascio (2000).

[18] Eck (2000a) provides a characteristically excellent survey.

of broadly defined functions into narrower ones. In the end, this prepared the ground for a more formally hierarchical system, thus foreshadowing rationalizations of later centuries, but it also raised the cost of running the system, not least by opening up more opportunities for enrichment. This creeping administrative expansion favored the equestrian order, whose members not only benefited from the numerical increase in posts but also came to hold offices that had originally emerged within the imperial household and used to be held by the ruler's freedmen. At the same time, although equestrians eventually came to control almost all higher-tier administrative posts, they were frequently paired with imperial freedmen, who acted as their senior associates or could even hold the same titles as their equestrian counterparts. We can only guess at the reasons for this effective duplication: beyond workload as such, we may suspect "a system of reciprocal checks" among peers of different social status that was meant to address rulers' anxiety about predatory behavior in the handling of financial affairs.[19]

The farming of regular direct taxes on output and people to rich contractors or their associations (see Chapter 6) was replaced by tax assessment and collection by the leaders of individual local communities. For land and poll taxes, this process was based on censuses conducted by city governments and supervised by imperial officials.[20] These governments were chosen by election or appointment from within the councils of self-governing communities, which usually consisted of a city and its hinterland. In this period the central authorities were not directly involved in the selection of city officials or community management. Autonomous city councils and their officials consequently assumed an even more important role than beforehand.

While we know that the registers compiled from census data were supposed to be quite detailed, we have little knowledge of how this process worked in practice.[21] Two elements in particular remain obscure: whether tax obligations expressed in proportions of output were meant to represent a share of actual yields or were derived by estimating likely yield from assessed capital values, and if and how assets beyond land (and people) were captured by registration – a potentially important issue given that liquid wealth and income from manufacturing, trade, and finance may have been

[19] Ibid.: 254–6. See also below.

[20] For provincial censuses and cadasters, see Neesen (1980: 30–61) and Brunt (1990: 329–35).

[21] Neesen (1980: 44–53). Le Teuff (2012) now provides the most comprehensive study of the imperial census.

easier to conceal.[22] To add further to our uncertainties, the actual spread of poll taxes beyond Egypt and a few other areas is unclear.[23]

State officials charged with the oversight of local assessments are unevenly documented, and the extent to which they and their rudimentary support staffs would have been able to monitor these procedures should not be overrated.[24] Much hinged on local compliance; as the jurist Ulpian observed regarding the local censuses, "[H]e who declares anything must value it."[25] This means that compliance levels were primarily determined by the importance the local communities themselves attached to the accurate declaration of their members' property. The apparent absence of regular direct taxation of local assets for the city's own coffers can be seen as a disincentive to full compliance.[26] It is true that property qualifications for council membership (and the more rarefied equestrian order) were key determinants of social standing and political power within each civic community. Once a given wealth threshold had been cleared by an individual, however, there was no compelling incentive to declare further assets, and the payments to their cities (*summae honorariae*) that officials were required to make in exchange for the honor of being appointed were fixed and unrelated to actual individual wealth.[27] The strongest structural incentive for local elite compliance with imperial registration mandates should perhaps be sought in the universal Roman practice of liturgies – obligations that the propertied had to perform for their communities both for local purposes and on behalf of the state, most notably in connection with fiscal matters.[28] As the wealthiest citizens of a given community were the first in line for fiscal liturgies, it would have been in their own interest to declare all their assets when these tasks were lucrative. The state's practice of converting tax liabilities that had been determined by tallying up individual assessments into lump sums that were then imposed en bloc on an entire community may have enabled local holders of tax collection

[22] Scope of census coverage: Brunt (1990: 335–9); concealment of liquid assets, citing Apuleius, Golden Ass 4.9: ibid.: 533–4. A more generalized property tax may but need not be reported for Syria and Cilicia (Neesen 1980: 54–5, 63) but is not documented in records from nearby Arabia. A more comprehensive attempt to capture such income was undertaken only in the fourth century CE.

[23] Neesen (1980: 117–20).

[24] See Eck (2000b: 286–8), Brunt (1990: 532–3), and the collection of references given by Le Teuff (2007). For compliance problems in the context of more substantial proto-bureaucracies, see Bang, Chapter 18.

[25] Ulpian, Digest 50.15.4. [26] Liebenam (1900: 22); Schwarz (2001: 363–9).

[27] Census thresholds: Duncan-Jones (1982: 147); *summae honorariae*: ibid.: 82–8, 148–55.

[28] For the character of different *munera* and their link to officials' standing, including seniority and assets, see Langhammer (1973: 237–62).

liturgies to distribute the actual burden to their own advantage.[29] And, even if such positions were not normally profitable, they may at least have offered the best available insurance policy; as Brunt suspects, it would still have been "in the interest of the rich. . .to assume. . .the actual tasks of assessment and collection, which gave them the best chance of protecting themselves and their friends."[30] Conversely, if fiscal liturgies had been unattractive under any circumstances, for instance because of personal liability for covering shortfalls, local elites would have had a powerful incentive to prevent free-riding by their richest peers – an avoidance strategy that would have forced others to assume heavier burdens; in this scenario, monitoring at the local level would have been driven by self-interest – a potent check on tax evasion by those best able to bear fiscal obligations.[31] This suggests that the quality of local self-assessment and tax collection was primarily a function of local elite relations rather than its impact on the community as a whole. Overall, local checks on evasion appear to have been sufficiently powerful to ensure acceptable returns for the state.

Moreover, the move away from tax-farming was limited in scope.[32] City governments could assess only local assets and not those located in areas beyond their reach, such as unincorporated tracts of land (*saltus*), public land, and imperial estates, revenues from which were handled by tax farmers or tenants. More generally, even as state offices connected to revenue collection grew in number, tax farmers remained active alongside those salaried elite agents with respect to a whole range of taxes and revenue sources, such as internal tolls, legacies, manumission, and mining. This development resembles the aforementioned duplication of responsibility among elite agents and imperial freedmen, in this case with procurators and tax farmers acting side by side.[33] Once again, we may surmise a desire to curtail rent-seeking, and a concomitant increase of mouths at the trough.

This leaves us with the question as to why autocratic rulers curbed taxfarming at all, and, more specifically, for regular direct taxes only. Among other factors, Levi notes the very short time horizons of

[29] For later examples of this practice, see Corbier (2005: 371–2).

[30] Brunt (1990: 339–43, 534–7; quote: 535). See also below, note 75.

[31] Severe state penalties attached to tax evasion (Brunt 1990: 337–8); enforcement was cheap whenever local informers had sufficiently strong incentives to report cases.

[32] The best discussion is provided by Brunt (1990: 354–432).

[33] Eck (2000b: 283–6). In one case a procurator was also a tax farmer: Brunt (1990: 407–8), revealing the density of mutual enmeshment.

Republican office-holders, which raised discount rates and encouraged ad hoc predation. Kiser and Kane explain extensive and predatory tax-farming in the late Republic with reference to the collective action problem posed by multiple principals and various forms of elite collusion. Tan sidesteps the issue of the principal controlling agents by arguing that the late Republic lacked genuine antagonism between Senate and officials because the former did not desire to increase public revenue at the expense of private profit.[34] Whichever explanation we favor, autocracy altered each of these variables. The presence of a unitary principal constrained intra-elite collusion in rent-taking and caused the interests of principal and agents to diverge, even if we allow for compromises arising from the principal's continuing dependence on cooperation with members of the wealth elite. Moreover, there can be little doubt that discount rates dropped under the monarchy: the emperor Tiberius's rebuke of a governor who presented him with excess tax receipts – "I want my sheep shorn, not shaven" – may well be apocryphal but the underlying sentiment makes sense.[35] Together, these changes reduced the state's incentive to rely on tax-farming; it was abandoned for regular direct taxes, a sphere in which this practice was in any case rare in global historical terms, and limited to more suitable types of taxation. Comparatively speaking, Republican tax-farming had been "overextended": this reform made Roman arrangements less unusual.[36]

It is worth asking how this change relates to the general logic of different strategies of revenue collection. As noted in Chapter 1, scholars distinguish between three types of revenue collection, which tend to be associated with specific configurations of contextual circumstances.[37] Share contracts work best if revenue can be measured cheaply, which was rarely the case: they appear in imperial mining, in which contractors and the state split the yields.[38] Wage contracts are suitable when the cost of measuring the tax base or actual revenue are high and variance in the tax base and the cost of measuring collection efforts are low. Several of these conditions applied

[34] See Levi (1988: 93), Kiser and Kane (2007: 199–200), and Tan, Chapter 6.

[35] Dio 57.10.5. See the related anecdote of Tiberius resisting frequent rotation of provincial governors since they would behave like fresh and hungry flies sucking on a sore: Josephus, Jewish Antiquities 18.6. Kiser and Kane (2007: 198–9, 205) are mistaken in denying greater ruler security under the monarchy, given that, nowithstanding frequent assassinations, emperors could expect to hold power for much longer than late Republican officials, and that we also need to take account of kinship ties, especially among the early emperors, and view the monarchy as a (very durable) complex, not just as a series of individuals.

[36] Ibid.: 208.

[37] For the three types, see most clearly Coşgel and Miceli (2009: esp. 401–4); for their implications, ibid. (408–15). See also Kiser (1994: 290–3).

[38] For Vipasca, see Hirt (2011: 262; also 90–3).

under the monarchy, as imperial agents merely had to ensure that fixed amounts of tribute were actually delivered (that is, variance was low). Actual revenue did not need to be measured, but it would have been costly to do so. Monitoring of the collection effort was a critical variable; agents were few in number and often closely attached to the ruler's household, which ought to have facilitated both supervision and sanctions for transgressions, even if that potential was not properly realized.[39] In any case, this mode remained relatively rare prior to late antiquity.

Fixed-rent contracts work well if the cost of assessing the tax base is low and its variance and the cost of measuring the collection effort and actual revenue are high. Variance was high for flow taxes but not for land and poll taxes, for which the cost of measuring collection efforts and actual revenue was nonetheless high. Under the Republic, the auctioning of tax-farming contracts had kept assessment costs at close to zero for the state, but they remained low for the locally organized censuses of the early monarchy. But where does liturgical tax collection fit into this taxonomy?

I suggest that local self-assessment and tax collection under a regime of collective responsibility should be viewed as analogous to fixed-rent contracts. In this reading, the Roman state maintained fixed-rent contracts throughout, defined as arrangements "under which the contractor would pay the government a fixed amount (based on the tax base) in exchange for the right to collect the taxes and keep the residual after taxes are collected."[40] Auction, which determined the appropriate fixed amount, was replaced by an implicit compact between state and local elites that required the latter to determine the appropriate amount through self-assessment and collect it on their own. This arrangement made sense if, as it did, it greatly lowered the cost (for the state) of measuring the tax base, the cost of measuring the collection effort and actual revenue were high (which they were), and variance in the tax base was low (which it was, making it feasible to rely on occasional updates of local registers – hence the introduction of provincial censuses at the beginning of the monarchy). This configuration differs from that for tax-farming only with regard to variance in the tax base, which helps explain why tax-farming was abolished specifically for regular direct taxes on land and people. Otherwise, the two systems are very similar, as in both of them collectors (tax farmers or local officials) were responsible for delivering predetermined amounts regardless of actual revenue.

[39] See below, note 68. Agent malfeasance could be addressed by subsequent confiscation of their ill-gotten gains (Suetonius, Vespasian 16.2), or might indeed best be regarded as an integral part of the power structure that implicitly rewarded key subordinates.

[40] Coşgel and Miceli (2009: 402).

The long-term success of the revised system depended on two preconditions: that it did not greatly harm economic development, and that local elites displayed an adequate commitment to self-monitoring and compliance. Whereas late Republican governors had been the ultimate roving bandits, officials drawn from local elites were quintessentially stationary bandits acting under powerful constraints of peer pressure; lowered rates of predation and increased long-term strategies ought to have ensued.[41] Inasmuch as this made the system more efficient and sustainable, it would have conformed to the interests of lifelong autocrats and their administrative apparatus.[42] As discussed above, opportunities for profiteering and self-protection, as well as peer sanctions against free-riding, would have discouraged extreme forms of evasion or iniquity. These vital constraints suggest that, in the absence of strong state intervention, a system that relied on both self-assessment and self-collection might function in the specific context of autonomous communities only where the concept of liturgical obligations for the community was deeply entrenched.

It is important to note that, despite the abiding heterogeneity of tax demands, the system of municipal self-assessment and collection became near-universal across the empire, including those areas where city-based communities had be created first. The result (and, arguably, also the motive) of this was an equilibrium of satisficing profits for both the state and different elite strata. Rulers and their key constituencies in the military and the capital enjoyed stable income (net of remissions) gathered with low overheads from supervision efforts. Upper-tier intermediaries were provided with opportunities for enrichment. Local elites were recognized as indispensable allies of the state, and may have reaped sufficient benefits to cover their risk, though not enough to starve the state of revenue or foster disruptive internal oppression.[43] In political terms, this mode of revenue collection empowered the state: instead of contracting with a small number of powerful intermediaries who were organized in associations, it relied

[41] Unlike short-term tax farmers (Kiser 1994: 291), local elites could not easily have sought to maximize (gross) revenue collection.

[42] See above. Tax-farming can be unsuited to the direct taxation of land because of the adverse effects of overexploitation on capital assets (Kiser 1994: 291), which means that the shift to assessment and collection by local elites may have increased long-term efficiency; see the use of lifetime contracts in the farming of late Ottoman land taxes: ibid.: 297.

[43] See Monson (2012: 262–72) for the argument that Augustus favored urban elites in Egypt at the expense of supporters of the previous Ptolemaic regime in order to forge alliances that were meant to sustain Roman rule.

more on large numbers of spatially dispersed local leaders overseen by agents on fixed-wage contracts who were closely attached to the rulers and socially detached from these local leaders. Economically, this arrangement would have favored cities and especially their elites, potentially at the expense of the tributary rural population, and constrained the state's ability to respond to changes in demand for revenue.

This scenario logically entails predictions about outcomes that can be tested against empirical evidence. For it to be accepted as a reasonably close approximation of historical reality, we may expect to observe the following: that state spending did not greatly increase in real terms during the first two centuries of the monarchy (indicating a preference for stable revenue); that net receipts from regular direct taxes on land and people fell short of nominal rates (indicating deficient assessment and/or frequent remission); conspicuous growth of local spending in and on the cities of the empire; evidence of rent-seeking by waged state agents; and immediate budgetary strains whenever unusual demands arose. I have already briefly noted in the second section that the first condition does seem to have applied, and I argue in the remaining sections that all the other predictions are similarly consistent with the evidence.[44]

The scale and distribution of state expenditure

No relevant government statistics of overall state revenue or expenditure have survived from this period, even though we know they once existed.[45] The size of the imperial budget (if this is an appropriate term) is usually estimated from the expenditure side, because its main components are better documented or less difficult to guess than on the income side. The key item was military spending, which can be estimated with a fair degree of confidence on the basis of information about army size and the pay and bonus rates of rank and file. By the middle of the second century CE annual military compensation, including discharge benefits, may have reached as much as 700 million sesterces – a notional total that would in practice have been affected by the countervailing consequences of allowing units to fall below full strength (which would have lowered actual costs)

[44] The following sections are all closely based on my more detailed and richly referenced analysis (Scheidel 2015), to which readers are referred for supporting argument and bibliography. Earlier accounts include those by Duncan-Jones (1994: 33–46) and Wolters (1999: 202–34).

[45] Tantalizing hints are provided by Suetonius, Augustus 101; Statius, Silvae 3.3.85–108; and Appian, Roman History, preface 15.

and the additional expenses associated with procurement and campaigning (which would have raised them).[46]

Other outlays covered a wide range of items. The salaries of officials and periodic handouts to the metropolitan population and the military may have averaged a little over 100 million sesterces per year.[47] The scale of investment in civilian infrastructure, which is sometimes held to have been very considerable,[48] is empirically unknown; our estimates are necessarily constrained, however, by the extant evidence for the scale and cost of certain types of construction in this period. Rough calculations indicate that, even under deliberately maximizing assumptions, this kind of spending was, on average, highly unlikely to have accounted for more than a relatively modest fraction of military spending, perhaps of the order of 100 or 150 million sesterces per year.[49] The grain distributions in the city of Rome represented expenditure in the (high?) tens of millions, and the cost of spectacles and rulers' gifts to their associates would have fallen in a comparable range.[50] Taken together, these estimates yield, at the low end, a conservative total of less than 600 million sesterces in annual military spending, a bit over 100 million in salaries and handouts, and around 250 million for all other expenses, making a total of close to 1 billion sesterces; or, at the high end, a more generous budget of 700 million sesterces for the army, 200 million for salaries, handouts, and the grain supply, 100 to 150 million for construction, and another 100 to 150 million for other discretionary spending, adding up to somewhat more than 1 billion sesterces. With the empire's GDP perhaps approaching 20 billion sesterces, this would have translated into a state share equivalent to some 5 to 7 percent of GDP in net revenue – comparable to eighteenth-century France and plausible for a stable premodern state, especially since we also need to allow for municipal taxation and agents' rent-taking, which would

46 Duncan-Jones (1994: 33–7) says 600 to 700 million; Wolters (1999: 211–18, 223) 535 million; and Rathbone (2007: 174) up to 680 million, in theory. On understrength, see Bang (2013: 420–1); on non-salary costs, Herz (2007: 314–19); on war costs, Rathbone (2007: 174–5). The fact that military compensation was partly in kind does not affect these calculations, which are based on monetary equivalents rather than cash proper.

47 Duncan-Jones (1994: 37–41).

48 In relation to military spending, see, for example, Rathbone (1996: 311–12; 2007: 175), Wilson (2009: 81), and Katsari (2011: 37–8).

49 Scheidel (2015: esp. 157–8 nn. 28 & 29).

50 Scheidel (2015: 158): gifts averaging 150 million sesterces per year under Nero were considered extravagant; c. 400 kg of wheat per capita and year for 200,000 dole recipients would have cost in the low tens of millions at source but considerably more in the capital; a few million could buy lavish games.

have raised the share of gross revenue extraction in GDP by a non-trivial margin.[51]

The sources of state revenue

As already noted, the state derived income from a wide variety of sources. Their relative weight is of considerable importance for our understanding of the configuration of power within the empire. Pride of place is conventionally given to regular direct taxes on assets, output, and persons. Yet the actual contribution of these obligations is impossible to measure, because we lack information about net revenue. Tax rates of one-tenth, one-eighth, one-seventh, and one-fifth of agricultural output are reported for different regions but their precise meaning is often obscure.[52] Land taxes in Egypt effectively amounted to one-tenth or one-eighth of the grain harvest for privately owned land and more (30 to 40 percent) for public land.[53] To this we need to add poll taxes wherever they existed. Admittedly crude estimates suggest that, had nominal tax rates of anywhere from 10 to 20 percent just of agrarian output resulted in comparable rates of *net* revenue, they would have been sufficient to cover most – or perhaps even all – of state expenditure all by themselves.[54] High levels of taxpayer compliance combined with low levels of graft would therefore have eliminated the need for both contingent or irregular taxes and other sources of state revenue.

This notion is impossible to reconcile with the apparent significance of those categories. Taxes on trade included internal tolls (recorded at rates of 2, 2.5 and 5 percent in different provinces, and perhaps more for the city of Rome itself), and much higher border tolls (of 25 percent in Egypt). Net intake from internal tolls depended on the volume of trade, compliance, and agency costs but need not have been very large: revenue of 100 million sesterces would require up to a quarter of total GDP to have been traded inter-regionally – an unlikely amount for an agrarian economy. Border

[51] GDP: Scheidel and Friesen (2009: 73–4) (17 to 19 billion sesterces). France: Goldstone (1991: 205). For municipal revenues, see Liebenam (1900) and Schwarz (2001).

[52] Neesen (1980: 68–70) gathers the scarce references.

[53] Duncan-Jones (1990: 47–55). If public land had accounted for one-third of all land, the overall tax take would have been over 20 percent: ibid.: 48. See also Monson (2012: 159–208).

[54] See Scheidel (2015: 160 n. 40). A very rough calculation: if GDP was close to 20 billion sesterces, 20 percent of total output was off limits because of tax immunities, and farming accounted for a half of (taxable) GDP, a simple tithe on agrarian output alone would have raised 70 to 80 percent of an imperial budget of 1 to 1.2 billion sesterces. If we also allow for some poll and non-agrarian asset taxes even at low percentage rates, this would have been enough to cover the entire budget or more.

tolls may have been more lucrative – an impression we derive not only from sweeping and unreliable claims about the cost and volume of Asian imports but, more specifically, from the fact that a single shipload of luxury goods from India was capable of generating tax revenue of 1.4 million sesterces.[55] Total revenue from this source may well have been in excess of 100 million, and possibly even higher. Tolls alone could therefore have covered a significant share of total state expenditure: at least one-eighth, and possibly up to twice as much. The yield of the inheritance tax imposed on Roman citizens cannot be properly quantified but, as it was originally meant to fund military discharge bonuses of at least 40 million per year and was much later considered important enough to be portrayed (however rhetorically) as a motive for the enfranchisement of much of the remaining non-citizen population of the empire in 212 CE, it cannot have been trivial either.[56] Taxes on the sale and manumission of slaves may have yielded tens of millions unless they were poorly enforced or evaded, and, although an official reference in 177 CE to a heavy tax on the sale of gladiators yielding 20 or 30 million annually may be hyperbole (meant to emphasize the benefice of its abolition), this chance bit of information suggests that even relatively revenue obscure sources may have played a non-trivial role.[57] Overall, these indirect taxes were at least capable of generating several hundred million sesterces per year, and even if enforcement was uneven they would have greatly contributed to annual expenditure set at the order of more than 1 billion sesterces.

The same is true of income from mining and quarrying. Reports of the production of gold and silver mines, especially in the Iberian Peninsula, are impressive, but they were not always contemporaneous, and we cannot be certain whether they refer to gross output or the share of the state, although the latter is commonly assumed. Even so, factoring in additional resources that we know to have been important but that are not quantified at all in the record, such as precious metal deposits in Dacia, as well as income from lesser mines and quarries (especially marble), it would seem hard to escape

[55] Rathbone (2001) (on P.Vindob. G 40822). Pliny, Natural History 12.41, speaks of an annual outflow of 100 million sesterces to Arabia, India, and China, but imported goods would have been assessed at higher levels upon entering the empire (see 6.26.101–2); 120 ships involved in the Indian Ocean trade (Strabo 2.5.12) could have generated 170 million sesterces in toll revenue, but only if both this number is true and the one papyrus record we have is somehow representative. These are many "ifs," and modern conjectures consequently vary wildly; see Rathbone (2001: 48–9), Young (2001: 210), McLaughlin (2010: 164), and Sidebotham (2011: 218), with Scheidel (2015: 160 n. 44). We are left to conclude that revenue was probably quite substantial, especially as toll income from imports via land routes into Syria also has to be taken into account.

[56] Discharge costs: Duncan-Jones (1994: 35–6); inheritance tax: Dio 78.9.5.

[57] Carter (2003).

the conclusion that mineral exploitation accounted for a sizeable share of total state income: perhaps anywhere from one-tenth to a quarter.[58] This impression is highly consistent with the observation that the rapid deterioration of the imperial silver currency coincided with a strong decline in mining activity from the late second century CE onward (Chapter 8); while other factors such as rising state spending may well have contributed, these concurrent developments suggest at least some connection between mining yields and fiscal health, which in turn points to the former's overall importance.

As the emperor became by far the biggest landowner in the empire, domain income would also have mattered. And, while it would be unwise to include sporadic income from plunder in long-term estimates, it is worth noting that legacies to rulers (partly meant to offset imperial gifts) and at times even confiscations could easily have contributed in excess of 5 percent of average state income.[59]

There is no denying that the process of adding up multiple guesstimates with varying margins of error cannot produce a solid tally of the revenue derived from all these sources. Nevertheless, considering that major revenue streams (from import tolls levied at a few choke points to mining and domain income) were easy to control by state agents (who were in turn relatively easy to monitor), it seems to me unlikely that net yield dramatically fell short of estimated potential or occasionally reported gross figures. Overall, net revenue would have been in the hundreds of millions of sesterces, and could readily have accounted for half the billion-plus budget.[60]

This does not mesh well with the notion of high compliance for taxes on land and people. The most economical solution to this problem is to allow for the possibility that net revenue from these taxes was considerably lower than nominal rates would imply. Two alternative explanations cannot bear much weight: much higher discretionary spending (resulting in a bigger budget), or the accumulation of large fiscal reserves. Neither one of them is compatible with the evidence.[61] There is no indication that reserves ever

[58] Scheidel (2015: 161–2).

[59] Suetonius, Augustus 101 (1.4 billion sesterces in legacies for Augustus over 20 years); see Millar (1977: 153–8). Confiscations: see Burgers (1993) for a minimum of 800 million sesterces under Claudius (41–54 CE) following ancient reports of the number of elite convictions; see also Millar (1977: 163–74).

[60] See Scheidel (2015: 163 n. 58) for schematic calculations.

[61] The notion of massively greater civilian spending cannot readily be reconciled with what we know about the cost of certain types of buildings: Scheidel (2015: esp. 157 n. 29). For what it is worth, a budget estimate of the order of 1 billion sesterces is also logically consistent with reported revenues in

rose beyond a few billion sesterces; alleged savings under rulers who shunned costly wars and extravagant construction projects averaged no more than about 100 million a year.[62] This observation is also relevant for assessments of actual discretionary spending: if conservative spending policies merely yielded savings on this scale, customary annual civilian discretionary spending is unlikely to have been in the many hundreds of millions. The notion of huge routine discretionary outlays is likewise inconsistent with the fact that extraordinary expenses, such as the rebuilding of Rome after the fire of 64 CE or the wars of the 160s and 170s CE, immediately triggered significant coin debasement. If the state had normally enjoyed huge profit margins it could simply have reined in discretionary spending instead, especially considering the relatively modest windfall such debasements produced; if they were nevertheless thought desirable, state income in excess of more or less fixed spending requirements cannot have been enormous.[63]

The evidence therefore consistently supports the impression of significant constraints on civilian discretionary spending. If regular military spending is regarded as fixed and able to be reduced only by allowing units to become understrength (an inelastic remedy), and much civilian expenditure was in effect mandatory once introduced (such as the grain dole, salaries, and even games, and, at least to a certain degree, court expenses), the scope of genuinely discretionary spending was modest: it would in the first instance have taken the form of ad hoc largess (as gifts or for construction projects), which would have been appreciated but was not formally expected or effectively enforceable. The scale of this kind of spending would have had to rival that of military expenditure, however, in order to produce imperial expenditure far in excess of 1 billion sesterces, and thus the larger net revenue required for us to conjecture strong compliance with nominal tax demands on land and people.

the eastern empire of the sixth century CE (Scheidel 2015: 159 n. 36); for long-term continuity, see Bransbourg, Chapter 8.

62 Suetonius, Caius 3.37; Dio 74.8.3, for reserves of 2.7 billion sesterces. While this figure is probably symbolic (3 X 3 X 300 million, or "an awful lot": see Scheidel 1996), the only thing that matters here is the order of magnitude – a few billion rather than hundreds of million or tens of billion. Despite numerical stylization, reported orders of magnitude are usually sound.

63 Silver coin debasements under Nero and Marcus Aurelius amounted to a little over 10 percent each (Duncan-Jones 1994: 217), although more invasive coin analysis suggests a somewhat higher rate. Even if hundreds of millions worth of new silver denarii had been struck per year (in itself a dubious notion), this would not have yielded more than tens of millions in extra revenue. Would this have made sense in the context of a multi-hundred-million discretionary budget?

Cui bono, or the "skeleton of empire"

A scenario of deficient net revenue collection from fixed assets is plausible in the context of low pressure on the state's performance and moderate discretionary spending. If fiscal needs were moderate (relative to the tax base), predictable, and stable, the state was likely to focus on revenues it could obtain reliably and with the least effort. This situation favored reliance on domain income in the broadest sense of the term, covering revenue from estates as well as mining and quarrying. It also favored tapping into high-value trade flows that passed through specific choke points. Mildly predatory strategies, such as the occasional (re-)absorption of the private assets of what was in many ways a thoroughly captive wealth elite (through legacies or confiscations), belong in the same category. Applying the same logic to annual direct taxes, we may expect the state to have concentrated its extraction efforts on those parts of the empire where, for locally specific reasons, monitoring was relatively easy and compliance relatively high. Egypt is a classic example, with its deeply entrenched institutions of tracking and taxing an ecologically "caged" population and its assets.[64] In such areas, even nominally lowered demands would have produced ample revenue. The large increase in state income in the 60s BCE and other references suggest that much the same applied to the eastern provinces of the empire more generally.[65]

The disproportionate importance of revenue from key regions – a characteristic of all kinds of income, from tax on land to tax on trade or mineral wealth – helps explain the frequent practice of conferring tax immunity on sometimes sizeable communities, a process that (even if sometimes reversed) would have removed a growing portion of total output from the state's grasp. Such imbalances were firmly rooted in the logic of imperial rule under the Republic, as shown by the successive abolition of *tributum* and tolls in Italy and the long-standing unequal treatment of subject territories, but had come to spread across what had grown into a very large empire. This suggests that in many areas full compliance with nominal demands for regular direct tax may have been less than vital to the functioning of the state. The notion of limited compliance that was so persistent as to be a structural feature of the fiscal regime chimes well with recurrent evidence for the remission of tax arrears and temporary tax relief.

[64] At the same time, reports of the flight of taxpayers in Egypt shows that we must not overestimate compliance even in that region: see, for example, Braunert (1964: 158–79) and Link (1993).

[65] See above, the section entitled "Change in extraction and spending levels." See also Duncan-Jones (1994: 254) for other parts of the East.

The emperor Hadrian's remission of reportedly 900 million sesterces – not far short of a whole year's budget – may (as I phrase it elsewhere) merely have been the tip of an iceberg of forgone state revenue.[66]

This iceberg was made up of two main components. As noted in the section entitled "Fiscal organization and agency problems," the concealment of taxable assets or claims of output shortfalls were viable options for local elites put in charge of both assessment and collection. In Brunt's words, "Communal deficits probably meant almost always that it was the class responsible for assessments and collection who had evaded or postponed their own payments, and they were the chief gainers from remissions."[67] Rent-seeking behavior by intermediary state agents was another source of attrition. This problem (or compromise) is well illustrated by references to the extravagant wealth of such agents, and it is probably also reflected in the aforementioned expansion and duplication of fiscal posts.[68]

The budget has rightly been called "the skeleton of the state stripped of all misleading ideologies."[69] This is even truer of the actual flows of state revenue, whether or not it reached the state's coffers: these flows reveal the distribution of power and enable us to identify winners and losers. Depending on the scenario we prefer, in the middle of the second century CE military spending accounted for between one-half and two-thirds of total state expenditure.[70] Maybe around 15 percent went to the population of the capital via free food, handouts, construction, and entertainment, and a comparable share was absorbed by emperors, courtiers, and the ruling class via court expenses, salaries, and gifts. Beyond the umbrella benefit of "protection" sustained by military and administrative outlays, this leaves only a fairly thin sliver of overall spending on the general provincial population, mainly via infrastructure projects and other benefactions. The imperial system was therefore massively redistributive in both spatial and social terms. Expenditure in Rome and along the military frontiers may have reached 80 or even 90 percent of the total, directly

[66] Scheidel (2015). Dio 69.8.1 (possibly also a symbolic figure, 3 X 300 million: see above, note 62). For tax arrears and remissions, see Kloft (1970: 122–5), MacMullen (1987), and Duncan-Jones (1994: 60). See also Brunt (1990: 343).

[67] Ibid.: 537.

[68] For examples of (sometimes extreme) enrichment of agents of all statuses from servile to equestrian, see ibid.: 539. For the underlying logic, see Kiser (1994: 291).

[69] Schumpeter (1954 [1918]: 100), translating Goldscheid (1917).

[70] Some 600 to 700 million sesterces of 1 to 1.2 billion; see above, the section "The scale and disibution of state expenditure."

benefiting some 3 percent of the imperial population – soldiers and their families, metropolitan residents, and the top tier of the ruling class.[71]

Looked at more closely, imbalances were even more pronounced. Although the military as a whole was the biggest recipient of net revenue, ordinary soldiers were not particularly well compensated, and their income need not have risen in real terms; in the 160s CE a hypothetical legionary earned one-third more than 200 years earlier in nominal terms (which only represented a real increase if annual inflation remained below 0.15 percent) but would have received less than a quarter more in actual gold if he had been paid in newly minted gold coin, and, indeed, slightly less than two centuries earlier in actual silver if he had been paid in new silver coin.[72] We may suspect that, on top of repeatedly resorting to conscription, the state maintained adequate staffing levels by capitalizing on nominal price differences across the empire; recruits increasingly appear to have hailed from provincial areas rather than Italy, where non-reciprocal inflows of money rents likely drove up nominal prices and wages.[73] Real benefits for the Roman populace may likewise have been more modest than the size of the free rations might suggest; while the grain dole would have curbed hunger, it may have depressed market wages and effectively subsidized employers and landlords, just as modern food subsidies have been known to do. Large benefits (in terms of access to net revenue and illicit gains alike) accrued only to a chosen few, most notably the imperial court, the officer corps, and agents drawn from the wealth elite and the imperial household.[74]

Finally, tangible material benefits could be derived not only from the receipt of funds but also from the non-payment of dues. Italy's immunity is the most prominent example, accompanied by a growing number of other beneficiaries, ranging from entire communities to groups of individuals such as veterans and well-connected individuals. The apparent shortfall in net revenue from annual direct taxes points to the existence of yet another favored constituency, which I assess to have been the ruling class of the

[71] See Scheidel (2015: 177 n. 101) for the numbers. Some spending may have occurred elsewhere (such as for food transports), but the effective beneficiaries were mostly concentrated in these zones and groups.

[72] Estimated from the data given by Duncan-Jones (1994: 217 tab. 15.3). In reality, soldiers received a mix of older and newer coins alongside payments in kind.

[73] See Brunt (1990: 188–214, 512–13) on recruitment (and now also Eck 2010 on conscription), and von Freyberg (1989) on prices.

[74] Military officers were disproportionately well paid, with a commander of a mere eighty men receiving ten times base pay, presumably in order to ensure loyalty to rulers. Salaries for senior officials were much higher than in Han China, with its tighter controls on aristocratic privilege: Scheidel (2015: 168). For the enrichment of governors, see Brunt (1990: 53–95, 487–506); for other agents, above, note 68. See most recently Bang (2012: 208–9; 2013: 441).

local communities, for all the reasons identified above.[75] State demand for tax competed not only with the local elites' desire to capture surplus by means of collecting rent but also with municipal revenue demands.[76] Both private elite and public municipal income benefited urban development: the more taxable assets could be shielded from the state, the more was available for investment in urban infrastructure, institutions, and services. While municipal taxes underwrote these directly, the strong urban focus of the local ruling classes likewise encouraged this type of spending, either through outright benefactions ("euergetism") or through city-centered elite expenditure on private goods and services.[77] The conspicuous flourishing of cities, and especially their often ambitious building projects, in this period should perhaps at least in part be attributed to the successful retention of local surpluses.[78]

It is more challenging to get a sense of the overall distribution of fiscal extraction. Generally speaking, the probable importance of state income from tolls and mines points to a strong local concentration of revenue sources, with a modest number of key locations generating a considerable share of total receipts. This impression is reinforced by the aforementioned geographical imbalances in revenue collection, placing tribute-exempt Italy at one end of the spectrum and Egypt and a few other high-yield regions at the other. If Blanton and Fargher are right to posit a connection between broadly based public revenue collection and beneficial developments such as the provision of public goods and control on principals, the multiple imbalances of the Roman taxation regime may have acted as a serious constraint on successful state formation.[79] Above all, these imbalances reveal the genuinely skeletal underpinnings of the state: the system was highly spatially extensive and critically dependent on long-range connectivity. Although local supplies played an important role, especially in the provisioning of troops with staple foods and equipment, the

[75] My rough quantitative model of the relative importance of locally assessed land/poll taxes compared to other revenue sources therefore lends support to Brunt's intuition that "pressure on the city magnates was perhaps not so harsh in times of prosperity, especially if the communal liability could be met without enforcement of the full sums due from every individual" (1990: 343). For elites' success in competing with the state for surplus in this period more generally, see Hopkins (2002: 204–8).

[76] Fur urban revenues, see above, note 51. Moreover, fixed state demand allowed cities to retain excess revenue; for a telling example from Lycia, see Schwarz (2001: 282–3).

[77] Zuiderhoek (2009) argues for the importance of regular municipal income relative to euergetism. For the nature of the city-centered economic system in general, see especially Erdkamp (2001).

[78] This offers not so much an alternative as a complement to the modern thesis that the extraction and processing of state tax boosted urban growth: see below, note 83.

[79] Blanton and Fargher (2008); see also Monson and Scheidel, Chapter 1.

principal constituent elements of the state power structure relied on long-distance transfers of revenue in either cash or kind: the court, the army and especially its well-paid officer corps, and the city of Rome.[80]

The transfer of revenue raises several big questions that cannot be addressed here. One concerns the extent of the monetization of tax revenue: while cash payments were important, and arguably expanded in this period, tax in kind continued to exist.[81] The case of Roman Egypt illustrates the need to convert collected food surpluses into cash; because this region produced more tax grain than the state could have used, we may assume that part of it had to be sold and the proceeds transferred as cash revenue.[82] A related but even broader issue is the extent to which tax collection by the state boosted exchange, monetization, urbanization, and a measure of economic integration. This relationship lies at the heart of the "taxes and trade" model of the Roman economy developed by Hopkins, who regards the exaction of taxes and rents as the prime stimulus of (quite limited) economic growth. In this scenario, the ongoing flow of tax from net suppliers of revenue (the more developed and pacified provinces of the empire) to its net consumers (the capital and the militarized frontiers) required reciprocal flows of goods in order to counterbalance extractive transfers; inflows of tax and rent raised nominal prices in the center, encouraging the import of cheaper goods from elsewhere; and the concurrent huge increase in coined money reflected the commercialization of the surplus and hence the growing volume of trade.[83] This argument is tied up with even more fundamental debates about the nature of premodern economies, especially the question of how much inter-regional trade was sustained by tributary extraction.[84] Closer consideration of all this, as well as other forms of interaction between taxation and economic growth, would require a separate survey.

Conclusions

The first two centuries of the Roman monarchy unfolded in an environment of fairly limited state expectations. Rulers had to make sure they

80 We know little about how monetized tax transfers worked in practice: see de Ligt (2002). It is easier to track the movement of certain goods.

81 For discussion, see Brunt (1990: 531–2), Duncan-Jones (1990: 187–98), and Hopkins (2002: 215–17).

82 Ibid.: 216, to be amended using the lower yields above, note 3.

83 Developed by Hopkins (1980; 2002). For discussion, see Duncan-Jones (1990: 30–58), Howgego (1994), and de Ligt (2003).

84 See Bang (2007; 2008) and Wickham (2005).

gathered enough net revenue to fund a large army, mostly at conservative levels of compensation. Thanks in no small part to windfalls from mining and trade, they also disposed of enough resources to lavish benefits on the capital, the court, and select elite beneficiaries. But overall margins were slim, arguably thanks to the collective bargaining power of state agents and allies; the system left ample scope for enrichment in provincial administration, both via the generous compensation of elite officials and via tolerance (or impotence in the face) of certain levels of predation. It similarly left room for municipal elites to shield some of their surplus from the state, allowing it to be spent locally instead of being transferred to faraway troops or the capital, or being pocketed by intermediaries.

The fiscal regime of the imperial state during the first two centuries of the monarchy was satisficing, not maximizing, in its ambitions and outcomes; heterogeneous, not rationalized; and openly unfair, not consistent. The first of these characteristics owed much to the lack of strong competitive pressures from within or without. The other two originated in and perpetuated the circumstances of past conquest but were also, in the final analysis, sustained by the weakness of pressures that, alone, might otherwise have provided a sufficiently powerful incentive for the rebalancing and standardizing of fiscal obligations. Demographic and economic growth facilitated by unusually prolonged peace and lowered transaction costs further helped preserve these features insofar as previously less developed provinces and sectors of the economy were capable of contributing more revenue in real terms.[85]

Notwithstanding casual references to spendthrift emperors and depleted treasuries in hostile literary sources, the fundamental soundness of the imperial coinage throughout this period may serve as a rough proxy of fiscal stability. During the first 150 years CE gold and silver coins lost 7 and 20 percent of their intrinsic value, respectively; if it is correct that gold accounted for much the total value of the money stock, the overall degree of debasement need not have been much more than 10 percent. The state's ability to maintain both fineness and fixed exchange rates within a trimetallic coinage system speaks to the fiscal health of this period, and stands in striking contrast to the currency collapse of the following century.[86]

[85] Compare the low tribute imposed on Caesar's Gaul with the region's supposed tax obligations in the fourth century CE, as discussed by Bransbourg, Chapter 8.

[86] Based on Duncan-Jones (1994: 217 tab. 15.3); see ibid.: 168–70 for an estimate of the value ratio of gold to silver coinage, which probably overestimates both the former and the total money stock. Again, more recent metallurgical analysis points to somewhat stronger debasement. For subsequent developments, see Bransbourg Chapter 8.

The fiscal regime managed to reduce friction by accommodating the interests of multiple powerful constituencies. Yet this apparent virtue was also its biggest weakness: due to the system's lack of flexibility in responding to any kind of change, it proved sustainable only as long as conditions were stable and demands on state capabilities remained low. The extensive interdependences of the tributary system reinforced this weakness by rendering it vulnerable to localized shocks; the loss of mining or toll income or of particularly profitable areas was bound to have a disproportionate impact on revenues.

From the late second century CE, as foreign pressure rose, epidemics interfered with production, trade, and revenue collection, coups drove up the cost of the military, mining operations declined, and climate change may have begun to have adverse effects on output, state demand for revenue increasingly exceeded routine income. This posed serious problems not only because margins had always been relatively slim but also because the Roman Empire lacked mechanisms to take on public debt to compensate for revenue shortfalls.[87] Growing pressures therefore called for increases in net revenue yield per capita – a move resisted by entrenched elites that had long benefited from the more relaxed tax regime of the early monarchy. As discussed in Chapter 8, it took massive dislocations and regime change in the third century CE to make restructuring possible even to the limited extent that was in fact feasible.

References

Alpers, M. (1995) *Das nachrepublikanische Finanzsystem: fiscus und fisci in der frühen Kaiserzeit*. Berlin.

Andreau, J. (2006) "Existait-il une dette publique dans l'antiquité romaine?," in *La dette publique dans l'histoire*, ed. J. Andreau, G. Béaur, and J.-Y. Grenier. Paris: 101–14.

Bang, P. F. (2007) "Trade and empire: in search of organizing concepts for the Roman economy," *Past and Present* 195: 3–54.

(2008) *The Roman Bazaar: A Comparative Study of Trade and Markets in a Tributary Empire*. Cambridge.

(2012) "Predation," in *The Cambridge Companion to the Roman Economy*, ed. W. Scheidel. Cambridge: 197–217.

[87] See Andreau (2006) for the absence of public debt at the state level, at least in this period (at the end of the third century BCE some wealthy citizens had been reimbursed for extraordinary contributions to the war effort: ibid.: 104–5). See also Tacitus, Histories 4.47, for a comparable proposal, not realized. By contrast, local communities within the empire are known to have borrowed money to fund projects: Andreau (2006: 108–10); and see Mackil, Chapter 15.

(2013) "The Roman Empire, II: the imperial monarchy," in *The Oxford Handbook of the Ancient State: Near East and Mediterranean*, ed. P. F. Bang and W. Scheidel. New York: 412–72.

Bernhardt, R. (1980) "Die Immunitas der Freistädte," *Historia* 29: 190–204.

(1982) "Immunität und Abgabenverpflichtung bei römischen Kolonien und Munizipien," *Historia* 31: 343–52.

Blanton, R., and Fargher, L. (2008) *Collective Action in the Formation of Pre-Modern States*. New York.

Braunert, H. (1964) *Die Binnenwanderung: Studien zur Sozialgeschichte Ägyptens in der Ptolemäer- und Kaiserzeit*. Bonn.

Brunt, P. A. (1987) *Italian Manpower 225 BC – AD 14*, rev. edn. Oxford.

(1990) *Roman Imperial Themes*. Oxford.

Burgers, P. (1993) "Taxing the rich: confiscation and the financing of the Claudian Principate (AD 41–54)," *Laverna* 4: 55–68.

Carter, M. (2003) "Gladiatorial ranking and the *SC de pretiis gladiatorum minuendis (CIL* II 6278 = ILS 5163)," *Phoenix* 57: 83–114.

Corbier, M. (2005) "Coinage and taxation: the state's point of view, AD 193–337," in *The Cambridge Ancient History*, vol. XII, *The Crisis of Empire AD 193–337*, 2nd edn, ed. A. K. Bowman, P. Garnsey, and A. Cameron. Cambridge: 327–92.

Coşgel, M. M., and Miceli, T. J. (2009) "Tax collection in history," *Public Finance Review* 37: 399–420.

De Ligt, L. (2002) "Tax transfers in the Roman Empire," in *The Transformation of Economic Life under the Roman Empire*, ed. L. de Blois and J. Rich. Amsterdam: 48–66.

(2003) "Taxes, trade, and the circulation of coin: the Roman Empire, Mughal India and T'ang China compared," *Medieval History Journal* 6: 231–48.

Duncan-Jones, R. (1982) *The Economy of the Roman Empire: Quantitative Studies*, 2nd edn. Cambridge.

(1990) *Structure and Scale in the Roman Economy*. Cambridge.

(1994) *Money and Government in the Roman Empire*. Cambridge.

Eck, W. (2000a) "The growth of administrative posts," in *The Cambridge Ancient History*, vol. XI, *The High Empire AD 70–192*, 2nd edn, ed. A. K. Bowman, P. Garnsey, and D. W. Rathbone. Cambridge: 238–65.

(2000b) "Provincial administration and finance," in *The Cambridge Ancient History*, vol. XI, *The High Empire AD 70–192*, 2nd edn, ed. A. K. Bowman, P. Garnsey, and D. W. Rathbone. Cambridge: 266–92.

(2010) "Friedenssicherung und Krieg in der römischen Kaiserzeit: wie ergänzt man das römische Heer?," in *Die Verwaltung der kaiserzeitlichen römischen Armee: Studien für Hartmut Wolff*, ed. A. Eich. Stuttgart: 87–110.

Erdkamp, P. (2001) "Beyond the limits of the 'consumer city': a model of the urban and rural economy in the Roman world," *Historia* 50: 332–56.

Goldscheid, R. (1917) *Staatssozialismus oder Staatskapitalismus*. Vienna.

Goldstone, J. A. (1991) *Revolution and Rebellion in the Early Modern World*. Berkeley, CA.

Günther, S. (2008) *"Vectigalia nervos esse rei publicae": die indirekten Steuern in der Römischen Kaiserzeit von Augustus bis Diokletian*. Wiesbaden.
Herz, P. (2007) "Finances and costs of the Roman army," in *A Companion to the Roman Army*, ed. P. Erdkamp. Malden, MA: 306–22.
Hirt, A. M. (2011) *Imperial Mines and Quarries in the Roman World: Organizational Aspects 27 BC – AD 235*. Oxford.
Hopkins, K. (1980) "Taxes and trade in the Roman Empire (200 BC – AD 400)," *Journal of Roman Studies* 70: 101–25.
(2002) "Rome, taxes, rents and trade," in *The Ancient Economy*, ed. W. Scheidel and S. von Reden. Edinburgh: 190–230 [repr. from *Kodai: Journal of Ancient History* 6/7 (1995): 41–75].
Howgego, C. (1994) "Coin circulation and the integration of the Roman economy," *Journal of Roman Archaeology* 7: 5–21.
Katsari, K. (2011) *The Roman Monetary System: The Eastern Provinces from the First to the Third Century AD*. Cambridge.
Kiser, E. (1994) "Markets and hierarchies in early modern tax systems: a principal–agent analysis," *Politics and Society* 22: 284–315.
Kiser, E., and Kane, D. (2007) "The perils of privatization: how the characteristics of principals affected tax farming in the Roman Republic and Empire," *Social Science History* 31: 191–212.
Kloft, H. (1970) *Liberalitas principis: Herkunft und Bedeutung: Studien zur Prinzipatsideologie*. Cologne.
Langhammer, W. (1973) *Die rechtliche und soziale Stellung der Magistratus municipales und der Decuriones in der Übergangsphase der Städte von sich selbstverwaltenden Gemeinden zu Vollzugsorganen des spätantiken Zwangsstaates (2. – 4. Jahrhundert der römischen Kaiserzeit)*. Wiesbaden.
Le Teuff, B. (2007) "Les agents du recensement dans les provinces de l'empire romain d'Auguste à Dioclétien," mémoire de Master 2. Pantheon–Sorbonne University, Paris.
(2012) "*Census*: les recensements dans les provinces de l'empire romain d'Auguste à Dioclétien," doctoral thesis. Bordeaux University.
Levi, M. (1988) *Of Rule and Revenue*. Berkeley, CA.
Liebenam, W. (1900) *Städteverwaltung im römischen Kaiserreiche*. Leipzig.
Link, S. (1993) "*Anachoresis*: Steuerflucht im Ägypten der frühen Kaiserzeit," *Klio* 75: 306–20.
Lo Cascio, E. (2000) *Il princeps e il suo impero: studi di storia amministrativa e finanziaria romana*. Bari.
McLaughlin, R. (2010) *Rome and the Distant East: Trade Routes to the Ancient Lands of Arabia, India and China*. London.
MacMullen, R. (1987) "Tax-pressure in the Roman Empire," *Latomus* 46: 737–54.
Millar, F. (1977) *The Emperor in the Roman World (31 BC – AD 337)*. London.
(2002) *Rome, the Greek World, and the East*, vol. I, *The Roman Republic and the Augustan Revolution*. Chapel Hill, NC.
Monson, A. (2012) *From the Ptolemies to the Romans: Political and Economic Change in Egypt*. Cambridge.

(2013) "The Augustan threshold: imperial taxation and the European project," paper presented at conference "Römisches Reich und Europäische Union: Perspektiven eines Vergleichs," Konstanz, May 24.

Neesen, L. (1980) *Untersuchungen zu den direkten Staatsabgaben der römischen Kaiserzeit: 27 v. Chr – 284 n. Chr.* Bonn.

Rathbone, D. W. (1996) "The imperial finances," in *The Cambridge Ancient History*, vol. X, *The Augustan Empire 43 BC – AD 69*, ed. A. K. Bowman, E. Champlin, and A. Lintott. Cambridge: 309–23.

(2001) "The 'Muziris' papyrus (SB XVIII 13167): financing Roman trade with India," *Bulletin de la Société Archéologique d'Alexandrie* 46: 39–50.

(2007) "Military finance and supply," in *The Cambridge History of Greek and Roman Warfare*, vol. II, *Rome from the Republic to the Late Empire*, ed. P. Sabin, H. van Wees, and M. Whitby. Cambridge: 158–75.

Rickman, G. (1980) *The Corn Supply of Ancient Rome*. Oxford.

Scheidel, W. (1996) "Finances, figures and fiction," *Classical Quarterly* 46: 222–38.

(2001) *Death on the Nile: Disease and the Demography of Roman Egypt*. Leiden.

(2007) "A model of real income growth in Roman Italy," *Historia* 56: 322–46.

(2009) "In search of Roman economic growth," *Journal of Roman Archaeology* 22: 46–70.

(2015) "State revenue and expenditure in the Han and Roman Empires," in *State Power in Ancient China and Rome*, ed. W. Scheidel. New York: 150–80.

Scheidel, W., and Friesen, S. J. (2009) "The size of the economy and the distribution of income in the Roman Empire," *Journal of Roman Studies* 99: 61–91.

Schwarz, H. (2001) *Soll oder Haben? Die Finanzwirtschaft kleinasiatischer Städte in der Römischen Kaiserzeit am Beispiel von Bithynien, Lykien und Ephesos (29 v. Chr – 284 n. Chr)*. Bonn.

Sidebotham, S. E. (2011) *Berenike and the Ancient Maritime Spice Route*. Berkeley, CA.

Schumpeter, J. A. (1954 [1918]) "The crisis of the tax state," trans. W. F. Stolper and R. A. Musgrave, *American Economic Papers* 4: 5–38.

Von Freyberg, H.-U. (1989) *Kapitalverkehr und Handel im römischen Kaiserreich (27 v. Chr – 235 n. Chr)*. Fribourg.

Wallace, S. L. (1938) *Taxation in Egypt from Augustus to Diocletian*. Princeton, NJ.

Wickham, C. (2005) *Framing the Early Middle Ages: Europe and the Mediterranean, 400–800*. Oxford.

Wilson, A. (2009) "Indicators for Roman economic growth: a response to Walter Scheidel," *Journal of Roman Archaeology* 22: 71–82.

Wolters, R. (1999) *Nummi Signati: Untersuchungen zur römischen Münzprägung und Geldwirtschaft*. Munich.

Young, G. K. (2001) *Rome's Eastern Trade: International Commerce and Imperial Policy 31 BC – AD 305*. London.

Zuiderhoek, A. (2009) *The Politics of Munificence in the Roman Empire: Citizens, Elites and Benefactors in Asia Minor*. Cambridge.

CHAPTER 8

The later Roman Empire

Gilles Bransbourg

The limits of the tributarian regime

The satisficing Roman imperial fiscal regime of its first two centuries described by Scheidel, in Chapter 7, could operate as long as the potential resources easily at its disposal significantly exceeded its needs. As the second century CE unfolded, several mechanisms at the core of the imperial extraction structure became more and more problematic with, first and foremost, its essentially tributary nature.

As stressed by Tacitus in his version of the speech delivered by the emperor Claudius to the Senate in 48 CE, what made Rome different from any other city was its capacity to grant citizenship to foreign nations, foes and friends alike, explaining why Rome had succeeded in building a lasting empire where others had failed: "What else proved fatal to Lacedaemon and Athens, in spite of their power in arms, but their policy of holding the conquered aloof as alien-born?"[1] As a result of the progressive incorporation of foreign citizens into the Roman nation, provincial elites, predominantly concerned by this integration process, became embedded into a sense of joint community with Rome and its empire, as exemplified by the oration delivered in front of the Roman Senate in 155 CE by the wealthy Asia-Minor-born landowner and rhetorician Aelius Aristides, himself from a family who had been recently granted Roman citizenship.[2] There is little doubt that, even as local customs and cults remained well alive throughout the imperial history, inhabitants of the Roman dominions felt an increased sense of a shared belonging to a common society as peace, trade, the rule of law, the expanded use of Latin and Greek as shared languages, and the ever-expanding number of citizens progressed with time. Such a process was not limited to the elites, as shown by the role of the army as a major provider of Roman citizens throughout the empire.

[1] Tacitus, *Annals*, 11.24. [2] Aelius Aristides, *The Roman Oration*.

The tributarian aspects that had laid the foundation of the imperial revenue system had become harder to justify. Why should Italian soil remain immune from land tax and tolls while Africa, Spain, Gaul, or Greece should pay? Would the poll tax concern only some city or countryside dwellers and not some of their neighbors because of their privileged status? Why should some communities escape the tribute on the basis that their distant ancestors had sided with the Romans during the conquest, while most others would indefinitely pay the price of long-forgotten wrong choices? At a time when imperial rulers, senators, and bureaucrats increasingly originated from outside Italy, while the presence of Italians inside the army became marginal, such biases were deemed to have become more and more unsustainable. The modern historian should not let him- or herself be overwhelmed by the sense of stability and acceptance displayed by the Roman society of the first centuries at a distance of two millennia. Taxation is never popular, and even less so when it is restricted to those perceived as the distant descendants of the vanquished, and accordingly associated with the additional stigma of foreign appropriation. As stated by the emperor Claudius, the sheer evaluation of wealth conducted by the Romans in recently incorporated provinces was a perilous enterprise,[3] frequently leading to anger and revolt.[4]

The massive tax remittance granted by Hadrian in 118 CE, followed by several others during his reign and those of his immediate successors,[5] may be a sign that the Romans' discriminatory tax system was operating under a reduced degree of acceptance and facing increasing resistance by the middle of the second century. In this context, the granting of Roman citizenship to all free inhabitants of the empire by Caracalla in 212 CE cannot be reduced to a fiscal trick aiming at making everyone liable to the inheritance tax that only befell the Romans;[6] rather, it signifies the emergence of an empire-wide sense of community.

As Rome had traditionally shared with the provincial elites the task of supervising and allocating much of the tax levies, the entrenched interests of this privileged group was necessarily on a collision course with any policy that would have leveled tax privileges and established a more efficient, universal assessment system. As such, it took the third century's combination of growing domestic and external pressures to trigger a long-due transformation of the Roman state tax ideology.

[3] *Corpus Inscriptionum Latinarum* XIII.1668, col. II, lines 36–41.

[4] Such as the census conducted by Publius Sulpicius Quirinius in Judea in 6–7 CE: Flavius Josephus, *Jewish Antiquities*, 17.355.

[5] Duncan-Jones (1994: 60).

[6] As malignantly claimed by Dio Cassius 78.9.

The third century CE and the crisis of empire

Signs of economic crisis emerged during the reign of Marcus Aurelius: the so-called "Antonine plague" had maybe wiped out about a tenth of the population of the empire in the years between 165 and 180 CE.[7] Although any global assumption regarding such a wide and loosely integrated geographic area must be considered with caution, one cannot rule out the occurrence of Malthusian economic checks in some key areas of the empire during this period[8].

At about the same time prices in Egypt doubled. Several explanations have been suggested. It could be a possible consequence of a population-led agricultural production decline in an economy highly dependent on the maintenance of its water management system.[9] An alternative monetary explanation may also be sought, since the local currency lost about 50 percent of its silver content under Marcus Aurelius.[10] Accelerated coinage debasement seems to have become a general phenomenon by then. Outside Egypt, the imperial silver coinage's standards markedly declined during the later part of the second century CE. Under Trajan, in the early second century CE, *denarii* contained about 80 percent silver; Septimius Severus used bullion with a 46 percent silver content after 194/195 CE. The initial monetary reforms of Nero in 64 CE had been followed by an overall period of stability. This was no longer the case by the end of the second century, as debasement entered a downward spiral.[11]

A likely explanation lies in the relative exhaustion of the sources of new gold and silver that hit the empire during the century. Issues of silver and then gold coinage on a massive scale had been facilitated by the mining bonanza of the later Roman Republic and earlier Empire, particularly in Iberia, Dalmatia, Gallic and Alpine areas, and then Dacia with Trajan's conquest. As the precious coinage was quickly debased from Marcus Aurelius onward, a marked slowdown in mining activity is visible throughout the empire. Many of the important mines of the first and second

[7] Frier (2000: 813–14); Scheidel (2001: 162). [8] Scheidel (2012b: 9–11).

[9] Rathbone (1996: 330–3; 1997: 192, 215–16). Scheidel (2002: 2012a) advances a view doubted by Bagnall (2002). See Borsch (2005: 91–112) regarding the inflationary impact of the Black Death in fourteenth-century Egypt.

[10] See Caley (1958: 177) and Walker (1977: 114).

[11] Regarding the debasement of the silver coinage, Walker's three-volume series (1976; 1977; 1978) was a masterly synthesis at that time, but its results have been proved to be too optimistic. The overall profile retains some validity in its broadest sense; see Duncan-Jones (1994: 226 with fig. 15.4). For more accurate recent measures of fineness: Butcher and Ponting (2009); Gitler and Ponting (2003).

centuries CE were no longer active by the years 170 to 190.[12] Rich and accessible ores had been exhausted, while relative deforestation had increased mining costs. Since mining had significantly contributed to the state's income over the centuries by providing the precious metals used to issue new coins, their disappearance added to the new strains faced by the Roman state.

Finally, the Roman tributarian model had always incorporated a component of external predation as a mean to ensure its internal equilibrium when needed. The failure to secure Mesopotamia under Trajan and the subsequent retreat ordered by Hadrian probably highlighted the overextension of the empire from a logistical standpoint and the increasing marginal costs of additional conquests.

At the turn of the second and third centuries CE the financial strain increased as both Septimius Severus and Caracalla raised army pay and *donativa*.[13] The reasons given for such rises vary. The most conventional explanation is that the monetary debasement of the silver coinage triggered a general price increase that had to be compensated for so as not to alienate the military. An alternative – and not necessarily contradictory – view is that the army had become a less reliable actor by the end of the second century as increased military pressure from outside the Roman world, combined with the lack of potentially lucrative campaigns, decreased soldiers' incentive to look outside the empire for more wealth and power.[14] As a consequence, the army inevitably play an increased political role, as shown by the civil wars from 193 to 196 CE. Centrifugal forces had already been witnessed during the civil war of 69 CE. The Flavian dynasty and the Antonines had provided the soldiers with a pay increase and renewed opportunities for lootings and conquest in Judaea, northern Britain, Arabia, Dacia, and Mesopotamia. Septimius Severus and his son may

[12] In Spain, twenty-one mining sites were active beyond the third century, versus 173 under the earlier empire: Domergue (1990: 219–24). Spain was without doubt the main source of mined silver and gold for several centuries. The third quarter of the second century marked a step decline in mining activities: Jones (1980). Claude Domergue has noticed that some ore containing 15 percent silver was neglected, while poorer ores at 2 percent were mined, for the reason that they were more accessible: Domergue (1983).

[13] There is no scholarly consensus regarding the way the soldiers' salary was raised. Domitian had set the annual stipend at 300 *denarii* a year. Estimates of the pay rise during the period from AD 197 to 238 have produced a range of 600 to 1,500 *denarii* for the final annual salary: Carrié (1978: 229); Alston (1994: 115). The primary sources offer only very indirect and partial quantitative hints: Herodian 3.8.4; 4.4.7; *Augustan History, Life of Septimius Severus* 12.2; Dio Cassius 79.36.

[14] As shown by Septimius Severus's final campaign in remote and non-strategic Caledonia. Six new legions were created between Marcus Aurelius and Septimius Severus, leading to a 20 percent increase in army size.

have had this precedent in mind when they raised army pay again after more than a century of stability, and launched campaigns in Parthia and Caledonia.[15] The possibly apocryphal advice that Septimius Severus provided to his sons on his deathbed most likely represents a sour but realistic assessment of the situation at the onset of the third century CE: "Be harmonious, enrich the soldiers, and scorn all other men."[16] Failures to complete lucrative conquests logically led a cash-strapped Caracalla into some tax increases and the creation of an overvalued coin denomination between 212 and 215 CE.[17]

From the beginning of the third century onward the budget of the Roman state was no longer balanced. Domestic acceptance of the tributarian system declined, the tax base possibly shrank in the aftermath of the Antonine plague, the resources for precious metals mining disappeared, and external military pressures rose while lucrative external wars declined, increasing domestic military threats. Caracalla's policies make sense in this context: having to secure the support of the army, his tax increases and monetary debasements represent a familiar solution. They largely failed, however, as the imperial tax system displayed its limited resilience under pressure. Undermined by too many exemptions, including those that spared the wealthiest strata of the landowning class,[18] the increased recourse to currency debasement could prove no more than a short-term alternative. The only rational course of action was to move from a satisficing approach to a maximizing and widely shared system of fairer taxation. It would take the onslaught of the middle of the third century CE to lead the Roman state, on the brink of collapse, toward this new pattern.

Caracalla's murder in 217 CE and the futile attempt by his successor and the likely instigator of his murder, Macrinus, to return taxes and the praetorians' pay to their previous lower levels[19] finally paved the way for the political, monetary, and military anarchy that lasted until the final quarter of the century. As the old tax system could not securely function in the face of inflation, invasions, provincial secessions, and military

[15] Septimius Severus was actively seeking to enrich his soldiers, maybe by the complete enslavement of the local population. The fear of an unruly army is something that Dio Cassius hints at, speaking of the idleness of the legions as a motivation for that campaign – something Septimius Severus found undesirable: Dio Cassius 77.11.

[16] Dio Cassius 77.15.2.

[17] Dio Cassius suggests that the generalization of the Roman citizenship aimed at extending the scope of the inheritance and manumission tax, since only citizens were liable. The inheritance tax rate was increased and the "double-*denarius*" *antoninianus* coin incorporated only 50 percent more silver: Dio Cassius 78.9, 15.1. On the *antoninianus* reform, see Bland (1996).

[18] Bransbourg (2010: 33–140). [19] Dio Cassius 29.12.

insecurity, the so-called military emperors resorted to extreme measures, from straight confiscation to internal plunder,[20] and issued growing amounts of further debased and increasingly worthless currency. The *denarius* silver coin virtually disappeared after Gordian III (238–244 CE), replaced by the increasingly debased radiate *antoninianus*, while the bronze coinage was progressively withdrawn, hoarded, melted, or overstruck as its metal value exceeded that of the debased billon coinage. By the years 260 to 270 CE imperial "silver" coins contained only traces of silver while their minted quantity exponentially grew.[21] Huge amounts of counterfeit and imitative coins of all sources were added to official issues and contributed to the wreckage of the traditional Roman monetary system.[22]

Taxation and monetary reform from Aurelian to the Tetrarchy (273–305 CE – and beyond)

The emperors of the last quarter of the third century, who often emerged from the rank and file of the army, finally managed to restore the territorial integrity of the empire. Between 272 and 274 Aurelian recovered its richest provinces. Little to nothing is known about his fiscal policy, although there is some likelihood that it anticipated the future reforms undertaken by Diocletian at the end of the century. Visible changes affected the administrative organization of the taxation process in Egypt, and a special tax levy was set up to benefit the city of Rome, while the later literary and legal traditions acknowledge some form of tax amnesty; corruption among officials was punished with unusual harshness and the tax privileges of the landed elites were most likely curtailed, although it is impossible to assess how far this process went.[23]

The most visible reforms occurred in the monetary sphere. A heavier billon coin, most likely called *aurelianus*, was issued with marks advertising a 20:1 value ratio of silver to bronze in order to restore the public's

[20] Herodian 7.9 about Maximinus Thrax seizing the gold belonging to the cities of the empire.

[21] Depeyrot and Hollard (1987: 67); Estiot (2012: 544 fig. 29B).

[22] Regarding the exponential increase in coinage volume and correlated collapse in standards, see Depeyrot and Hollard (1987: 66). It may well be that by that time precious (that is, gold) coins were exchanged by weight and no longer by tale, stressing how broken the monetary system was; see Bland (1996), notably the charts showing the growing weights' dispersion of the mid-century *aurei*: ibid.: 92–8.

[23] *Augustan History*, Aurelian 39.3–5, 45.1; Ammianus Marcellinus, 26.6.7. See as well the Constantinian ruling from 337 CE that referred to a previous decision of Aurelian that had made the city councilors financially responsible for the tax burden associated with uncultivated lands: *Justinianic Code* 11.59.1. More generally: Carrié and Rousselle (1999: 142–4); Molin (1999).

confidence in the coinage. Modern metal analyses of the coins show a silver content of about 4 percent. Bronze coins were resurrected alongside few *denarii*, and heavier, metrologically more reliable gold coins were minted in considerable numbers.[24] Aurelian's intent appears to have been the restoration of the trimetallic Augustan monetary system, coupled with the withdrawal of the impoverished species circulating through the Roman monetary system as a result of the previous excesses.[25]

Modern scholars often offer a rather negative assessment of Aurelian's reforms. They suffer from being compared to the much better documented reforms of Diocletian, while the tenfold increase in Egyptian prices in *c.* 273/274 CE is considered as a failure to curb inflation.[26] As the new, reformed coinage failed to replace the old monetary stock west of the Alps and was successful mostly in the Balkans, there have been legitimate questions about its overall implementation.[27] Beyond the fact that Aurelian died early and that he might have inspired some of the innovations introduced by Diocletian,[28] his input deserves to be reevaluated. Issuing a new coinage anchored to its metal value effectively checked the inflationist pressure of the previous decade. The sudden increase in Egyptian prices was most likely a consequence of the devaluation of the old species as enacted by the monetary reform itself.[29] That the *aureus* is customarily valued at 1,000 *denarii* in the 270s in Palestine – something quite compatible with the price of the pound of gold in 300/301 CE[30] – speaks in favor of a widespread stabilization of the Roman price system during the last quarter of the third century. This is confirmed by the overall stability of Egyptian prices during the years 276 to 294 CE.[31] Last but not least, the valuation of the reformed coinage in terms of rarely issued *denarii*

[24] On Aurelian's monetary reform, see Estiot (1995a: 127–9; 1995b: 54–5; 2012: 545–8). The marks of value on billon coins had been previously interpreted as a conversion rate between the new coinage and *denarii, sestertii, assaria,* or asses: Callu (1969: 325–8); Crawford (1975); Harl (1985: 146; 1996: 146–7). The metallurgic analysis, the explicit "." found at Siscia between the "XX" and the "I," and the later issues of Tacitus and Carus with a double silver content and the mark of value XI/IA or X-ET-I have mostly discredited this scenario: Callu, Brenot, and Barrandon (1979); Bourne (1996). It is sometimes still advocated nonetheless: Weiser (2000: 314–15).

[25] Zosimus 1.61.3 [26] Egyptian prices: Rathbone (1996; 1997). [27] Callu (1969: 344–50).

[28] It was certainly Aurelian's intention to introduce a pure silver coin: Estiot (2012: 547). Interestingly, Zosimus wrongly attributes the silver *argenteus* not to Diocletian but to Aurelian: Zosimus 1.61.3. See Carrié (1993a: 291).

[29] Bransbourg (2010: 497–524).

[30] Sperber (1974: 38–9). With the *aureus* struck close or lower than one-fiftieth to the pound during this period, the implied price of the pound of gold must be somehow higher than 50,000 *denarii*. In the years 300 to 301 CE the official price of gold moved from 60,000 to 72,000 *denarii*: Bagnall (1985: 20, 61; 1989: 70 n. 9); Estiot (2012: 549–50).

[31] Rathbone (1996: 330).

opens the gates to the concept of "ghost currencies," whereby monetary values were expressed through a unit of account referring to physical coins that were no longer produced.[32] This provided the later Empire with an additional degree of flexibility in the conduct of its monetary policy.

The shortcomings of the reign of Aurelian undoubtedly lay on the fiscal side. As precious metals were increasingly hoarded or used as jewelry during the third century, the imperial authorities crucially needed to reintegrate them into the monetary circulation in order to restore a functioning monetary economy. The failure to introduce a new silver coinage, the debasement of the *aureliani* under his immediate successors, and the relative scarcity of gold issues are clear signs of this unmet need for precious metals.

The reforms of the years 287 to 312 CE initiated by Diocletian were much more far-reaching, though they could not have taken place without the precedent set by Aurelian. Diocletian's initial focus was on the tax system. The Roman tax system, like its Greek and Persian predecessors or Mughal and Chinese equivalents, strongly relied on the tributary extraction of the available agricultural surpluses, although indirect taxes and tolls certainly had a greater impact than in some other premodern empires.[33] During the earlier Roman Empire a multiplicity of exemptions, special regimes, and privileges granted to Italian soil and to various layers of local grandees had had the effect of impairing the overall efficiency of the taxation process.[34] Diocletian's conception of standardized taxable units of accounts enabling the state universally to assess the contributory potential of the land and of its workforce, human or animal, was unquestionably revolutionary. His reforms would necessarily harm the categories that had benefited most from the previous tributarian system, and it is more than likely that the humble social background of the emperor and his career through the military meritocracy were no obstacle to such a grand design.

There have been many controversies regarding the exact dating and functioning of this new tax system. It seems safe to assume that 287 CE

[32] It could be argued that the Ptolemies were the first rulers to introduce a ghost currency at the beginning of the second century BCE when they let the "bronze" drachm as a unit of account be decoupled from the physical bronze coins: Faucher and Lorber (2010: 54–9).

[33] Estimates of the agricultural share of the overall Roman economy usually average 80 percent or above: Hopkins (1980: 104). The share of land-related tax income in Egypt has been evaluated at 63.7 percent: Duncan-Jones (1994: 47–53, tab. 4.6). Regarding the importance of indirect taxes and tolls in the Roman tax system, see Scheidel (2015: 158–60; Chapter 7 in this volume). On the political economy of tributary empires, see Bang (2008). The overall tax extraction rate is customarily assessed at around 5 percent of "GDP": Scheidel and Friesen (2009: 68 n. 26). See Scheidel, Chapter 7.

[34] Bransbourg (2010: 33–140); Scheidel (2015: 162).

marks the beginning of its implementation, involving a census spanning two decades[35] by which taxable resources were assessed all across the empire. A variety of sources allowed Jean-Michel Carrié to restore the different steps of the implementation process.[36] By the time Diocletian abdicated, in 305 CE, the principles of the most rational taxation system ever operated on such a large scale in the Western world had been put in place to fund the later period of the Roman Empire.

Two main units of account assessed taxpayers' contributive capacity: the *iugum* and the *caput*. Legislative edicts from the fourth to the seventh centuries CE addressing land tax issues invariably refer to these *iuga, capita*, or *iuga sive capita* through the *capitatio* or *iugatio sive capitatio* process. They highlight the dual origin of added value in any agricultural economy: land and the workforce. The land tax, and the precious metals requisitions that took place between 300 and 329 CE, were spread among the inhabitants of the empire according to the number of units that had been allocated to them in the aftermath of the census process. One of the key questions that has been debated is the numerical relationship between these taxable units and actual land size and the number of people and animals. The *caput* had originally been understood in its classic sense, as one person. Several imperial edicts including the term *caput* effectively deal with individuals.[37] The Syro-Roman lawbook considers the *iugum* equivalent to 20, 40, or 60 *iugera*[38] of arable land according to its quality, with a separate schedule for vines and olive trees, while some of the tax registers produced in the early fourth century in the Aegean area seem to equate the *iugum* with 100 *iugera* of arable land.[39] As the same registers provide ratios between the *capitatio* and the *iugatio* ranging from 1.16 to 1.33, the implausibility of seeing a little over one farmer handling over 60 acres of arable land led to alternative readings, by which the *iugum* was reduced to roughly 14 *iugera*.[40] Striking progress in the understanding of these measurements was achieved when it was finally noticed that the *caput* in its sense as a tax unit had to represent a lot more than one or two individuals.[41] Since other documents prove beyond reasonable doubt the existence of a *iugum* of 100 *iugera*,[42] the obvious conclusion was that the *caput* was sometimes used as

[35] Lactantius, *On the Death of the Persecutors* 23. [36] Carrié (1994: notably 57).

[37] *Theodosian Code* 7.20.4 (325 CE), 7.13.7 (375 CE), 13.11.2 = *Justinianic Code* 11.48.10 (386 CE).

[38] The *iugerum* was a Roman measure of area close to 0.65 acres and 0.26 hectares.

[39] Déléage (1945: 182); Jones (1953; 1964: 62–3). [40] Duncan-Jones (1990: 199–210).

[41] Carrié (1994: 43–52, 61).

[42] Notably the identification of the tax rate in *Papyrus Oxyrhynchus* 16.1905 with *Theodosian Code* 7.6.3 (377 CE): Déléage (1945: 115); Carrié (1993b: 116–26).

an abstract workforce-related taxation unit representing well over one man. Further thorough studies have highlighted the fact that 100 *iugera* certainly constituted too big a unit to be consistent with the size of the civic territories addressed by the Aegean registers, implying a more complex reality.[43] Taking into account the different types of land, an equivalence between the *iugum* and around 40 *iugera* of land seems to represent a reasonable order of magnitude,[44] while it appears that "micro" and "macro" units coexisted at different levels, explaining part of the apparent contradiction of the sources. Local authorities would have used the small "micro" units in order to conduct their assessment duties, while larger "macro" units would have been consolidated at a provincial level in order to work out the allocation of the overall taxation burden among the constituencies of the empire.[45]

The second major area of implementation of the new tax system concerns the widespread compulsory requisition of precious metals – gold and silver. Precious metal contributions by the Senate and the cities were a well-attested practice of the earlier Empire that became more demanding in the third century.[46] The peculiarity of the Diocletianic reform, well attested by several Egyptian papyri,[47] was to generalize and standardize this practice to all ordinary taxpayers. The contribution amount was assessed on the size of the land in Egypt, as this province operated under a straightforward *iugatio* system. A given quantity of gold and silver was requested in exchange for a payment in billon coinage by the authorities at some undervalued rate.[48] As the official coinage's depreciation quickly accelerated against all precious metals after 324 CE, the purchase prices as set by the authorities dropped to a small fraction of the value of the requisitioned gold and silver, and these requisitions effectively became a levy of precious metals, finally integrated into a new tax whose principal aim was to fund the military budget, the *aurum comparaticium*.[49]

[43] Harper (2008). [44] Thonemann (2007). [45] Carrié (2007).

[46] Dio Cassius 78.9.2; *Augustan History, Severus Alexander* 39, 6; *Berliner Griechische Urkunden* 518, line 11; *Papyrus Oxyrhynchus* 14.1659.

[47] See notably *Papyri from Panopolis in the Chester Beatty Library* 2, lines 215–21, and T. C. Skeat's comments, as well as *Papiri della Società Italiana* 4.310, in Rea (1974).

[48] Bagnall (1977: 336); Carrié (1993b: 128–30). On the undervaluation of official prices of gold, see Bagnall (1985: 28).

[49] The last attested reimbursed requisitions would date from 324 or 329 CE: see Carrié (1994: 53) and Bagnall (1977), with *Papyrus Vindobonensis Graecus*, inventory 27879. On the *aurum comparaticium*, see Carrié (1993b: 126–7).

The standardization effort of the land tax, combined with the requisition of precious metals, clearly aimed at solving problems on the income side of the imperial budget while providing the state with the necessary metallic resources for its new coinage. The Diocletianic currency reform was implemented starting in 294 CE, when a new, heavier billon coinage was minted on top of a reformed gold coinage and a new silver coinage. Similarities with the first-century CE imperial coinage were considerable, with the simultaneous use of a one-sixtieth of a Roman pound gold *aureus*, an 80 percent silver one-ninety-sixth of a pound *argenteus*, and a heavier billion coin weighing about 10 g (one-thirty-second of a pound) alongside lighter copper fractions struck at 1/110th and 1/250th of a pound – 3 and 1.3 g.[50] The likely conversion values, with 1 *aureus* for 20 *argentei* or 80 billion *nummi*, thus 1 *argenteus* for 4 *nummi*, linked these coins by a relationship very similar to that of the old *aureus, denarius*, and *sestertius* of in the early Empire (1 *aureus* = 25 *denarii* =100 *sestertii*). The true innovation was the fact that the value of these coins was set as a given number of *denarii* and not through a set of reciprocal relationships. Since physical *denarii* were about to vanish from the circulation pool, this represented the use of an abstract unit of account, in the very same sense that medieval states would later use ghost currencies as a result of successive debasements.[51] These relationships were amended in 301 CE when the silver, billon, and copper coinages' face value was multiplied by two while gold was only slightly revalued in unit-of-account terms.[52] This way, the authorities purposely undervalued gold as a metal and as a coin, in order to facilitate their compulsory purchases against billion coins; this shows how fiscal and monetary reforms were interlinked. At the same time, and in order to fend off the obviously inflationary impact of overvaluing the base coinage, another edict was issued, aimed at capping hundreds of current prices of defined commodities, products, and salaries.[53]

Finally, a major process of administrative reorganization was initiated, aimed at the establishment of a true imperial bureaucracy. As seen in Chapter 7 of this volume, officials were mostly drawn from the equestrian order, and, with the help of limted numbers of imperial slaves and freedmen, they had operated the skeleton of an administrative system under the Principate. With the Severans, it is likely that this apparatus had been

[50] Estiot (2012: 548–50). [51] Cippola (1956: 38–51).

[52] Erim, Reynolds, and Crawford (1971); Estiot (2012: 549–50 tab. 29D).

[53] Crawford and Reynolds (1979); Reynolds (1989).

reinforced and its attribution enlarged, while the frame under which the legal system of the empire functioned was broadened and partially reshaped by the jurists Papinian, Ulpian, and Paul. Under Diocletian and then Constantine, new steps were accomplished, leading to the establishment of defined imperial structures. Provinces were broken down into smaller geographical entities and grouped under new praetorian prefectures; the military and civil taxes or *largitionalia*, managed by a distinct administrative structure, were directed toward the imperial *aerarium*, while the management of the emperors' patrimony was kept under the responsibility of the counts of the *res privata*. Even if civic structures retained a role in the tax collection process, there is little doubt that a massive redistribution of power was engineered at the expense of the traditional provincial elites, aiming at a higher degree of efficiency and fairness.[54]

The sweeping reforms of Diocletian have attracted little sympathy from generations of historians, who equated them with the forced implementation of corporatism and absolutism: "The system of Diocletian was accompanied with another very material disadvantage, which cannot even at present be totally overlooked: a more expensive establishment, and consequently an increase of taxes, and the oppression of people"; "The interests of the people were sacrificed for what seemed to be the interests of the state" and "Led directly to ruin and slavery."[55] Many contemporary or later Christian sources were similarly hostile to the Tetrarchy[56]. This judgment has been largely revised as a result of more recent scholarship, and a numerical comparison between the effective tax rates in the early and later Empire does not give much credence to the notion of massive tax increase but, rather, to an evolution that may have privileged farmers' shares of the agricultural added value at the expense of landlords' net income.[57] If anything, the reformed fiscal and monetary system aimed to restore the fiscal health of the earlier period without its patchwork of specific tax regimes, exemptions, privileges, and unequal conditions that the history of conquests had created. An obvious lack of transparency, the predatory powers of the local elites of autonomous communities, and the anachronistic exemption that Italy and various other polities enjoyed as a result of their involvement with the initial conquest process had always

[54] On the administrative structures of the fourth century, see Delmaire (1989). Regarding the struggle between the cities and the central bureaucracy, see Bransbourg (2008).

[55] Gibbon (1845 [1776]: 567–8); Rostovtzeff (1926: 461, 496).

[56] Eutropius, *Abridgment of Roman History* 9; Lactantius, *On the Death of the Persecutors* 7; 23, 31. See Carrié (1994: 35–6).

[57] Carrié (1997: 130–3).

characterized the early imperial system.[58] The Diocletianic reform violated many vested interests, and the hatred it triggered within many influential circles of the Roman elite may be a tribute to its relative efficiency and success. Without wishing to paint a rosy picture of the early fourth-century tax reform, some of the words used by the Prefect Aristius Optatus in 297 CE deserve to be quoted:

> [I]t has come about that the levies of the public taxes take place in such a way that some persons are being relieved, while other persons are being overburdened, and they [the emperors] have determined to eradicate this most evil and pernicious practice in their provincials' interest and to give a salutary standard to which the taxes shall conform. Therefore, it is possible for all persons to know the amount levied on each *arura* with respect to the quality of the soil, the amount levied on each head of the rural population, and the minimum and the maximum ages of liability from the published godlike edict and the schedule attached thereto, to which I have prefixed copies of this my edict for public display.[59]

As the succession regime initiated by Diocletian, with its carefully planned voluntary resignations of co-rulers, quickly failed, the monetary and fiscal systems proved unable to cope with the additional strain of renewed civil wars. The base coinage started to depreciate again, a clear sign that the imperial budget had remained unbalanced, whereas Constantine reformed the gold coinage. Nevertheless, the Diocletianic tax reforms were to have far-reaching consequences. They would survive the collapse of the Tetrarchic system of government, and even of the Western Empire, shaping the fiscal system of the Roman and then Byzantine states for several centuries. The late Roman tax system, with its universal reach toward land and productive forces encompassing aristocratic and public lands together, became the most comprehensive and rational fiscal regime in the Mediterranean world until modern times. It saved an empire that was to last another millennium in the East – a legacy that very few reformers have ever managed to achieve in history.

The end of unity (305–395 CE)

The years from 324 to 395 constituted the last period of imperial unity. The most visible economic developments of the period were the progressive debasement of the bronze coinage and the even faster inflationary process that drove the gold price from the range 60,000 to 72,000 *denarii* per

58 Bransbourg (2008: 262–7).

59 Johnson, Coleman-Norton, and Bourne (1961: 235 n. 298).

pound in 300/301 CE to some 3 billion by the years 380 to 390 CE.[60] This is equivalent to an average compounded annual inflation of about 13 to 14 percent. The bronze coinage, whose main module was initially a large and carefully designed billon coin of around 10 g with a silver content of about 4 percent, turned into a poorly struck piece of leaded bronze of around 1 g. Because of the instability of the bronze currency, gold became the natural anchor and store of value. The one-seventy-second of a pound gold *solidus* became the standard gold coin under Constantine in 312 CE, and was to remain unchanged for many centuries. The growing ubiquity of gold in the literary and legal sources of the last third of the century, combined with a major discontinuity within the chemical composition of the gold used by the imperial mints, points to new sources of gold at this time.[61] The most likely scenario is that significant discoveries of gold deposits were made, perhaps in the area of the Balkans, providing the empire with additional sources of revenue.[62] The contrast between an even more prevalent gold coinage and the increasingly debased base coins implies a sharp decoupling between two very distinct monetary circuits, one involving the upper strata of the Roman society, which used gold, while poorer individuals were left to deal with the inflationary consequences of the bronze currency's ongoing devaluations. Rather limited silver series and gold fractional coins provided an incomplete bridge across that wealth divide. A vivid papyrus describes how two brothers speculate around the exchange rate between copper and gold coins in order to intermediate (with profit) between the official fiscal requirements in gold and the final taxpayers.[63]

On the fiscal side, the Diocletianic land tax evolved into a dual system of levies involving a land tax proper, accounted for in wheat or other staple products and converted into cash as it suited the state, and a gold tax, both of them assessed on the standardized land and workforce fiscal units. The latter tax replaced the compulsory requisitions of gold and silver as well as

[60] On base currency debasement, see Callu (1989: 223–9). On gold prices as recorded by Egyptian papyri, see Bagnall (1985; 1989).

[61] On circulation of gold in the fourth century, see Banaji (1996; 2001). Regarding the changes in the chemical composition of gold by the second half of the fourth century, see Morrisson *et al.* (1985: 92–5) and Callu (1989: 231–2).

[62] A hint in that direction is the "Balkan" focus of some imperial edicts dealing with gold mining during that period: *Theodosian Code* 10.19.7 and 8 from 370 to 378 CE and *Theodosian Code* 1.32.5 (386 CE) and 11.28.9 (414 CE). The Goths were joined after Hadrianopolis by local (this is in the Balkans) miners who could no longer stand the imperial tax burden: Ammianus Marcellinus 31.6.4–5.

[63] *Papyrus Oxyrhynchus* 48.3401, datable from *c.* 355 CE with respect to the gold price.

the obligation for landowners or groups of taxpayers to provide equipped men and horses fit for military service. In doing so, the state adopted a strategy aimed at monetizing the military sector. The consolidated military tax, most likely called *aurum comparaticium*,[64] was the key means by which the "barbarization" of the army decisively progressed throughout the century.[65] The overall gold tax (including the military levy, to which an equivalent civilian component was added) was labeled *species ceterae* or *aes pecunia* by the legal edicts, and finally became known under the term *largitionales tituli* as it flowed toward the more discretionary and more centrally controlled imperial financial department called *aerarium*.[66] The basic land tax, classically called *tributum, species*, or *annonariae functiones*, fed the provincial treasury, the *arca*.[67] The provincial administration, under the leadership of the praetorian prefects, handled the current needs of the state (army supplies, road maintenance, ordinary expenses) while the *aerarium* was the true treasury of the emperor, divided between his private funds, the *res privata*, and the *largitionales*, which were in charge of financing the military levies.[68] State funds were thus divided into two normally very distinct financial bureaucracies, although limits of attribution did fluctuate among the various imperial officials, notably regarding the management and sharing of the income from civic lands.[69]

On top of the taxation based on land, various fiscal dues were assessed on commercial and artisanal assets, such as the infamous *chrysargyron* or *collatio lustralis*, created by Licinius or Constantine possibly between 314 and 318 CE, and abolished by Anastasius in 498 CE.[70] The fact a large city such as Edessa would have contributed only 140 pounds of gold every four years, while the sole military tax assessed on land areas of around 1,500 acres produced an annual payment of 1 pound of gold, has led many to discount it as a very marginal form of income for the state compared to the land taxes.[71] That said, it aroused passions and was universally resented by those

[64] Carrié (1993b: 127 n. 34); 1994: 59–60).

[65] Ammianus Marcellinus is wonderfully explicit in describing how Valens sought to use the cash proceeds of the military tax to incorporate into his army the Goths he had invited to cross the Danube in 376 CE: "[T]hat instead of the levy of soldiers which was contributed annually by each province, there would accrue to the treasuries a vast amount of gold" (31.4.4). He saw an opportunity to increase the value of his army with Gothic warriors, using to that effect the money provided by the provincials in lieu of local recruits.

[66] Refer to Haldon, Chapter 11, in the section entitled "The administration of taxation," for a more detailed analysis of the later Roman administrative apparatus.

[67] See, for example, *Theodosian Code* 11.9.2 (321 CE), 12.2 (362 CE), 28.9 (314 CE), and 28.14 (423 CE).

[68] Delmaire (1989: 6–7).

[69] Bransbourg (2008: 290).

[70] Jones (1964: 429–30); Delmaire (1989: 354–74).

[71] Hendy (1985: 174–5). Military tax computations from Carrié (1993b).

who had to pay it, to the extent that it is known to have contributed to urban rioting.[72] It seems that an average of about 1 to 2 *solidi* every four years per liable contributor is a fair estimate – a rather substantial amount for the lower strata of the urban population.[73] Custom dues are widely attested, as well as an annual tax levied on senators and specific offerings and payments linked to anniversaries or victories, following a practice well established since Hellenistic times.

There have been few attempts to quantify the amount of resources the later Empire managed to levy and spend. Revenue of the order of some 24,000 pounds of gold for Gaul and 8,333 pounds for Egypt, to which the grain tax would have to be added, has been estimated on the basis of local tax receipts and literary testimonies.[74] The restored Empire of Justinian would have enjoyed overall revenue of around 5 to 6 million *solidi* in the sixth century CE – that is, 70,000 to 85,000 pounds of gold the vast majority of which was provided by the eastern provinces.[75] Based on these estimates, the Roman Empire in the middle of the fourth century may have yielded tax revenues in the range of 150,000 to 200,000 pounds of gold. Attempts to estimate the overall budget of the Roman Empire during the first two centuries CE have typically led to a range of 800 million to 1.5 billion *sestertii* – 200,000 to 350,000 pounds of gold.[76] It is thus hard to accept the traditional argument that the later Empire inaugurated a period of tax oppression, at least on the basis of these necessarily incomplete numerical guesses.

If anything, the contrast between the level of private wealth, as testified by later fourth- and fifth-century sources, and public wealth points toward a rather low tax intake, at least with respect to the wealthiest citizens of the empire. If, as a possibly hyperbolic source claims, the richest Roman families were actually able to accumulate annual income of 40 *kentenaria* of gold (= 4,000 pounds = 288,000 *solidi*), to which income in kind of about one-third would have to be added,[77] then four such families would have earned the equivalent of

[72] Libanius, *Oration* 46.22–23; Zosimus 2.38; Priscian, *Panegyric of Anastasius* 153; Procopius, *Panegyric of Anastasius* 13.

[73] Jones (1964: 872); Delmaire (1989: 371).

[74] Carrié (1994: 61). These figures in gold equivalent do not imply that all this income was actually denominated in gold. Papyrological and legal sources show that silver was frequently used, while one edict even shows iron as a commodity that could settle tax dues: *Theodosian Code* 11.20.6 (430 CE).

[75] Hendy (1985: 171). See also below, as well as Haldon, Chapter 11, in the section entitled "The incidence of taxation."

[76] Duncan-Jones (1994: 45 tab. 3.7). 100 *sestertii* = 1 *aureus* at one-fortieth of a pound under Caesar, one-fiftieth under Caracalla.

[77] Olympiodorus of Thebes, *fragments* 44.

the entire tax proceeds of Gaul, the largest and one of the richest regions of the empire.

The triumphant East (395–476 CE)

The division of the empire in 395 CE is customarily considered as the start of the great divergence between the Western and the Eastern parts of the Mediterranean world. By 476 CE there were no more emperors in the West, while the Eastern Empire thrived to such a degree that Justinian was able to undertake the reconquest of the lost territories from 534 CE onward. Generations have speculated about the reasons why it was the West, and not the East, that fell. In this context it is worth noting that the most tax-productive regions of the Eastern part, Egypt and Syria, were located far away from the military pressure that fell on the Rhine/Danube border areas. At the same time the Persian Empire to the east had to deal with steppe threats (the White Huns or Hephthalites), and as a result the later fourth and fifth centuries represented a largely peaceful period between both empires.

The Western Empire was economically more vulnerable. Only Africa enjoyed a relatively secure situation. Gaul, by contrast, probably the wealthiest region of the West, was on the front line. Even if not conquered, its economic infrastructure could not have been left unimpaired by the repeated raids that materialized from the middle of the fourth century onward. Italy was barely in a better situation, easily accessible as it was from the Danube area or the Balkans.

Paradoxically, the East suffered the largest initial loss of tax income, as the Danube area was the first frontier to be decisively breached during the migration of the Goths from 376 to 378 CE, which enabled them to plunder the Balkans at will. As they failed to seize the eastern capital Constantinople, however, and became cornered in the relatively poor Balkans during the last two decades of the fourth century, it was only a matter of time until an ambitious leader turned westward toward Italy. Alaric's move culminated in the sack of Rome in 410 CE. Placed in a rather similar situation about a century later, Theodoric emulated Alaric, by unsuccessfully threatening Constantinople and similarly finding a safer option in following the "orders" of Zeno, which directed him to Italy in 488 CE. The easy spoils were located in the West, not in the East. With eastern "Danubian" invaders eventually moving westward while others invaders operated across the Rhine area, the Western Empire suffered greater pressure along a much longer frontier, while the Eastern authorities, after surrendering much of the Balkans, could focus on guarding access to Asia Minor, shielded by the fleet and the heavily fortified imperial capital of Constantinople, which effectively controlled the crossing to Asia. At the same time, Constantinople cashed in the tax proceeds of Egypt, Syria, and Asia Minor and used them to buy peace from the various potentially threatening foreign groups.[78] Their leaders were often induced into looking westward – a course of action duly followed by Attila's Huns once they realized that this was the line of least resistance.[79]

Imperial edicts and literary sources allow us to track the fiscal decline and eventual demise of the Western Empire. Limited ad hoc tax discounts are standard practice for any smart regime. As such, the 22 percent reduction of the taxable base in Autun in 311 CE as Constantine bid for supreme power, or the 20 percent discount offered to Antioch in 362 CE by Julian when he was about to embark on his Persian expedition, do not require specific comments.[80] The reduction of 72 percent apparently offered to Gaul by Julian in 355 CE is obviously of another nature,[81] regardless of whether Constantius II had raised taxes to unbearable levels or military activity had seriously disrupted the contributive capacity of the province. Both explanations may be defensible. In any case, the final rate of 7 *solidi* per taxable unit seems low: as 1 pound of gold was provided in the East for the sole military tax by groups of twenty or thirty taxable units, and as the civil component of the gold tax was equal to the military component,[82] it seems as if the entire Gallic tax has been reduced to the sole gold tax (7 × 20 = 140 = 2 pounds of gold), while the provincial base tax payment would have been suspended.[83]

Bad fiscal news accumulated in the West as it moved closer to disintegration. In 395 CE about 40 percent of the land of Campania, the most fertile region of ancient Italy, was exempted from tax arrears. In 413

[78] The empire paid an annual subsidy of 350 pounds of gold to the Huns from 422 CE onward, raised to 700 pounds in 437, and 2,100 pounds in 447; 2,000 pounds were annually paid to the Goths from 473 onward: Hendy (1985: 261). If Egypt alone could provide the imperial treasury with *c.* 8,000 pounds, none of these payments would have represented an existential threat to the revenues of the Eastern Empire.

[79] Attila failed to take Constantinople in 443 CE even though he had scored several victories over imperial armies. The Huns received hefty payments from Theodosius II and left the empire *c.* 445, to return in 447 for an indecisive campaign. In 450 Attila decided to look west, and successfully invaded Gaul and northern Italy. He considered renewed attacks against Constantinople before his death, in 453, since Marcian had suspended the payment of the tribute.

[80] Eumenius, *Panegyric* 8.5.5; Julian, *Misopogon ('Beard-hater')* 365b.

[81] Ammianus Marcellinus 16.5.54. [82] From Carrié (1993b).

[83] The use of *capitulum* in the manuscripts is most likely a corruption that stands for *caput*, as the numbers exactly fit in that case: Carrié (1994: 44). That no other tax is levied on the Gauls is explicated by the use of *munera universa* by Ammianus.

CE, just after the Goths left Italy for Gaul, a global tax exemption of 80 percent was granted to the entire peninsula for five years. In 418 CE, as the previous tax cut was about the expire, an extension was granted at a discount rate close to 90 percent for Tuscany, the region of Ancones, and Campania – in productive terms, most of peninsular Italy. After the Vandals invaded north Africa, 40 to 50 percent of all imperial lands were exempted from taxation in 422 CE. In 445 CE, after the empire had lost most of Africa, what was left of it was asked to contribute at a rate of only 12.5 percent of its former tax obligations. In 451 CE 85 percent of the remaining African land was allocated, tax-free, to whomever was in a position to handle its cultivation. In the East, only the Balkans benefited from a similar measure, in 424 CE. We also know about another tax rebate in the East, limited to 20 percent of imperial lands in a region close to the river Euphrates in the 440s CE.[84]

The literary and legal evidence is striking: as the lands of the Western Empire fall prey to invaders, starting with Gaul and ending with Africa, its financial resources shrink, impeding its capacity to maintain an adequate level of military strength. When Rome was forced to pay the Goths to avoid been sacked in 408 and 409 CE, 9,000 pounds of gold, 30,000 pounds of silver (around 2,500 pounds of gold), and 4,000 silk tunics were delivered in two installments. To achieve this, statues were melted down or stripped of their precious metals.[85] It is quite obvious that the deliquescent tax system of the West was no longer in a position to mobilize great wealth, whereas in 468 CE the Eastern Empire was able to spend 64,000 pounds of gold and 700,000 pounds of silver (equivalent to around 58,000 pounds of gold) on a botched attempt to recover north Africa.[86] The replacement of the western imperial state by the successor "barbarian" kingdoms accentuated this divergence further.[87]

Conclusions

By promoting the accession of the "Illyrian" emperors, drawn from the army and necessarily unsympathetic to the privileges of the traditional ruling elites, the military disorders of the third century CE allowed a decisive transformation of the Roman state. The later Roman Empire effectively evolved from a

[84] *Theodosian Code* 11.28.2 (395 CE); 7 (413 CE), 12 (418 CE); 13 (422 CE); *Valentinianic Novellae* 13.1 (445 CE), 34.2 (451 CE). In the East: *Theodosian Code* 11.1.33 (424); Theodoret, *Correspondence* 42.

[85] Hendy (1985: 261). [86] John Lydus, *On the Magistracies of the Roman State* 3.43.

[87] This is discussed further by Haldon, Chapter 11, particularly in the subsection entitled "Resources, revenues, and control."

tribute state toward a fiscal state. In order to achieve this, the reformers of the later third century and early fourth century CE targeted at the same time the exemptions that had maintained the distinction between allied and conquered peoples deep into the second century CE, the wide discrepancies in assessing and taxing wealth all around the empire, and the levying process that had been mostly delegated to provincial elites under the loose supervision of a skeletal embryo of a bureaucracy.

By about 310 CE a new contributory system had been extended to formerly privileged entities, mostly bypassing the local elites to whom the levying process had been formerly entrusted, a universal assessment mechanism had been applied to taxable wealth, and an official administrative apparatus had become functional all across the empire, supervising and organizing public funding and expenses. No such system could function without abuses, and ancient complaints cannot be summarily rejected. This said, it does not seem that the level of overall extraction went higher than during the previous period, while most opponents of the reforms were members of those categories that had lost out to the new state apparatus.

Judging by its historical consequences, the reformers achieved mixed results. On the one hand, the Roman state was not to last more than an additional century over most of the West. By 410 CE Roman control was effectively limited to Italy, north Africa, and a very few areas in Iberia and Gaul. By 450 CE the Western Empire had been reduced to Italy – at best. On the other hand, as shown in Chapter 11 in this volume, its Eastern half was to last another millennium, while the concept of a fiscal state had been pushed to new limits.

Finally, the thousands of imperial edicts and decisions gathered into the massive legislative compilations of the later Empire, notably the *Codex Theodosianus*, the *Codex Iuris Civilis* (*Codex Justinianus, Digest, Institutes*) and the *Novellae Constitutiones*, went on to have a deep influence over the way modern states defined their taxation powers once Europe started to emerge from its feudal fragmentation and rediscovered its Roman past.

References

Alston, R (1994) "Roman military pay from Caesar to Diocletian," *Journal of Roman Studies* 84: 113–23.

Banaji, J. (1996) "The circulation of gold as an index of prosperity in the central and eastern Mediterranean in late antiquity," in *Coin Finds and Coin Use in the Roman World: 13th Oxford Symposium on Coinage and Monetary History, 25–27/3/93*, ed. C. E. King and D. G. Wigg. Berlin: 41–54.

(2001) *Agrarian Change in Late Antiquity: Gold, Labour and Aristocratic Dominance*. Oxford.

Bagnall, R. S. (1977) "Bullion purchases and landholding in the fourth century," *Chronique d'Égypte* 52: 322–36.

(1985) Currency and Inflation: 4th Century Egypt. Durham, NC.

(1989) "Fourth-century prices: new evidence and further thoughts," *Zeitschrift für Papyrologie und Epigraphik* 76: 69–76.

(2002) "The effects of plague: models and evidence," *Journal of Roman Archaeology* 15: 114–20.

Bang, P. F. (2008) *The Roman Bazaar: A Comparative Study of Trade and Markets in a Tributary Empire*. New York.

Bland, R. (1996) "The development of gold and silver coin denominations, AD 193–253," in *Coin Finds and Coin Use in the Roman World: 13th Oxford Symposium on Coinage and Monetary History, 25–27/3/1993*, ed. C. E. King and D. G. Wigg. Berlin: 63–100.

Borsch, S. J. (2005) *The Black Death in Egypt and England: A Comparative Study*. Austin, TX.

Bourne, R. J. (1996) "The XXI coinage of Aurelian *et al.*," *Numismatic Circular* 104: 84.

Bransbourg, G. (2008) "Fiscalité impériale et finances municipales au IVe siècle," *AnTar* 16: 255–96.

(2010) "Politique fiscale et enjeux de pouvoir dans le monde romain," unpublished doctoral thesis. École des Hautes Études en Sciences Sociales, Paris.

Butcher, K., and Ponting, M. (2009) "The denarius in the first century," in *Proceedings of the XIV Numismatic International Congress, Glasgow 2009*, ed. N. Holmes. Glasgow: 557–68.

Caley, E. R. (1958) "Chemical composition of Alexandrian tetradrachms," in *Centennial Publication of the American Numismatic Society*, ed. H. Ingholt. New York: 167–80.

Callu, J.-P. (1969) *La politique monétaire des empereurs Romains de 238 à 311*. Paris.

(1989) "Analyses métalliques et inflation: l'Orient romain de 295 à 361/368," in *Hommes et richesses dans l'Empire byzantin,* vol. I, *IVe – VIIe siècles,* ed. J. Lefort and C. Morrisson. Paris: 223–33.

Callu, J.-P., Brenot, C., and Barrandon, J.-N. (1979) "Analyse de séries atypiques (Aurélien, Tacite, Carus, Licinius)," *Numismatica e Antichità Classiche: Quaderni Ticinesi* 8: 241–54.

Carrié, J.-M. (1978) "Finances militaires et fait monétaire," in *Les "devaluations" à Rome: époque républicaine et impériale (Rome, 13–15 novembre 1975)*. Rome: 227–48.

(1993a) "Le riforme economiche da Aureliano a Constantino," in *Storia di Roma,* vol. III, part 1, *L'età tardoantica,* ed. A. Momigliano and A. Schiavone. Turin: 283–322.

(1993b) "Observations sur la fiscalité du IVe siècle pour servir à l'histoire monétaire," in *L'"inflazione" nel quarto secolo DC: atti dell'incontro di studio, Roma 23–25 giugno 1988*. Rome: 115–54.

(1994) "Dioclétien et la fiscalité," *AnTar* 2: 34–64.

(1997) "L'arithmétique sociale de l'économie agraire: prix de la terre, rente foncière et prix des céréales dans l'Égypte romano-byzantine," in *Économie antique,* vol. II, *Prix et formation des prix dans les économies antiques*, ed. J. Andreau, P. Briant, and R. Descat. Saint-Bertrand-de-Comminges, France: 103–24.

(2007) "Du sommet à la base et retour: les circuits de la fiscalité tardoimpériale," in *Poteri centrali e poteri periferici nella tarda antichità: confronti, conflitti: atti della giornata di studio, Messina, 5 Settembre 2006*, ed. R. Pintaudi. Florence: 51–66.

Carrié, J.-M., and Rousselle, A. (1999) *L'Empire romain en mutation: des Sévères à Constantin.* Paris.

Cipolla, C. M. (1956) *Money, Prices, and Civilization in the Mediterranean World: Fifth to Seventeenth Century.* Princeton, NJ.

Crawford, M. H. (1975) "Finance, coinage and money from the Severans to Constantine II," *Aufstieg und Niedergang der romischen Welt* 2: 560–93.

Crawford, M. H., and Reynolds, J. M. (1979) "The Aezani copy of the prices edict," *Zeitschrift für Papyrologie und Epigraphik* 34: 163–210.

Déléage, A. (1945) *La capitation du Bas-Empire.* Mâcon.

Delmaire, R. (1989) *Largesses privées et res privata: l'aerarium impérial et son administration du IVe au VIe siècle.* Rome.

Depeyrot, G., and Hollard, D. (1987) "Pénurie d'argent métal et crise monétaire au 3è siècle après J-C," *Histoire et Mesure* 2: 57–85.

Domergue, C. (1983) *La mine antique d'Aljustrel (Portugal) et les tables de bronze de Vipasca.* Bordeaux.

(1990) *Les mines de la péninsule ibérique dans l'antiquité romaine.* Rome.

Duncan-Jones, R. (1990) *Structure and Scale in the Roman Economy.* Cambridge.

(1994) *Money and Government in the Roman Empire.* Cambridge.

Erim, K. T., Reynolds, J. M., and Crawford, M. H. (1971) "Diocletian's currency reform: a new inscription," *Journal of Roman Studies* 61: 171–7.

Estiot, S. (1995a) *Ripostiglio della Venèra: nuovo catalogo illustrato,* vol. II, part 1, *Aureliano.* Rome.

(1995b) "Aureliana," *Revue Numismatique* 150: 50–94.

(2012) "The later third century," in *The Oxford Handbook of Greek and Roman Coinage*, ed. W. E. Metcalf. Oxford: 538–60.

Faucher, T., and Lorber, C. (2010) "Bronze coinage of Ptolemaic Egypt in the second century BC," *American Journal of Numismatics* 22: 35–80.

Frier, B. (2000) "Demography," in *The Cambridge Ancient History,* vol. XI, *The High Empire AD 70–192*, 2nd edn, ed. A. K. Bowman, P. Garnsey, and D. W. Rathbone. Cambridge: 788–816.

Gibbon, E. (1845 [1776]) *The History of the Decline and Fall of the Roman Empire,* vol. I. London.

Gitler, H., and Ponting, M. (2003) *The Silver Coinage of Septimius Severus and His Family (193–211 AD): A Study of the Chemical Composition of the Roman and Eastern Issues.* Milan.

Harl, K. W. (1985) "Marks of value on Tetrarchic *nummi* and Diocletian's monetary policy," *Phoenix* 39: 263–70.

(1996) *Coinage in Roman Economy, 300 BC – 700 AD*. Baltimore.

Harper, K. (2008) "The Greek census inscriptions of late antiquity," *Journal of Roman Studies* 98: 83–119.

Hendy, M. F. (1985) *Studies in the Byzantine Monetary Economy* c. *300–1450*. Cambridge.

Hopkins, K. (1980) "Taxes and trade in the Roman Empire (200 BC – 400 AD)," *Journal of Roman Studies* 70: 101–25.

Johnson, A. C., Coleman-Norton, P. R., and Bourne, F. C. (1961) *Ancient Roman Statutes: A Translation with Commentary, Glossary and Index*. Austin, TX.

Jones, A. H. M. (1953) "Census records of the later Roman Empire," *Journal of Roman Studies* 43: 49–64.

(1964) *The Later Roman Empire 284–602: A Social, Economic and Administrative Survey*. Oxford.

Jones, G. D. B. (1980) "The Roman mines at Rio Tinto," *Journal of Roman Studies* 70: 146–65.

Molin, M. (1999) "Haud dissimilis Magno Alexandro seu Caesari dictatori: l'empereur Aurélien," *Cahiers du Centre Gustave Glotz* 10: 347–54.

Morrisson, C., Brenot, C., Callu, J.-P., Barrandon, J.-P., Poirier, J., and Halleux, R. (1985) *L'or monnayé*, vol. I, *Purification et altérations de Rome à Byzance*. Paris.

Rathbone, D. W. (1996) "Monetisation, not price-inflation, in third-century AD Egypt?," in *Coin Finds and Coin Use in the Roman World: The Thirteenth Oxford Symposium on Coinage and Monetary History*, ed. C. E. King and D. G. Wigg. Oxford: 321–39.

(1997) "Prices and price formation in Roman Egypt," in *Économie antique*, vol. II, *Prix et formation des prix dans les économies antiques*, ed. J. Andreau, P. Briant, and R. Descat. Saint-Bertrand-de-Comminges, France: 183–244.

Rea, J. R. (1974) "P.S.I. IV 310 and imperial bullion purchases," *Chronique de'Égypte* 49: 163–74.

Reynolds, J. M. (1989) "Imperial regulations: 231 – the prices edict," in *Aphrodisias in Late Antiquity*, ed. C. Roueché. London: 265–318.

Rostovtzeff, M. I. (1926) *The Social and Economic History of the Roman Empire*. Oxford.

Scheidel, W. (2001) *Death on the Nile: Disease and the Demography of Roman Egypt*. Leiden.

(2002) "A model of demographic and economic change in Roman Egypt after the Antonine Plague," *Journal of Roman Archaeology* 15: 97–114.

(2012a) (contrib. Sutherland, J. W.) "Roman wellbeing and the economic consequences of the Antonine Plague," in *L'impatto della "peste Antonina,"* ed. E. Lo Cascio. Bari: 265–95.

(2012b) "Approaching the Roman economy," in *The Cambridge Companion to the Roman Economy*, ed. W. Scheidel. Cambridge: 1–21.

(2015) "State revenue and expenditure in the Han and Roman Empires," in *State Power in Ancient China and Rome*, ed. W. Scheidel. New York: 150–80.

Scheidel, W., and Friesen, S. J. (2009) "The size of the economy and the distribution of income in the Roman Empire," *Journal of Roman Studies* 99: 61–91.

Sperber, D. (1974) *Roman Palestine 200–400: Money and Prices*. Jerusalem.

Thonemann, P. (2007) "Estate and the land in late Roman Asia Minor," *Chiron* 37: 435–78.

Walker, D. R. (1976) *The Metrology of the Roman Silver Coinage*, vol. I, *From Augustus to Domitian*. Oxford.

(1977) *The Metrology of the Roman Silver Coinage*, vol. II, *Frem Nerva to Commodus*. Oxford.

(1978) *The Metrology of the Roman Silver Coinage*, vol. III, *From Pertinax to Aemilian*. Oxford.

Weiser, W. (2000) "Nominale römischer Münzen des 3. – 5. Jahrhunderts n. Chr: Nummus, Binio, Bicharactus, Follis, Pecunia maiorina, Centenionalis, Myris, Monas, Argyron, Decargyrus," *Geldgeschichtliche Nachrichten* 35: 311–27.

CHAPTER 9

Early imperial China, from the Qin and Han through Tang

Mark E. Lewis

Introduction

The term "early imperial China" conventionally applies to the period from the establishment of the first Chinese empire (BC 221) through the fall of the Tang Dynasty (906 AD). Like the term "premodern," the phrase "early imperial" is defined by what it lacks: no examination system, no state-defined orthodoxy, no elaborate system of water-based transport, no regional economic specialization based on such a system, and no distinctive urban culture defined by distinctive commodities and entertainment. Given the absence of any real unity to the period, the history of the fiscal regimes divides into several major epochs: the early empires (Qin and Han), the era of division (Northern and Southern Dynasties), and the middle empires (Sui and Tang). There are also several enduring features that characterize the entire period. In this chapter I focus on the latter, while also sketching the changes that emerged in each epoch. As the most enduring features first appeared under the early empires, I devote more attention to this period, while the treatment of subsequent periods focuses on their distinctive practices or institutions and on the transition to the later empires.

I will first enumerate the key features of the early imperial Chinese fiscal regime. First, as in the later imperial period described by Deng in Chapter 10, early imperial China featured a relatively low-tax regime concentrated largely on the small peasantry. The state extracted land taxes, capitation taxes, and labor service from peasant households, and these were the primary sources of the government's wealth. Attempts to tax the urban population and merchants, which were technically difficult and provoked elite resistance, were largely abandoned. Since the taxes levied on each peasant household were comparatively low, the state needed as many households as possible to be registered and taxed. Taxes were kept relatively low not because of any ideological commitment but because the peasants lacked a sufficient surplus to pay more without being ruined. Even the low rates set proved to be sustainable only in normal times, and the natural and man-made calamities that inevitably occurred pushed ever-larger numbers of peasants into bankruptcy. This resulted in the conversion of free peasants into sharecroppers, which steadily reduced the number of households liable to taxes. This ultimately destroyed the fiscal foundations of the Han state and played a major role in its collapse.

A second feature was that the state's chief rivals for the collection of resources were the state's own agents, rather than a nobility or urban merchants. Officials were rivals in two ways. First, the imperial Chinese state was constantly worried that officials would become powerful enough in their local administrations to threaten the court. As we will see, this had a major impact on the fiscal regime. Second, throughout the early imperial period and the rest of Chinese history, the greatest threat to fiscal stability was the degree to which the officials converted the temporary bonanza of a salary and bribes into the enduring security of landownership. It was the steady extension of officials' landholdings (and of those of temples and monasteries in the era of state-sponsored religious institutions) that constantly reduced the number of taxable peasant households and that, consequently, successively destroyed the early empires.

A third key feature of the early fiscal regimes, and one whose disappearance marked the shift toward the later empires, is what I would call its "tight spatial circumscription." Given the absence of an extensive system of water transport, bulk commodities (above all grain) could not be shipped in high volume for great distances. This meant that all cities, including the imperial capital, were provisioned primarily by their own regions. The bulk of grain and labor services were absorbed by local and provincial governments, with only a limited amount being shipped on to the capital, and most of that probably as cash. The imperial capital itself, with its population swollen by the court and those who provided for the courtiers, was largely fed and clothed by the products of its hinterland, the Guanzhong region. This meant that the early imperial state focused its efforts to improve irrigation and transport entirely on the capital region, and also tended to concentrate the armed forces there.

A fourth and final feature was that in the early empires, again in contrast with the later ones, state-owned land played a key role. It is important to note, however, that the reliance on state-owned land was largely a feature of government weakness. When the state was strong it extracted wealth through taxation, and only when it grew weak and lost administrative capacity did it shift to amassing land and a servile population to work it. These features are all elaborated below.

The early empires: Qin and Han

We have little documentation on the fiscal regime of the Qin Empire, and for the moment it is probably best understood by examining the early Han Empire, which was its direct heir. Two features of the history of Warring States China (the period in which Qin rose to dominance) had a major impact on the fiscal structure of the early empires, however. First, states as bureaucratic entities organized around a single supreme ruler emerged through a process of the ever-wider incorporation and mobilization of the rural population as payers of taxes and providers of military service. The earlier states had been dominated by a warrior nobility based in cities (which were initially city states), so the emergence of the Warring States entailed a revolution in which the cities were geographically and politically swallowed up into territorial states. Power in this era depended on the extraction of income and service from the countryside, which became the foundation of the state, in order to control the cities. This suspicion of the city and endorsement of rural villages as the basis of any proper society was elaborated in the so-called "legalist" philosophical texts (notably *The Book of Lord Shang* and the *Master Han Fei*, which both associated themselves with the Qin state) that advocated a state based on "agriculture and war." It was also to some degree expressed in Qin (and early Han) legal discrimination against merchants and the urban population.[1]

The period was also marked by the emergence of intensive agriculture involving large labor inputs to extract higher yields from relatively small plots of land. By the late Warring States period texts already discuss the importance of fertilization, the need for careful preparation of soil and seeds, techniques for conserving moisture in the soil, and above all the supreme importance of careful timing. The clearest articulation of these came in the chapters on agriculture at the end of *The Springs and Autumns of Master Lü*, an encyclopedic work produced under the patronage of Qin's chief minister when the later First Emperor was still under-aged. This emphasis on labor-intensive methods to extract the maximum crop from small plots was further elaborated in Han texts on agriculture, and manifested in the introduction of new methods.[2]

This emphasis on labor-intensive agriculture, which distinguished Chinese agriculture for the rest of its history, affected the fiscal regime in several ways. First, it made the individual peasant household (with two to

[1] Lewis (1990: chs. 1 & 2); Schwartz (1985: 330–43); Bodde (1986: 38, 52, 59, 76); Kern (2000: 26, 42–3); Hulsewé (1985).

[2] Hsu (1980: 5–14, 109–29, 279–303); Lü (2000 [239 BCE]: 650–67). See also Kiser and Cai (2003).

three laborers) working relatively small plots of land (the typical household had about 10 acres) the basic unit of rural society, and thus the core unit for the extraction of taxes. This produced a high population density, which facilitated the policy of trying to distribute a low average tax load across the largest possible number of payers. Second, the need for hard and skillful labor militated against the development of large estates worked by slave or servile labor that would have had no motivation for the necessary exertions or the acquisition of the necessary skills. Third, as the population expanded and the size of family plots was steadily reduced, each household worked closer and closer to the level of minimal subsistence.

The taxes and labor services extracted from the Han peasantry (which were adapted from those of the Qin) consisted of several major forms that continued across the four centuries of Han rule, others that were important for substantial periods, some that lasted only for one reign, and many minor exactions. Several sources provide details, so here I will only sketch the major forms and their ramifications.[3]

One significant feature of the Han fiscal regime is that financial administration was divided between the Ministry of Agriculture, which handled public finances, and the Lesser Treasury, which handled the personal finances of the emperor and the imperial court. The former primarily collected taxes from the rural population, and managed expenditures for officials' salaries, public works, flood control or irrigation, and military actions. The latter derived income from taxes on the natural products of the mountains, forests, rivers, lakes, and marshes (all non-cultivated land and all bodies of water being the property of the emperor), as well as from the taxes on registered merchants. The income from natural products primarily came from taxes on timber and fish, as well as the income from the gigantic imperial hunting parks. The primary expenditures of the Lesser Treasury were for the costs of running the imperial court and for gifts of gold and silver that the emperor bestowed on officials and meritorious commoners.[4] The shifting division of income and expenditure between the two treasuries is touched on further below.

The primary tax was that on land. While this was supposedly a percentage of the harvest, in practice it was levied on the amount of land multiplied by a notional average yield. The rate was fixed at the beginning of the dynasty as one-fifteenth of the yield, which was described as a reduction

[3] A good summary in English is given by Nishijima (1986: 591–607). The most detailed treatment in Chinese is that by Ma (1983). Useful treatments are also provided by Sun (1996: 26–49; 2003: 67–103; 1988: 27–56).

[4] The classic discussion is that by Katō (1952: 35–156).

from the Qin rate. From 168 to 156 BC the abundance of stored grain allowed the court to remit this tax, although titles were granted to those who presented grain. In 156 it was restored at the rate of one-thirtieth, at which rate it continued until the civil war triggered by the usurpation of Wang Mang in AD 9. After a brief period with an emergency rate of one-tenth, the tax was restored in AD 30 to the level of one-thirtieth until the end of the dynasty. Moreover, it was routine to remit the land tax in any region struck by natural disasters; remissions were also given to reward certain behavior, such as resettling at the frontier.

In addition to the land tax, which was apparently paid in grain, the Han government also levied a cash poll tax on all men and women between the ages of fifteen and fifty-six. For most of the dynasty the rate was 120 cash, which in the first century of the Han would have represented the price of one picul (about 20 liters) of grain, and in the second century somewhat less. Children between three and fourteen, or later seven and fourteen, were taxed at 20 cash, with some small variations. Variations in the rate of taxation were also introduced for purposes of social engineering, with merchants and slaves being charged double the rate of free peasants, unmarried women between fifteen and thirty (the notional age of fertility) being briefly charged five times the normal rate, and families with someone over the age of eighty receiving an exemption of 240 cash. In the Eastern Han for certain periods women who gave birth received a three-year remission.

In comparison, the yield of a typical small farm was estimated in Han sources at about 100 piculs per year. Since a normal household would have consisted of between two and four adults (when children had reached the age of fifteen but not yet moved out), and one or two children, the poll tax would vary from around 3 percent to 6 percent of a household's average annual yield in good times, in addition to the land tax of between one-fiftieth and one-thirtieth (3 percent to 7 percent). Thus payments in cash and grain would have hovered at around 10 percent of a household's notional average yield.

In addition to these taxes, and a couple of minor charges, Han peasant households also owed labor service. This consisted of work on government projects and military service. The former entailed one month's work per year for all males between fifteen and fifty-six on tasks for local governments. This would generally take place in periods of low demand for agricultural labor. Most work was in the peasant's locality, but if he was required to travel long distances then the state provided food. In the Western Han all young men were also obliged to give one year of military service in their localities, and were mustered for an annual training session after the fall harvest. Finally, some males were obliged to provide a further year of service either in the capital or at the frontier. In the second century of the Han these military obligations were gradually replaced by a cash payment to hire long-term professionals. After the civil war to overthrow Wang Mang the obligation for regular military service was abolished in AD 32, although emergency levies were still employed, particularly near the frontier.

These taxes and labor services were the primary payments demanded from a peasant household, and the only ones that lasted for the four centuries of the Han Dynasty (excluding the military obligation, which was abolished). Merchants were also liable for the poll tax, and those registered to buy and sell in the urban markets (generally smaller vendors) had to pay an annual fee, as well as a small fee on each notarized contract. Goods in transit were taxed at stations along the road network. In addition, there were substantial taxes or means of extracting income from merchants that were imposed for shorter periods. The most important were the property or wealth tax and the monopolies on salt and iron. Both were initiated by Emperor Wu (who reigned from 141 to 87 BC) to provide money for his foreign wars, and their impact was largely in his reign, although the monopolies were usually in force during the rest of the Western Han.

The wealth tax was an annual tax levied on all cash reserves and physical assets. It was instituted early in the dynasty in association with the poll tax. It became prominent under Emperor Wu, however, who in 119 BC raised the rates on merchants and artisans. This was intended not only to provide money for wars and to tap the substantial amounts of urban wealth otherwise beyond the reach of the state but also to discourage pursuit of the "peripheral enterprises" of trade and manufacture, and to facilitate the destruction of leading local families. To achieve these ends, Emperor Wu raised the rates on non-registered merchants to as high as 10 percent of declared wealth and those on artisans to just under 5 percent. By contrast, the rate for the general population was 1 to 2 percent. At the same time the Han government introduced a vehicle tax aimed at the wagons and boats used to transport goods.

The wealth tax was based on a declaration of total holdings by the head of each household. Failure to report all wealth was punished by complete confiscation and the exile of the malefactor. Compliance was secured through a system of bounties by which anyone who reported an omission in declared wealth would be given one-half of the confiscated property.

Encouraging such informing by employees or servants became a major weapon in the campaign waged by Emperor Wu's specially appointed legal agents, who were charged with the task of destroying locally powerful families. Sources describe the fabulous amounts of wealth that were confiscated in this period, and the destruction of much of what had hitherto been the local elite throughout the empire. It is unclear how long this tax was in force, but references to it disappear after the reign of Emperor Wu.[5]

The second of the two great attempts to tap merchant wealth, launched in 119 BC, was the establishment of state monopolies on iron and salt. Archaeological finds show that some feudal lords who ruled substantial regions of China in the first half-century of the Han had established such offices, and the Qin Dynasty may have done so earlier. Prior to 119 BC, however, the Han state had simply taxed merchants who gained wealth through the sale of iron and salt, which were natural products that belonged to the emperor. Interestingly, whereas these earlier taxes had gone into the emperor's Lesser Treasury, income from the new monopolies went to the Ministry of Agriculture, signaling that it was public income to be devoted to the army.

Details of the administration of the two monopolies, and the history of their sporadic terminations and revivals, are provided in numerous scholarly works. The essential points are that the iron monopoly entailed the establishment of government iron-manufacturing agencies that mined ore, produced implements, and sold them to the people. Labor was largely provided by convicts, with some professional craftsmen and slaves also participating. The salt monopoly, in contrast, left manufacture in the hands of the earlier producers, who were simply required to sell the salt to the state's agents, who resold it. Given that iron was widespread, and that the products of the state workshops were of poor quality, private manufacture seems to have continued with some degree of official toleration. Furthermore, after the abandonment of the monopoly at the end of the Western Han, it was never again significant for any dynasty. Salt, on the other hand, was both indispensable and produced in only a small number of easily controlled sites, so every subsequent major dynasty employed some form of state manufacture or monopoly.

One final form of exaction that was essential to the fiscal regimes of the Qin and Han Dynasties was convict labor. Elaborate legal codes produced

[5] In addition to Nishijima (1986: 599), see Barbieri-Low (2007: 127–8). For a translation of a chapter describing Emperor Wu's campaign against the powerful families of his day, see Sima (1961 [109 BCE]).

tens of thousands of convicts, who were exploited for labor that cost only the food needed to keep them alive. Whereas the peasants' corvée labor was concentrated in their own localities, and the pressure to have them home for the agricultural seasons was acute, convicts could be transported across great distances and kept working for years until they died of exhaustion or malnutrition, or were executed for any breach of discipline. Thus convicts provided a substantial pool of labor for major imperial construction projects, such as palaces, temples, imperial tombs, roads, canals, and irrigation channels. Convicts also did the more dangerous and exhausting labor in the iron monopoly, such as mining and smelting. They also provided manpower in the frontier garrisons, and after the abolition of universal military service they became the primary source for such men. Thus, just as convict labor was a major resource for the states of early modern Europe, it was also crucial to the early Chinese empires.[6]

While Emperor Wu's attempts to finance his wars led to a tremendous increase in the amount of wealth extracted by the state, these policies were anomalous. The wealth tax seems not to have endured in practice, and the monopolies were largely abandoned in the Eastern Han, as were the most burdensome aspects of labor service. The enduring fiscal regime consisted of the land tax, the poll tax, and some forms of labor in the locality, or fees to escape such service. As noted above, these taxes constituted a fairly low percentage of what is described as the average income of a household. The rest of this section tries to explain the rationale for such a "low-tax" regime.

Ideology seems to have played little role. Conventional Chinese histories attribute a low-tax regime in the first half-century of the Han to a supposed minimalist theory of the state that dominated the court's intellectual life under the rubric of "Huang-Lao." Apart from the tenuous textual base indicating the existence, influence, and contents of such an intellectual tradition, this account in no way fits the actual history. As noted above, the Han was a relatively low-tax regime throughout its four centuries, with the exception of the heavy burdens imposed by Emperor Wu. While the dominant ideology of the court supposedly shifted from Huang-Lao to Confucianism, the tax regime remained consistent. In fact, in spite of the myth of an early low-tax period, the rate of land tax declined over the course of the dynasty, and the capitation tax remained fairly constant. The Chinese idea of an early era marked by notably low taxes because of a Huang-Lao ideology stems entirely from Sima Qian's history. This history was written under Emperor Wu, however, who was the veiled target of its

[6] Barbieri-Low (2007: ch. 6); Lewis (2007: 248–52); Sellin (1976).

most scathing critiques. Sima Qian died during Emperor Wu's reign, and thus his idea of a low-tax regime being supplanted by a high-tax one resulted from his truncated perspective. Over the full sweep of the Han, the low-tax regime endured through all ideological shifts in the court and society.

Given the fact that ideological changes explain nothing, what factors account for the enduring low-tax regime? First, political unification left Han China facing no peer states. As several writers in this volume have noted in comparable cases, this meant that preparations for and the conduct of war, with its extraordinary fiscal demands, were not necessary. While we have no way of contrasting Han taxation rates with earlier ones, the size of Warring States and Qin armies necessitated a vastly greater levy of labor/military service, and the cost of weapons, walls, and so forth certainly entailed higher levies. The tremendous temporary increase in taxation to pay for Emperor Wu's campaigns, and the subsequent resumption of a low-tax regime when the expeditions ceased, support this hypothesis.

Moreover, several Han observers cited excessive exactions as a major reason for the rapid collapse of the Qin Empire.[7] The speed and violence of this collapse after centuries of Qin victories and expansion evoked general wonder and perplexity, so the dangers of levying high taxes and labor service, particularly in a world in which continuous warfare was no longer necessary, were widely acknowledged among the Han elite.

A third factor, especially in the early decades of the dynasty, was the relative weakness and instability of the regime. The fall of Qin cast a shadow over the very idea of a united empire – itself a recent innovation. Many called for restoring a multi-state system, which had endured for centuries, or reviving the Zhou practice of dividing the state into fiefs – a practice that had preserved the Zhou monarchy for more than a millennium. The Han ruling house was also weakened by its humble origins as middling landowners who had served in only low official posts. The decisions to locate their capital in the secure geographic confines of the old Qin state, although they came from the southern state of Chu, and to establish fiefs over the rest of the empire indicate the insecurity of the initial position of the Han ruling house. Although the defeat of the feudatories in 154 BC had considerably strengthened the Han Dynasty by the time that Emperor Wu ascended the throne, the social strains and fiscal bankruptcy brought about by his expeditions once again called into disrepute the idea of an aggressive fiscal policy in the service of warfare.

[7] For a list and evaluation of early and recent explanations of the Qin collapse, see Bodde (1986: 85–90).

A fourth explanation is that, in terms of the resources of peasant households, the so-called "low-tax" regime was actually set at the limits of what was bearable, and perhaps beyond those limits. This was elaborated in a memorial by Chao Cuo submitted in 178 BC[8] After conventional arguments that agriculture was the basis of all wealth, and that sufficient clothes and food for the common people were essential to maintain social order, Chao then described the life and financial circumstances of a typical household of five. He posited an average harvest of 100 piculs, traced all the labor involved in producing this, sketched the expenses faced by such a household, and noted the impact of the state's fiscal demands. Apart from subsistence, the family had to pay for sociability with acquaintances, religious needs, and possibly caring for sick or orphaned neighbors. Moreover, they faced the threat of floods or droughts, and irregular taxes were sometimes imposed at short notice that required the sale of grain or cloth at reduced prices. While bumper harvests might occur, although Chao does not mention the possibility, these would be of limited benefit since the price of grain would be reduced, meaning that more would have to be sold to pay the poll tax and other expenses. Disasters, on the other hand, would require the borrowing of money, and the high interest rates charged in the period meant that it was nearly impossible for such people to escape from debt. Instead, they would inexorably fall deeper into debt, lose their land, and be reduced to the status of sharecroppers.

Chao Cuo's analysis is supported by figures found in archaeologically recovered government documents for monthly grain rations for garrison soldiers, their families, convict men, and convict women. While the figures vary, they indicate that a man would consume somewhat over three piculs per month, a woman about two and a half, a child one and a half, and an infant about one.[9] These figures indicate that, for a typical family of four or five people, the average annual harvest posited by Chao Cuo (and routinely given elsewhere as a notional figure) would just meet the consumption needs of the family. They might have eaten less than soldiers or convicts, and could have supplemented grain with vegetables or with food purchased with cloth produced by the female members of the household. (Chao suggests that the average peasant needed only one new set of coarse clothing per year, so producing surplus cloth would have been possible.) Nevertheless, a 10 percent tax in such a situation, which would not include

[8] This is translated by Hsu (1980: 160–3).

[9] For figures regarding soldiers and their families, see Loewe (1967: 93–5). On convicts, see Barbieri-Low (2007: 236–7).

labor services, would have represented a colossal burden. Any bad harvest, inevitable on occasion, would have spelled disaster. Thus the circumstances of the Han peasant anticipated R. H. Tawney's famous image of the late imperial Chinese peasant as a man standing in water up to his chin, so that the smallest wave would drown him.

Chao Cuo's account and these crude calculations are supported by the history of the Han peasantry. From early in the dynasty, but particularly beginning with the reign of Emperor Wu and carrying on until the end, authors note that more and more peasants were losing their land. This was bought up by wealthy families, who kept the farmers as sharecroppers, paying a third – or even a half – of their harvest as rent. Although these figures are highly polemical, it is possible that, if the sharecroppers escaped state registration and the demands of the local government, they might have been able to pay a larger fixed percentage of their harvest to the landlord.[10] It is also likely that the rent, unlike the land tax, was based on actual harvest and not just size of holdings multiplied by a notional yield. In any case, the incontrovertible evidence of the ruin of a significant percentage of the Han peasantry, in spite of repeated government attempts to protect small peasants and limit wealthy families' landholdings, supports Chao Cuo's account of the straitened circumstances of the Han farmers and their inability to pay higher taxes.[11]

A fifth factor militating against more aggressive taxation was the government's distrust of local administrators. Throughout imperial Chinese history the court suspected the loyalties of local officials, who all too easily identified their interests with the regions that they regulated. This led to the policies of dividing local administrations into small units and of depriving these administrations of sufficient income to threaten the court, which often meant lacking the income to perform even their assigned functions. This problem was greater still in the early empires, which inherited what for centuries had been a multi-state world and where, consequently, loyalties to regions (which had been states) often surpassed those to a newly founded empire.[12] The cache of Qin legal documents discovered at Yunmeng clearly shows that even prior to the foundation of the empire, when Qin was still only one state among several, the central court was far more concerned with guarding against its own officials than against the peasant masses.[13] The importance of this issue in Chinese

[10] The drop of about one-quarter in the number of registered households and people in the eastern Han probably reflects the non-registration of most tenants; see Nishijima (1986: 596).

[11] On these government policies, see Hsu (1980: ch. 1). [12] Lewis (2006: ch. 4; 2007: ch. 1).

[13] Lewis (1999: 21–8).

history demonstrates once again that fiscal regimes are defined not only by the issue of extraction but also by the distribution of wealth between those participating in tax collection.[14]

Given the state's inability to guarantee the loyalty of its local administrators, any increase in taxation would have enriched potential rebels. All taxes passed through the hands of local administrators in the first instance, and most grain and cash collected stayed at the local level, just as peasants' labor services were largely concentrated in their own localities. The amounts passed up to the court would in part have depended on reported population, and would have been modified to allow for cases of local flood or famine. All this gave local administrators some leeway in how much income they sent to the court, and how much remained at the local level. As is discussed below, the court relied primarily on the produce of its own Guanzhong region, so there was little advantage in pressing officials to gather more taxes throughout the empire. The worry over loyalty, in this case the loyalty of the peasants, was decisive in the abolition of universal military service. This clearly shows that the court sometimes chose to limit the resources that it extracted because it doubted its ability to control their use.[15]

A related problem that might have led the central court to extract as few taxes as possible was the fact that many of the people who were buying up the lands of ruined peasants, and thereby reducing the fiscal foundation of the Han state, were Han local officials. Even as many powerful families who had dominated local society under the late Warring States and the first decades of the empire were being destroyed by Emperor Wu's policies, many officials were securing their long-term futures by buying land. While salaries and "gifts" that officials received produced a windfall, such income often lasted only for a few years. The most secure form of turning this into permanent income was to buy up land, particularly when Emperor Wu's wealth tax placed a heavy burden on money invested in trade or usury. While many merchants also bought up land, both as an investment and to secure a lower tax rate, the surviving records suggest that most emergent landlords in this period were officials.[16]

By the late first century AD this process had created a new form of elite in which great families combined office-holding (secured through recommendations), substantial landholdings (dispersed among kin and sharecroppers), and trade or moneylending.[17] While these families were still ideologically and financially tied to the Han, from the second quarter of

[14] Beik (1985: ch. 11); Sandberg (2010: 240–51). [15] Lewis (2000: 40–2). [16] Yu (1956).
[17] Yang (1972).

the second century AD many were increasingly alienated from a court dominated by imperial affines and eunuchs. The triangular battle among these parties constituted the political history of the last half-century of Han rule. This hostility between the court and the elite it had helped to create, along with the diminished tax base produced by the elite's ability to remove its tenants from the population registers, were key features in the collapse of the Han Dynasty.

This tension between the central court and local powers also probably explains another feature of the early imperial tax regime: the relative failure to extract tax income from the urban population and from mercantile wealth. This could in part be explained as a result of the path-dependent formation of institutions. As noted earlier, the Warring States and the empires in which they culminated were based on using wealth and services extracted from the peasant population to defeat a city-based nobility. The institutions thus created relied on the taxes and service of peasants, while ignoring the cities. (I might note here that, for this reason, the passage cited at the beginning of Bang's contribution, Chapter 18, could not have been written by an early Confucian literatus. The invocation of the cities as witnesses and as sources of income is alien to Qin/Han China.) Institutional inertia was furthered by the fact that urban wealth in cash and manufactured products was highly mobile, and thus far harder to track and assess than was land.

This would not explain why for centuries no dynasty extracted substantial income from the cities, however. It particularly would not explain why, as noted by Deng, after the late Tang, Song, and Yuan states had relied on extracting higher taxes from the cities and the urban population, the subsequent Ming and Qing Dynasties reverted to the older pattern of relying primarily on a land tax. I would argue that cities represented the most extreme form of the dangers posed by local governments. Any local administrator who could mobilize a city's large concentrations of population and wealth would have posed a major threat to the court. Whereas large regions or provinces were made controllable through division into small administrative units, cities were less liable to such treatment. Nevertheless, the Ming and Qing practice of dividing major urban agglomerations between several counties to keep them administratively weak suggests that the problem of cities was like that of the regions. Any extraction of substantial taxes from the merchant wealth in cities would have been a bonanza for local administrators, who would therefore become far more powerful than the court desired.

It is also worth noting that in Ming and Qing China the tension between the court and the urban sector was particularly great because of the geographic structure of the late imperial state. The capital was located in Beijing, in the far northeast, for strategic and military reasons, while all the greatest cities – which together formed the demographic, economic, and cultural center of China – were in the south, particularly in the Yangzi delta. This radical divergence of the political and economic centers, made possible first by the Grand Canal and later by sea shipments, produced a situation in which the political center was so far from the greatest centers of wealth and talent that Qing emperors (notably Kangxi and Qianlong) made expeditions to the south with much of their court in order to assert the unity of their realm. While the lower Yangzi may have been almost on a par with the more advanced regions of western Europe in the eighteenth century, China's division between the political and economic centers meant that such wealth was more a threat than a resource for a suspicious court, and that the court did little to further the economic development of the south.[18] The problems created by this geographic structure thus support Stasavage's contribution (Chapter 17) arguing for the critical importance of the unification of economic resources and political control in early modern city states.

This issue of the economic relations of the capital to the empire leads to the third feature of the early fiscal regime: its tight spatial circumscription. Between 85 and 90 percent of the registered Han population lived in the drainage basin of the Yellow River, but the seasonal character of this river's flow made water transport along its length quite difficult. Consequently, although the flood basin of the Yellow River in the east was the most productive and populous region, the capital, at Chang'an, was provisioned largely from its own poorer hinterland in Guanzhong (primarily the modern province of Shaanxi and northern Shanxi). I will now sketch the evidence for this highly regional character of the Han court's resource base.

For the first half-century of Han rule the court directly administered and extracted income only from Guanzhong, Sichuan, and the area immediately along the Yellow River as far as Sichuan. Horses could not be exported from the capital region, people moving in and out required special passports, and those born outside the capital region could not obtain appointments at court. After the defeat of the feudatories in 154 BC and their suppression under Emperor Wu, the court first attempted to build canals to facilitate the shipment of grain from the eastern Yellow River valley and the Fen River valley. Shipments proved difficult, however, and the court

[18] This issue, without any focus on the divergent political center, is discussed by Pomeranz (2000), and in the literature inspired by his book.

sponsored several major irrigation projects to improve the productivity of its own region. By contrast, only a single irrigation project was built elsewhere, and a major break in the dyke in the eastern flood plain was ignored for years while work proceeded on irrigation in the capital region. Moreover, leading families from throughout the empire were forcibly resettled in a row of suburban cities adjacent to the capital, and these cities became the major source for recruiting officials.[19]

When the Han Dynasty was restored after the overthrow of Wang Mang, in AD 25, the capital was moved east to Luoyang, where the flood plain abutted the loess highlands. The capital was moved both because the dynasty had been restored by a coalition of landlords with estates and local bases in the east, and because the city was much easier to provision from the more productive eastern regions. Furthermore, the city had been the capital under the Eastern Zhou, and escaped the taint of Qin and its military traditions.

Shifting the capital transformed the distribution of public works. Irrigation works and transport canals around the old capital were allowed to fall into disrepair, while those nearer to Luoyang were repaired and expanded. Surrendered barbarian tribes were resettled in the old capital region, and during the Qiang rebellions in the first half of the second century AD a significant party at court even advocated abandoning Guanzhong.[20] Although there was a brief attempt under the Western Han to supplement the provisioning of the capital with grain, timber, and other goods shipped from a distance, in the second half of the dynasty this was abandoned, restoring the principle that the capital should rely economically on its own regional hinterland.

This practice of regionally provisioning the capital also encouraged the policies described above of minimizing taxes on peasants and eschewing them in the cities in order to sharply restrict the income that passed through the hands of local officials. Since the court did not significantly depend on income derived from most of the empire, it had no interest in maximizing taxes but, instead, reduced them so as to keep significant wealth out of the hands of potential rivals. This distinction between the capital and the rest of the empire found administrative expression in the aforementioned division between the Lesser Treasury and the Ministry of Agriculture. While the latter – which depended on taxes – paid for official salaries, public works, and the military, the former – which derived its

[19] See Lewis (2009b: 8–9), Chi (1936: 79–88), Shi (1996: ch. 5), and Lewis (2006: 178–9).

[20] Chi (1936: 89–95); Lewis (2000: 67–9).

income from the emperor's monopoly of natural resources, his personal estates and hunting parks (which contained many workshops for craft production), the income from minting coins, and (for unknown reasons) the capitation tax on children – provisioned the court.

To summarize the key points of the fiscal regime of the early empires: it was largely based on extracting a light tax load distributed across the maximum number of individuals, primarily peasants. In addition to trying to preserve the greatest number of free peasant households, the low-tax regime sought to minimize the wealth that flowed into the hands of local officials whose loyalties were uncertain. This same principle led the state, except during Emperor Wu's fabulously expensive military expeditions, to avoid tapping the mercantile wealth of the cities, which, once again, would have excessively empowered local administrators. This policy of reducing the income of local administrative offices (income that largely met local needs) was facilitated by the practice of provisioning the imperial capital from its own hinterland. While this policy was also attributable to the difficulty of moving bulk commodities across great distances, it facilitated an enduring policy of strengthening the imperial center not by maximizing the wealth transferred there but by keeping all potential local rivals, primarily the state's own officials, so weak that the modest powers that the court gathered for itself could still overawe them.

A final feature, in this case a negative one, that recurred in later periods was that the chief intra-elite rivalry for resources of the kind discussed by Goldstone was between the state and its officials.[21] The rivalry resulted not from officials' resistance to the imperial center but, rather, from their attempt to secure their own economic futures. Facing frequently brief but highly lucrative careers that had to be translated into enduring wealth, most officials opted for secure and prestigious investments in land. Since wealth was divided among sons, however, landholdings broke up within a couple of generations, and consequently required more purchases made possible by further state service. This constant purchase of lands reduced the number of free peasants and, consequently, the state's tax income. Thus the state expended much of its income on salaries, which were then turned into land purchases that constantly reduced that income. Peasants could provide taxes to the state or rent to a landlord, but they could not in the long run afford to do both. And, as the rents gradually drained off the taxes, a direction determined by the superior local knowledge and influence of the landlords, the Han state and many that followed it were

[21] Goldstone (1991: ch. 1).

gradually starved of the wealth that they needed to survive. This rivalry for the small surpluses produced by millions of peasant households meant that the state's officials, however loyal they might have been in service, were repeatedly the executioners of the regimes that they served.

The Northern and Southern Dynasties

This rubric identifies the four centuries after the fall of the Han, when no single dynastic house was able to unite the territory of the early empires. In the third century it was divided into the so-called Three Kingdoms. In the next century the north (the Yellow River valley) was a chaos of short-lived regimes (largely ruled by nomadic tribesmen) while the south (the Yangzi valley) was under a weak imperial court dominated by powerful landlord families. Finally, in the fifth and sixth centuries the north and the south were each united under dynasties founded by military men.

On paper, the fiscal regimes of these short-lived states continued many Han practices, relying on a land tax, labor services, and secondary levies on trade.[22] There were significant changes, however. First, cash largely disappeared, so the capitation tax measured and paid in cash was replaced by a household tax paid in cloth. The reasons for the disappearance of cash are uncertain, but it seems to have been primarily a result of the absence of a strong government that controlled the quality of coins and guaranteed their value. Some scholars have speculated that the rise of Buddhism and the consequent frenzy for casting statues of divinities led to a shortage of metal. A temporary revival of a cash economy in the lower and middle Yangzi regions in the first half of the sixth century AD, a period marked by a fluorescence of Buddhism and image worship, suggests that the question of political authority was more significant, however.[23] Nevertheless, the inability of the state to produce enough cash after the long-term reunification of China under the Tang Dynasty suggests that a shortage of metal was also an issue.

The single greatest change was that, because the states were unable reimpose an effective administration, they increasingly relied on the direct ownership of land worked by a servile population. State-owned land had been a minor feature of the Han fiscal regime, when small quantities of land belonging to local administrations provided grain and cloth. As states lost administrative control of much agricultural land, however – on

[22] Sun (2003: 104–35; 1988: 57–77; 1996: 50–76); Ministry of Finance (1991: 132–246).
[23] Lewis (2009a: 116–17).

account of military weakness, opposition by powerful families, or the abandonment of land by peasants fleeing war and floods – they had to supplement taxes and labor service through owning land worked by state tenants. The earliest forms of this were military and agricultural colonies in the north in the third century, where soldiers and peasant refugees were settled on abandoned land. While these colonies were gradually broken up and absorbed back into the general population, all attempts to reassert state power until the eighth century entailed direct state ownership of land, often worked by servile tenants.[24] The imperial state thus survived only in a seriously reduced form through becoming, in effect, the greatest landlord with the biggest army in a world of powerful landlords with private armies.

A second change was the reliance of several states in the north on the simple pillage of the peasant population. These states, founded by non-Chinese tribesmen primarily in the fourth century, often attempted to set up an administration run by surrendered Chinese, but in practice banditry remained the leading form of securing wealth. Needless to say, such states did not last more than a generation or two, but they represent an element in state formation that figures in many parts of the world. They also confirm that rulers sometimes are, as Olson describes them, merely bandits who have become stationary (which is simply a variation of Augustine's definition of states as bandit gangs acting with justice).[25]

A third change in this period relates to the practice of provisioning capitals from their own hinterlands. After the fragmentation of the Han Empire, many states ruled only one physiographic region (an area demarcated by surrounding highlands and united by a central river valley). Consequently, the areas from which capitals could extract wealth were even more restricted. Many rulers in the north resorted to the forcible resettlement of large numbers of people within or immediately around their capitals. This is best documented for the Northern Wei capitals of Pingcheng and Luoyang, which were filled with populations moved from elsewhere, while peasants and pastoralists were resettled around them. Even the military population of this dynasty (and the subsequent Sui and Tang Dynasties) was settled around the capital.[26]

A final change in these centuries was a new form of the intra-elite rivalries sketched at the end of the preceding section. While the problem of allocating between taxes and rents remained central, and the power of

[24] Ibid.: ch. 2; Crowell (1979). [25] Olson (1993; 2000); Passerin d'Entrêves (1969: 28–9).

[26] Lewis (2009a: 114–15); Jenner (1981: 19–37, 103–26); Han (1964: part 2, ch. 4); Miyakawa (1964: ch. 8).

local landlord families limited the state's ability to extract resources from the peasantry, the question of allocating military service between powerful families and the state also came to the fore. Throughout this period many powerful families raised private armies and constructed forts with which they could protect their followers, sometimes several villages, from all but the largest attack. At the same time the servile military populations associated with military colonies, as well as later soldiery drawn from tribesmen in the north and refugees in the south, proved essential to any attempt to establish a state or empire. The ability to command the service of such populations allowed a partial revival of imperial power by new dynasties in the north and the south in the fifth century, and ultimately facilitated the reunification of China under the Sui and Tang Dynasties.[27]

The restored empire: Sui and Tang

The fiscal regime of the Sui and the first century and a half of the Tang continued the pattern of the preceding centuries: state-owned lands, labor services, and a household cloth tax. The system of state-owned land, the "equal-field system," was the last and the best-known form in Chinese history of direct state control of land. It was probably practiced only in north China, which at this time represented between 60 and 65 percent of the population. Under the equal-field system each married couple received a grant of land from the state for the period of their working lives. In some regions additional land could be given for adult males in the family, slaves, or even flocks. When the couple was no longer liable for taxes or labor service, the land was returned to the state. Additional land, in theory for the growth of mulberry trees for silk, was given in perpetuity, since such trees required decades of cultivation to be productive. Such permanent "mulberry land" provided a rubric under which influential families accumulated ever-larger holdings.

In return for land grants, households paid taxes in grain and cloth, and performed labor service. These levies were standardized for all households, which in theory held equal land, and did not reflect actual ability to pay. In distant regions distinctive local commodities were substituted for more conventional payments, and it was not uncommon to transform grain payments into cloth, for ease in shipping and preservation. The labor service was gradually replaced by a payment to hire substitute labor. In the early Tang the state also introduced taxes based on rating households

[27] Lewis (2009a: ch. 2).

into nine categories on the basis of wealth, but these remained minor adjuncts to the system.[28]

The Tang state also continued to levy the standard taxes on merchants. First, as in earlier times merchants had to pay a fee to engage in trade in the official markets. While in theory no trade was allowed outside these markets, in practice businesses developed in the residential wards of major cities, and these may have avoided taxes. Second, control stations were placed along the imperial road system. Merchants passing through these stations paid a tax on the assessed value of their goods. These remained minor taxes, however.

This fiscal regime lasted, with modifications, until the An Lushan Rebellion (755–763) nearly destroyed the empire and led to many major changes. Politically, the Tang court lost control of most of the northeast to semi-independent military governors, who collected their own taxes and paid a negotiated share to the court. The court also lost much land in the northwest to Tibet. The loss of much of the north, where the equal-field system had functioned, and the destruction of land records meant that this taxation system, already declining because of the rise of large estates, ceased to function. It was replaced by new institutions, which marked the fiscal transition to later imperial China.

The most important change was the promulgation of the "two-tax system" in AD 780. This marked the final abandonment of the idea that China's countryside was composed of roughly identical peasant households that should owe roughly identical taxes. It also adopted the principle that all households in China, without distinction between rural and urban, should participate in a single tax system. The two-tax system combined the taxes based on ratings of household wealth – taxes whose importance had been growing over the decades – so that all households were ranked on the size and quality of their landholdings, as well as any other forms of wealth. The total tax burden was divided into two payments (hence "two-tax"), one in the summer after harvesting the winter wheat, and the other in the fall after the millet harvest (or rice in the south). The tax was measured in cash, but largely paid in cloth or grain. All other taxes, which had accumulated in confusing variants in different parts of the empire, were abolished.[29]

This reform had several important ramifications. The most significant was the abandonment of any idea of a "standard" peasant household paying a standard tax burden. Instead, taxes were levied on wealth,

28 Lewis (2009b: 54–7); Twitchett (1970: 1–11; 1959a; 1959b).
29 Lewis (2009b: 80–1); Twitchett (1970: 39–46).

which meant that the fiscal regime would adapt to major discrepancies in landholding. The assessment in cash became significant, but only when standardized cash became more readily available and fiduciary currency was introduced. (Early forms of fiduciary currency appeared in the late Tang, but they were not widespread.)[30] A final major feature was that the central court simply imposed quotas for taxes on local administrations (both those it controlled and those under the semi-independent generals). Local authorities set taxes at whatever rate – and collected them in whatever form – allowed them to meet the quota. This abandonment of a standard empire-wide rate and the recognition of clear regional variations marked an important development in Chinese fiscal practices.

The late Tang fiscal regime also made significant changes in levies on markets and trade. The regulated markets that had characterized the early imperial period largely broke down in the eighth and ninth centuries, with shops appearing throughout the city. At the same time the southward shift of the demographic and economic center of the empire greatly increased the amount of long-distance trade along the waterways, including bulk commodities such as grain and timber. Numerous cities in the lower Yangzi region (such as Jingkou, Suzhou, Hangzhou, and Nanjing), at key junctures on the Grand Canal (Jiangdu and Bianfeng), and in Sichuan (Chengdu) developed into huge commercial entrepôts where tens of thousands of ships moved goods from all over the empire. At the same time periodic markets emerged at key transit points in the countryside, and they soon developed into permanent commercial settlements. This huge expansion in trade meant that taxes on goods in transit became much more significant.[31] In association with the taxation of urban wealth under the two-tax system, mercantile wealth for the first time became a significant element of state finance, especially in the south. This culminated in the tremendous expansion of taxation under the Song described by Deng.

Another development was the reestablishment of the salt monopoly as a major source of income. With income from the north greatly reduced after the An Lushan Rebellion, the court depended heavily on the south, where salt became a major source of state wealth. The late eighth and ninth centuries witnessed a regional division of the fiscal administration, with income in the north being largely handled by the Public Revenue Department, which controlled the two-tax system, and that in the south

30 Lewis (2009b: 118–20); Twitchett (1970: ch. 4).

31 Lewis (2009b: 113–18); Twitchett (1966); Kiang (1999).

under the control of the Salt and Iron Commission, which handled the monopolies and transit taxes. Indeed, the commission extended its remit to income from minting, mining, and taxation on the newly booming tea trade. For a few decades at the end of the eighth century the salt commissioners also assumed concurrent posts as civil administrators over the wealthy provinces of the lower Yangzi, leading to the emergence of a shadow state in the south controlled by the empire's leading financial administrators. Only a bungled rebellion in 805 brought an end to this danger.[32] This confirmed the wisdom of avoiding concentrations of wealth in the hands of local or urban administrators.

These developments had at least two major impacts on later Chinese fiscal regimes. First, the Salt and Iron Commission, and to a lesser extent the Public Revenue Department, pioneered fiscal professionalization. All the statesmen who controlled these departments rose through financial posts. Thus, expertise in fiscal matters, rather than in conventional government affairs, became the avenue by which men ascended to the most powerful posts in government. The patterns of professional training and patronage in these departments were reinforced by intermarriages, creating a "fiscal aristocracy" that dominated the Song government in the eleventh century.[33]

Second, for the first time the capital was largely provisioned from long-distance shipments of grain and other bulk materials. The Sui and Tang, for considerations of security, built their capitals just south of Han Chang'an. This region had for centuries suffered major environmental degradation, however, because of deforestation and erosion. Consequently, its ability to supply a court was seriously reduced, while the Tang capital's population grew much larger than that of its Han predecessor. In the seventh century the court moved several times to Luoyang for sustenance, and at the end of the century Empress Wu established Luoyang as her capital. Although policies of resettling Guanzhong allowed the court to move back to Chang'an in the early eighth century, the An Lushan Rebellion left it once again without sufficient supplies from its own region. Only the prior development of agricultural surpluses in the lower Yangzi, the existence of the Grand Canal, and the administrative skill of the Salt and Iron Commission allowed sufficient resources to be extracted from the southeast and shipped to the capital. This geopolitical structure, with a wealthy but demilitarized south

32 Lewis (2009b: 81–2); Twitchett (1970: chs. 3 & 6; 1954).

33 Lewis (2009b: 82–3); Hartwell (1971).

sustaining a capital located in the north for strategic reasons, set the pattern for later imperial China. The only difference was that subsequent courts were located in the northeast rather than the northwest.[34]

Conclusions

The chief characteristic of the fiscal regimes of both early and late imperial China was the attempt to distribute a relatively light tax burden across the greatest number of peasant households. This policy reflected the fact that the peasants were too poor to bear a heavier burden. Greater exactions would ruin the peasants and thus reduce the tax base. The commitment to a low-tax regime also grew out of the imperial center's suspicion of local officials, which led the court to try to keep administrators weak by severely limiting the resources at their disposal.

Another feature of the early imperial fiscal regime was its commitment to the ideal that rural society consisted of "normal" households that were roughly comparable in their wealth and labor resources. Taxes, whether levied on individuals or on the household, were based on this idea of rough equality and made little effort to reflect the differential wealth of households. This idea was abandoned with the introduction of the two-tax system in AD 780, and never figured in the later imperial dynasties

Levies in this period were collected in the form of grain, cash, cloth, and labor. Cash was significant only under the Han Dynasty; in subsequent periods the shortage of cash resulted in reliance on taxes in kind. Although labor services existed throughout the period, they were frequently commuted by payment of a tax that allowed the hiring of substitute labor. These practices continued into the later dynasties, with cash reappearing as a major form of payment.

The period was also marked by the fact that the imperial capital, like all cities, was routinely provisioned from its own hinterland. Taxes primarily provided income for use at the local level, with only a limited amount of cash and goods being shipped to the court. This reflects the inadequacy of water transport, which meant that bulk materials could not efficiently be transferred to the capital. It meant that in reality there were a number of regional fiscal systems, greatly resembling the old Warring States, and that the encompassing imperial structure did not create an empire-wide financial system. The emergence of the lower Yangzi in the late Tang as the

[34] Lewis (2009b: 10–13); Elvin (2004: 12–26); Shi (1998: 63–87, 104–6, 111–30, 318; 1996: 277–85, 439–43, 537–40).

economic and demographic center of the empire, along with the Grand Canal at the center of a network of waterways, made possible the formation of the first imperial structure in which the capital was provisioned through long-distance shipments. This created the first true empire-wide economic and fiscal systems in which certain areas produced wealth that provisioned the strategic and political centers. This pattern defined the late-imperial political order with its political capital at Beijing and its economic, demographic, and cultural center in the lower Yangzi.

The early imperial fiscal regime also failed to extract significant income from trade, wealthy merchants, and the urban population. This was in part a result of the difficulty of measuring the highly fungible and mobile wealth held by such people. It was also because merchants were sufficiently wealthy to buy off the officials who would have been responsible for taxing them, and the fact that many officials' families relied on trade to secure their economic situation. A third reason was that cities constituted the most extreme version of the threat posed by local societies. A vigorous urban tax regime would have produced officials commanding such extraordinary resources that they could challenge the imperial center. The tremendous power of the salt commissioners at the end of the seventh century and early in the eighth was just such a threat.

A final feature of the fiscal regime of the early empires was that the state's own agents invariably came to constitute its chief rivals in the allocation of economic surpluses and labor services. The primary version of the former was the struggle over the distribution of the peasants' small surpluses between taxes for the state and rent for landlords, whose families also relied on income from offices to maintain local bases in the face of the practice of partible inheritance. As for labor services, the greatest tension between the state and its servants was the issue of who would control the military services of the relevant population. Over time, in each dynasty, those who had direct control of the armies evolved into challengers to the imperial court, and in some cases ended by founding their own dynasties.

References

Barbieri-Low, A. J. (2007) *Artisans in Early Imperial China*. Seattle.

Beik, W. (1985) *Absolutism and Society in Seventeenth-Century France: State Power and Provincial Aristocracy in Languedoc*. Cambridge.

Bodde, D. (1986) "The state and empire of Ch'in," in *The Cambridge History of China*, vol. I, *The Ch'in and Han Empires 221 BC – AD 220*, ed. M. Loewe. Cambridge: 20 102.

Chi, C. (1936) *Key Economic Areas in Chinese History as Revealed in the Development of Public Works*. London.
Crowell, W. G. (1979) "Government land policies and systems in early imperial China," PhD dissertation. University of Washington.
Elvin, M. (2004) *The Retreat of the Elephants: An Environmental History of China*. New Haven, CT.
Goldstone, J. A. (1991) *Revolution and Rebellion in the Early Modern World*. Berkeley, CA.
Han, G. (1964) *Nanbeichao jingji shitan*. Shanghai.
Hartwell, R. M. (1971) "Financial expertise, examinations, and the formulation of economic policy in northern Sung China," *Journal of Asian Studies* 30: 281–314.
Hsu, C. (1980) *Han Agriculture: The Formation of Early Chinese Agrarian Economy*. Seattle.
Hulsewé, A. F. P. (1985) "The influence of the 'legalist' government of Qin on the economy as reflected in the texts discovered in Yunmeng County," in *The Scope of State Power in China*, ed. S. R. Schram. London: 211–36.
Jenner, W. F. J. (1981) *Memories of Loyang: Yang Hsüan-chih and the Lost Capital (493–534)*. Oxford.
Katō, S. (1952) *Shina keizaishi kōshō*, vol. I. Tokyo.
Kern, M. (2000) *The Stele Inscriptions of Ch'in Shih-huang*. New Haven, CT.
Kiang, H. C. (1999) *Cities of Aristocrats and Bureaucrats*. Honolulu.
Kiser, E., and Cai, Y. (2003) "War and bureaucratization in Qin China: exploring an anomalous case," *American Sociological Review* 68: 511–39.
Lewis, M. E. (1990) *Sanctioned Violence in Early China*. Albany, NY.
(1999) *Writing and Authority in Early China*. Albany, NY.
(2000) "The Han abolition of universal military service," in *Warfare in Chinese History*, ed. H. van de Ven. Leiden: 33–75.
(2006) *The Construction of Space in Early China*. Albany, NY.
(2007) *The Early Chinese Empires: Qin and Han*. Cambridge, MA.
(2009a) *China between Empires: The Northern and Southern Dynasties*. Cambridge, MA.
(2009b) *China's Cosmopolitan Empire: The Tang Dynasty*. Cambridge, MA.
Loewe, M. (1967) *Records of Han Administration*, vol. I. Cambridge.
Lü, B. (ed.) (2000 [239 BC]) *The Annals of Lü Buwei*, trans. J. Knoblock and J. Riegel. Stanford, CA.
Ma, D. (1983) *Han dai caizheng shi*. Beijing.
Ministry of Finance (1991) *Zhongguo nongmin fudan shi*, vol. I. Beijing.
Miyakawa, H. (1964) *Rikuchō shi kenkyū: seiji shakai hen*. Kyoto.
Nishijima, S. (1986) "The economic and social history of Former Han," in *The Cambridge History of China*, vol. I, *The Ch'in and Han Empires 221 BC – AD 220*, ed. M. Loewe. Cambridge: 545–607.
Olson, M. (1993) "Dictatorship, democracy, and development," *American Political Science Review* 83: 567–76.

(2000) *Power and Prosperity: Outgrowing Communist and Capitalist Dictatorships*. New York.
Passerin d'Entrêves, A. (1969) *La Notion de l'état*. Paris.
Pomeranz, K. (2000) *The Great Divergence: China, Europe, and the Making of the Modern World Economy*. Princeton, NJ.
Sandberg, B. (2010) *Warrior Pursuits: Noble Culture and Civil Conflict in Early Modern France*. Baltimore.
Schwartz, B. (1985) *The World of Thought in Ancient China*. Cambridge, MA.
Sellin, J. T. (1976) *Slavery and the Penal System*. New York.
Shi, N. (1996) *Zhongguo gu du he wenhua*. Beijing.
(1998) *Tang dai lishi dili yanjiu*. Beijing.
Sima, Q. (1961 [109 BC])) "The biographies of the harsh officials," in *Records of the Grand Historian: Han Dynasty*, vol. II, rev. edn, trans. B. Watson. New York: 379–407.
Sun, Y. (ed.) (1988) *Jianming Zhongguo caizheng shi*. Beijing.
(ed.) (1996) *Zhongguo fushui shi*. Beijing.
(ed.) (2003) *Zhongguo caizheng shi*. Beijing.
Twitchett, D. C. (1954) "The salt commissioners after the rebellion of An Lu-shan," *Asia Major* 4: 60–89.
(1959a) "Lands under state cultivation during the T'ang Dynasty," *Journal of the Economic and Social History of the Orient* 2: 162–203.
(1959b) "Lands under state cultivation during the T'ang Dynasty: some central Asian documents concerning military colonies," *Journal of the Economic and Social History of the Orient* 2: 335–6.
(1966) "The T'ang market system," *Asia Major* 12: 202–48.
(1970) *Financial Administration under the T'ang Dynasty*, 2nd edn. Cambridge.
Yang, L. (1972) "Great families of the Eastern Han," in *Chinese Social History: Translations of Selected Studies*, ed. E. Z. Sun and J. DeFrancis. New York: 103–34.
Yu, Y. (1956) "Dong Han zhengquan zhi jianli yu shizu daxing zhi guanxi," *Xinya Xuebao* 1: 209–80.

CHAPTER 10

Imperial China under the Song and late Qing

Kent Gang Deng

China had a long history of being a land-based empire run by well-trained bureaucrats who were selected from the male population of the general public. As a non-feudal society, China adopted a set of values for the maintenance of the empire. The key concept was benevolence: benevolent rule of the state. This had profound implications in how the state should behave, including how to tax the economy and how to finance the government projects. In this context, a Confucian benevolent state aimed to run a small and balanced budget with a light tax burden on the population. Such a state may be called an "anti-fiscal state," because a fiscal state tends to maximize tax revenues. Occasional deviations from the Confucian norm appeared under the Song Period and the late Qing (after 1850), however, when heavy taxes were imposed against all the odds. Both periods were revolutionary in some ways in Chinese history. This chapter explores the causality of the rise of a one-off fiscal state in China.

Views on state governance and capacity

The conventional wisdom on the *raison d'être* of the state is threefold. First, it has the exclusive authority to maintain social order within a territory. Second, it has the exclusive right to shield off external interference. Third, it monopolizes violence and information to ensure social order. All these aspects (or "services") require resources (or "inputs"), and hence taxation.

When one looks at this services/taxation equation, there are three interlinking issues that a society faces: first, the problem of "willingness" to deliver services by the state and to pay taxes by the general public; second, the question of efficiency (quality and quantity per unit of time) in service provision and tax collection; and, third, the matter of a strong (necessarily forceful and intrusive) or weak state (often lethargic and benevolent).

In an ideal world, the exchange between services and taxes should be market-like, with voluntary entry and exit and equal and reciprocal rights. This is the classical and neoclassical view. Unfortunately, few societies have ever behaved this way in human history. The reason is simply that the "traders" in this market are never voluntary or equal. The state power-holder is able to impose taxes unilaterally by force, and remains unpunished – at least in the short run. Of course, there are strategies to constrain the despot, via "exit" or "voice."[1]

Thus, Max Weber had no illusion about the state. For him, state power yields monetary returns (including taxes) for the power-holders.[2] This is also the reason why thinkers such as Douglass North, Mancur Olson, Stephen Haggard and R. R. Kaufman view the state as a predator or bandit: it robs society without providing it proportionately with services.[3] Charles Tilly simply calls state-building an "organized crime."[4]

Even so, a fiscal state becomes a necessary condition when a society wishes to make changes. Gerschenkronism and Neo-Gerschenkronism intentionally downplay the importance of the market; they maintain that the state is able to substitute for the market.[5]

European perceptions of China and governance in China

Political theories and debate on polities and state formation aside, so far as can be ascertained, two opposite views on society and governance in traditional China have been in circulation – views that can be crudely labeled as "Sinophile" and "Sinophobe". What separates them is the view of how China is seen to be ruled.

The Sinophile view was the mainstream one for a long time after a series occasional contacts between the two civilizations at the opposite ends of Eurasia. Much credit should go to legendary individuals such as Marco Polo (1254–1324).[6] The most prominent Sinophile messengers were Jesuits in the seventeenth and early eighteenth centuries. Many eventually ended in Beijing (see Table 10.1). In the capital city, Jesuits mingled with the *crème de la crème* of the empire. Some, such as von Bell, Verbiest, Bouvet, and Gerbillon, became close to Emperor Kangxi (who reigned from 1662 to 1722). Some obtained official appointments and ranks. Castiglione

[1] For a good review, see Rosenthal and Wong (2011: 186–96). [2] Gerth and Mills (1946: 117–28).
[3] North (1990: 140); Olson (2000); see also Haggard and Kaufman (1992: 139–81).
[4] See Evans, Rueschemeyer, and Skocpol (1985: 169–91).
[5] Gerschenkron (1962); Amsden (1989: 139–55); Alam (1989); Wade (1990). [6] Wright (1968).

Table 10.1 *Jesuits working in China, seventeenth and eighteenth centuries*

Name	Date of entry into China
Matteo Ricci (1552–1610)	1582 (Macao), 1601 (Beijing)
Nicolas Longobardi (1565–1655)	1597 (Macao), 1609 (Beijing)
Diego de Pantoja (1571–1618)	1599 (Macao), 1601 (Beijing)
Giulio Aleni (1582–1649)	1610 (Macao), 1613 (Beijing)
Sabbatino de Ursis (1575–1620)	1606 (–)
Johannes Schreck (1576–1630)	1619 (Macao), 1623 (Beijing)
Johann Adam Schall von Bell (1592–1666)	1620 (Macao), 1623 (Beijing)
Jacques Rho (1593–1638)	1622 (–), 1630 (Beijing)
Ferdinand Verbiest (1623–88)	1658 (Macao), 1660 (Beijing)
Domingo Navarette (1618–86)	1658 (Macao)
Philippus Maria Grimaldi (1639–1712)	1659 (Macao), 1671 (Beijing)
Thoma Pereira (1645–1708)	1672 (Macao), 1673 (Beijing)
Jean Francois Gerbillon (1654–1707)	1687 (–), 1688 (Beijing)
Bernard-Kiliam Stumpf (1655–1720)	1695 (Beijing)
Joachim Bouvet (1656–1730)	1687 (Ningbo), 1688 (Beijing)
Ignatius Koegler (1680–1747)	1716 (Macao), 1717 (Beijing)
Joseph Giuseppe Castiglione (1688–1766)	1715 (Beijing)
Andre Pereira (1690–1743)	1716 (Beijing)
Augustin de Hallerstein (1721–74)	1738 (Beijing)

achieved the Third Rank, while von Bell climbed to the First Rank Proper (*zheng yipin*), at the very top of the bureaucratic ladder.

On China's side, although the elite oozed confidence (in Ricci's phrase, "The Chinese believe that they themselves are the only people to possess real sciences and technology"),[7] they showed huge interest in and great tolerance toward Jesuits, with the notions of "complement Confucianism with Christian learning" (*tianxue bu ru*) and "Chinese knowledge as the foundation and Western knowledge for utility" (*zhongxue we ti, xixue wei yong*). For the record, three Ming government ministers were converted to Catholicism in 1610.[8] Many European books were translated into Chinese, and European scientific tools and devices were copied.[9]

As a result, these individuals saw China only in the best light possible at the time. Meanwhile, cultural assimilation began. Ricci proudly called himself a "Western Confucian" (*xi ru*) in order to identify himself with the Chinese code of conduct.[10] Early Jesuits all learned and mastered the

[7] Ricci (1983 [1610]: 94).
[8] They were later called the "Three Pillars of the Catholic Church in China" (*tianzhujiao san zhushi*).
[9] At least 120 such titles were produced: Hou (1960: 1254).
[10] See Xu (2000: 90) and Brockey (2007).

Chinese language and customs. Chinese law was observed by most foreigners.[11] The Europeans needed to be sinicized and to ingratiate themselves with the Confucian elite if they wanted to get anywhere in China.

In this top-down context, the seventeenth century was an era of Sinophilia, represented by the thoughts of Voltaire (1694–1778) and François Quesnay (1696–1774), who were well informed about China's "despotism" but hitherto viewed China, especially its institutions and governance, overwhelmingly positively.[12] In the scientific field there was Gottfried Leibniz (1646–1716), who kept direct contact with Jesuits in China and drew inspiration from Chinese culture and practices. On a societal level, Sinophilia was responsible for the fad of *chinoiserie* in Europe. To the European elite, China meant good taste and good life. Institutionally, however, this phase ended in 1775 when the Pope suspended Jesuit missionaries to China.

In contrast to this shared good life with the Mandarins, another group of Europeans saw a different China, at the grass-roots level. Once commercial links with the empire had increased and strengthened, foreign traders frequently contacted and dealt with Chinese merchants who did not command a high social status legally. There is little surprise that the imperial court did not treat European traders the same way it did Jesuits; this is illustrated by the most cited episode of China's arrogance, shown by Emperor Qianlong's letter of 1793 to the British king, George III, to the effect that the Celestial Dynasty of the Qing was so productive that it relied on no goods from the Western countries.[13] No one seemed to dispute Qianlong's conclusion at the time. Even so, China's hostility toward foreign trade planted the seed of Sinophobia. In a nutshell, it was not China that changed, but European perceptions.

This coincided with the European Age of Enlightenment in the eighteenth century. Thinkers such as Montesquieu (1689–1755), a contemporary of Quesnay, began to play the dichotomy of republicanism versus despotism, democracy versus dictatorship.[14] David Hume (1711–76) followed suit, advocating freedom and democracy. Adam Smith (1723–90) was among the first group of European thinkers to acknowledge China's wealth and laissez-faire economic structure, but he also questioned the Chinese

[11] The Portuguese were very impressed by fair trial in the Chinese court: Boxer (1953: xxix). The Ming state created an incentive by treating the Portuguese differently from other Europeans so long as the Portuguese were "well behaved" by Chinese standards: Morse (1926: 29, 47); see also (Schurz 1938: ch. 3).

[12] See Voltaire (1990 [1756]), Quesnay (1767), Maverick (1946), and Hobson (2004).

[13] Anon. (1964b [1799]: vol. 1435, 15). [14] Lai (2009).

labour-intensive model of the economy.[15] Gradually, the center of gravity of desirable polities shifted inward to Europe in the hands of Georg Hegel (1770–1831), who asserted explicitly that the Prussian state system was superior and God-chosen.[16] Thus began modern political Eurocentricism, and a string of followers lined up behind Hegel. Some launched frontal attacks on China. Karl Marx (1818–83), who never visited Asia, was self-assured enough to write disparagingly, though falsely, about an "Asiatic mode of production." Karl Wittfogel took up the baton, and went even further with his hypothesis of "Oriental despotism."[17] With little supporting evidence from the history of China since about 1000 CE (apart from the short-lived and brutal Mongol Yuan), these two hypotheses had no historical bearing on China at all. Unlike Marx and Wittfogel's falsifications, the hypothesis of Max Weber (1864–1920) was based on some serious research into Asians' thinking. In contrast to the "Protestant ethic," which led directly to capitalist triumph, Weber was however pessimistic about any positive impact from Confucianism and Taoism on modern growth.[18] These thinkers all embodied the trend to stigmatize traditional China. The murderous totalitarianism of Mao Zedong, which was imported from the Soviet Union, did not help China's historical image.

It was only from 1954 onward that a different voice was found, in Joseph Needham's works on Chinese science and civilization.[19] His research demonstrated that, until the arrival of the Jesuits, China had been a donor of technology to Europe, at least indirectly.[20] Then, arising in the 1980s, there was the "California School," which began to talk about traditional China politically with approval, in Voltaire/Quesnay terms. Since 2000 the "Great Divergence" debate has helped put traditional China back in the global mainstream in terms of governance and economic growth, thereby undermining the moribund, low-level Eurocentricism prevalent since Hegel.[21] A counterattack has been launched on the Californians, however, on the fronts of "science and technology" and "real wages" against the newly emerged Sinocentricism.[22]

[15] Smith (1977 [1776]). [16] Hegel (1977 [1807]). [17] Pryor (1980); Wittfogel (1957).
[18] Weber (1951 [1915]; 1958 [1905]).
[19] According to Needham, China did not need European knowledge in most areas, and developed independently a cluster of technologies that allowed it to lead the world from *c.* 100 BCE to *c.* 1550 CE. Needham in 1954 initiated a series of books edited by himself entitled *Science and Civilisation in China*, the last volume being published in 2008.
[20] See Needham (1998: 214). [21] Deng (2000). [22] Mokyr (1990); Allen (2001; 2005).

A long-term pattern for state finance in the Chinese Empire

By the time the Jesuits entered China the empire had already become very experienced and mature, having experienced a long evolution for about two millennia. The Chinese Empire took shape in the third century BCE, after an era of protracted conflict on the East Asian Mainland known as the "Warring States," from 475 to 221 BCE. Among the warring states, some had a mixed economy with a considerable degree of commercialization, especially those on the east coast. At that time there were no uniform taxes or a uniform fiscal approach. But the fighting required all kingdoms to maximize their revenue just to survive. Indeed, according to Mencius, the second most important leader of the Confucian School (*rujia*) in Chinese history who lived through this period, heavy taxation, described as "ferocious as man-eating tigers," was not uncommon. The Confucian School, which advocated benevolence as the way of life, unconditionally condemned wars and heavy taxes alike. Predictably, the school was not favored by most power-holders at the time, simply because adopting a policy of low taxes and benevolence would have meant suicide during the wars.

Over time, however, it became clear that it was not the amount of cash revenues that guaranteed a kingdom's survival; rather, it was the amount of disposable food and loyal soldiers that ultimately determined a kingdom's fate. In the process of military competition and confrontation, the East Asian Mainland was unified politically for the first time when the marginal kingdom of Qin (841–220 BCE), a farming economy in the Northwest Plateau, triumphed against all its wealthier rivals.

The key to Qin's success in 221 BCE in unifying China was a state–peasant alliance, built upon private landholding rights in exchange for a heavy tax burden to finance an army of bureaucrats, who were selected and appointed by a single political center to run an ever-increasing territory. Old feudal elements within the Qin domain were ruthlessly crushed.[23]

But the Qin rulers, the first successful empire builders in Chinese history, soon ruined the economy through heavy taxes (including a corvée) for unsustainable public works such as the Great Wall and the terracotta army. The peasant partners of the Qin state rebelled and ended Qing rule in 206 BCE. From then on, tax-cum-rebellion became the sword of Damocles hanging over the head of all power-holders in imperial China.

[23] Deng (1999: chs. 2 & 3).

In the following Han period (206 BCE to 220 CE) a new norm was established, with which tax ceilings and tax cuts became the main means to gain legitimacy to rule, together with the full adoption of Confucian ideology as the state philosophy. The benevolent golden rule of "light taxes and undemanding corvée" (*bofu qingyao*) was born in order to maintain the state–peasant alliance, and hence to maintain social order in a private economy made up of an ocean of landholding farmers. To secure such an alliance, sons from landholding families were encouraged to enter officialdom through competition and selection. Officials were then subject to regular assessment for promotion in a meritocracy. This eventually led to a system of imperial examinations based on Confucian teachings, including the ideology of light taxation on the general public.

By the Tang period (from 618 to 907) such a system had been so systematically refined that government legitimacy depended on how light the tax burden was compared with China's best track record. Coupled with this approach, the imperial government in various periods consistently committed itself to a balanced budget. Overspending beyond the predicated revenue was considered unethical and politically dangerous.

The regime most devoted to "light taxes and undemanding corvée" was the Qing period (from 1644 to 1911). Before 1850 China's "Confucian-state finance" went to the extreme. First, the Qing tax burden was lower than that of the Ming norm, even when the Qing had extensive military operations during the seventeenth century in China's western regions. Second, the Qing ruler decided unilaterally to curb future taxes. In 1715 Emperor Kangxi announced a policy of "freezing the tax revenue forever" (*yongbu jiafu*) as a benevolent gesture to society.[24] It meant that the annual tax revenue for the Imperial Treasury was frozen at 30 million taels of silver (1,125 tonnes) from the direct tax called the land poll tax (*diding yin*). When this policy was decided, China had just doubled its territory, so strong growth in the farming population (and hence the number of taxpayers) was actually expected by the Qing ruler. Even so, this policy remained valid until 1840. And, contrary to what is commonly believed, this tax did not have to be paid in silver to make taxpayers' lives easier. Third, there was then the highly visible tax called "stipend rice" (*caomi, caoliang*) of 4.5 million piculs per year imposed on six provinces in 1850 (see Table 10.2).[25]

As far as we can tell, the provincial rice quotas were also fixed. Given that the price for rice varied from 0.94 to 2.18 taels of silver per picul in the

[24] Zhao (1986: 9261). [25] Li and Jiang (1995: 410–17, 422, 428).

Table 10.2 *Shares of stipend rice tax in six provinces*

	Stipend rice (piculs)
Anhui	277,634
Hubei	297,412
Hunan	130,000
Jiangsu	2,029,174
Jiangxi	760,000
Zhejiang	1,000,418
Total	4,494,638

Yangtze and Pearl Deltas during the seventeenth and eighteenth centuries,[26] if we take the higher price as the proxy, the total tax in the stipend rice could be another 9.8 million taels (367.5 tonnes). The final total of direct taxes was therefore in the region of 40 million taels (1,500 tonnes). The tax burden was 0.1 taels (3.75 grams) per capita (in 1840),[27] or 28.6 taels per square mile of land under cultivation.[28]

Of course, these 40 million taels were the net income for the Imperial Treasury. It was not the total cost of the Qing taxation. Related to the land poll tax, there was the "currency loss surcharge" (*haoxian*) of 12 percent on top of the land poll for the wear and tear of the currency in the taxation process.[29] Thus, another 4.8 million taels (180 tonnes), or 0.01 tales per head of the population, had to be extracted. Moreover, there were indirect taxes, of which the most cited were the salt levies (*yanke*). Given that one can only eat a limited amount of salt, the total revenue from this tax was inelastic. In the 1840s 10 million taels of silver (375 tonnes) were collected annually from salt levies.[30] The per capita tax burden of salt was 0.025 taels. It is reasonable to assume that on average each citizen paid 0.14 taels (5.3 grams) in taxes to Beijing. Considering that fact that both the land poll and stipend rice came from the farming communities, they selectively benefited the rural population for the sake of the state–peasant alliance.[31]

[26] Marks (1991: 102); Wang (1992: 40–7).

[27] The size of the population is based on figures given by Liang (1980: 10).

[28] This is to use the 1920s figure of 1.4 million square miles as a proxy: Buck (1937: 30).

[29] See Liang (1980: 419, 426–7) and Wang (1973: 70).

[30] Zhou (1981: 419–21, 426); compare with Tang (1992: 126–8).

[31] According to William Skinner, China's urbanization rate was 5.1 percent in 1843 and 6.0 percent in 1893; even in the most affluent region, Jiangnan, the rate was merely 7.4 percent in 1843 and 10.6 percent in 1893: Skinner (1977: 228–9).

Putting the Qing tax burden into perspective, according to Gamble the average daily wage during the 1807–50 period for unskilled laborers in Beijing remained at around 80 copper coins (in sluggish seasons), or 0.05 to 0.08 taels of silver, and 150 copper coins (in busy seasons), or 0.09 to 0.15 taels of silver. Thus, the annual tax burden was about one to two days' wages for an unskilled worker.[32] Similarly, in the nineteenth century a Qing cavalryman had a cash allowance of 36 taels a year plus stipend rice.[33] The per capita tax burden was, again, 1.5 days' pay maximum for a soldier. On the official record, the lowest annual land poll tax burden per head under the reign of Emperor Qianlong reign (from 1736 to 1795) was merely 0.006 taels in Zhejiang.[34] If so, this was less than 10 percent of one day's wages in a sluggish reason.

Comparatively, the Qing per capita tax burden in 1766 was merely 8 percent of the 1381 level under Ming rule (1368–1644).[35] Declines in the tax burden went hand in hand with the Qing population explosion: between 1715 and 1840 the Chinese population increased around 5.7 times (as from 1721 to 1833),[36] but the enlarged population paid roughly the same 40 million taels in taxes a year. In per capita terms, the direct tax burden fell a massive 79 percent; per unit of land, it fell between 30 and 50 percent, as arable land also expanded.[37]

There has been a notion that a Confucian state often treated the commercial sector harshly. We know roughly how much was traded (see Table 10.3), and assume that an aggressive 30 percent tax rate was applied to all trading goods. In this regard, once a farming household became involved in commerce, its lower taxes from land could be compensated for by a much heavier tax regime.[38] This would yield the Qing state a handsome 120 million taels (4,500 tonnes). Even so, this does not change the fact that the Qing state claimed a tiny share of China's total GDP (see Table 10.4)[39] – much lower than that of the Meiji state in Japan, which taxed away 30 to 50 percent of all agricultural income, worth about 20 percent of Japan's total GDP.[40]

[32] For the wage data, see Gamble (1943: 62); for the money exchange rate, see Yu (2000: 860).

[33] He and Wei (1992: 868). [34] Liang (1980: 419); Wang (1973: 513).

[35] This is the only available datum for the Ming Empire as a whole: Liang (1980: 428).

[36] Deng (2004: appendix 2).

[37] Liu and Fei (1977: 373, 375–6); Liang (1980: 380, 428); Deng (2004: appendix 2).

[38] According to Perkins, one-third of post-tax agricultural output was marketed: Perkins (1969: 115). A more recent study indicates that Qing grain growers sold regularly 30 to 35 percent of their post-tax output to the market, those growing both grain and cotton 35 to 40 percent, and those growing cash crop 60 to 70 percent: Li (1993).

[39] For similar conclusions, see Perkins (1967: 492), Feuerwerker (1984: 300, 322), Will (1990), and Deng (1999: appendix 7).

[40] Francks (1992: 30, 103).

Table 10.3 *Marketed goods in total value, 1830s*

	Value (in million silver taels)	%
Grain	163.3	41.0
Cotton fiber and cloth	107.4	27.0
Salt and tea	90.5	22.7
Silk yarn and textiles	26.6	6.7
Porcelain and metals	10.5	2.6
Total	398.3	100.0

Source: Based on Wu (2001: 148–9).

Table 10.4 *Tax revenues vis-à-vis GDP, 1880s*

Estimates	Chang	Feuerwerker	Liu *et al.*	Average
Total GDP (A)	104,300	125,200	131,600	120,370
State total revenue (B)				6,180
Land poll and stipend rice				*1,500*
Currency loss surcharge				*180*
Taxes on trade (including the salt levies)				*4,500*
B/A (%)				5.1

Note: Figures are in tonnes of pure silver, converted from silver taels.
Sources: Based on information from Chang (1962: 296); Feuerwerker (1995: 16); Liu, Wang, and Zhao (1999: 66).

With limited revenues, it was rational for the Qing state to sell nominal official titles to individuals who had money to spend (*juanshu, juanguan*). These purchased titles had no more than vanity value and did not lead to any official appointment.[41] This is similar to "cash for peerages" in modern-day Britain. Buying a title was commonly considered as a donation for a worthy cause to help the state finance – a good Confucian deed that was widely respected. If this helped buyers' businesses, it was a result of the externalities of the donation. If so, it was not a source of political corruption, as one might think. Moreover, it has not been widely appreciated that the actual income from the trade of nominal official titles was

[41] See Xu (1917: 27).

trivial. In the late seventeenth century a report to the throne indicated that the state coffers yielded just 2 million taels this way in a three-year campaign; this was equivalent to 2 percent of the land poll revenue in the same period.[42]

Additionally, there were irregular business donations (*juanxiang*). Prior to 1840 the business donations mainly came from chartered maritime traders in Canton (*hangshang*) and licensed salt merchants (*yanshang*). Both groups made monopolistic fortunes but were at the mercy of the Qing state. A large proportion of the chartered maritime traders were made bankrupt as a result of forced donations.[43] The actual amount of revenue from these donations has remained very unclear, however. Overall, Qing taxation was so light that ordinary Chinese "barely noticed the tax system, almost as if they suffered no tax burden at all."[44] If so, a fiscal state was absent in China. Such a judgment is fully justified for the era before 1850.

The Qing approach differed fundamentally from Meiji Japan, where the 1873 Land Tax Reform set the tax at the rate of 3 percent of the land's market value for each farm.[45] If the land's value was equivalent to twenty years of the agricultural gross output, the annual tax rate would be 60 percent of the gross output.[46] In absolute terms, the Meiji land tax allowed the Meiji state to scoop 76,528,000 yen (or 48.7 million taels, 1,826 tonnes) per annum (in 1875).[47] This amount was close to the Qing revenues from the land poll and salt levies combined. Given that Japan had a population (34 million in 1875) that stood at 9 percent of China's (377.6 million in 1887), the per capita tax burden in Japan was eleven times the Qing level.

On the other side of the equation were the Qing government expenditures. As far as one can tell, to maintain the Qing standing army cost 20 million taels a year.[48] This sum was by far the largest single item in the Qing state budget.[49] Qing officials were known to be paid generously after the 1724 Regulations for Virtuousness and Uprightness Bonuses.[50] This

[42] In comparison, in France under Henri IV (r. 1589–1610) and Louis XIV (r. 1643–1715) real official positions, not just vanity titles, were actively traded: Moore (1966: 57–9).

[43] Deng (1997: 112). [44] Mann (1987: 16). [45] Yamamura (1986).

[46] My estimation is based on a simple formula 0.03 nq/q, where 0.03 is the percentage of the current land value, n is the number of years it took for the peasant to pay off the market value of his or her land with the gross output from the same land, and q, is the annual gross output.

[47] Editorial board of *Journal of World History* (1981: 53).

[48] It was documented that the total monthly salary bill for the Qing military was 1.5 million taels: Xu (1917: 1); see also Zhao (1986: 9283).

[49] He and Wei (1992: 867).

[50] The bonuses ran on a progressive scale: the country magistrate got 600 to 1,000 taels on top of his meagre basic salary of 45 taels, while the Governor General got a bonus of 15,000 to 20,000 taels on top of his basic salary of 180 taels: Cheng and Ying (1968); see also Zuo (1976) and Zelin (1984).

practice was confirmed by foreign observers of the time: the Shanghai superintendent (*daotai*) had an annual basic salary of 4,000 taels but earned, quite openly, 335,000 taels a year after allowing for all expenses.[51] This scheme was designed exclusively for officials serving outside Beijing, where bureaucrats possessed a great deal of power. These bonuses, up to 100 times the basic salary, effectively discouraged officials from preying on the peasantry – a policy known as "high salaries nurturing virtue" (*gaoxin yanglian*). Bureaucrats who worked in the capital city, Beijing, were not eligible for bonuses because they had no one to prey on. In contrast to their wealthy colleagues in provinces, many officials in Beijing could hardly break even without a second income.[52]

Even after the introduction of these bonuses, however, the total salary bill for Qing bureaucracy remained incredibly small. During the entire eighteenth century the annual salary bill for a province, including all the bonuses, varied from 44,700 taels (Guizhou) to 184,300 taels (Jiangsu).[53] If we take the higher figure as a proxy, the aggregate salary bill for all eighteen provinces cost the Imperial Treasury around 3.3 million taels (124 tonnes) per year,[54] equivalent to a mere 0.1 percent of the Qing GDP during the 1880s (see Table 10.4).

Paradoxically, individual officials were well paid, but the Qing state as a whole remained cheap. This was because the absolute size of the bureaucracy was so minute. It employed fewer than 30,000 civilian officials and military officers: 24,150 in *c.* 1700 and 26,355 in 1850.[55] There were merely 2,546 key officials in Beijing (Table 10.5).

This left 20,000 administrators to run an army of between 600,000 and 1 million men plus eighteen provinces (*sheng*), divided into 190 prefectures (*fu*) and 1,672 counties (*xian*).[56] As officials in Beijing worked very long hours to keep the vital departments running,[57] a county magistrate on average served a population of 214,710 (in the 1830s).

[51] See Williams (1856: 257–8).

[52] Middle-ranking bureaucrats living in the capital, Beijing, constantly needed financial support from their relatives, and sometimes had to quit their positions: Zhang (1970: 46–54).

[53] Zelin (1984: ch. 4).

[54] Chung-li Chang's estimate for the 1880s is higher, but not prohibitory, at 4.7 million: Chang (1962: 320 tab. 36).

[55] Yang (1992: 420–1). According to Chang, the number of officials varied from 12,000 to 22,830: Chang (1962: 42, 197, 329–30).

[56] Yang (1992: 420–1). Note that, after 1882, Fengtian, Jilin, Heilongjiang, Xinjiang, and Taiwan became full provinces. Also, if all the 402 county-equivalent units are counted, there were 2,074 counties: Zhao (1986: 9071–131).

[57] Officials in the Qing central government worked very long hours to keep the vital departments running twenty-four hours a day: Wanyan (2005: 172–81).

Table 10.5 *Officials in the Qing central government*

		Number of officials
1. Cabinet (*neige*)		288
2. Six ministries (*liubu*)		1,964
Personnel (*libu*)	224	
Revenue (*hubu*)	362	
Rites (*libu*)	145	
War (*bingbu*)	221	
Punishments (*xingbu*)	407	
Public works (*gongbu*)	317	
3. Other departments		582
Total		2,546

Sources: Based on Yang (1992: 420–1); Zhang (2001: 6, 39, 43, 57, 79, 106, 127).

If one combines soldiers' living allowances and bureaucrats' salaries, the total expenditure was well below 30 million taels in a normal year. Another main expense was the maintenance of the state granary system for disaster relief. This system routinely stored a stockpile of over 30 million piculs of unhusked rice (2.2 million tonnes) for at least a century until 1847.[58] A more optimistic estimate is 45 million piculs (3.3 million tonnes), ready to be sent off when disasters struck.[59] The total value of such a stockpile was about 60 to 90 million taels (2,250 to 3,375 tonnes) if the aforementioned price level applies, excluding costs of labor and capital (such as buildings).

This was a large-scale, ongoing operation of government granaries across China, affecting the health and stability of the economy. With China's 756.4 million *mu* farmland in 1851,[60] its total food output can be estimated as around 105,900 million *catties* (53 million tonnes).[61] The amount of 2.2 to 3.3 million tonnes of reserves was therefore equivalent to 4 to 7 percent of China's annual grain output.[62] According to the Ming standard, it required 30 *sheng* of unhusked rice to help an adult to survive a famine;[63] the 2.2 to 3.3 million tonnes of could, accordingly, save the

[58] Liang (1980: 251–4). [59] Myers and Wang (2002: 602). [60] See Liang (1980: 380).

[61] On the assumptions that (1) the average land yield level across the board was 200 *catties* per *mu* and (2) 30 percent of land suffered total crop failure each year.

[62] For similar estimates, see Li (1982: 697), Myers and Wang (2002: 602), and Shiue (2005: 40).

[63] Zhang (1986: 7791, 7807).

Table 10.6 *End-year budget surpluses (percentage of total revenue), 1885–1894*

1885	5.7
1886	2.2
1887	2.5
1888	5.7
1889	6.2
1890	6.4
1891	9.3
1892	6.4
1893	8.0
1894	0.6

lives of between 110 and 165 million adults, roughly one-third of China's population at its nineteenth-century level.[64]

What is remarkable is that the Imperial Treasury often managed to make budget savings. This applies even to the 1880s and 1890s, when China was in serious economic straits (Table 10.6).[65] In comparison, although the Meiji state in Japan took in tax 10 times more than its Qing counterpart, its revenues covered only 10 percent of its expenditures.[66] The rest came from public debt.

Overall, the Qing state showed a high degree of persistent self-discipline in minimizing its budgets against government spending sprees, on the one hand, and the lowering of taxes to allow the population to keep their surpluses, on the other. Such self-restraint in behavior could come only from the Confucian benevolence adopted by the Qing rulers: the view that a good government was one that taxes the economy as little as possible. Without the mounting debts caused, directly or indirectly, by the attacks by foreign powers and internal unrest, such a "feather-light" tax regime could have continued indefinitely. In this context, any development toward a fiscal state, a state that maximizes its revenue, became a tall order.

Exceptional periods tending toward a fiscal state

Generally speaking, there was little movement toward a fiscal state in China despite its long history. Two periods can be identified in Chinese history when a quasi-fiscal state did stand out, however. One was the Song period (from 960 to 1279), and the other was the late Qing period, after

[64] Deng (2004: appendix 2). [65] Liu (1901). [66] Wan (1984: 68).

1850. In both cases China's political and economic conditions were drastically different from usual, forcing state finances to change.

The Song deviation

The Song period has been commonly viewed as an age of medieval economic revolution in China's long history. It was marked by an unprecedented degree of industrial and commercial activities. First of all, there was strong growth in heavy industry in terms of iron- and steel-making, in which China's output led the rest of the world with a large margin in both total and per capita terms. According to Hartwell, in a typical fashion for mass production, China's output of iron and steel increased by 385 percent from 998 to 1078 while their prices relative to grain dropped by over 70 percent at the same time.[67] Such growth in heavy industry was highly visible in the period painting *Scenery along the Bian River during the Qingming Festival* (*qingming shanghe tu*) by Zhang Zeduan (1085–1145). In the painting, heavy cargo is being loaded onto large carts with wheels as tall as adult men, pulled by three to four cattle. The painting also reveals the extensive use of iron rivets on clinker-built ships' hulls, to hold overlapping planks firmly together in a wood/iron structure. This is compatible with the use of iron for mass-produced coins as currency, and for the large statues of Song times.

Moreover, commercial engagement was no longer something that decent people frowned at. Professional merchants played a leading role in the economy, including an experiment with paper currency. Bureaucrats were no longer satisfied with their fixed salaries, despite the fact that Song officials received the highest nominal salaries in China's history. Official profiteering was common.

In addition, there was a full-scale "green revolution" in the wake of a state-sponsored scheme in the eleventh century to promote an early-ripening rice variety imported from Champa (current-day Vietnam).[68] This new type of rice was able to mature in as quickly as forty to fifty days, making multi-cropping possible. It significant enlarged the Song food supply, to overcome a Malthusian threat to the population for centuries to come in China.

With the rise of industry, commerce, and new rice-farming, China's economic base vigorously expanded. Although the then entrenched Confucian ideology would make light taxation a *chose jugée*, this economic

[67] Hartwell (1966: 29–58); see also Shiba (1970). [68] Ho (1956).

Table 10.7 *Comparison in Tang and Song taxes on grains*

	Tang (750 CE)	Song nominal (1021 CE)	Song actual
Total (million piculs)	12.5	32.8 (262)	36.7 (294)
Per household (piculs)	1.4	3.8 (271)	4.2 (300)

Note: Figures in brackets show growth index, taking as base year 750 CE = 100.

Table 10.8 *Song customs revenues*

	Maritime customs dues	All taxes
1049–53	530	36,800
1127–61	2,000 (377)	60,000 (163)

Note: Figures in brackets show growth index, taking as base period 1049–53 = 100.

boom left the state two choices: either to leave the economy alone, for the sake of China's internal peace, or to tax it more, risk the state's legitimacy. The Song state chose the later. The Song tax burden is reported to have been "twice as much as its predecessor of the Tang period" (from 618 to 907).[69] Not only did the Song authorities increase the tax rate, they also changed official standards for volume and measuring, purely for taxation purposes: the Song grain unit (*sheng*) was 12 percent greater in volume than that of the Tang; and the Song cloth unit (*sansi chi*) was 5.4 percent longer than that of the Tang.[70] They became "stealth" taxes, to cash in on the green revolution. Table 10.7 sheds light on the situation.[71]

Moreover, Song taxes leaned heavily toward taxing non-farming activities. Song maritime customs revenue increased nearly fourfold – more rapidly than the growth in total taxes (in million coins); see Table 10.8.[72]

Furthermore, large budget deficits began to appear (see Table 10.9).[73]

[69] Liang (1980: 297). [70] Ibid.: 544–5. [71] Ibid.: 6, 284, 288.
[72] Yan (1994: 107); Liang (1980: 297). [73] Ibid.: 289.

Table 10.9 *Deficits on selected items (percentage of total revenues), 1085*

Silver	–105.0
Hay (as fodder)	–103.0
Silk cloth	–11.3
Bronze coins	–3.8

The question is: what made the Song state change so fundamentally? The main trigger turns out to have been the increase in external pressure from nomads along the northern borders of the Song territory – mainly the Khitans and Jurchens, who had military supremacy over the Chinese. Over the course of a century these nomads steadily annexed China's territory. By 1127 the entire north of China had fallen into their hands. Soon the threat from the Mongols loomed large. In 1234 CE the rule of the Jurchens was replaced by that of the Mongols in north China. Later, in 1279, the Mongols conquered south China too.

In the process, large ransom amounts were demanded annually by the Khitans and Jurchens in the form of silver and silk. Unless they were paid generously, Khitans and Jurchens would resume their war against the Songs. As it happens, they never intended to honor their promises of peace; but their military strength allowed them to change the rules of the game unilaterally.

The Song state, which was militarily weak and thus at the mercy of the nomads,[74] had no other choice but to increase taxes in order to meet the external demand, as the political survival of the Song Empire overruled the Confucian taboo against heavy taxation. The pressure to tax more heavily reached its climax when half the Song territory, together with a large chunk of China's farmland, markets, and overland silk roads, was lost to the Jurchens early in the twelfth century.

Trade – especially that with the outside world – was singled out by the Song state simply because it had much the greatest capacity to add value. In addition, China was known for its poor silver endowment. Trade was essential to obtain the metal needed to pay the nomads. Finally, China's traditional silk roads to central Asia, India, and beyond were completely lost to the nomads long before the fall of the Songs' capital city, Kaifeng, in 1126. Alternative routes at sea had to be established as a matter of national

[74] For the reasons and mechanisms, see Deng (1999: ch. 6).

emergency. In this context, to extract more revenue from commerce became the core of the Song economic reforms. To show how maritime trade was being vigorously promoted, customs officials paid personal visits to rich merchants to urge them to go overseas. On some occasions officials even picked up names from the list of government registrants and sent reluctant merchants out from China, in the fashion of military service.[75] This was a type of mercantilism, by which a merchant–state alliance was forged. It worked. From 1056 to 1127 the share of income from maritime trade jumped from 1.7 percent to 20 percent of total government revenue, in a more than tenfold increase.[76]

It was during this period that large port cities came into being along China's east coast. Among them, Quanzhou, also called "Zaitun," was the best known port in the continent of Asia at the time, with a population of about 100,000 households (in 989 CE).[77] In 976 CE alone Quanzhou passed on to the Song state 176,000 *catties* of goods (105 tonnes), either as taxes or as government procurements, including 10,000 *catties* of ivory (10 tonnes), 61,000 rolls (*pi*) of cloth, and 27,000 taels of silver (1 tonne). It also paid 2,000 million bronze coins as taxes that year.

There were a range of linkage effects. To facilitate seagoing trade, for profit and taxes, the Songs invented the "Fuzhou Ship" (*fuchuan*) in the middle of the twelfth century, exclusively to handle deep-sea traveling. The new type could be built quickly and cheaply with the use of wooden planks and iron rivets. This ship design remained unchanged in East Asian waters until the end of the eighteenth century. According to some official records, a fleet of forty-two of them was built in a short space of time in coastal Ningbo in 1169 CE. The demand for seagoing ships in turn fueled the growth in iron and steel.

Meanwhile, maritime technology was developing rapidly. The first-ever installation of a maritime compass in world history was on Song ships in 1119 CE, as a vital device for navigation on cloudy days. From the recorded foreign locations, the Song sailors seem to have had a fairly good grasp of sea routes to South and Southeast Asia. Maritime activities in the following Yuan (1279–1368) and Ming (1368–1644) periods were, in effect, the icing on the cake.[78]

In addition, with more and more people engaging in trade and trade-related services, the pace of urbanization increased. Such a trend was intensified by a steady flood of refugee-immigrants from the regions lost

[75] Xu (1957: chs. "Zhiguan," "Xingfa"). [76] Ye (1991: 104); Zhang (1992). [77] Liang (1980: 135).
[78] See Deng (1995).

to the nomads. The northern refugees, known as the *Hakka* (or *kejia*), had little prospect of owning their own land in the south. They either became farming tenants or gave up farming for other businesses. Many chose the latter. Making a living outside farming was encouraged by the Song state. As a result, Song urbanization proceeded at a double-digit rate, the highest in the entire premodern era of China.[79] Against this backdrop, large cities emerged. For instance, between 1165 and 1173 CE the population in Hangzhou, the capital of the Southern Song, more than doubled from 550,000 to 1,240,000, with an annual increase of 10.7 percent.[80] It was the second "millionaire city" under Song rule, after Kaifeng prior to 1126.

Not only that, but the total population in south China grew from 16.8 million in 1159 CE to 28.3 million in 1223.[81] All the new growth under the Song was ultimately underpinned by the windfall of the green revolution, through which the food supply was maintained within Song territory. The loop was complete.

The British economic historian Eric Jones has famously suggested, in his book *The European Miracle*, that China during the Song period was just a "hair's breadth" away from a genuine industrial revolution.[82] Counterfactually, if the standoff between the nomads and the Songs had continued for another 200 to 300 years, China might indeed have become a capitalist economy.

As the Song economy prospered, though, it attracted the Mongols, the most efficient raiders in the world before 1500 CE. The Mongols not only captured the Jurchen domain in north China but also conquered south China. In the process, Song mercantilism was brought to a sudden stop, in 1279. Under Mongol rule, the Songs' merchant–state alliance was destroyed with the policy that all commerce was to be conducted exclusively by Mongol-trusted foreigners from Central Asia and beyond (*semu ren*). The Confucian ideology was systematically banned, and so were the imperial examinations (for eighty out of the eighty-nine years of Mongol rule);[83] the bureaucracy of the empire was manned by Mongols and their mercenaries from Central Asia, while a large proportion of the Song population was eliminated by the well-documented Mongol genocide.[84] In this context, contrary to the well-circulated fantasy, the alleged political stability and commercial growth under *Pax Mongolica* did little for the Han Chinese, who were systematically excluded from politics and foreign trade.

[79] Rozman (1973: 102, 279–82). [80] Lin (1990: 138). [81] Liang (1980: 130–1).
[82] Jones (1981: 160). [83] Deng (1993: 24).
[84] Song (1371); see also Wright and Twitchett (1962: 19–20, 189–216).

The dark age of the Mongol apartheid, under which Middle Easterners and Europeans were purposely brought in, was ended in 1368 when the Chinese finally rebelled to expel the Mongols out of China proper.

In the following Ming period there was a full-scale political and economic renaissance of "Chinese-ness" and Confucian orthodoxy. Farming was re-enshrined. The old peasant–state alliance, private landholding property rights, and a low-tax regime were systematically re-established.[85] Consequently, the conditions that had nurtured the Song mercantilism, namely the right amount of pressure from the external threat and from internal population density, were removed; so, too, was a fiscal state.

The Ming trend of "Chinese-ness" and Confucian orthodoxy continued right throughout much of the Qing, despite the fact that the ruling Manchus were ethnically non-Han. What was so special about the Manchus was that they actively avoided taking the ill-fated Mongol path in ruling China. Chinese remained as an official language; Confucianism remained as the state philosophy; all Manchu emperors were strictly educated from a very young age by top Chinese scholars; the Ming administration (including the crucial institution of the imperial examinations to recruit bureaucrats) and judiciary were maintained; most ex-Ming officials were re-hired, such that political power and administrative responsibilities were openly shared between the Manchus and the Han Chinese.[86] In addition, the centerpiece for Ming communication, "memorials to the throne" or "palace memorials" (*zoubao*), was expanded and perfected, allowing courtiers and provincial officials to openly discuss how to manage the empire.[87] In most cases the emperor acted only as the final arbitrator, with most decisions being made by various officials at different levels.[88] Such a bureaucratic monarchy, in which the head of state had a very limited role to play, not only resumed China's historic traditions but also developed the idea of "people as the foundation" to its extreme. Therefore, it is not at all surprising that the Qing tax burden per capita was the lightest on record. Life for the population in China became good again.

The late Qing divergence

The Qing Empire doubled its territory and quadrupled its population. But the bureaucracy was kept disproportionately small. As mentioned earlier, it

[85] Deng (1999: chs. 1–4; 2003). [86] Metzger (1973). [87] Wu (1970); see also Metzger (1973).

[88] See anon. (1964a [1741]; 1964b [1799]; 1964c [1824]). For the most revealing record in the English language, see Dunstan (1996). See also Wu (1970).

employed fewer than 30,000 civilian officials and military officers to run the empire: Qing China was under-governed.

Such under-governance produced two results. First, regarding ordinary people's material lives before 1800, Qing rule was by far the best to date in China's long history.[89] Second, the under-governance made China exceptionally vulnerable to external threat and internal chaos, which duly took place in a big way in the middle of the nineteenth century: the 1839–40 Opium War and the 1850–70 empire-wide social unrest, with turmoil involving the Taiping, the Nians, and Muslims occurring across all the main geographic regions.[90] The only regions that the rebels did not touch were Manchuria, Mongolia, and Tibet, where the locals were under alternative rule.

The 1839–40 Opium War and its reparations apart, the immediate consequence of the unrest was the loss of virtually all the Qing incomes – up to 90 percent. It caused Qing state finances to collapse in around 1850. The fact that there was no official datum for central government revenues for thirty-five years from 1850 to 1885 supports such a judgment.[91] If the state finances had not been re-established, the dynasty would have met its demise there and then.

The response from Qing officials was to declare war on the rebels and rebuild law and order after military victory. But all wars need money to be prosecuted. For example, to maintain a local army of 100,000 against the Taipings in Hunan cost 1 million taels of silver minimum a year.[92] How to extract such a sum on a regular basis from alternative sources became a life or death issue for the Qing regime. The Qing elite came up with two solutions: targeting commerce for indirect taxes, and raising public debt from overseas borrowings. The move was unprecedented in the history of the empire, whether in terms of scale (indirect taxes) or of initiative (foreign debts).

Before 1850, however, alternative ways to raise revenue were limited to indirect taxes on salt and on commodities subject to long-distance trade.[93] In the 1840s only 10 million taels of silver (375 tonnes) were collected annually from salt levies (*yanke*) together with internal customs

[89] Pomeranz (2000).

[90] Yi and Zhu (1968a: vols. 1–40); Yi and Zhu (1990: vols. 1–320); Yi and Zhu (1968b: vols. 1–50); Yi and Zhu (1965: vols. 1–420). See also Michael (1966: 216), Liu and Smith (1980: 216), and Spence (1999: 187). Additionally, see Li, Qian, and Lai (1958), Zhang and Zheng (1983), and Atwill (2006).

[91] Liang (1980: 415–16). [92] Luo (1984: 121); Zhao (1986: 9311).

[93] See Zhao (1986: 9269–74, 9282–3).

duties (*guanshui*).[94] Indirect taxes were equivalent to just 2.5 percent of the aggregate value of marketed goods (see Table 10.3). China's population at the time was about 400 million (in 1833). The empire had 60,000 local markets and thirty-four national trade routes.[95] This meant that the annual burden of indirect taxation was merely 0.025 taels (0.94 g) per head or 168 taels per market. Heavy taxation remained politically taboo. Discontinuity did not come until 1853, when a new transit duty called *lijin* (or *likin*), at a rate of 1 to 2 percent of the value of goods, was introduced for the first time to raise money to maintain the Qing troops in the Taiping-infested Yangzhou region (Jiangsu).[96]

The *lijin* began its life cycle merely as a temporary one-off measure at the provincial level with Beijing's tacit consent. It differed from the conventional taxes on long-distance trade by making all market exchanges legitimate targets for taxation. This freed the Qing state from the previous self-imposed constraint regarding sectors, locations, and frequency for taxes. It was based on the principle of "paying as you trade," and thus fairer than any direct tax. Logically, the new tax began in the Yangtze Valley, where local commerce was most active. It soon took China by storm, shaking China off its long tradition of the "low taxation trap." To facilitate the new tax regime, each province began to run its own tax networks, and hence ushered in the era of local fiscal autonomy.

It is crucial to understand that this new transit tax was fully compatible with Confucian ideology of physiocracy and so politically acceptable, as stated by Li Hongzhang (1823–1901), who was in charge of Anhui Province at the time:

> Each day I am in charge of an office and an army, I impose the *lijin*. It is better to harm commerce than damage agriculture.[97]

In this context, in Hunan Province, under the leadership of Zeng Guofan (1811–72), a new bureaucracy was established from scratch. Zeng's taxmen aggressively expanded their *lijin* agencies where possible. In 1856 there were 480 such agencies inside Hubei Province alone.[98] By 1864 they were running 123 offices in five other provinces (Anhui, Jiangsu, Hubei, Hunan, and Jiangxi) too. This practice was confirmed by Lindley, writing:

94 Zhou (1981: 419–21, 426); compare with Tang (1992: 126–8).

95 For population size, see Deng (2004: appendix 2); for the number of markets, see Skinner (1977: 24); for trade routes, see Feuerwerker (1980: 42).

96 Zhao (1986: 10178); see also Beal (1958). 97 Li (1921: 164). 98 Zhao (1986: 9281).

"[W]ithin 30 miles there are no less than 15 *lijin* checkpoints."[99] The *lijin* revenue was devoted to run Zeng's Hunan Army (*xiangjun*).

Zeng was not alone. Other powerful officials, such as Zuo Zongtang (1812–85) and Li Hongzhang, also established their independent provincial taxes, bureaucracies, and armed forces.[100] At their peak, these three provincial armies totaled at least 150,000 troops.[101] They jointly crushed the Taipings in 1864. Afterwards, Zuo's army marched further afield, to Shaanxi and Gansu in west China, to put down the Muslim riots in 1867. Zuo and Li went on and eliminated the Nians in north China in 1868, marking the end of all unrest in China proper. Zuo went on to retake Xinjiang in 1878. This episode of military triumph is commonly called the "Tongzhi Renaissance" (*tongzhi zhongxing*).

Before long, Beijing saw the merit of this new institution. In 1855 the Ministry of Revenue (*hubu*) issued a memorandum to all provincial governors that the governors warring with rebels were allowed to impose the *lijin* to pay for the war.[102] By 1862 the *lijin* had joined the mainstream; all provinces, apart from remote Yunnan, Heilongjiang, and offshore Taiwan, were subject to the new levy.[103]

The result was remarkable. It has been estimated that, between 1853 and 1864, total *lijin* revenue was in the region of 100 million taels.[104] All these sums had previous been left untapped by the Qing state. Now they played a vital role in rescuing Qing rule across the empire. In the following decades China had multiple provincial armed forces (*fangjun*, literally "local defense forces"). The aggregate number of these forces reached about 360,000 men, costing 20 million taels of silver per year (see Table 10.10).[105]

In addition, from the 1870s to the 1900s there were thirteen provincial waterborne forces (*shuishi*). They boasted 2,530 traditional ships and 44,900 marines.[106] Not surprisingly, with their newly found stable revenues, Qing provinces became truly autonomous administratively, militarily, and fiscally.

Such provincial autonomy reduced Beijing's financial burden. From the available data, from 1885 to 1894 Beijing managed to record an average budget surplus of 6 million taels a year.[107] Less known, but more importantly, the new local resource backlog was unavailable to either Beijing or the Taipings. As already mentioned, the Taipings were crushed. In Beijing's case, in the 1890s the Green Standard Army (*lüying*) had to be

[99] Lindley (1866a: 43–4; 1866b: 296).
[100] They were the New Hunan Army (*chujun*) in 1860 and the Anhui Army (*huaijun*) in 1861.
[101] Zhao (1986: 9311). [102] Luo (1936: 20, 308). [103] Zhou (1981: 168). [104] Luo (1936: 38).
[105] Zhao (1986: 9311). [106] Ibid. (9318–24); Zhang and Gao (2006: 418). [107] Liu (1901).

Table 10.10 *Numbers of troops in provinces, 1870s*

Province	Troops
Anhui	11,290
Fujian	10,540
Gansu	12,500
Guangdong	11,800
Guangxi	16,940
Guizhou	9,486
Henan	9,190
Hubei	13,783
Hunan	12,970
Jiangsu	29,960
Jiangxi	9,360
Manchuria	32,407
Shaanxi	14,450
Shandong	13,950
Sichuan	15,698
Sshanxi	4,900
Xinjiang	30,277
Yunnan	15,033
Zhejiang	21,300
Zhili	63,400

disbanded, while the Eight Banners (*baqi*) of 120,000 men remained only as beneficiaries of Qing social welfare, instead of as a fighting force.[108] With it, the center of political and military gravity shifted from Beijing to the provinces.

Although the *lijin* effectively freed the Qing state from its previous low-taxation trap, it still presented an upper limit of 100 million taels a year. On the other hand, the demand for revenues kept increasing steadily with the new ideology of "Westernization" – a synonym for modernization nowadays. In a three-decade pursuit known as the "Westernization Movement," from the 1860s to the 1890s, foreign technology was introduced, foreign technicians were hired, factories were built, telegraph and railways were constructed, and new institutions – government departments, schools, and academies – were tried out. All cost money. When the *lijin* was no longer enough, and while heavy taxation on agriculture was still a taboo politically as long as Qing rule continued, China's only hope was external finance.

[108] Zhao (1986: 9307).

Thanks to the 1839–40 Opium War, China's door had been prised open, and foreign borrowing became not just possible but attractive to power-holders. Meanwhile, individual provinces had had the taste of freedom and choice in raising money. It was only natural for them to look at the international capital market. This was partly because no Chinese merchant was willing to lend money to the Qing establishments, as Zuo Zongtang explained:

> To borrow money by a government for wars is common in the West. Foreign traders are willing to lend money [to us], unlike Chinese merchants who are reluctant [to lend for wars]. Also, the more one borrows from foreigners the lower the interest he pays. This is also very different from the Chinese merchants' practice [who charge more if they lend more].[109]

Such differences in lending behavior can only mean that, in China, the supply of capital was very inelastic. In other words, the amount of capital available for lending in China was extremely limited, making it a "sellers' market," in which the creditor calls the shots. In contrast, the West had abundant capital supply and hence a "buyers' market," in which the debtor calls the shots. But this suited the Qing power-holders, whether in Beijing or in the provinces, fine. This was the beginning of government deficit finance, or public debts (Table 10.11).[110]

Not until 1891 did the Ministry of Revenue send a memo to all foreign embassies in Beijing saying that all public debts raised by provincial officials needed Beijing's endorsement.[111] This was mere lip service, as Beijing had no control over foreign financiers.

After 1911 foreign debt became the lifeline of power-holders in China, and public debt was the norm in government finance (see Table 10.12).[112]

Table 10.11 *Total foreign borrowing, c. 1890*

	Millions of taels	%
Beijing	121.0	53.2
Provinces	106.4	46.8
Total	227.4	100.0

[109] Zuo (1890: 12).

[110] Excluding foreign borrowings for China's railway projects because of the ambiguity in ownership: Li Y. (2000: 133, 184, 217–9, 223–7, 230–8, 244, 252–5, 265, 278, 326, 340, 360, 376, 393, 452, 464, 474, 482–9, 513, 528, 537, 548, 566, 627, 630, 640, 651, 730, 807, 823, 833, 845, 867, 881, 902, 916, 943, 964–6, 980, 1003, 1023, 1053–6, 1065, 1073, 1094, 1099, 1109, 1119, 1130–44, 1150–8, 1164–9, 1170–5).

[111] Ibid.: 587.

[112] Wang (2000: 1370, 1375, 1378, 1380–6, 1405); Qu and Bai (2006: 57–8, 92–3, 100, 103).

Table 10.12 *Government finances (million yuan, current prices), 1912–1937*

	Revenues	Expenses	Borrowings	Balance
1912	2.6	–	400.0	–
1914	358.5	357.0	24.0	1.5
1916	462.1	471.5	10.0	0.6
1919	647.7	647.7	238.7	0.0
1925	461.6	634.4	–	−172.8
1927	–	–	70	–
1929	483	584	198	97
1931	619	749	446	336
1933	689	836	124	−23
1935	817	1,073	330	74
1937	870	1,167	578	281

Similarly, during the Second World War, when the Japanese destruction and occupation deprived the Nanjing government of its usual tax base by a massive 99.9 percent,[113] a total of US$935 million had to be borrowed from the West and the Soviet Union to keep the government afloat.[114]

Foreign debts reveal a symbiotic relationship between foreigners and domestic power-holders in China. Students of China's history are all familiar with the terms "carving up China" and "foreign spheres of influence in China." Conventional wisdom asserts that the whole process was entirely driven by foreign greed and that China was merely a passive victim. This notion is completely flawed. What it overlooks is that, after 1850, real power was possessed by China's provinces, which were heavily armed. Foreign powers could not just stroll into a province, especially in coastal China, without permission. In this context, foreign powers had to be invited in. Unless there was a strong and persistent demand from China's provinces for foreign involvement, however, foreigners had no spheres of influence in China. So, foreign powers did not carve up China. Rather, the Chinese provincial governors carved up China between themselves first, and then invited foreigners in. The acid test was provided during the Second World War: when the Japanese were rash enough to use their forces against China's provinces from 1931 to 1945, they faced the stiffest armed resistance and suffered the heaviest causalities anywhere in

[113] It was worth 54 million yuan in 1945 prices: ibid.: 108, 125.

[114] Ibid.: 121, 125. It was worth another 18.7 billion yuan, based on the 1942 exchange rate of US$1 – 20 yuan; see http://www.globalfinancialdata.com/index.

Asia, despite the fact that the Chinese forces never had an efficient chain of command.[115]

The impact of the post-1850 changes was profound. The combination of the *lijin* and foreign debts gave the Qing state a new lease of life to overcome the major challenge from the domestic rebels in the 1850s and 1860s. The *lijin* and foreign debts also planted the seed of provincial financial and military independence, however. By around 1870 a centralized Qing state existed, but only in name. The empire was now organized with the new principle of "provincial federalism," under which the Qing court was marginalized as a symbol while provincial governors became de facto "governor-lords," who were no longer the old-fashioned Confucian civil servants but armed-to-the-teeth, battle-hardened military commanders. These military strongmen ran provinces independently, in areas ranging from finance and recruitment to foreign diplomacy. The provinces thereby became mini-states. This was the opposite process to Tokugawa Japan, where a feudal system was bureaucratized, the feudal lords (*daimyo*) were converted into "lord-governors," and their independent, militarized mini-states became subordinate prefectures (*han*).

The most obvious sign of this federalism was the provincial power over personnel. Governor-lords appointed their protégés to official posts, while Beijing simply rubber-stamped the appointments.[116] About 80 percent of members of Zeng Gufan's personal bureaucracy gained official posts this way.[117] In particular, Zeng helped twenty-six of his men on 134 occasions to become governors and Governors General (*xunfu, zongdu*).[118] Given that the Qing bureaucracy had, in all, twenty-five Governor and Governor General posts available, Zeng became a powerful patron in the Qing bureaucracy, competing with the Qing imperial examination system. Such patronage became the fast track to get into the already overcrowded Qing bureaucracy. The imperial tradition of open recruitment from Confucian scholars to be deployed anywhere across the empire and to be promoted by their deeds was now severely undermined. To work in imperial ministries and become courtiers in Beijing was no longer an attractive career path. Highly qualified people preferred to stay in the provinces where their political, military, economic, and human resources lay. The subtlety of this change was that these militarized mini-states were all run by Confucian officials who were, seemingly, loyal to the same Qing

[115] The Japanese official line so far has been that, during the Second World War, the Japanese army "entered" China, as if China was a no-man's-land, and there was no need for an invitation. Clearly, they have not learned the lesson.

[116] Porter (1972: 87–91). [117] Li Z. (2000: 163). [118] Ibid. (138).

regime. There was no legal reason for Beijing to reject them. Instead, Beijing had to accept them as its own. In return, all the governor-lords accepted the Qing emperor as their overlord.

After 1870 the Qing regime became highly fragmented from within and from the bottom up. China seemed to be heading for federalism ("the united provinces of China") if not downright feudalism (the break-up of the empire).[119] A single command center in Beijing gave way to multiple centers in the provinces; one army was substituted by several armies; one budget was replaced by many budgets; and one diplomatic voice became many voices. Such a situation is clearly shown in a Qing record from July 1895, when Beijing begged all the governors to report their plans and measures regarding railway construction, coinage, weapon production, mining operations, stipend rice, post service, army training, naval formation, and school reforms,[120] as all these activities were no longer centrally controlled.

To reflect these changes, during the 1880s and 1890s there were open complaints from the Confucian gentry that "[n]owadays, a governor is like a king during the Warring States period [475–221 BCE]."[121] Kang Youwei (1858–1927), one of the leaders of the ill-fated "100-Day Reform" in 1898, put it bluntly that China's eighteen provinces had already become eighteen kingdoms. He urged China to abandon provinces altogether (*feisheng*) in order to uproot the governor-lords.[122]

In this context, it becomes easy to understand how the so-called "1911 Nationalist Revolution" came about from a mutiny by a few hundred army cadets on a small scale in October in Wuhan. Within a few months most provincial governor-lords had decided to support a new Beijing government headed by Yuan Shikai (1859–1916), who was one of the governor-lords of the time. It was Yuan who forced the last Qing emperor, Puyi (1906–67; r. 1909–12), to abdicate in February 1912 so as to give way to a republic called "the Nation of the Han Chinese" (*zhonghua minguo*).[123] Then, in the election held in April 1913, when 760 "representatives" (selected by negotiations among various social groups) voted for a new head of state, Yuan Shikai won 62 percent of the votes (471), followed by

[119] A recent book suggests that, before 221 BCE, China had sovereign territorial states similar to Europe in the early modern period: Hui (2005).

[120] Anon. (1987 [1921]: 23); Deng (2009). [121] Wang (1927: 21).

[122] See Jiang and Wu (1987: 347–8); Tang (1981: 133).

[123] This was done in a highly publicized fashion when forty-six of Yuan's army officers stationed near Beijing put forward a petition for the emperor to step down. It turned out to be far more effective than Sun's Republican rebellions in the south.

General Li Yuanhong with 20 percent (151).[124] Yuan's new presidency did not bring peace to China, however, with the provinces remaining heavily armed.

Thus the post-1850 fiscal reforms were the savior of Qing rule only in the short run. Eventually they wrecked the Qing Empire from within and from the bottom up. In the end, only an empty shell of an empire remained in China.[125]

Final remarks

These two one-off cases – the Song and the late Qing periods – were two eras when a fiscal state was created in China, with the aim of maximizing revenues. The problem is, these two periods were half a millennium apart (from 1279 to 1860); there was no clear trend of continuity. The unmistakable fact is that, in both cases, the fiscal state was the product of extraordinary circumstances of external threat and/or internal unrest. In other words, a fiscal state emerged only in response to such challenges. This passive nature and exogeneity of a fiscal state in China's long-term history sheds some light on our understanding of the country's growth potential, but also highlights the developmental limits that China faced.

References

Alam, M. S. (1989) *Governments and Markets in Economic Development Strategies.* New York.

Allen, R. C. (2001) "The great divergence: wages and prices from the Middle Ages to the First World War," *Explorations in Economic History* 38: 411–47.

(2005) "Real wages in Europe and Asia: a first look at the long-term patterns," *Living Standards in the Past: New Perspectives on Well-Being in Asia and Europe*, ed. R. C. Allen, T. Bengtsson, and M. Dribe. Oxford: 111–30.

Amsden, A. H. (1989) *Asia's Next Giant: South Korea and Late Industrialization.* New York.

Anon. (1964a [1741]) *Qing Shizong Shilu [Veritable Records of Emperor Shizong of the Qing Dynasty].* Taipei.

(1964b [1799]) *Qing Gaozong Shilu [Veritable Records of Emperor Gaozong of the Qing Dynasty].* Taipei.

(1964c [1824]) *Qing Renzong Shilu [Veritable Records of Emperor Renzong of the Qing Dynasty].* Taipei.

(1987 [1921]) *Qing Dezong Shilu [Veritable Records of Emperor Guangxu of the Qing Dynasty]*, vol. 369. Beijing.

[124] Li (2004: 109). [125] Doyle (1986: 40–5); Colás (2007: 5–11); Münkler (2007: 4–8).

Atwill, D. G. (2006) *The Chinese Sultanate: Islam, Ethnicity and the Panthay Rebellion in Southwest China, 1856–1873*. Stanford, CA.

Beal, E. G. (1958) *The Origin of Likin, 1853–1864*. Cambridge, MA.

Boxer, C. R. (ed.) (1953) *South China in the Sixteenth Century*. London.

Brockey, L. M. (2007) *Journey to the East: The Jesuit Mission to China, 1579–1724*. Cambridge, MA.

Buck, J. L. (1937) *Land Utilization in China: Statistics*. London.

Chang, C. (1962) *The Income of the Chinese Gentry*. Seattle.

Cheng Qi and Ying Jie (eds.) (1968) *Qinding Hubu Zeli [Regulations of Ministry of Revenue, Made by Imperial Order]*, vol. LXXIII. Taipei.

Colás, A. (2007) *Empire*. Cambridge.

Deng, K. G. (1993) *Development versus Stagnation: Technological Continuity and Agricultural Progress in Premodern China*. New York.

(1995) "An evaluation of the role of Admiral Zheng He's voyages in Chinese maritime history," *International Journal of Maritime History* 7: 1–19.

(1997) *Chinese Maritime Activities and Socioeconomic Consequences, c. 2100* BC – *1900 AD*. New York.

(1999) *The Chinese Premodern Economy: Structural Equilibrium and Capitalist Sterility*. London.

(2000) "A critical survey of recent research in Chinese economic history," *Economic History Review* 53: 1–28.

(2003) "Development and its deadlock in imperial China, 221 BC – 1840 AD," *Economic Development and Cultural Change* 51: 479–522.

(2004) "Unveiling China's true population statistics for the pre-modern era with official census data," *Population Review* 43: 1–28.

(2009) "Movers and shakers of knowledge in China during the Ming–Qing period," *History of Technology* 29: 151–71.

Doyle, M. W. (1986) *Empires*. Ithaca, NY.

Dunstan, H. (1996) *Conflicting Counsels to Confuse the Age: A Documentary Study of Political Economy in Qing China, 1644–1840*. Ann Arbor, MI.

Editorial board of *Journal of World History* (ed.) (1981) *Mingzhi Weixinde Zai Tantao [Reevaluation of the Meiji Reform]*. Beijing.

Evans, P. B., Rueschemeyer, D., and Skocpol, T. (eds.) (1985) *Bringing the State Back In*. Cambridge.

Feuerwerker, A. (1980) "Economic trends in the late Ch'ing empire, 1870–1911," in *The Cambridge History of China*, vol. XI, *Late Ch'ing 1800–1911: Part 2*, ed. J. K. Fairbank and K.-C. Liu. Cambridge: 1–69.

(1984) "The state and the economy in late imperial China," *Theory and Society* 13: 297–326.

(1995) *The Chinese Economy, 1870–1949*. Ann Arbor, MI.

Francks, P. (1992) *Japanese Economic Development: Theory and Practice*. London.

Gamble, S. D. (1943) "Daily wages of unskilled Chinese laborers, 1807–1902," *Far Eastern Quarterly* 3: 41–73.

Gerschenkron, A. (1962) *Economic Backwardness in Historical Perspective*. Cambridge, MA.

Gerth, H. H., and Mills, C. W. (eds.) (1946) *From Max Weber: Essays in Sociology*. New York.

Haggard, S., and Kaufman, R. R. (eds.) (1992) *The Politics of Economic Adjustment*. Princeton, NJ.

Hartwell, R. (1966) "Markets, technology, and the structure of enterprise in the development of the eleventh-century Chinese iron and steel industry," *Journal of Economic History* 26: 29–58.

He Changling and Wei Yuan (eds.) (1992) *Huangchao Jingshi Wenbian [Collection of Documents of the Qing Administration]*. Beijing.

Hegel, G. W. F. (1977 [1807]) *Phenomenology of Spirit*, trans. A. V. Miller. Oxford.

Ho, P.-T. (1956) "Early-ripening rice in Chinese history," *Economic History Review* 9: 200–18.

Hobson, J. M. (2004) *The Eastern Origins of Western Civilisation*. Cambridge.

Hou Wailu (1960) *Zhongguo Sixiang Shi [A General History of Thought in China]*, vol. IV. Beijing.

Hui, V. T. (2005) *War and State Formation in Ancient China and Early Modern Europe*. Cambridge.

Jones, E. L. (1981) *The European Miracle: Environments, Economies and Geopolitics in the History of Europe and Asia*. Cambridge.

Jiang Yihua and Wu Genliang (eds.) (1987) *Kang Youwei Quanji [The Collected Works of Kang Youwei]*, vol. I. Shanghai.

Lai, C.-L. (2009) "A contrast between Montesquieu's and Quesnay's thoughts of China's despotism: a methodological reflection," PhD dissertation. National Sun Yat-sen University, Taipei.

Li Guangbi, Qian Junye, and Lai Xinxia (1958) *Zhongguo Nongmin Qiyi Lunji [On Chinese Peasant Rebellions]*. Beijing.

Li Hongzhang (1921) *Li Wenzhonggong Quanji [Collected Works of Li Hongzhang]*, vol. I. Shanghai.

Li Jie (2004) *Wenwu Beiyang [Achievements of the "Northern Modern" Elite]*. Nanning, China.

Li Wenzhi (1993) "Lun mingqing shidai nongmin jingji shangpinlü [Marketing rates of the peasant products in Ming–Qing times]," *Zhongguo Jingjishi Yanjiu [Study of Chinese Economic History]* 1: 21–42.

Li Wenzhi and Jiang Taixin (1995) *Qingdai Caoyun [Stipend Rice during the Qing Period]*. Beijing.

Li Yunjun (ed.) (2000) *Wanqing Jingji Shishi Biannian [A Chronicle of Late Qing Economic History]*. Shanghai.

Li Zhiming (2000) *Wanqing Sida Mufu [Four Major Personal Bureaucracies in the Late Qing]*. Shanghai.

Li, L. M. (1982) "Introduction: food, famine and the Chinese state," *Journal of Asian Studies* 41: 687–707.

Liang Fangzhong (1980) *Zhongguo Lidai Huko Tiandi Tianfu Tongji [Dynastic Data for China's Households, Cultivated Land, and Land Taxation]*. Shanghai.

Lin Shimin (1990) *Haishang Sichouzhi Lude Zhuming Haigang Mingzhou [Ningbo: A Well-Known Port for the Silk Routes]*. Beijing.

Lindley, A. F. (1866a) *Ti-Ping Tien-Kwoh: The History of the Ti-ping Revolution*, vol. I. London.
(1866b) *Ti-Ping Tien-Kwoh: The History of the Ti-ping Revolution*, vol. II. London.
Liu Foding, Wang Yuru, and Zhao Jin (1999) *Zhongguo Jindai Jingji Fazhanshi [A History of Economic Development in Early Modern China]*. Beijing.
Liu, K.-C., and Smith, R. J. (1980) "The military challenge: the north-west and the coast," in *The Cambridge History of China*, vol. XI, *Late Ch'ing 1800–1911: Part 2*, ed. J. K. Fairbank and K.-C. Liu. Cambridge: 202–68.
Liu Yueyun (1901) *Guangxu Kuaiji Biao [Government Accounting Book of the Guangxu Reign]*. Shanghai.
Liu, T. J., and Fei, J. C. H. (1977) "An analysis of the land tax burden in China, 1650–1865," *Journal of Economic History* 37: 339–81.
Luo Ergang (1984) *Xiangjun Bingzhi [A History of the Hunan Army]*. Beijing.
Luo Yudong (1936) *Zhongguo Lijin Shi [A History of the Transit Surcharge in China]*, vol. I. Shanghai.
Mann, S. (1987) *Local Merchants and the Chinese Bureaucracy, 1750–1950*. Stanford, CA.
Marks, R. B. (1991) "Rice prices, food supply, and market structure in eighteenth-century south China," *Late Imperial China* 12: 61–116.
Maverick, L. A. (1946) *China: A Model for Europe*. San Antonio, TX.
Metzger, T. A. (1973) *The Internal Organization of Ch'ing Bureaucracy: Legal, Normative, and Communication Aspects*. Cambridge, MA.
Michael, F. H. (1966) *The Taiping Rebellion: History and Documents*, vol. I, *History*. Seattle.
Mokyr, J. (1990) *The Lever of Riches: Technological Creativity and Economic Progress*. Oxford.
Moore, B. (1966) *Social Origins of Dictatorship and Democracy: Lord and Peasant in the Making of the Modern World*. Boston.
Morse, H. B. (1926) *The Chronicles of the East India Company Trading to China, 1635–1834*, vol. I. Oxford.
Münkler, H. (2007) *Empires*. Cambridge.
Myers, R. H., and Yeh-chien Wang (2002) "Economic developments, 1644–1800," in *The Cambridge History of China*, vol. IX, *The Ch'ing Dynasty to 1800*, ed. W. J. Peterson. Cambridge: 563–647.
Needham, J. (ed.) (1998) *Science and Civilisation in China*, vol. VII, *The Social Background*, part 1, *Language and Logic in Traditional China*. Cambridge.
North, D. C. (1990) *Institutions, Institutional Change and Economic Performance*. Cambridge.
Olson, M. (2000) *Power and Prosperity: Outgrowing Communist and Capitalist Dictatorships*. New York.
Perkins, D. H. (1967) "Government as an obstacle to industrialization: the case of nineteenth-century China," *Journal of Economic History* 27: 478–92.
(1969) *Agricultural Development in China, 1368–1968*. Edinburgh.

Pomeranz, K. (2000) *The Great Divergence: China, Europe, and the Making of the Modern World Economy*. Princeton, NJ.
Porter, J. (1972) *Tseng Kuo-fan's Private Bureaucracy*. Berkeley, CA.
Pryor, F. L. (1980) "The Asian mode of production as an economic system," *Journal of Comparative Economics* 4: 420–42.
Qu Shaohong and Bai Lijian (2006) *Zhongguo Jindai Caizheng Jianshi [A Short History of Government Finance in Early Modern China]*. Tianjin.
Quesnay, F. (1767) *Le Despotisme de la Chine*. Paris.
Ricci, M. (1983 [1610]) *Limadou Zhongguo Zhaji [Matteo Ricci's Diary on China]*. Beijing.
Rosenthal, J.-L., and Wong, R. B. (2011) *Before and beyond Divergence: The Politics of Economic Change in China and Europe*. Cambridge, MA.
Rozman, G. (1973) *Urban Networks in Ch'ing China and Tokugawa Japan*. Princeton, NJ.
Schurz, W. L. (1938) *The Manila Galleon*. Manila.
Shiba, Y. (1970) *Commerce and Society in Sung China*, trans. M. Elvin. Ann Arbor, MI.
Shiue, C. H. (2005) "The political economy of famine relief in China, 1740–1820," *Journal of Interdisciplinary History* 1: 33–55.
Skinner, G. W. (1977) *The City in Late Imperial China*. Stanford, CA.
Smith, A. (1977 [1776]) *An Inquiry into the Nature and Causes of the Wealth of Nations*. Chicago.
Song Lian (1371) *Yuan Shi [History of the Yuan Dynasty]*, vol. 153, entry no. 146. Place unknown.
Spence, J. D. (1999) *The Search for Modern China*. New York.
Tang Xianlong (1992) *Zhongguo Jindai Haiguan Shuishou He Fenpei Tongji [Data for Customs Revenue and Its Distribution in Modern China, 1861–1910]*. Beijing.
Tang Zhijun (ed.) (1981) *Kang Youwei Luzheng Ji [Essays of Kang Youwer on Politics]*, vol. I. Beijing.
Voltaire (1990 [1756]) *Essai sur les moeurs et l'esprit des nations*. Paris.
Wade, R. (1990) *Governing the Market: Economic Theory and the Role of Government in East Asian Industrialization*. Princeton, NJ.
Wan Feng (1984) *Riben Zibenzhuyi Yanjiu [Analysis of Japan's Capitalism]*. Changsha, China.
Wang Jingyu (2000) *Zhongguo Jindai Jingjishi, 1895–1927 [An Economic History of Early Modern China, 1895–1927]*, vol. II. Beijing.
Wang Kaiyun (1927) *Xiangqilou Riji [Diary from the Xiangqi Studio]*, vol. V. Shanghai.
Wang Yeh-chien (1973) *Late Taxation in Imperial China, 1750–1911*. Cambridge, MA.
(1992) "Secular trends of rice prices in the Yangtze Delta, 1638–1935," in *Chinese History in Economic Perspective*, ed. T. G. Rawski and L. M. Li. Berkeley, CA: 35–68.
Wanyan Shaoyuan (2005) *Dao Yanmen Shangbanqu [Go to Work in Government Offices]*. Taipei.

Weber, M. (1951 [1915]) *The Religion of China: Confucianism and Taoism*, trans and ed. H. H. Gerth. New York.

(1958 [1905]) *The Protestant Ethic and the Spirit of Capitalism*, trans. T. Parsons. New York.

Will, P.-E. (1990) *Bureaucracy and Famine in Eighteenth-Century China*. Stanford, CA.

Williams, S. W. (1856) *A Chinese Commercial Guide, Consisting of a Collection of Details and Regulations Respecting Foreign Trade with China, Sailing Directions, Tables, Etc.* Guangzhou.

Wittfogel, K. A. (1957) *Oriental Despotism: A Comparative Study of Total Power*. New Haven, CT.

Wright, A. F., and Twitchett, D. (eds.) (1962) *Confucian Personalities*. Stanford, CA.

Wright, T. (ed.) (1968) *The Travels of Marco Polo, the Venetian*, trans. W. Marsden. New York.

Wu Chengming (2001) *Zhongguode Xiandaihua: Shichang Yu Shehui [China's Modernization: Market and Society]*. Beijing.

Wu, S. (1970) *Communication and Imperial Control in China: The Evolution of the Palace Memorial System, 1693–1735*. Cambridge, MA.

Xu Haisong (2000) *Qingchu Shiren Yu Xixue [Chinese Literati and Western Knowledge during the Early Qing]*. Beijing.

Xu Ke (1917) *Qing Bai Lei Chao [Collection of Antidotes of Qing Times]*, vol. XVIII, book 4. Shanghai.

Xu Song (1957) *Song Huiyao Jigao [Edited Administrative Statutes of the Song Dynasty]*. Beijing.

Yamamura, K. (1986) "The Meiji land tax reform and its effects," in *Japan in Transition: From Tokugawa to Meiji*, ed. M. B. Jansen and G. Rozman. Princeton, NJ: 387–92.

Yan Huicong (1994) "Songdai taociye xingshengde yuanyin [On the rise of the ceramics industry during the Song period]," *Nanchang Daxue Xuebao [Bulletin of the University of Nanchang]* 2: 105–10.

Yang Zhimei (1992) *Xhongguo Gudai Guanzhi Jiangzuo [Bureaucracy of Premodern China]*. Beijing.

Ye Tan (1991) "Songdai gongshangye fazhande lishi tezheng [Features of the development of industries and commerce in the Song period]," *Shanghai Shehui Kexueyuan Jikan [Quarterly Bulletin of Shanghai Academy of Social Sciences]* 2: 103–11.

Yi Xin and Zhu Xueqin (1965) *Qinding Pingding Yuefei Fanglue [Strategies and Tactics to Suppress Guangdong Taiping Bandits, Made by Imperial Order]*. Taipei.

Yi Xin and Zhu Xueqin (1968a) *Qinding Pingding Guizhou Miaofei Fanglue [Strategies and Tactics to Suppress Miao Bandits in Guizhou, Made by Imperial Order]*. Taipei.

Yi Xin and Zhu Xueqin (1968b) *Qinding Pingding Yunnan Huifei Fanglue [Strategies and Tactics to Suppress the Muslin Bandits in Yunnan, Made by Imperial Order]* Taipei.

Yi Xin and Zhu Xueqin (1990) *Qinding Pingding Shaangan Xinjiang Huifei Fanglue [Strategies and Tactics to Suppress the Muslin Bandits in Shaanxi, Gansu, and Xinjiang, Made by Imperial Order]*. Lanzhou, China.

Yu Yaohua (2000) *Zhongguo Jiage Shi [A History of Prices in China]*. Beijing.

Zelin, M. (1984) *The Magistrate's Tael: Rationalizing Fiscal Reform in Eighteenth-Century Ch'ing China*. Berkeley, CA.

Zhang Dechang (1970) *Qingji Yige Jingguande Shenghuo [Life of a Qing Official in Beijing]*. Hong Kong.

Zhang Deze (2001) *Qingdai Guojia Jiguan Kaolue [The State Apparatus of the Qing Period]*. Beijing.

Zhang Shaoliang and Zheng Xianjin (1983) *Zhongguo Nongmin Geming Douzhengshi [A History of Revolutionary Struggle of the Chinese Peasantry]*. Beijing.

Zhang Shen (1992) "Xifeng bianfa shiqide haiwai maoyi [Sino-foreign trade during the Song reforms in 1068–85 CE]," *Hebei Xuekan [Hebei Journal]* 5: 79–84.

Zhang Tiemiu and Gao Xiaoxing (2006) *Zhongguo Gudai Haijun Shi [A Naval History of Premodern China]*. Beijing.

Zhang Tingyu (1986) *Ming Shi [History of the Ming Dynasty]*, vol. X of *Er-shi-wu Shi [Twenty-Five Official Histories]*. Shanghai.

Zhao Erxun (1986) *Qingshi Gao [Draft of the History of the Qing Dynasty]*, vol. XI of *Er-shi-wu Shi [Twenty-Five Official Histories]*. Shanghai.

Zhou Bodi (1981) *Zhongguo Caizheng Shi [A History of State Finance in China]*. Shanghai.

Zuo Bofu (1976) *Qingdai Yongzhengchaode Yanglianyin Yanjiu [A Study of "Honesty and Uprightness Bonus" under the Yongzheng Reign, 1723–35]*. Taipei.

Zuo Zongtang (1890) *Zuo Wenxianggong Zoushu Chubian [Zuo Zongtang's Memorials to the Throne]*, vol. LIX, no. 11. Shanghai.

PART III

Divergent Trends among Established Regimes

CHAPTER 11

Late Rome, Byzantium, and early medieval western Europe

John Haldon

Introduction

"The financial system was set up to take care of matters of public importance that arise on occasion, such as the building of ships and of walls. But it is principally concerned with paying the soldiers. Each year most of the income of the public revenues are spent for this purpose."[1]

This brief but telling remark is taken from an anonymous ninth-century Byzantine handbook on strategy, and gives us some idea of how medieval east Romans or Byzantines understood their own fiscal system – a system that had evolved uninterrupted out of the later Roman Empire in the east, with its capital and imperial court at Constantinople, modern Istanbul. From the sixth to the twelfth centuries this Byzantine Empire dominated the eastern Mediterranean, vying for political and military preeminence with the Islamic powers to the east and with new polities in the Balkans, and during the tenth century going over to an offensive that enabled it to expand into the Caucasus, recover considerable territories in northern Syria, and crush the Bulgarian state, which was incorporated for almost two centuries into the empire itself. But by the later twelfth century the rise of western and central European powers that could match the Byzantines in terms of technology, resources, and organization, culminating in the Fourth Crusade of 1204 and the sack of Constantinople itself, put an end to Byzantine preeminence. While the constantly changing international situation played a crucial contributory role in determining the empire's potential for survival, the power and authority – and therefore the effectiveness – of the government at Constantinople was largely founded on the

[1] Anon. (1985 [*c.* 850]: sect. II, 18–21). The text has traditionally been dated to the sixth century, but several scholars have now shown that, in the form in which is has come down to us, it should most probably be assigned to the ninth century, as a number of internal features would suggest. The possibility that it is at origin a sixth-century document reworked and expanded in the ninth century should be borne in mind: Zuckerman (1990); Cosentino (2000); Rance (2007). For our purposes, the material point remains valid. For general discussion on resources, see Haldon (1995).

degree to which it was able to exercise control over the resources necessary to its continued existence and to the maintenance of its army and its administrative machinery. Integral to the ways in which it achieved this were also certain social/economic and ideological interests. It is the fluctuating relationship between these elements and the extraction and redistribution of resources that determined both the internal limits and the extent of state power. Since the ways in which states exercise power and authority vary along a scale that alternates between two poles – extreme centralization and extreme decentralization – such changes and fluctuations are essential to understanding why the empire evolved in the ways it did.

The history of taxation – or, perhaps better, the history of resource extraction, redistribution, allocation, and consumption by political systems in the western Eurasian world from the sixth to twelfth centuries CE – is one of complexity, of hybridity, of failed initiatives and successful crisis management, of consummate bureaucratic manipulation, and of power struggles, all within a framework that may best be described as one of competitive selection. Although "best practice" and "fit for purpose" might be part of contemporary Western management-speak, they are phrases that might equally apply, in their essence, to the process of the evolution or abandonment of fiscal management structures in the early medieval European world. If it is possible to extrapolate from a range of case studies a common causal theme in the evolution of fiscal and political structures across several historical polities, then it will be possible to construct a model, a heuristic tool, that will help us to understand systemic transformation across a wide range of historically variable conditions and contexts, and thus offer possibilities for answering the question of why some systems ultimately failed to thrive or transform while others did not.

This chapter does not attempt this larger task, but it does examine in particular the case of the medieval eastern Roman Empire, and place it in the context of developments in central and western medieval Europe, as well as in the Balkans. Beginning with a descriptive account of different fiscal practices across these cultures and across the period in question, I then attempt to isolate some of the underlying structures that generated these forms, to see whether some broader elements were indeed present and shared across the political-economic systems in question. While the descriptive model of fiscal adaptive change for European political systems set out by Bonney and Ormrod[2] can be substantially modified in many respects, it does provide a useful summary of a number of key features of

[2] Bonney and Ormrod (1999).

different type of state: fiscal system associations; and, while none of the arrangements I look at in this chapter can be fitted neatly into one category of "tribute," "domain," "tax," or "fiscal" state, the typology does provide a useful framework, I think, for considering how to investigate the question.

The later Roman and Byzantine world from *c.* 500 to 1204: context

The first priority for the government at Constantinople was the maintenance of its territorial integrity; without territory there was no state. To achieve this end it required two things: an army, with which to defend itself against external foes and to maintain order internally; and a fiscal system, through which the resources to achieve this, as well as to support the other apparatuses of government, could be extracted from the producing population. Late Roman and Byzantine society was an agrarian society of peasants and rural artisans, and they were the only realistic source of surplus wealth production.[3] Trade and commerce flourished across the Mediterranean world, and even after the collapse of east Roman power in the middle of the seventh century and the rise of the new Arab Islamic Empire the evidence suggests that it continued, if on a more regionally nuanced and in places much more fragile basis, until a recovery set in during the ninth century and beyond. Calculating the proportion of total government revenues from agriculture, on the one hand, and trade and commerce, on the other, is very difficult, because there is little in the way of quantifiable data. At the height of the period of economic expansion, during the middle and later twelfth century, the state's gross revenue from the non-agricultural sector has been estimated at little more than a fifth of that from the agrarian sector; substantial enough in a premodern agrarian society, it is true, but still relatively modest compared with, say, the trading cities of northern Italy at the same period. This situation remained until after the Fourth Crusade in 1204, when the consequent dramatic territorial shrinkage of the empire shifted the balance dramatically. As the ratio of landed income to commercial income changed in favor of the latter, trade become a significant element in the state's economy, as well as in its awareness.[4]

[3] For general overviews of the Byzantine economy, see Laiou (2002b), Lefort and Morrisson (1989), Kravari, Lefort, and Morrisson (1991), and Oikonomidès (2002).

[4] See Laiou (2002b) for a survey of the evidence, emphasizing also the rise in the importance of trade and commerce after the ninth century.

It would still be broadly true to say, therefore, that, while the government derived some fiscal benefit from commerce through customs and transportation levies, exacted at certain key points, this may have been as much an aspect of the enforcement of political authority along the frontiers as a purely revenue-generating exercise. Until its last century and a half, Byzantine society was dominated throughout by a system of extracting resources characterized by the appropriation of wealth through a variety of forms of tax and rent imposed on land – agrarian and pastoral production. This does not mean that they were the only forms of surplus appropriation; slavery continued to exist, but even as early as the fourth century in the East seems to have played only a very limited role in direct production and, more importantly, in the production of the wealth of the dominant class, being restricted for the most part to the domestic or industrial sphere – certainly, therefore, an aspect, and a significant aspect, of the productive process. Indeed, during the late Roman period agricultural slaves came to approximate more and more, to various degrees, to tied but free tenants, and the result was that the economic reality of slavery faded away in many contexts. However important slavery may have been, therefore, as a general means of exploiting human labor power, rent and tax – not the intensive, plantation-based exploitation of chattel-slaves – was the main form of surplus appropriation from the later third century and afterward in the eastern Roman world.[5]

Surplus appropriation could take many different forms. Private landlords normally collected rent in cash or kind, according to the nature of the contract or lease and according to the economic conditions of the time or area, or both. The existence or not of a market for each locality, and thus of the potential for producers to exchange their surplus goods for cash, determined the form. The state exacted surplus in both cash and kind, from the regular taxes on land, for example, as well as through a variety of labor services – the maintenance of the postal stations and horses, or the production of iron ore, woven cloths, and so on – that would be calculated according to centrally determined tables of equivalence. By the same token, local communities were on occasion required to help with the building of roads and bridges or fortifications, and to billet and feed soldiers and their officers, imperial officials and messengers, and so on. By the ninth century the state demanded the production of weapons and various items of

[5] See McCormick (2001: 244–54, 733–77) for a detailed analysis of the slave trade in the period from about 600 to 900, and Wickham (2005: 259ff.) for an argument for the diminishing importance of slavery as a form of exploitation of agrarian labor. See also Banaji (2010), and the older discussion given by Wickham (1984).

military equipment from provincial craftsmen, imposed as additional corvées. Extraordinary levies in food or grain were common. Military service always brought with it exemption from these extra demands, but did not merit exemption from the chief state taxes on land. All these forms of surplus appropriation were obtained through "customary" obligations and the force of law, as in most cases, backed up ultimately by imperial military might, or by simple threats and bullying, by state officials, churchmen, or private landlords. Only at the very end of the Byzantine period, when the state was reduced to a few districts in the southern Balkans and the Aegean islands, did commerce become a significant element in the state economy. But by then, as we have seen, the Byzantine Empire was itself an insignificant political force in the east Mediterranean.

Coinage and money

The late Roman and Byzantine state was always relatively highly monetized, though it is also the case that there were strong regional as well as chronological variations in the availability and use of coin. Areas in which urban or rural markets existed and were secure from hostile attack, such as the metropolitan regions around Constantinople, were generally supplied not only with gold but also with bronze coinage, for example. The physical evidence is largely derived from casual finds of bronze, but it should also be remembered that the imperial administrators, tax officials, and military received their salaries in gold, and, depending on circumstances, would have spent some of this in the provinces. The extent to which the economy of an area remained monetized depended upon several factors: the structure of rural exploitation, for example, was a key element, and the contraction of the available supply of gold would have impacted in several ways.[6] The army or other state-funded activities, such as the *dromos* or courier and transport service, played an important role in enabling the population of some areas to obtain gold for taxation, even when fixed tariffs for certain commodities, such as wheat, were enforced – and, in this respect, even quite small urban centers that had a military and

[6] See Banaji (2001: 6–22, 39–88), with the critical comments of Sarris (2001). Banaji somewhat overestimates the liquidity of the monetized economy after the middle of the seventh century, however, by assuming that the conditions that pertained before the Islamic conquests continued to hold in respect of both the issue of gold coin and the nature and structure of the Byzantine state elite. For changes in landlord–tenant relations across the period from the sixth to the eighth centuries, see Haldon (1997: 132–41) and Kaplan (1992: 161–9, 186–218); for estate management and labour in the sixth century, see Sarris (2006: 29–70 [50–68 on credit]; 2004).

administrative presence would have remained foci for money-based exchange.[7] The usual constraints on a generalized system of monetary exchange became more pronounced in difficult political and military conditions, but such constraints had always operated in remoter localities, or areas where the activities of the state did not promote such monetized activity.[8]

Moving wealth around the empire was thus easiest in the form of coin, and the state always preferred to use coin when possible, though the existence of isolated regions without market possibilities meant that some resources always had to be raised in kind or services. At the same time, it meant that the state could use the presence of soldiers in particular (who were usually paid in coin) as a sort of mobile market, and it was frequently the case that, by demanding that local populations sold goods to the army at artificially low prices, the state benefited at the cost of the producers when there was no access to a normal market. Transport of bulk goods overland was very costly, and was practicable only for the state, which invested in a system of fast and slow transportation to serve its own requirements, in particular supplying the army with equipment and food, and moving news and information. The role of the state transport system, the Roman *cursus publicus* or, in Greek, *dromos*, remained crucial throughout the empire's history. During the period from the fourth century to the middle of the sixth it was organized in two divisions, regular (*cursus clabularis* or *platys dromos*) and fast (*cursus velox* or *oxys dromos*), responsible, respectively, for the transportation of goods in bulk, whether by oxcart or by mule and packhorse, and for the rapid movement of messengers and imperial officials of all kinds around the empire. Some changes to these arrangements were made by reforms carried through in the middle of the sixth century. But, even though it may have been trimmed and reduced from its original extent, a system of post stations, with small teams of riding and pack animals, continued to be supported. The system was maintained by state-funded purchases of provisions or impositions on particular groups or individuals, who received exemption from certain taxes in return; the animals were originally supplied by the state ranches on which they were bred and raised, later by a combination of state and private supply. The use of the animals attached to the post stations was strictly controlled by the issue of state warrants, issued either by the

[7] See, for example, Ireland (2000), Ashton, Lightfoot, and Özme (2000: 171–92), Lightfoot (2009), and Dagron (2002).

[8] See Hendy (1985: 294–305; 1989), Haldon (1994), Morrisson (2002: 954ff.), and Laiou (2002a) for a general discussion of the balance between economic and non-economic exchange (although the question might better be presented in terms of monetized and non-monetized exchange).

praetorian prefects of the appropriate prefecture – who were responsible for the administration of the system – or the office of the *magister officiorum* (the "master of offices," who was in charge of the state's messengers and couriers). By the 760s, and following upon the changes that occurred in the administration of the state during the later seventh century, this transport and postal system was an independent department under its *logothete* ("accountant"), a high-ranking officer; numerous seals for the position survive.

Put very simply, the state financed its operations through a straightforward redistributive mechanism that worked through the issue of gold coin, by which state officials and, above all, the army were paid, and through which they then purchased their foodstuffs and other requirements. The state then collected this gold via money taxes. It is apparent that such a system operates most efficiently when a plurimetallic system exists – that is, if a petty coinage (in this case, bronze) is available through which day-to-day exchanges can be carried out, change given, and so on. Such a coinage, if it is to function at all, must have a stable rate of exchange with the precious metal coinage, so that in this respect the government always faced two problems: first, to estimate how much gold coinage should be produced to maintain the cycle of redistribution and to service the demands of its own personnel; second, to know how much bronze coinage was required to facilitate this cycle at the lower level, the overissue of which generally had inflationary consequences and, when the relationship with precious metal coinage broke down, the bronze coinage became marginalized.[9] When the precious metal coinage was also scarce, price inflation – followed by hoarding – usually ensued, and, so far as state fiscal requirements were concerned, a fairly rapid move from the extraction of fiscal revenues in cash to one in which actual produce was collected, with all the consequences for the distribution of goods and personnel that that entailed. But a regular, reliable gold issue sufficient to cover the needs of the military and the bureaucracy, put into the market through purchases of the supplies, goods, and services to meet these needs, maintained the stability of the system, if not its former flexibility.[10] The incidence of taxation – raising resources – in kind thus varied regionally. There may have been occasions when the empire's resources were collected almost entirely in this form, but such occasions were not very frequent. There was a strongly regionalized pattern, which in its turn depended on longer-term

[9] See Hendy (1985: 297–9); see also Curta (2005: 120f.; 2001: 170–6), with literature.

[10] The evidence from hoards of gold coin is generally taken to confirm this; see, for example, Morrisson (1980; 1985; 1991; 2002). On prices, see Morrisson and Cheynet (2002).

patterns of the availability of coin, the political conditions in each area, and the relation of towns and the larger population centers to their hinterlands and major routes of communication, military needs, and so forth.[11]

The administration of taxation

The main function of the late Roman and Byzantine administration was the assessment, collection, and redistribution of fiscal resources, in whatever form, toward the maintenance of the state.[12] The amount of tax required by the government varied year by year according to the international political situation and according to internal requirements. From the early fourth century CE state finances had come to be controlled and administered through three departments: the praetorian prefectures, the "sacred largesses" (*sacrae largitiones*), and the "private fisc" (*res privata*). The most important was the praetorian prefecture, through which the land tax assessment was calculated, collected, and redistributed. Each prefecture comprised a specific territory, although they were reorganized and redistributed on several occasions. In the 320s there were three major prefectures: Oriens (stretching from Moesia and Thrace in the Balkans around to Upper Libya in Africa); Illyricum, with Italy and Africa; and the Gauls, including Britain and Tingitana in North Africa. By the 440s these had been rearranged into four prefectures: the Gauls, Italy with North Africa, Illyricum, and the East (Oriens). The Gallic, Italian, and much of the North African prefectures were lost during the middle and later fifth century, leaving Illyricum and Oriens only, but with Justinian's reconquests in the period from about 530 to 550 new prefectures for Italy and for Africa were established. Each prefecture was subdivided into dioceses (the Roman form of the term was *dioecesae*, "directorates"), under a deputy – *vicarius* – of the praetorian prefect; and each diocese was divided into provinces under provincial governors. The lowest unit of administration was then the city – *civitas* or *polis* – each with its district – *territorium* – upon which the assessment and collection of taxes ultimately devolved. Taxes were raised in a variety of forms, but the most important regular tax was the land tax. This could be raised in money, and traditionally had

[11] For some useful discussion of the relationships between urban centers and their *territoria* up to the middle of the seventh century, see Trombley (2001). For coinage, see especially Reece (2003).

[12] The following paragraphs are based on material expounded by Jones (1964), Haldon (1997), Brandes and Haldon (2000), Brandes (2002), Brubaker and Haldon (2011: 665ff.), and Oikonomidès (1996; 2002). For the older literature on Byzantine fiscal administration, see Dölger (1927), Ostrogorsky (1927), Karayannopoulos (1958; 1966), and Svoronos (1959).

been; but during the financial crisis that the state suffered in the later third century, and as a result of the restructuring of finances and military arrangements under Diocletian and Constantine, much of it was actually raised in kind – grains, other foodstuffs, and so forth – and deposited in a vast network of state warehouses, where it could be drawn on by soldiers and civial administrators alike, who received a large portion of their salaries in the form of rations (*annonae*). As the financial situation of the government improved during the fourth century and into the fifth, so these rations could be commuted once again for cash – assuming the producers were able to obtain it – but the government always kept available the option of raising revenues in kind, especially when military requirements demanded it. The prefectures, through their diocesan and, more particularly, their provincial levels of administration, were also responsible for the maintenance of the public post, the state weapons and arms factories, and provincial public works. The latter – the maintenance of roads, bridges, and granaries, and the provision of crafts and skills for particular tasks – were provided through special levies or impositions upon the population, or specific groups within the population, depending on the task in hand.

The other finance departments, the sacred largesses and the private fisc, had evolved out of earlier Roman palatine departments, and had more limited functions. The sacred largesses were responsible for bullion from mines, minting coin, state-run clothing workshops, and the issue of military donatives – regular and irregular gifts of coin to the troops for particular occasions such as an imperial birthday, accession celebration, and so forth. This department had local branches in each diocese, and representatives in the cities and provinces to administer the revenues drawn from civic lands (which it administered after the middle of the fifth century) and from other income, such as the cash for the commutation of miltary service or the provision of horses for the army. The *res privata*, under its *comes*, was essentially responsible for the income derived as rents from imperial lands, whatever their origin (from confiscation, for example, of by bequest or escheat). It was as complex as that of the *comes sacrarum largitionum*, with different sections responsible for its various tasks. During the sixth century its responsibilties were divded between income destined for state purposes and that employed to maintain the imperial household, and a new department, the *patrimonium*, was established.

During the course of the sixth century both the sacred largesses and the private fisc were further altered: the various estates administered by the latter were organized into five sections, each independent (including the original *res privata*), responsible for different types of estate and expenditure, while the diocesan level of the activities of the sacred largesses was gradually subsumed by the provincial level of the praetorian prefectures. The situation of the seventh century speeded up this process. Under Heraclius, a major centralization of minting took place, involving the retention of mints at Ravenna, Carthage, and Alexandria, apart from Constantinople, and the closure of the remaining six provincial mints. During his reign, and over the following twenty years or so, the *sacrae largitiones* disappeared as a separate department. Over the same period the praetorian prefecture of the East (that of Illyricum effectively disappeared with the loss of imperial control over most of the Balkans) was broken up, so that each of its subsections became an independent bureau, mostly under its own *logothetes*, or accountant. These *logothetai* were quite senior officials, subordinated in the first instance to the supervision of the *sakellarios*, and then the emperor himself.

The role of the *sakellarios*, as superintendant of the imperial household finances, illustrates the changes. His close association with the emperor and the imperial household shows that a process of centralization was taking place in which the emperors played a much more active managerial role – a reflection of the crisis in the empire's financial and political situation in the years from 640 on. By the middle of the eighth century the new structures are more apparent in the sources. A *logothete* for the general finance office (*genikon logothesion*) was responsible for the land tax and associated revenues; similarly, a department for military finance (*stratiotikon logothesion*) dealt with recruitment, muster rolls, and military pay, while another department, the *idikon*, or special *logothesion*, dealt with armaments, imperial workshops, and a host of related miscellaneous requirements. The various departments that were once part of the *res privata* became similarly entirely independent and placed under their own officials. The public post, previously under the *magister officiorum*, the master of offices, became independent under its own *logothete*. Other departments that had originally been part of the imperial household, such as the sacred bedchamber, evolved into special treasuries and storehouses for special state requirements, while the bedchamber itself, known as the *koitôn*, evolved its own personal imperial treasury for household expenditures. The result of the political changes and massive loss of territory of the seventh century, and the consequent fiscal crisis that affected the empire during this period, was thus to generate a transformed fiscal organization, evidenced by the appearance of provincial fiscal officials – *dioiketai* – responsible for collecting the taxes, which were assessed and verified by *epoptai* and *exisotai*, all under the general authority of the *genikon logothesion*. Provincial fiscal affairs and the coordination of military and fiscal arrangements constituted the sphere of the *protonotarios*, an official who appears during the 820s and who was responsible to the central financial department of the *sakellion*.

These structures remained in force with minor modifications, until the later eleventh century. From this time onward tax collection and assessment came increasingly to be in the hands of a single official for each province, the *praktor*, originally a low-ranking fiscal agent but, by the twelfth century, a tax farmer who worked in conjunction with another assessment official, the *apographeus*, who was responsible for drawing up detailed accounts of the taxable lands in a *praktikon* – a statement of the taxes owing on each fiscal unit or group of units and of tenants' obligations to their landlord. From the 1090s into the first decade of the twelfth century the emperor Alexios I was responsible for a series of major reforms in the central and provincial fiscal administration of the empire. New supervisors of the central bureaux were created: the *logothetês* of the *sekreta* (i.e. of the "departments") who acted as a general overseer; the grand *logariastês*, to supervise the administration of taxation; and the grand *logariastês* of the imperial domains and related institutions (including charitable houses). At the same time, he ordered a fundamental reassessment of all basic taxes, and began to issue a reformed coinage, with a greater number of fractional denominations, to meet the increased demand for precious-metal coin in commercial and day-to-day transactions.

A major change in the ways in which resources were administered occurred during the twelfth century, with the expansion of the institution known as *pronoia* – literally "care" or "forethought." The term referred to the concession by the state of the right to receive the revenues from certain public (i.e. fiscal, or taxed) districts; or of certain imperial estates, and their tenants, along with part or all of the rents and taxes raised from them. Such grants were made to individuals by the emperors for a variety of reasons. They took the form of personal grants from the ruler, who represented the state in the institutional sense; and, while there was also a more general meaning of the term *pronoia*, the most important involved *pronoia* grants in return for military service. This was a new departure, and, involving as it did – for the first time – the temporary alienation of state revenues to private individuals, it marked a further move along the line from absolute to devolved state power referred to in the opening sections of this chapter. It is important to emphasize that *pronoia* grants were at first limited to members of the extended family of the imperial clan, the Comneni; and that, although the emperor Manuel I appears to have employed them a little more liberally, they first appeared on a wider scale after the events of

1204 and the introduction into many areas of the Byzantine world of Western, feudal arrangements. These no doubt had an influence on the Byzantine way of doing things, and may have speeded up the development of *pronoia* on a more generalized basis. But such grants were given not only on a large scale to individuals but also to groups, and sometimes on a very small scale, while the government, at least in theory, always retained the right to revoke such a grant. They rarely became hereditary in the proper sense.

Taxation: demand, assessment, and collection

A fundamental principle of late Roman and Byzantine taxation was to ensure the maximization of exploitation, and hence of revenues. In the later Roman period this was achieved by a system whereby land registered for taxation but not cultivated was attributed for assessment to neighboring landlords – a process known as *adiectio sterilium*. Tax was assessed according to a formula tying land, determined by area, quality, and type of crop, to labor power – a formula referred to as the *capitatio–iugatio* system. Land that was not exploited, either by agriculture or for pasturage, was not taxed directly. The tax burden was reassessed at intervals, originally in cycles of five, then of fifteen, years, although in practice it took place far more irregularly. From the seventh or eighth centuries a number of changes were introduced. Each tax unit was expected to produce a fixed revenue, distributed across taxpayers, who were as a body responsible for deficits, which they shared. The tax unit – the community, in effect – was jointly responsible for the payments due from lands that belonged to their tax unit but were not farmed, for whatever reason. Remissions of tax could be requested or bestowed to compensate for such burdens, but, if the community took over and farmed the land for which they had been responsible, they had also to pay the deficits incurred by the remission. During the same period the cities lost their role as crucial intermediaries in the levying of taxation, which was now devolved for the most part upon imperial officials of the provinces and upon the village community.

The most important change that took place after the seventh century seems to have been the introduction of a distributive tax assessment, whereby the annual assessment was based on the capacity of the producers to pay, rather than on a flat rate determined by the demands of the state budget. This involved, of course, accurate records and statements of property, and one important result was that the Byzantine Empire evolved one of the most advanced land registration and fiscal assessment systems of the medieval world, as well as one of the most sophisticated bureaucracies for administering it. It also appears to have been associated with the ending of the connection between the land tax and the poll tax: instead of a combined *capitatio–iugatio* assessment, the land tax, or *kanon*, was now assessed as a separate item, with the replacement for the poll tax, known as the *kapnikon*, or "hearth" tax, raised on each household. These changes may not have happened overnight, and there is no imperial legislation to give us a clue as to when and how they occurred, but they had been completed by the middle of the ninth century, and probably long beforehand. The regular taxation of land was supplemented by a wide range of extraordinary taxes and corvées, noted already, including obligations to provide hospitality for soldiers and officials, maintain roads, bridges, and fortifications, and to deliver and/or produce a wide range of requirements such as charcoal or wood. These continued unbroken into the middle and later Byzantine periods, although their Latin names were mostly replaced with Greek or Hellenized equivalents. But certain types of landed property were always exempt from many of these extra taxes, in particular the land owned or held by soldiers, and that held by persons registered in the service of the public post, in both cases because of traditional favored conditions of service, and because they depended to a degree on their property for the carrying out of their duties (see below on soldiers). Although the basic land tax and the accompanying hearth tax now became the fundamental elements of the tax system, the situation was complicated by the addition of a vast range of extra and incidental impositions: quite apart from the extraordinary taxes in kind or services mentioned already, government tax officials began to add more and more extras to their demands, in the form of fees for their services and demands for hospitality (which could then be commuted for money), so that the system became immensely ramified. During the second half of the eleventh century depreciation of the precious-metal coinage, combined with bureaucratic corruption, led to the near-collapse of the system.

Further real changes were not made until the early twelfth century, when the emperor Alexios I was forced by inflationary pressures and the complexity and ad hoc nature of the old system to introduce important changes. The older charges were rationalized, standard rates were established, and the bureaucracy was trimmed. Increasingly, however, as the wealthy and powerful managed to extract exemptions for themselves and their lands from many fiscal burdens, the weight of the state's demands fell upon an ever more hard-pressed peasantry, so that the social divisions within the empire, which had grown with the evolution of the new, middle Byzantine elite as it gradually turned itself into an aristocracy of office and birth, became more and more apparent. During the later ninth century the system of communal responsibility for untilled lands was transformed into a system in which land could be temporarily exempted from taxation, removed from the fiscal district to which it originally belonged, and administered separately, or granted special reductions in taxation. Such interventionist measures seem to have been intended to maintain as close a degree of control as possible over fiscal resources in land. Yet over the same period, and in order to retain control over its fiscal base and to compete with the elite and the powerful, the government itself began to transform fiscal land into state lands, so that rents to the government in its capacity as a landlord now became indistinguishable in many respects from taxation. The evolution of *pronoia* represented an alternative means of redistributing resources by the government, but also encouraged this overlap.

Until the end of the twelfth century the government was able to retain a fairly effective control over fiscal resources. But the growth of the aristocracy, which had first challenged the state in the tenth century, had continued; it was from members of this elite that the emperors from the later eleventh century were drawn, and whose hold on power was determined largely by their ability to maintain a series of family alliances – through marriage, governorships, and so on – with their peers. After 1204 in particular the devolution of imperial authority became the chief means by which emperors governed and administered, and through which imperial resources were mobilized. Central taxation – the land tax and its associated impositions – remained the basis of government finance; but, as the empire shrank territorially, so commerce came to play a more important role, yet one that was already limited by the strength and dominant position in the carrying trade of Italian merchants and maritime power. The fact that the *kommerkion* on trade was, by the end of the empire, a more important source of income than the land tax illustrates the insoluble problem faced by the emperors of the last century of Byzantium.[13]

So far I have described the later Roman and Byzantine Empire in the period from the sixth to the twelfth century as though it were an effective bureaucratically managed medieval state system, very different from its western and northern neighbours, and with a non-aristocratic elite managing fiscal resources and the army efficiently (or less so) for the benefit of the imperial state. That this bureaucracy was to some degree compromised by vested interests, and by the existence of an imperial court at Constantinople and the network of patronage radiating from it, is

[13] See the summary given by Haldon (2013), and the detailed account by Harvey (1989).

generally admitted. But we should bear in mind both that this bureaucracy was not fully professional (it bears no comparison, for example, to the later Chinese mandarinate) and that it was heavily mediated by familial connections and local or regional loyalties. A good proportion of the resources extracted through money taxes were actually consumed by the extracting imperial officials themselves – a point recognized by the government in its estimates of revenues required.

In 1694 the Bank of England was established on the basis of a mutual share issue with a guaranteed 8 percent return. Within a year it had raised over £1.5 million, enough to fund a vast new programme of warship construction. Within ten years the revived and reequipped Royal Navy had confronted and defeated the French and begun to transform the military-political balance of power in western Europe. Much more significantly, though, the demands of the navy stimulated over the following half-century a vast increase in industrial output, as well as a host of new industries, promoting both technological innovation and improved construction and production techniques.[14] The Byzantine state had no such option at its disposal. It had no opportunity to raise loans or generate credit. Credit certainly existed, but only at the level of individual transactions and trading relationships. When the government needed additional revenues, it had three basic options: (1) impose an additional round of taxation (nominally set against future annual levies, but this debt was often "forgotten," either empire-wide or across the provinces where the resources were required; (2) "borrow" funds from the Church (usually plate to be melted down for cash) or other private persons (members of the government establishment or the aristocracy/elite, monastic houses); or (3) temporarily debase the coinage. Had the option to raise loans on such a massive scale existed, we can be sure Byzantine rulers would have taken them – and we would then confront a very different eastern Mediterranean economic and financial world, in which state borrowing to invest in military and naval warfare may well have stimulated a dramatic transformation of economic, and thus social and political, relationships.

Or not: for the structural constraints imposed by the Byzantine "thought world" or symbolic universe, by medieval social relations, by political ideologies, and by the availability of certain key natural resources, iron ore in particular, would almost certainly have meant that such changes in finance would only gradually have effected the sort of transformative change that occurred in England after the 1690s. In other words, historical

[14] See Roseveare (1991: 34) and Roberts and Kynaston (1995).

context plays a crucial role – obviously – in determining the possibilities for transformation, and the mere fact of the existence of a particular social, economic, or political institution, in and of itself, is no guarantee of such change. It has long been recognized, for example, that various forms of capitalist enterprise existed in the Roman and medieval worlds – indeed, that such enterprises often dominated their market sector and that they impacted in various significant ways on the social relations with which they came into contact. But we cannot speak of capitalism as the dominant means of generating social wealth until a whole range of other changes had also occurred – changes that were far broader geographically and economically than the economic sector in which these limited forms had evolved.[15] By the same token, I would suggest that, even if credit and loan investment arrangements had existed (and in Roman law the legal and institutional framework for their existence was already present), we would have seen the Byzantine state invest its funds quantitatively rather than qualitatively. Increased military investment and recruitment would have generated expanded markets for a range of agrarian and artisanal produce – foodstuffs, livestock, warhorses, arms and armor, leather goods, and so forth – and this would have stimulated economic growth in some areas, and perhaps resulted in further victorious warfare and the incorporation of new and taxable lands. But this would have been an expansion in quantity, as noted already, liable to collapse in on itself very rapidly, since neither the technological nor the intellectual structures to support it yet existed.

The incidence of taxation

Attempts to calculate the percentage burden of output taken in tax from the producing population face a number of methodological problems, and are likely to founder for lack of adequate statistical evidence, although some efforts have been made.[16] But that the burden was heavy, and that it swallowed up much – in some cases perhaps most – of the surplus[17] generated by the rural population every year, is very probable; it is clear that, once they had acquitted their basic land tax and rents, peasant producers had little extra to give in the event of the imposition of an

[15] Banaji (2010); Sarris (2006; 2009). [16] See Treadgold (1982), and the review by Lilie (1987).

[17] A "surplus" is, of course, a flexible quantity. In its simplest form, I take it to refer to what remains after the subsistence consumption needs of the producer are taken into account; but, since subsistence needs can be fixed along a spectrum ranging from minimum nutritional requirements (to permit biological reproduction and labor) upward, it is obvious that there may often be a very considerable degree of variation in the percentage of gross product characterized as "surplus."

extraordinary levy, for military purposes, for example.[18] Documents dating from the tenth to twelfth centuries suggest that the basic land tax amounted to some 4.5 to 5 percent, or one-twenty-fourth, of the value of the land, the calculation of value being based on the average "normal" sale price, while rents represented usually double this amount. The percentage of the annual crop that the former reflected varied, of course, but it seems that about 10 to 12 percent would be a reasonable average, although it may have been higher at times and in particular regions; the absolute burden was very considerably increased, both by the rent extracted by landlords and by the addition of a number of regular supplementary impositions, as well as by the extraordinary levies (which were often raised on a yearly basis, particularly in regions where the armies were active). A global rate of taxation of between 15 and 23 percent has been proposed for the empire in the period from the eighth century onward, for example, varying by time and place, degree of monetization, and other related factors.[19] From the evidence of the eighth to tenth centuries, the basic rent for a leased holding was 10 percent of the crop.[20]

There are one or two cases of evidence surviving from which one can infer the ratio between tax paid to the state and rents paid to a landlord. From calculations based on information about imperial and ecclesiastical revenues from Sicily in the later seventh and early eighth centuries, for example, it can be inferred that tax revenue and rent represented more or less equivalent values.[21] But this total represented less than 100 percent of the gross produce or market value from the estates in question, since the same documents show that at least a further 3 percent of the combined total of rent and tax was generated in grain, the equivalent of a wheat ration per person for some 1,250 adults.[22] Some scholars have argued that imperial taxation was heavier than comparable rates in the Islamic world

18 Haldon (1994: 140–2; 1992).

19 For calculations of basic land taxes, see Schilbach (1970: 248–63), Oikonomidès (1991), Morrisson (1991: 295; 2002: 949–50), and Morrisson and Cheynet (2002: 821f). The middle Byzantine rates are much higher than those of the Roman Empire in the first and second centuries (see Hopkins 1980; 1995), but much lower than the very high rates suggested for the later Roman Empire in the sixth century by Wickham (2005: 64–6).

20 See Kaplan (2001: 370; 1992: 262), Laiou (1977), and Lefort (2002).

21 Haldon (1997: 313), with literature; Zuckerman (2005: 95–104).

22 On the basis of an annual per capita requirement of 40 *modii* per person: Rickman (1980: 156–97); Duncan-Jones (1976). Garnsey (1991: 77–9) – followed by Carrié (2003: 164) – uses a per capita ration of 25 *modii*, however (suggesting a total of 2,000 persons in this case), while Kislinger (1995) uses a ration of 49 *modii*, resulting in a much lower number of persons. The problem of which *modios* is used in which context has been resolved for the period from the middle of the sixth century in favor of the *modius castrensis*, of 8.94 kg. With a shift in the weight of the Byzantine pound, the Byzantine equivalent is referred to in later texts as the *annonikos modios* (= 8.5 kg); see Haldon (1998).

or with the Carolingians, but this is not supported by the evidence: taxes in eighth-century Egypt appear to have been as high as they had been before the conquest, and possibly higher; when the Franks occupied Istria at the beginning of the ninth century, taxes went up; and it is known that taxes in the Lombard territories were higher than in neighboring Roman (imperial) territories. Yet we should be extremely cautious in interpreting these statistics. The figures give us absolute figures for state revenue and private income, but tell us nothing about the gross income from the land. The late antique evidence for parts of Syria and Palestine shows that, even with relatively high levels of taxation, rural communities producing particular crops for a local market – such as wine or oil, for example – could be fairly well off.[23] The extent to which we can generalize from such material is problematic. Yet the Italian evidence does give some broad indications of imperial revenue in the period from the 660s to the 720s, and it has been argued that the total revenue accruing from the taxes on the island of Sicily, as distributed across the estates of Ravenna, those of the papal patrimonial properties, and the rest, in the proportion 21.1 percent: 33.3 percent: 45.6 percent would yield, approximately, a cash revenue of some 120,000 *solidi* plus a revenue in wheat of some 300,000 *modii*.[24]

As noted already, the state managed its fiscal affairs on the basis of a three-sided redistributive model: (1) the state, minting coin and issuing it to (2) the bureaucracy/army, which spent it on food, raw materials, livestock, etc. purchased from (3) producers, who were then taxed in gold (change was given only in the petty coinage, not in precious-metal coins) so that as much as possible of the gold released to the bureaucracy and army was recouped back to (1) the state. But this arrangement could not operate in a monetary vacuum; even when the state's fiscal interests did generally predominate (thus until the reforms of the later eleventh and early twelfth centuries), coins were inevitably drawn into the market. A fourth point, above the triangle, thus created in effect a three-dimensional spatial metaphor of the dialectic between the state and its needs, the producing population, and the movement of wealth by means of market exchange, especially through the activities of the

[23] The useful discussion given by Kingsley (2003), with relevant literature, should serve as a healthy guide in this respect; see also Foss (1997), emphasizing regional variations. Price fluctuations could be considerable, however, depending on levels of production and a range of related factors: Morrisson and Cheynet (2002: tab. 5).

[24] See Zuckerman (2005: 103–5).

state elite – which, as we shall see, received very considerable quantities of gold in the form of annual salaries and occasional largess.[25]

Calculating revenues is a very difficult business. As noted, a total (probable) income for Sicily and parts of southern Italy from about 680 to 730 can be calculated, but there are virtually no figures for other parts of the empire until the twelfth century and later. One estimate for the Eastern Empire in the sixth century, including the North African and Italian prefectures, puts the total income in cash at about 5 to 6 million *solidi*, much of this drawn from Egypt and the eastern prefecture. Recent work suggests a really dramatic collapse after the loss of the eastern provinces in the middle of the seventh century, down to less than 1.5 million *solidi* and rising only gradually to about 3 million or a little above by the middle of the ninth century. Recovery was thus very slow, lasting well into the ninth century. By the middle of the twelfth century it had risen again – although Anatolia was only partially under imperial control – to something around 60 percent of the sixth-century total. These are, of course, extremely crude estimates, subject to a large number of caveats. In addition, we must allow for the fluctuating value of resources extracted in kind and in labour through various state corvées, for example, the proportion of which to cash revenues must have risen considerably from the middle of the seventh to the middle of the eighth century, even if it then subsided again. Such figures are, inevitably, subject to very considerable qualification, and represent only what can be calculated, sometimes very crudely, from a combination of evidence from the die analysis of coins and the rate of production, textual references, and mathematical modeling of economic indicators for pre-industrial economic systems.[26]

By the same token, a calculation of imperial expenditures is equally hazardous, although there is no doubt that, for much of the period between the reigns of Justin II and Basil II (565 to 1025), the army and related military costs swallowed up the largest part of the state's annual income in

[25] See Corbier (1989), who modifies the "state fiscality" model in this respect for the Roman world, and Banaji (2001: 39ff.), for the later Roman world up to the early seventh century. See also Banaji (2006).

[26] Hendy (1985: 157–73, with 173–201); Morrisson (2002: 936–46, with tab. 6). Although there were some fluctuations across the period from the early sixth century to the middle of the eleventh, the Byzantine gold coinage was remarkably stable – and was dubbed by the economic historian Robert Lopez "the dollar of the Middle Ages": Lopez (1951). The basic full-value coin, the *solidus* or *nomisma*, was minted at a standard of just under 22 carats, and there were seventy-two such coins to 1 lb weight. See Morrisson (1985) for detailed discussion. The dies from which coins were struck, representing the obverse and reverse of the coin, had variable lives and were recombined in ways that permit a mathematical/statistical analysis, thus facilitating the calculation of approximate values for the numbers of each issue that were minted.

one form or another, at an absolute minimum some 35 percent – probably much more – in the sixth century, and an even greater proportion in the reduced circumstances of the seventh and eighth centuries.[27] The court spent money on building activity, largess to the army, and subsidies to neighboring or more distant states, in the last case often very substantial sums. For example, Hugh of Provence, the king of Italy, was paid some 7,200 *nomismata* (100 lbs by weight in gold) in cash, quite apart from gifts of silks and plate, to support imperial interests against Lombard rebels there in 935/936; throughout the empire's history the court paid out substantial amounts in gold or silver to foreign rulers, particularly leaders of nomad peoples, for support or neutrality, as the evidence of coin hoards dateable to the later seventh and eighth centuries from the steppe and the region north and northwest of the Danube suggests.[28] It also invested in the complex system of *rogai* or state pensions tied to the ranks and titles of the palatine hierarchy; it has been calculated plausibly that the bill for the salaries of the leading sixty imperial officials at court and in the provinces in the tenth century amounted to some 60,000 to 80,000 *nomismata* per annum (around 835 to 1,110 lbs gold), to which must be added a sum possibly two to three times greater for the *rogai* attached to imperial titles.[29] Although the acquisition of landed wealth was always important, many members of the elite, with the exception of a few important families in the metropolitan area, depended heavily on the very considerable sums they received in the form of salaries in gold coin and precious silks. This reflected the nature of the centralized imperial political hierarchy and the cultural domination of the court and palace, as well as a range of other factors, such as the fact that during the later seventh to ninth centuries substantial districts even in the well-defended inner provinces were subject to hostile and economically disruptive activity, so that the returns on investment in land were not always promising. Loyal servants of the emperors were rewarded with senior military posts and the granting of imperial estates.[30] The annual salary attached to senior military and civil positions ranged from 10 to as much as 40 lbs of gold, in coin, per annum, so that very substantial fortunes in liquid assets could be amassed over a relatively short period. The Italian observer Liudprand of Cremona in the middle of the tenth century remarked on the vast sums carried off by various senior officials on the occasion of the annual payment of state

[27] Hendy (1985: 158–9, 168–72); Oikonomides (2002: 1010–16).
[28] Ibid.: 1016; Laiou (2002a: 692f.); Curta (2005). [29] Oikonomides (2002: 1010ff.).
[30] Kaplan (2006).

salaries before Easter, many of whom needed the assistance of servants to take their gold away.[31]

Then came the costs of the annual payments to the various provincial armies for the soldiers, their officers and staffs, and associated support, which were considerable. In the early ninth century the pay of the Armeniakon army amounted to some 93,600 *nomismata* (1,300 lbs gold); for the army of Macedonia it amounted to some 79,200 *nomismata* (1,100 lbs gold) There were at this time at least twelve such military provinces, albeit of very different extent (the Armeniakon and Anatolikon regions were certainly two of the largest and most costly), but this nevertheless indicates the nature of the expense incurred in their maintenance. In addition, there were centrally maintained mercenary units paid substantially more per person than the provincial armies, though at first these were quite limited in numbers. To this must then be added the costs of the remaining bureaucratic and administrative departments of the government in Constantinople and in the provinces, alongside the incidental costs they would have attracted as part of their standard running requirements.[32] To the regular costs of maintaining the army and the imperial fleet should then be added the costs of a range of (quite frequent) expeditionary forces, and these were often very expensive additional burdens on the treasury and on the population; military expeditions to Syria in 910/911 and to Crete in 949 cost something over 203,000 *nomismata* (around 2,820 lbs gold) and 127,000 *nomismata* (some 1,765 lbs gold), respectively, and these are minimal figures in both cases. Other expeditions cost even more, such as that against the Normans of Sicily in 1155, which required an additional 2,160,000 gold coins or *hyperpera*.[33] Few emperors were known to have built up substantial reserves. Theophilos (829 to 842) is supposed to have left just under 7 million *nomismata*, (97,220 lbs gold) and Basil II (976 to 1025) over 14 million, but much of the latter derived from loot in the eastern campaigns and in Bulgaria, from confiscations, and from tribute exacted from neighboring protectorates.[34]

For the most part the state's income was more or less balanced by its outgoings, although, again, we must bear in mind the substantial amount of wealth that it consumed directly in the form of supplies for the army on campaign, the functioning of the *dromos* or state courier and transport service, and various services exacted in kind, mentioned above: road and bridge maintenance, the production of certain types of weapon such as

[31] Oikonomides (1997: 202–3; 207–8). [32] Hendy (1985: 181–201). [33] Ibid.: 221–3.
[34] Oikonomides (2002: 1016–18).

arrowheads, or of equipment such as nails and cut wood for the fleet, and so forth. None of these considerations takes into account the gross "national product" of the empire, of course. Considerable revenues were taken by private individuals and institutions such as monasteries and the church. Furthermore, it must not be forgotten, first, that the state's income was only a part of the total amount of wealth generated through agriculture, trade, and industry, and, second, that the state's economy remained in many respects separate from, if not independent of, the economic activities of the society at large.[35]

The activities of the state in the process of extracting and redistributing wealth can thus be summed up as the "fiscal economy," and the relationship between this economy and that of elite society – and, indeed, society at large – varied according to both internal political and international economic circumstances. The state extracted agrarian produce, skills, and labor power, and then redistributed them according to its own needs, including the payment of considerable quantities of gold coin to its leading officials. This redistributive process could occur centrally and indirectly, through the collection of taxes in gold and the recirculation of some of that gold to the army and members of the elite; or directly and locally, either through the imposition on the producers of the transportation of the goods to state depots, or through the direct consumption of the resources by state officials and the military at the point of collection/production. The imperial postal and heavy transport service, with its network of way stations, stables and stud farms, hostelries, and ancillary services (farriers, leatherworkers, etc.), represented a direct consumer of fiscal resources throughout the regions where it was established.[36] Units of soldiers en route to a military base or a campaign were provisioned by direct levies of foodstuffs on the districts through which they passed, and the goods and services consumed were then written off against that year's or the following year's tax demands (in theory; the system generally worked to the disadvantage of the producers). It could also occur trans-regionally, through the conversion of those resources into cash (gold coin), its collection through regular fiscal assessments at the local and provincial level, and its forwarding to Constantinople. The state might assist the process, insofar as it regularly established "artificial" markets through which the produce in question could be purchased for coin, which could then be collected through the fiscal system. The presence of state officials and the army, who were paid in

[35] Hendy (1985); Morrisson (2002); Laiou (2002a; 2002b); Oikonomides (2002).
[36] See Hendy (1985: 603–13; also 294–6) and Oikonomidès (1972: 311–12).

gold, represented the most obvious way in which this could be attained, and there is good evidence not only that this happened as a matter of course but also that it could have significant distorting effects on the price structure of the local markets it affected; indeed, the continuous presence of administrative and military officials salaried in gold enhanced local economies and attracted both production and commerce. The use of a system of compulsory purchase was an alternative means of introducing cash through an artificially imposed price structure on provincial populations and redistributing locally produced goods.[37]

Given its difficult and often precarious political-geographical situation, its relatively impoverished resource base (especially when compared with the immensely wealthier Islamic states to the east), its limited manpower, and the fact that it was almost constantly at war with one or more of its neighbors from the early seventh century through to the twelfth century, one may reasonably ask: how did the Byzantine Empire survive as long as it did? The answer is, of course, a complex one, but one thing is absolutely clear: without the effective and relatively efficient fiscal administrative machinery it maintained, it could have resourced neither the military capacity to resist aggressive warfare nor the diplomatic wherewithal to deal with its enemies and allies on an equal footing. The Byzantine Empire exemplifies the potential for a territorially relatively small state to maintain an independent status in a hostile political world – provided it has the ability to manage its resources effectively, to allocate them as befitted the needs of the times, and to maintain an effective central authority that can respond appropriately to stresses and challenges. In these respects the Byzantine Empire represents a mix of characteristics typical of both domain system and tributary system, yet with some attributes of tax and fiscal systems; its fiscal and military administration were able to plan in advance, and public – Romano-Byzantine – law was applied through a formal judicial structure, open to all members of society, even if access to justice was not always easy for the poorer or less privileged. In most other respects it singularly fails to fit neatly into any of the categories listed by Bonney and Ormrod; rather, it represents a hybrid version of tax, domain, and tribute states: kinship and familial relationships continued to play a key role throughout, yet many members of the middling and lower staffs of administrative offices constituted, in effect, a specialized body.

Byzantine political theory (perhaps better described as political theology) established the emperor as God's vice-gerent on earth, the Romans as

[37] Stein (1949: 440); Haldon (1994: 118–22).

the new Chosen People, and the Roman Empire as co-terminous with the civilized world, its mission to defend and extend orthodoxy. The emperor was both the law incarnate and guarantor of the law, defender of his subjects and protector of the rights of Christians – both implicit in his role as God's representative on earth and made explicit in written (Roman) law. Central control, even if somewhat compromised by kinship and elite politics, remained throughout; but political participation was entirely confined to members of the provincial and metropolitan elites. This might include also ecclesiastical as well as monastic leaders and their followers, but they, like secular officials and post- and title-holders, were involved in the imperial system of titles, offices, and precedence, which were the only recognized means of social – and therefore political – advancement. Taxation was regular and based on complex cadastral accounting, taking into account type of crop, quality of land, and output – although the wealthy were always able to minimize their tax burdens (and maximize rents) through various means, legal and illegal; and censuses and revisions were built into the system. It was also highly monetized, except where market or political-military conditions made it difficult; but tax was always calculated on the basis of money equivalences; and taxation formed the basis of the state's finances, even though imperial private estates made a contribution. Expenditure was heavily slanted toward the military, of course, but imperial endowments of orphanages and other charitable institutions (mirrored by private and ecclesiastical institutions of like character) were an important part of the Byzantine Christian philanthropic self-image. Yet there was no established model of public credit and loan, and shortfalls in income in difficult situations could be met only by confiscations, the temporary cashing in of church plate, the withdrawal of privileges, and the like. In terms of the wider economy, the state apparatus, in particular the army, played a key role in the distribution of coin, but the state itself invested very little in non-military productive enterprise or industry. Until the eleventh century, for example, the state silk-weaving workshops produced largely for state purposes, with an independent entrepreneurial silk industry evolving to meet market demand only from the eleventh century. It did occasionally intervene in sectoral markets in particular provinces to manage prices or imports and exports of particular goods, largely grain.

Yet, in spite of its apparent structural and organizational advantages, the Byzantine state found itself increasingly compromised by neighbors whose dynamism, social and economic, was beginning to outstrip it. The reasons for this are the subject of further discussion below.

Western Europe: the Frankish kingdoms and the western medieval state

Historical overview: western Europe c. *500 – 1100*

As a useful comparison for the Byzantine state, it will be helpful to turn our attention to other polities that evolved out of the late Roman world, in particular those that became the kingdoms of France and Germany.[38] The polities that succeeded Rome during the fifth and sixth centuries in the west all have their origins in the tumultuous changes that affected the western Eurasian world in the two preceding centuries, yet they had very different histories and outcomes. The loose confederacy of Suevi, Alans, and Vandals who crossed the Rhine in 406 spent the next three years extracting tribute and booty from Gaul, before crossing the Pyrenees in 409 and entering Spain. Here, the Suevi established their own kingdom in Galicia. The Visigoths, who had moved from the Balkans into Italy and thence (from 412) into southern Gaul after the sack of Rome and subsequent death of their leader, Alaric, in 410, had established their own state around Toulouse by about 418 – a move encouraged by the imperial government, which pitted the Visigoths against a rival emperor set up under Frankish and Alamannic influence. In 416 the Visigoths then advanced against the Vandals and Alans in southwestern and southern Spain, whom they crushed, before being "offered" an independent kingdom in southwestern Gaul. This saved the remaining Suevi and Vandals in the northwestern regions and Galicia, but by the late 420s the latter were on the move again, crossing in 429 into north Africa. Threatened by the establishment of a Vandal kingdom with naval power at its disposal and with the potential fatally to disrupt the grain supplies of Rome, the imperial government was forced to accept and to recognize formally the king of the Vandals, Gaiseric, as an independent ruler. Germanic raiders from the Danish peninsula and the North Sea coastlands had meanwhile transformed the political landscape in the British provinces. In 410 Rome appears officially to have conceded to local British authorities the right to organize their own defenses, in view of the lack of substantial imperial forces. Although the history of the British provinces is clouded in obscurity at this time, local polities led by Romano-British nobles and by Celtic warlords appear to have evolved, competing with one another and with

[38] For the general political background, see Halsall (2007), Costambeys, Innes, and MacLean (2011), Fouracre (2005), Wood (1993), Ewig (1997), Pohl (2002), and the useful essay of Becher (2011). Older literature: Geary (1988); McKitterick (1983); James (1982).

raiders from Ireland, from the Pictish lands to the north, and from the Saxons, Jutes, and Angles in northwest Germany, Denmark, and the Low Countries. The latter were also employed as mercenaries, and by the later fifth century certain groups had a firm foothold and would, during the sixth century, succeed in establishing a political dominance in much of the southern and central lowlands.

Various Frankish groups had been officially permitted to reside on Roman territory along the Rhine by Honorius in 410 as a result of the pressures he faced elsewhere. Several other Frankish groups remained in Franconia. Those Franks who settled within the empire supplied federate troops to the Roman armies. In central and northern Gaul the Salian Franks, having moved first into the Low Countries, were then able to establish themselves, precariously at first, in the valleys of the Moselle and Rhine, and by the last years of the century had succeeded in defeating the last remnants of independent Roman rule in the Seine Valley, defeating and incorporating into their territory the Ripuarian Franks (settled originally on the right bank of the Rhine but occupying territory on the "Roman" side during the fifth century), and driving off the Alamanni, who threatened them from the southeast in the late 490s. Frankish control was broad; the valleys of the Loire and Seine and the central French plain were the heartland, but Frankish rule extended down to the Visigothic lands stretching from the Pyrenees into northern Italy, across to the valleys of the Main and Rhine in the east, and down to the Burgundian lands about the headwaters of the Rhone in the southeast. The conversion to orthodox Christianity of the Frankish king Clovis in 506 won the Franks the support – or at least disarmed the opposition of – the Gallo-Roman elite and the Church, facilitating the consolidation of Frankish power under Clovis and his successors, the dynasty of the Merovingians, gaining diplomatic and political support from the Eastern emperor Anastasius against the Visigoths and Ostrogoths, as well as the support of the papacy and thus political legitimacy.

During the sixth century the division of the kingdom into eastern and western portions (in 511, and then in 561) was probably a compromise among the sons of the previous ruler; by the middle of the seventh century the Frankish kingdom had fallen into three territorial zones, Neustria, Austrasia, and Burgundy, and these reasserted themselves time after time in the internecine squabbles of the Merovingian dynasty. The last time an effectively unified kingdom was achieved was under King Dagobert I (who reigned from 629 to 639), and thereafter division and inter-factional strife became the norm. Only with the rise to power of the family of Pippin I, *major domus* ("mayor of the palace") of the kings of Austrasia, was a degree of stability and precarious consensus gradually reestablished. Pippin was able to defeat the rival mayor of the palace of the kings of Neustria and Burgundy in 687, thereby bringing the two kingdoms together once more and establishing the basis for a consolidation of his own power and the administrative unity of the realm.[39] Under his son and successor Charles "Martel" (who had to fight first to become Pippin's successor and then to retain the unity won by his father), the Alamanni and Thuringians, who objected to what they saw as Charles' usurpation of authority, were subjugated, Bavaria was reduced to dependency, and the struggle with the Saxons began in earnest. From 737 he ruled without a Merovingian king, the latter dynasty having been reduced to the status of "shadow kings" (the last of the line, Childerich III, reinstated in 743, was formally removed, with papal sanction, in 751). Charles died in 741, but divided the kingdom – following Frankish tradition – between his sons Carloman and Pippin the Younger, though Carloman retired to a monastery and Pippin became sole ruler in 751. Pippin again divided the kingdom on his own death in 768, but of the two sons, Charles and Carloman, the latter died soon afterward and Charles inherited the whole kingdom. Charles the Great, as he is known, turned the Frankish kingdom into an empire. Between 772 and 804 he defeated and subjugated the Saxons, whose leaders converted to Christianity; he conquered and incorporated the Lombard kingdom in Italy; Bavarian independence was effectively ended and the duchy incorporated into the Frankish kingdom; the remaining Avar strongholds in what is now western Hungary were attacked and the Avars reduced to a tenuous dependency. Already recognizing the power and potential of Carolingian support, the papacy had endowed Charles with the title of *patricius Romanorum* in 774; and on December 24 in the year 800 he was crowned by the pope as emperor and "ruler of the territory of the Romans." It took the Byzantines twelve years to recognize the eastern emperor, however: only in 812, by the Treaty of Aachen, did the emperor Michael I recognize Charles' title (and then only in return for territory in northern Italy and the Adriatic).[40]

Charles' empire can be said to have lasted in name and in respect of certain institutional arrangements until it was dissolved by Napoleon in 1806! But as early as 842–3 his grandsons had divided the empire into three parts: the eastern, middle, and western kingdoms. While factional conflict and mismanagement thereafter resulted in the division of the empire, and

[39] See Wood (2004). [40] See the short account given by Becher (2011: 183–94).

while a host of "tribal" duchies (re)asserted their relative autonomy, the three kingdoms all took as their frame of reference the original empire – even if the political division between eastern (German) and western (French) territories became permanent, with Burgundy (with or without the kingdom of Italy, representing Carolingian conquests from the Lombards) caught between the two. In the east, the emperors of the Saxon dynasty, which came to power in 919 in the person of Henry I, were able to progressively extend the frontiers of their kingdom to the east and maintain their power in Italy, putting constant pressure also on the Byzantine territories in the south. In the east, the campaigns against the various Slav peoples were accompanied by successful missionary activity; the defeat of the Magyars in 955 halted their incursions into royal territory and, in turn, stimulated the development of a settled Hungarian kingdom. Although facing frequent and constant challenges from the dukes and independent lords upon whose power their own authority in part depended, papal support and the Carolingian imperial tradition lent the German Empire of the Ottonian and Franconian dynasties a degree of continuity that made it the paramount power in central Europe, able to treat as an equal with the Byzantines and to play a key role in the international politics of the period. The existence of the East Frankish/Ottonian Empire radically transformed the political and diplomatic world in which the Byzantine Empire existed. These relationships were then further complicated during the eleventh century by the arrival of Norman adventurers in Italy, where some served the empire as mercenary cavalry.

Structures

The Merovingian kingdom of the sixth century was in many respects a proto-state: the exercise of royal authority was based on traditional lineage and warfare loyalties, with a legal basis founded in an oath of fealty to the kings.[41] But there was no real possibility of royal control being enforced through the kings' representatives, the counts (or *comites*, originally the warrior companions and members of the war band of the ruler, then their provincial representatives and plenipotentiaries),[42] without an effective fighting force or royal support. The war band of the kings themselves constituted a key component in the nascent royal nobility. It was these latter whom the kings appointed to the administrative-military positions throughout the early kingdom, giving them land in return for their service.

[41] See Esders (2009). [42] See Donat (1988), Schulze (1985: 47ff.), and Grahn-Hoek (1976).

At the same time, however, the posts and the properties attached to the duties of such posts tended often to be dispersed, so that the higher-ranking members of the leading groups often held lands and exercised functions simultaneously in different parts of the kingdom at once.[43] The officials, who belonged also to the king's retinue, had their various centres of authority and power dispersed across the whole kingdom, and might be drawn from a variety of ethnic backgrounds, not necessarily Franks, and certainly including Romans. Their positions were remunerated by grants of land, which in some cases may have been temporary, and, while in most cases they were probably for life or longer, this was legally enshrined only from the 870s. By virtue of placing members of his family and retinue as officials throughout his lands, the king was able to draw upon a wide network of loyalty, and enforce his authority wherever he found himself. In theory, this system, which was based ultimately on purely personal ties, both enabled the kings to remove power from traditional tribal or clan leaders and provided the ideological justification for punishing those who challenged their authority. In practice, the mixed Frankish-Germanic and Gallo-Roman elites of the different regions that made up the Frankish kingdom possessed an independent ideological identity as "nobles" or leading families, often accompanied by allodial (private) landed property, so that royal power was less solidly based than might at first seem to be the case. In addition, Frankish identity was bound up with the notion of freedom from "taxation," so that in the course of the seventh century the kings' revenues had to come increasingly from a range of fines and related impositions for dereliction of various duties vis-à-vis the kings, the more so as new "Frankish" identities – especially in the areas north of the Loire – began to evolve. Tax collection became increasingly marginalized, although even in the later seventh century seems still to have played a significant role in revenues.

This picture is nuanced by the somewhat different nature of the relationship between the Franks and the Gallo-Roman notables of the south, where lineage and kinship played a less prominent role. Nevertheless, as long as the kings were active and popular campaigners, were orthodox Christians (see below),[44] and their war hosts took to the field every year, they could enforce compliance by the threat or application of direct coercion, and this seems generally to have been sufficient to maintain a

[43] See especially Steuer (1987).

[44] "Orthodox" means here, literally, "right-believing" – i.e. in communion with Rome and the Roman Church – as opposed to Arianism, the "heretical" religion of the neighboring Germanic peoples until later in the sixth century (when most converted to Rome).

degree of order and obedience – enough at least to maintain internal order and the continued appropriation of revenues. Even as local elites came increasingly to replace the older urban communities or cities as the foci of administration, and as city fiscal obligations were transferred to or taken over by such local elites, there seems to have been substantial continuity in the ability of the royal administration to control established taxes. Revenue collection was only very gradually transformed into a private system of customary dues and impositions, raised at first largely through those with royal positions and functions, but increasingly through members of their wider kinship circles. As long as the Merovingian kings could maintain peace and some form of order to the extent that the interests of the magnates upon whom they depended were assured, then they received the support of those magnates. Once this military activity declined, however, the threat of coercion and the ability of the kings to maintain order receded, an independent source of substantial royal revenues withered away, and so royal authority receded also. And royal coercion began to fail as magnates and wealthy lords found the wherewithal to oppose the kings, even if passively, simply by not turning up or not sending soldiers or warriors, or enough of them, when the kings demanded. It would be incorrect to see the rise of the lords and magnate class in general as a result of royal weakness; on the contrary, the two developments were inextricably connected. Yet continuity – territorial as well as ideological and political – also inhered in the Church, which survived the disappearance of Roman political authority with an unbroken ecclesiastical administrative tradition, and rapidly became embedded within the new arrangements. Already by the time of the Frankish occupation the bishops had become key figures in secular administration within their sees – a tendency that was only reinforced in the following period, especially as kings began increasingly to appoint their own candidates to sees, thus further strengthening ties between the court, the episcopacy, the Church, and royal rule.[45] Thus, regardless of the struggle for power between different factions of the Frankish elite, institutional stability and a rootedness of the Frankish kingdom in society at large gave it an important degree of permanence and continuity.

Administration in the Merovingian kingdom was based on the Roman cities, headed locally now by a royally appointed count, who was responsible for both civil and military administration. Some evidence suggests that elements of the late Roman military administration of the Gallic

[45] Gauthier (2000); Heinzelmann (1976).

provinces continued to function at certain levels under Merovingian royal authority, declining only as central power itself began to recede from the middle of the seventh century. The kings appointed their counts, but counts were in many cases checked more by the presence of a local bishop or a regional duke than by any centralized supervisory procedures. Bishops often provided the crucial link between the older, indigenous population and the newcomers, whether Franks, Burgundians, or Goths. They were a source of justice as well as of charity, and their spiritual and economic power made of them formidable potential opponents of secular administrators. Dukes were likewise royal appointments, at least at first, before such titles became hereditary during the later sixth century and afterward, and, because they were associated directly with the royal retinue, they had probably a great deal more power than the counts. The latter were more numerous but had authority usually over relatively small districts and numbers of soldiers, and were often selected from local men. But, again, while initially in charge of revenues destined to maintain a royal administration and military capacity, the latter soon became effectively privatized, their use entirely at the disposal and discretion of the counts and their subordinates or related members of local elites.[46]

To characterize the Merovingian kingdom as a proto-state seems problematic, given the pattern of institutional arrangements inherited from Roman administration. Just as importantly, the early acceptance of orthodoxy by Clovis at the beginning of the sixth century (sometime between 496 and 508),[47] followed by the relatively rapid acceptance of Christianity by the Franks across the next half-century, meant a fairly quick coming together of Franks and Gallo-Romans. While the Frankish kingdom was a patrimonial polity, dependent upon the royal household, certain lineage solidarities, and the king's role as war leader – as well as the older fiscal institutions – for its cohesiveness, this added ideological element was of fundamental importance in permitting the evolution of a new hybrid identity, at least among the elite, and lent the Frankish kingdom a certain stability that the neighboring Germanic kingdoms lacked until somewhat later. It was a state form that represented the result of the imposition of a compromised tribal kingship upon a rural peasantry and its landlords. The Roman structures that survived, particularly in the realm of royal justice

46 On the structure of the Merovingian kingdom, see Wallace-Hadrill (1967; 1962) and Geary (1988: 88ff., 12–139). For the role of bishops and dukes, see especially Heinzelmann (1975), Wood (1977: esp. 24), James (1982), and Lewis (1976). There is an excellent short summary of these processes from Innes (2007: 290–303).

47 Shanzer (1998).

and taxation, permitted the Merovingian kings to maintain a degree of administrative continuity for a long time. But, even though the very notion of statehood in its Roman form meant for the Germanic successor states the ability to raise tax on the basis of non-personal, institutionalized relationships, royal taxation was regarded as both heavy and an unjustifiable additional burden. Its continued existence served to emphasize the supreme authority of the kings, as well as to recall the shadowy past of a Roman state authority that they had inherited. But bishops and laymen fought, often successfully, for exemption; and tax rapidly became only one element among many, of the royal resources, to be granted away in immunities to royal favorites or to those whose support the king needed. It continued to be raised until the end of the seventh century in a number of localized forms, but this reflected as much the institutional stasis of tradition – aas embodied in the activities of local counts – as it did central control.[48]

The replacement of the Merovingian dynasty by the Carolingians in 751 (with papal support – a key ideological prerequisite) was a problem only in respect of traditional attachments to an old dynasty. In real terms, the mayors of the palace had succeeded in monopolizing access to the kings, thereby putting an end to the regional consensual balance between local and central networks of power, exploiting a radically different and much more effective network of power relations, and it was this establishment of successive layers of dependence that cut the ground from under the old royal household and its provincial representatives. Carolingian and later French and German rule all remained patrimonial and highly dependent upon the ruler's personality for its efficacy. The structures of subordination and vassalage that developed in the Merovingian period constituted the basic framework of power relations, within the terms of which both "private" and "state" political power and authority were constrained. Indeed, the Carolingian kingdom hardly fared better in the end than its Merovingian predecessor, succumbing to the strains engendered by an overstretched geopolitical structure administered by an underresourced royal administration. For, in spite of the early successes of the system of *missi dominici*, royal messengers sent out to supervise the local powers of the king's realm, effective power still depended ultimately on royal

[48] See the summaries by Innes (2007: 268ff.) and Wickham (2009: 111–29, 170–202). Durliat (1990) argues that the basic elements of late Roman land tax remained in place throughout the Merovingian period into that of the Carolingians, and, while this view has not met with general agreement, it does seem nonetheless that there was substantial continuity in many respects, albeit with changes in both form and practice.

campaigning and the regular assertion of royal rights and vassals' obligations.[49] Under Charlemagne the court issued capitularies, sets of instructions directed at regional leaders representing the king, but these did not represent any bureaucratic apparatus; royal authority was expressed through the counts, who in turn, as representatives of the king, presided over assemblies of local notables and lords. But authority thus managed depended largely on the connections and kinship relations among the regional elites and the ability of the counts to persuade their peers that following a royal command was also in their best interests. The *missi*, after the early 800s generally despatched in pairs – one layperson and one ecclesiastic – to implement royal demands or instructions (such as raising troops), were also members of the regional elites, and their authority also depended at base on local ties and persuasion.

Patrimonial power and charismatic leadership were not adequate bases for a permanent and effective bureaucratic administrative apparatus, the more so in view of the lack of any real, centrally controlled fiscal system that would give the ruler a permanent, independent, and legally enshrined "state" income. It is true that individual rulers were able, either through force of personality and/or the loyalty of vassals, local counts, and their *missi*, to maintain control over a good deal of the royal revenues from a range of sources. But the gradual alienation of royal lands, for example, reduced this resource. In the longer term, the inability to establish a bureaucracy is perhaps one of the most important points in this respect. Intermediate agencies such as bureaucracies generally evolve, through their own, culturally specific institutionalized practices and rituals, an ideology of service, on the one hand, and are able both to recruit new members through the appropriately determined channels and effectively to reproduce themselves (and are thus at least partly independent of the ruler or the dominant elite), on the other hand. Without such an agency, it was clearly impossible for the Frankish rulers to act autonomously or to pursue policies that in any serious way diverged from the interests of the dominant political elite. The reasons for the failure lie in the intensely personalized nature of political power relationships, in which service was to an individual rather than to a corporate body or conceptually reified institution such as the state – in contrast, for example, to the situation in the Eastern or Byzantine Empire. They also lie in the human and social sources of Charlemagne's administrators, who, for the most part, were drawn from the ranks of the powerful, and represented the same element as the ruling

[49] See Reuter (1978) and Becher and Jarnut (2004).

elite of the Merovingian period. Literacy – a prerequisite for any effective administrative apparatus – may have been more common under the Carolingians, an education more usual for such persons, and the rulers may have relied to a far greater extent on written legislative acts to further their policies. But familial loyalties and entrenched and interlocking relationships of both patronage and vassalage, together with the entirely personal nature of the relationship between Charlemagne and his *missi dominici* (in most cases only marginally dependent upon the king for their economic security), meant that an organized bureaucracy, independent of such personal relationships, had really no chance. The failure of any such structure to develop, combined with traditional Frankish inheritance practice, promoted the fragmentation of Charlemagne's empire. Yet, even though the unitary Carolingian state broke up into its constituent political-geographical parts during the ninth century, it was precisely the presence of the Church, and the relationships between court, Church, and local elites, that provided the dynamic elements in the slow evolution of the kingdom of France, on the one hand, and the conflicts between the German emperors and the duchies or principalities of Swabia, Saxony, and Bavaria, on the other.[50]

Resources, revenues, and control

Thus, it was the combination of the alienation of state (royal) lands to the servants of the kings, reducing the power of the former to raise revenues and control their own service nobility, with the superficiality of the royal administration and the fragmented and localized patterns of loyalty and social solidarity that rendered an effective, self-regenerating, non-personalized mode of rulership and a centralized administration more or less unviable, much though the Franks admired Roman institutions. Patrimonial rule can be highly effective in a state formation with a sophisticated bureaucratic tradition – as in the Eastern Roman or Byzantine Empire, for example; but the extensive and fragmented patterns of power in post-Roman Gaul deprived it of any long-term, regenerative efficacy.[51] The Frankish kingdom was thus never entirely centralized nor properly bureaucratic. It relied upon traditional loyalties (that is to say,

[50] For details and further literature, see the useful summary given by Innes (2007: 429–50); there is more detailed discussion from de Jong (2003), Innes 2005), Pohl and Wieser (2009), and Werner (1980).

[51] Wood (1977); on the Carolingian system, see in particular McKitterick (1983); and, for Carolingian administrative structures, see Werner (1980), and the literature cited in the discussion below.

upon established ideological practices) to a specific dynasty or ruler, which in the case of the early Merovingians extracted revenues simply by imposing upon a preexisting structure of taxation and corvées a group of officials with local powers. What did change were the officials who carried out the collection of revenues (and even here there may well have been substantive continuities, especially in respect of the tenants of Gallo-Roman landlords) and the authority for whom the surplus was extracted. Royal officials merely collected a raked-off surplus, but their diffused power in society as a whole came to be as much based on personal relationships of patronage and, later, vassalage as it was on royal authority. This was not in itself in strong contrast to the early Carolingian regime, whose lords, won over by warfare or by other means, represented the first and most obvious level of the ruler's reach into the social relations of production. The Carolingians recognized the nature of their power, which evolved out of just such relationships, combined with the fruits of successful warfare and the incorporation of new lands and resources, and exploited the situation accordingly.[52] Charles the Great was able to impose a more centralized political and fiscal management, through the counts and the *missi*, in parallel with his military successes. But it was these same structural features that prevented the Carolingian kingdom from expanding its basic fisc into a more complex administrative apparatus. The Visigothic kingdom of Spain offers close parallels.[53] Yet the fact that the Merovingian and Frankish kingdoms did have a fisc should not be forgotten. The Frankish fisc consisted chiefly of revenue sources – land – that were permanently within the remit of the kings, that were transferred from king to king regardless of family association, and that therefore clearly attached to the kingdom, not the person of the ruler. The relative autonomy of this structure (or, rather, this accumulation of landed properties distributed throughout the kingdom) lent the Carolingian kingdom(s) in particular their "state-ness" and, at the same time reinforced, the authority and the image of the kings as monarchs.[54] By the same token, the state was

[52] See Reuter (1985; 1990), who argues that the prime resource of the Carolingian state under Charlemagne was plunder and booty – a position that has been substantially modified in subsequent debates, but that retains some validity in understanding the sources of royal power and wealth; see especially Fouracre (2009: 293–4).

[53] On Visigothic Spain, see Collins (1983: esp. 102ff.), Thompson (1969), Murphy (1952), Innes (2007: 219–29), and Wickham (2009: 130–9). It needs to be emphasized, of course, that the Catholic Frankish elite found a degree of social and political acceptance among the indigenous Gallo-Roman population more readily and more rapidly than their Arian counterparts in Spain, who remained isolated linguistically, culturally, and ideologically for longer.

[54] Barbier (2009).

intimately bound up with the Church as a landowner, borrowing ecclesiastical lands and then leasing them out in return for military service, so that the (usually token) rents accrued to the Church and the military benefits to the state (although, in granting immunities from various royal impositions to Church lands, the balance between the two was probably maintained).[55]

While the process of state formation may have been differed between the Merovingian and Carolingian cases, both suffered from the same fundamental problems of control over resources and their distribution – ssential to their further existence and to the power and authority of their rulers. Both succumbed, in effect, to the same fate, resulting from the same general structural causes. Both can reasonably be described as "segmentary states," signifying territorially sovereign polities, with nominal central yet patrimonial rule, with a number of peripheral centres of power and administration; with a ruler's monopoly over force, yet with the legitimate use of coercion open also to peripheral authorities; and with the potential for the more peripheral powers to detach and transfer their allegiance from one "center" to another.[56] The absence of any strong bureaucracy or administrative institutions through which the kings could maintain institutionalized control over the direct appropriation of surplus to their own advantage meant that the process of delegation and the fragmentation of state authority inexorably promoted the collapse of central rule, and made anything more than a relatively short-term autonomy of royal politics – reflecting successful warfare: the incorporation of new territory – a structural impossibility. As Carolingian rulers became less well resourced during the later ninth century, so their dependence on regional elites increased and their political and military independence declined. In the centuries that followed, the political shape of western and central Europe was dictated largely by the forms of rulership and territorial management that evolved during the Carolingian period. The disposition of the successor kingdoms that arose from the plan for succession established by Charles in 806, with, first, the division of the kingdom among the sons of Louis the Pious in 817 and, later, the partition after 843 and afterward, played a key role in shaping the polities that evolved following the disappearance of Carolingian power east of the Rhine in the early tenth century. Rulers depended increasingly on alliances with the Church, powerful monasteries, and groups of related

[55] Fouracre (2009: 291–2); de Jong (2003; 2009).

[56] See the useful remarks of Fouracre (2009) on the inherent structural weaknesses of Merovingian and Carolingian polities. On the concept of a "segmentary" state, see Southall (1956; 1965).

notables; the notion of a royal fisc never disappeared, and in some cases rulers were able to expand their resources by conquest, expropriation, collecting fines, and inheritance. At the same time, the notions of "stateness" that evolved with the Carolingians, however diluted by the fact of powerful regional rulers such as the dukes of Bavaria and Saxony in the eastern parts of the former empire, were kept alive in imperial ceremonial, political-ideological tradition and ritual, and the association between Church, state, and Christianity.[57]

Some conclusions

The first – and perhaps most obvious – point to be made is that the existence of an effective bureaucratic fiscal management structure is not a prerequisite for a successful territorial polity that can survive over several generations or centuries; the Carolingian and Ottonian kingdoms depended on a combination of public, private, and ecclesiastical or monastic resources in conjunction with what I would call a political theology – an ideology – of kingship that offered both a broader identity under the umbrella of a single political-ideological entity, "the kingdom," and effective autonomy at the regional and local levels for the majority of those who, in one form or another, represented royal power.[58] The second point is that there is no such thing as a simple "domain" or "tax" state – at least, not in the later ancient and medieval world of western Eurasia. The political formations I have dealt with here, including the Byzantine, represent hybrid versions of resource management involving greater or lesser degrees of fiscalization of resources, of "private" versus "public" elements of control (and, for the medieval West, this dichotomy has in any case been shown to be extremely problematic), of centralized and decentralized political and fiscal authority. A third point, it seems to me, is that modeling fiscal structures, or modeling states and the fiscal structures that they maintain, is certainly conducive to generating a typology; but whether such typologies can have more than a very broad heuristic value remains doubtful. If we define taxation as entailing the extraction of resources directly by a central authority, then of course we may include a whole range of resource appropriation, including the conscription of labor power, the production of weapons or clothing, and so forth, as taxation. But we could not include the moral-ideological pressure on local nobles or elites to provide warriors and other resources for warfare as such, even if it is quite clear, empirically,

[57] See Deutinger (2009), Zotz (1995), and Reuter (1992). [58] See Pohl (2009) and Kaschke (2009).

that political systems that relied heavily on such means to raise military forces were just as capable of sustained military campaigns and of holding their own against neighboring regimes with more sophisticated fiscal resource management (for example, the conflicts between the Byzantine state and neighboring Bulgaria or Hungary in the period from the ninth century to the twelfth). What a complex fiscal structure does offer, it seems, is greater flexibility in responding to fiscal crisis, at least so long as the resources are actually available to be collected and redistributed.

Any discussion of fiscal systems is predicated, reasonably enough, on the basic proposition that the problem faced by all states, however we define the term, is that of the control of resources. Whether bureaucratic means of doing this evolve or whether rulers come to rely on the loyalty of individuals to the throne or the person of the ruler, perhaps also mediated through a range of ideological mechanisms, in administrating such resources, the problem of supervising or controlling such agents inevitably arises. Given the pre-industrial levels of communications, transport, and surveillance at their disposal, medieval states or rulers were confronted with the need both to effectively extract resources from the producing population and to ensure the effective appropriation of surplus to reproduce their apparatus. The inherent contradiction between the need for the state to collect sufficient resources to fulfill its various functions, political/military as well as ideological, on the one hand, and the inevitable process of delegation and the competition over surplus offered by dominant social-economic elites, on the other, establishes certain limits on the autonomy of states and rulers. In pre-industrial societies there is no alternative to this, and the process brings them into potential conflict with the producers as well as with the aristocracies, or the group of agents or intermediaries established or selected by the state for this purpose (or both). The latter constitutes an element that, by virtue of its position, either within society outside the state center or within the state apparatus itself, can be transformed into a major competitor for the control of resources – competition manifested in struggles over the appropriation and, politically, the distribution and redistribution of surplus wealth. Constraints on state power (and autonomy) were therefore determined both by the limits of exploitation of pre-capitalist rural production (which is obvious) and, more importantly, by the nature of the social and political relations of distributing the surplus. The issue of control over the collection and distribution of surplus thus determined both the political relationships (power relations) within states and that pertaining between states and the ruling class, as well as the possibility for states to act independently of the interests of such a ruling class. But its functioning was then directly affected by the inflections of each specific state and social formation, and the institutions, both social and administrative, that evolved.

References

Anon. (1985 [*c.* 850]) "On strategy," in *Three Byzantine Military Treatises*, trans. and ed. G. T. Dennis. Washington, DC: 1–135.

Ashton, R., Lightfoot, C., and Özme, A. (2000) "Ancient, Byzantine and Islamic coins in the Bolvadin municipal museum," *Anatolia Antiqua* 8: 171–92.

Banaji, J. (2001) *Agrarian Change in Late Antiquity: Gold, Labour, and Aristocratic Dominance*. Oxford.

(2006) "Precious metal coinages and monetary expansion in late antiquity," in *Dal* Denarius *al* Dinar*: l'Oriente e la moneta romana*, ed. F. De Romanis and S. Sorda. Rome: 265–303.

(2010) *Theory as History: Essays on Modes of Production and Exploitation*. Leiden.

Barbier, J. (2009) "Le fisc du royaume franc: quelques jalons pour une réflexion sur l'état au haut moyen âge," in Pohl and Wieser (2009): 271–85.

Becher, M. (2011) "The Franks: Rome's heirs in the west," in *The Roman Empire in Context: Historical and Regional Perspectives*, ed. J. P. Arnason and K. Raaflaub. London: 179–98.

Becher, M., and Jarnut, J. (eds.) (2004) *Der Dynastiewechsel von 751: Vorgeschichte, Legitimationsstrategien und Erinnerung*. Münster.

Bonney, R., and Ormrod, W. M. (1999) "Introduction: crises, revolutions and self-sustained growth: towards a conceptual model of change in fiscal history," in *Crises, Revolutions and Self-Sustained Growth: Essays in European Fiscal History, 1130–1830*, ed. W. M. Ormrod, M. Bonney, and R. Bonney. Stamford, UK: 1–21.

Brandes, W. (2002) *Finanzverwaltung in Krisenzeiten: Untersuchungen zur byzantinischen Administration im 6. – 9. Jahrhundert*. Frankfurt.

Brandes, W., and Haldon, J. F. (2000) "Towns, tax and transformation: state, cities and their hinterlands in the east Roman world, *c.* 500–800," in *Towns and Their Hinterlands between Late Antiquity and the Early Middle Ages*, ed. G. P. Brogiolo, N. Christie, and N. Gauthier. Leiden: 141–72.

Brubaker, L., and Haldon, J. F. (2011) *Byzantium in the Iconoclast Era,* c. *680–850: A History*. Cambridge.

Carrié, J.-M. (2003) "L'institution annonaire de la première à la deuxième Rome: continuité et innovation," in *Nourrir les cités de Méditerranée: antiquité – temps modernes*, ed. B. Marin and C. Virlouvet. Paris: 153–211.

Collins, R. (1983) *Early Medieval Spain: Unity in Diversity*. London.

Corbier, M. (1989) "Dévaluations, inflation et circulation monétaire au IIIe siècle," in *Hommes et richesses dans l'Empire byzantin,* vol. I, *IVe – VIIe siècles*, ed. J. Lefort and C. Morrisson. Paris: 195–211.

Cosentino, S. (2000) "The Syrianos's 'Strategikon': a ninth-century source?," *Bizantinistica* 2: 243–80.

Costambeys, M., Innes, M., and MacLean, S. (eds.) (2011) *The Carolingian World.* Cambridge.

Curta, F. (2001) *The Making of the Slavs: History and Archaeology of the Lower Danube Region, c. 500–700.* Cambridge.

(2005) "Byzantium in Dark-Age Greece (the numismatic evidence in its Balkan context)," *Byzantine and Modern Greek Studies* 29: 113–46.

Dagron, G. (2002) "The urban economy, seventh–twelfth centuries," in *The Economic History of Byzantium: From the Seventh through the Fifteenth Century*, vol. II, ed. A. E. Laiou. Washington, DC: 393–461.

De Jong, M. (2003) "*Sacrum palatium et ecclesia*: l'autorité religieuse royale sous les carolingiens," *Annales: histoire, sciences sociales* 58: 1243–69.

(2009) "The state of the Church: *ecclesia* and early medieval state formation," in Pohl and Wieser (2009): 241–54.

Deutinger, R. (2009) "Staatlichkeit im Reich der Ottonen: ein versuch," in Pohl and Wieser (2009): 133–44.

Dölger, F. (1927) *Beiträge zur Geschichte der byzantinischen Finanzverwaltung besonders des 10. und 11. Jahrhunderts.* Munich.

Donat, P. (1988) "Gentiladel-Feudaladel: Forschungen in der BRD zur Adelsentstehung," *Jahrbuch für die Geschichte des Feudalismus* 11: 9–27.

Duncan-Jones, R. P. (1976) "The size of the *modius castrensis*," *Zeitschrift für Papyrologie und Epigraphik* 21: 53–62.

Durliat, J. (1990) *Les finances publiques de Dioclétien aux Carolingiens.* Sigmaringen, Germany.

Esders, S. (2009) "Rechtliche Grundlagen frühmittelalterlicher Staatlichkeit: der allgemeine Treuid," in Pohl and Wieser (2009): 423–32.

Ewig, E. (1997) *Die Merowinger und das Frankenreich.* Stuttgart.

Foss, C. (1997) "Syria in transition, AD 550–750: an archaeological approach," *Dumbarton Oaks Papers* 51: 189–269.

Fouracre, P. (2005) "Francia in the seventh century," in *The New Cambridge Medieval History, vol. I, c. 500 –c. 700*, ed. P. Fouracre. Cambridge: 371–96.

(2009) "Comparing the resources of the Merovingian and Carolingian states: problems and perspectives," in Pohl and Wieser (2009): 287–97.

Garnsey, P. (1991) "Mass diet and nutrition in the city of Rome," in *Nourrir la plèbe: actes du colloque tenu à Genève les 28 et 29 IX 1989 en hommage à Denis van Berchem*, ed. A. Giovannini. Basel: 67–99.

Gauthier, N. (2000) "Le réseau de pouvoirs de l'évêque dans la Gaule du haut moyen-âge," in *Towns and Their Territories between Late Antiquity and the Early Middle Ages*, ed. N. Gauthirer, G. P. Brogiolo, and N. Christie. Leiden: 173–207.

Geary, P. J. (1988) *Before France and Germany: The Creation and Transformation of the Merovingian World.* Oxford.

Grahn-Hoek, H. (1976) *Die fränkische Oberschicht im 6. Jahrhundert.* Sigmaringen, Germany.

Haldon, J. F. (1992) "The army and the economy: the allocation and redistribution of surplus wealth," *Mediterranean History Review* 7: 133–53.

(1994) "*Synônê*: re-considering a problematic term of middle Byzantine fiscal administration," *Byzantine and Modern Greek Studies* 18: 116–53.

(1995) "Pre-industrial states and the distribution of resources: the nature of the problem," in *States, Resources and Armies: Papers of the Third Workshop on Late Antiquity and Early Islam*, ed. A. Cameron. Princeton, NJ: 1–25.

(1997) *Byzantium in the Seventh Century: The Transformation of a Culture*, 2nd edn. Cambridge.

(1998) "The organisation and support of an expeditionary force: manpower and logistics in the middle Byzantine period," in *Byzantium at War, 9th – 12th Centuries,* ed. N. Oikonomidès. Athens: 111–51.

(2013) "The Byzantine successor state," in *The Oxford Handbook of the State in the Ancient Near East and Mediterranean*, ed. P. F. Bang and W. Scheidel. New York: 475–97.

Halsall, G. (2007) *Barbarian Migrations and the Roman West, 376–568.* Cambridge.

Harvey, A. (1989) *Economic Expansion in the Byzantine Empire, 900–1200.* Cambridge.

Heinzelmann, M. (1975) "L'aristocratie et les évêchés entre Loire et Rhin jusqu'à la fin du VIIe siècle," *Revue d'Histoire de l'église de France* 62: 75–90.

(1976) *Bischofsherrschaft in Gallien: zur Kontinuität römischer Führungsschichten vom 4. bis zum 7. Jahrhundert: soziale, prosopographische und bildungsgeschichtliche Aspekte.* Zurich.

Hendy, M. F. (1985) *Studies in the Byzantine Monetary Economy,* c. *300–1450.* Cambridge.

(1989) "'Byzantium, 1081–1204': the economy revisited twenty years on," in *The Economy, Fiscal Administration and Coinage of Byzantium*, ed. M. F. Hendy. London: 1–48.

Hopkins, K. (1980) "Taxes and trade in the Roman Empire (200 BC – AD 400)," *Journal of Roman Studies* 70: 101–25.

(1995) "Rome, taxes, rents and trade," *Kodai: Journal of Ancient History* 6/7: 41–75 [repr. in W. Scheidel and S. von Reden (eds.) *The Ancient Economy.* Edinburgh (2002): 190–230].

Innes, M. (2005) "Charlemagne's government," in *Charlemagne: Empire and Society*, ed. J. Storey. Manchester: 71–89.

(2007) *Introduction to Early Medieval Western Europe, 300–900: The Sword, the Plough and the Book.* Abingdon, UK.

Ireland, S. (2000) *Greek, Roman and Byzantine Coins in the Museum at Amasya (Ancient Amaseia), Turkey.* London.

James, E. (1982) *The Origins of France: From Clovis to the Capetians.* London.

Jones, A. H. M. (1964) *The Later Roman Empire 284–602: A Social and Administrative Survey.* Oxford.

Kaplan, M. (1992) *Les hommes et la terre à Byzance du VIe au XIe siècles: propriété et exploitation du sol.* Paris.

(2001) "Quelques remarques sur la vie rurale à Byzance au IXe siècle d'après la correspondance d'Ignace le Diacre," in *The Dark Centuries of Byzantium*, ed E. Kountoura-Galaki. Athens: 365–76.

(2006) "Quelques aspects des maisons divines du VIe au IXe siècle," in *Byzance: villes et campagnes*, ed. M. Kaplan. Paris: 138–56.

Karayannopoulos, I. (1958) *Das Finanzwesen des frühbyzantinischen Staates.* Munich.

(1966) "Fragmente aus dem Vademecum eines byzantinischen Finanzbeamten," in *Polychronion: Festschrift F. Dölger zum 75. Geburtstag*, ed. P. Wirth. Heidelberg: 318–34.

Kaschke, S. (2009) "Zur Trennung von Reich und Herrscher in der Vorstellungswelt des 9. Jahrhunderts," in Pohl and Wieser (2009): 451–69.

Kingsley, S. (2003) "Late antique trade: research methodologies and field practices," in *Theory and Practice in Late Antique Archaeology*, ed. L. Lavan and W. Bowden. Leiden: 113–38.

Kislinger, E. (1995) "Pane e demografia: l'approvigionamento di Constantinopoli," in *Nel nome de pane*, ed. O. Longo and P. Scarpi. Trento: 159–76.

Kravari, V., Lefort, J., and Morrisson, C. (eds.) (1991) *Hommes et richesses dans l'Empire byzantin*, vol. II, *VIIIe – XVe siècles*. Paris.

Laiou, A. E. (1977) *Peasant Society in the Late Byzantine Empire: A Social and Demographic Study*. Princeton, NJ.

(2002a) "Economic and non-economic exchange," in *The Economic History of Byzantium: From the Seventh through the Fifteenth Century*, vol. II, ed. A. E. Laiou. Washington, DC: 681–96.

(2002b) "The Byzantine economy: an overview," in *The Economic History of Byzantium: From the Seventh through the Fifteenth Century*, vol. III, ed. A. E. Laiou. Washington, DC: 1145–64.

Lefort, J. (2002) "The rural economy, seventh–twelfth centuries," in *The Economic History of Byzantium: From the Seventh through the Fifteenth Century*, vol. I, ed. A. E. Laiou. Washington, DC: 231–310.

Lefort, J., and Morrisson, C. (eds.) (1989) *Hommes et richesses dans l'empire byzantin*, vol. I, *IVe – VIIe siècles*. Paris.

Lewis, A. R. (1976) "The dukes in the 'Regnum Francorum' AD 550–751," *Speculum* 51: 381–410.

Lightfoot, C. (2009) "Excavations at Amorium: results from the last ten years (1998–2008)," in *Archaeology of the Countryside in Medieval Anatolia*, ed. T. Vorderstrasse and J. Roodenberg. Leiden: 139–53.

Lilie, R.-J. (1987) "Die byzantinischen Staatsfinanzen im 8./9. Jahrhundert und die *stratiôtika ktêmata*," *Byzantinoslavica* 48: 49–55.

Lopez, R. S. (1951) "The dollar of the Middle Ages," *Journal of Economic History* 11: 209–34.

McCormick, M. (2001) *Origins of the European Economy: Communications and Commerce AD 300–900*. Cambridge.

McKitterick, R. (1983) *The Frankish Kingdoms under the Carolingians, 751–987*. London.

Morrisson, C. (1980) "Un trésor de *solidi* de Constantin IV de Carthage," *Revue Numismatique* 22: 155–60.

(1985) "La monnaie d'or byzantine à Constantinople: purification et modes d'altérations (491–1354)," in *L'or monnayé*, vol. 1, *Purification et altérations de Rome à Byzance*, ed. C. Brenot, J.-N. Barrandon, J.-P. Callu, J. Poirier, R. Halleux, and C. Morrisson, Paris: 113–87.

(1991) "Monnaie et finances dans l'empire byzantin Xe – XIVe siècle," in Kravari, Lefort, and Morrisson (1991): 291–315.

(2002) "Byzantine money: its production and circulation," in *The Economic History of Byzantium: From the Seventh through the Fifteenth Century*, vol. III, ed. A. E. Laiou. Washington, DC: 909–66.

Morrisson, C., and Cheynet, J.-C. (2002) "Prices and wages in the Byzantine world," in *The Economic History of Byzantium: From the Seventh through the Fifteenth Century*, vol. II, ed. A. E. Laiou. Washington, DC: 815–78.

Murphy, F. X. (1952) "Julian of Toledo and the fall of the Visigothic kingdom in Spain," *Speculum* 27: 1–21.

Oikonomidès, N. (1972) *Les listes de préséance byzantines des IXe – Xe siècles*. Paris.

(1991) "Terres du fisc et revenu de la terre aux Xe – XIe siècles," in Kravari, Lefort, and Morrisson (1991): 321–37.

(1996) *Fiscalité et exemption fiscale à Byzance (IXe – XIe s.)*. Athens.

(1997) "Title and income at the Byzantine court," in *Byzantine Court Culture from 829 to 1204*, ed. H. Maguire. Washington, DC: 199–215.

(2002) "The role of the Byzantine state in the economy," in *The Economic History of Byzantium: From the Seventh through the Fifteenth Century*, vol. III, ed. A. E. Laiou. Washington, DC: 973–1058.

Ostrogorsky, G. (1927) *Die ländliche Steuergemeinde des byzantinischen Reiches im X. Jahrhundert*. Stuttgart.

Pohl, W. (2002) *Die Völkerwanderungen*. Stuttgart.

(2009) "Regnum und gens," in Pohl and Wieser (2009): 435–50.

Pohl, W., and Wieser, V. (eds.) (2009) *Der frühmittealterliche Staat: europäische Perspektiven*. Vienna.

Rance, P. (2007) "The date of the military compendium of Syrianus Magister (formerly the sixth-century Anonymus Byzantinus)," *Byzantinische Zeitschrift* 100: 701–37.

Reece, R. (2003) "Coins and the late Roman economy," in *Theory and Practice in Late Antique Archaeology*, ed. L. Lavan and W. Bowden. Leiden: 139–68.

Reuter, T. (trans. and ed.) (1978) *The Medieval Nobility: Studies on the Ruling Classes of France and Germany from the Sixth to the Twelfth Centuries*. Amsterdam.

(1985) "Plunder and tribute in the Carolingian empire," *Transactions of the Royal Historical Society* 35: 75–94.

(1990) "The end of Carolingian military expansion," in *Charlemagne's Heir: New Perspectives on the Reign of Louis the Pious*, ed. P. Godman and R. Collins. Oxford: 391–405.
(1992) *Germany in the Middle Ages, 800–1056*. London.
Rickman, G. (1980) *The Corn Supply of Ancient Rome*. Oxford.
Roberts, R., and Kynaston, D. (eds.) (1995) *The Bank of England: Money, Power and Influence 1694–1994*. Oxford.
Roseveare, H. (1991) *The Financial Revolution 1660–1760*. London.
Sarris, P. (2001) "Review article of *Agrarian Change in Late Antiquity: Gold, Labour, and Aristocratic Dominance* by Jairus Banaji," *Historical Materialism* 13: 207–19.
(2004) "Rehabilitating the great estate: aristocratic property and economic growth in the late antique east," in *Recent Research on the Late Antique Countryside*, ed. W. Bowden, L. Lavan, and C. Machado. Leiden: 55–71.
(2006) *Economy and Society in the Age of Justinian*. Cambridge.
(2009) "Aristocrats, peasants and the transformation of rural society, *c*. 400–800," *Journal of Agrarian Change* 9: 3–153.
Schilbach, E. (1970) *Byzantinische Metrologie*. Munich.
Schulze, H. K. (1985) *Grundstrukturen der Verfassung im Mittelalter*, vol. I, *Stammesverband, Gefolgschaft, Lehnswesen, Grundherrschaft*. Stuttgart.
Shanzer, D. (1998) "Dating the baoptism of Clovis: 1886–1993," *Early Medieval Europe* 3: 97–116.
Southall, A. (1956) *Alur Society*. Cambridge.
(1965) "A critique of the typology of states and political systems," in *Political Systems and the Distribution of Power*, ed. M. Barton. New York: 113–40.
Steuer, H. (1987) "Archäologie und die Erforschung der germanischen Sozialgeschichte des 5. bis 8. Jahrhunderts," in *Akten des 22. Deutschen Rechtshistorikertages: Studien zur Europäischen Rechtsgeschichte*. ed. D. Simon. Frankfurt: 443–53.
Svoronos, N. (1959) *Recherches sur le cadastre byzantin et la fiscalité aux XIe et XIIe siècles*. Athens.
Thompson, E. A. (1969) *The Goths in Spain*. Oxford.
Treadgold, W. T. (1982) *The Byzantine State Finances in the Eighth and Ninth Centuries*. New York.
Trombley, F. R. (2001) "Town and *territorium* in late Roman Anatolia (late 5th to early 7th c.)," in *Recent Research in Late-Antique Urbanism*, ed. L. Lavan. Portsmouth, RI: 217–32.
Wallace-Hadrill, J.-M. (1962) *The Long-Haired Kings, and Other Studies in Frankish History*. London.
(1967) *The Barbarian West 400–1000*. London.
Werner, K. F. (1980) "Missus – Marchio – Comes," in *Histoire comparée de l'administration (IVe – XVIIIe siècle)*, ed. W. Paravicini and K. F. Werner. Munich: 191–239.
Wickham, C. J. (1984) "The other transition: from the ancient world to feudalism," *Past and Present* 103: 3–36.

(2005) *Framing the Early Middle Ages: Europe and the Mediterranean, 400–800.* Oxford.
(2009) *The Inheritance of Rome: A History of Europe from 400 to 1000.* London.
Wood, I. (1977) "Kings, kingdoms and consent," in *Early Medieval Kingship*, ed. P. Sawyer and I. Wood. Leeds: 6–29.
(1993) *The Merovingian Kingdoms, 450–751.* London.
(2004) "Usurpers and Merovingian kingship," in Becher and Jarnut (2004): 15–31.
Zotz, T. (1995) "Zur Grundherrschaft des Königs im Deutschen Reich vom 10. bis zum frühen 13. Jahrhundert," in *Grundherrschaft und bäuerliche Gesellschaft im Hochmittelalter*, ed. W. Rösener. Göttingen: 76–115.
Zuckerman, C. (1990) "The military compendium of Syrianos magister," *Jahrbuch des österreichischen Byzantinistik* 40: 209–24.
(2005) "Learning from the enemy and more: studies in 'dark centuries' Byzantium," Millennium: Jahrbuch zu Kultur und Geschichte des ersten Jahrtausends n. Chr. 2: 79–135.

CHAPTER 12

The Middle East in Islamic late antiquity

Hugh Kennedy

The concept of "Islamic late antiquity," first developed, I believe, in the work of the late Tom Sizgorich,[1] has now achieved a general currency among historians as a hermeneutic device for interpreting and explaining the first three centuries of Islam rule in the Middle East, roughly from the time of the Prophet until the middle of the tenth century.[2] Sizgorich uses the term to describe a pattern of inter-communal relations and the role played by religious violence in maintaining the boundaries between different sects and groups – a pattern that he saw extending from late antiquity (as described in the accepted Peter Brown model) into the early Islamic period, with more communities and actors entering the fray. As such, his work played an important part in undermining those sharp but unhelpful barriers that still separate the world of late antiquity from the world of early Islam, both inside the academy and outside.

In this chapter I argue that the concept also has a value and validity in looking at the world of administrative and, above all, fiscal systems in the early Islamic world. I argue that the early Islamic state, alone of the polities that succeeded Roman rule in the Mediterranean world, preserved and exploited an effective system of public taxation, especially a regular system for the taxation of agricultural land. It was preserved not because of any sentimental or ideological commitment to an old and – as far as the early Muslims were concerned – largely irrelevant imperial model, nor yet because there was a bureaucracy already in place that they continued to use out of a sort of institutional inertia, but because these structures were of immediate use and were, indeed, indispensable.

To understand why this should be we need to look at the course of the Muslim conquests of the third and fourth decades of the seventh century,[3] and the consequences that followed from them. This fiscal system was first

[1] Sizgorich (2009). [2] For the general political history of this period, see Kennedy (2004a).
[3] On which, see Donner (1981) and Kennedy (2007).

developed in Iraq, and, above all, the alluvial lands between Baghdad and the head of the Gulf that the Arabic sources refer to as the Sawad from 636 on. Only later, from the time of the Umayyad caliph ʿAbd al-Malik (685–705), was this system rolled out in the rest of the caliphate, and even then the implementation was patchy.

There were good reasons for this. According to the records of taxation that could be expected from the different provinces of the caliphate in the late eighth and ninth centuries, the Sawad of Iraq contributed approximately four times as much revenue as the next most productive area, Egypt, and five times as much as all the provinces of Syria and Palestine put together.[4] The fiscal politics of the Sawad were central to the maintenance of the Islamic caliphate up to the environmental and administrative collapse of the early tenth century.

The conquest of Iraq by the Muslim armies was swift and decisive. There was no prolonged period of uncertainty and disruption between the collapse of the Sasanian *ancien régime* and the establishment of some form of Muslim rule. This swift transition meant that a significant number of the *fonctionnnaires* of the Sasanian administration took service almost immediately under the new Muslim administration, bringing with them, we must presume, much of the expertise that they had previously used under the old empire.[5]

None of these skills and none of this accumulated knowledge would have been of any use, however, had it not served the purposes of the new Muslim masters of the country; it would simply have withered and died, as Roman administrative expertise did in sixth-century northern Italy, when the conquerors were rewarded with grants of land that made the land tax both redundant and uncollectable. With the disappearance of the land tax there also disappeared the state bureaucracy and apparatus that had collected it.[6]

The key to understanding this is the pattern and mechanisms of Muslim settlement in Iraq. Iraq was largely conquered by tribesmen from northern and eastern Arabia who joined the Muslim force in large numbers, and who continued to emigrate from the desert after the major battles had been won in the hope of participating in further campaigns in Iran and sharing in the resulting booty. In this respect, the conquest of Iraq was very different from that of Syria, which was largely conquered by members of the Quraysh, the tribe of the Prophet, and other tribes from the Hijaz, which formed the elite of the of the early Muslim umma. They were also

[4] See Kennedy (2004b: 11–12). [5] See Morony (1984). [6] As described by Wickham (1984).

assisted by members of Arab tribes who had lived in the desert margins of Syria and Palestine before the coming of Islam.[7]

The Islamic tradition[8] explains that the caliph Umar I (634–44) decided not to divide the lands of Iraq among the Arab conquerors, nor to allow them to settle the agricultural lands and effectively become a landowning elite, as the Persian dehqans had been before them. Instead, they were to be settled in newly established garrison towns, notably Basra and Kufa,[9] on the fringes of the agricultural lands of the Sawad. The Arabic sources explain this policy as a way of protecting the religious qualities and the martial prowess of the settlers, so enabling them to defend the conquered lands and, increasingly, to participate in later campaigns of conquest. There were other ideological factors at work here too. The idea of *hijra* was crucial. *Hijra* means "migration," but, in particular in the early Islamic context, it means migration from the desert to the towns and from paganism to Islam. The Prophet himself had made the most famous *hijra* of all, from pagan Mecca to now Muslim Medina, in 622, and there was a strong current of belief among the Muslim leadership that, if the Bedouin tribesmen were going to be good Muslims, loyal to the caliphate, they should be encouraged, even compelled, to leave their nomad lifestyles and become citizens of the newly established cities.

Although the exact chronology and mechanisms remain to some extent uncertain, it seems as if this is basically what happened. Attempts by a few notables to take over areas as private domains were prevented, and the pattern of urban settlement was established with a decade of the initial conquests, or probably in even less time.

Whatever the reasons for this government-enforced pattern of settlement, it immediately gave rise to major and very pressing problems – problems that could not be put off for a year or two until administrative arrangements had been debated and refined. The Bedouin who came to these towns were effectively obliged to abandon their pastoral way of life. We do not know what happened to their sheep, goats, and camels; many of them must have remained with those Bedouin who chose not to undertake this *hijra*, but for those who did migrate to the cities it was clear that urban

[7] One is reminded of the comment about British settlement in east Africa in the first half of the twentieth century, explaining that "officers went to Kenya, other ranks to Rhodesia." We can perhaps read Syria for Kenya, Iraq for Rhodesia. In both cases, it can be argued, the social stratification of settlement had a lasting effect on the political future of the areas.

[8] See, for example, al-Ansari Abu Yusuf (1967 [*c.* 795]: 68).

[9] These garrison towns were called *miṣr* (pl. *amṣār*). A *miṣr* was a city (*madīna*) in which pensions and salaries were paid out to the Muslims. For the early history and development of Kufa, see Djait (1986). There is no comparable work on Basra, but see Pellat (1953).

life was, in general, incompatible with a pastoral lifestyle. There was a further consideration. Some of the areas of Arabia where the conquerors of Iraq and the emigrants who followed them came from were the areas, notably in northeast Arabia, that had broken away from the Muslim umma after the death of the Prophet. The so-called *ridda* wars against these elements had been hard fought and, were, in many ways, the first of the Muslim conquests. These people could not be allowed to slip back into their old, recalcitrant ways.

In short, there are good reasons to accept, in broad terms, the picture painted by the early Muslim sources, even if the texts, in their present form, were not written down for a century or more after the events they describe. This "big bang" explanation of the earliest phases of Muslim administration is both textually attested and heuristic, in the sense that it provides a clear and logical explanation for what happened. We can even propose with some confidence that the man who devised the scheme of payment that was to form the foundations of the distinctive early Islamic fiscal system was Ziyād b. Sumayya, also known as Ziyād b. Abī Sufyān or Ziyād b. Abīhi (*c.* 622–673).[10]

The system for paying the newly settled inhabitants of the new towns of Iraq was based on the idea that they should be paid at regular intervals so that they could provide for their own needs and also those of their families and dependants. They would then be able to purchase foodstuffs and the necessities of life, and, presumably, some luxuries as well. There is evidence that in the early stages of this process there were some payments in kind, known in the Arabic sources as *rizq*, but these were gradually discontinued, and payments were almost entirely made in coined money.

These payments were known as *ʿaṭāʾ*, or "gift." Originally they seem to have been made once or twice a year, often before the Muslim armies set out on campaign.[11] They were also paid on a sliding scale. Members of the Muslim elite and those who could claim to have participated in the first great battle against the Persians were awarded the highest rates of *ʿaṭāʾ*. Those who had come later and joined the Muslims after the first fighting was over, especially those who had joined in the *ridda* rebellion against the authority of the first caliphs, were awarded a much lower level of compensation.

Fundamental to the understanding of this system, at least among those who benefited from it, was the fact that it was hereditary. As the years

[10] For Ziyad, see Hasson (2002).

[11] The payment of the military in the early Islamic period is discussed by Kennedy (2001: 59–95; 2002).

passed and the original participants in these heroic events died out, their heirs claimed to inherit the privileged status of their fathers and grandfathers: the *'aṭā'* was theirs by right. This claim to right was reinforced by the quasi-religious force that these arrangements came to acquire. The system had had the blessing of the greatest of the early caliphs, 'Umar I, and 'Ali (who reigned from 656 to 661). After the Prophet Muhammad, who had of course died before the conquests, 'Umar was the greatest early Muslim legislator, particularly among those who can be described as proto-Sunnis, and it was he whose authority had established the system. 'Ali was the cousin and son-in-law of Muhammad and undisputed leader of the family of the Prophet, who, it was claimed, had given the system his blessing during his attempts to establish his authority in Iraq during his short and troubled caliphate. The system the settlers cherished so much had acquired the support of the greatest authorities in the early Islamic umma after the Prophet himself. The system was, in the Arabic terminology, not just part of their earthly rights, their *dunyā*, but part of their *dīn*, or religion. In defending their rights, they claimed, they were not just defending their material possessions but their very faith.

This system clearly required a continuing supply of money. According to narrative sources, the number of military settlers in Basra around 670 – that is, a generation after the initial conquests – was some 80,000, with around 120,000 in their families, while in Kufa at the same time there were some 60,000, with 80,000 dependants. Even if all the fighting men had been paid only the lowest rate of *'aṭā'*, 200 dirham per year, this would still have meant that an enormous amount of coined money was in circulation. The other figures we have from the same period are broadly in agreement with these.[12] One consequence of this was the high degree of monetization of the early Islamic economy. Like the late Roman and Sasanian Empires, but unlike contemporary western Europe and even contemporary Byzantium, coined money was in regular use for all types of transactions at all levels of society, except possibly the very poorest in remote rural areas.

This is where the existing bureaucracy proved essential to the early Islamic project. Without a regular supply of coined money, the new structure would very quickly disintegrate, and the tribesmen would soon go back to the desert or end up by fighting with their fellow citizens. It was essential to continue and adapt Sasanian methods to new Islamic purposes. As Morony, whose work on early Islamic Iraq remains essential, notes, "The process was inaugurated by a circle of bilingual Persian and Arab

[12] Further details and discussion of these figures: Kennedy (2001: 19–21, 71–4).

administrators at Basra, where the main institutional forms of Sasanian civil and military administration were adapted by the newly formed Islamic state."[13] In reality, as Morony observes, our knowledge of late Sasanian and early Islamic tax administration is very limited and largely derived from Arabic writers such as al-Yaʿqūbī and al-Jahshiyārī writing in the early Abbasid period. Nonetheless, it seems clear that a land tax, based on the cultivated area, was regularly collected under the Sasanians, who forwarded the records of taxes collected to the monarch. We also know of named individuals, such as Zādhānfarrukh and his sons, who had been involved with Sasanian fiscal administration and continued to work for the new Muslim administration. They were joined by prisoners of war with administrative experience, and they developed an early Islamic tax system.

A similar process occurred with expenditure, the other main branch of Sasanian administration. According to al-Yaʿqūbī, there were registers (he uses the Arabic word *dīwān* for these registers) in which the names and equipment of the professional military were recorded. Again, it is highly likely that the Islamic administrators of Basra and Kufa used the expertise of Persian administrators to compile their *dīwāns* or pay lists, though, given that, at this stage, virtually all those entitled to payments were Arabs with Arabic names, the language of these registers must have been in Arabic from the beginning.

Although the evidence is slight, it clearly suggests that Persian administrative systems, along with skilled Persia personnel, were used by the first Islamic governors of Iraq from a very early stage. The key point in understanding this development was that this administrative apparatus survived because it was useful – indeed, vital – for the running of the early Islamic system. If the Muslims had been encouraged or even allowed to settle the lands of Iraq as farmers and landlords, and live off the proceeds of their estates, this Sasanian administration would have atrophied and finally died, as Roman administrative systems did in most of western Europe in the post-imperial stage.

During the course of the Umayyad century (661–750) this system was modified, and in many ways it was transformed, sometimes violently, into a real system of state[14] financial management.

13 Morony (1984: 51).

14 The term used in many early Arabic sources is *sulṭān*. By the eleventh century this term had acquired its familiar usage as a title for a ruling individual, such as the Ottoman sultan for example. In earlier sources, however, it is an abstract noun meaning "the authorities," unattached to any individual and persisting from one caliph to another. I believe we can with some confidence translate it as "state," or at least "state apparatus."

One aspect of this development was the spread of this Iraqi model into other areas of the caliphate, which at this time stretched from Spain and Morocco in the west to central Asia and what is now southern Pakistan in the east. The position that emerged in Egypt in the years following the conquest of 640–1[15] was in some ways similar to the position in Iraq. Until the end of the Umayyad period there is very little evidence of Arab Muslims settling outside the main cities of Fustat (Old Cairo) and Alexandria. Tax collection remained, at a local level, in the hands of Greek- speaking and -writing officials, though we have a very significant number of bilingual documents. What distinguished the Egyptian model from the Iraqi was that the number of Arab Muslim settlers was much smaller and the rate of conversion to Islam much slower in Egypt. There is evidence of Coptic revolts, driven by fiscal pressure, but much less of discontent among the Muslims themselves, who retained the position of a small privileged elite until the end of the eighth century.

The position in Syria is much more obscure. It is one of the more frustrating problems of the history of the Umayyad period that, while Syria was the seat of caliphal power and Syrians dominated the upper ranks of government and the military, we have very little evidence for the working of the system, how Syria was governed and taxed, and how they used Byzantine administrative legacies. We have evidence of continuity of personnel, notably in the family of St John of Damascus, who had worked for both late Byzantine and early Islamic administration. We know something of this family, however, not because of their administrative importance but because of his sanctity. It is likely that many of the *mawālī*,[16] who formed the core of the Umayyad administration in Syria, were Greek converts familiar with administrative practice, but their biographies are virtually unknown, and even their names give no hints as to their background.

The only area of Syria where we can get below the surface of the narratives is in the little town of Nessana in the Negev. Here the dryness of the climate allowed the survival of a small, but nonetheless valuable, collection of administrative papyri from the 680s.[17] Some of these are bilingual *entagia* in Greek and Arabic, ordering the people of the town to make payments of wheat and olive oil to local Bedouin tribes. This may

[15] Kennedy (1998).

[16] The word *mawlā* (pl. *mawālī*) was used at this stage to describe freedmen or non-Arabs who attached themselves as clients to Arab tribes in order to become part of the Muslim community. This practice had died out by the end of the Umayyad period, and the word acquired other meanings.

[17] Published by Kraemer (1958).

have been only part of a much more extensive administrative system, but, on the basis of the surviving material, we can conclude that the administration, and the transfer of resources from the local inhabitants to the Arabic tribes, was, at this stage, much simpler and on a much smaller scale than in contemporary Iraq. The documents give little evidence for the use of coin, and none of any central administrative apparatus. But it would be rash to extrapolate from this to the rest of Syria. Nessana was always a small town on the margins of the desert. The taxation system in a developed agricultural area near the center of power – the Ghuta of Damascus, for example – might well have been much more developed.

The practices of Basra and Kufa were no doubt exported to some areas of Iran, especially to Khurasan and other frontier areas in the northeast where Arabs from Iraq had settled in quite large numbers.

Finally, in the case of distant al-Andalus, where the surviving evidence has been thoroughly examined, we find a very different picture.[18] Here the pattern of the initial Arab/Muslim settlement was very different. There were no military towns or major concentrations of settlers. Instead, the newcomers were dispersed in the landscape and seem to have become property owners, supporting themselves on the proceeds of farming and trade. There was little in the way of bureaucracy or evidence of any system of universal land tax. In some ways, the pattern of fiscal administration in eighth- and ninth-century al-Andalus may be more similar to that of contemporary Merovingian and early Carolingian France than of Umayyad or Abbasid Baghdad. That is too big a topic to discuss here, however.

Another feature of the fiscal structure developed in the Sawad of Iraq should be noted: there was very little role for the "central" government – that is, the government of the caliphs in Damascus. There seems to have been only a very modest transfer of resources from the province to Syria, and even this transfer was the subject of the most vigorous controversy. In what we can perhaps describe as the classical model elaborated in Iraq, it was held that the resources of Iraq constituted the *fay* of Iraq, which should be distributed among those Muslims in Iraq who were entitled to it: the conquerors and their descendants. If there was any surplus, there were many in the province who held firmly that it should remain in the province and be distributed there.

This clearly left little or no freedom of action for the caliphal government, and such evidence as we do have suggests that the government sustained

[18] Chalmeta (1975).

itself largely on the revenues of the Syrian provinces: fiscally, if not religiously or politically, the early caliphate was a sort of federation of provinces.

This position was not to last. After the death of the caliph Yazīd I in 683, the caliphate was torn apart by a series of civil wars, which came very close to destroying it altogether. The epicenter of this struggle was Iraq, where the Syria-based regime of the Umayyads was vigorously rejected. When some measure of unity began to be restored by the Umayyad ʿAbd al-Malik from 685 onward, he and his advisers, a bit like the Roman emperors of the late third century, seem to have been convinced that the decentralized quasi-federal system with which the early caliphs and Muʿāwiya had ruled was no longer viable. A much more centralized system was required that would give the caliphs much more real political and, above all, financial power.

In 694 ʿAbd al-Malik appointed the celebrated Hajjāj b. Yūsuf as governor of Iraq and all the east – a post he was to retain until his death in 714. ʿAbd al-Malik and Hajjāj seem to have agreed on a common approach to the *fay* of Iraq: that it should be used to pay a standing professional military, obedient to the government of the caliphs. This was a fundamental change. Payment of the *ʿaṭāʾ* was no longer to be dependent on descent from the conquering army but on actual service to the current administration: if you did not fight you did not get paid. Hajjāj made things tougher, by instructing the army of Iraq to undertake long and hazardous expeditions to places such as eastern Sistan and Zabulistan, essentially the Helmand area of modern Afghanistan – never an easy place for alien armies. The upshot of these campaigns, and the suppression of the rebellion among the Iraqi troops that inevitably followed, was that the Iraqis were effectively excluded from the army and, consequently, from the *ʿaṭāʾ* payments that many of them continued to believe strongly they were entitled to.

This did not mean that all the revenue was now forwarded to Syria, though no doubt some of it was. Instead, the Umayyads attempted to solve the problems of resource and entitlement by exporting the Syrian army to Iraq, where they could keep order but also have more immediate access to the *fay* of the country. This led to the foundation of the third major Islamic new town at Wasit, effectively halfway between Basra and Kufa. This new city became the seat of the governor, and the effective capital of Iraq until the send of the Umayyad period. It also became by far the most important mint for silver dirhams, which were the currency of the eastern caliphate, reflecting its importance as the center where the (now almost exclusively Syrian) army was paid.

One result of the caliph's determination to take control of the fiscal administration was the standardization of administrative practice throughout the caliphate. This was demonstrated in two conspicuous and lasting changes. The first was the issuing of a new and radically different type of coinage. Until this point, around 700, the Muslim authorities had used coins based on Byzantine and Sasanian models: the gold dinar of the Byzantines and the silver dirham of the Sasanians. Both sorts of coins were embellished with human images but were sometimes overstruck with short Arabic inscriptions. The new coins, though based on the weights and materials of the previous ones, were entirely epigraphic, giving religious inscriptions, names of rulers, and the date and place of minting. For the purposes of this discussion, the important thing was the imposition of a form of monetary standardization, albeit still based on the gold standard of the west and the silver standard of the east.

The second main change was a decree that all administrative functions should be conducted exclusively in Arabic, rather than the Greek or Pahlavi (Middle Persian) that had previously been employed by bureaucrats educated in the Byzantine and Sasanian traditions. Like all such administrative changes, the process occurred more completely in some areas than others, and the papyri show that Greek and Coptic were still both being used in the local administration of Egypt for some time after the changeover was supposed to have occurred. Nonetheless, the changes led to a standardized fiscal terminology throughout the Islamic Middle East, reflecting the breakdown of the local fiscal autonomies that had characterized the first seventy years after the conquests.

After 750 the Abbasids essentially built on the fiscal system that ʿAbd al-Malik and Hajjāj had established, but used it for slightly different purposes and to enrich a different elite, though a number of the bureaucrats who had served the later Umayyads also worked for the early Abbasids,[19] leading to a continuity of personnel as well as policy. The most fundamental point was that the Abbasids continued to raise a general land tax; indeed, their administrators in the Sawad and other central areas seem to have been more thorough than the Umayyads were. The receipts of this taxation were partly used to support the increasingly numerous and luxurious court, but, as under the later Umayyads, the bulk of the tax revenues were devoted to the financing of an increasingly professional and well-paid military, now receiving salaries – still called *ʿaṭāʾ* – every month. In contrast to the

[19] For administrative continuity between the Umayyad and early Abbasid governments, see Bligh Abramski (1988).

Umayyads, however, the early Abbasid military were largely recruited from Khurasan (northeast Iran and the western parts of central Asia).

This process was given added impetus by the foundation of Baghdad, which led to a further centralization of government and fiscal policy. Although wages were still paid to troops on the *diwan* lists in Basra, Kufa, Fustat, and Merv, as well as smaller provincial centers such as Mosul, by far the most important part of the revenues were taken to Baghdad and dispersed to the military elite and an increasingly numerous and well-rewarded bureaucracy. The new city expanded very rapidly. By the early ninth century it may well have had a population of some 500,000, and it was the largest city in western Eurasia – and possibly on the entire planet. The payment of salaries to a large number of military and civil personnel generated a huge market for goods and services and attracted merchants, artisans, poets, and intellectuals from all over the Muslim world.[20]

After the death of Harun al-Rashid, in 809, the caliphate was plunged into another protracted civil war, which finally resulted, from around 830 onward, in the reestablishment of Abbasid rule based on yet another new military elite, recruited among the Turkic and Iranian horsemen of the northeast of the empire and the steppes that stretched beyond. Many of these new troops were mounted horse archers, very effective on the field of battle but significantly more expensive to pay and maintain than the foot soldiers who had formed the main part of the armies of the early Abbasids. The presence of this new military led, in turn, to the development of a new capital in which they could be stationed and rewarded.[21] While the armies of the later Umayyads and early Abbasids were Arabic-speaking and no doubt engaged in trade and commerce to supplement their salaries., the new troops were Persian- or Turkish-speaking, without any family or tribal connections in Iraq and the west of the caliphate, and so entirely dependent on their pay for their survival. They became increasing militant in defense of their income, and, unlike the inhabitants of early Islamic Iraq, they had control of the person of the caliph, who they could threaten or murder if he did not respond to their wishes. From 861 to 870 the caliphs were effectively taken prisoner in the vast palatial-bureaucratic complex at Samarra.

There can be no doubt that the semi-captivity of the caliphs in Samarra inflicted lasting damage on the fiscal system. Some provinces, such as Khurasan, effectively drifted out of any sort of caliphal control, never to return, with a lasting loss of revenue to the treasury. Others, such as Egypt,

[20] For estimates of the population of Baghdad, see Lassner (1970: 155–60).
[21] For the built-up area of Samarra, see Northedge (2005).

had to be reconquered, and never yielded the sorts of revenue they had previously. Most damaging was the revolt of the Zanj in the southern part of the Sawad from 869 to 883.[22] Zanj was the name given to black slaves of east African origin who worked as agricultural laborers on the estates of the area, clearing salt off the fields. Twice beforehand they had risen in violent revolt against this miserable work and the conditions they were obliged to endure, but this uprising was much more violent and prolonged than its predecessors. Not only was much of the most productive land in the area rendered barren and useless but the great city of Basra itself was sacked, with huge loss of life and destruction of buildings.

The revolt of the Zanj points to another long-term factor in the decline of the resource base of the state: the salinization of the topsoil caused by continuous irrigation and lack of proper drainage. It is possible to suggest that the agriculture of this area was bound to follow a cyclical development, with periods of intensive development inevitably being followed by salinization and the consequent loss of fertile land.

The first four decades of the tenth century saw the effective collapse of the system of public taxation, and, with it, the resource base of the *sulṭān*. We are comparatively well informed about this process, because it was described by a number of chroniclers, notably Miskawayh (d. 1040), who collected information from sources in the bureaucracy. We do not need to follow the process in detail but the main developments were the repeated shortages of cash to fund government expenditure, primarily, of course, the military, but also a luxurious court. These pressures led to the introduction, first, of large-scale tax-farming, but soon afterward the dispersal of state revenues and assets as *iqṭāʿ*.[23] The granting of *iqṭāʿ*. meant that important figures, almost always members of the military elite, were entitled to collect government taxes and rents directly from the agricultural producers, and use them to pay for their "table" and to reward their followers and secure their loyalty.

As a result, the *sulṭān* lost control over both the collection of taxes and the payments of salaries, leading, inevitably, to a weakening of the administration, which was almost redundant in this new situation. This privatization of taxation resembled the processes of change and decay that characterized the end of imperial administration in much of fifth-century Gaul and sixth-century northern Italy. It represented, in a very real sense, the end of Islamic late antiquity, and the disappearance of that most important legacy of the ancients: the system of public taxation.

22 On the Zanj, see Popovic (1998). 23 For the classic account of *iqṭāʿ*., see Cahen (1953).

For the three centuries in which it lasted, this fiscal system provided the economic underpinning for the cultural developments of the period – cultural developments that had a profound effect on the development of Muslim civilization. The system supported the precocious development of urban life, especially in Iraq but also in cities such as Fustat in Egypt and Merv in Turkmenistan. The revenues may have been collected as taxes on agricultural land but they were disbursed in cities, and it was to cities that the people who wanted a share of this wealth came. It was in cities such as Basra and Baghdad that the salaried elites of the seventh and eighth centuries spent their surplus income on patronizing the poets who were the most esteemed cultural figures of their time. It was in Baghdad and Samarra in the ninth century that the same sorts of elites gave gifts and pensions to those who translated the works of classical Greek erudition into Arabic. It was the bureaucrats who bought the newly manufactured paper that, from the end of the eighth century, democratized writing, and it was they who pioneered the new sorts of rapid, fluid but nonetheless elegant Arabic scripts that were the stock in trade of the refined court secretaries of the Abbasid period. And it is arguable that it was in the well-attested book suqs of Baghdad that, for the first time in human history, a "Grub Street" writer could make a living without patronage or institutional support, by selling his or her works to a passing public with money to spend on such frivolities.[24]

References

Al-Ansari Abu Yusuf, I. (1967 [*c.* 795]) *Kitāb al-kharāj [Book of Taxation]*, trans. A. Ben Shemesh as *Taxation in Islam*, vol. III. Leiden.

Bligh-Abramski, I. (1988) "Evolution versus revolution: Umayyad elements in the ʿAbbāsid regime, 133/750–320/932," *Der Islam* 65: 226–43.

Cahen, C. (1953) "L'évolution de l' iqtaʿ du IXe au XIIe siècle," *Annales: Économies, Sociétés, Civilisations* 8: 25–52.

Chalmeta, P. (1975) "Concesiones territoriales en al-Andalus," *Cuadernos de Historia* 6: 2–87.

Djait, H. (1986) *Al-Kūfa: naissance de la ville islamique*. Paris.

Donner, F. M. (1981) *The Early Islamic Conquests*. Princeton, NJ.

Hasson, I. (2002) "Ziyād b. Abīhi," in *Encyclopaedia of Islam,* 2nd edn, vol. XI, *V–Z*, ed. P. J. Bearman, T. Bianquis, C. E. Bosworth, E. van Donzel, and W. P. Heinrichs. Leiden: 519–22.

[24] For the authors of this period, see Toorawa (2005).

Kennedy, H. (1998) "Egypt as a province in the Islamic caliphate, 641–868," in *The Cambridge History of Egypt*, vol. I, *Islamic Egypt, 640–1517*, ed. C. F. Petry. Cambridge: 62–85.
(2001) The Armies of the Caliphs: Military and Society in the Early Islamic State. London.
(2002) "Military pay and the economy of the early Islamic state," *Historical Research* 75: 155–69.
(2004a) *The Prophet and the Age of the Caliphates*, 2nd edn. London.
(2004b) "The decline and fall of the first Muslim empire," *Der Islam* 81: 3–30.
(2007) *The Great Arab Conquests*. London.
Kraemer, C. J. (1958) *Excavations in Nessana*, vol. III, *Non-Literary Papyri*. Princeton, NJ.
Lassner, J. (1970) *The Topography of Baghdad in the Early Middle Ages*. Detroit.
Morony, M. (1984) *Iraq after the Muslim Conquest*. Princeton, NJ.
Northedge, A. (2005) *The Historical Topography of Samarra*. London.
Pellat, C. (1953) *Le milieu basrien et la formation de Djahiz*. Paris.
Popovic, A. (1998) *The Revolt of African Slaves in Iraq in the 3rd/9th Century*. Princeton, NJ.
Sizgorich, T. (2009) *Violence and Belief in Late Antiquity: Militant Devotion in Christianity and Islam*. Philadelphia.
Toorawa, S. M. (2005) *Ibn Abī Ṭāhir Ṭayfūr and Arabic Writerly Culture: A Ninth-Century Bookman in Baghdad*. London.
Wickham, C. (1984) "The other transition: from the ancient world to feudalism," *Past and Present* 103: 3–36.

CHAPTER 13

The Ottoman Empire

Metin M. Coşgel

As empires expand into new territories, they face the problem of how to tax the newly conquered resources, which were most likely taxed under a different regime. An expanding state has a choice between preserving the existing system of taxation in newly conquered lands and changing it to conform to the system prevailing in other parts of the empire. The choice may depend on the relative efficiency of the two systems, particularly if one system is vastly superior to the other owing to a lower cost of collection or higher productivity benefits. Political constraints are also important, since taxpayers generally resent taxation, and may even join a revolt because of exorbitant rates or drastic changes. In the same vein, the ruler may not have sufficient legitimacy to collect the tax revenue. To acquire legitimacy and avoid the risk of revolt, the conqueror has to evaluate his options carefully in light of the new political realities.

To examine the problem of how an expanding state might establish a fiscal regime, this chapter focuses on the tax system of the Ottoman Empire during its expansion between the fourteenth and sixteenth centuries. Starting as a small tribe settled in northwestern Anatolia at the end of the thirteenth century, the Ottomans kept expanding in the next three centuries, and eventually built a vast empire that spanned the area from the Black Sea in the north to Egypt and the Arabian Peninsula in the south, and from the Persian Gulf in the east to central Europe and north Africa in the west. Conquering land from multiple predecessor states, they inherited the tax systems of various legal and political traditions, which needed to be molded into a coherent whole and applied to local conditions.

The chapter is organized as follows. In the next section, I outline the general structure of the Ottoman system of taxation. Using information from Ottoman tax registers of the fifteenth and sixteenth centuries, I categorize taxes into a coherent whole and discuss briefly how the central government assigned tax revenues to different recipients. Second, I develop a simple theoretical framework to analyze the basic parameters of an expanding state's choice of a fiscal regime. Using a political economy model of choice, I identify how the net surplus available to a ruler would depend on not just the available gross revenue but also his legitimacy and the likelihood of a successful revolt against his regime. In the third section, I examine the political economy of this system in a specific context, namely the question of how the choice of tax bases and rate structures depended on the cost of measurement. The fourth section analyzes the interaction between rates and bases in a more specific context, namely the system of discriminatory taxation that the Ottomans inherited in the Fertile Crescent. Discussing the reasons as to why the Ottomans continued this system, I use data from tax registers to study quantitatively how discriminatory rates affected production and tax revenue. Finally, I use the theoretical framework to explain how the political economy constraints affected the regional variation of the Ottoman tax system.

The general structure of the Ottoman system of taxation

Studies of the Ottoman system of taxation have typically used the detailed information recorded in imperial registers (*defter-i hākanī*) for their source. Upon conquering new lands, the Ottomans typically surveyed all taxable resources and activities and recorded the information in tax registers commonly known as the *tahrir defterleri*.[1] As circumstances changed over time, they conducted subsequent periodic surveys in order to update the information on the empire's current sources of revenue. The registers were used for a variety of purposes, including serving as official records to establish legal claims to land, assessing the empire's expected tax revenues, and appropriating some of the revenues to the military and administrative officials as remuneration for their services. Fortunately, many of these registers have survived to the present, making it possible to study the Ottoman system of taxation in great detail.

At the beginning of each district's register was its tax code, a document called a *kānūnnāme*, which showed the bases and rates that prevailed in that district. Tax codes show that the Ottomans did not use complicated tax instruments such as income tax or a value added tax for public finance, because they faced various constraints in their capacity to gather the information required to administer taxes. Instead, they relied on simpler and more feasible taxes, such as lump-sum taxes on shops, personal taxes with standard rates within a district or province, and production taxes

[1] Coşgel (2004).

that were collected as simple proportions of output or based simply on the amounts of land or another input. Because taxes were levied on numerous groups of persons and activities, however, the resulting system was still inevitably complex. The types and rates of taxes could also vary significantly between regions, making the system yet more complicated. It must have been complicated enough, even perhaps for the government's own agents, that the government felt obligated to carefully lay out the basic tax regulations of each district in a formal code and to specify the rates at which each tax was to be collected in different circumstances.

Despite the enormous complexity of the Ottoman system of taxation on the surface, it had a simple basic structure. To understand the fundamental elements of this structure, we can use simple insights and concepts from the economic theory of taxation and follow the usual analytical procedure of classifying taxes according to their base. A tax base is simply the item on which the tax is levied. Ottoman tax bases can be grouped into three major categories: personal taxes levied on the persons or households, trade taxes on the goods and services brought to market for sale, and production taxes on various farming and manufacturing activities.[2]

Legally, personal taxes resulted from the dependent status of the subjects.[3] Although the names and rates of personal taxes could vary among regions, they were commonly levied on the persons or households. The tax rates could vary between taxpayers, depending on their observable characteristics, such as land ownership and marital status, which served as an index of their ability to generate income and pay taxes. For example, under the conventional system of taxing subjects, a married subject who held farm land workable by a pair (*çift*) of oxen paid the *çift* tax, which was higher than the amount paid by bachelors (*resm-i mücerred*) and those possessing less than a *çift* or no land (*resm-i bennāk*). Those unable to work, such as the elderly and the disabled, were exempted from personal taxes.[4]

[2] Ottoman budgets included other sources of revenue, such as tributes from vassal states, profits from government-owned enterprises, and revenues from various fees and fines, such as marriage fees and criminal fines. Because of the focus on tax revenues, other sources are excluded from this classification. Extraordinary levies to the state, called avarız-ı divaniyye, are also omitted, because of their irregular nature during the fifteenth and sixteenth centuries. For Ottoman state revenues, see İnalcık and Quataert (1994: 55–76); for revenues as fees and fines from marriages and misdemeanors, see Singer (1996: 113–52).

[3] For a detailed account and the historical origins of personal taxes, see İnalcık (1959).

[4] Because the amount of land also affected these taxes, İnalcık and Quataert insist that "[t]his was actually a system assessing peasants' labor and land in combination": İnalcık and Quataert (1994: 149). That the tax rates also depended on one's age and marital status, however, suggests that the taxpayer himself was the broader tax base. Although those who owned land paid at a higher rate, even landless subjects were responsible for paying the personal tax.

Table 13.1 shows examples of personal taxes in the Ottoman Empire during the fifteenth and sixteenth centuries. Representing the differences in rates and the geographical diversity of the empire during this period, the table includes information from such diverse districts as Jerusalem in the eastern Mediterranean, Budapest in Europe, Bursa in western Anatolia, Erbil in northern Iraq, and Antep and Malatya in eastern Anatolia.[5] Personal taxes were typically levied in cash. The rates for the *çift* tax, for example, were specified in terms of the Ottoman currency of the *akçe*, and varied from being 33 *akçes* in Bursa in 1487 to 50 *akçes* in Erbil in 1542 and Malatya in 1560.

The second general category of Ottoman taxes was the trade taxes, which applied to market exchanges of goods and services. Trade taxes included customs dues and the general market tax, exacted on items brought for exchange into towns and villages that hosted the periodic markets. The tax base was the item brought in for trade. The tax codes, especially of districts with large markets, specified the rates at which various goods, spices, animals, slaves, and agricultural products were to be taxed. In some places trade taxes took the form of gate dues, which applied to items in transit or brought in for local consumption. Items could also be taxed at ports or river crossings. Although most trade taxes were levied in cash, the tax rates for some items were specified in kind. In the Jerusalem district, for example, whereas fruits brought to market were taxed at the rate of one-thirtieth, linens were taxed at twenty *akçes* per camel-load.

In the third category were the production taxes, which applied to various productive activities in agriculture and manufacturing. These taxes can be further divided into three subcategories depending on the tax base: output taxes, levied on the total output of an activity; input taxes, levied on one of the inputs used in production; and enterprise taxes, levied on the activity as a whole.

Output taxes consisted of the tithes (*öşür*), applying primarily to grains, legumes, and fibers. Taxes on these products were to be collected in kind, as a share of the total output. The usual rate was one-tenth, typically with an additional one-fortieth, called *salāriye*, collected as fodder for the horses of the fief-holder. As Table 13.1 shows, the rates could vary significantly between regions, sometimes even between villages within a region. Despite such variations, however, output taxes throughout the empire had the common property of being based on the harvested product and collected at rates specified as a percentage share of the total output. The usual rate of one-tenth, for example, meant that the tax collector

[5] For the complete tax codes of these and other districts, see Akgündüz (1990) and Barkan (1943).

Table 13.1 *Examples of taxes and tax rates in Ottoman districts*

	Personal taxes			**Input taxes**		**Trade taxes**	**Output taxes**
Region (year)	Yoke tax	Bachelor tax	Gate tax	Animal products	Vineyards	Goods brought to market	Tax rate
Antep (1574)	40	6	–	0.5 per animal	0.02 per vine	1 per camel-load of miscellaneous goods	1/8th
Budapest (1562)	–	–	50	0.5 per animal	4 per *dönüm*	4 per wagon-load of pots and cups	1/10th
Bursa (1521)	33	9 or 12	–	0.5 per animal	3, 5, or 10 per *dönüm*	–	1/10th
Erbil (1542)	50	6	–	0.5 per animal	–	10 per load of butter and honey	–
Jerusalem (1562)	–	–	–	0.5 per animal	0.1 per vine	20 per camel-load of linen	Variable between 1/7th and 2/5ths
Malatya (1560)	50	6	–	0.5 per animal	0.03 per vine	–	1/5th

Notes: All monetary values are in the Ottoman currency of *akçe*. A *dönüm* is a measure of land. Some cells are blank either because the tax code did not specify the rate for those items or because the description was too detailed and complex to be summarized in a single entry. Because of the customized nature of lump-sum enterprise taxes, their rates are not reported.
Sources: Ottoman provincial tax codes, published by Akgündüz (1990); and Barkan (1943).

could claim his share immediately after the harvest as 10 percent of the output of wheat, barley, lentils, and so on.

Input taxes applied primarily in the taxation of fruits, vegetables, and animal products. Taxes for these items were levied on the land, trees, or other inputs used in their production, rather than on total output. For example, taxes on the production of fruits, nuts, and dates depended on the number (sometimes also the age, height, and type) of trees. Similarly, taxes on vineyards typically depended on the number of vines, taxes on vegetables depended on the amount of land allocated to them, and taxes on animal products depended on the numbers of animals or other inputs, such as beehives.

Enterprise taxes were levied not on the total output or one of the inputs used in production but on the activity as a whole. In towns, they applied to retail stores and manufacturing enterprises, such as dye-houses, tanneries, juice-makers, slaughterhouses, and soap-makers.[6] This method was also used in the taxation of agricultural production in uninhabited lands, called *mezra'as*, and in some small or remote villages. The tax rate for enterprise taxes was specified as a lump-sum payment, presumably determined by some estimate of the profitability of the enterprise. Because enterprise taxes were customized to activities, the tax codes typically did not codify standardized rates for these activities (except for some rare occasions, such as when they specified the tax rates for retail stores as "per store"). Because the lump-sum rates thus showed great variability in the tax registers, they are not reported in Table 13.1.

The Ottomans allocated tax revenues within a multi-tiered governmental system that divided the empire into provinces, provinces into districts, and districts into fiefs. Combining elements from the customs and administrative practices of previously existing states and the basic principles of Islamic taxation, they developed a system of government finance that assigned tax revenues to various recipients, including the central treasury, provincial and district governments, military personnel, and various non-governmental groups such as tribes and pious foundations. Although in principle all revenue belonged to the central government, tax revenues from some sources could be assigned exclusively to other levels of government in order to minimize transaction costs.[7] Because the Ottoman system of tax assignment differed significantly from less centralized European systems, the central government's share of overall tax revenues were lower in the Ottoman Empire than in

[6] Urban taxes and activities in Anatolia: Faroqhi (1979). [7] Coşgel and Miceli (2005).

European states.[8] But the overall tax burden, including all types of taxes paid to all levels of government, could still be very high.

Legitimacy, revolt, and taxation

The Ottoman system of taxation described in the previous section was the outcome of a long process during which the state expanded significantly from a small tribe to a vast empire that spanned three continents. To study the fiscal regime of such an expanding state in an abstract political economy framework, consider a ruler whose primary objective is to extract as much surplus from the population as possible for his own consumption. The citizenry produces a gross surplus equal to S, which the ruler can extract as taxes levied on persons, wealth, production, or trade.

The ruler has to rely on agents for tax collection, who act as intermediaries between him and the subjects. The agent could represent a religious authority, a military authority, or an aristocratic class (the nobility). His role is to support, or legitimize, the ruler and collect taxes on his behalf.[9] If he legitimizes the ruler, the latter is able to extract a fraction β of the gross surplus, which reflects the degree to which citizens view the ruler as legitimate; a higher value of β means that the ruler is seen as being more legitimate, which makes citizens less resistant to paying taxes. If the citizens revolt against the new ruler, he receives no surplus. Let p be the probability that the revolt succeeds in deposing the ruler.

The resulting expected revenue to the ruler is given by

$$\beta (1 - p)S$$

To maximize his income, the ruler would thus have to set up a fiscal regime that (1) maximizes the available surplus and (2) adjusts to local conditions in ways that can boost his legitimacy and reduce the probability of a successful revolt. Although the ruler may have no direct control over these variables, he can affect them indirectly through his choices of tax bases, rate structures, and collection schemes.

How to maximize the surplus: the economics of choosing tax bases and rates

To maximize the available surplus, the ruler would have to set up a system of taxation that minimizes the cost of collection and the loss due to

[8] Karaman and Pamuk (2010).

[9] Legitimacy can come from various sources. For analyses of force and loyalty as sources of legitimacy, see Coşgel, Miceli, and Rubin (2012; 2012b).

distortion. For a simple analysis of whether a tax system achieved these goals, we need to identify the two basic components of the system, namely the tax base(s) and the rate structure(s). As already noted, the tax base is simply the item on which the tax is levied, and the rate structure refers to how the rates change corresponding to variations in the type and magnitude of the base. By examining how the cost of collecting taxes changed among alternative types of bases and whether the rate structure caused distortion due to changing behavior, we can determine the efficiency of the bases and rates that were used to tax specific resources and productive activities.

Consider, first, the question of whether the tax bases were chosen efficiently. As described in detail above, Ottoman tax bases consisted of three major categories: personal taxes, trade taxes, and production taxes.[10] To examine the efficiency of this structure, we need to identify its purpose – the principles behind why the tax on some items or activities were levied on one type of base and others on another type. Why were taxes on grains typically levied on the output, while those on fruits and vegetables levied on one of the inputs? Similarly, why were trade taxes levied on items brought to the market for trade, rather than on the revenue or profits from the trade, or as a personal lump-sum payment on the trader him- or herself?

To explain the organizational forms observed in history, economic historians have found it useful to examine the transaction costs of available alternatives. In market exchange, the transaction costs include the time, effort, and other resources used in locating parties to trade with, negotiating the terms of the trade, and drawing up and enforcing contracts. In the transaction cost approach to the analysis of organizations and institutions, their presence and form are treated as the results of choice, subject to the constraints of transaction costs. In a hypothetical world without transaction costs, it would not matter how production or exchange is organized, because the organization of activities would not affect the use of resources. But, if transaction costs are positive, for example if the information required for an activity or exchange is costly and imperfect, the organization of activities can make a big difference in solving the problem. The efficiency principle would require that the form that best economizes on these costs should be adopted. By focusing on transaction costs, economic historians have explained various organizational arrangements, including the firm, sharecropping, and manorial contracts, as outcomes of how the costs varied among alternatives.

[10] Coşgel (2005).

Although the transaction cost approach has been used primarily in the analysis of private organizations and institutions, it can easily be extended to the analysis of the public sector and tax systems. If the transaction costs are zero, it would make no difference which base the government uses to tax an economic activity. In taxing production, for example, the government can raise the same amount of revenue by any combination of input, output, or enterprise taxes, ranging from levying the amount on only one of them to an equal amount or varying amounts of each. But, in a world complicated by transaction costs, the cost may vary significantly among taxable activities and bases, making it costlier for the government to collect taxes by some methods than others. In this case, the difference in transaction costs may explain why some activities are taxed by one type of a base rather than another.

The transaction cost that is most relevant in studying taxes is the cost of measuring the tax base.[11] This is simply the time and resources required to determine the value of the tax base, such as those that would be needed in classifying different types of items constituting the base (possibly varying in shape, size, ripeness, and so on), quantifying the total amount in each category, and estimating the monetary value. By focusing on measurement, we are able to explain both the choice of taxable economic activities and the choice of a base for their taxation. Efficiency in tax collection typically restricts states to taxing only observable activities, and the Ottoman state was no exception. Consumption, for example, was generally not taxed because it was difficult to observe. Non-market exchange and productive activities that took place at home, such as cleaning and cooking, were similarly not taxed. Instead, easily observable activities, such as market exchange and agricultural and manufacturing production, were taxed. Once the state decided to tax an activity, it was also important to choose a tax base that could be easily measured. It would not have been sufficient for the cost of measurement to be low to the taxpayer himself, because he had an incentive to hide revenue whenever possible. The state or its agents who received the taxes had to be able to measure the tax base independently at low cost. Moreover, hiring a tax collector introduced a principal–agent problem to tax collection, accompanied by agency costs. For example, the tax collector could make side agreements with the tax payer to collect reduced taxes in return for a transfer payment to himself (a bribe).

[11] For the importance of measurement costs in agricultural contracts and market organization, see Allen and Lueck (2005) and Barzel (1982).

Examining differences in the cost of measurement in light of the Ottoman economy of this period helps us to understand the structure of the tax system as a whole. Trade taxes, for example, were based on observable items such as the goods brought for exchange, rather than the costlier-to-observe exchange itself, which is consistent with our knowledge of the institutions and technology surrounding exchange at this time. Similarly, because the state could not directly observe the marginal product of labor or the income-generating capacity of individuals, personal taxes were based on the household as a whole or on observable characteristics such as marital status and land ownership.

To illustrate the importance of the cost of measurement in detail, let us focus on production taxes and explain the choice between the output, input, or enterprise as the base in taxing a productive activity. Comparing the cost of measurement helps us understand the observed subcategories of production taxes, with taxes on grains levied on the output, those on fruits and vegetables on one of the inputs, and taxes on manufacturing activities on the enterprise itself. Once again, if the output of activities could have been measured at no cost, they could all be taxed under the category of, say, output taxes and there would have been no need for input or enterprise taxes. The total output would have been the tax base, and the tax amount would have been determined either as a proportion of the output or as its cash equivalent. In reality, however, the cost of measurement varied significantly between activities. Whereas the producer and the tax collector could both easily measure the output of some activities, for other activities the tax collector had to incur significant cost in determining the quality and/or the quantity of the output.[12]

The cost to the tax collector was probably the lowest for products such as cereal grains, whose characteristics and harvest technologies made it easy to determine both the quality and the quantity of output at low cost. Because the harvested crop was fairly homogeneous for these items, the tax collector did not have to incur high cost by inspecting the whole output closely in determining its quality. The quantity of cereal grains could also be determined at low cost. The technology for harvesting these products and the brevity of their harvest period made it easy for the tax collector to observe the output, and difficult for the taxpayer to underreport it.[13] The division of the

[12] Court records show frequent disputes arising from the division of the harvest, which support the importance of measurement costs for division. For harvest-related disputes in the Jerusalem court records, see Singer (1994: 90–9).

[13] For the relationship between the harvest and tax collection schedules in the Aleppo region, see Venzke (1981: 135–9).

grain output could be a fairly simple matter of, for example, first threshing all the cut grain together and then dividing it between the parties, or, similarly, loading every Nth wagon (with 1/N being the tax ratio) of the harvested grain as the share of the tax recipient.

The cost of measuring the output could be considerably high for other products such as fruits and vegetables, because the total output could include products with significant variations in size, taste, shape, and ripeness. Even when the tax collector might have observed the quantity, the taxpayer could still increase his share of the output simply by keeping the best ones to himself. Given the taxpayer's incentive to underreport the quality by such means, tax collectors had to incur cost by physically being present (or hiring an agent) for close inspection of the quality of output. Not just the quality but also the quantity of total output could be difficult to determine for some products, in particular those with harvests lasting for a long time. Because continual harvests created opportunities for such concerns as overnight theft, the tax collector would have had to incur cost in trying to prevent any crop from being withdrawn from division, which would have resulted in a high cost of determining the quantity independently.

Whenever the cost of measuring the output of an activity was prohibitively high, the next best alternative for the state could be to choose one of the inputs as the tax base. For the input tax method to be an efficient alternative, however, the quality and quantity of the base had to be easily observable. Land and trees, for example, were better candidates than seed, water, fertilizers, and labor. The taxpayer could not evade taxes by underreporting the amounts of trees and land used in production, because their amounts remained fixed during the production period, and the tax collector could easily observe them. The production tax on fruits was thus typically levied on the number of trees, and the tax on vegetables was levied on the amount of land allocated to them. Whenever it was expensive to measure the output of an activity but cheap to measure one of the inputs, the activity was taxed by the input tax method.

When neither the output nor any of the inputs were easily observable, the last resort for the state was to tax the activity as a whole. This was typically the case for manufacturing enterprises such as juice-makers and soap-makers in towns and agricultural production in remote villages or uninhabited fields.[14] Because the cost of measuring the output or one of the inputs of these activities would have been very high, the state

[14] Evidence of increasing cost of measurement in distant villages: Kunt (1983: 19).

determined the tax amount as a lump-sum payment that was levied on the enterprise itself.

How the rate structure affected the tax base

Let us now turn to the question of how to choose the tax rate. The answer may not be as simple as choosing the rate to be as high as possible, subject to the subsistence constraints of the population, because taxpayers might respond to the rate change by cutting back production, thus reducing the tax base. As the ruler increases the tax rate, beyond a certain point he might actually see his total revenue start to fall – a phenomenon known in economics as the Laffer curve. As the tax rate increases, the total revenue may fall depending on the rate elasticity of the tax base.

To set the tax rate that maximizes the government's revenue, the ruler thus needs to know whether and how the taxpayers will respond to changes in the tax rate. The basic behavioral assumption of the Laffer curve is that rational taxpayers would produce less income in response to an increase in the tax rate because they would have reduced incentives to generate the same income. Whereas economists have variously studied this assumption, as well as other testable implications of the Laffer curve, for modern societies, little is known quantitatively about how taxpayers responded to rate changes in history, particularly in premodern societies. Although the behavior of taxpayers has been the subject of numerous historical debates, data limitations have prevented systematic quantitative studies of these issues.

The information contained in Ottoman tax registers makes it possible to examine how producers responded to tax incentives quantitatively. Although we do not have time series data that would have allowed us to isolate instances of how behavior changed over time in response to changes in tax rates, the discriminatory rate structure that prevailed in the Fertile Crescent offers an indirect test of this behavioral response. The tax system of this region included output tax rates that could vary significantly from one village to the next, as can be seen from the distribution of tax rates in Ottoman Palestine, southern Syria, and Transjordan in the late sixteenth century (Table 13.2).[15] By studying how villagers chose productive activities in response to the variation in tax rates, we can determine their response to taxation.

Taxes were mandatory, but taxpayers were free to adjust their behavior in an effort to increase their net (after-tax) income. They could shelter

[15] See Coşgel (2006) for a quantitative analysis of the reasons, distortionary effects, and distributional consequences of discriminatory rates in this region.

Table 13.2 *Discriminatory tax rates in Ottoman Palestine, southern Syria, and Transjordan*

		Distribution by tax rate					
	All villages	1/7th	1/6th	1/5th	1/4th	1/3rd	2/5ths
Number of villages	1,348	1	4	38	704	451	150
Households per village	31.7	10	21.0	23.6	28.7	37.6	30.9
	(38.2)		(10.1)	(23.4)	(36.2)	(42.0)	(33.5)
Total taxes per village (in *akçes*)	6,874.8	2,000	3,522.7	5,112.9	6,194.5	7,240.6	9,535.9
	(7,190.1)		(730.2)	(4,236.3)	(6,891.5)	(6,435.1)	(10,138.1)

Note: Figures in parentheses are the standard deviations.
Sources: Ottoman *Tahrir Defterleri* numbered 72, 100, 112, 181, 185, and 192 in the Cadastral Office in Ankara; Hütteroth and Abdulfattah (1977).

some of their income from taxation by shifting resources toward non-taxed activities, such as domestic production. Another opportunity was created by the difference between the rate structures of output and input taxes in the Fertile Crescent. Whenever the rates differed between producers for output-taxed activities but were uniform for input-taxed ones, taxpayers could adjust to their own rates by changing the composition of output between these two types of activities. For example, a village could adjust to a high output tax rate by shifting resources from items subject to the output tax to those subject to the input tax, such as by converting a grain field to a vegetable garden. Although regulations may have prevented producers from altering their product mix significantly in any one year, they could have nevertheless achieved the desired changes in the long run as cumulative outcomes of small yearly adjustments. We would thus expect taxpayers with higher output tax rates than others to produce less of the output-taxed products, all else being the same. As a corollary, the amounts of input-taxed products would be expected to be higher for high-rate producers than others.

To test these expectations about the distortionary effects of discriminatory taxation, I have performed a regression analysis of how tax rates affected output-taxed and input-taxed products.[16] The data come from the tax registers of the Ottoman districts of Quds (Jerusalem), Nāblūs, Gazza, Lajjūn, 'Ajlūn, Safad, and Hawran for the year 1595–6. I omitted fiscal units that made a single lump-sum payment for taxes (rather than itemized taxes) and those with missing information on inhabitants or taxes. Of the 1,559 fiscal units (excluding uninhabited fields called *mazra'as*) reported by two analysts,[17] 211 observations were thus dropped, and the remaining 1,348 villages constitute the observations in the data set.

Regression analysis (in Table 13.3) includes two equations with the revenue from output-taxed products and input-taxed products as the dependent variables. To calculate the dependent variable of the first equation, we can simply multiply the taxes listed in the registers for output-taxed products by the taxation factor (the inverse of the tax rate). Although the tax codes have no similarly direct information on the revenue from input-taxed products, we can nevertheless calculate the dependent variable of the second equation by estimating the relationship between inputs and outputs from more recent information about the productivities and production processes of some of the items listed in the registers.[18]

I use the same set of independent variables in both equations because the same set of factors could have potentially, if differently, affected

[16] Ibid. [17] Hütteroth and Abdulfattah (1977). [18] Coşgel (2006: 349–50).

Table 13.3 *Distortionary effects of discriminatory taxation*

	Effect on output-taxed products	Effect on input-taxed products
Tax rate	-0.52	0.38
	(< 0.0001)	(0.063)
Labor (number of adult males)	0.57	0.65
	(< 0.0001)	(< 0.0001)
Village is near irrigation water	-0.009	0.008
	(0.823)	(0.888)
Village has a mill	0.25	0.43
	(0.004)	(< 0.0001)
Village has press for oil or juice	0.17	0.03
	(0.005)	(0.732)
Distance to nearest market town	-0.002	-0.014
	(0.854)	(0.444)
Village pays urban/market taxes	0.11	1.17
	(0.552)	(< 0.0001)
Multiple recipients share tax revenue	0.18	0.24
	(< 0.0001)	(< 0.0001)
Recipient of tax revenue is a provincial soldier Commander, or Governor	-0.11	-0.37
	(0.042)	(< 0.0001)
Recipient of tax revenue is a pious foundation	0.08	-0.13
	(0.256)	(0.167)
Constant	9.04	4.96
	(< 0.0001)	(< 0.0001)
N	1,348	1,348
F	22.9	22.1
R2	0.48	0.47

Notes: Figures in parentheses are the p-values. The dependent variables are the natural logarithms of the revenue from output-taxed products (equation 1) and input-taxed products (equation 2). "Tax rate" and "Labor" are also in natural logarithms. The omitted variable is "Recipient of tax revenue is the central government." Because of space constraints, the results of the dummy variables that account for unobservable differences between the forty-two subdistricts are not reported.
Sources: Ottoman *Tahrir Defterleri* numbered 72, 100, 112, 181, 185, and 192 in the Cadastral Office in Ankara; Hütteroth and Abdulfattah (1977).

output-taxed and input-taxed products. The independent variable of primary interest is the tax rate. Among the other variables that could have also affected production, perhaps the most important are the inputs used in production. Although the tax registers did not directly record the quantities of inputs, they did record the numbers of adult males in each village, which we can use to generate a general proxy for all inputs.

Assuming the number of adult males to be proportional to the agricultural labor force and input proportions to be similar among villages, this measure would represent the units of the input bundle used in production.

I have also included variables to control for the physical characteristics of a village, namely the availability of irrigation water in a village, its distance to the nearest town, and the recipients of its tax revenue. I used the information from tax registers to create three dummy variables that represent other economic activities in a village. To consider the effects of commercial activities, I created a dummy variable based on whether the village hosted the periodic regional market or pursued any urban activities (1 if the village paid *bāj bāzār* or other urban taxes). The other dummy variables capture the effects of making investments in manufacturing activities. One is whether the village had a water mill (1 if the village paid taxes for *tāhūn*), whose presence would indicate a lower cost of converting grain to final products and could thus have had a complementary, positive effect on grain production. The other dummy variable is whether the village had a press for grape syrup or olive oil (1 if the village paid taxes on *ma'sara*), which would similarly indicate a lower cost in the processing of fruits and olives into final products.

To control for unobservable differences between regions in rainfall, climate, prices, soil quality, and other local factors, I generated dummy variables for the forty-two administrative subdistricts represented in the data set.

Table 13.3 reports the ordinary least squares (OLS) estimates of influences on the revenues of output-taxed and input-taxed products separately.[19] The results show interesting relationships between the control variables and the revenues from output-taxed and input-taxed products. The number of adult males affected the quantities of the two types of products positively, as one would expect. Being close to irrigation water had an insignificant effect on these products, probably because it affected more the cost of production than its revenue. Villages with a water mill produced more of both types of products than other villages. Although the positive effect of mills on output-taxed products confirms expectations about their complementarity, it is difficult to explain why the same type of positive relationship existed between mills and input-taxed products. Consistent with grape syrup and olive oil being output-taxed products,

[19] See ibid.: 350 1 for a discussion of the consistency of these results with two-stages least squares (2SLS) estimates of the same equations.

having a press for grape syrup or olive oil affected the production of output-taxed products (but not input-taxed products) positively. The presence of urban and commercial activities in a village, on the other hand, affected the input-taxed products (but not output-taxed products) positively, indicating a complementary relationship between them. Although the distribution of tax revenue also affected production in interesting ways, it is beyond the scope of this chapter to examine them in detail.[20]

The coefficients of the tax rate in the two equations show how taxes distorted output by changing the behavior of producers in response to differences in tax rates. The negative coefficient of the tax rate in the first equation confirms the expectation that, all else being the same, taxpayers adjusted to higher rates by producing less of the output-taxed products (and substituting by others). The positive coefficient of the tax rate in the second equation shows the other side of the substitution effect: taxpayers substituted output-taxed products with input-taxed ones as those with higher rates produced more of the latter. The magnitudes of these effects are also interesting. Because both variables are in logs, the coefficients of the tax rate reflect the tax elasticities of the two types of products. The tax elasticity of supply was low in both cases, possibly caused by the immobility of resources and restrictions on changing the composition of products. At any rate, these results show that Ottoman villagers in the Fertile Crescent behaved rationally in responding to the rate structure of the Ottoman tax system in the late sixteenth century.

Going back to the question of whether the ruler could simply raise the tax rates to raise revenue, the results indicate that he was constrained by the reactions of taxpayers. He had to consider these reactions carefully in setting the rate that could maximize his revenue from taxation.

Regional variation: political economy constraints on change

To maximize his overall expected net revenue, the ruler had to not only maximize the surplus he could extract from the population *(S)* but also to adjust to local conditions in ways that would reduce the probability of a successful revolt (p) and boost his legitimacy (β). Political economy constraints were thus also important in choosing the tax bases and rate

[20] Because of space limitations, the results of the dummy variables that control for the differences among the forty-two subdistricts are not reported in Table 13.3. A majority of these variables affected output significantly, confirming the importance of local factors in production decisions.

structures and in appointing agents for tax collection. An empire expanding into new territories inevitably faced the question of whether to preserve the previous system of taxation or to change it in ways that enhanced efficiency.

The structure of the Ottoman system of taxation shared many elements with those of preceding and contemporary states, suggesting the presence of a selection process that caused these structures to converge toward an efficient ideal. Output and input taxes, for example, were similar in principle to the basic categories of Islamic taxation of production known as the *muqāsama* and *misāḥa* methods.[21] Enterprise taxes were also similar to the *maqṭū'* method of assessment (sometimes also called *dīmūs*, a word of Greek origin from the pre-Islamic period). These categories typically formed the basic structure of the production taxes observed in various Islamic states that the Arab, Persian, Turkish, and other rulers had established in the Middle East before the Ottomans. Ottoman personal taxes also resembled those of predecessor states, in particular the Byzantine Empire. The *çift* tax, for example, was similar in principle to the Byzantine tax called *zeugaratikion*.[22] These commonalities clearly support the view that the observed structure of Ottoman taxes had efficiency properties that made it more desirable than its alternatives.

But the vast empire that the Ottomans had built by the middle of the sixteenth century had inherited not only common elements but also various idiosyncrasies from the customs and administrative practices of preceding states. The tax system that the Ottomans developed in each region also reflected these idiosyncrasies, indicating that some things were harder to change than others and that political economy constraints also played an important role in shaping the final outcome. In what follows, I describe some of the significant regional differences in tax bases, rate structures, and collection methods, and discuss how political economy constraints shaped these differences.

Tax bases and rate structures varied significantly among regions, as can be seen in personal taxes. Under the conventional system observed in Anatolia, personal taxes were based on adult males, and the tax rate varied by marital status and land ownership. The subjects in Hungary, on the other hand, paid personal taxes in terms of the gate (*kapı*) tax, for which the unit of taxation was the household, rather than adult males, and

21 Mamluk and Ottoman taxation in Muslim lands: Johansen (1988); Bakhit (1981); Lapidus (1969); Petersen (2005); Poliak (1977); Kark (1997).

22 For the relationship between Byzantine and Ottoman taxation, see Bryer and Lowry (1986) and İnalcık (1960).

the tax amount did not change by marital status or land ownership. Moreover, personal taxes were not even fully implemented in all areas (though non-Muslim subjects throughout the empire paid a poll tax called *cizye*). In Jerusalem and surrounding districts, for example, the Ottomans did not introduce the *çift* tax or any other form of personal tax systematically levied on individuals or households.[23] Some of these differences during the fifteenth and sixteenth centuries can be seen in Table 13.1.

Trade taxes also varied a great detail between regions. In some places they took the form of gate dues that applied to items in transit or brought in for local consumption. Items could also be taxed at ports or river crossings. Although most trade taxes were levied in cash, the tax rates for some items were specified in kind. In the Jerusalem district, for example, whereas fruits brought to market were taxed at the rate of one-thirtieth, linens were taxed at 20 *akçes* per camel-load.

In the same vein, production taxes varied among regions. Although the usual output-tax rate was one-tenth, a higher rate of one-fifth was applied in some of the provinces annexed after the middle of the sixteenth century. As discussed above, the rates varied even among villages in the Palestine, southern Syria, and Transjordan regions. Activities taxed under one category in one region could be taxed in another category in another region. Whereas beehive taxes were levied on the output of honey as an output tax (under some circumstances) in Hungary, they were based on the hive itself as an input tax in other regions. Similarly, there could even be differences within the same type of an activity within a region, as was the case for the taxation of olive products in the Arab lands. A clear distinction was made between the products of *rumānī* trees (generally interpreted as referring to aged trees), taxed based on output, and *islāmī* trees (younger trees), taxed on the basis of the number of trees.

Although one might be tempted to explain these differences as economically optimal outcomes of some sort, it is difficult to explain all the components of the Ottoman tax system with economic principles alone. If efficiency was the sole driving force in tax design, then the truly efficient system would have replaced all others, and regional differences would have been mere adaptations of this system to local conditions. But there are numerous other regional differences that are difficult to explain with economic principles or with an efficiency view of institutions.

23 The system of remunerating government employees from tax revenues was also different in this region's history. For example, as Kennedy (2002) has shown, soldiers were paid in cash, rather than tax revenues, in the early Islamic state (c. 650–900).

Consider some of the differences in tax bases and rate structures observed in the empire. Among personal taxes, for example, numerous differences existed between regions not just in the local names of personal taxes but also in their bases and rate structures, raising the question of why the more efficient ones did not replace others. If it was more efficient to vary the rates of personal taxes on the basis of the characteristics of adult males (because of, for example, varying abilities to pay), as was the case under the *çift* tax system, then one would have expected personal taxes observed in the Balkans (where the payment was based on the household as a whole, rather than individuals) to be replaced by the *çift* tax system. Similarly, if a uniform rate for output taxes was more desirable, one would have expected it to have replaced the rate structure observed in parts of the Fertile Crescent with rates that varied between villages. But in both cases the Ottomans simply adopted the prevailing taxes and rate structures, making no systematic attempt to change things one way or another. They did not extend the *çift* tax system to the Balkans or the Fertile Crescent. Neither did they change the output tax rates that varied between villages in the Fertile Crescent to a uniform-rate system that prevailed in the rest of the empire. It is difficult to explain such continuities of sharply different rate structures merely as efficient adaptations of the tax system to local conditions.

Political constraints were significant because of the way taxpayers react to change. Opposition to taxes has been one of the most common reasons in history for popular uprisings.[24] Taxpayers naturally resist higher taxes, and they prefer stable, secure incomes. This type of resistance may also have been most evident during conquests. Unless changing taxes clearly eliminated excessively oppressive elements of the previous tax system (as may have been the case for labor services), the general population would have been likely to prefer the status quo over change, for fear that change might mean higher taxes and worse conditions. And they could have even fled the land or revolted against the new regime if the changes were perceived to be too burdensome. Even if an existing tax system was known to be inefficient, therefore, the Ottomans had to carefully weigh their desire to change the system against the possibility of political instability and a rise in the probability of a successful revolt against their regime. An inefficient tax system could have thus survived if political rigidities prevented a ruler from changing it.

[24] Burg (2003); Goldstone (1991).

Given the political realities surrounding conquest, assimilation, and stability, the Ottomans were not free to change the tax codes as they wished. Even if they could have increased tax revenues in Hungary by changing personal taxes from being based on the household as a whole to a differential rate structure based on the characteristics of its individual members, they would have met stiff resistance from those who would have paid higher taxes. Because of this resistance, they could not have implemented the change easily. Similarly, they could not have easily changed the rate structure of output taxes in the Fertile Crescent from discriminatory rates to a uniform rate, because this would have meant higher rates for some villages. Political obstacles existed not just in newly conquered lands but in well-assimilated regions as well. Once the tax code of a region had been adopted, changing it would have been difficult, because the general population, accustomed to paying taxes under a familiar system, and powerful groups with vested interests in this system would have continued to resist the change and initiate a revolt against the Ottoman government.

These examples indicate that certain institutions were more flexible than others, and political constraints were more binding in some areas than in others. Although the Ottomans' ultimate objective in designing the tax system may have been to maximize tax revenues, they could not seek efficiency and minimize transaction costs as they wished. They needed to work within the parameters of various institutional constraints.

Economic and political variables similarly worked together in determining how the Ottomans appointed agents to collect taxes and allocated tax revenues among these agents. Organized in a multi-tiered system, the Ottoman government consisted of multiple hierarchical levels that, as mentioned, divided the empire into provinces, the provinces into districts, and the districts into fiefs or other administrative units. To support offices at lower levels, the central government assigned some of the tax revenues directly to governors of provinces (variously denoted in the registers as *mīr mīrān*, *paşa*, *beylerbeyi*), district officials (*mīr liwā*, *sancakbeyi*), and holders of small and large fiefs *(tımār and za'āma)*.[25] In the resulting system of tax collection and revenue allocation, you could have one village paying taxes to the central government, their neighbors in the next village paying taxes to the provincial government,

[25] For the organization and financing of the Ottoman government, see Coşgel and Miceli (2005), Darling (1996), İnalcık and Quataert (1994), and Kunt (1983).

and those in other villages paying taxes to the district government, or a local fief-holder (a cavalryman or military commander).

In addition to this system of tax collection and revenue allocation, which was commonly observed in all parts of the empire, there were numerous idiosyncrasies that seemed to complicate the assignment of agents in some regions. Most prominent among these were the tribal leaders who somehow possessed the right to collect the tax revenues of some villages, and the landholders who similarly held the rights to collect taxes privately (*mülk*), or jointly with the government (under a system called *mālikāne dīvānī*). Typically, these were rights the Ottomans had preserved from the system that they inherited upon conquest or assigned through negotiations with power-holders.

The system of allocation was determined in part by economic factors, such as the variability of the tax base or the cost of measuring the tax base or the collector's effort.[26] A quantitative analysis of tax assignment in the Ottoman Empire has indeed shown that the sources of revenue allocated to local government officials included a higher proportion of variable taxes than those allocated to the provincial and central treasury, indicating that the variance of the tax base affected the allocation.[27] Economic factors have also influenced the government's decision as to which contractual form (rent, wage, share) to adopt in employing agents for tax collection.

Purely economic factors do not explain, however, why the Ottomans granted tax revenues to private landholders, tribal leaders, or others who acquired rights through special arrangements. For a more complete explanation, we also need to consider political economy constraints on the allocation; more specifically, how tax collectors could affect the ruler's legitimacy. In general, tax collectors acted not only as government officials in their districts but also as legitimizing agents who could enhance the ruler's ability to extract the surplus. This ability gained even greater significance in newly conquered lands. Acting as local representatives of the new ruler, carefully chosen tax collectors could solidify his legitimacy and raise the share of the gross surplus (β) that he could extract from the general population for his own consumption.

Tax collectors could affect the legitimacy of the Ottoman sultans through either force or loyalty during this period – the two main sources of legitimacy.[28] If a newly conquered population included powerful individuals who could be bribed into using their power for tax collection if

[26] Coşgel and Miceli (2009). [27] Coşgel and Miceli (2005).
[28] Coşgel, Miceli, and Rubin (2012b).

necessary, in some cases this ability could be of better use to the Ottomans than that of military officials appointed from the center. In the same vein, if the local population included individuals with leadership qualities who could generate loyalty by encouraging the citizens to accept the Ottoman ruler's right to rule and his ability to provide protection and other public goods and services, this ability too could provide legitimacy through loyalty more effectively than an Ottoman official appointed from the center but unknown in this region. If the local leaders in newly conquered areas thus had superior ability to provide legitimacy through force or loyalty, these qualities could supersede economic considerations in the assignment of tax revenues, and the Ottomans could be better off using them as agents to raise the share of the surplus the public would pay voluntarily as taxes.

By including political constraints in the analysis, we can thus offer a more complete explanation as to why the Ottomans appointed tribal leaders and private individuals as tax collectors in some areas. They preserved the rights of some landholders to collect taxes after conquest under the *mālikāne dīvānī* system in eastern Anatolia because, in these regions, these leaders had a comparative advantage in force and loyalty that was essential to collect taxes on behalf of the Ottomans – a right that was granted in exchange for a share of the tax revenue. The Ottomans similarly appointed tribal leaders in some regions as tax collectors so that Ottoman rule would be established within the institutional constraints of conquest politics. They assigned some of the tax revenues to Bedouin tribes in the Fertile Crescent, for example, so as to establish Ottoman rule in the desert frontiers. They allocated a share of the tax revenues to the leaders of the Bani ʻAta and ʻArab Sawalma tribes in the Gaza district in exchange for their collaboration in providing security in the region and their support in legitimizing the Ottomans' rule.[29] Although purely economic concerns from expanding into new territories might have suggested to the Ottomans that they should replace previous systems of taxation and collection with more efficient schemes that could be adopted from other parts of the empire, political constraints sometimes required them to work within the parameters of existing orders and capitalize on the comparative advantages of local agents who could better legitimize their regime through force and loyalty.

[29] As Etkes (2006) has shown.

References

Akgündüz, A. (ed.) (1990) *Osmanlı Kanunnāmeleri ve Hukukī Tahlilleri [Ottoman Law Codes and Their Legal Analysis]*. Istanbul.

Allen, D. W., and Lueck, D. (2005) "Agricultural contracts," in *Handbook of New Institutional Economics*, ed. C. Menard and M. M. Shirley. Dordrecht: 465–90.

Bakhit, M. (1981) "Sidon in Mamluk and early Ottoman times," *Abhath* 29: 51–64.

Barkan, Ö. L. (1943) *XV ve XVIıncı Asırlarda Osmanlı Imparatorluğunda Ziraî Ekonominin Hukukî ve Malî Esarları [The Legal and Fiscal Foundations of the Ottoman Agricultural Economy in the 15th and 16th Centuries]*. Istanbul.

Barzel, Y. (1982) "Measurement cost and the organization of markets," *Journal of Law and Economics* 25: 27–48.

Bryer, A., and Lowry, H. W. (1986) *Continuity and Change in Late Byzantine and Early Ottoman Society: Papers Given at a Symposium at Dumbarton Oaks in May 1982*. Washington, DC.

Burg, D. F. (2003) *A World History of Tax Rebellions: An Encyclopedia of Tax Rebels, Revolts, and Riots from Antiquity to the Present*. New York.

Coşgel, M. M. (2004) "Ottoman tax registers (*tahrir defterleri*)," *Historical Methods* 37: 87–100.

(2005) "Efficiency and continuity in public finance: the Ottoman system of taxation," *International Journal of Middle East Studies* 37: 567–86.

(2006) "Taxes, efficiency, and redistribution: discriminatory taxation of villages in Ottoman Palestine, southern Syria, and Transjordan in the sixteenth century," *Explorations in Economic History* 43: 332–56.

Coşgel, M. M., and Miceli, T. J. (2005) "Risk, transaction costs, and tax assignment: government finance in the Ottoman Empire," *Journal of Economic History* 65: 806–21.

(2009) "Tax collection in history," *Public Finance Review* 37: 399–420.

Coşgel, M. M., Miceli, T. J., and Rubin, J. (2012a) "The political economy of mass printing: legitimacy and technological change in the Ottoman Empire," *Journal of Comparative Economics* 40: 357–71.

(2012b) "Political legitimacy and technology adoption," *Journal of Institutional and Theoretical Economics* 168: 339–61.

Darling, L. T. (1996) *Revenue-Raising and Legitimacy: Tax Collection and Finance Administration in the Ottoman Empire, 1560–1660*. New York.

Etkes, H. (2006) "Legalizing extortion: containing armed tribes by state regulated 'protection payments' in Ottoman Gaza (1519–1582)," working paper. Hebrew University, Jerusalem.

Faroqhi, S. (1979) "Taxation and urban activities in sixteenth-century Anatolia," *International Journal of Turkish Studies* 1: 19–53.

Goldstone, J. A. (1991) *Revolution and Rebellion in the Early Modern World*. Berkeley, CA.

Hütteroth, W.-D., and Abdulfattah, K. (1977) *Historical Geography of Palestine, Transjordan and Southern Syria in the Late 16th (Sixteenth) Century*. Erlangen, Germany.

İnalcık, H. (1959) "Osmanlılarda raiyyet rüsumu [The taxation of subjects in the Ottoman Empire]," *Belleten* 23: 575–610.

(1960) "The problem of the relationship between Byzantine and Ottoman taxation," in *Akten des XI. Internationalen Byzantinisten-Kongresses*, ed. M. A. Cook. Munich: 237–42.

İnalcık, H., and Quataert, D. (1994) *An Economic and Social History of the Ottoman Empire*, vol. I, *1300–1600*. Cambridge.

Johansen, B. (1988) *The Islamic Law on Land Tax and Rent: The Peasants' Loss of Property Rights as Interpreted in the Hanafite Legal Literature of the Mamluk and Ottoman Periods*. New York.

Karaman, K., and Pamuk, Ş. (2010) "Ottoman state finances in European perspective, 1500–1914," *Journal of Economic History* 70: 593–629.

Kark, R. (1997) "Mamluk and Ottoman cadastral surveys and early mapping of landed properties in Palestine," *Agricultural History* 71: 46–70.

Kennedy, H. (2002) "Military pay and the economy of the early Islamic state," *Historical Research* 75: 155–69.

Kunt, İ. M. (1983) *The Sultan's Servants: The Transformation of Ottoman Provincial Government, 1550–1650*. New York.

Lapidus, I. M. (1969) "The grain economy of Mamluk Egypt," *Journal of the Economic and Social History of the Orient* 12: 1–15.

Petersen, A. (2005) *The Towns of Palestine under Muslim Rule: AD 600–1600*. Oxford.

Poliak, A. N. (1977) *Feudalism in Egypt, Syria, Palestine, and the Lebanon, 1250–1900*. Philadelphia.

Singer, A. (1994) *Palestinian Peasants and Ottoman Officials: Rural Administration around Sixteenth-Century Jerusalem*. Cambridge.

(1996) "Marriages and misdemeanors: a record of 'resm-i`arus ve bad-i hava,'" *Princeton Papers: Interdisciplinary Journal of Middle Eastern Studies* 4: 113–52.

Venzke, M. L. (1981) "The sixteenth-century Ottoman sanjaq of Aleppo: a study of provincial taxation," PhD dissertation. Columbia University, New York.

CHAPTER 14

Early modern Japan

Philip C. Brown

Wages of peace: fiscal perspectives on early modern Japan

Traditionally defined from 1600 to 1868, Japan's early modern period was marked by a massive outbreak of peace. For two and half centuries no foreign conflict embroiled the land. Only in the early seventeenth century did two major domestic conflicts erupt. Japan's circumstances thus present a clear contrast to those that marked both eastern and western Europe, and much of Asia too. Japan was relatively isolated from other states, not just limiting war but restricting taxpayer flight to purely domestic options.

The financial pressures created by war are widely acknowledged, and, for scholars such as Charles Tilly, they become the major stimulus to the centralization of state authority and state-building.[1] Domestic violence is also sometimes seen in a similar light.[2] In the early modern context, developments often associated with state-building in Europe – the development of formal budgets (including techniques such as double-entry bookkeeping), developing state plans for economic expansion, and borrowing strategically to promote economic growth – are also associated with state efforts to command more financial resources, and use them more efficiently in response to pressures generated by military expenditures. Bonney and Ormrod indicate appropriately that the development of fiscal regimes need not be unidirectional, though the development of the major European states shows little significant regression from state-strengthening tendencies.[3] Beyond this framework explaining the rise of a modern fiscal regime, Tilly characterizes premodern forms of tax assessment and collection as burdened by inefficiencies and extra investments of labor or other costs.[4] This said, New Fiscal Sociology finds that, even in modern contexts, it is a mistake to assume that the taxed lack power to contest their assessors,

[1] Tilly (1992). [2] Bonney and Ormrod (1999). [3] Ibid. [4] Tilly (1992: 87–8).

and exactions involve an element of compromise.[5] This perspective suggests that the effectiveness of taxation must always be considered in the context of a variety of power, cultural, and other constraints, including the ability of people being taxed to flee.[6]

Japan's long-term premodern development, virtually free from invasion, provides a fascinating mirror in which to reflect on the experience of early modern European fiscal development. To begin with, it presents a picture of state-building very different from countries such as France and Britain, for which we can portray a long-term movement toward stronger state structures from late medieval times through the nineteenth century. Japan moved toward centralization in the seventh to ninth centuries, but, in a premodern parallel to Bates' analysis of late twentieth-century Africa, retreated from central state-building over time – a devolution that it did not reverse until the 1870s.[7] When state-building did occur again, it was in the mid- to late sixteenth century, to advance regional leaders' ability to prosecute wars with each other; the effort never went as far as European state-building in the late eighteenth and early nineteenth centuries.

The most frequent and broad-based changes in state-building and state finance took place during the domestic wars of the sixteenth century and in the middle of the seventeenth century, immediately following the establishment of peace, but at the regional level of baronial domain organization. (Since these changes lay the foundation for the Pax Tokugawa, I include the late sixteenth century within the purview of early modern Japan rather than treating it as a separate era, which is Japanese custom.) Knowledge of taxable resources improved within domain lands, subordinate fief-holders lost autonomy and became increasingly dependent for revenues on their daimyo overlords. Tax efficiency improved and compromises were made with villagers to eliminate absconding. Daimyo invested in expanding arable land and protecting it from both drought and flood, creating greater wealth to tax. Those who did not follow this path could not marshal the kind of military power that gave them a chance to survive incessant battles.

With the restoration of peace, movement toward a nationally centralized fisc ground to a halt. While we might expect the absence of invasion, and even revolutionary movements, in early modern Japan to permit

[5] Martin, Mehrotra, and Prasad (2009); Kiser and Barzel (1991); Barzel and Kiser (1997).
[6] Hirschman (2004); Scott (1985). [7] Bates (2008).

alternative, socially productive state investments, this did not occur on any broad scale for most of the era. Practices commonly associated with modern governments did not develop. Formal budgets did not develop and double-entry bookkeeping or its functional equivalent did not become standard practice. Borrowing in order to invest was absent; cash flow documents suggest the use of loans to cover intermittent shortfalls (not the common trope of historians: widespread budgetary red ink and borrowing), at modest levels. What fiscal records we have can conceal as much as they reveal about finances, but they suggest a long-standing pattern of daimyo consumption focused on personal, not public, expenditures.

In the end, we find a state organization in which multiple bandits (regional lords, the daimyo) contracted with villages, trade, commercial, and other groups via a mechanism akin to an (unbalanced) collective bargaining based on a combination of custom and values linked to images of good rulership, with the organizations subject to taxation having substantial autonomy to administer their own activities in return for assuming much of the administrative burden of allocating taxes to individuals and administering tax collection. Tax revenues came overwhelmingly from internal exactions. Taxes (including license fees) were based on well-known standards that specified what the lord was due, and, in combination with the use of salaried tax administrators, limited (but did not eliminate) practices that undermined revenue collection.

These methods were efficient, in the context of the resources available, and cost-effective – not inefficient, as Tilly has suggested. The preceding notwithstanding, daimyo bore an opportunity cost – one that, along with other circumstances, suggests a measure of "satisficing" rather than "maximization."[8] Nonetheless, institutional constraints on overlords' knowledge compromised their efforts to capture the gains of a growing economy, and left room for bribery, extortion by tax officials, and other diversions of revenues from domain treasuries.

I begin with an overview of the long-term trends through which a centralized fiscal regime lost its control and fiscal authority devolved to regional politico-military forces. This overview illustrates the long-term reversion from central control. As background, it also highlights the significant role of late sixteenth-century innovations in constructing the foundation of Japan's early modern order.

[8] Simon (1957: 204–5).

Loss of the center: seventh to sixteenth centuries

Japan's political history is often explained by reference to a sequence of national central administrations, beginning with the establishment of the Yamato court in the seventh century (and its Heian successor), the Kamakura *Bakufu* in the late twelfth century, the Ashikaga shogunate in the fourteenth century, and the early modern regimes of Oda Nobunaga, Toyotomi Hideyoshi, and their Tokugawa successors in the late sixteenth and seventeenth centuries. Only two periods – that prior to the efforts of the sixth- and seventh-century Yamato elites to mimic Chinese administration, and the century of intense civil wars of the late fifteenth through mid-sixteenth centuries – are described in ways that suggest the lack of a broadly functioning central government and intense conflict. Yet any overview of Japanese history that focuses on successive central administrations is badly misleading in several respects, and reveals a clearly non-linear trajectory.

First, even in periods of clearly functioning central governments, such as the Yamato/Heian eras (seventh to eleventh centuries), the exercise of military-administrative control could be highly fragmented at the national level, even when the same people were in charge of both private and public revenue streams. State apparatus under an emperor had developed significantly by the eighth century, with the creation of a Sinified central authority in the seventh century. While the emperor typically reigned rather than ruled, in his or her name advisers ran a nationwide administration that collected national taxes, maintained a national conscript army (through the eighth century), and created a nationwide administrative structure of provinces, counties, and towns, with provinces and counties led by imperial appointees.

Yet this centralizing movement had critical limitations that, from the eighth century, slowly permitted a rotting of the fiscal structure of the state. First, powerful court families with connections to provincial governors used their positions to pilfer the national treasury, arranging tax-exempt status for many properties, in return for which they received a share of the revenues that these lands produced. They acted as the lynchpin of an intricate, stratified system of rents called *shōen*, often translated as "manors." These arrangements ultimately diverted an estimated one-third of imperial revenues into the hands of courtier families. Although these same families occupied key posts in the central government, oversaw tax collections, and therefore had a solid understanding of how these private arrangements beggared the national treasury, they preferred to line their own pockets over maintaining the fiscal soundness of the imperial apparatus that legitimated their political authority.

Second, from the eighth century, at lower levels of public administration, locally powerful military leaders – the samurai – emerged to replace the national conscript army, gradually fragment military command, and provide the muscle that gave force to provincial and lower-level revenue-raising structures. They vied to capture what amounted to tax-farming rights, and fought openly to compromise the demands of the overlords they nominally served. Over time, these local groups formed regional alliances of substantial reach and politico-military power. The imperial government bought the allegiance of local military bands to enforce its policies and maintain its position, adding increasing paths for the emergent samurai to enhance their authority and wealth. At the end of the twelfth century local utilitary forces had organized into two large and complex alliances led by Minamoto Yoritomo and Taira Kiyomori, each of which drew revenues from a combination of tax-free estates, public office, and their service as utilitary protectors. In the ensuing conflict, Yoritomo's forces defeated the Taira and established the Kamakura Bakufu (a utilitary organization paralleling the civilian regime), in 1192.

The founding of the Kamakura shogunate signaled the transformation of autonomous local and provincial military power into a unified national structure that functioned in parallel with the old aristocratic national regime.[9] Initially the regime exercised the most stringent control of warrior bands that Japan had witnessed in some time. Nonetheless, it shared national administrative responsibilities with the old imperial order and guaranteed revenue flows to the court. Rather than a dramatic replacement of civilian with military rule, the old civilian order continued largely intact.[10]

Full samurai preeminence over the aristocratic administration came after Japan's response to the Mongol invasions of 1274 and 1281. Financial strains created by increased defense efforts exacerbated tensions within the samurai class and encouraged the shogunate to exert greater control over the imperial court. The self-seeking tendency of local warrior bands became more pronounced. Local deputies (*shugo-dai* and *jitō*) of regional lords (*shugo*) competed among themselves as well as with their

[9] Scholars disagree about the degree to which central administrators were in charge of emerging regional samurai during the Heian era; see Farris (1992); and Friday (1992).

[10] Mass (1985).

overlords.[11] Emperor Godaigo, chafing under constraints on imperial prerogatives, led the last significant effort to reclaim imperial political primacy. He rallied disaffected samurai and marshaled elements of the imperial administration, but failed when his key, erstwhile military ally, the Ashikaga, set up their own competing candidate for emperor and took the title of shogun, in 1338.

From the outset, the Ashikagas' position was more tenuous than that of the early Kamakura regime. Conflict persisted for a half-century after the Ashikaga family took the title of shogun; they ultimately reached an accommodation with the rival claimant to the throne (1390), and dominated the emperor, whose symbolic and cultural authority they exploited. Even then, Ashikaga rule did not constitute a truly dominant political-military force. The family shared power with fewer than a dozen powerful regional samurai leaders, the military governors of the provinces (*shugo*), and they controlled no national treasury with which to finance a national military or administrative system. Even the military governors found themselves in a precarious position, challenged not only by other governors but also by subordinates who often resisted their demands (consequently, Japanese historians call the period the era of *gekokujō*, or "the low topple the high"). Conflicts in Kyoto among the Military Governors ultimately led to the Onin War (1467–77), during which the shogun and the governors both found their control over their multi-province domains eviscerated. The war's end was marked by a descent into pervasive small-scale warfare. While the Ashikaga continued to claim the title of shogun, it meant little in practice. The average size of the domains effectively controlled by the samurai lords shrank dramatically, and Japan was largely ruled by many dozens of locally powerful military figures.

Up to this time one can argue that taking and controlling territory did not constitute the principal goal of military activity; instead, samurai leaders fought to gain control of streams of revenue, typically without other major administrative accoutrements.[12] Their efforts were not quite the same as raiding nomadic groups such as the Mongols; they sought a regular flow of revenues, often those associated with the *shōen* manors. Nonetheless, there were elements of a "raiding/plunder" mentality, in the form of willful efforts to conscript labor and/or compel individuals to work as servants, as well as to capture revenues from neighbors.[13]

[11] For an overview of how this process played out in what is now Ishikawa Prefecture, see Shimode (1979: 67–95).

[12] Friday (2004). [13] Ibid.

No linear progression in fiscal regime is evident here. All the changes described to this point can be summarized in two broad trends: first, the long-term evisceration of national imperial administrative capacity; second, the parallel emergence of regional and local political forces who held real fiscal authority and under whom military power ultimately stabilized in the late sixteenth and early seventeenth centuries. Especially regarding the earlier centuries, scholars still discuss exactly when specific classes of regional authorities took on particular roles, but their rise in importance and role as fiscal powers is broadly acknowledged.[14] In the long term, a centralized fisc dissolved.

Reconsolidation of regional power in the sixteenth century

From the middle of the sixteenth century energetic, creative, forceful local leaders known as daimyo restructured domains to provide a foundation for a new national political order and strengthen local-regional fiscal control. These men gradually encroached on the autonomy of their enfeoffed retainers. They invested in new weapons, hand-held firearms, and created a salaried military corps. These and other steps were independently undertaken by daimyo whose names constitute the stuff of Japanese lore: Oda Nobunaga, Toyotomi Hideyoshi, Takeda Shingen, Uesugi Kenshin, Tokugawa Ieyasu, Date Masamune, and Maeda Toshiie, among others. The regional leagues these men organized fought among each other, and the victors effectively transformed their regional alliance into increasingly large units. Oda, collaborating with other daimyo, resuscitated the imperial institution, secured its finances and pomp, and restored its glory; he then employed the emperor's restored luster to legitimate his own power.[15] When Oda died in 1582, he and his allies controlled about a third of Japan and had laid out many of the contours of the new, peaceful, early modern order that his successors elaborated, first under Toyotomi Hideyoshi (from 1590) and, later, under Tokugawa Ieyasu and his heirs (1600–1868). In the Toyotomi and Tokugawa regimes, administratively autonomous but militarily subservient daimyo all pledged allegiance to the hegemonic power but ceded no regular fiscal responsibilities to them.

All the preceding changes required a strong, expanded fiscal base. The new daimyo fiscal regimes accomplished five basic objectives.

[14] For examples of local/regional contests that exemplify the critical role of these levels of authority, see Ferejohn and Rosenbluth (2010).

[15] Tilly (1992: 87–8).

(1) They reestablished more effective land taxation, initially in their own directly controlled lands, over time extending into controls over the revenue flows of enfeoffed retainers too.
(2) They invested in land reclamation, irrigation, and flood control to increase output of their key economic resource: agricultural lands.
(3) They took direct control of key natural resources, notably gold, silver, and copper, as well as forest reserves.
(4) They struck a bargain with villagers, promising them considerable autonomy over day-to-day affairs in return for the regular delivery of tax revenues. This point will be elaborated later, but it is important to stress that daimyo and shogun alike established increasingly direct relations with villages under their control, squeezed out enfeoffed retainers, and restricted their subordinates' administrative, tax, and judicial powers.[16]
(5) More and more, daimyo collected taxes for, and dispensed salaries to, increased proportions of their samurai, rendering subordinates economically dependent.

Limited fiscal consolidation: state-building and domain finance in early modern Japan

The socio-economic setting

The late sixteenth century and the Pax Tokugawa witnessed a burgeoning and increasingly diverse economy, which supported dynamic population growth, but was largely isolated from international trade. One must single out the long-term importance of the peace dividend paid to all classes of society. With the end of internecine warfare, and the creation of a long period free from invasion, war no longer destroyed wealth. Returns on any long-term investments were more secure. In addition, sixteenth- and early seventeenth-century fiscal policy was clearly intended to stimulate economic growth; in the high Tokugawa, such efforts were more limited, but economic diversification continued. Apart from direct stimulative policies, programs designed to serve political and security functions also fostered commercial growth, economic diversification, and national economic integration.

Daimyo castle town construction created some of the world's largest urban centers, with transformative economic impacts. By the end of the

[16] See Birt (1985: 381), Brown (1993: 11), and Hall (1961).

seventeenth century even some provincial towns such as Kanazawa boasted populations of about 100,000. As part of efforts to secure control over their domains, daimyo typically brought their samurai into their castle towns, where they could be closely supervised, and, in combination with the daimyos' own substantial expenditures, these policies created urban economic magnets throughout Japan.

By the late seventeenth century truly national markets had formed for key commodities such as rice, which was an outgrowth of two developments.[17] First, daimyo regularly spent extended time in the Tokugawa's castle town, Edo, either on military duty or as hostages to assure daimyo loyalties. Daimyo travel with large retinues stimulated trade and economic growth along major highways linking castle towns to Edo. Second, much of the major agricultural taxation collected in kind was shipped to Osaka for conversion to cash, further linking regional to national markets.

Over the eighteenth and nineteenth centuries the impact of these patterns multiplied. Urbanization, initially focused on the castle towns consciously designed by both daimyo and shogun, shifted to more rustic nodes of craft production and commerce. Castle town growth stagnated in the eighteenth century as rustic periodic markets shortened their intervals and were transformed into permanent markets. Small villages and towns metamorphosed into larger towns and cities that served commoner, not samurai, populations. Day labor markets proliferated, replacing contracts of servitude with wages, and the cash economy expanded dramatically. Commoners increasingly engaged district, regional, and even nationwide trade networks, producing more, and a more diversified range of crops. They processed agricultural goods to sell in the marketplace. They consumed more locally produced niceties (*sake*, better roofs, etc.) as well as urban-produced luxuries (books, artwork, etc.). International trade was limited to Nagasaki, indirect trade with China via the Ryukyu Islands, frontier trade with Hokkaido, and some trade with Korea via Tsushima Island.

In combination, the preceding economic stimuli fueled a robust seventeenth-century economy that supported a premodern population explosion of remarkable proportions. Population estimates for Japan in about 1600 vary widely, from some 12 million to 18 million. Regardless of which base one takes, by around 1720 a national estimate conducted under shogunal auspices counted the population at 26 million, excluding

[17] Takase (1975a; 1975b).

samurai. Demographic historian Hayami Akira estimates that, with samurai, the population was around 30 million at this time, and grew modestly to about 33 million in the early nineteenth century. After the early eighteenth century, regional variation is marked. The population in the northeast retracted, that in the north central and southwest grew, and in the south-central region it was largely unchanged.[18]

The challenge for the early modern ruling classes lay in finding a reasonably efficient tax structure capable of capturing some portion of an expanding, diversifying economy. If they could not capture all the gains, can we judge their efforts to be ineffective in some sense? The discussion that follows focuses on the largest segment of the economy: agriculture.

The early modern political orders

Despite the creation of a nationally stable political order from 1590 on, what Hideyoshi and his Tokugawa successors established was a hegemony, an order that was something less than what moderns consider a fully developed state.[19] While Hideyoshi and the Tokugawa shoguns stood preeminent as leaders of nationwide military bands, they could not perform key government functions. On the "statist" side of the ledger, for example, they oversaw diversity disputes – legal claims that transcended domain boundaries. On the "weak state" side, there was no national administrative structure that extended down even to the provincial level.

Daimyo owed military service to the hegemons, but they were not bureaucratically subordinate. Barring a major disturbance of civic order, their domains were their private territory to administer. They created their own governing structures and laws, some of which might voluntarily draw on shogunal models, but they were not compelled to adopt them.[20] Put plainly, the shogun possessed access to adequate force to keep the great barons from open opposition, but not sufficient strength to impinge greatly on daimyo administrative authority within their domains.

The hegemons' most notable deficit as a country-wide political authority was that they lacked any regularized national tax regime. Hideyoshi, and the Tokugawa shoguns who succeeded him, could make demands on daimyo for irregular contributions to defense efforts, to the political

[18] We lack any national demographic data for the seventeenth century: Hayami (2010). Hayami earlier estimated 1600 population at 12 million, Fam's (2006) were recently estimated up to 17 million.

[19] Only two major conflicts among daimyo marked the early half-century of the period: competition between Hideyoshi's followers in 1599–1600 and 1614–15.

[20] Botsman (2005).

marriages that increasingly bound major samurai families to the shogunal and imperial families, and increasingly in the eighteenth and nineteenth centuries to fund other projects, such as flood control efforts, that crossed domain boundaries. For example, after the Osaka campaigns (1614–15), which defeated the last of Tokugawa Ieyasu's opponents, daimyo throughout the land made contributions of men and materials to the reconstruction of Osaka Castle.[21] In the eighteenth century daimyo contributed to large riparian works near Nagoya.[22] In some instances, the shogun coordinated daimyo suppression of commoner protests when they spilled across domain boundaries.[23] None of these developments led to the creation of a *national* treasury, tax system, or budget. There were advocates for a stronger shogunate, but until Commodore Matthew Perry's arrival there was no pressure, domestic or foreign, sufficient to spawn these institutions; Hideyoshi and his Tokugawa successors were successful military leaders and the largest individual landholders in Japan, but the ordinary revenues they commanded came solely from their own directly administered domains.[24]

Some implications

This brief sketch holds implications for the nature and structure of the fiscal regimes of early modern Japan, and ultimately for whether we find that the resulting patterns constituted modern fiscal regimes.

First, largely absent from the preceding summary is the story of a need to defend Japan from outsiders. Japan's disengagement from foreign wars did much to support its early modern polity. No external pressure forced a nationwide consolidation of administrative and fiscal control. With the exception of the Mongols, Japan faced no invasions. To be sure, there were threats and the perception of threats, such as the arrival of Western warships in the late eighteenth and early nineteenth centuries, and military adventures in Korea in the 1590s, but Japan had no persistent need for massive, sustained defense appropriations.[25] Even early Japanese frontier expansion relied on relatively low-scale warfare, and, once that had been completed (in medieval times), other efforts at conquest were infrequent, of limited duration, and not very costly. Focused largely on Hokkaido and

[21] Hauser (1985). [22] Totman (1992). [23] White (1988).

[24] On efforts to strengthen the Bakufu, see Bodart-Bailey (2006) and Nakai (1988). Much of Tokugawa control over daimyo was exercised via their role as family heads (e.g. marriage) and warrior subordinates who were called to military duty, not a national administrative obligation. See, among others, Vaporis (2008).

[25] Farris (1992); Toby (1984); Sansom (1977).

Okinawa, early modern adventures generally involved short campaigns against peoples with limited capacity to wage high-intensity, extended wars of resistance.[26]

Second, after backsliding from Heian fiscal centralization, the administrative authority of the center was never reestablished until after the Meiji Restoration (1868) and the creation of Japan's first modern government. While some regional problems that transcended daimyo domains came under shogunal purview, within the early modern order no near-modern integrated bureaucratic regime emerged nationally. Fiscal control was exercised by daimyo in their own territories. In this sense, the shogun was just the largest of domain lords.

Third, the implication of this characterization is that we must look at sub-national levels to explore the development of early modern Japanese fiscal regimes. To modify Olsen's characterization, here we witness a political order comprised of multiple, largely stationary bandits operating with great autonomy, and without an overarching superior making regular fiscal demands on them.[27] In a sense, we have multiple natural states, and, within daimyo realms, no competition from others to control the fiscal order (although there were those who sought to milk it.).[28]

Fourth, the development of fiscal regimes showed considerable variation across Japan during the early modern era. Basic numbers tell the story. Japan was fragmented into some 260 to 280 daimyo domains. Domain characteristics varied greatly in ways that influenced fiscal goals, methods, and administrative apparatus. They varied considerably in size, from small realms of the "just barely" daimyo to domains of putative rice yields of 100,000 *koku* (one *koku* is just under five bushels), to the largest domains, which ruled one or more provinces (e.g. Kaga, at 1.2 million *koku*), to the shogunal realms several times larger than the biggest daimyo. Since daimyo divided up some 580 counties (*kōri*), the vast majority were small to medium-sized domain-holders controlling one or two counties or fewer; only a handful of "province-holding" (*kuni-mochi*) daimyo oversaw a dozen or more counties. Further, the daimyo's territory might be either largely contiguous or widely scattered. The latter circumstance clearly presented administrative challenges, whether the domain was of average size or, like the shogunal domains, very large.

While some presume that large domains with contiguous territory exercised more independence than smaller domains or those with scattered

[26] Sakai (1968); Walker (2001). [27] Olson (1993). [28] North, Wallis, and Weingast (2009).

lands, such a guideline should be taken with a healthy dose of salt.[29] To cite one example of a small domain exhibiting independent patterns, one need only look at the small daimiates that comprised much of modern Shimane prefecture, just across the mountains from Hiroshima. The Matsue (186,000 *koku*), Hirose (30,000 *koku*), Mori (10,000 *koku*), Hamada (51,000 *koku*), and Tsuwano (43,000 *koku*) domains controlled most of the region, supplemented by shogunal lands of some 45,000 *koku*.[30] In shogunal lands, local administration was structured just as textbooks tell us it should be: rural administration was under the command of a samurai official called a *daikan*, who supervised commoner officials called elders, village headmen, and lesser administrative figures. In Matsue and the other domains, however, a county magistrate (*kōri bugyō*) who supervised general affairs, including taxation, oversaw the *daikan*, who were in charge of collecting land taxes, and other local officials, who were in charge of inspecting harvests as part of the tax assessment and collection. Commoners from the upper-class villages also worked in the county magistrate's offices, not samurai. Moreover, while there was typically only one village headman in shogunal realms, there were typically two or three in Matsue, with a similar number of group heads within the village (this has a parallel in some shogunal domains). Most of these offices bore local titles distinct from those used in shogunal domains.[31] Thus, even small and medium-sized domains could exhibit a significant degree of autonomy in their administrative structures.

Variation was evident in policies, too, not just structures. The so-called fixed tax rate (*jōmen*) system, discussed in more detail below, is widely thought to have been enacted broadly after its implementation by the shogunal administration in the eighteenth century. In fact, a number of daimyo had employed this method from the seventeenth century.[32]

Fifth, to the degree that anything provided a "do or die" stimulus to strengthening fiscal regimes in Japan, it typically had to have operated at the local and regional level, not at an erstwhile national level of an imperial or shogunal administration. Military pressures provided a push in the sixteenth century, but these ceased quite early in the early modern era, with the last intra-daimyo conflict ending in 1615, and the last outright military threat that called for coordinated multi-daimyo response, the Shimabara rebellion, being snuffed out by 1638. Although it would be several decades before everyone could be confident that the Pax Tokugawa

[29] Ravina (1999). [30] Naitō (1980: 81). [31] Ibid.: 89–90.

[32] See Brown (1988; 1993); both touch on this issue.

would hold, violent outbreaks were almost entirely limited to modest disturbances within the retainer bands of individual daimyo (*oie sōdō*) and protests of villagers or townsmen that typically were controlled readily.[33] Even demographic pressures, while arguably present, did not generate pressures for an integrated nationwide fisc through the end of the era. To the degree that they engendered administrative or policy change, it was within daimyo domains.

Sixth, daimyo and shogunal fiscal arrangements were quite stable after the middle of the seventeenth century, experiencing reform but not radical change. Only Perry's "opening" of Japan generated pressures for change – pressures that the Tokugawa order ultimately failed to accommodate.

Common trends in taxation

Despite the devolution of fiscal authority to the domain level, there were broad trends that cut across daimyo realms.

Domain taxation was overwhelmingly weighted toward *internal exactions*. There were tariffs between domains, but the revenues generated were tiny. While some international trade may have contributed to revenues in the southwest during the late sixteenth to early seventeenth centuries, that revenue shrank and disappeared for most domains other than the shogunate and a tiny handful of daimyo. European trade dwindled to that with the Dutch, the outcome of a combination of the Japanese ordering Spain and Portugal out, the English losing interest, and the Dutch being restricted to Nagasaki. Nagasaki, managed by the shogun, was also home to the major port for trade with China, although additional trade came through Satsuma's domination of the Ryukyu Islands. Trade with Korea came through Tsushima, and small-scale trade took place with Ainu and other communities in Hokkaido.[34] In total, this represented a very small portion of GDP and tax revenues.

Heavy emphasis on internal revenue sources involved something of a social contract. The ideal of the *good lord* (key exemplars were Ikeda Mitsumasa, Tokugawa Yorinobu, and Abe Tadaaki) became a part of the ruling class's self-image. Even protesting villagers resorted to elements of that paradigm in pressing their demands on the authorities.[35] From the villagers' point of view, the obligations of the good lord were to reduce

[33] See Fukuda (1999; 2005) and White (1995). [34] Walker (2001).

[35] On villager invocation of benevolent rule, see Scheiner (1973); on protests generally, see White (1995).

taxes in crop shortfalls, be a court to adjudicate disputes (including those over tax issues), curtail extreme cases of mercantile predations, and the like. While rulers and ruled may, nominally, have embraced the same ideals, this did not mean that that villager and domain administrations necessarily agreed on what the limits of fair taxation were. From a village perspective, perhaps the largely hands-off role of the daimyo within village administration was most important: the less the ruler (daimyo) was involved in village affairs, the less he knew about the village's circumstances, and the more secure village control was over its own resources and activities.

While the diversity of practice and pace of change were clearly evident, the late sixteenth and early seventeenth centuries were a period of state-building for domains, including the shogunate as lord of its own domains. Daimyo and shogun alike experimented with policies and tactics designed to stabilize their control over retainers, make rural administration – including tax collection – more efficient, and secure their relationship with each other. As compared to later periods, major revisions in domain policy and structure were common.

During the first decades of the early modern era domain administration was bare-bones. Even in a growing domain such as Kaga, the daimyo himself signed off on tax receipts, but during the early seventeenth century a well-articulated bureaucracy developed.[36] From this time through the end of the era organizations developed sufficiently to promote specialized expertise. In their administrative (as opposed to military) realms, samurai often served in an office as part of a team of three or more who rotated time on duty over the course of a month. This provided a measure of continuity, as well as the opportunity to consult with others familiar with official duties, obligations, and techniques. Serial office-holding data indicate that people served long enough to gain credible expertise in financial offices (for example).[37]

Despite their elevated social status, only a fraction of the samurai numbers actually participated in civilian administrative activities. Generally thought to number about 8 percent of the total population, samurai constituted a hereditary standing army. As a rule, daimyo and their senior retainer families occupied all the highest domain offices. Middle-class samurai competed for appointment to generally mid-level appointments, and the vast majority of low-level samurai competed for the lowest tiers of offices, scraping by as best they could. Appointments to administrative office were in high demand, for they brought salaries to supplement

[36] Brown (1993). [37] Yasuzawa (2000).

the modest hereditary stipends of middle-class samurai and the inadequate income received by their lower-class brethren.[38]

Tilly notes that, in a somewhat less monetized economy, rulers rely on a larger administrative force and less efficient processes to extract revenues from more resistant subjects than in a more monetized economy; does the Japanese case support this observation?[39] In the late sixteenth century, certainly, Japan was a relatively unmonetized society, particularly in the rural areas. The broadest levy on the population was the land tax, assessed on agricultural communities. Land taxes were paid overwhelmingly in kind, most often rice and soybeans, though there is evidence that cash became increasingly important over the eighteenth and nineteenth centuries. If Tilly is right, then there should have been a relatively large organization to assess and collect these dues.

Arguably, a different picture emerges. Domain administrators simplified and regularized administrative structures over the later decades of the sixteenth century and the seventeenth in three areas: (1) landed retainers' roles in taxation and rural administration were restricted, and commonly eliminated completely; (2) the reorganization of local administration simplified tax collection and limited costs; and (3) tax assessment procedures were restructured so as to reduce costs.

The first major trend saw domains creating relationships with villagers and townsmen that made them unpaid tax collectors. Whole villages became the sole unit of taxation, not individuals. The village as a whole was responsible for collecting and delivering taxes, and responsibility for allocating taxes among villagers devolved to village leadership. In other words, the expense of tax allocation to individuals and collection from them was pressed on villagers, with expenses paid in time, not cash. In the monetized sections of economic activity, merchants and craftsmen were either organized into formal groups based on their trade, which paid fees to the domain, or, in the case of some very large merchants, individually granted licenses, which were often exclusive. As with villages, trade groups apportioned shares of the responsibility among members, collected dues, and forwarded them to domain authorities.

Villages, initially grouped into small districts of twelve to twenty villages, were often reorganized into larger groups. In the large domain of Kaga, for example, villages were organized into groups that often numbered well over 100, reducing the number of district officials who helped oversee tax assessments and collection, the encouragement of agriculture,

[38] Craig (1961); Katsu (1988). [39] Tilly (1992: 87, 89).

the tracking of cultivation rights, and other matters. Since village group leaders were typically paid with tax exemptions and similar emoluments, enlarging groups reduced administrative expenses for the domain. With a domain consisting of several thousand villages, the expense was still significant, but a fraction of what it had been earlier.[40]

Second, landed retainers' relationship to villages was restricted or ended entirely, reducing the duplication of administrative effort through consolidation. Prior to the creation of a well-grounded, stable administration, much of the land in each domain was parceled out to enfeoffed retainers, who were directly responsible for assessing and collecting the land tax. As a rule, the percentage of domain lands held in fief and the proportion of retainers holding fiefs gradually declined from the 1570s to the early seventeenth century. Their fiefs typically consisted of both whole villages and villages they taxed in concert with other landed retainers. In these circumstances there was much duplication of effort. Each retainer (and the daimyo) sent officials to inspect crops, assess taxes, and arrange for villager transport of tax goods.

Not only did multiple bureaucracies create waste, they also led to disputes with villagers and samurai abuse of them as part of the extraction process.[41] The late sixteenth and early seventeenth centuries were marked by many examples of tax officials trying to coerce payments from individuals. Such efforts often proved destructive of civil order and raised costs.

Abuse of villagers during taxation provided a rationale for daimyo to extend their direct supervision of villages, often removing landed retainers' rights in fief, in fact if not in name.[42] As part of this process, from the late sixteenth century into the seventeenth, samurai residences were widely removed from rural villages and towns to daimyo castle towns. In addition, most daimyo progressively intruded on retainer prerogatives, eliminating all, including their right to independently assess and collect taxes, and to conscript labor. Domains frequently took these tasks on themselves, dispensing annual stipends to the disenfranchised retainers.[43] Tax rates for each village were assessed and collected by only one set of officials, reducing administrative costs overall.

A third labor-saving change came with the simplification of land tax assessment. From the start, taxation was structured as a crop-sharing arrangement in which tax officials invoked two separate processes. In general terms the case of Kaga was typical. The first step, initiated in the 1580s, but undertaken in two systematic domain-wide efforts in the early

[40] Brown (1993). [41] Ibid. [42] Ibid. [43] Ibid.

seventeenth century, was a campaign to assess the agricultural productivity of each village in the domain to establish its putative yield as the village land tax base. Survey teams went to each village to consult its leadership about the area of land under cultivation and its agricultural output, taking actual measurements as needed. The estimated area and per-hectare yield were multiplied to produce a yield standard for the village, expressed as a volume of rice: its *kokudaka*, its assessed yield. The value was a standard, an artifice not entirely unrelated to average village output, but not tightly linked to it, either.

Standard descriptions of the process for establishing tax value nationally ascribe it to orders from Toyotomi Hideyoshi, especially after 1590, which purportedly established a national standard for the actual measurement of village arable land; in fact, the situation was far from simple, and, even when measurements were actually made, standards varied. Unlike land measurement in western Europe, procedures were subject to such great variation in judgment that replication through resurvey was impossible, creating opportunities for bribery, extortion, and much strife between official and villagers.[44] Even if measurements were actually taken (dubious in many cases, given the time needed to complete actual measurements), there was much daimyo manipulation of output per hectare, so that nationally no consistent standard was applied.[45] Nevertheless, within a domain, the standards were typically clear and uniform.[46]

After these surveys, typically undertaken by the middle of the seventeenth century, few domains felt the need to do more than make adjustments to villages' assessed values. When new land was brought under the plow or converted from dry field to paddy, it was surveyed, and the authorities adjusted the village's assessed value. When lands were permanently lost due to floods or landslides, the assessed value was reduced based on a survey. This approach to assessing village value greatly limited the costs involved in the very time-consuming process of calculating the tax base.

The calculation of each village's tax rate was based on crop-sampling. For each village, tax officials sampled the yields of different kinds of fields, paddy and dry, and different grades of land within these types. Typically, a rate of 40 percent or 50 percent was multiplied by the sample yields of paddy, and that amount of rice was then converted to a proportion of

[44] Brown (1987; 1989; 1998). [45] See Brown (1993) and Berry (1982).

[46] Kaga domain actually treated some counties differently, but standards were uniform within the counties.

the village putative yield (dry fields included such a variety of crops that their output was formulaically based on desktop calculation, not sample cuttings).

At the start of the Tokugawa era such a process was conducted on an annual basis throughout Kaga and other domains. It was time-consuming and required the labor of many commoners and samurai officials. A large domain might consist of several thousand villages, and even a small or modest one of hundreds, making annual crop inspections a demanding chore.

Depending on the fields chosen for sampling, the outcome could vary considerably – an outcome that generated strife in villages. On the one hand, with the widespread removal of samurai from the land, samurai officials lost familiarity with agriculture and the ability to judge differing qualities of land. As a result, they often felt they were not getting their due, especially when they compared rates extracted by their brethren when a village was taxed by multiple overlords. In these circumstances, samurai tax collectors resorted to violence against villagers in efforts to collect taxes they felt were their due. On the other hand, since outcomes varied by overlord, villagers often felt that some exactions had been unfairly harsh. Consequently, while this arrangement had the potential to keep up with increased per-hectare yields in principle, it came with a significant administrative burden that exacted a high price in both labor and social strife.[47]

As a result of all these troubling issues, domains widely moved to establish a base tax rate that would be altered only when (1) there was a significant crop shortfall (e.g. a more than 20 percent reduction from average years) or (2) when better irrigation or riparian works were introduced that improved average yields. This was the so-called "fixed" (*jōmen*) system of taxation.[48] Kaga provides an example. A major administrative change, initiated in 1652, stopped annual inspections of every village in order to reduce administrative costs. In its place, a "fixed" tax rate was established, on the basis of a review of recent tax collections, and supplemented by additional crop samplings. This rate was to hold for all but significant crop shortfalls (over 20 percent). Crop inspections would be undertaken only when villages claimed that a very poor harvest had befallen them.[49]

Serial tax data for the late sixteenth to mid-seventeenth century are not common but suggest an intriguing trend. For Kaga, the proportion of assessed village value (*kokudaka*) paid as tax in the 1580s ranged between

[47] Brown (1993). [48] Brown (1988). [49] Ibid.

60 and 80 percent. At this time samurai, including the daimyo, had had significant experience observing agriculture because they spent much time living in small towns or villages, not castle towns. As samurai were pulled from the land, however, retainers and domain tax officials alike struggled to collect what they thought they were due. Rates in the early seventeenth century declined to the 30 to 40 percent range. They then moved gradually upward, but there was no major change until domain-wide implementation of fixed tax rates began in mid-century. At this point average rates hovered around 48 percent of assessed village yield, close to where they had been in the 1580s.[50] Rates typically did not rise thereafter for Kaga or other domains after the adoption of fixed tax rates.[51]

After this time land tax rates did not keep up with widespread improvements in agricultural output. Whether this outcome resulted from villager opposition, the manipulation of yield-sampling, the inability of an urbanized samurai to make proper judgments, bribery by villages, or some other factor cannot be judged with certainty. (As the case of Kaga illustrates, however, annual inspections also had failed to track yields, and generated even worse collections than fixed rates.) The failure to capture a growing surplus fostered the growth of rural markets and rustic urbanization over the eighteenth and nineteenth centuries.

Kaga's pattern of administrative cost-cutting typified much of Japan. It took the shogun another seventy years to move to fixed tax rates; other domains changed earlier. Kaga's district reorganization was more extreme than that I have seen in shogunal domains, but the effort to simplify tax assessment and collection by restricting retainer prerogatives and simplifying tax assessment was widespread. In principle, the implementation of fixed rates brought the land tax closer in form to many of the commercial taxes, which were also fixed fees, not calculated on the basis of revenues or profits, which were challenging to work out.

The degree to which the use of fixed tax rates represented daimyo satisficing and the degree to which it was a function of constraints on land taxation cannot readily be assessed. I have argued that information constraints played an important role, given the nature of survey techniques, the rapidity with which yield assessments were made, and the increased unfamiliarity of samurai administrators with agriculture as they moved from village to castle town.[52] White has noted a decline in village protest over taxation after the seventeenth century.[53] Surely such protests weighed on the daimyo in the seventeenth century, but then, and in the

[50] Brown (1993). [51] Smith (1958). [52] Brown (1988; 1987; 1993). [53] White (1995).

early eighteenth century, high levels of protest did not stop domain lords from aggressively reassessing land tax rates as the fixed tax rate system was implemented. The decline in protests over taxation may have reflected village recognition that the new rates could be reduced by their ability to convince agriculturally ignorant samurai that crop shortfalls they claimed were real and merited reduced rates. The increased productivity of land over time may also have ameliorated pressures from below. Even with the decline in tax rate protests, other commoner outbursts continued, and even grew, serving as a constant reminder to domain lords of the risks they faced if they sought to aggressively raise rates. Whether constrained, satisficing, or a combination of the two, the outcome was a failure to raise land taxes, even as the secular price of rice, the principal tax good, stabilized or declined.[54]

Revenues, expenditures, and the private realm

I have referred to the processes above as "taxation," a public assessment to raise funds for public purposes, and this has become common practice in English-language literature; but it was not always the case. Both English-language and Japanese authors used to refer to collections as "rents" or "feudal dues." John Hall began to treat Japan's early modern era as more bureaucratic than "feudal," a function of the degree to which a political order that was originally based on personalistic lord–vassal ties forged in war became highly routinized during the Pax Tokugawa.[55] One implication of treating levies as taxes is that agricultural produce belonged to the villagers, but a portion was taken by the domain lord in return for the provision of some public good. The discussion of lordship above certainly suggests that daimyo rulers and villagers acknowledged this as an ideal that rulers should strive to attain.

Financial documents from domains provide a mixed picture, however. Late sixteent-century tax receipts from Kaga domain, for example, provide evidence for characterizing rulers' exactions as "rents" or "dues." Thereafter the early seventeenth-century version of these documents suggests a shift in perspective. In the former case, the documents state the putative yield of the village in terms that indicate the village's whole crop belonged to the domain lord, who then exempted (*men*) for villagers a certain share of the crop in return for their work as cultivators – a form of sharecropping. By the early seventeenth century the relationship was reversed, with

[54] Yamamura (1974). [55] Hall (1966).

statements that a proportion of the putative yield was to be collected by the daimyo or his landed retainers, while the residual output remained with the village.[56]

It is not clear how widespread this apparent shift in conceptualization from rent or dues to taxation was; evidence from some domains indicates that the presumption of daimyo ownership of all land continued into the nineteenth century, however. In Saga domain, such a premise remained in place into the 1840s. Its budgets identify as daimyo revenue the full assessed productive value of the domain, and then list an "exemption" from that revenue to be left for villagers.

Other budget elements further suggest that daimyo viewed their domain as a private possession, not as a public charge. Despite bearing broadly acknowledged public responsibilities, budget data from Matsue and Saga domains suggest overwhelming concern with the daimyo's private family expenditures. We have precisely the confounding of public and private that characterizes regimes commonly identified as feudal. Budget disbursements for individual daimyo family members, ceremonials, travel expenses, and the like utterly dominate any list of expenditures. In addition to disbursements for family expenses, those for retainer salaries constituted a major expense. Retainer salaries should be classified as private household expenditures too, since they were a commitment to the daimyo's hereditary "housemen" (*kenin*), not distinct from office salaries.

Line items for expenditures such as flood relief and infrastructure investment were seldom detailed. They appear to have been lumped together in the modest expenditure lines for domain office-holders generally (in some instances the "office salary" covered operational expenses as well, not simply compensation for the employee). These budgets do not include lines for investments in infrastructure, economic expansion, and similar activities associated with the promotion of public welfare or an expansion of domain economic activities. We know that such activities were all part of domain activities, and if we were to find budgets for individual offices we might well get a different picture. Nonetheless, it is significant that, viewed from the top down, budget categories reflected a heavy emphasis on the private character of domain administration.

The confounding of personal expenditures with those we today treat as public outlays leads to another significant observation: budgeting was far from modern or rigorous. Merchants had developed bookkeeping methods and circulated handbooks that might have been adapted for domain

[56] See Brown (1993).

budgets, but they were not. Even among merchants, such practice was not broadly consistent even in the late Tokugawa era.[57] (Full-fledged double-entry bookkeeping was not even introduced into commercial practice until the middle of the nineteenth century.)[58]

Deficits

Much scholarship, Japanese and English-language, focuses on what domains did in financial straits, what steps they took to boost revenue. For the shogun, currency manipulation was one approach to relieving financial stress – an option that was also open to domains that issued their own notes. Trade in copper with China also affected currency – a trade in which exchange rates, especially in the eighteenth century, badly distorted the market relationship between silver and copper. The manipulation of this trade, conducted through Bakufu-controlled Nagasaki, also influenced budgets.[59]

More broadly, however, scholars focus on (1) steps to promote agriculture and special local products, such as land reclamation, improved irrigation and flood control, and the cultivation of special crops under a domain license or monopoly, or (2) how increased imposts harmed villagers, forcing them into increasingly intensive forms of agriculture.[60] Major projects to extend arable lands and irrigation networks were heavily concentrated in the seventeenth century.[61] By the eighteenth century the average scale of such investments had declined substantially, the best opportunities exhausted. The emphasis in the eighteenth and nineteenth centuries was on the development of special products, often based on agriculture but including lacquer, pottery, and other manufactured goods. The daimyo's hand was commonly present in these endeavors, but major growth sectors (e.g. the production of *sake*) lay outside their ken.[62]

[57] Hirai discusses one Matsue example and compares it to double-entry bookkeeping methods, while Chiba presents a more recent exploration of this and other examples: Hirai (1936); Chiba (2009).

[58] Shimme looks at Western double-entry bookkeeping, concentrating on the importation of Western-language texts after 1868: Shimme (1937).

[59] Innes (1980). An entire series of books in Japanese studies the development of special local products, especially those associated with domain monopolies: Chihōshi Kenkyū Kyōgikai (1959).

[60] Ravina presents examples of local product development, and efforts to settle samurai in villages in order to ease their financial pain and staunch the red ink on domain budgets: Ravina (1999). Hanley and Yamamura review the Japanese literature that stresses injury to villagers: Hanley and Yamamura (1977).

[61] Yamamura (1981). [62] Pratt (1999).

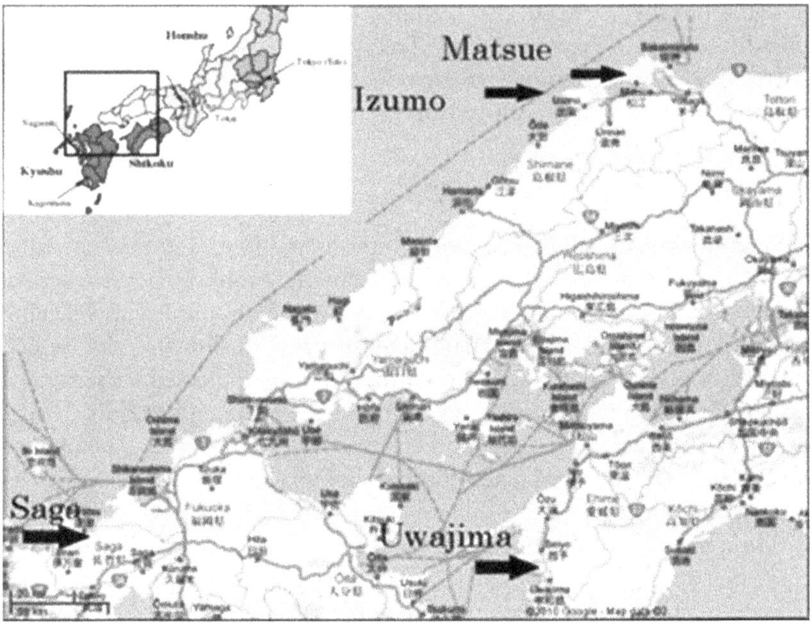

Figure 14.1 Matsue and Saga regions

Financial problems intensified in the middle and late Tokugawa eras, when domain budgetary straits are thought to have reached significant proportions. Certainly, red ink had besmirched balance sheets well before this time, but financial crises during the middle and late Tokugawa periods have been seen as so pervasive that only a few domains found a way out of them, enabling them to participate in the Meiji Restoration movement.[63]

Closer examination of long-term budgetary records suggests a more complex picture of domain finance. Long-term domain budget data are rare. The following paragraphs examine two exceptional series of data from Matsue and Saga domains. Their castle town locations are noted on the map shown in Figure 14.1. In addition to showing rather low ratios of debt, they show no use of debt to invest in new wealth-generating endeavors.

Both domains were located south and west of Osaka/Kobe. This is the region in which demographic historian Hayami Akira has indicated that the population continued to grow after the seventeenth century. Domain

[63] Chōshū, with the development of commercial crops, and Satsuma's monopoly of sugar cane production are the principal cases cited.

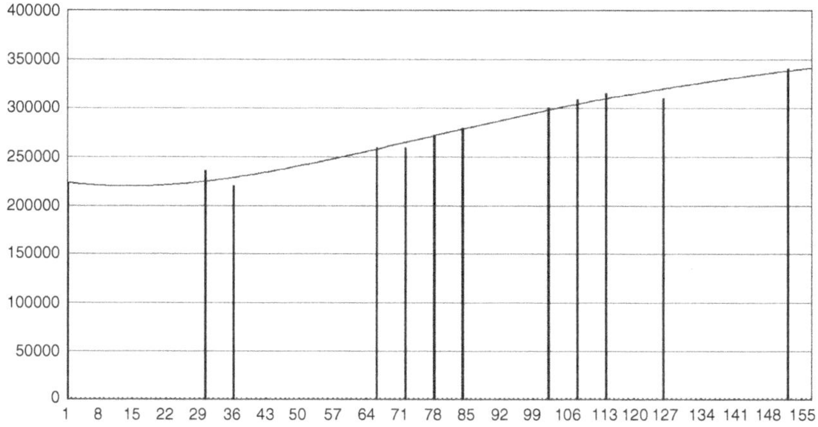

Figure 14.2 Izumo population trends, 1721–1877

records from Izumo, Matsue, and Uwajima (on Shikoku) all suggest that this was the case (see Figures 14.2 to 14.4).

Population data for Saga, per se, is missing, but eighteenth- and nineteenth-century figures for the four provinces from which the domain drew territory – all of Hizen and Chikugo provinces, and parts of Chikuzen and Higo provinces – show population growth. There is no reason to assume that it differed from the Matsue/Izumo and Uwajima districts.[64]

The budget data for Matsue and Saga were compiled for particular purposes, both related to reporting to the shogunate on their potential service obligations to the Bakufu. Each set of documents was designed to make a particular case, and to do so in a way that was convincing to shogunal officials, but also in a way so as to mask as much private information as possible. Although modern corporate financial statements have a similar orientation, the Financial Accounting Standards Board (FASB) would not have approved of the budget reporting of these two domains; the data are often opaque. Yasuzawa Shūichi, editor and compiler of late eighteenth- and early nineteenth-century financial data for Matsue domain, *Deiri yōran*, as well as that for Saga, *Saga han kanjōsho daimeyasu*, stresses that these long-term records of domain income and expenditures

[64] Hanley and Yamamura (1977: 54).

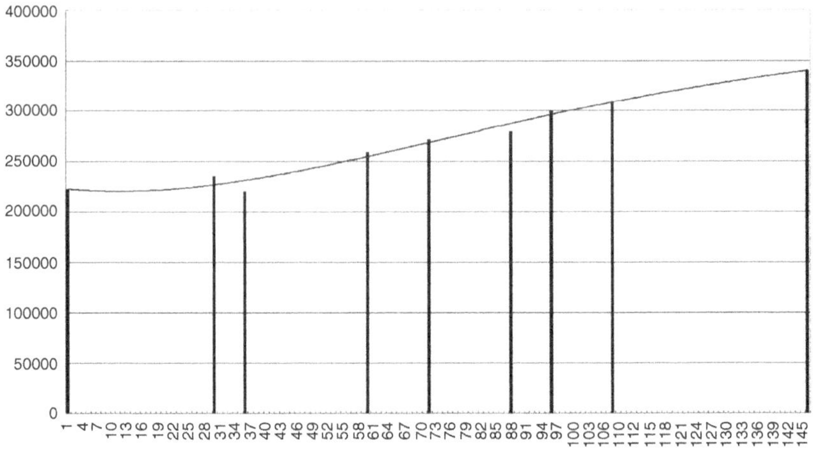

Figure 14.3 Matsue domain population trends, 1721–1877

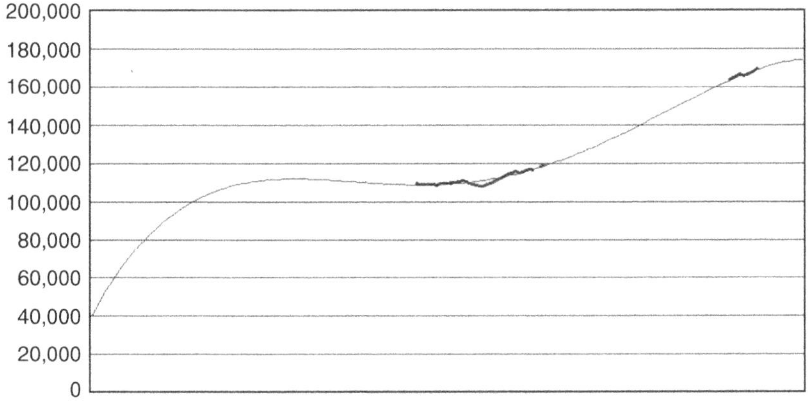

Figure 14.4 Uwajima domain population, 1680–1867

were not compiled for use in managing finances year to year. The Matsue data were created as a project in the 1830s, a summary for use in reporting to the daimyo the payoff of some 500,000 gold *ryō* in debt taken on in 1767.[65] As the years proximate to the compilation were recorded, the number of errors in entries increases, giving a sense that a project deadline was

[65] Yasuzawa (1999).

nearing, and the compiler was under pressure. The last entries in the document focus on a time after the repayment of the loan; they are associated with the major nationwide crop failures of the 1830s, the Tenpō crisis.[66] The Saga data were compiled for a similar purpose, but one that suggested the domain was already financially strained and could not take on more duties for the shogun than it already bore: the duties to post men at the port of Nagasaki and other ports under Bakufu control in the southwest.[67] The Matsue records show modest efforts at something akin to double-entry bookkeeping. Its unusual balance sheet format bears some similarity to the "Izumo chōai" ("Izumo Account Book"), which reflected the multiple-entry format of townsmen in the domain. The Saga data do not reflect a similar practice.

Both sets of documents show a dual system of record-keeping, one for cash and one for rice (the chief form for payment of agricultural land taxes). Transactions for each were kept distinct in the original documents (to combine the figures presented in the graphs, rice transactions were converted to cash values on the basis of rice purchase/sale data included in the documents). This practice reflected the way that tax obligations were collected and disbursed in all domains, and the routine collection of goods in kind by itself presented a significant challenge to maintaining a true, double-entry account book. Early in the era the situation would have been more complicated, since a broader array of non-rice agricultural products were also commonly collected in kind, especially soybeans and textiles. While that practice continued most broadly for payments in soybeans, it became less common.[68] In some domains cash transactions were handled by one official or set of officials, and agricultural transactions in kind were handled by different people, clearly implying the need for specialized skills to deal with each type of transaction.[69]

Reflecting the specific financial arguments that each domain sought to make, the constituent budget elements of the data are quite different for Matsue and Saga. Both documents record income sources fairly well, classifying them largely by income form – rice or coin – as well as major revenue category, but not providing details of lesser cash revenues from commoner populations. As noted, expenditures were most detailed for

[66] Ibid.: 13–14. [67] Personal communication, April 26, 2010.

[68] Over time, many daimyo converted smaller tax levies from collections in kind or labor to cash.

[69] Yasuzawa (2006).

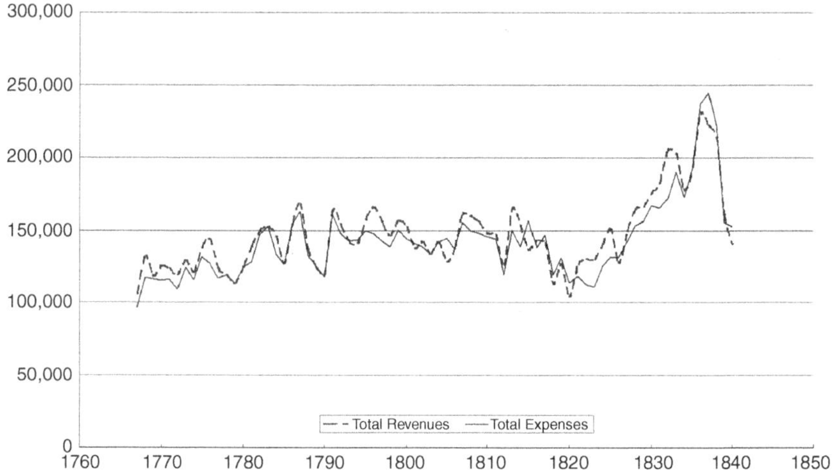

Figure 14.5 Matsue domain expenditures versus income, in gold *ryō*, 1760–1850

items associated with daimyo, their families, samurai retainer expenditures, and loans. Listings of temporary expenditures provide increased detail, and often reflected further expenditure for the domain lord, ceremonials, and the like.

Matsue domain, at least during the early 1670s, suffered the financial straights widely presumed to be typical. Expenditures outstripped treasury receipts by about 30 percent.[70] Later data suggest a very different, more favorable picture, however.

Figure 14.5 presents the trends in total domain revenues and expenditures over more than sixty years later in the era. These data have a significant limitation, however, in that each year's data begins from scratch, with no carryover from the previous year. If there was a surplus or deficit, the record does not explicitly record how that revenue or expense was handled.[71] Data for Matsue indicate that, during the eighteenth century to the 1840s, domain budgets did not hemorrhage red ink. Expenditures exceeded revenues in very few years. Only rarely, notably around 1816 and 1839, were revenues outpaced significantly. Indeed, throughout the high Tokugawa, expenditures and revenues were pretty well aligned.

[70] Naitō (1980: 107).

[71] Personal communication, Yasuzawa Shūichi, April 14, 2010. On *Izumo chōai*, see Hirai (1936).

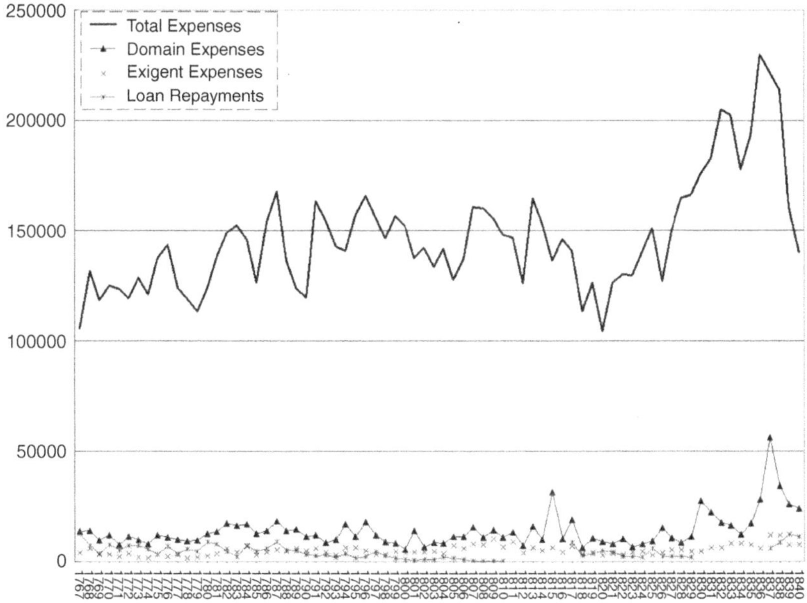

Figure 14.6 Matsue domain internal domain expenses versus total expenses, 1767–1840

Examination of the degree to which loan repayments comprised domain expenditures can be seen in Figure 14.6. Loan repayments, represented by the dark line closest to the X-axis, were a consistent, if not universal element of the domain budget, but they were a very small portion of overall expenditures. Despite the loans, this series of data shows a generally healthy balance of income and expenditures.

Despite these data, historians widely see, and contemporaries saw, Matsue was impoverished. One widely available survey of prefectural history, *Shimane-ken no rekishi (A History of Shimane Prefecture)*, explicitly titles one subsection of the domain's early modern history "The impoverishment of domain finances."[72] More importantly, this evidence of fiscal probity (from our perspective) cannot gainsay the domain administrator's concerns of the time. That perspective appears to be reflected in the purpose for creating this document: demonstrating to the daimyo how a large loan was paid off. There is no indication that administrators were acclimated to the idea of borrowing as a positive, beneficial fiscal tool,

[72] Naitō (1980: 107).

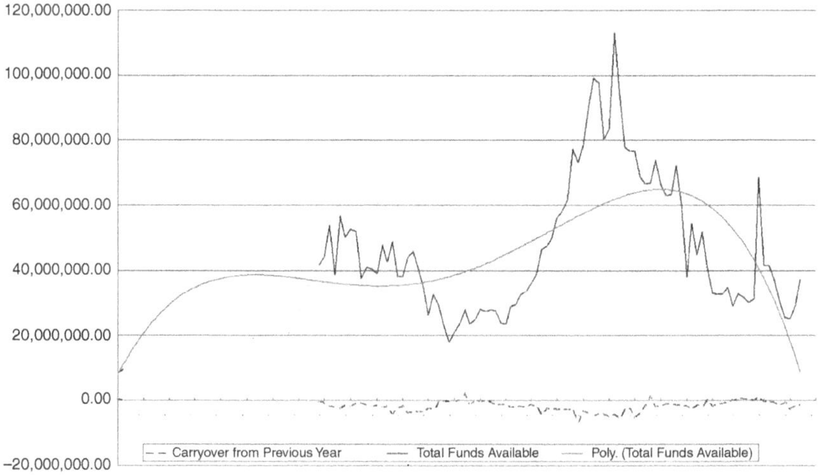

Figure 14.7 Saga domain deficit/surplus, 1764–1857

much less as a means of investing in economic growth. The premise appears to have been "Debt is bad – all debt."

Saga domain data are a bit more difficult to parse. Constructing a database from the documentary records is still in process, however, as Figure 14.7 indicates via the lower line tracing the surplus or deficit from year to year; in most years, even when income rose substantially, the domain ran a deficit. While each year's deficit may not have been great, the cumulative effect of loans plus interest was likely quite significant. (Note that the case for heavy expenses vis-à-vis expenditures as part of duty for the Bakufu is made largely through tracking domain expenditures for travel and living expenses associated with duty posts such as Nagasaki.)

If a European scholar were to read a direct translation of the Matsue and Saga expense records, one of the first characteristics that would strike him or her is the absence of any large category associated with military or defense expenditures. There are expenses for Edo residence (a military duty required by the shogun), travel from the domain to Edo and back, disbursements to retainers, and other similar categories. Given that samurai warriors represented some 7 percent of Matsue's population, about the same percentage as townsmen, this seems terribly odd.[73] In fact, most such expenditures were masked under the categories associated

[73] Yasuzawa (2006: 152).

with retainer stipends (samurai received a base income in return for which they provided military service). Samurai were expected to provide their own weapons, armor, and related equipment, and office "salaries" were often expected to cover the expenses of office as well as provide compensation.

In the absence of major military conflicts, the absence of emergency expenditures for military purposes is not surprising. During the years documented by the Matsue and Saga data, the only major period of military pressure came with Perry's arrival in 1853. Although greater efforts to strengthen coastal preparedness preceded his arrival (a response to petulant Russian coastal raids and earlier European/American efforts to establish trade relations with Japan) sustained efforts began in earnest only after Japan signed a treaty with the United States in 1858. Domains, independent of shogunal efforts, began their own experimentation with military reforms during this time.

Matsue data do not cover this time period, but those for Saga extend into the first years after Perry's arrival. Budget items for Western steam ships and provision for the casting of cannon reflect the domain's leadership role in exploring the adaptation and production of new military technologies. Nonetheless, such temporary military expenditures comprise less than 5 percent of all expenses for 1858.[74]

Conclusions

A very long-term view of Japan's fiscal structure from the seventh century into the modern age would show four distinct periods of non-linear fiscal development. A long classical age, approximately from the seventh century through the thirteenth, witnessed the rise and persistence of a relatively strong, truly national fisc. Centrifugal forces were in operation to be sure, but their full impact was not felt until some time after the Mongol invasions of the mid-thirteenth century – the start of a second, medieval, period during which Japan moved with accelerating speed from a national fiscal regime to regional and local control of taxation as the country collapsed into chaos in the late fifteenth century. The incessant civil wars of the sixteenth century, which marked the latter part of this third era, ultimately generated pressures to create a more stable, but still dispersed, early modern fiscal order. The new approaches had matured by the middle

[74] This calculation focuses on extraordinary expenditures. Saga domain's ordinary expenditures included guard duties in Nagasaki, Japan's major international port, and funded a large samurai population, but these routine expenditures did not reflect the impact of the Western threat.

of the seventeenth century, and lasted until the third quarter of the nineteenth century. The Meiji Restoration of 1868 marked the dawn of a modern fiscal system: the fourth era, and the one that finally restored the financial foundations of a truly national administrative regime. My focus in this chapter has been on the third stage, but it is important to recall this longer trajectory, especially the existence of the fourth stage, which highlights just how successful the Japanese ruling classes were in maintaining a peaceful and stable regime without ever creating many of the rudiments of a national political administrative system *à la* China, large European states, and other contemporary governments.

Peace brought stability and economic transformation to early modern Japan, but it did not restore any semblance of the national fiscal order of the Yamato/Heian eras. At the domain level, military conflict ultimately led to better fiscal controls and improved mechanisms to extract income from agriculture. These initiatives contributed to daimyo ability to succeed in war, expand their domains, and join in leagues with others. They constituted the building blocks of the Toyotomi, and later the Tokugawa, alliances that encompassed all Japan. The onset of peace removed a major stimulus for Japanese leaders to create and strengthen a national fisc. Significant movement toward centralized administration stagnated early in the seventeenth century, and resumed only with the Meiji Restoration of 1868.

By the mid-seventeenth century domains had established the basic patterns of administration and taxation within which they lived for the next two centuries. Daimyo generally had achieved fiscal centralization. Domains had become stable internally, with the problem of landed retainers brought under daimyo control. While there were reforms in later years, the core structures had been established.

In contrast to Tilly's hypotheses, much of the pattern that emerged was arguably quite efficient, especially considering in the context of the times. Daimyo successfully cut administrative expenditures. Village group consolidation reduced district administrative expenses. At the local level, villages as a corporate unit took (uncompensated) responsibility for the allocation of land taxes among their members and they collected taxes from their residents for delivery to tax officials. These measures enabled daimyo to work with a smaller, samurai-staffed bureaucracy. They typically reduced duplicative labors by taking over all tax collection entirely or rationalizing and standardizing landed retainer efforts.

Tax assessment procedures were simplified to reduce administrative costs and labors. After the broad land surveys domains undertook in the late sixteenth and early seventeenth centuries, there was no similar effort. Early measurements were supplemented only by much smaller investigations designed to assess land added to or removed from tax registers. Through the fixed-rate tax system, the tax assessment process was simplified. Although this appears to have had an opportunity cost – giving up the chance to capture increases in agricultural yields – data were introduced to show that the annual inspection of crops in Kaga actually produced worse results than the fixed-rate system. The labor demands, complexity, the inability of urbanized samurai to understand and assess crop losses and productivity, and the speed required for inspections all interfered with effective tax assessments. Further, procedures such as surveying were not precisely replicable, leaving room for bribery and extortion that compromised tax yields and assessment. In effect, all these circumstances limited the state's ability to "see" the object of its extractions. All these efforts reduced administrative costs, yet ultimately provided a reliable, if not ideal, foundation for revenues under existing technical, political, and administrative constraints.

This tax settlement was supported by some key values held by villagers and administrators alike. The image of the "good lord," shared by both parties, placed broad constraints on exactions. In principle, through flight or protest, cooperation or non-cooperation, villagers could negotiate, remonstrate, and argue with tax assessors or manipulate inspection processes. While Tokugawa villages did all of these, it is telling that by the late seventeenth century the bulk of tax protests had peaked and were replaced by protests focused on other issues. A rough modus vivendi had been reached between lord and subject. Early on, this solution may have been rendered more acceptable to daimyo because of the successful investments they had made to reclaim and improve arable land, ameliorate flood damage, and exploit precious metals in the late sixteenth and early seventeenth centuries. Nonetheless, it is fair to say that assessors and assessed both satisficed in considerable measure.

That we label the late sixteenth to mid-nineteenth-century period "early modern" implies an affinity with the modern era, yet Tokugawa Japan failed to move toward a modern fiscal regime. First, it never developed a national structure or fiscal order. But within domains, too, there was little movement toward modern attitudes and practice. Domain rulers continued to rely on premodern land survey techniques. Financial records indicate that daimyo often thought of revenues in very personal terms: as rents, not taxes. Most expenditures were for them and their family. Most of the rudimentary public goods we moderns expect from government do not appear in these documents. Collections were only partially monetized; the vast majority of land tax revenues were collected in kind down to 1868. Domain accounting practice did not even keep pace with advances in the most progressive merchant establishments.

Attitudes toward debt also reveal the absence of a modern fisc. The baronial domains did not borrow in order to make investments in the economy or to boost revenues. Borrowing subsidized daimyo household expenses. While the two budgets we have examined show very modest levels of debt (lower than most historians of Japan typically presume), the attitudes of contemporaries and those reflected in the documents indicate that debt – all debt – was considered bad. At the least, examination of these budgets indicates that borrowing did not reach proportions so great as to provide a stimulus to a major restructuring of the fiscal order.

Mid-nineteenth-century foreigners, as investors in Japan's daimyo debt and, later, national debt instruments, complained about the quality of Japan's first national budgets. The first financial statements were welcomed, but they also generated significant criticism and skepticism.[75] It took Japan some time to develop a consistent modern budgetary structure.[76] When it did, budgets, taxation, and assessments moved away from Tokugawa practices to adopt European-inspired practices in order to strengthen the military, defend Japan from European colonialism, and promote the economic transformations that would enable Japan to accomplish those objectives.

References

Barzel, Y., and Kiser, E. (1997) "The development and decline of medieval voting institutions: a comparison of England and France," Economic Inquiry 35: 244–60.

Bates, R. H. (2008) *When Things Fell Apart: State Failure in Late-Century Africa*. New York.

Berry, M. E. (1982) *Hideyoshi*. Cambridge, MA.

Birt, M. P. (1985) "Samurai in passage: the transformation of the sixteenth-century Kanto," *Journal of Japanese Studies* 11: 369–99.

75 English-language newspapers covered the publication of the first national financial statement; see *Japan Gazette Mail and Shipping and Market Report*, June 21, 1873 (Yokohama), reprinted by Suzuki (1997: 148); *Japan Weekly Mail*, June 21, 1873, reprinted by Kitane and Suzuki (1995b: 436–7); and the full translation published in *Japan Weekly Mail*, June 14, 1873: Kitane and Suzuki (1995a: 407–11).

76 Budgetary data over the first years of the new Meiji government show significant variation in budget structure and the organization of government administrative offices: Meiji Zaisei Shi Hensankai (1971 [1904]).

Bodart-Bailey, B. M. (2006) *The Dog Shogun: The Personality and Policies of Tokugawa Tsunayoshi*. Honolulu.

Bonney, R., and Ormrod, W. M. (1999) "Introduction: crises, revolutions and self-sustained growth: towards a conceptual model of change in fiscal history," in *Crises, Revolutions and Self-Sustained Growth: Essays in European Fiscal History, 1130–1830*, ed. W. M. Ormrod, M. Bonney, and R. Bonney. Stamford, UK: 1–21.

Botsman, D. (2005) *Punishment and Power in the Making of Modern Japan*. Princeton, NJ.

Brown, P. C. (1987) "The mismeasure of land: land surveying in the Tokugawa period," *Monumenta Nipponica* 42: 115–55.

(1988) "Practical constraints on early Tokugawa land taxation: annual versus fixed assessments in Kaga domain," *Journal of Japanese Studies* 14: 369–401.

(1989) "Never the twain shall meet: European land survey techniques in Tokugawa Japan," *Chinese Science* 9: 53–79.

(1993) *Central Authority and Local Autonomy in the Formation of Early Modern Japan: The Case of Kaga Domain*. Stanford, CA.

(1998) "A case of failed technology transfer: land survey technology in early modern Japan," *Senri Ethnological Studies* 46: 83–97.

Chiba, J. (2009) "Kinsei edo-ki ni okeru keizai shisō to kaku shōka no naibu hōkoku kaikei jissen," *Keizai shirin [Housei University Economic Review]* 76: 269–93.

Chihōshi Kenkyū Kyōgikai (1959) *Nihon sangyōshi taikei*, 8 vols. Tokyo.

Craig, A. M. (1961) *Chōshū in the Meiji Restoration*. Cambridge, MA.

Farris, W. W. (1992) *Heavenly Warriors: The Evolution of Japan's Military, 500–1300*. Cambridge, MA.

Ferejohn, J. A., and F. M. Rosenbluth, F. (eds.) (2010) *War and State Building in Medieval Japan*. Stanford, CA.

Friday, K. F. (1992) *Hired Swords: The Rise of Private Warrior Power in Early Japan*. Stanford, CA.

(2004) *Samurai, Warfare and the State in Early Medieval Japan*. New York.

Fukuda, C. (1999) *Bakuhanseiteki chitsujo to oie sōdō*. Tokyo.

(2005) *Oie sōdō: daimyōke o yurugashita kenryoku tōsō*. Tokyo.

Hall, J. W. (1961) "Foundations of the modern Japanese Daimyo," *Journal of Asian Studies* 20: 317–29.

(1966) *Government and Local Power in Japan, 500 to 1700: A Study Based on Bizen Province*. Princeton, NJ.

Hanley, S. B., and Yamamura, K. (1977) *Economic and Demographic Change in Preindustrial Japan, 1600–1868*. Princeton, NJ.

Hauser, W. B. (1985) "Osaka Castle and Tokugawa authority in western Japan," in *The Bakufu in Japanese History*, ed. J. P. Mass and W. B. Hauser. Stanford, CA: 153–73.

Hayami, A. (2010) *Population and Family in Early-Modern Central Japan*. Kyoto.

Hirai, Y. (1936) "Izumo chōai no seishitsu," *Kokumin keizai zasshi* 61: 319–46.

Hirschman, A. O. (2004) *Exit, Voice, and Loyalty: Responses to Decline in Firms, Organizations, and States*. Cambridge, MA.

Innes, R. L. (1980) *The Door Ajar: Japan's Foreign Trade in the Seventeenth Century*. Ann Arbor, MI.
Katsu, K. (1988) *Musui's Story: The Autobiography of a Tokugawa Samurai*. Tucson, AZ.
Kiser, E., and Barzel, Y. (1991) "The origins of democracy in England," *Rationality and Society* 3: 396–422.
Kitane, Y., and Suzuki, Y. (1995a) *Nihon shoki shinbun zenshū: hen'nen fukuseiban 53*. Tokyo.
(1995b) *Nihon shoki shinbun zenshū: hen'nen fukuseiban 54*. Tokyo.
Martin, I. W., Mehrotra, A. K., and Prasad, M. (eds.) (2009) *The New Fiscal Sociology: Taxation in Comparative and Historical Perspective*. New York.
Mass, J. P. (1985) "What can we not know about the Kamakura Bakufu?," in *The Bakufu in Japanese History*, ed. J. P. Mass and W. B. Hauser. Stanford, CA: 13–31.
Meiji Zaisei Shi Hensankai (1971 [1904]) Meiji zaisei shi, 15 vols. Yoshikawa.
Naitō, S. (1980) *Shimane-ken no rekishi*. Tokyo.
Nakai, K. W. (1988) *Shogunal Politics: Arai Hakuseki and the Premises of Tokugawa Rule*. Cambridge, MA.
North, D. C., Wallis, J. J., and Weingast, B. R. (2009) *Violence and Social Orders: A Conceptual Framework for Interpreting Recorded Human History*. New York.
Olson, M. (1993) "Dictatorship, democracy, and development," *American Political Science Review* 83: 567–76.
Pratt, E. E. (1999) *Japan's Protoindustrial Elite: The Economic Foundations of the Gōnō*. Cambridge, MA.
Ravina, M. (1999) *Land and Lordship in Early Modern Japan*. Stanford, CA.
Sakai, R. K. (1968) "The Ryukyu (Liu-Ch'iu) Islands as a fief of Satsuma," in *The Chinese World Order: Traditional China's Foreign Relations*, ed. J. Fairbank. Cambridge, MA: 112–34.
Sansom, G. B. (1977) *The Western World and Japan: A Study in the Interaction of European and Asiatic Cultures*. Rutland, VT.
Scheiner, I. (1973) "The mindful peasant: sketches for a study of rebellion," *Journal of Asian Studies* 32: 579–91.
Scott, J. C. (1985) *Weapons of the Weak: Everyday Forms of Peasant Resistance*. New Haven, CT.
Shimme, S. (1937) "Introduction of double-entry bookkeeping into Japan," *The Accounting Review* 12: 290–5.
Shimode, S. (1979) *Ishikawa-ken no rekishi*, 2nd edn. Tokyo.
Simon, H. A. (1957) *Models of Man, Social and Rational: Mathematical Essays on Rational Human Behavior in a Social Setting*. New York.
Smith, T. C. (1958) "The land tax in the Tokugawa period," *Journal of Asian Studies* 18: 3–19.
Suzuki, Y. (1997) *Nihon shoki shinbun zenshū: hen'nen fukuseiban hokan 2*. Tokyo.
Takase, T. (1975a) "Zenkoku shijō kakuritsu ni tomonau Kaga-han no taiō sakū," *Kanjishi kenkyū* 25: 15–36.

(1975b) "Bakuhanseika no zenkoku shijō no keisei to Kaga-han: nishi mawari senro no kaitaku," *Nihonshi kenkyū* 159: 33–61.
Tilly, C. (1992) *Coercion, Capital, and European States: AD 990–1992*, rev edn. Malden, MA.
Toby, R. P. (1984) *State and Diplomacy in Early Modern Japan: Asia in the Development of the Tokugawa Bakufu*. Princeton, NJ.
Totman, C. (1992) "Preindustrial river conservancy: causes and consequences," *Monumenta Nipponica* 47: 59–76.
Vaporis, C. N. (2008) *Tour of Duty: Samurai, Military Service in Edo, and the Culture of Early Modern Japan*. Honolulu.
Walker, B. L. (2001) *The Conquest of Ainu Lands: Ecology and Culture in Japanese Expansion, 1590–1800*. Berkeley, CA.
White, J. W. (1988) "State growth and popular protest in Tokugawa Japan," *Journal of Japanese Studies* 14: 1–25.
(1995) *Ikki: Social Conflict and Political Protest in Early Modern Japan*. Ithaca, NY.
Yamamura, K. (1974) *A Study of Samurai Income and Entrepreneurship: Quantitative Analyses of Economic and Social Aspects of the Samurai in Tokugawa and Meiji Japan*. Cambridge, MA.
(1981) "Returns on unification economic growth in Japan, 1550–1650," in *Japan before Tokugawa: Political Consolidation and Economic Growth, 1550–1650*, ed. J. W. Hall, N. Keiji, and K. Yamamura. Princeton, NJ: 327–72.
Yasuzawa, S. (1999) *Matsue-han deiri shōran*. Tokyo.
(ed.) (2000) *Saga han kanjōsho daimeyasu*, 4 vols. Place unknown.
(2006) "Han zaisei," in *Kinsei hansei hankō daijiten*, ed. M. Oishi. Tokyo: 151–7.

PART IV

Fragmented Political Ecologies and Institutional Innovation

CHAPTER 15

The Greek polis *and* koinon

Emily Mackil

Historical background

In the course of the twelfth century BCE the Greek world stumbled into a so-called "Dark Age," characterized by the collapse of early, palace-based states, the contraction of rural settlement, indicating population decline, and drastic reduction in the intensity of long-distance trade.[1] Recovery was slow and varied regionally, but it is only in the eighth century (the onset of the Archaic period) that we begin to see the reemergence of recognizable state entities. By the early sixth century most such entities had become *poleis* (pl., sing. *polis*), city states usually comprised of an urban center, increasingly fortified, and a rural territory, ranging in total size from a few square kilometers to about 2,500 km^2. By the fourth century there were more than 1,000 *poleis* in the Greek world.[2] They were for the most part quite small, ranging in size from a few hundred inhabitants to a few thousand, with one or two outliers (such as Athens, a special case treated by Ober in this volume) home to perhaps a hundred thousand individuals. The total population of the Greek world in the fourth century has recently been calculated to have been about 7 million.[3]

These *poleis* exhibited an astonishing variety of political systems, arrayed on a bell-shaped curve from monarchy or tyranny to radical democracy. Extreme forms were rare, and looser forms of oligarchy and democracy predominated; by the fourth century monarchy had been virtually eradicated from Greece proper, although it persisted in neighboring areas, such

[1] All non-bibliographic dates are BCE unless otherwise stated. Thanks are due to my research assistant, Lisa Eberle, for her help.

[2] Hansen and Nielsen (2004).

[3] On territory sizes, see Hansen and Nielsen (2004: 70–3). The total population in Athens is an extrapolation from isolated figures for male citizens (Herodotus 5.97.2; Athenaeus 6.272c); see Hansen (1986; 1988). For the total population of the Greek world, see Hansen (2006).

as Macedonia, Thrace, and Cyprus.[4] In mainland Greece, during the classical period, groups of mostly small *poleis* sharing a sense of identity and bound together by patterns of economic and religious interaction, often combined with a shared threat posed by hostile neighbors, chose to formalize their cooperation by forming confederations, which they called *koina* (pl., sing. *koinon*). By the end of the fourth century nearly half of the *poleis* of mainland Greece had joined one of a dozen *koina*.[5] Political rights and obligations, together with fiscal responsibilities, were distributed among the member *poleis* and the central government in accordance with a basic principle of subsidiarity, but these allocations of power were subject to constant negotiation.

The three major periods of Greek antiquity, as traditionally defined, are bounded by interstate wars: the archaic period (800–479) ended with the Greek victory in the Persian Wars; the classical period (479–323) ended with the eastern conquests of Alexander III (the Great) of Macedon and his death in Babylon; and the Hellenistic period (323–331), marked by the development of competing territorial kingdoms in Greece, Egypt, and Asia Minor, ended with the Roman defeat of Cleopatra, the last monarch of the last Hellenistic kingdom, at Actium. Despite the power amassed by these kingdoms (which are treated by Monson in this volume), the *polis* remained a highly viable form of state in this period, and, while some were subjected to the kings, many remained independent.[6] If warfare was always endemic to the Greek world, it is certain that both its scale and its frequency increased in the Hellenistic period, while small, local conflicts persisted.[7] The struggle to fund these hostile interactions was perpetual, and – as we shall see – the Greek states directed significant public revenues to the financing of war, but it will be difficult to argue, as has been done for early modern Europe, that war was a significant motor of state development.[8] The world of the Greek *polis* and *koinon* was, then, a world of more or less democratic states on a small scale that engaged in constant and intensive interaction with one another, participating in a broader city-state culture.[9] The character of these interstate interactions was peaceful at least as frequently as it was not, despite the absence in all periods of any formal state or legal structure governing them.

[4] Hansen and Nielsen (2004: 80–6, 1338–40). [5] Mackil (2013a: 305–6; 2013b: 1).

[6] *Contra* Runciman (1990). On the vitality of political discourse in *poleis* being subjected to a monarch, see Ma (1999).

[7] Ma (2000); Chaniotis (2005). [8] Tilly (1992). [9] Hansen (2000).

Distinctive features

One of the most prevalent forms of interaction between these states, and a prominent cause for dispute, was trade. Evidence for both short- and long-distance trade in the Greek world goes back into the prehistoric period, but in the world of the *polis* and the *koinon* it was tremendously facilitated by the development of coinage. The earliest coins were produced in Asia Minor, in the late seventh century; they were made of electrum, a naturally occurring alluvial alloy of gold and silver. The metallic ratios were easy to manipulate, making it a simple matter to break the connection between content and face value that tends to make precious-metal coinage so stable. As a result, when separate gold and silver coinages were developed in Lydia by the middle of the sixth century, by virtue of the great stability of their value and consequent utility the bimetallic coinage system spread rapidly throughout the Greek world.[10] By 480, the transition from the archaic to the classical period, more than 100 *poleis* were issuing coinage (mostly silver) in small denominations – an indication that coinage was used by the Greeks, from very early in its history, for small transactions as well as larger ones.[11] While the right to issue coins was reserved exclusively for states (with heavy penalties for counterfeiting), the act of minting was not necessarily a sign of absolute sovereignty.[12] The introduction of coinage to the Greek world had profound cultural effects, but its economic impact is difficult to assay.[13] Studies of the scale of Greek coin production allow us to determine that, in some times and places, there was not enough coinage in circulation, while in others there was too much. Yet, in aggregate, for the Hellenistic period it has been estimated that only perhaps 10 percent of all the gold and silver available in the Greek world was converted into coin.[14] Other financial needs were met by credit and by the extensive use of silver bullion as money throughout the period under consideration.[15] There is no doubt, however, that even the incomplete monetization experienced by the

[10] Greek tradition (Herodotus 1.94.1) held that gold and silver coinage first developed in Lydia, and this is confirmed by archaeolgical evidence. See Cowell and Hyne (2000) for the impact of gold-refining techniques at the Lydian capital, Sardis, on the production of coinage, and Cahill and Kroll (2005) for recent archaeological evidence confirming the mid-sixth-century date for the development of the bimetallic Lydian coinage.

[11] Kim (2001).

[12] For penalties for counterfeiting, see, for example, Thür and Stumpf (1989); for minting and sovereignty: Martin (1985).

[13] See Kurke (1999) on the cultural impact of the introduction of coinage.

[14] See de Callataÿ (2011: 20–3).

[15] For the use of bullion as money, see de Callataÿ (2006; 2008) and Kroll (2008). More will be said about credit below.

Greek world triggered important economic changes, including greater specialization of labor, more sophisticated financial planning, and the development of complex structures of credit and debt.

The most distinctive feature of the fiscal regimes of the Greek *polis* and *koinon* may be the scale at which fiscal autonomy occurred. The citizens of these states had a direct influence on their own revenue strategies, from the levying of taxes to collection mechanisms to determination of how revenues would be spent. This feature is highlighted by comparison with the experience of the Greek cities subject to the Achaemenid Empire; here, cities were subject to taxes and other mandatory contributions levied by the king as well as by his regional governors (satraps), and they had little or no ability to bargain. Demands of this kind – for tribute, taxes, corvée labor, and gifts – were unknown in Greek states outside the empire, except in those few *poleis* that were governed by tyrants.[16] The closest we come to it in the oligarchic and democratic *poleis* and *koina* is compulsory borrowing by the state from its citizens, which was highly unusual and came in the context of extreme crisis.[17]

It is tempting, based on this contrast, to assume that democratic states in the Greek world essentially voted tax freedom for themselves. Indeed, scholarly orthodoxy within the field of ancient history holds this to be true: since the subject was first studied in the early nineteenth century, it has been widely believed that Athenians (and, by extension, other Greeks) shunned direct taxation as a mark of tyranny.[18] This largely unsubstantiated conclusion has finally begun to be rejected, principally through detailed studies of epigraphic evidence for public finance surviving from *poleis* throughout the Greek world. Overall, however, the Greeks displayed a marked preference for indirect taxation, and it was once suggested that this could be explained in environmental terms: maritime cities had the luxury of collecting only indirect taxes, while inland communities were forced to levy direct taxes on agricultural produce.[19] Yet we can now document the fact that independent Greek cities taxed their citizens directly, and did so quite regularly, in patterns

[16] For the Achaemenid taxation system, see Jursa and Moreno García, Chapter 4 in this volume, and Briant (2002: 67–70, 399–406). [Aristotle], despite recognizing a distinctive "satrapal economy" (*Oeconomica* II.1.4), attributes to Anatolian satraps (II.2.13–14) and Sicilian tyrants (II.2.20) similarly extortionate methods.

[17] Migeotte (1984: 366).

[18] Boeckh (1828 [1817]: 297); Francotte (1909); Andreades (1933: 128); Finley (1985); Hudson (2000).

[19] Pleket (1973: 252).

that do not conform to this hypothesis.[20] What is clear, particularly from a comparative perspective, is that they extracted these revenues in quite distinctive ways. In this chapter I attempt to sketch the outlines of these distinctive patterns, and offer a preliminary explanation for the shape they took.

I suggest that the following six features describe the major characteristics of the fiscal regimes of the Greek *polis* and *koinon*.

(1) While Greek states were willing regularly to levy taxes directly on land and its produce, they preferred other methods of raising revenue when possible.
(2) Direct taxes were also levied episodically to raise revenues for war.
(3) Most indirect taxes were essentially taxes on mobility.
(4) The payment of taxes by citizens was closely associated in Greek thought with the provision of services by the state.
(5) Public debt was widespread in the Greek world, but it cannot be explained simply as a function of crisis or failure in financial planning.
(6) The tax regimes of the independent Greek states were subject to constant negotiation by their citizens.

I discuss each of these characteristics in turn, and then posit an explanation for the distinctive Greek fiscal regime that is (I hope) both theoretically informed and historically situated.

First, a few caveats. The evidence we have for the fiscal practices of the Greek *poleis* and *koina* is extremely uneven and fragmentary. We do not have enough information about any single state (Athens, perhaps, excepted) to describe its fiscal system in detail. We do know a little about a lot of states, however. It is impossible to generate a complete picture of Greek fiscal practices that is correlated to specific political arrangements, therefore, so, instead, I shall outline the fiscal regimes of a *type* of state. Nor do we have quantitative data that can be aggregated to produce a picture of total revenues and expenditures in a particular year, or period, for any single state. And, while there is plentiful evidence for fiscal crises in particular *poleis* and *koina*, it is typically not possible to see whether these crises prompted major changes within the state's fiscal system or prompted fiscal revolution.[21]

[20] Gauthier (1976: 307–10; 1991: 66 n. 84); Gallo (2000); Migeotte (2003). Although direct and indirect taxation are not fiscal categories recognized by the Greeks themselves (Chankowski 2007), I retain them as analytically useful, particularly in a comparative historical volume such as this.

[21] Bonney and Ormrod (1999).

Direct taxation

Taxes levied on a regular basis should contribute to political stability and to fiscal welfare, insofar as they create the potential for financial planning and the calibration of expenditures to revenues. So they represent an important starting point. Independent Greek states regularly levied direct taxes on three things: agricultural produce; livestock and its produce; and, sometimes, people.

Each of the major agricultural products of the Mediterranean was subject to direct taxation in some communities. On Thasos, in the late fifth century, taxes were collected on harvests and vines, though it is unclear whether the land on which they were produced was privately held or public property leased out to farmers; in the latter case the tax could be construed as rent.[22] In the third century the island *polis* of Samos in the eastern Aegean levied a 5 percent tax on grain produced in a territory that it controlled on the opposite mainland, whose inhabitants were almost certainly Samian citizens. The tax was paid in kind, and the grain thus collected was purchased by the state, via elected officials in charge of the grain supply, and distributed to citizens (and no one else) starting around the time of the summer solstice.[23] Citizens, in short, produced the grain, paid the tax, and received free grain, though not in quantities sufficient to meet all their dietary needs.[24] The coastal *polis* of Iasos in Asia Minor levied an 8⅓ percent (one-twelfth) tax on wine produced in its territory.[25] In addition to grain and wine, oil was also normally taxed at inland Pidasa, not far north of Iasos.[26] Citizens cultivating and harvesting tree fruits, including olives, were taxed at a rate higher than 10 percent of their harvest at Telmessos in southern Asia Minor; they also paid out some portion of their grain harvest. Both taxes were probably collected in kind.[27]

Direct taxes on livestock are attested in several cities in Asia Minor, but we do not know whether these were taxes on the animals themselves,

[22] See Salviat (1986: 152–3) (*Supplementum Epigraphicum Graecum* 36.792), with Pleket (1973: 251–2).

[23] *Inscriptiones Graecae* XII(2) 6.1.172 with English translation in Austin (2006: no. 135). See also Migeotte (1989; 1991), Gargola (1992), and Bresson (2000: 254–5). On the status of the dependent territory, Anaia, in the Hellenistic period, see Hallof and Mileta (1997) and Schuler (1998: 177–9). The Athenian grain tax law, which collected tax in kind on grain producers from the dependent islands of Lemnos, Imbros, and Skyros and provided grain (at a price) to Athenian citizens, is in some ways comparable; see Stroud (1998), with more recent discussion by Moreno (2003) and Ober (2008: 260–3).

[24] Migeotte (1991). [25] *Supplementum Epigraphicum Graecum* 41.929.

[26] So we infer from a clause exempting these products from taxation for a short time while Pidasa was integrated politically into the larger *polis* of Miletos in 187: Kawerau and Rehm (1914: no. 149, lines 18–21) = Chandezon (2003: no. 57).

[27] Dittenberger (1903–1905: II, 55).

treated as capital, or on the young they bore during the year, treated as revenue.[28] Elsewhere it is clear that taxes on pastoralists were levied on the revenues derived from herds, including young animals and wool.[29]

Capitation taxes were rare in the Greek world, but that imposed on resident foreigners (metics) at Athens was not the only attested instance, although it is the one about which we are best informed. Elsewhere we find taxes on slaves, but it is possible that, like the taxes on pastoralists, these were taxes on the revenues deriving from the labor of others, in this case slaves.[30] Poll taxes on citizens in Greek cities were unknown.[31]

These examples of direct regular taxation indicate that the phenomenon was somewhat more restricted than indirect taxation (as we shall see in the next section), but the evidence for taxes on agricultural and pastoral produce is widespread enough to cause us to dismiss the old argument that direct taxation was shunned as a mark of tyranny. Direct taxes were also levied by Greek states on an occasional basis in order to meet particular expenses. Most frequently these were associated with war, as in the case of the Athenian *eisphora*, or "contribution."[32] At Potidaia, in northern Greece, a majority voted in a democratic assembly to raise funds for war by a direct tax on citizens based on property assessments; those citizens who did not own any property (land) were obligated to pay a fixed sum of 2 *mnai* (200 drachmas) per head – certainly a rate lower than that levied on property owners.[33] The Achaian *koinon*, a confederation of *poleis* in the Peloponnese (southern Greece), also raised an *eisphora* to meet the expenses of war. In this case, it appears that member *poleis* rather than individual citizens were obligated to contribute, but we do not know whether this meant simply that the *koinon* effectively farmed out the responsibility for collection from citizens to its member *poleis* or whether the tax was paid out of the public treasuries of the *poleis* themselves. What is clear is that the *poleis* expected, having paid this tax, to be defended by the confederate army; when the *koinon* failed to meet this responsibility in the midst of the costly Social War of the late third century, several member *poleis* that were attacked by the enemy refused to pay their taxes to the *koinon* and used the money instead to hire a mercenary force to protect

[28] Chandezon (2003 nos. 53 [Teos], 55 [Priene], 57 [Pidasa], with 313–16).

[29] Ibid.: nos. 39 [Kos], 51 [Aigai/Olympenoi], 53 [Teos]).

[30] See, for example, Dittenberger (1915–1924: no. 1000) for a female slave working in vineyards. See also Bussi (2003).

[31] Gauthier (1991). [32] See Ober, Chapter 16. [33] [Aristotle], *Oeconomica* II.2.5.

their territory.[34] They were not shirking or free-riding; they regarded the federal government as having failed to uphold its side of a bargain. The tax burden of each *polis* may have been determined, as in the case of the citizens of Potidaia, by the collective wealth of the city, determined at least in part by size. In the early fourth century the Boiotian *koinon* in central Greece collected *eisphorai* from its member *poleis* in proportion to the size of their population; and, in third-century Aitolia, *poleis* paid taxes to the *koinon* on a proportional basis tied to representation in the Aitolian council.[35]

Such efforts to correlate a community's tax burden with the combined wealth of its citizens were clearly made in the interests of fairness. Yet, despite these scrupulous arrangements, states sought to avoid imposing the burden of an *eisphora* or other form of direct tax at all if they could find alternative means of funding the war in which they were engaged. The Achaians, still struggling to fund the Social War, were elated when a windfall in the form of plunder allowed them to relieve the *poleis* of the burden of an *eisphora*.[36] This preference for revenues deriving from sources other than direct taxation is further exemplified by the *polis* of Mende in northern Greece, which did not regularly collect property taxes but did keep a register of property owners, who could be taxed in arrears in the event that revenues were needed beyond those provided by harbor and other taxes.[37]

There was one final way in which the Greek states extracted resources directly from their citizens, though it is usually considered a liturgy rather than a form of taxation. When a state needed funds, it sometimes had recourse to an *epidosis*, a contribution. A proposal was made in the democratic assembly to open what has been called a subscription, an account accepting donations to fund a particular project by the state.[38] Following a majority vote in the assembly in favor of the proposal, the fund was opened and contributions were accepted on a voluntary basis from citizens, and occasionally from women and foreigners as well.[39] This

[34] Polybius 4.60.4–5, 10. The mercenaries thus hired by the *polis* of Dyme appear to have been granted citizenship as an additional reward: Rizakis (2008: 49–54 no. 4).

[35] Mackil (2013b: 296–7).

[36] Polybius 5.94.9. The sale of plunder was a widespread, if highly opportunistic, means of funding war; see, for example, Polybius 4.6.3 (Aetolians); Xenophon *Hellenica* 4.1.26, *Lacedaemonian Constitution* 13.11 (Spartans).

[37] [Aristotle], *Oeconomica* II.2.21.

[38] The phenomenon has been studied in detail by Migeotte (1992; see also 1985).

[39] On occasion, contributions were accepted *only* from women, as in second-century Tanagra (Boeotia), where the funds were used to build a temple to the goddesses Demeter and Kore

strategy for raising revenues was adopted primarily in times of peace and prosperity to fund the construction or restoration of fortification walls and temples, or for the purchase of grain by the state. Occasionally, however, it was used like an *eisphora*, to raise funds to meet wartime expenses.[40] The practice is widely attested, from Sicily to Asia Minor, and persisted from the classical period into the Roman Empire. The *epidosis* differed from a tax only in that payment was entirely voluntary; but, like the *eisphora* and other forms of mandatory revenue collection, the decision to raise the revenues had to be approved by a majority in a democratic assembly.

I refer back to my list of principal characteristics of the fiscal regimes of Greek *poleis* and *koina*. This section has illustrated the claims that (1) they were willing regularly to levy taxes directly on land and its produce, but preferred other methods of raising revenue where possible, and that (2) direct taxes were also levied episodically to raise revenues for war. The most widespread alternative method for raising state revenues was indirect taxation.

Indirect taxation

Virtually every Greek city with a decent harbor (and there were many) collected what are generally called harbor taxes – a name that included both import and export taxes. The practice is attested as early as the late seventh century, when the temple of Artemis at Ephesos in Asia Minor recorded among its income "33 mnas of silver from the harbor [tax]."[41] In the classical period the *polis* of Mende in northern Greece, as we have seen, preferred to use the regular income from its harbor taxes and other forms of indirect taxation to fund "the administration of the *polis*" rather than

(Persephone); see Dittenberger (1915–1924: no. 1185), with Knoepfler (1977) for date and Migeotte (1985: 311–13) for discussion.

[40] This may be the mechanism behind the collection of funds and gifts recorded in a fifth-century Spartan inscription, the so-called Spartan War Fund (Meiggs and Lewis 1988: no. 67; Loomis 1992), and in a fourth-century inscription from Thebes (Rhodes and Osborne 2003: no. 57), both of which include gifts from outsiders, including individuals and entire communities, such as the Achaean *epidosis* of 146 (*Inscriptiones Graecae* IV.757) (Maier 1951: no. 32). Defense and other forms of military services were the purpose of the *epidosis* in 24 percent of attested cases, but most of them come from Athens in the form of literary sources, which are not as plentiful for other states, so the figure may be distorted: Migeotte (1992: 327, 346–7).

[41] See Wankel (1979: no. 1A), with recent discussion by Kroll (2008). Collected before the development of coinage, this tax was clearly paid in silver bullion. The harbor and the revenues it generated appear to have remained in the control of the temple: Athenaeus 8.361. For an excellent overview of taxes associated with inter-*polis* exchange, with much more detail than can be offered here, see Bresson (2008: 72–97).

levying property taxes on its citizens.[42] In the third century the island *polis* of Delos charged a 2 percent harbor tax, which certainly included imports and exports, and may also have included transit taxes. For several years we have figures for the total amount of tax revenue thus collected: in 279 almost 14,200 drachmas, and in the following year almost 17,900 drachmas.[43] These figures appear to represent the relatively modest revenues deriving from a small port whose only real significance was that it provided access to the Panhellenic sanctuary of Apollo on the island. By comparison, at a moment when commercial traffic in Athens was depressed by defeat in the Peloponnesian War, the Athenian harbor tax was farmed for 21,600 drachmas, which represented the minimum amount the tax farmers could reasonably expect to collect.[44] Arguably the busiest harbor in the Hellenistic Mediterranean, the island *polis* of Rhodes farmed out its annual harbor dues for 1 million drachmas, a figure that was reduced to 150,000 when, in 167, the Romans diverted commercial traffic away from Rhodes by declaring Delos a free port.[45] This drastically reduced number indicates, by comparison with the Athenian and early Delian figures, a still vigorous trade from which the state derived significant revenues. These are only a few examples of a practice that was so widespread in the Greek world that a coastal *polis* that failed to collect harbor taxes was ridiculed for its stupidity.[46] Import and export taxes could also be levied on goods crossing political boundaries by land.[47] The rationale of taxing one's own exports is less difficult to grasp when we recognize the Greeks' own close association of exports with imports: a city exported what it did *not* need only in order to import what it *did* need.[48] Both activities were vital to a state's survival.[49]

In addition to standard import and export taxes, some states levied transit taxes on commercial goods simply being moved through a port or

[42] [Aristotle], *Oeconomica* II.2.21.

[43] 279: *Inscriptiones Graecae* XI.2.161A ll. 25–6. 278: *Inscriptiones Graecae* XI.2.162A ll. 29–30. See Reger (1994: 254–5).

[44] Andocides, *On the Mysteries* 1.133–4.

[45] Polybius 30.31.10–12.

[46] Strabo 13.3.6 on Aeolian Cyme: "Cyme is ridiculed for its stupidity, owing to the repute, as some say, that not until three hundred years after the founding of the city did they sell the tolls of the harbor, and that before this time the people did not reap this revenue. They got the reputation, therefore, of being a people who learned late that they were living in a city by the sea." See also Purcell (2005: 207–8).

[47] See, for example, *Inscriptiones Graecae* IX.1.98, a treaty between Phocis and Boeotia concluded sometime between 228 and 224, that exempts from these taxes goods being deposited in the other state's territory as a safety measure; clearly, the right is exceptional.

[48] Polybius (4.38.9) praises the Byzantines, who, because of the position of their city, "can readily export all their superfluous produce and import whatever they require on advantageous terms and without any suffering or danger."

[49] Bresson (2000: 109–30).

territory. The *koinon* of the Chalkidians imposed both export and transport taxes on goods purchased from their territory in the early fourth century.[50] The movement of animals across state boundaries in transhumant pastoralist practices was frequently subject to taxation as well.[51] States enjoying a particularly strategic position could profit by taxing merchants who wished to pass through their territory. Corinth, situated on a narrow isthmus that separates the Aegean from the Corinthian Gulf and the Ionian Sea, controlled two harbors, one on each side of the isthmus, and profited handsomely from the trade that passed in both directions. The Corinthians built a stone track (*diolkos*) across the isthmus for hauling goods, and although in literary sources it is described as being used for the transport of warships, it is highly likely that its original purpose was the transport of cargo from one harbor to the other.[52] Those in control of the Bosporus, the narrow body of water from which the Black Sea debouches into the Aegean, could profit similarly from the traffic in goods.[53]

From the beginning of their history Greek *poleis* upheld private property rights and at the same time demarcated some land as public. Such public property became a source of revenue for the state when taxes were levied on its use. Harbor taxes ultimately fall under this rubric. Other examples include taxes charged for the use of public pasturage, for fishing in public waters, and even for the dedication of statues on public land.[54]

While it is impossible to quantify the proportion of revenues derived in any given city from direct and indirect taxes, we have much more evidence for the latter, and, combined with evidence that Greeks avoided direct taxation when there was an alternative means of raising needed revenues, it is probably safe to conclude that indirect taxes were more widespread. And,

[50] Rhodes and Osborne (2003: no. 12). Overland transit taxes were also normally levied by the Thracian kings on goods being exported from their territory toward the sea – a practice attested by exemption in a treaty between a Thracian king and the Greek *emporion* (trading post) at Pistiros; see *Supplementum Epigraphicum Graecum* 43.486, with Chankowski and Domaradzka (1999).

[51] Chandezon (2003: no. 51); this practice is attested by exemption according to the terms of the treaty between the Aeolian *polis* of Aigai and the neighboring Olympenoi (middle of the third century). Elsewhere we find taxes levied on slaves and asses engaged in hauling wood, again attested by special exemption: ibid.: no. 53 line 7).

[52] Strabo (8.6.20). For the commercial uses of the *diolkos*, see Wiseman (1978: 45–50, 74), Cook (1979), MacDonald (1986), and Raepsaet (1993).

[53] The *polis* of Byzantium itself is said to have instituted a 10 percent tax on the profits of its own merchantmen, as well as a 10 percent sales tax, in the late Classical period: [Aristotle], *Oeconomica* II.2.3. During a period of imperial strength the Athenians established a customs house at the Bosporus; see Xenophon, *Hellenica* 1.1.22, 4.8.27, and Ober, Chapter 16. See above, note 48.

[54] Pasturage: Chandezon (2003: nos. 7–9 [Boeotia], 30 [Delos]). Fishing: *Inscriptiones Graecae* XI.2.161A ll. 26–7, 287A ll. 9–10 (Delos); [Aristotle], *Oeconomica* II.2.3 (Byzantium). Statues: Sosin (2005) (Laodicea by the Sea).

while there were a dizzying array of minor, indirect taxes, of which I have tried to give only a sample, the majority of such tax revenues came from harbor and transit taxes. The Greek states, in short, filled their coffers by charging a percentage tax on goods being moved across their boundaries. These were essentially taxes on mobility, (3) in my list of characteristics – a feature of Mediterranean taxation that has recently been highlighted by Nicholas Purcell, and to which I return below.[55]

Revenues, expenditures, and accounting

Despite their preference for avoiding direct taxation when possible, Greeks did not generally regard taxation as a form of theft.[56] Instead, they associated the payment of taxes by citizens with the provision of services by the state – (4) in my list of characteristics. This assumption – or perhaps it was a demand – may explain why the revenues deriving from particular taxes were sometimes earmarked to meet specific expenditures. This is obviously true for the irregular direct taxes levied to fund military efforts, but the phenomenon is particularly significant when it attaches to taxes that were extracted on a regular basis. While the earmarking mentality is at least partly responsible for the huge number of different taxes levied by Greek states, it seems also to be an attempt to stave off fiscal irresponsibility. In an essentially democratic world, a populace will agree to a particular tax only if the majority has been persuaded that the revenues raised thereby will fund some valuable service. Earmarking those revenues was a way of ensuring that would in fact happen. So, in Delphi and in Teos, we know that the revenues deriving from the "doctor tax" (*iatrikon*) were used to provide a salary for a public doctor.[57] On the island of Samos, the revenues of the tax on agricultural producers in a piece of public property on the mainland opposite the island were to be used only for the purchase of grain to be distributed to the citizens.[58] And on Delos, where an

[55] Purcell (2005).

[56] The basic assumption that taxation is theft underlies the influential account of Brennan and Buchanan (1980). Problems and complaints arose particularly when taxes were collected by farmers; see, for example, *Supplementum Epigraphicum Graecum* 48.1404, with Étienne and Migeotte (1998) and Migeotte (2001). Tax-farming was widespread in Greek antiquity, but space constraints prevent me from addressing here the impact of this practice on the broader fiscal regimes of the independent Greek *poleis* and *koina*. My claim does not imply that the Greeks *liked* paying taxes; there is indeed evidence that they sometimes resented it: Heracleides Criticus reviles the taxmen of Oropos (*Brill's New Jacoby* 369A F I.7).

[57] Teos: Chandezon (2003 no. 52, ll. 10–11); Delphi: Dittenberger (1915–1924: no. 437 lines 4–7). See Samama (2003: 50–1) for discussion of this tax, which she argues was probably quite widespread.

[58] See above, note 23.

unusually high number of fiscal records have been preserved, cash was actually placed in pots that were labeled for particular expenditures; most varied from year to year, but both defense and the purchase of grain by the state received permanent earmarks.[59]

The Delian example richly illustrates a broader point: in many, if not all, cases, expenditures were at least in principle limited by revenues. This arrangement certainly led to a straitened ability to spend, which itself sparked a search for other means to fund necessary and desired activities, but it mitigated the politically pernicious problem of high expenditures leading to increased taxation levels. We see this fundamental principle at work in those few public accounts that do survive. An early second-century account kept by the head of the cavalry at Thebes lists revenues and then expenditures; at the end of the year his account was in the black, and the balance was distributed among the cavalry.[60] Several documents from third-century Miletos in Asia Minor point to more complex budgetary practices that make clear the determination of expenditures by known levels of revenue.[61] Such allocations were carefully and rigorously protected.[62] Examples can be multiplied, and have recently been studied to argue, contrary to many scholarly claims, that the finances of Greek cities were *not* hopelessly disorganized.[63] But the evidence seems to me to point toward a much more significant fact: that the Greek cities did not generally raise taxes in order to meet expenses to which they had previously committed themselves, with the exception of wartime levies. This should mean that they avoided that form of fiscal crisis that arises when rulers simply cannot collect revenues adequate to meet their expenditures.[64]

Public debt and credit

The claim that the Greek states linked revenues with expenditures, and more generally planned their budgets, does not mean, however, that such

59 Migeotte (2005; see also 2008). Earmarking was extremely common in the context of euergetism, private gifts to the city that frequently came with specifications about exactly how the funds were to be used, for example to provide oil for the gymnasium or to provide pay for public teachers: Dittenberger (1915–1924: no. 577); Polybius 31.31.1–3. I leave the issue of euergetism aside as ancillary to present concerns, but point out that the mentality is the same in the cases of benefaction and taxation, though in the former it is much easier to implement because the giver can act unilaterally.

60 *Inscriptiones Graecae* VII.2426. See also Roesch (1965: 177–8) and Grandjean (1995).

61 Dittenberger (1903–1905: no. 213); Migeotte (1984: no. 97); Dittenberger (1915–1924: no. 577).

62 Ibid.: no. 577 lines 64–5); Migeotte (1984: no. 97 lines 21–48).

63 See Migeotte (2006), *contra*, for example, Will (1998: 446–52).

64 A major feature of the premodern European public economies studied by Bonney (1995; 1999).

conservative measures were always successful. Evidence for public debt in ancient Greece is plentiful.[65]

Greek states sometimes borrowed money in order to meet the elevated expenses associated with warfare, when regular tax revenues, occasional wartime levies, and public subscriptions either were not options or were insufficient. After two decades of fighting against the Athenian naval empire the Spartans finally agreed to borrow the money they needed to build the fleet that would be necessary to inflict a decisive defeat, and the loan came, awkwardly enough for the Spartans, from an agent of the Persian king.[66] At the end of the fourth century Peloponnesian Argos borrowed from the island *polis* of Rhodes to meet the expense of restoring its fortification walls and rebuilding its cavalry during a war.[67] Loans were usually made for fixed terms, and, though many lenders were honored by cities as benefactors for forgiving part or all of the loan, or for extending the term of repayment, they did in general expect to be repaid. When cities defaulted on their loans, creditors could and did seize the assets they had offered as security, including public revenues and buildings.[68]

War was not the only pressure that drove Greek states to borrow money, however. The provision of grain was another major public expense that sometimes caused them to incur debts. The *polis* of Klazomenai in Asia Minor, experiencing a shortage of both grain and cash, resolved that all private citizens with stores of olive oil should lend it to the *polis* at interest. This stored oil was then used by the state as security for the purchase of grain from abroad on credit. The same city, whether at the same time or not, was so strapped for cash that it persuaded its wealthiest citizens to exchange the local silver coinage in their possession for an iron coinage of the same face value. This was, in fact, a loan, for the city did over time return the silver and recall the iron currency. But it is certain that those who voted in favor of this proposal were not necessarily going to be subject to the demand themselves.[69] The loan of stored oil made the city a credible borrower when it needed to acquire grain for its citizens. The small

[65] *Contra* Hudson (2000: 6, 16–20). The evidence has been collected by Migeotte (1984).

[66] See Thucydides 8.58.5–6 for the loan from Tissaphernes in 412: Migeotte (1984: no. 23). The Spartans and their allies had considered the possibility of borrowing the funds laid up in the panhellenic sanctuaries at Delphi and Olympia in order to build a navy at the outset of the war (432), but rejected the idea: Thucydides 1.121.3, 143.1 (Migeotte 1984: no. 22).

[67] Ibid.: no. 19 = Maier (1951: no. 33).

[68] Migeotte (1980; 1984: 395–6).

[69] [Aristotle], *Oeconomica* II.2.16.

Boiotian *polis* of Chorsiai accepted loans of both grain and cash from a foreigner, and the city of Samos twice took out loans from a wealthy private individual for the purchase of grain for the city.[70]

Arkesine, a small *polis* on the Aegean island of Amorgos, borrowed repeatedly over a period of perhaps fifty years. Its creditors, when we know about them, were private individuals from other *poleis*. Six loan contracts from Arkesine survive, some in highly fragmentary states, but one preserves plentiful details: Arkesine borrowed a large sum of cash at an annual interest rate of 10 percent. The loan was, remarkably, guaranteed on "all the public property of the polis, and all the private property, terrestrial and maritime, of the citizens and residents of Arkesine."[71] The fact that so much collateral was offered explains why the loan made by the creditor is described as "entirely lacking in risk." But the cumulative value of such property must have been considerably higher than the principal and the interest combined, and this in itself suggests that Arkesine was actively leveraging its debt, borrowing money only to lend it out at a higher interest rate than that paid to the initial creditor.[72] Of course, leveraging debts is a risky strategy, and it is not surprising to find that another creditor of Arkesine imposed a higher interest rate – 12 percent – probably as a risk premium.[73] Four of the six surviving contracts state explicitly that the state had other outstanding debts.

Does this dossier reflect crisis? Unlike the cases of Sparta, Argos, Klazomenai, Samos, and Chorsiai, we know of no specific expense that drove Arkesine to borrow money. The hints that Arkesine was in fact borrowing money from private individuals only in order to lend it out again at a higher interest rate points to an innovation that was highly significant in the history of Greek fiscal regimes: during the Hellenistic period, states began to realize that they could generate revenue by making loans, just as private bankers and entrepreneurs had been doing for centuries.[74] In other words, the Arkesine dossier suggests that cities sometimes borrowed money not because they were experiencing crisis but because they were seeking an opportunity to generate revenues. It is not clear that this innovation was ever institutionalized in a formal way at Arkesine, but in other cities it took the form of a public bank. Our clearest

[70] Migeotte (1984: no. 10 [Chorsiai], no. 67 [Samos]). [71] Ibid.: no. 49 lines 8–9.

[72] The same conclusion is reached by Gabrielsen (2005), on the grounds that the officials in charge of the borrowing were called *daneistai*, which means not *borrowers* but *lenders*.

[73] Migeotte (1984: no. 50).

[74] Chankowski (2008) emphasizes that public officials must have learned the accounting techniques that we begin to see in the Hellenistic period from private entrepreneurs; her case study is Delos.

example comes from Miletos in Asia Minor.[75] At the end of the third century capital was accumulated by inviting citizens to make permanent, interest-bearing deposits in the public bank. After meeting deficits in current public expenditures, the bank put the money to work.[76] We do not know what interest rates they charged, but we can calculate that they would have broken even, or indeed made a profit, by charging the prevailing interest rates of 10 to 12 percent. The case of the public bank at Miletos reveals a problem that appears to have been faced by an increasing number of cities in the Hellenistic period: public revenues were falling short, but citizens themselves had plenty of money, and were willing to loan it out. The development of a public bank allowed states to increase revenues that were not subject to interest and repayment, and to regularize their payment.[77] This had the additional advantage of facilitating financial planning insofar as such credit operations yielded regular streams of revenue.[78] So it is true that public debt – (5) in my list of principal characteristics – was widespread in the Greek world, but it is not always to be explained as a function of crisis or failure in financial planning.

Fiscal negotiations

The decree of Miletos by which the public bank was established preserves the motives for the innovation: there were deficits in public revenues for the current year, but the citizens were unwilling to fill them by raising an *eisphora* or by reducing the wages of public employees. Accumulating capital reserves and lending money at interest became an alternative to direct taxation not because the latter was impossible but because the people of Miletos, who had sovereignty over their own financial affairs, preferred it. At the end of the third century the Lykian *polis* of Xanthos in Asia Minor had resolved not to levy any new taxes for nine years; the city was at the time heavily indebted and had recently raised an *eisphora*.[79] Clearly, the citizens' willingness to pay taxes had reached its limit. What is interesting is

[75] Migeotte (1984: no. 97).

[76] Migeotte (1984: 309) suggests that, after meeting their deficits, the Milesians left the money sitting in the bank. But, as Gabrielsen (2005: 148–9) has pointed out, the payment of annuities to those who had made the initial deposits would have depleted the entire fund in only ten years. We know that in subsequent years Miletos was lending money: Wiegand (1958: nos. 488.3–5, 19–32).

[77] Gabrielsen (2005: 147).

[78] Faraguna (2008) has shown that such calculations were possible even before the development of public banks; smaller, less formal credit operations essentially worked in the same way, and can be traced back at least to the fifth century.

[79] Bousquet (1988: lines 53–5).

that they were simply able, having reached their limit, to draw a line and insist that, when additional revenues were needed, they would have to be found by some other means. These are negotiations about citizens' willingness to pay, embedded in contexts of financial strain. Two episodes in the history of the Achaian *koinon* show that negotiations about the payment of taxes also touched on issues of justice, however.

The first is an episode I have already mentioned: several *poleis* of western Achaia were invaded by hostile forces during a war in the late third century, and appealed for defensive assistance to the federal government. Their request was refused, on the grounds that the entire federal army had already been mobilized, while the state (*koinon*) was behind in paying its mercenaries from a previous war. The *poleis* that had been attacked resolved not to pay their *eisphorai* to the *koinon*, instead using the money to pay a mercenary force of their own.[80] By withdrawing their tax revenues, these *poleis* effectively held the *koinon* to account for failing to provide the services they were obligated to render when it received those revenues from its member *poleis*. Far from sparking the breakdown of the Achaian *koinon*, the cities' refusal clearly prompted a round of negotiations, for we know that they were quickly restored to full membership in the *koinon*, which implies that amends were made. A few decades later, Messene, a city in the southern Peloponnese, revolted from the Achaian *koinon*, which waged a bitter war to regain this strategically vital member. When the city was restored as a member of the *koinon*, the terms of the settlement included the grant of "tax immunity for three years, so that the destruction of the territory [of Messene inflicted during the war] would harm the Achaians no less than the Messenians."[81] The federal tax regime thus became subject to the negotiations by which a rebel city was restored. The war waged against Messene had been costly, and the *koinon* was eager to demonstrate that it treated its member states with equity rather than imperiousness.

Thus, for purely financial reasons as well as for reasons of justice and equity – (6) in my list of characteristics – the tax regimes of the independent Greek states were subject to constant negotiation by their citizens, the principals of the government who both "control and benefit from the organization of the state."[82] They bargained with each other, and, when they chose to forestall the collection of additional taxes, they were effectively choosing to limit their own power by limiting the power of the state.

[80] Polybius 4.60.1–5, 10. [81] Polybius 24.2.3. [82] Levi (1988: 3).

Explaining Greek fiscal regimes

The extent to which the levels and manner of taxation by Greek states was subject to frequent negotiation by their citizens is striking, particularly from a comparative perspective. Decrees prohibiting additional tax levies, or ruling them out as possible remedies for shortfall, point to the power of the citizens as constituents of the state, which can be said, with Margaret Levi, to act as a constraint on the ruling majority.[83] What is unusual in early fiscal history, it seems, is the identity of the constituents and the ruling majority. That identity is partly a function of democracy, which explains several of the distinctive characteristics of Greek fiscal regimes: the constant negotiation ((6) in my list of characteristics); the preference for raising revenue by means other than direct taxation (1) except when war threatened the very existence of the state and made direct taxation more acceptable (2); and the close association of the payment of taxes with the provision of services by the state (4). Bound up in these characteristics were the democratic practice of citizen administration and the value of accountability. Like the audits to which magistrates who handled public funds were subject at the end of their term of office, the insistence that tax revenues should be deployed to provide services deemed beneficial by the majority was a product of a culture of governmental accountability. It was, furthermore, a stated aim of democratic public officials to balance revenues and expenditures.[84] The democracies of the Greek world were, for the most part, remarkably stable – a fact that seems to contribute, as Levi has suggested in theoretical terms, to their relatively low levels of taxation (low discount rates).[85]

Democracy does not on its own explain all the characteristics of Greek fiscal regimes, however. The fact that most tax revenues derived from indirect taxes, which in their particular manifestations (import, export, and transport) were essentially taxes on mobility ((3) in my list), can be accounted for only by the intersection of two further conditions: the extreme political fragmentation of the Mediterranean (over 1,000 *poleis*) and its extreme ecological fragmentation, which mandated exchange, transhumance, and other economic strategies requiring movement beyond the bounds of a single *polis*.[86] The need to import, export, and transport goods was universal, and this very fact presented an opportunity for the

[83] Levi (1988). [84] Xenophon, *Memorabilia* III.6; Aristotle, *Rhetoric* I.4.1359b.

[85] I have intentionally excluded from this chapter consideration of the tax regimes of Greek tyrants, but this material would further support Levi's model of the predatory ruler.

[86] Horden and Purcell (2000).

Greek states to generate revenue in a way that was consistent with the democratic principle of providing services in exchange for revenues: taxes could be collected in exchange for the use of harbor facilities, which had to be developed in any case for defensive purposes as well as to enable the trade on which Greek cities relied. This opportunism may have built upon the fact that collecting taxes at the point of production – i.e. collecting direct taxes – was both difficult and unpredictable, in a world in which agricultural yield varied greatly from year to year. The political and ecological fragmentation of the Mediterranean also, I submit, spurred the development of the credit markets that made public debt, in contexts of both crisis and opportunity, a feasible fiscal strategy.

References

Andreades, A. M. (1933) *A History of Greek Public Finance*. Cambridge, MA.

Austin, M. M. (2006) *The Hellenistic World from Alexander to the Roman Conquest: A Selection of Ancient Sources in Translation*. Cambridge.

Boeckh, A. (1828 [1817]) *The Public Economy of Athens; To Which Is Added, A Dissertation on the Silver Mines of Laurion*, 4 vols., trans. and ed. G. Cornewall Lewis. London.

Bonney, R. (ed.) (1995) *Economic Systems and State Finance*. Oxford.

(ed.) (1999) *The Rise of the Fiscal State in Europe* c. *1200–1815*. Oxford.

Bonney, R., and Ormrod, W. M. (1999) "Introduction: crises, revolutions and self-sustained growth: towards a conceptual model of change in fiscal history," in *Crises, Revolutions and Self-Sustained Growth: Essays in European Fiscal History, 1130–1830*, ed. W. M. Ormrod, M. Bonney, and R. Bonney. Stamford, UK: 1–21.

Bousquet, J. (1988) "La stèle des Kyténiens au Létôon de Xanthos," *Revue des études grecques* 101: 12–53.

Brennan, G., and Buchanan, J. M. (1980) *The Power to Tax: Analytical Foundations of a Fiscal Constitution*. Cambridge.

Bresson, A. (2000) *La cité marchande*. Bordeaux.

(2008) *L'économie de la Grèce des cités*, vol. II, *Les espaces de l'échange*. Paris.

Briant, P. (2002) *From Cyrus to Alexander: A History of the Persian Empire*. Winona Lake, IN.

Bussi, S. (2003) "Schiavi: prezzi e tasse sul lavoro," in *Donna e lavoro nella documentazione epigrafica*, ed. A. Buonopane and F. Cenerini. Faenza, Italy: 277–86.

Cahill, N., and Kroll, J. H. (2005) "New archaic coin finds at Sardis," *American Journal of Archaeology* 109: 589–616.

Chandezon, C. (2003) *L'élevage en Grèce (fin Ve – fin Ier s. aC): l'apport des sources épigraphiques*. Bordeaux.

Chaniotis, A. (2005) *War in the Hellenistic World: A Social and Cultural History.* Oxford.

Chankowski, V. (2007) "Les catégories du vocabulaire de la fiscalité dans les cités grecques," in *Vocabulaire et expression de l'économie dans le monde antique*, ed. J. Andreau and V. Chankowski. Bordeaux: 299–331.

(2008) "Banquiers, caissiers, comptable: à propos des methods financiers dans les comptes de Délos," in *Πιστοὶ διὰ τὴν τέχνην: Bankers, Loans, and Archives in the Ancient World: Studies in Honour of Raymond Bogaert*, ed. K. Verboven, K. Vandorpe, and V. Chankowski. Leuven: 77–91.

Chankowski, V., and Domaradzka, L. (1999) "Réédition de l'inscription de Pistiros et problèmes d'interprétation," *Bulletin de Correspondance Hellénique* 123: 247–58.

Cook, R. M. (1979) "Archaic Greek trade: three conjectures," *Journal of Hellenic Studies* 99: 152–5.

Cowell, M. R., and Hyne, K. (2000) "Scientific examination of the Lydian precious metal coinages," in *King Croesus' Gold: Excavations at Sardis and the History of Gold Refining*, ed. A. Ramage and P. Craddock. Cambridge, MA: 169–74.

De Callataÿ, F. (2006) "Réflexions quantitatives sur l'or et l'argent monnayé à l'époque hellénistique: pompes, triomphes, réquisitions, fortunes des temples, orfèvrerie et masses métalliques disponibles," in *Approches de l'économie hellénistique*, ed. R. Descat. Saint-Bertrand-de-Comminges, France: 37–84.

(2008) "La monnaie de compte à l'époque hellénistique: le nécessaire réexamen des textes (en particulier du sense du terme argurion) à la lumière de la documentation numismatique," *Annali del Istituto Italiano di Numismatica* 54: 19–34.

(2011) "Quantifying monetary production in Greco-Roman times: a general frame," in *Quantifying Monetary Supplies in Greco-Roman Times*, ed. F. de Callataÿ. Bari: 7–29.

Dittenberger, W. (1903–1905) *Orientis Graeci Inscriptiones Selectae*, 2 vols. Leipzig.

(1915–1924) *Sylloge Inscriptionum Graecarum*, 3rd edn, 4 vols. Leipzig.

Étienne, R., and Migeotte, L. (1998) "Colophon et les abus des fermiers des taxes," *Bulletin de correspondance hellénique* 122: 143–57.

Faraguna, M. (2008) "Calcolo economico, archivi finanziari e credito," in *Πιστοὶ διὰ τὴν τέχνην: Bankers, Loans, and Archives in the Ancient World: Studies in Honour of Raymond Bogaert*, ed. K. Verboven, K. Vandorpe, and V. Chankowski. Leuven: 33–57.

Finley, M. I. (1985) *The Ancient Economy*. London.

Francotte, H. (1909) *Les finances des cités grecques*. Paris.

Gabrielsen, V. (2005) "Banking and credit operations in Hellenistic times," in *Making, Moving, and Managing: The New World of Ancient Economies, 323–31 BC*, ed. Z. H. Archibald, J. K. Davies, and V. Gabrielsen. Oxford: 136–64.

Gallo, L. (2000) "L'imposte dirette nelle *poleis* greche: un istituto tirannico?," *Minima Epigraphica et Papyrologica* 3: 17–36.

Gargola, D. J. (1992) "Grain distributions and the revenue of the Temple of Hera on Samos," *Phoenix* 66: 12–28.

Gauthier, P. (1976) *Commentaire historique des Poroi de Xénophon*. Geneva.

(1991) "*Ἀτέλεια τοῦ σώματος* [Exemption of the person]," *Chiron* 21: 49–68.

Grandjean, C. (1995) "Les comptes de Pompidas (*IG* VII 2426): drachmes d'argent symmachique et drachmes de bronze," *Bulletin de correspondance hellénique* 119: 1–21.

Hallof, K., and Mileta, C. (1997) "Samos und Ptolemaios III: ein neues Fragment zu en samischen Volksbeschluß AM 72, 1957, 226 nr. 59," *Chiron* 27: 255–85.

Hansen, M. H. (1986) *Demography and Democracy: The Number of Athenian Citizens in the Fourth Century BC*. Herning, Denmark.

(1988) *Three Studies in Athenian Demography*. Copenhagen.

(ed.) (2000) *A Comparative Study of Thirty City-State Cultures*. Copenhagen.

(2006) *The Shotgun Method: The Demography of the Ancient Greek City-State Culture*. Columbia, MO.

Hansen, M. H., and Nielsen, T. H. (eds.) (2004) *An Inventory of Archaic and Classical Poleis: An Investigation Conducted by the Copenhagen Polis Centre for the Danish National Research Foundation*. Oxford.

Horden, P., and Purcell, N. (2000) *The Corrupting Sea: A Study of Mediterranean History*. Oxford.

Hudson, M. (2000) "Mesopotamia and classical antiquity," in *Land-Value Taxation around the World*, 3rd edn, ed. R. V. Andelson. Oxford: 3–25.

Kawerau, G., and Rehm, A. (1914) *Ergebnisse der Ausgrabungen und Untersuchungen seit dem Jahre 1899*, vol. III, *Das Delphinion in Milet*. Berlin.

Kim, H. (2001) "Archaic coinage as evidence for the use of money," in *Money and Its Uses in the Ancient Greek World*, ed. A. Meadows and K. Shipton. Oxford: 7–22.

Knoepfler, D. (1977) "Zur Datierung der großen Inschrift aus Tanagra im Louvre," *Chiron* 7: 67–87.

Kroll, J. H. (2008) "The monetary use of weighed bullion in Archaic Greece," in *The Monetary Systems of the Greeks and Romans*, ed. W. V. Harris. Oxford: 12–37.

Kurke, L. (1999) *Coins, Bodies, Games, and Gold: The Politics of Meaning in Archaic Greece*. Princeton, NJ.

Levi, M. (1988) *Of Rule and Revenue*. Berkeley, CA.

Loomis, W. T. (1992) *The Spartan War Fund:* IG *V.1.1 and a New Fragment*. Stuttgart.

Ma, J. (1999) *Antiochos III and the Cities of Asia Minor*. Oxford.

(2000) "Fighting *poleis* of the Hellenistic world," in *War and Violence in Archaic Greece*, ed. H. van Wees. London: 337–76.

MacDonald, B. R. (1986) "The Diolkos," *Journal of Hellenic Studies* 106: 191–5.

Mackil, E. (2013a) "The Greek *koinon*," in *The Oxford Handbook of the State in the Ancient Near East and Mediterranean*, ed. P. F. Bang and W. Scheidel. New York: 304–23.

(2013b) *Creating a Common Polity: Religion, Economy, and Politics in the Making of the Greek Koinon*. Berkeley, CA.

Maier, F. G. (1951) *Griechische Mauerbauinschriften*. Heidelberg.

Martin, T. R. (1985) *Sovereignty and Coinage in Classical Greece*. Princeton, NJ.

Meiggs, R., and Lewis, D. M. (1988) *Greek Historical Inscriptions to the End of the Fifth Century BC*, rev. edn. Oxford.

Migeotte, L. (1980) "Engagement et saisie de biens publics dans les cités grecques," in *Mélanges d'études anciennes offerts à M. Lebel*, ed. J.-B. Caron, M. Fortin, and G. Maloney. Quebec: 161–71.

(1984) *L'emprunt public dans les cités grecques: recueil des documents et analyse critique*. Quebec.

(1985) "Souscriptions publiques en Béotie," in *La Béotie antique: Lyon–Saint-Étienne 16–20 mai 1983*, ed. P. Roesch and G. Argoud. Paris: 311–16.

(1989) "Distributions de grain à Samos à la période hellénistique: le 'pain gratuit' pour tous?" *Sacris Erudiri: Jaarboek voor Godsdienstwetenschappen* 31: 297–308.

(1991) "Le pain quotidien dans les cités hellénistiques: à propos des fonds permanents pour l'approvisionnement en grain," *Cahiers du Centre Gustave Glotz* 2: 19–41.

(1992) *Les souscriptions publiques dans les cités grecques*. Geneva.

(2001) "Quelques aspects légaux et juridiques de l'affermage des taxes en Grèce ancienne," in *Symposion 1997: Vorträge zur griechischen und hellenistischen Rechtsgeschichte*, ed. E. Cantarella and G. Thür. Cologne: 165–74.

(2003) "Taxation directe en Grèce ancienne," in *Symposion 1999: Vorträge zur griechischen und hellenistischen Rechtsgeschichte*, ed. G. Thür and F. J. F. Nieto. Cologne: 297–313.

(2005) "La διάταξις de Délos durant l'indépendance: un budget pour la cité?," *Les études classiques* 73: 27–38.

(2006) "La planification des dépenses publiques dans les cités hellénistiques," in *Studi ellenistici XIX*, ed. B. Virgilio. Pisa: 77–97.

(2008) "La comptabilité publique dans les cités grecques: l'exemple de Delos," in Πιστοὶ διὰ τὴν τεχνήν: *Bankers, Loans, and Archives in the Ancient World: Studies in Honour of Raymond Bogaert*, ed. K. Verboven, K. Vandorpe, and V. Chankowski. Leuven: 59–76.

Moreno, A. (2003) "Athenian bread-baskets: the grain-tax law of 374/3 BC reinterpreted," *Zeitschrift für Papyrologie und Epigraphik* 145: 97–106.

Ober, J. (2008) *Democracy and Knowledge: Innovation and Learning in Classical Athens*. Princeton, NJ.

Pleket, H. W. (1973) "Economic history of the ancient world and epigraphy: some introductory remarks," in *Akten des VI. internationalen Kongresses für griechische und lateinische Epigraphik München 1972*. Munich: 243–57.

Purcell, N. (2005) "The ancient Mediterranean: the view from the customs house," in *Rethinking the Mediterranean*, ed. W. V. Harris. Oxford: 200–34.

Raepsaet, G. (1993) "Le diolkos de l'isthme à Corinthe: son tracé, son fonctionnement," *Bulletin de correspondance hellénique* 117: 233–61.

Reger, G. (1994) *Regionalism and Change in the Economy of Independent Delos, 314–167 BC.* Berkeley, CA.

Rhodes, P. J., and Osborne, R. (2003) *Greek Historical Inscriptions, 404–323 BC.* Oxford.

Rizakis, A. D. (2008) *Achaïe III: les cités achéennes: épigraphie et histoire.* Athens.

Roesch, P. (1965) *Thespies et la confédération béotienne.* Paris.

Runciman, W. G. (1990) "Doomed to extinction: the *polis* as an evolutionary dead-end," in *The Greek City: From Homer to Alexander*, ed. O. Murray and S. Price. Oxford: 347–67.

Salviat, F. (1986) "Le vin de Thasos: amphores, vin et sources écrites," in *Recherches sur les amphores grecques: actes du colloque international organisé par le Centre national de la recherche scientifique, l'Université de Rennes II et l'École française d'Athènes*, ed. J.-Y. Empereur and Y. Garlan. Athens: 145–96.

Samama, E. (2003) *Les médicins dans le monde grec: sources épigraphiques sur la naissance d'un corps médical.* Geneva.

Schuler, C. (1998) Ländziche *Siedlungen und Gemeinden im hellenistischen und römischen Kleinasien.* Munich.

Sosin, J. (2005) "Unwelcome dedications: public law and private religion in Hellenistic Laodicea by the sea," *Classical Quarterly* 55: 130–9.

Stroud, R. S. (1998) *The Athenian Grain-Tax Law of 374/3 BC.* Princeton, NJ.

Thür, G., and Stumpf, G. (1989) "Sechs Todesurteile und zwei plattierte Hemidrachmen aus Dyme: zu Syll.3 530, Munzkabinette Athen nr. 4046 und München, Dyme 12," *Tyche* 4: 171–83.

Tilly, C. (1992) *Coercion, Capital, and European States: AD 990–1992*, rev edn. Malden, MA.

Wankel, H. (1979) *Inschriften griechischer Städte aus Kleinasien,* vol. XI, *Die Inschriften von Ephesos: Teil Ia, nr. 1–47 (Texte).* Bonn.

Wiegand, T. (1958) *Didyma,* vol. II, *Die Inschriften von Albert Rehm,* ed. R. Harder. Berlin.

Will, E. (1998) *Historica Graeco-Hellenistica: choix d'écrits 1953–1993.* Paris.

Wiseman, J. (1978) *The Land of the Ancient Corinthians.* Gothenburg.

CHAPTER 16

Classical Athens

Josiah Ober

Athenian public finance has been the object of intensive study ever since August Boeckh's classic work of the early nineteenth century; this chapter offers an overview of major issues in the scholarship, but does not pretend to be a comprehensive literature review. The classical period encompasses the fifth and fourth centuries BC. All non-bibliographic dates are BC, unless otherwise specified.[1]

Economic and political background

In the relatively well documented fourth century there were around 1,000 to 1,100 city states (*poleis*); the greater Greek world (Greek mainland and eastern Mediterranean islands, many coastal areas of the Black and Mediterranean Seas), had a population of about 8 to 10 million persons.

[1] Important studies (focusing chiefly on those published in the last thirty years) on Greek, and especially Athenian, public finance include works by the following authors: Boeckh (1828 [1817]) – a general survey, defining the field; Andreades (1933) – still in some ways the most complete survey; Brun (1983) – direct taxes; Migeotte (1984) – documents related to taxation; (1992) – voluntary contributions to public projects; Burke (1985); French (1991) – the Athenian economy and finances in the fourth century; Kallet (1993; 2001) – Thucydides and Peloponnesian War finances; Vannier (1988) – discourse on public finance and private wealth; Gabrielsen (1994) – naval finance; (2013) – survey of finance in Greek cities; Langdon (1994) – sales of goods confiscated from convicted criminals; Lambert (1997) – sales of public assets; Bresson (2000: 243–61) – indirect taxes; Loomis (1998) – welfare costs; Samons (2000) – fifth-century imperial finances, with special reference to temple funds; Davies (2004) – fiscal expertise; Blok (2010) – local deme finances; Williams (2011) – the leasing of sacred properties by state and cult associations; Ismard (2010) – the finances of local associations; Wilson (2008; 2010) – festival expenses; Oliver (2007) – grain imports; Pritchard (2007; 2012) – military and festival spending; Bissa (2008) – government intervention in foreign trade; Kyriazis (2009) – a survey from the perspective of social science; Christ (2007) – direct taxes; Lyttkens (2012) – taxation and expenses; and Rhodes (2013) – a general survey of the evidence. The essays collected by Osborne and Hornblower (1994) have much of value. A collection of essays tentatively entitled *The Business of State: Public Finance in Ancient Athens, 594 BC to AD 14*, edited by H. v. Wees, P. J. Rhodes, D. M. Pritchard, P. Fawcett, and G. J. Oliver, has been announced. My thanks go to Alain Bresson, François de Callataÿ, Vincent Gabrielsen, Paulin Ismard, Nikolaos Kyriazis, Carl Hampus Lyttkens, David Pritchard, and P. J. Rhodes for sharing work in advance of publication, bibliography, and guesses/estimates of Athenian expenses and income.

Mainland Greece and the Aegean islands (*c.* 3 to 3.5 million persons) were densely populated, well above the likely carrying capacity of *c.* 2.2 million, meaning that substantial food imports were essential. The Greek world was highly urbanized by the standards of premodern societies: By the fourth century probably at least 30 percent of Greeks lived in towns of 5,000 inhabitants or larger. The ancient Greek *polis* world appears to be among the most urbanized regions of the world in premodernity.[2]

This dense and urbanized population was made possible by 500 years (*c.* 800 to 300) of sustained economic growth. In this period Greece experienced substantial demographic growth (at least one order of magnitude) and relatively high per capita GDP growth (estimated at 0.15 percent per annum), resulting in aggregate growth that probably approached 1 percent per annum. These rates are higher than those estimated for most other premodern societies.[3]

Compared to most premodern polities, Greek states were unusually egalitarian, in terms of both cultural norms and institutional rules.[4] The most common form of state government was some version of citizen republic: moderate oligarchy (franchise limited by wealth, with perhaps one of three to five native males enfranchised) to democracy (full native male franchise with minimal or no property qualification).

Democratic Athens was among the largest of the *poleis*, and by far the best documented. Athens was also, by various measures, the highest-performing of the *poleis* in terms of security, wealth, and cultural influence.[5] The total Athenian population in the fourth century was in the region of 250,000; of these, around 30,000 were citizens (adult native males); some 15,000 were resident foreigners; and perhaps 80,000 were slaves.[6] Athenian wealth and income distribution were strikingly egalitarian, with some 40 to 60 percent of the total Athenian population (including slaves) living at a decent "middling" level above subsistence.[7] By comparison, some 6 to 12 percent of the population of the Roman Empire lived at a similar "decent middling" level.[8]

Greek states existed in conditions of vigorous interstate competition, both between *poleis* and with predatory imperial states on the frontiers (especially Persia to the east, Carthage to the south, and, later, Macedon to the north and Rome to the west). State death was a relatively common result of competition among *poleis* and with extra-Greek rivals. The

[2] Hansen (2006b; 2008). [3] Morris (2004); Bresson (2007); Ober (2010). [4] Runciman (1990).
[5] Ober (2008). [6] Hansen (2006a; 2006b). [7] Scheidel (2010); Ober (2010).
[8] Scheidel and Friesen (2009).

destruction of urban infrastructure was even more common. *Poleis* could also be severely weakened by civil conflict, especially between factions favoring oligarchy or democracy. Darwinian pressure drove adaptive efficiency in the domain of state governance, as individual *poleis* sought innovative institutional solutions to a constantly shifting menu of external and internal threats. Meanwhile, the Greek world was a fairly homogeneous culture zone, featuring shared language and religion, as well as shared disease pools and similar climatic conditions. Communication across state borders was easy, and interchange (trade, diplomacy, religious cult) was constant, even in time of war. Interstate learning was thus relatively seamless; there is considerable evidence for both material technology and social institutions spreading very quickly through the Greek world and beyond.[9]

Fiscal regimes in the classical Greek world, and especially in Athens, were shaped by the imperative for adaptive efficiency in an environment that was at once highly competitive and marked by high levels of institutional innovation and interstate learning. Athens' fiscal institutions changed substantially over the course of the classical period (from about 500 to 300) and appear to have been an important contributory cause (though not the unique cause) of the relative success of Athens in the competitive city-state environment. Both in the imperial fifth century and in the post-imperial fourth century innovative fiscal institutions enabled the Athenian state to secure revenues adequate to provide a relatively high level of public goods, including security and welfare. The operation of the Athenian fiscal system was essential to sustaining the socio-political stability of the state. Especially in the fourth century, Athens depended on the regular direct taxation of wealthy citizens. Taxation of the rich ensured national security, sustained the state religion, and kept the government running. Taxation served a distributive function, in that poorer citizens were paid to serve in the military, to attend festivals, and to fulfill various civic and governmental functions. The role of taxation and redistribution in preserving the Athenian social equilibrium is discussed in the section entitled "Revenues, taxes, and the Athenian social equilibrium."

Athenian history

Athens had emerged from a long "dark age" by about 750 as a distinct region of central Greece whose residents shared a local identity marked by a

[9] Ober (2008; 2010).

shared dialect and cults. The eighth-century Athenian elite failed to establish a stable rent-extracting "natural state,"[10] in part because of egalitarian norms/aspirations that had crystallized by the end of the dark age and were retained in the centuries that followed.[11] The upshot was a series of political/legal reforms between about 600 and 500 BC, culminating in an Athenian political order in which all adult males were enfranchised citizens, ergo *dêmokratia* in fact (if not yet in name).

Athens' new democratic government performed remarkably well. High levels of citizen mobilization enabled Athens to push back threats from regional rivals Sparta, Chalcis, and Aegina. Athens later allied with key rivals (Sparta, Aegina, Corinth) to defeat a large-scale invasion launched by imperial Persia. After 478, in the aftermath of the Persian Wars, Athens built up a defensive league of states. This "Delian League" quickly morphed into an Athenian Empire. At the height of the empire Athens dominated perhaps 30 percent of Greeks. Athens' imperial age, which lasted until the final years of the fifth century, was prosperous, in part because of rents extracted from subject states. During the imperial era Athens also engaged in extensive military activity and public building, expanded the provision of public goods, and elaborated democratic institutions. The years 431 to 404 witnessed a struggle between imperial Athens and Sparta (at the head of a Peloponnesian coalition), famously recorded by Thucydides. Ultimately Athens lost the war, and with it the empire.

In the aftermath of the Peloponnesian War Athens suffered a brief, intense, period of civil strife, and a longer period during which its population and economy were reduced in size. Yet recovery, political and economic, was relatively quick. Athens retained a few overseas possessions (see below) from which rents were extracted via tax-farming, and for a time engaged in quasi-imperial rent-seeking in the northern and central Aegean. This culminated in the financially debilitating "Social War" of the mid-350s. Yet throughout the fourth century most Athenian revenues were raised through indirect taxes (notably harbor dues and a head tax on resident aliens), resource revenue (notably from silver mines: the government owned mineral rights), and direct taxes on wealth (levied uniquely upon the wealthiest Athenians).

Athens' democratic political institutions evolved in the post-imperial era, as did its fiscal institutions. The results (by the 330s) were state revenues and prosperity rivaling those of the era of the high empire. Athens was defeated militarily by Macedon in 338 and (along with almost

[10] North, Wallis, and Weingast (2009). [11] Morris (1987).

all other mainland Greek states) joined the Macedonian-led League of Corinth. By the end of the fourth century the Macedonians had ended Athens' democratic government. With the new conditions of the Hellenistic world, the context of public finance in Athens and the other Greek states, like much else in the Greek world, had changed in substantial ways.[12] Some fourth-century innovations in Athenian public finance were adopted, however, and adapted to a much larger scale, by the Hellenistic kingdoms of the third and second centuries.[13]

Athenian government

In the imperial fifth century and post-imperial fourth century alike, Athens was governed by a participatory democracy. Legislation was passed by majority vote of a citizen assembly, meeting (in the fourth century) forty times each year and attended by some 6,000 to 8,000 citizens.[14] The administration of government was, in the main, by citizen-amateurs, serving on collegial boards and chosen in lotteries for (typically) one-year terms. A key body relevant to fiscal administration was the agenda-setting Council of 500 citizens; its membership was selected in a lottery designed to ensure representation from all parts of Attica – Athens' home territory. The council had limited decision authority, but considerable executive authority and primary responsibility for managing (though not setting) the state budget.[15]

Boards of magistrates (typically ten individuals) handled much of the day-to-day administration of public funds. In the fourth century funds were disbursed to the various magisterial boards according to a distribution rule (the *merismos*):[16] this will have had the benefit (intended or otherwise) of reducing the time spent on strategic legislative micro-managing. Accountability for all magistrates handling state monies was, in principle, strict. All magistrates were subject to annual end-of-year audits; suspected malefactors were tried before People's Courts.[17]

By the middle of the fourth century different revenue streams were being earmarked for specific purposes, military (the Stratiotic Fund) and domestic (including the Theoric Fund); constitutional rules forbade the diversion of revenues from one of these major areas to another, limiting state policy flexibility but increasing financial predictability. Fiscal regularity was

[12] See Ober (2008: 55–70) for details of history and references. [13] Davies (2004).
[14] Hansen (1999) provides a very useful survey of all aspects of Athenian government.
[15] Rhodes (1985). [16] Hansen (1999: 152, 158). [17] Roberts (1982).

further promoted by the mandatory discussion of specific fiscal issues at certain meetings of the assembly.

A key question about Athenian financial administration concerns how expert knowledge was developed and accessed by the government.[18] Well-known public speakers (*rhêtores*) developed expertise in various areas of public finance. In the fifth century Pericles' political preeminence rested in part on his reputation as an expert on imperial sources of revenue.[19] In the fourth century public speakers became expert in the areas of tax-farming[20] and the grain trade.[21] Expertise also resided in state-paid secretaries to the various magisterial bodies; these included citizens (such as the orator Aeschines, early in his career) and state-owned slaves, who were in at least some cases purchased by the state specifically for their specialized expertise.[22]

The fourth century saw an augmented role for elected financial officials; there is reason to believe that at least some of these officials developed high levels of expertise. In the 350s, in the immediate aftermath of the Social War, the politician Eubulus succeeded in consolidating important financial powers in the office of the manager of the Theoric Fund.[23] In the 350s the orator Lycurgus acquired a similarly influential position in state finances.[24]

Coinage and monetary value

By the fifth and fourth centuries the Greek world was quite highly monetized; many (perhaps most) commercial exchanges were in the form of silver coins. Most major Greek city states issued a "national" coinage; some states were involved in cooperative coining arrangements.[25] Athenian coinage was very prominent in the Greek world; it is by far the most common *polis* coinage in coin hoards from across the Greek world.[26] The Attic weight standard was used in Athens and in much of the Greek world.

- 1 Attic drachma = *c.* 4.3 g of silver: one day's wage for a soldier or unskilled laborer in the later fifth century BC.
- 4 drachmas = 1 tetradrachm: the standard high-denomination coin of the classical Greek world. This is the typical Athenian "owl."
- 6,000 drachmas = 1 Attic talent (T) = *c.* 26 kg of silver: very approximately twenty-five years of gross wages (at the late fifth century rate of 1

[18] Davies (2004). [19] Kallet (1993; 1994); Samons (2000). [20] Stroud (1998); Moreno (2003).
[21] Oliver (2007); Moreno (2008). [22] Rhodes and Osborne (2003: no. 25); Ismard (2013).
[23] Cawkwell (1963). [24] See Humphreys (1985) and Burke (1985).
[25] Mackil and van Alfen (2006). [26] Flament (2007); Ober (2008: ch. 2).

drachma per day, and assuming 250 working days per year). 1 talent may be very roughly equated to the gross income of an ordinary working man's life (assuming an average age at death of those who lived to adulthood to have been in the mid-forties). Elite (liturgical) fortune in classical Athens = 3 to 4 talents (and up).

State expenditures

The Athenian state undertook considerable annual expenditures. Military expenses (maintaining armed forces and military construction) were in most (perhaps in all) years by far the largest item of the state budget.[27] Other important items included government and law, domestic welfare programs, festivals, and public building. The figures discussed in this section are summed up in Table 16.1. The numbers are necessarily speculative, but should be in the right order of magnitude. Note that the expenditures discussed here are limited to those incurred by the central state government. Substantial public expenditures were also incurred at various "sub-state" local levels as well: certainly at the level of the village (deme), and perhaps at the level of the tribe. Deme expenditures on public goods included festivals, public buildings, and administrative record-keeping.[28]

Military

The primary expenses included in this category were paying men who served in the armed forces (land and sea; citizen and mercenary) and building and maintaining warships. Costs can be roughly divided into the fixed costs of upkeep and homeland security, estimated by Pritchard at *c.* 130T/yr in the 370s, and highly variable costs of land and sea military expeditions.[29]

Pritchard's estimates:[30]

- 431 to 423 (Archidamian War): 1,500T per year.
- Later Peloponnesian War: 900T per year.
- 370s to 360s: 500 T per year for "public and private expenses" (my guess for public expenses alone – less private expenses for cavalry and trierarchic liturgies: 350T per year).

27 Wees (2000: 81); compare with Pritchard (2007: 125–6; 2012).

28 Jones (1999). Compare the relatively high levels of public spending by American states and local governments, especially before the 1930s: Wallis (2000).

29 Pritchard (2012: 55).

30 Pritchard (2007; 2012).

Table 16.1 *Athenian state spending and income (estimates)*

	c. 435	c. 425	c. 370	354	c. 340	330s
Spending						
Military	400	1500	350	130	200	400
Government/law	100	100	100	75	100	120
Festivals	100	100	100	100	100	150
Welfare	50	50	40	30	50	100
Building	350	100	75	0	50	200
Total	*1,000*	*1,850*	*665*	*335*	*500*	*970*
Income						
General	1,000	1,500	600	130	400	1,200
Mint (maximum)	300	100	50	150	100	150
Total	*1,300*	*1,600*	*650*	*280*	*500*	*1,350*
Loans (internal)	250					
Surplus/deficit	*300*	*0*	*-15*	*-55*	*0*	*380*

Notes: "General" income is as reported in ancient sources except for *c.* 370, which is a guess. Minting fees are not included in "General" income, but mine leases are included. One-time windfall minting profir from coinage recall in 355 is included in 354. Pritchard's (2012) estimate for *c.* 425 military expenses is adopted here, but his estimate for 370s–360s "public and private" expenses is reduced to reflect public only. My estimate for 330s government expense (Hansen 1999) is increased by 20 to 30T (Gabrielsen 2013). Sub-state (deme, tribe) spending and income are excluded.
Sources: Pritchard (2012); Hansen (1999); Gabrielsen (2013).

My guesses:

- 430s, before Peloponnesian War: 400T per year.[31]
- Late 350s to mid-340s (austerity era): 130 to 200 T per year.[32]
- Mid-330s (rebuilding era): 400T per year.

Democratic government, law

The primary cost borne by government was paying citizens for service, and paying the secretaries who aided them. In the fourth century citizens were paid a daily stipend to attend meetings of the assembly, to sit on juries, and to serve on the Council of 500. The greatest imponderable is whether ordinary (not council) magistrates were paid in the fourth century, as they certainly were in the fifth century; I assume, with Gabrielsen,[33] that magistrates were paid in the fourth century. Total costs were somewhat lower in the fifth century (before the introduction of assembly pay), and

[31] Unz (1985) estimates military expenses in the period 478–433 at some 300T per year. This calculation is criticized by Pritchard (2012: 55).
[32] See, further, Cook (1990). [33] Gabrielsen (2012).

during the austerity period of the mid-fourth century, when some government services were curtailed.[34]

Hansen's estimate for total costs in the 330s: 92 to 112 T per yr.[35] Adding 20 to 30T per year to include magistrates' salaries[36] gives a total of about 120T per year.

Festivals: state religion

Festivals were thought of as public goods, not just because they were essential for sustaining the right relationship between mortals and the gods but also because they were a significant source of food redistribution. Rosivach calculates that, in the period from 334 to 331, a citizen could receive a portion of meat at a public sacrifice every eight or nine days, meaning perhaps forty to fifty times each year.[37] Costs included the purchase of sacrificial animals and stipends for some participants.

Pritchard's estimate:[38] 100 T per year from about 450 to 350; expenditures may have been higher in the 330s and 320s. Note that, although the costs of festivals were paid for in part by private sources, here they are treated entirely as state expenses.[39]

Domestic welfare programs

These included programs for the rearing of children of citizens who died fighting in the armed forces (certainly in the infantry, and, plausibly, in the navy as well) and handicapped citizens. After around 350 the state subsidized admission to the great theatrical festivals through the Theoric Fund; under the financial administration of Eubulus, surplus state income was paid directly into the Theoric Fund and became a very significant part of the Athenian fiscal regime.

My guess (fourth century): 30 to 150 T per year.

[34] Rhodes (2010: 328–30) estimates considerably higher costs for running the Athenian government, with totals approaching 250T (assembly: 45T; council: 26T; courts: 150T; and other expenses for other magistrates and incidentals).

[35] Hansen (1999: 315–16). [36] Gabrielsen (2012).

[37] Rosivach (1994: 1966). There is regrettably little evidence other than this for the frequency of meat-eating in the Greek world: Tsoukala (2009).

[38] Pritchard (2012).

[39] This number includes direct costs to the state and some private expenditures on state-run festivals by private individuals.

Public building

This expense varied considerably over the course of Athenian classical history. In the high imperial building boom from 447 to 425, Athens spent in the neighborhood of 8,000T on public buildings (notably the great acropolis project) and their furnishings – including the extraordinary cult statue of Athenian in the Parthenon.[40] This came to an annual expenditure of over 350T per year. Obviously, this was exceptional. The Athenian rate of public building varied considerably,[41] as did the purpose of public building, which in various periods was devoted to city walls, temples and other primarily religious buildings (keeping in mind that there was considerable overlap between government and religious architecture), rural fortifications, and government buildings of various sorts.

My guess (fourth century): 25 to 200 T per year.

Conclusions on state expenditures

The Athenian state provided its residents, and especially its citizens, with a very extensive basket of public goods; the basket was, at least anecdotally,[42] regarded as more generous than in other Greek *poleis*. A mean figure of 700 to 800T for annual state expenditures in the fourth century seems reasonable. Throughout the Peloponnesian War, and probably for some periods of intense military activity and public building (especially on fortifications) in the fourth century, expenses must have been much higher. In the early phase of the Peloponnesian War state expenses may have been around 2,000 T per year.

Expenditures as a percentage of GDP

Estimating the gross domestic product of Athens requires drawing plausible inferences from admittedly noisy data. Based on what we can reasonably posit about gross domestic income (here taken as a proxy for GDP), GDP likely fell somewhere in the range of 5,000 to 7,500 T per year, with the high in the 430s and the low in the austerity period of the middle of the fourth century. For income calculations, see Table 16.2. Note that these figures would need to be raised considerably, especially for the 430s, if the higher figure for silver mine revenues (see section entitled "Resource

[40] Zimmern (1931: 412). [41] See Ober (2008: 292–3) for guesses about rates.
[42] Ps-Xenophon, *Constitution of Athens*.

Table 16.2 *Model of Athenian gross domestic income*

	Elite	dr/day	Middling	dr/day	Subsistence	dr/day	Total/day
430s "neutral"							
Citzen men	400	16	34,500	1	15,000	0.5	48,400
Citizen women	400	0	34,500	0.25	15,000	0.25	12,375
Children of citizens	1,000	0	86,250	0.25	37,500	0.25	30,937.5
Metic men	200	16	4,500	1	5,500	0.5	10,450
metic women	200	0	2,250	0.25	1,100	0.25	837.5
Children of metics	500	0	5,625	0.25	2,750	0.25	2,093.75
Slaves (total)	0	0	0	1	100,000	0.75	75,000
Total dr/day		9,600		71,156		99,338	180,094
Percent of GDP		**0.05**		**0.40**		**0.55**	
340s "neutral"							
Citzen men	400	16	19,500	1	10,000	0.5	30,900
Citizen women	400	0	19,500	0.15	10,000	0.25	5,425
Children of citizens	1,000	0	48,750	0.15	25,000	0.25	13,562.5
Metic men	200	16	4,500	1	5,500	0.5	10,450
Metic women	200	0	2,250	0.15	1,100	0.25	612.5
Children of metics	500	0	5,625	0.15	2,750	0.25	1,531.25
Slaves (total)	0	0	0	1	80,000	0.75	60,000
Total dr/day		9,600		35,419		77,463	122,481
Percent of GDP		**0.08**		**0.29**		**0.63**	
330s "optimistic"							
Citizen men	400	16	24,500	1.5	5,000	0.5	45,650
Citizen women	400	0	24,500	0.25	5,000	0.25	7,375
Children of citizens	1000	0	61,250	0.25	12,500	0.25	18,437.5
Metic men	200	16	7,500	1.5	2,500	0.5	15,700
Metic women	200	0	3,750	0.25	500	0.25	1,062.5

Children of metics	500	0	9,375	0.25	1,250	0.25	2,656.25
Slaves (total)	0	0	8,000	1.5	72,000	0.75	66,000
Total dr/day		9,600		84,719		62,563	156,881
Percent of GPD		**0.06**		**0.54**		**0.40**	
330s "pessimistic"							
Citzen men	400	16	19,500	1	10,000	0.5	30,900
Citizen women	400	0	19,500	0.15	10,000	0.25	5,425
Children of citizens	1000	0	48,750	0.15	25,000	0.25	13,562.5
Metic men	200	16	4,500	1	5,500	0.5	10,450
Metic women	200	0	2,250	0.15	1,100	0.25	612.5
Children of metics	500	0	5,625	0.15	2,750	0.25	1,531.25
Slaves (total)	0	0	0	1	80,000	0.75	60,000
Total dr/day		9,600		35,419		77,463	122,481
Percent of GDP		**0.08**		**0.29**		**0.63**	

Table 16.3 *Income and spending as a percentage of GDP*

	T/yr GDI	General income	Fraction GDI	Spending	Fraction GDI
430s	7,504	1,000	0.13	1,000	0.13
340s	5,103	400	0.08	500	0.10
330s "optimistic"	6,537	1,200	0.18	970	0.15
330s "pessimistic"	5,103	1,200	0.24	970	0.19

Notes: GDP is taken as a proxy for GDI. T(alents)/year based on Table 16.2 income model, and 250 working days per year. General income and total spending from Table 16.1. 340s estimate is 330s pessimistic with lower general income assumption.

revenues: minting and leases") is correct. This would have the effect of lowering the estimates of spending as a percentage of GDP.

Based on the estimates of state expenditures in the preceding section, state spending would seem to fall between 10 and 15 percent of GDP (assuming the "optimistic" scenario for the fourth century in Table 16.2); see Table 16.3. Spending as a percentage of GDP undoubtedly spiked in the early Peloponnesian War era, perhaps approaching 25 percent of GDP. Assuming the income model of Table 16.2 is roughly correct, to is difficult to see how Athenian spending could have dropped much below 10 percent of GDP for long periods, because some expenses, notably those required for state religion and homeland security, were inflexible.

By way of a modern-world comparison, in the United States, from 1903 to 2010, median central government spending stood at about 29 percent of GDP, with lows of around 7 percent early in the twentieth century, an early spike to 22 to 29 percent in 1918 and 1919, and all-time highs of over 50 percent in the Second World War years of 1944 and 1945. It is important to keep in mind that these figures include only federal government spending; they are non-inclusive of state and local spending. State provision of public goods, relative to federal government, was considerably higher before the 1930s, so the very low early twentieth-century figures are not reflective of total public goods provision.[43] Likewise, the Athenian figures do not include the substantial spending on public goods by sub-state governments (deme, tribe), or non-state associations. Moreover, the figures

[43] See http://www.usgovernmentspending.com/us_20th_century_chart.html.

do not include all "private" contributions to state spending. The military spending figure for the 370s and 360s, for example (Table 16.1), excludes private contributions by the cavalry and extra-liturgical expenses for maintaining triremes. Including these sources would have the effect of increasing spending for state purposes as a percentage of GDP.

General state income: snapshots

In a conversation between Socrates and the would-be political leader Glaucon, reported by Xenophon,[44] Socrates begins his inquiry into Glaucon's fitness for his intended role by asking if Glaucon will attempt to make the city richer. Glaucon agrees that of course this will be his goal. Socrates points out that the *polis* would be richer if it had a larger income, and asks if Glaucon knows the sources and total of the *polis*'s revenue or expenditures, noting that reducing unnecessary costs would have the same enriching effect. Glaucon proves his lack of fitness for leadership by his ignorance of the facts and figures related to public spending and revenue – numbers that (at least, so Xenophon would have us believe) a diligent would-be leader would have at his fingertips. The story is probably a fiction, but its plausibility depends upon the reader's agreement that the numbers in question were knowable and that Glaucon demonstrates lack of fitness for leadership by not knowing them.

Our Athenian sources do record several figures for total state income over the century from the 430s to the 330s. We do not know how accurate these figures are (the numbers are very round), nor do we know, in most cases, exactly what is being included in or left out of revenue estimates. But the very fact that there *are* figures for total state revenue in our sources (reported by historians, and public orators, and extrapolated from inscribed and publicly displayed imperial documents: the Athenian Tribute Lists) suggests that Xenophon was not being facetious: at least some Athenians thought that they did know the total annual income of the state, and thought it was worth writing about. As in the case of expenditures, this is presumably only central state income. Local governments (demes, tribes) had their own sources of income, including common lands, which could be leased.[45]

We have no meaningful figures for total state income before the later fifth century.[46] Herodotus's story[47] about the politician Themistocles' plan

[44] Xenophon, *Memorabilia* 3.6.4–6. [45] Jones (1999); Blok (2010); Williams (2011).

[46] Thucydides 1.96 says that the total contributions of the original Delian League, in 477, was 460T – a figure doubted by Meiggs (1972: 62–3).

[47] Herodotus 7.144.1–2.

to use a windfall profit from the silver mines to build ships against Persia in 483, rather than simply distributing the "surplus" money as one-time cash payments to the citizenry, suggests that there may not have been a regular state revenue stream, and no serious thought about balancing state income and expenditure, before the imperial era of the mid-fifth century.

The ancient figures for Athenian state income are as follows, and listed as "General income" in Table 16.1. As noted earlier, we do not know the sources of income that a given number includes or excludes, nor the extent to which the figures from different periods include and exclude the same sources.

- 432/431 (eve of the Peloponnesian War): estimated imperial income – tribute, imperial rents and internal revenues: 1,000T per year.[48] This is more or less consistent with figures reported by Thucydides (600T per year)[49] for the tribute of subjects alone and with the figures extrapolated from the Athenian Tribute Lists (*c.* 400T per year) for imperial tribute alone.[50]
- 355 (immediate aftermath of the debilitating Social War, in a period of serious financial difficulty for Athens, on which see below): 130T.[51]
- late 340s (after Eubulus's financial reforms): 400T.[52]
- 330s (era of the financial leadership of Lycurgus): 1,200T per year.[53]

Athenian sources of state income may be, somewhat arbitrarily, divided into direct taxes on wealth, indirect taxes on exchange, state rents, extraordinary measures, and state borrowing (see the next six sections below). The relative importance of these various sources of income varied considerably over the course of classical Athenian history. Direct and indirect taxes were always important sources of revenue, but the income from rents, leases, extraordinary measures, and state borrowing varied substantially over time. In Table 16.1 I have assumed that there were considerable annual revenues from minting (see below), and that these were not included in the ancient figures, reported above. This assumption helps to bring spending into balance with income, but it is, admittedly, no more than a speculation.

Income certainly exceeded expenditures in some years. Thucydides claims[54] that Pericles reported to the Athenians in 431 BC that there was a state reserve of 6,000T of coined silver (this was not counting uncoined

[48] Xenophon, *Anabasis* 7.1.27. [49] Thucydides 2.13.6.
[50] For various ways of reconciling Thucydides, the Athenian Tribute Lists, and Xenophon, see Pritchard (2012). In the 420s the tribute from the empire was somewhat higher; Meiggs (1973: 325, 343) estimates 800T in 428 and 1,500T in 425 BC.
[51] Demosthenes 10.37. [52] Demosthenes 10.38.
[53] [Plutarch], *Ten Orators*, 842F: with Burke (1985). [54] Thucydides 2.13.6–7.

precious-metal reserves and sacred objects owned by the state), and that the reserve fund had formerly been as high as 9,700T. In order to achieve a surplus of that size, income had to exceed expenses by a substantial margin, over a considerable period of time. If we assume, for the moment, that the state did not receive interest on surplus funds, we must assume an average annual surplus revenue of around 300T over the thirty plus years from the mid-460s to the late 430s. This is compatible with the estimates, above, of ordinary expenditures of some 700 to 800T per year, and total imperial-era revenues of about 1,000T per year, although, if we assume that high military and extremely high building expenditures in those years came to around 850T, and government, festival, and welfare expenses to another 250T, we have an unaccounted shortfall of 400T per year (1,100T expenses, 300T surplus, minus 1,000T income). Again, revenues from the silver mines would help to explain the difference.

Athens' substantial reserves were a key factor in the democratic state's capacity to fight the Peloponnesian War. There cannot have been regular surpluses of revenue in the first half of the fourth century BC, but in the third quarter of the fourth century there was a vigorous debate among Athenian politicians as to whether annual surpluses ought to be paid to the Stratiotic (Military) Fund or to the Theoric Fund, which in practice seems to have funded various sorts of citizen welfare.[55] In many years expenses exceeded income, which, when there was no reserve fund available, necessitated extraordinary measures and/or state borrowing (see sections on extraordinary measures and state loans below, in which I consider the question of sovereign debt and state deficits).

Direct taxes

The simplest form of direct taxes known from Athens was a "head tax" (*metoikion*), levied on non-natives resident in Athens (*metoikoi*) for longer than a short period (according to a late source, one month). The tax amounted to 1 drachma per month on men and 0.5 drachma per month on adult women. Based on what we know of Athenian wages,[56] for an unskilled laborer in the late fifth or late fourth century this might have amounted (for men) to a tax of something in the range of 3 to 5 percent on annual income from wages. It would have been less, of course for more highly paid skilled laborers or successful merchants. The total revenue to the state from the *metoikion* would have amounted to roughly 25T per year,

[55] Hansen (1976). [56] Loomis (1998).

assuming that there were something in the range of 10,000 male and 4,500 female metics paying the tax. A tax on prostitutes (*pornikon*) is reported in late sources; Lyttkens suggests that it may have been a head tax, and that it could have produced at least 15T per year, and perhaps much more than that.[57]

There has been considerable discussion among scholars about whether metic status was a privilege or a burden, and the costs of the metic tax to individuals and its value to the state. For our present purposes, what is important is that the burden to individuals was not too great to preclude Athens from having a famously large population of resident foreigners; it seems plausible (see below on indirect taxes) that the Athenian state kept the metic head tax (and perhaps also the prostitute tax) relatively low in order to make Athens a somewhat more desirable destination for workers and (especially) traders, and that the Athenians therefore believed they would reap more from indirect taxes and other economic benefits than they would by charging a more extortionate head tax.[58]

The most important direct taxes were imposed uniquely on wealthy citizens and metics. Liturgies were occasional requirements on the part of individuals to provide important public goods. The *eisphora* was a tax on property, used especially to finance the military. Initially both were occasional impositions, but by the fourth century these payments were substantial and frequent enough to be regarded as regular taxation, whether or not they were included in ancient estimates of state income. Liturgies were notionally voluntary, but in practice mandatory payments by the wealthiest 1 to 4 percent (depending on period) of the Athenian population.[59] Liturgies were levied on individual estates, for a given year, and at least notionally based on a rotation, such that individuals were not ordinarily required to perform a liturgy in consecutive years. The two primary forms of liturgy were, first, financing some aspect of a state religious festival (for example, by serving as producer [*choregos*] for a group of tragedies at the Dionysia) and, next and more frequent and costly, outfitting a warship (as "ship-master" [*trierarchos*]). Liturgies were expensive, costing from 1,500 to 4,000 drachmas in the early fourth century.[60] Liturgical payments were essential for sustaining state-funded festivals[61] and for the maintenance and deployment of the navy.[62] The *eisphora* was an occasional (though increasingly regular) tax on property, meant to fund special needs of military

[57] Lyttkens (2012: 107).

[58] For detailed discussion, and very different conclusions, about the conditions of the lives of metics and the payment of the *metoikion*, see Whitehead (1977) and Cohen (2000).

[59] Davies (1971; 1981). [60] Ibid.: xxii–xxiv. [61] Wilson (2000). [62] Gabrielsen (1994).

security. It appears to have been levied on the wealthiest 6 to 8 percent of the population, and the cost was slight, per household, compared to the liturgies.[63]

Given the many variables involved, it is difficult to determine the average annual percentage of a wealthy man's income that would have been paid in liturgies and *eisphora*, but it was not negligible. Given the frequent revisions of the systems employed for levying liturgies and *eisphora* taxes, and in light of anecdotal evidence from forensic oratory, the burden seems to have been regarded as heavy and yet tolerable by wealthy Athenians. There were no significant direct taxes on most (i.e. non-elite) Athenian citizens.[64]

Indirect taxes

Indirect taxes, in the form of tolls and harbor taxes, and typically farmed via an auction system, were major sources of Athenian revenue in the imperial era, and became increasingly important in the post-imperial fourth century. In the imperial era the Athenians temporarily suspended the regular tribute upon their allies (see section after next) in favor of a 5 percent tax on all imports and exports throughout the empire; this tax seems not to have been successful, as it was withdrawn after a few years. Likewise, late in the Peloponnesian War (from about 410 to 405), and again in the early fourth century (from the mid-390s to 387), the Athenians established a toll tax at the Bosporus of 10 percent; again, this was of relatively short duration.[65]

More enduring (and certainly more important to Athenian finances in the long run) was the 2 percent tax on imports and exports from the Athenian port of Piraeus. This tax was farmed for two years at the very beginning of the fourth century for the fairly meager amounts of 30T and 36T.[66] It seems likely that, by the prosperous era of the 330s, the revenues from the port tax were very substantially higher.

In the course of the fourth century the Athenian government developed a number of initiatives that appear to be aimed specifically at increasing the level of trade and number of traders using Athens markets: the state provided expert "approvers of coins" (*dokimastai*) charged with ensuring

[63] Christ (2007).

[64] Athenian farmers paid a tiny "first fruits" tax (1/1,200th to 1/600th of the grain harvest) to the Eleusinian goddesses – which provides useful evidence of grain production, but is not significant in assessing tax burdens: Jardé (1925); Cavanaugh (1996).

[65] Andreades (1933: 294–9). [66] Andocides 1.133–34, with Andreades (1933: 298–9).

the quality of the coinage being exchanged in Athenian markets. Other market officials were charged with preventing fraud and enforcing the use of standard measures. The laws regulating commercial exchange were revised to enable non-citizens to enforce written contracts without fear that their status would put them at a systematic disadvantage relative to citizens. Port facilities were improved, and the Athenian state deployed its navy to suppress piracy. All these measures would have served to lower transaction costs, and thus to increase the value of exchanges – and appear to be self-consciously so designed. Xenophon, in a mid-fourth century essay *Revenues* (*Poroi*), advocated some of these measures (among others) as a solution to the problem of low state revenues in the aftermath of the Social War. As was the case with the ongoing series of changes in direct taxes, the democratic government appears to have adapted institutions to a changing environment. Policy was shaped with an eye toward the state's need to provide public goods, and toward the preferences of individuals whose behavior determined the state's capacity to collect revenue.[67]

Rents

Throughout the classical period, but especially in the imperial fifth century, rents (income extracted from others as uncompensated value, by a superior power, through manipulation of the exchange environment, often by enforcing an monopoly)[68] were an important source of Athenian state revenues. The most obvious imperial rents were in the form of the tribute (*phoros*) levied by imperial Athens on its subjects, but the empire enabled Athenians to extract rents in other ways as well, such as through the confiscation of property, fees for the maintenance of garrisons, and legal fees. Thucydides claimed[69] that, by 431, the income from the empire averaged 600T per year; since this is half again the roughly 400T per year listed as direct *phoros* in the Athenian Tribute Lists, it is at least possible that Thucydides was attempting to sum up various forms of imperial rent extraction. The 5 percent and 10 percent indirect taxes on trade within the empire and as a toll at the Bosporus, discussed above as "indirect taxes," can, obviously enough, be regarded as rents accruing from a monopoly – since the imperial subjects and traders through the Bosporus had no alternatives (unlike traders paying the 2 percent tax at Piraeus, who were free to trade in other markets if they chose).

[67] On these various measures, see Ober (2008: ch. 6). [68] Krueger (1974).
[69] Thucydides 2.13.3.

In the fourth century Athens lost most of its overseas holdings, but retained three Aegean islands: Lemnos, Imbros, and Skyros. These islands were subject to an 8.3 percent (one-twelfth) tax on grain production; a document detailing the mechanisms of the tax has survived, in the form of a law passed in 375 BCE. It is evidently the administration of the tax, rather than its rate, that was changed by the new law. The grain tax was farmed; the winning bid took the form of a certain volume of grain, the tax auction, conducted before the harvest, thus constituting a sort of futures market in grain. The syndicate that won the concession was required by law to deliver the grain (weighed to ensure quality) to the port at Piraeus by a certain date. Having arrived at Athens, the grain was put up for sale by a board of magistrates; the revenues went directly into the military budget. The price at which the tax grain was sold was set not by the market but by a vote of the citizen assembly. Clearly, rent extracted from the subject islands was treated by the Athenian government as a fungible public good. Each year the assembly made a simple "guns versus butter" choice by setting the price of the grain taken as rent. A lower price meant that more heavily subsidized food was available, and thus the good was the welfare of the poorer residents; higher prices meant more money in the military fund, meaning that the preferred good was military security. Once again, we see a democratic government designing fiscal institutions that would flexibly and dynamically adapt to a changing environment.[70]

Resource revenues: minting and leases

We have one very notable example of natural resource revenue from Athens. Whereas much of the surface land of Attica was in private hands (with strong private property rules to protect its owners), subsurface mineral rights were retained by the state. The Laurion/Thorikos region of southern Attica had relatively rich silver mines; these mines provided the silver for Athenian (and probably much non-Athenian) coinage. Each year the state leased mineral rights to private individuals, and fragments of the leases have survived. The individual lessor was responsible for both mining and refining the ore; it is generally assumed that the silver produced was then sold to the state (as primary, but perhaps not sole, buyer) at something like market rates: according to one plausible scenario the state would receive bullion from the mine lessors and return minted coins to them – presumably charging a minting fee.[71]

[70] The inscription: Stroud (1998); discussion: Moreno (2003); Ober (2008: 260–3).

[71] Flament (2007); van Alfen (2011).

In forthcoming work, Andrew Meadows[72] estimates that Athenian silver coin production in the middle of the fifth century BCE stood anywhere between 700T and 6,000T per year.[73] At the lower end of this range, profits would presumably be small in light of the fixed production costs (labor and capital investment); at the upper end, the potential state and private profit and state income from the mines would be great. Hypothetically setting state profit margin for minting fees at 5 percent means a state income of 35T to 300T per year. At the upper end of the range, this goes a long way toward explaining the substantial mid-fifth-century annual surplus mentioned above.

Mines were leased by the shaft. Established, productive shafts were leased at rates higher than new, unproved shafts (exactly how the expert knowledge of productivity was transferred from lessor to the state officials responsible for setting lease rates is unknown). By the most probable reconstruction, the mines were very productive in the middle of the fifth century, which was a period characterized by huge issues of Athenian "owls"; somewhat less productive in the later phases of the Peloponnesian War and the early fourth century; and quite productive again in the mid- to late fourth century – the period from which our lease evidence comes. By the likeliest method of calculating, the leases alone (apart from any revenues accruing from minting) would have brought the state, per annum, between 20T (in 367/366) and 160T (in 341/340). At the upper range, this would have been an important part of total annual state revenues. The revival of the silver mines, perhaps driven by new leasing strategies that incentivized new exploration, goes some way toward explaining one source of the post-Social-War recovery in Athenian finances.[74]

In addition to the property owned by individuals, substantial amounts of real estate were owned by the Athenian state, by local governmental units (demes, tribes), and by private and quasi-public associations of various sorts. Some of this land was leased out, and the profits of these leases were made available for public purposes, at the state and local levels. We cannot quantify this income.[75]

[72] Reported by van Alfen (2011: 127 n. 1).

[73] Domergue (2008) estimates total Laurion silver production (across more than two centuries) at 3,500 tons. This comes to *c.* 4 million drachma per year, or 680T per year, which is not far off Meadows' low estimate for the middle of the fifth century. If we assume 2,000T to 4,000T for the high fifth century (in the middle of Meadows' range), we could plausibly model Athenian silver production at 200T to 400T in the earlier fourth century, perhaps up to 700T to 1,000T in the later fourth century.

[74] Ober (1985: 28–30); Faraguna (2006); Bissa (2008).

[75] For the leasing of sacred and public lands, by the state, local governments, and associations, see Blok (2010) and Williams (2011); for voluntary associations and their finances, see Ismard (2010).

Extraordinary measures, gifts, fines, confiscation

The main topic of the (probably) late fourth-century pseudo-Aristotelian text *Economica* is clever strategies used by state governments to raise revenues through extraordinary (and in some cases clearly unscrupulous) measures. Some "extraordinary" forms of income may have been fairly regular – that is, the state's share of fines levied by the People's Courts, and the confiscation of property of convicted individuals who had fled from Athens or were unable to pay their fines. The existence of a regularly appointed magisterial board of "sellers" (*poletai*) responsible for disposing of confiscated property points to the regularization of this form of extraordinary revenue.[76] The state (along with various sub-state governmental entities) could – and on occasion did – sell off public assets (such as dedications to Athena, public lands) to private buyers.[77] Windfalls came to the state in the form of donations of money, grain, or cash (to subsidize the sale of grain) from internal and external benefactors; non-citizens who were particularly generous were, in some instances, rewarded with citizenship and other honors.[78]

Given the importance of silver and silver coinage in the Athenian economy, adjustments to the coinage offered a particularly attractive means of raising funds quickly, but the Athenians were aware that the "brand" of their distinctive "owl" coinage was extremely valuable. The general conservatism of Athenian coinage is striking: the coinage of Athens remained standard in weight and iconography, and archaizing in artistic type, throughout the classical era – during a period in which, as we have seen, the democratic government proved willing to experiment regularly with relatively substantial institutional changes. Experiments with gold and "clad" coins at the end of the Peloponnesian War were quickly discontinued, and the emergency war issues were eventually demonetized.[79] In the fourth century, during an era when many other states (especially in Egypt and Syria-Palestine) began striking imitation "owls," the Athenians sought to reassure traders and to protect their brand by establishing the office of the "Approvers".[80]

Yet there is one very striking example of a major intervention in the coinage by the Athenian state, dating to the immediate aftermath of the Social War – a period that has figured heavily in earlier parts of this chapter. John Kroll demonstrates that the very large, so-called "*pi* series" of

[76] (Langdon (1991; 1994). [77] Harris (1995); Lambert (1997).
[78] Migeotte (1992); Allen (2003); Moreno (2008). [79] Flament (2007). [80] Van Alfen (2005).

Athenian tetradrachmas, dated to the mid- to late fourth century BC, is best understood as a massive reminting project.[81] In his convincing reconstruction (based on numismatic evidence and a still unpublished inscription from the Athenian agora), in 353 there was a state recall of all large-denomination silver coinage in Attica; old "owls" were brought to the mint, and new "*pi*-style" coins of a similar weight were returned to the owners. Although there is no positive evidence of the profit made by the state from this operation, Kroll suggests that a reminting fee of around 5 percent would have been charged; this would amount to a one-time tax on Athenian wealth held in the form of large-denomination coins. It is impossible to say how much revenue such a tax would have netted, but it might have been in the hundreds of talents – perhaps enough to help get the state out of the deep hole represented by the immediate post-Social-War income low of 130T (above). Kroll points out that this bold move is typical of the innovative approach to state finance that characterized Athens in the middle of the fourth century BC. Notably, the recall did not lead to a devaluation of Athenian coinage; as Kroll notes, demand for Athenian owls remained "insatiable."

State loans and sovereign debt

In the fifth century BC, in the era of the high empire, the Athenian state successfully sought to create a large strategic reserve; this amounted to about 8,000T in 454 and 9,700T in 447. These large reserves were held, at least in part, as "sacred" funds officially owned by Athena and the other Athenian gods. These funds were, for example, partly in the form of removable plates of gold on the cult statue of Athena in the Parthenon and were assumed to be (as they in fact were) readily available to the state in time of crisis.[82] As Thucydides makes eminently clear, this massive and unique (within the Greek world) strategic reserve was an essential element in Athenian planning in advance of the Peloponnesian War;[83] epigraphic evidence makes it very clear that very substantial funds were in fact borrowed by the state in the course of the war.[84] The reserve, along with the new revenue-collecting efforts sketched above, sustained the Athenian war effort at a high level through much of the long and extremely expensive war.

In the post-imperial period, although precious items were still stored in sacred treasuries,[85] there is no evidence of great reserves of money in

[81] Kroll (2011a; 2011b). [82] Samons (2000). [83] Kallet (1993).
[84] Pritchard (2012: 42–3), with earlier literature cited. [85] Harris (1995).

Athenian sacred treasuries that might be tapped by the state in times of need. As we have seen, some state expenses were more or less fixed, and expenditures must have exceeded income fairly often. The extraordinary measures noted above served to cover some of the shortfall, but probably not all. Another source for covering the shortfall was for the state to borrow money from other states or from private lenders. Ismard suggests that a series of inscribed financial transactions from the later fourth century (the so-called *rationes centesimarum*) record loans to the Athenian state secured by land owned by Athenian civil associations.[86] Other explanations of the series of inscriptions remain possible, however.[87] Regrettably, we still know relatively little about the mechanisms of sovereign debt in the period before the Hellenistic era.[88]

Aristotle states with strong approval that the restored democratic government of Athens paid back money borrowed from Sparta by the anti-democratic "Thirty Tyrants" during a coup of 404/403;[89] he contrasts this Athenian example of fiscal responsibility with the bad tendency of other democratic governments to confiscate private property. Writing in the period of post-Social-War financial crisis, Xenophon notes, almost casually, that it would be possible for Athens to make substantial infrastructures improvements (which would encourage traders to choose Athens' market) by borrowing the necessary capital from private sources. The state could offer high rates of interest, and, at least as important, loans would be guaranteed by the credibility of the state itself, "which is to all appearances the safest and most durable of human institutions."[90] Despite the lack of positive evidence for classical-era state loans from private sources,[91] Xenophon's comment, along with the apparent Athenian concern to maintain a good reputation for repayment of loans in the incident discussed by Aristotle, might point to an Athenian "democratic advantage" in gaining access to private credit.[92]

Revenues, taxes, and the Athenian social equilibrium

The payment of significant direct taxes (other than head taxes by resident foreigners) uniquely by the wealthiest residents was a potential, and at times actual, source of conflict among the wealthy elite and the masses of

[86] Ismard (2010: 175–6). [87] Lambert (1997).
[88] On private credit in the Greek world, see Cohen (forthcoming).
[89] Aristotle, Constitution of Athens 40.3. [90] Xenophon, Revenues 3.9.
[91] Cohen (1992: 143 n. 134).
[92] For the concept and modern examples, see Schultz and Weingast (2003).

ordinary citizens. The success of Athenian democracy, in terms of its relative stability, longevity, and prosperity, depended on strategic agreement between masses and elites. If elites came to believe that paying taxes was oppressive enough to justify defection from the implicit compact, or if the masses used their majoritarian power to push the level of taxation to an extortionate level, the system would crash. As, except at the end of the fifth century, under the stress of the Peloponnesian War, the Athenian democracy proved to be remarkably stable, an equilibrium was achieved. Cooperation was chosen over defection by both the citizen masses (who could defect by confiscating wealth through the exercise of majoritarian political power) and the elite (who could defect by seeking to topple the democratic government in an oligarchic coup).

The robust democratic equilibrium emerged from a "game" in which the masses granted generous elites, qua public benefactors,[93] certain honors and privileges (including positions of political and military leadership), and elites could reliably count on the masses for mobilization (in both land forces and the navy) against outside threats to state security and to the trade interests that were important to many, if not all, Athenian elites. The strategic balance was sustained via public ideology and discourse[94] and democratic institutions that adapted dynamically – through the ordinary decision-making processes of the democratic state – to changes in the environment.[95] The result was that the direct tax burden was recalibrated (within a smaller or larger percentage of the relatively well-to-do population), based on changing state needs and the economic climate.[96]

The direct taxation system potentially suffered from a serious enforcement problem, in that much elite wealth was "invisible" – i.e. held in cash or other liquid assets rather than in the form of real estate or other easily monitored assets.[97] The Athenian system of government by amateur officials was ill-suited to investigating individual assets. The solution was to encourage elites to monitor one another: the legal mechanism of *antidosis* (property exchange) enabled any wealthy individual assigned a liturgy to challenge any other wealthy individual to pay the liturgy (on the premise that the second individual's estate had been less heavily taxed in the past), or, failing that, to exchange estates. If the second individual refused to pay the liturgy or to exchange, he could be legally indicted by the first man. The People's Court then decided who had to pay. Thus, every wealthy Athenian had a strong incentive to learn what he could about the

[93] Domingo Gygax (2006). [94] Ober (1989). [95] Ober (2008).
[96] Christ (2006) traces the relevant changes in the tax system. [97] Gabrielsen (1986).

wealth of other wealthy Athenians, and – if necessary – to disclose his knowledge to the democratic government.[98]

While the rich complained about paying taxes and while tax avoidance, including some level of overt cheating, was no doubt quite common,[99] Athens' decentralized and non-bureaucratic approach to distributing the tax burden among the wealthy seems on the whole to have worked. Athens' social equilibrium was characterized by political equality between citizens but economic inequality. Economic inequality was mitigated by a limited redistribution of wealth to the poorer citizens. This in turn lowered the incentive of the poor to seek a more thoroughgoing redistribution. The Athenians created a complex fiscal system, and annually expended a large (by premodern standards) percentage of GDP for public purposes, without creating an elaborate state bureaucracy. Athens was, in sum, able to raise enough revenue to maintain its security needs, its democratic government, and its religious rituals while sustaining a generally stable and strongly democratic form of government.

Conclusions

The Athenian fiscal regime was a very highly developed form of a system that probably pertained in other Greek *poleis*, both in the classical and Hellenistic eras.[100] Key features of the Athenian regime included the background conditions of high levels of interstate competition within a fairly homogeneous culture zone that featured high levels of urbanization, per capita economic growth, and aggregate growth. The comparatively high-performing Athenian economy was characterized by a relatively egalitarian (though far from equal) distribution of income among citizen households, and most Athenians paid no direct taxes. The system was, overall, stable, characterized by a social equilibrium from which neither relatively wealthy elites nor the masses of ordinary citizens had reason to defect.

The Athenian fiscal system provided relatively high levels of public goods, especially in terms of security and welfare: public spending probably accounted for some 10 to 15 percent of annual GDP. The Athenian fiscal system was dynamically adaptive; state institutions changed, especially from the imperial fifth century to the post-imperial fourth century, in response to changing state needs and a changing interstate environment. State revenues in the imperial era were heavily dependent on rent

[98] Christ (1990). [99] Christ (2006). [100] See Mackil, Chapter 15 in this volume.

extraction, but in the post-imperial era revenues depended more on indirect taxes paid by traders attracted to Athenian markets by low transaction costs.

Revenues, in both the fifth and the fourth centuries, came from a variety of sources, including direct taxes, indirect taxes, rents, leases, extraordinary income of various sorts, and loans – the last from quasi-public sacred treasuries, from other states, and perhaps from private individuals. Among the most important questions that remain to be answered in Athenian fiscal policy is how important and regular borrowing by the state was in the overall picture of state finance. It seems possible that among the reasons for Athens' continued high comparative performance in the post-imperial period was an ability to borrow money readily, and that this ability was related to the credibility of the democratic state as a debtor.

References

Allen, K. H. (2003) "Intercultural exchanges in fourth-century Attic decrees," *Classical Antiquity* 22: 199–246.

Andreades, A. M. (1933) *A History of Greek Public Finance*. Cambridge, MA.

Bissa, E. M. A. (2008) "Investment patterns in the Laurion mining industry in the fourth century BCE," *Historia* 57: 263–73.

Blok, J. (2010) "Deme accounts and the meaning of *hosios* money in fifth-century Athens," *Mnemosyne* 63: 61–93.

Boeckh, A. (1828 [1817]) *The Public Economy of Athens; To Which Is Added, A Dissertation on the Silver Mines of Laurion*, 4 vols., trans. and ed. G. Cornewall Lewis. London.

Bresson, A. (2000) *La cité marchande*. Paris.

(2007) *L'économie de la Grèce des cités*. Paris.

Brun, P. (1983) Eisphora, Syntaxis, Stratiotika: *recherches sur les finances militaires d'Athènes au IVe siècle av. J-C*. Paris.

Burke, E. M. (1985) "Lycurgan finances," *Greek, Roman, and Byzantine Studies* 26: 251–64.

Cavanaugh, M. B. (1996) *Eleusis and Athens: Documents in Finance, Religion, and Politics in the Fifth Century BC*. Atlanta.

Cawkwell, G. L. (1963) "Eubulus," *Journal of Hellenic Studies* 83: 47–67.

Christ, M. R. (1990) "Liturgy avoidance and antidosis in classical Athens," *Transactions of the American Philological Association* 120: 147–69.

(2006) *The Bad Citizen in Classical Athens*. Cambridge.

(2007) "The evolution of the *eisphora* in classical Athens," *Classical Quarterly* 57: 53–69.

Cohen, E. E. (1992) *Athenian Economy and Society: A Banking Perspective*. Princeton, NJ.

(2000) *The Athenian Nation*. Princeton, NJ.

(Forthcoming) "Credit institutions in Greece," in *Oxford Handbook of Economies in the Classical World*, ed. E. Lo Cascio, A. Bresson, and F. Velde. Oxford.

Cook, M. L. (1990) "Timocrates' 50 Talents and the cost of ancient warfare," *Eranos* 88: 69–97.

Davies, J. K. (1971) *Athenian Propertied Families, 600–300 BC*. Oxford.

(1981) *Wealth and the Power of Wealth in Classical Athens*. New York.

(2004) "Athenian fiscal expertise and its influence," *Mediterraneo Antico* 7: 491–512.

Domergue, C. (2008) *Les mines antiques: les productions de métaux aux époques grecque et romaine*. Paris.

Domingo Gygax, M. (2006) "Les origines de l'évergétisme: échanges et identités sociales dans la cité grecque," *Mètis: anthropologie des mondes grecs anciens* 4: 269–95.

Faraguna, M. (2006) "La città di Atene e l'administrazione della miniere del Laurion," in *Symposion 2003: Vorträge zur griechischen und hellenistischen Rechtsgeschichte*, ed. H.-A. Ruprecht. Cologne: 141–60.

Flament, C. (2007) *Le monnayage en argent d'Athènes: de l'époque archaïque à l'époque hellénistique (c. 550 – c. 40 av. J-C)*. Louvain-la-Neuve, Belgium.

French, A. (1991) "Economic conditions in fourth-century Athens," *Greece and Rome* 38: 24–40.

Gabrielsen, V. (1986) "*Phanera* and *aphanes ousia* in classical Athens," *Classica et Mediaevalia* 37: 99–114.

(1994) *Financing the Athenian Fleet: Public Taxation and Social Relations*. Baltimore.

(2013) "Finance and taxes," in *A Companion to Ancient Greek Government*, ed. H. Beck. Oxford: 332–48.

Hansen, M. H. (1976) "The Theoric Fund and the *graphê* paranomon against Apollodorus," *Greek, Roman, and Byzantine Studies*. 17: 235–46.

(1999) *The Athenian Democracy in the Age of Demosthenes: Structure, Principles and Ideology*. Norman, OK.

(2006a) *Studies in the Population of Aigina, Athens and Eretria*. Copenhagen.

(2006b) *The Shotgun Method: The Demography of the Ancient Greek City-State Culture*. Columbia, MO.

(2008) "An update on the shotgun method," *Greek, Roman, and Byzantine Studies* 48: 259–86.

Harris, D. (1995) *The Treasures of the Parthenon and Erechtheion*. Oxford.

Humphreys, S. C. (1985) "Lycurgus of Butadae: an Athenian aristocrat," in *The Craft of the Ancient Historian: Essays in Honor of Chester G. Starr*, ed. J. W. Eadie and J. Ober. Lanham, MD: 199–252.

Ismard, P. (2010) *La cité des réseaux: Athènes et ses associations, VIe – Ier siècle avt. J-C*. Paris.

(2013) "Public slavery, politics and expertise in classical Athens," *Center for Hellenic Studies Research Bulletin* 1: http://nrs.harvard.edu/urn-3:hlnc.essay:IsmardP.Public_Slavery_Politics_and_Expertise_in_Classical_Athens.2013.

Jardé, A. (1925) *Les céréales dans l'antiquité grecque*. Paris.
Jones, N. F. (1999) *The Associations of Classical Athens: The Response to Democracy*. New York.
Kallet, L. (1993) *Money, Expense, and Naval Power in Thucydides' History 1–5.24*. Berkeley, CA.
(1994) "Money talks: *rhetor*, *demos*, and resources of the Athenian Empire," in Osborne and Hornblower (1994): 227–52.
(2001) *Money and the Corrosion of Power in Thucydides: The Sicilian Expedition and Its Aftermath*. Berkeley, CA.
Kroll, J. H. (2011a) "Athenian tetradrachm coinage of the first half of the fourth century BC," *Revue Belge de Numismatique* 157: 3–26.
(2011b) "The reminting of Athenian silver coinage, 353 BC," *Hesperia* 80: 229–59.
Krueger, A. O. (1974) "The political economy of the rent-seeking society," *American Economic Review* 64:291–303.
Kyriazis, N. (2009) "Financing the Athenian state: public choice in the age of Demosthenes," *European Journal of Law and Economics* 27: 109–27.
Lambert, S. D. (1997) Rationes Centesimarum: *Sales of Public Land in Lykourgan Athens*. Amsterdam.
Langdon, M. K. (1991) "Poletai records," in *The Athenian Agora,* vol. XIX, *Inscriptions*. Princeton, NJ: 53–143.
(1994) "Public auctions at Athens," in Osborne and Hornblower (1994): 253–68.
Loomis, W. T. (1998) *Wages, Welfare Costs, and Inflation in Classical Athens*. Ann Arbor, MI.
Lyttkens, C. H. (2012) *Economic Analysis of Institutional Change in Ancient Greece: Politics, Taxation and Rational Behaviour*. London.
Mackil, E., and van Alfen, P. G. (2006) "Cooperative coinages," in *Agoranomia: Studies in Money and Exchange Presented to John Kroll*, ed. P. G. van Alfen. New York: 201–46.
Meiggs, R. (1972) *The Athenian Empire*. Oxford.
Migeotte, L. (1984) *L'emprunt public dans les cités grecques: recueil des documents et analyse critique*. Quebec.
(1992) *Les souscriptions publiques dans les cités grecques*. Geneva.
Moreno, A. (2003) "Athenian bread-baskets: the grain-tax law of 374/3 BC reinterpreted," *Zeitschrift für Papyrologie und Epigraphic* 145: 97–106.
(2008) *Feeding the Democracy: The Athenian Grain Supply in the Fifth and Fourth Centuries BC*. Oxford.
Morris, I. (1987) *Burial and Ancient Society: The Rise of the Greek City-State*. Cambridge.
(2004) "Economic growth in ancient Greece," *Journal of Institutional and Theoretical Economics* 160: 709–42.
North, D. C., Wallis, J. J., and Weingast, B. R. (2009) *Violence and Social Orders: A Conceptual Framework for Interpreting Recorded Human History*. New York.
Ober, J. (1985) *Fortress Attica: Defense of the Athenian Land Frontier, 404–322 BC*. Leiden.

(1989) *Mass and Elite in Democratic Athens: Rhetoric, Ideology, and the Power of the People*. Princeton, NJ.
(2008) *Democracy and Knowledge: Learning and Innovation in Classical Athens*. Princeton, NJ.
(2010) "Wealthy Hellas," *Transactions of the American Philological Association* 140: 241–86.
Oliver, G. J. (2007) *War, Food, and Politics in Early Hellenistic Athens*. Oxford.
Osborne, R., and Hornblower, S. (eds.) (1994) *Ritual, Finance, Politics: Athenian Democratic Accounts Presented to David Lewis*. Oxford.
Pritchard, D. (2007) "Costing the armed forces of Athens during the Peloponnesian War," *Ancient History* 37: 125–33.
(2012) "Costing festivals and war: spending priorities of the Athenian democracy," *Historia* 61: 18–65.
Rhodes, P. J. (1985) *The Athenian Boule*. Oxford.
(2010) *A History of the Classical Greek World: 478–323 BC*, 2nd edn. Malden, MA.
(2013) "The organisation of Athenian public finance," *Greece and Rome* 60: 203–31.
Rhodes, P. J., and Osborne, R. (2003) *Greek Historical Inscriptions: 404–323 BC*. Oxford.
Roberts, J. T. (1982) *Accountability in Athenian Government*. Madison, WI.
Rosivach, V. J. (1994) *The System of Public Sacrifice in Fourth-Century Athens*. Atlanta.
Runciman, W. G. (1990) "Doomed to extinction: the *polis* as an evolutionary dead-end," in *The Greek City: From Homer to Alexander*, ed. O. Murray and S. Price. Oxford: 347–67.
Samons, L. J. (2000) *Empire of the Owl: Athenian Imperial Finance*. Stuttgart.
Scheidel, W. (2010) "Real wages in early economies: evidence for living standards from 1800 BCE to 1300 CE," *Journal of the Social and Economic History of the Orient* 53: 425–62.
Scheidel, W., and Friesen, S. J. (2009) "The size of the economy and the distribution of income in the Roman Empire," *Journal of Roman Studies* 99: 61–91.
Schultz, K. A., and Weingast, B. R. (2003) "The democratic advantage: the institutional foundations of financial power in international competition," *International Organization* 57: 3–42.
Stroud, R. S. (1998) *The Athenian Grain-Tax Law of 374/3 BC*. Princeton, NJ.
Tsoukala, V. (2009) "Honorary shares of sacrificial meat in Attic vase painting: visual signs of distinction and civic identity," *Hesperia* 78: 1–40.
Unz, R. K. (1985) "The surplus of the Athenian *phoros*," *Greek, Roman, and Byzantine Studies* 26: 21–42.
Van Alfen, P. G. (2005) "Problems in ancient imitative and counterfeit coinage," in *Making, Moving, and Managing: The New World of Ancient Economics, 323–31 BC*, ed. Z. Archibald, J. K. Davies, and V. Gabrielsen. Oxford: 322–54.
(2011) "Hatching owls: Athenian public finance and the regulation of coin production," in *Quantifying Monetary Supplies in Greco-Roman Times*, ed. F. de Callataÿ. Bari: 127–49.

Vannier, F. (1988) *Finances publiques et richesses privées dans le discours athénien aux Ve et IVe siècles.* Paris.

Wallis, J. J. (2000) "American government finance in the long run: 1790 to 1990," *Journal of Economic Perspectives* 14: 61–82.

Wees, H. van (2000) "The city at war," in *Classical Greece, 500–323 BC*, ed. R. Osborne. Oxford: 81–110.

Whitehead, D. (1977) *The Ideology of the Athenian Metic.* Cambridge.

Williams, A. (2011) "Leasing of sacred land in 4th-century Athens: a reassessment of six inscribed fragments," *Hesperia* 80: 261–86.

Wilson, P. (2000) *The Athenian Institution of the Khoregia: The Chorus, the City and the Stage.* Cambridge.

(2008) "Costing the Dionysia," in *Performance, Iconography, Reception: Studies in Honour of Oliver Taplin*, ed. M. Revermann and P. Wilson. Oxford: 88–127.

(2010) "How did the Athenian demes fund their theatre?," *Bryn Mawr Classical Review* 04.21: 37–82.

Zimmern, A. E. (1931) *The Greek Commonwealth: Politics and Economics in Fifth-Century Athens.* Oxford.

CHAPTER 17

Why did public debt originate in Europe?

David Stasavage

Today we take it as a given that, in order to function effectively, a government needs to have the ability to borrow, and to borrow over long time horizons. Yet, in the long history of fiscal states, public borrowing is a relative recent innovation. This is a puzzle demanding explanation. Perhaps even more puzzling is the fact that a generalized form of long-term public borrowing first emerged in medieval Europe, an economic backwater in many respects. In this short chapter I suggest why public debt first originated in Europe, and what this tells us more generally about the political conditions necessary for a state to gain access to long-term credit. The initial development of public credit in Europe depended heavily on a particular political institution: a representative assembly that monitors and intervenes in the area of state finance. The emergence of representative political institutions itself depended on a deeper causal factor, however: the long-standing trend in Europe for certain cities to be able to govern themselves autonomously. In an era of high travel and transport costs it was initially possible to sustain the institutions necessary for public credit only in a small polity, such as an autonomous city. It was only over time that rulers in Europe's larger territorial states would learn to establish access to credit precisely by working through their cities.

In what follows I develop my argument in the following sequence of steps. Beginning with an abstract consideration of the factors that condition the development of public credit, I then chart the evolution of public borrowing in Europe over a period of five and a half centuries between 1250 and the French Revolution. This is then followed by an exploration of why city states were the pioneers with regard to credit, why they eventually died out, and, finally, how territorial rulers eventually learned to harness the power of their cities.[1]

[1] The account here derives from material in my recent book (Stasavage 2011), as well as from two recent papers (Stasavage 2010; 2014).

What factors conditioned the development of public credit?

If we are to ask why public credit first emerged in Europe, then it makes sense to first think in abstract terms about the factors necessary for a government to be able to borrow. There were four necessary preconditions for public credit to emerge.

A first and most obvious condition is that a government must have a monetary source of revenue that can be used to repay any debt that is contracted. Some of the states considered in this volume had fiscal systems – sometimes even advanced ones – that were not monetary in form, and therefore this condition was not satisfied.[2] In Europe, however, even in the early medieval era when state capacity was weak at best, polities had access to monetary forms of revenue.

A second condition for public credit to emerge – or, more exactly, to be necessary – is that a state must be faced with expenditure shocks. For modern states, such expenditure shocks can come in a number of different forms, involving the need to respond to economic crisis, sudden needs for infrastructure, or even those arising from natural disasters. For the polities considered in this volume, in which modern forms of social protection were absent, wartime needs constituted the almost exclusive form of expenditure shock. Once we take this into account, we can understand why a full-fledged public debt did not develop in a place such as Tokugawa Japan. With the problem of civil violence solved and external threats kept at a safe distance, there were no wartime expenditure shocks, and therefore no need to establish a highly developed system of public credit.[3] The situation in Europe could not have been more different, of course. Warfare was prevalent from a very early date and only increased in intensity as time progressed. It is a matter of debate whether war was the prime causal factor that drove European state development. What is certain, though, is that, were it not for the demands of war, European polities would have faced far fewer needs to borrow.

Even if a polity is faced with a sudden expenditure shock, there remains an alternative to borrowing if it is possible to suddenly increase revenue in dramatic fashion. The problem is that doing this with monetary revenue involves very significant political and economic costs. It is also possible for

[2] For an example, see D'Altroy, Chapter 2 in this volume, on the Inka fiscal regime.

[3] For further elaboration, see Brown, Chapter 14, on the Tokugawa fiscal regime.

polities to levy a tax in kind for war purposes, however, and the most common tax of this sort has been military conscription. A number of the polities in this volume had effective systems of military conscription that avoided the need to offer soldiers monetary compensation for their services, and that therefore reduced the need for developing a system of public credit. Once again, the situation in Europe could not have been more different. For European territorial states, a system of conscription did initially exist in the form of feudal service. This system evolved toward one of monetary compensation for paid mercenaries, however. This development took place for the simple reason that those bound only by feudal obligation often failed to show up when summoned. In the autonomous cities of Europe a different set of circumstances prevailed, though the end outcome was the same. Initially cities defended themselves and waged war by drafting citizen militias. Over time, however, it became apparent that a much more efficient strategy was the hiring of mercenaries. In autonomous cities and territorial states alike, then, the move away from waging war by obliging citizens or subjects to serve for free made it necessary to raise money, and often on short notice.

The above three conditions helped dictate why it was necessary and useful for European polities to have access to public credit. The presence of monetary revenues also explains why European rulers could repay debts. There is, however, a fourth critical condition that is of course necessary for a system of public credit to emerge: there must be some expectation that rulers will *want* to repay their debts. Given the immediate financial advantages of defaulting, there has to be some constraint on a ruler's incentive to exercise this option. One possibility is the fear for one's reputation. Failure to prioritize debt servicing may make it difficult or impossible for a ruler to obtain credit from lenders in the future. While reputational constraints can be binding, it is also well known that in times of crisis, with pressing and immediate needs, the risk of future sanctions may be insufficient to constrain a ruler.

Given the potential inadequacy of reputation as a constraint, a large body of work suggests that access to credit will depend above all on having a good set of institutions that offer creditors the assurance that debts will be repaid. In the context of medieval and early modern Europe, it has been suggested that representative assemblies could play this role, constraining rulers to repay debt when they might otherwise have preferred not to do so.[4] There

[4] This is an idea that is, of course, most closely associated with the seminal piece by North and Weingast (1989).

are two important questions about this, however. First, why would a representative assembly itself prefer debt servicing to default?[5] Second, if representative assemblies served this useful function, then why didn't they emerge in all European polities?

The other attractive feature of the argument emphasizing representative assemblies is that long-term credit and political representation were both innovations that saw their most extensive early development in Europe. Along with the other factors listed above, the relative absence of strong representative institutions in other world regions may provide further reason why European polities were the first to develop an extensive system of public credit. This said, even without representative assemblies as they existed in Europe, we should not ignore the possibility for rulers in other regions to establish alternative institutional forms that might have helped sustain a system of public credit.

The rise of European public credit in one picture

As part of the research for my recently published book, *States of Credit*, I collected an extensive new data set that charts the development of public credit in Europe from the thirteenth through the eighteenth centuries. This expands on the prior important work of Stephan Epstein for his book *Freedom and Growth*.[6] For a set of thirty-one European polities, my data set pools together observations from many disparate sources that report the year in which a polity contracted a long-term debt and the nominal interest rate on this debt. In the vast majority of cases these were actually life or perpetual annuities, as opposed to true debts. While the Catholic Church in Europe deemed that charging interest on debt was usury, it did not make the same judgment with regard to annuities for which a regular payment was made but the "borrower" in effect never returned the principal.[7]

Figure 17.1 presents each of the observations in the data set, distinguishing between two types of polities: autonomous cities and territorial states. This single picture is in fact very instructive about the evolution of public credit in Europe over this period of roughly five and a half centuries. There is an obvious and immediate distinction here between the fortunes of city states and territorial states. If city states began issuing long-term debt as early as the thirteenth century, at the height of the medieval commercial revolution, the first territorial states did not take this step until more than

[5] This is a point emphasized and considered by Stasavage (2003). [6] Epstein (2000).

[7] See Munro (2003) for an extensive and enlightening discussion of this point.

Figure 17.1 Interest rates on public credit in European polities, 1250–1789

two centuries later. This requires an explanation. Likewise, during periods when city states and territorial states both issued debt, we can see clearly from the figure that city states were, on average, able to do so on more favorable terms. This too requires an explanation.

One possible explanation for the above pattern is that rulers of territorial states simply had neither need nor desire to borrow prior to the beginning of the sixteenth century. This is implausible, however, given that the demands of war placed financial strains on monarchs from a much earlier date. Another possibility is that European monarchs preferred to contract short-term loans, such as those taken out by Edward III with various Italian bankers, rather than incur long-term obligations. The problem with this argument is that these short-term loans almost invariably came at very high rates of interest that reflected the risk involved.

Given the weakness of these above explanations, the most logical conclusion is that rulers of large territorial states would have benefited from establishing long-terms loans at an earlier date, but they found it difficult to gain access to credit. The key question, then, is: what were the underlying factors that differentiated territorial states from city states in this regard?

What was the secret of Europe's city states?

At first glance we might think that city states had an advantage in terms of access to credit because of their economic structure. These were economic dynamos involving long-distance commerce and light industry (i.e. textiles), and it is only logical that there would have been an available pool of lenders in such places. The problem with this argument is that large territorial states also had numerous, vibrant commercial cities under their rule that could have supplied a pool of capital. This raises the possibility that there was something particular about governance in city states, and this may explain why they were so successful in obtaining access to credit.

In *States of Credit* I report the results of an econometric analysis in which it was asked both what factors were associated with early access to credit and what factors were associated with access to credit at lower cost. The results of this analysis present a puzzle. We do indeed see clear evidence that the presence of a representative assembly that had strong financial prerogatives, and that met frequently, was associated with better access to credit. Once we introduce a dummy variable into the analysis to distinguish between city states and territorial states, however, we see, not surprisingly, that city states had better access to credit, but also that the representative institutions variables lose any statistical significance. Does this mean that representative institutions simply did not matter? No; what it suggests instead is that an intensive form of political representation did favor access to credit, but that this type of political representation existed almost exclusively in the autonomous cities of Europe. Why would this be the case? In what follows I suggest that, on one level, it was the intensive form of political representation within city states that was the key to their success in gaining access to credit. This form of political representation was itself dependent on two underlying factors, however: compact geography and merchant dominance.

Compact geography and political representation

Political representation is often presented as a necessary adaptation to a problem of scale. If the population of a polity is too numerous for direct democracy, then choose a set of representatives. If the population of a polity is spread too widely across the terrain, then adopt the same solution. If representation is an adaptation to problems of scale, however, then, ultimately, it should be recognized that representative systems are also constrained by scale. In medieval and early modern Europe geographic scale posed a major constraint for any and all who sought to maintain an intensive form of political representation within their polity. This fact has been cogently argued in a series of publications by Wim Blockmans.[8] In an era of high transport and communications costs in large polities it was costly to send representatives to an assembly. It was also costly for constituents to then monitor the actions of representatives once they were in place. Under these conditions, autonomous cities had an obvious advantage when compared with their larger territorial state neighbors. In a recent article I provide econometric support for the argument first made by Blockmans.[9] Based on an original data set on the functions and prerogatives of representative assemblies in a broad set of European states, I find very strong evidence of a negative correlation between geographic scale and the intensity of political representation. Moreover, this negative correlation continues to hold even when we exclude the set of city states from the sample. This rules out the possibility of a spurious correlation between geography and representation that was driven by some other feature of city states that led them to have an intensive form of political representation.

The "virtues" of merchant oligarchy

I suggested above that a representative assembly might constrain a government or ruler to service debt, but it is certainly also plausible that a representative assembly might express exactly the opposite preference. For example, on several occasions when it met the members of France's Estates General expressed a desire to see the monarchy defer or default on debt payments so as to avoid what would otherwise be a significant increase in taxes. Why did the representative assemblies of city states not follow this same course of action? The fundamental reason was that, in most cases, merchants dominated the membership of these assemblies and of the executive committees that most often ran them. These were the same individuals who had liquid capital and who purchased public debt. To see this we can consider what happened when a mercantile oligarchy lost power, such as in Siena after 1355. When this took place, public credit suffered.

The pattern of merchant dominance in autonomous cities was itself dependent on another underlying factor that was specific, if not unique, to Europe. As documented by Wickham, from an early date a pattern was established for most regions of Europe, in which merchants were located in cities and the members of the landed nobility resided in the countryside.[10]

[8] Blockmans (1978; 1998). [9] Stasavage (2010). [10] Wickham (2007).

This was a distinctive pattern that set the stage for merchants to become dominant in the governance of cities in a way that was not always or often replicated in other world regions.

How city states became obsolete

If urban autonomy was crucial in leading to the development of public credit in Europe, there nonetheless seems to be a curious twist to the story. As a number of authors have observed and attempted to explain, over the long run it was the territorial states, and not the city states, of Europe that became predominant. For some, such as Tilly and Bean, this had to do with economies of scale in war fighting.[11] In other words, city states died out because they couldn't raise the large armies nor afford new and expensive types of fortification or weaponry. In *States of Credit*, however, I argue that city states maintained a financial advantage over their territorial state neighbors for longer than is often realized, and this allowed a number of them to serve well after 1500 AD – a date that is sometimes offered as the beginning of the era of the territorial state in Europe. So why, then, did city states not retain their preeminence?

The secret of the financial success of city states was that the same merchants who provided the funds for public credit also controlled all the levers of political power, ensuring adequate servicing of debt. Merchant oligarchy was therefore good for access to credit. The problem with merchant oligarchy in city states was that, if it had unambiguously good implications for credit, the implications of this political system for long-run growth were considerably more mixed. One of the features of an oligarchy in which oligarchs are themselves engaged in economic activities is that it can provide very secure property rights for those on the inside of the political system. This can therefore be favorable to economic growth if those on the inside, so to speak, have access to the most advanced production technologies. A serious problem can then emerge, however, if in order to sustain the process of economic growth it is necessary to have a continuous inflow of new entrepreneurs bringing new techniques. As long as an oligarchy establishes barriers to entry into markets – and this was certainly the case for urban oligarchies in medieval and early modern Europe – then this poses an obvious problem for sustaining economic performance over the long run.[12]

[11] Tilly (1992); Bean (1973).

[12] This problem has been discussed in the European historical context by Mokyr (1990), and in a more abstract form by Acemoglu (2008).

In a recent paper I provide evidence consistent with the above theoretical mechanism; an oligarchic form of rule was good for city-state economic performance in the short term but bad for the long term.[13] Using population growth as a proxy for economic growth, I show econometrically that, during the first century in which they were politically independent, autonomous cities in Europe on average grew substantially more quickly than non-autonomous cities. After roughly a century of independence, however, autonomous cities stagnated relative to those cities subject to princely domination. This robust finding points to a new explanation as to why Europe's city states eventually became marginalized despite their excellent access to credit. The same political institutions that gave them access to credit also condemned them over time to economic obsolescence.

How territorial rulers harnessed the credit of their cities

The initial development of public credit in Europe was highly dependent on the existence of a particular form of polity: an autonomous city. This same pattern of urban autonomy would continue to influence the development of public credit when the territorial monarchies of Europe first established systems of long-term borrowing. Just as the autonomous cities of Europe issued annuities for which payment was backed by future municipal revenues, subject cities within territorial monarchies also often issued similar financial instruments. Initially territorial rulers used this as an ad hoc finance mechanism for their own purposes. Subsequently territorial rulers began to do this more systematically, resulting in the creation of the first true national debts. In France this practice was initiated with the creation of royal *rentes sur l'hotel de ville* in 1522. Through this system, annuities were issued in the king's name but were managed by the municipality of Paris, and the *rentes* were paid using revenue streams monitored by that same body – or, at least, initially so. In Castile a different system emerged. The monarchy had a representative assembly that was dominated by eighteen towns. Each of these towns issued annuities that were then used for royal finance.

The lesson of the French and Spanish experiences is clear. Lacking the state capacity to have a true, unified system of national debt, complete with the institutions to sustain this, large monarchies found that the optimal solution was to piggyback off the forms of governance that had been established by cities within their territories. Though the case of England

[13] Stasavage (2014).

after 1688 is often, and rightly, hailed as a very successful system of public credit, England was actually something of an exception among European territorial states. Compared to other states in this category, its core territory was quite small. A feature that went hand in hand with this is that England's fiscal system was centralized from a very early date, in fact from the Norman conquest.

Conclusions

In this chapter I have attempted to explore the reasons why a true system of public credit first emerged in Europe during an era when, paradoxically, the economic and administrative strength of European polities was considerably weaker than that in many other world regions. The combination of a monetary economy, sudden expenditure demands due to war, and the lack of a system for mobilizing manpower without payments made it very useful for rulers of European polities to have access to credit. Access to credit also depended on a critical fourth condition, however: an expectation on the part of creditors that debts would actually be repaid. It is now well established that one method for establishing this expectation is to adopt a good set of institutions for managing debt. Yet this raises a paradox, because medieval Europe was a place in which institutions of governance and state capacity were undoubtedly weak. Drawing on my work published elsewhere, I have argued that the answer to this puzzle can be provided by investigating the autonomous city phenomenon in Europe. Europe's autonomous cities were islands of state capacity that had the institutions and political composition necessary for the development of a system of public credit. Ultimately, however, the same institutions that gave city states a financial advantage put them at a long-run disadvantage, and ensured that they would become obsolete.

References

Acemoglu, D. (2008) "Oligarchic versus democratic societies," *Journal of the European Economic Association* 6: 1–44.

Bean, R. (1973) "War and the birth of the nation state," *Journal of Economic History* 33: 203–21.

Blockmans, W. (1978) "A typology of representative institutions in late medieval Europe," *Journal of Medieval History* 4: 189–215.

(1998) "Representation (since the thirteenth century)," in *The New Cambridge Medieval History, vol. VII, c. 1415 – c. 1500*, ed. C. Allmand. Cambridge: 29–64.

Epstein, S. (2000) *Freedom and Growth: The Rise of States and Markets in Europe, 1300–1750*. London.

Mokyr, J. (1990) *The Lever of Riches: Technological Creativity and Economic Progress*. Oxford.

Munro, J. H. (2003) "The late-medieval origins of the modern financial revolution: overcoming impediments from Church and state," International History Review 25: 505–62.

North, D. C., and Weingast, B. R. (1989) "Constitutions and commitment: the evolution of institutions governing public choice in seventeenth-century England," *Journal of Economic History* 49: 803–32.

Stasavage, D. (2003) *Public Debt and the Birth of the Democratic State: France and Great Britain 1688–1789*. Cambridge.

(2010) "When distance mattered: geographic scale and the development of European representative assemblies," *American Political Science Review* 104: 625–43.

(2011) *States of Credit: Size, Power, and the Development of European Polities*. Princeton, NJ.

(2014) "Was Weber right? The role of urban autonomy in Europe's rise," *American Political Science Review* 108: 337–54.

Tilly, C. (1992) *Coercion, Capital, and European States: AD 990–1992*, rev. edn. Malden, MA.

Wickham, C. (2007) *Framing the Early Middle Ages: Europe and the Mediterranean*. Oxford.

PART V

Comparative Perspectives and New Frontiers

CHAPTER 18

Tributary empires and the New Fiscal Sociology: some comparative reflections

Peter F. Bang

> "Imperator Caesar M. Aurelius Severus Alexander. . .proclaims. . . in order that through their desire to express the joy they have in my accession to the imperial office they not be forced into contributions greater than they can afford. . . Therefore, let all men in the cities both throughout Italy and among the other peoples be my witness: for other 'gold crowns', even though occasioned by my accession as emperor. . .I must cancel the claims made upon the cities. . . It is necessary that I. . .repair the declining state of things, not by searches for revenue, but by economy alone. . .to see the emperor administering the duties of kingship with so much orderliness and moderation and restraint."[1]

If we did not know better, this document might almost be thought to have issued from a chancellery staffed by Confucian literati. Certainly, the basic idea that the good emperor would remit taxes to spare the population and instead attempt to govern through an exemplary show of personal economy, self-restraint, and virtuous conduct seems to read almost like a textbook expression of the model of sage rulership espoused by generations of Chinese imperial monarchs. But, of course, the context is Roman, and the ideology fashioned in the crucible of Greek philosophy. There is a welcome reminder from 222 CE that for much of recorded history the question of "rule and revenue" played itself out within a constellation of social powers dominated by monarchs and landowners. This basic configuration produced a set of constraints and patterns of conduct that invite comparison across Eurasia, and beyond.

[1] Oliver (1989: no. 275) (Greek text, English translation [gently modified by me], and basic commentary). I am much obliged for helpful comments and suggestions from the editors, the conference participants, and the anonymous peer reviewers in writing up this essay – not least the advice that my conference paper be turned into a historical synthesis of sorts for the entire volume. I hope not too much violence has been done to the other contributions in this exercise.

But our example is also paradigmatic of the problems that this chapter seeks to address in a more narrow sense. The "tax" Alexander Severus remitted in a gesture of ostentatious magnanimity was not quite one of the regular taxes.[2] The so-called *aurum coronarium* was, in appearance, a voluntary contribution spontaneously sent or voted by the individual cities and provinces to congratulate the ruler, sometimes even delivered in the form of a golden wreath by an official delegation. Suitable occasions might, for instance, be military victories, accession to the throne, or jubilees. There is an almost "feudal" air about this tax, presenting itself as a gift from the subjects to the emperor. Even after centuries of imperial rule and permanent tribute extraction, taxation was still tinged, however faintly, with a sense of illegitimacy. It was often perceived as a mark of oppression. This feeling lay behind the trick question that the Gospels famously pose to Jesus, whether it was legitimate for the Jews to pay tax to the emperor, which elicited the famous, but elusive answer "Render therefore unto Caesar the things which are Caesar's; and unto God the things that are God's."[3] It is surely revealing that Eusebius in his *History of the Church* should have chosen to hold measurement of agricultural lands against the emperor Licinius in an attempt to smear and saddle the defeated rival of his hero, Constantine, with a reputation for tyranny.[4]

With regard to the *aurum coronarium*, an ironic observer pierced through the ceremonial facade and remarked how cities had to dread the arrival of imperial letters announcing victories, sometimes even fictitious, because such joyous occasions had been turned into a means of wringing extra tax payments out of the wretched subject communities.[5] Taxes might well appear acts of predation. The correspondence of a late antique member of the high Roman nobility reveals that it was not even beyond the emperors to specify how much was expected under this heading of a special contribution – by then, "a deafening silence" had fallen on the assembled senators. At the same time, however, the decision to postpone debate on how to bring about the desired sum also raised the prospect that

[2] See Ando (2000: 175–90) for a recent discussion of the *aurum coronarium*, emphasizing the element of ceremonial exchange. Klauser (1944) has collected most of the evidence, and notes how the initially voluntary contributions of the subject communites with time tended to become a regular tax, only then to prompt new voluntary gifts celebrating the successes of the ruler.

[3] Matthew 22.21 (King James version).

[4] Eusebius, *Ecclesiastical History* 10.8.12. See Mann (1986: 289), quoting Lactantius for similar objections to census registration.

[5] Ammianus Marcellinus, *Roman History* 16.12.69 (concerning Constantius); Dio Cassius, *Roman History* 78.9.1–2 (on Caracalla).

perhaps an element of negotiation was possible.[6] So does the edict of Alexander Severus, which envisages that not all cities had yet gone through with the voting of gold for his crowns. Occasionally subject communities were able to obtain a regular tax concession by offering crown gold instead.[7] But all such negotiation took place within limits. An open refusal of payment of the celebratory contribution would be tantamount to a declaration of disloyalty, effectively an act of rebellion. Legitimacy of taxation, predatory extraction, and the negotiation of payment: the *aurum coronarium* raises a number of issues that speak directly to the questions addressed by the so-called New Fiscal Sociology, which serves as a broad framework for this volume. How does the experience of pre-industrial societies, represented by the articles assembled here, and more widely, square with this body of theoretical work – modify, broaden, and identify alternative paths of development – that will be the topic of this chapter, particularly in relation to vast agrarian or tributary empires.

Tributary empires in the New Fiscal Sociology

Two tenets are at the heart of the New Fiscal Sociology: (1) that taxation is held to be the key to understanding society and the body politic, as in it is concentrated the social contract; and (2) that taxation is always the result of a negotiated process.[8] Unsurprisingly, hailing as it does from the social sciences, the New Fiscal Sociology has focused predominantly on the modern world and on demonstrating the crucial role played by taxation in developing its underpinning institutions. This is both weakness and

[6] Symmachus, *Letters* 2.57.2–3: "vastum silentium." In the thirteenth of his *Relationes*, Symmachus informs the emperor of the size of a contribution voted to him by the Roman Senate, but also explains why it is not even bigger: "[N]o riches. . .could match the goodwill of our love towards you" [author's translation].

[7] See *Theodosian Code* 13.4 (an imperial ruling, contemplating among other things that subjects might volunteer contributions in gratitude for a tax remission). Synesius's speech, *De Regno*, is generally seen as occasioned by just such an attempt to promise gold crowns in return for a reduction in the regular tax burden of the city of Cyrene; see Ando (2000: 180) and Cameron, Long, and Sherry (1993: 133–5).

[8] See Martin, Mehrotra, and Prasad (2009: 1 – social contract; 3–4, 23, 26 – social negotiation and bargaining): "Taxation enmeshes us in the web of generalized reciprocity that constitutes modern society. . . The form of tax obligations is constantly changing as different taxpayers and different rulers seek to renegotiate the relationship to their advantage. . . Because social order depends on the state and the state depends on the resources provided by taxation, this relationship may be renegotiated, but it will not be severed. The possibility of tension will be continually reproduced rather than resolved" (ibid.: 3–4). "[T]axpayer consent is best explained not as coercion, predation, or illusion, but as a collective bargain in which taxpayers give up resources in exchange for collective goods. . . [T]hat multiplies a society's infrastructural power" (ibid.: 14; inverse order of quotes).

strength, but most of all a great opportunity for constructive dialogue to develop. Students of premodern societies cannot merely be satisfied to take on the role of passive subscriber, but also have to modify and expand this new body of theory to cover the type of historical experience that we deal with. In this respect, the role of the contributions to this volume resembles that of the development economists. A recent collection of essays dedicated to the New Fiscal Sociology, for instance, contains a chapter advocating the adoption of tax-farming as a viable strategy for African states.[9] This method of taxation, normally thought of as less modern, might, the authors – Kiser and Sacks – argue, produce beneficial results in a setting in which the economy is insufficiently productive and the state too weak to sustain the elaborate, but costly, bureaucracies familiar from the more affluent parts of the modern world. Some premodern scholars are likely to object here to what they perceive as a primitivizing thrust in my argument. That rests on a misunderstanding. In terms of the size of their bureaucracy, level of taxation, and amount of infrastructure, most of the African examples dealt with by Kiser and Sacks compare favorably with pre-industrial societies.

As will emerge below, the need for modification relates particularly to the tenet of taxation as a negotiated process. The first principle, on the other hand, seems more than congenial as the basis on which to proceed. One of the key distinctions characteristic of pre-industrial, complex societies is that between the lord and the peasant. Much, not to say most, of the agricultural surplus was mobilized through the political extraction of dues from peasants and other primary producers. The effects of this process were profound, and resulted in some of the biggest cities and market concentrations of pre-industrial history, when vast agrarian empires formed as the result of conquest and fashioned rulers with command of resources on a staggering scale in a world otherwise characterized by small numbers. Wickham has dubbed this the tributary mode of production, in a classic article; opposed to this form of surplus extraction, he identifies a feudal mode based on the localized extraction of rents.[10] Haldon has attempted to modify this scheme: noticing that both modes of surplus appropriation were rooted in the political subjection of the peasantry, he prefers to treat them both as one; the tributary mode was the prevalent social form among complex pre-industrial societies.[11] Both variations of this scheme have their merits. By insisting on unity, Haldon is able to highlight how many local landlords owed their holdings to the privileged position they enjoyed

[9] Kiser and Sacks (2009). [10] Wickham (1985).
[11] Haldon (1993); Goldstone and Haldon (2009).

within a wider tributary political system. Likewise, Wickham's conceptualization identifies a potential conflict between local aristocracies and members higher up in the hierarchy of political elites more closely tied to the interests of a central, imperial government. It also facilitates an understanding of why the taxation of a central state apparatus remained contested for centuries, and might even be rolled back almost completely, as happened in Europe during the early Middle Ages. The crucial variable to explain this development is identified as changes in the form of military organization.[12] In spite of the overt Marxist credentials, there is little here to separate the approaches of Wickham and Haldon from the Weberian sociology of modes of power, of *Herrschaft*. The structure of rule, type of military mobilization, and mode of taxation are treated as inseparably linked. For much of history, military power served as a tool of domination to impose taxes on subject communities. This was the business of empire.

It is necessary to take note of an alternative, but very widespread, usage of the concept of tribute. Among social scientists, in particular, and several contributors to this volume, Smith most notably (Chapter 3), the term is often employed to denote payments that are only intermittent, rather than permanent, to an imperial overlord. To such terminological issues there is no solution, only reasons to prefer one definition instead of the other. Often the understanding of tribute as evanescent is accompanied by a view that sees it as a primitive form of extraction. As soon as the state develops, more permanent, institutionalized forms – in short, taxation – take over. Such a developmental view is not unequivocally borne out by the wide number of historical cases on parade here, however. Certainly, as remarked by several of the contributors, there was no general move toward a fiscal-military type of state. Chinese imperial history, for instance, confronts us with the paradox that at the pinnacle of success, when the Qing emperors had finally brought their arch-enemy, the nomads of central Asia to heel, the government was losing ground in society and saw its capacity to tax diminished.[13] To be sure, one may detect a modest evolutionary – or, perhaps better – accumulative trend. In the examples of early complex societies, such as the Incas, Mesopotamia, and Egypt described by D'Altroy (Chapter 2 in this volume) and Jursa and Moreno García (Chapter 4), control of labor and the formation of royal domain lands seem initially to be more important

[12] Wickham (2005).

[13] See Lieberman (2009: 504–24) for an excellent overview of late imperial Chinese history – in many ways the culmination of universal empire, but also, as Deng points out in Chapter 10 in this volume, an era when government taxation was hollowed out.

than a general collection of part of the produce of the peasant majority. But the introduction of "taxation" proper by more "mature" agrarian states does not render the other forms obsolete. Rather, they remain as forms of resource mobilization within a widened repertoire of extractive strategies. An imperial organism such as the Roman Empire, which I know best, or the Mughal Empire, to name an example among the early modern Muslim empires, would normally combine several types of exaction, from stable collection to chance extraction. It is not the "level of development" or institutionalization of the imperial governmental apparatus that was crucial.[14] Decisive for the mode of "exploitation" was, instead, the character of the territory. The population density, patterns of primary production, and the form of political organization were the crucial variables determining what kind of domination an area could sustain. To the Romans, tribute became the mark of imperial subjection, whether made manifest by the imposition of regular (land) taxes or articulated in ceremonies of defeated foes offering the resources of their territories as gifts of submission to the imperial lords.[15] Tribute reminds us of the element of domination behind the collection of dues in a way that "taxation," in the usage of the New Fiscal Sociology, with its emphasis on negotiation and collaboration, does not.

A good example of the latter approach is Glete's *War and the State in Early Modern Europe*. Taking his cue from Lane, he perceives the state as a seller of protection, and tax as the price it receives from its subject customers. A very important aspect of Lane's crisp and innovative conceptualization is left out of the analysis, however. States are not simply sellers of protection; they are also producers of violence. The market in protection is not constituted by groups of freely transacting and negotiating agents. States and ruling groups generally hold superior means of coercion, and thus offer their "goods" from a monopolistic position; they get to collect a surcharge, monopoly profit, or – as Lane calls it – a tribute

[14] See Alam and Subrahmanyam (1998: 15–16) for some brief observations on the limits to uniformity in the tax regime of the Mughal Empire. For Rome, apart from the contributions to this volume, see, for example, Duncan-Jones (1990: ch. 12).

[15] See Statius, *Silvae* 4.1.39–42; Tacitus, *Agricola* 31.1–2, for a graphic passage linking slavery and tribute; *Histories* 4.71: tribute an imposition tolerated by the Gauls; and *Histories* 4.74: the precondition of the imperial peace. Further, Cicero, *Against Verres* 2.3.6, 12–15, though using *stipendium* and *vectigal* instead of *tributum*, for a passage describing provincial taxation generally as the punishment for war, the prize of victory. *Digest* 50.15.8.7 (Paul, responses to the census) illustrates clearly how, when provincial communities were lifted to a more privileged status, this immediately brought up the question of freeing them from *tributum*. See Landskron (2006) on the representation of provinces in Roman imperial reliefs. Lavan (2013) analyzes slavery as a metaphor of imperial subjection in ancient Rome; chapter 3 is dedicated to Tacitus.

in excess of their production costs.[16] At heart, the state developed as a predator, and none more so than the vast agrarian and tributary empires of Eurasian history.[17] But, as Levi has taught us, naked predation is impractical and unstable. Successful state formation and imperialism require acceptance and compliance to develop; a measure of collaboration – and hence social negotiation – has to be fostered.[18]

For long, the form of British parliamentary politics developing out of the so-called "Glorious Revolution" has served as the model case of the growth of the collaborative fiscal-military state: a pure instance of taxation as negotiation.[19] Clearly, there is a lesson to be learned from this experience, and it seems to inform much of the literature on the New Fiscal Sociology. Even so, the crucial matter remains how we should go about generalizing the insights to be had from English history. Ottomanists, for instance, have been struggling to overcome the stereotype of Oriental despotism and the statist emphasis of Kemalist ideology, both projecting an image of "total power" and corrupt government onto the empire of the sultans. Developing an idea of Kafadar, Tezcan has most recently objected to this totalizing and inflated image of Ottoman "despotic" state power by identifying, among others, the janissaries as an influential group that limited and curbed the activities of the sultan. They could effectively be paralleled with the British parliament, he contends, similarly imposing a need on the government to reach negotiated arrangements with its subject community.[20] This is an inspired interpretation; and there is a long and distinguished pedigree for its way of thinking.[21] In the indictment of Warren Hastings, returned governor of India, Edmund Burke equally railed in the House of Lords against the exaggerated powers ascribed to Oriental despots and tirelessly proclaimed the virtues of the so-called "Institutes of Tamerlane," a treatise on statecraft cherished by the Mughals.[22] Government in India also recognized arrangements, parallel to

[16] Lane (1958). It is noticeable that the notion of a monopoly profit or tribute in Lane's theory is absent from Glete's (2002: 54–5) discussion. Of course, Glete knows well that people living in a territory are not absolutely free to choose from whom to buy protection; nevertheless, it is their bargaining power that is emphasized, and the prospect that states compete on a market to offer cheaper and more efficient protection. See Bang (2007) for an attempt to analyze the Roman imperial economy in terms of Lane's theories of protection costs and tribute.

[17] See Bang (2012) for a discussion of the role of predation in the Roman Empire.

[18] Levi (1988).

[19] Brewer (1988) provides the classic modern discussion.

[20] See Tezcan (2010), developing the interpretation of the janissaries presented by Kafadar (2007) – a paper presented as early as 1991. I am much obliged to Baki Tescan for providing me with a copy of the latter.

[21] Well analysed for the Ottoman Empire by Tezcan (2011), for early modern Sicily by Salmeri (2011).

[22] Published in parallel Persian and English translation in 1783, a few years before the trial started: *Institutes political and military, written originally in the Mogul language by the Great Timour, improperly called Tamerlane. It was first translated into Persian by Abu Taulib Alhusseini, and*

the British constitution, that reined in the activities of the ruler through grants of privileges and liberties to the subjects.[23] Absent from this comparison, though, is an important fact: British state capacity was not merely curtailed by parliament; it was vigorously expanded, and its penetration of society intensified. Paving the way for the negotiated compromises that constitute the success of British state formation was the relentless external pressure of ever-intensifying military competition. Other contemporary states found it difficult to match the response of Britain to this challenge. France, for instance, had to go through a social revolution to catch up. Polish elites never accepted the necessary compromises with government and instead found themselves under new masters. Rather than accepting to pay the rising costs of protection, they saw their king go out of business, as it were, and themselves become the subjects of foreign imperialisms.[24] In short, Tezcan's conception of the problem is correct, in that all social power is negotiated, but his solution seems too narrowly predicated on the British model.[25] Even for early modern Europe, the British arrangement cannot simply be taken as paradigmatic – a point well made by Stasavage (Chapter 17). Other forms of statecraft and strategies were possible.

This volume identifies two major such alternatives from the Bronze Age onward: small city states and vast agrarian imperial domains.[26] The former constitute something of a counter-example to the extensive land empires, the main focus of this chapter. Small scale – as pointed out in various ways by Mackil (Chapter 15), Ober (Chapter 16), and Stasavage – meant closer, but also more accountable, government. Equally, it facilitated more egalitarian societies, and therefore societies with a preference for types of indirect taxation rather than direct land taxes. Many city states developed

thence into English with marginal notes by Major [William] Davy, the original Persian transcribed by Joseph White.

23 Burke (2000: 257–81]) sums up Edmund Burke's analysis of the various kinds of law and custom that in the Mughal Empire served to rein in the monarch. On Burke, the ancient Mughal constitution, and early company rule in Bengal, see Travers (2007: 214–23; further, 1–30 [introd.], ch. 3).

24 Tilly's (1992) book remains the best synthesizing version of this argument.

25 Toward the end of his study, Tezcan (2010: 240–3) does touch briefly on the differences between the janissaries and the British parliament. Both served to curb absolutist state power, but, since this function in the Ottoman case was performed by a privileged section of the military, this made modernizing reforms of the army impossible. But the problem goes much beyond new forms of military equipment and organization; the key issue is that the Ottoman mode of social negotiation did not permit the enormous expansion in state spending power that the British parliamentarian system facilitated. Not all forms of social development should be shoehorned into a proto-modern mold.

26 See Scheidel (2013: 27–32) for a typological discussion of these two main forms of premodern statehood. Bang and Bayly (2011: 6–7) define and delineate the group of pre-colonial agrarian or tributary empires.

quite dynamic commercial economies and credit institutions, and experimented with public debt. But, in a world of continuous warfare, their small scale put them at a disadvantage in the long run. Both in the ancient world, and in Europe, city states ended up being subjected by the larger polities. This brings us to the other, perhaps more prominent, option: imperialism. If one may impute to rulers and governments a desire to maximize state income, this impulse seems commonly to have been articulated in conquest rather than any attempt systematically to improve the yield of territories already held.[27] Ottoman taxation, as studied by Coşgel (Chapter 13), reveals a concern to make provinces pay, but always constrained by pragmatic adjustment to preexisting arrangements in the interest of social peace.[28] Profits from conquest, on the other hand, may finance an expansion of a military apparatus and its expenditure rather than intensified taxation. Tan (Chapter 6) shows how the income from conquests made it unnecessary for the Roman Republic to build up state capacity at home. Indeed, the Roman *civitas* could even forgo much domestic taxation, as it increasingly came to enjoy the bounty of empire.

It is precisely this basic condition that changed decisively with the early modern military revolution, however. In the sixteenth century, during its first phase, two powers stood poised to gain hegemony in the greater Mediterranean world: the Ottomans and the Habsburg dynastic conglomerate. To contemporaries it looked as if they were on the path described by Rome centuries beforehand to win so-called universal empire.[29] Both powers certainly toyed with the idea, and in terms of state capacity were probably not far off from their Roman predecessor. With a military of some 100,000 to 150,000 and a population one-third or even less of that ruled by the old Roman Caesars, by the second half of the sixteenth century, the establishment of the Habsburg Spanish monarchy seems on a comparable scale, in relative terms, to that of the ancient emperors.[30] But neither the Habsburgs nor the Ottomans managed to absorb their rivals, and their conquests ground to a halt. Instead, the military revolution continued to roll on, relentlessly increasing the demands for resource mobilization made

[27] Oppenheimer (1990 [1929]: 56–63) is still worth consulting on this point.

[28] The claim made here is a guarded one. History is full of examples of rulers attempting to develop the capacity of their territories. Two prominent examples would be that of the early Ptolemies in Egypt (see Manning 2009) and the great Sassanian canal-building projects in Mesopotamia (see Christensen 1993). In the long run, though, satisficing strategies seem to predominate. See also Brown, Chapter 14.

[29] See, for example, T. Campanella, *De Monarchia Hispanica Discursus*, Ludovicus Elzevirius: Amsterdam 1640, ch. 30; see also Necipoğlu (1989) and Ágoston (2007).

[30] Bang (2013: 419–22).

on the great players in the game of power politics, generation by generation. In time, the predominant position enjoyed by the two would-be Roman powers began to erode, before it was finally lost. The response made by both governments to the rising costs of warfare produced surprisingly parallel results. Negotiating with the Spanish elites, the Habsburg government had increasingly to strengthen the position of local and regional aristocrats and their control of society's resources to receive the funds and men necessary for the military effort.[31] The regionalization of imperial power was, equally, a prominent theme of seventeenth- and eighteenth-century Ottoman history, where we know the phenomenon as the rise of the *ayan*, great provincial potentates farming imperial taxes. As time went by, and the need for centralizing and modernizing reform became urgent, these solutions came to look increasingly inefficient.[32] But it is worth emphasizing that an empire such as the Ottoman was still able to hold its own well into the eighteenth century. Failure, if we may use that term, was relative, not absolute. Without the pressure continuously to increase military capacity and intensify the collection of taxes, the more decentralized imperial solution would have been quite durable.

Having conquered and subjected most of its rivals, the Roman Empire, as argued by Monson (Chapter 5), Scheidel (Chapter 7), and Bransbourg (Chapter 8), was able to run a stable, low-tax regime for centuries on end. When the imperial state had to rebuild its tributary tax base during the fourth and fifth centuries, the government did engage in a period of seeming intensification. But in practice the later Caesars never managed to push revenues significantly beyond the level on which their predecessors had settled at the beginning of our era.[33] This state of affairs was only decisively ruptured when the modus vivendi established with the Sasanian Empire broke down at the turn of the sixth century. The ensuing set of all-out wars shook the foundations of the two monarchies and left them as easy prey for the Arabs, their former allied auxiliary soldiers, who seized the moment and conquered the major part of both realms.[34] Under the caliphate, Kennedy observes (Chapter 12), many of the old late antique systems of taxation were continued in a loosely structured empire resting lightly on the backs of its subjects. The purest example of the combination of stable imperial hegemony and moderate tribute extraction must be that of late imperial China, however. Proclaiming the Confucian ideology of

[31] Glete (2002: 121–36). [32] Karaman and Pamuk (2010).

[33] See Bang (2013) for an attempt to synthesize the entire span of the Roman imperial monarchy in terms of state formation.

[34] Sarris (2011: ch. 7).

virtuous rule and low taxation, the Ming and, even more, the Qing dynasties were both able to fund their activities by making very low, even decreasing, demands on the population. This was a social "contract" from which the Qing government was never able effectively to break out. As Deng argues (Chapter 10), when defeat in the Opium Wars and the cataclysmic Taiping Rebellion made it imperative to reverse the overall trend, the response came from the provinces, largely bypassing the court.

In short, accepting that taxation is the result of social negotiation, we need to differentiate our understanding of this process and distinguish different types and degrees of institutionalized collaboration, apart from the parliamentary model of evolving direct administration. Incidentally, this was a main concern of the British historical sociologists in the 1980s. John Hall's *Powers and Liberties* can be read as just such an attempt.[35] The first part of his book seeks to explore the various arrangements of socio-political collaboration within the four major pre-industrial civilizations. The present volume steers a slightly different course, however, by employing a cross-cultural typology. For our "tributary empires," Michael Mann, the other leading historical sociologist, has coined the notion of compulsory cooperation. Instead of the increasingly intense, negotiated power of modern statehood, he characterizes this form of power as extensive and indirect, rule being based on the collaboration of a small government elite apparatus with provincial and local aristocracies. Conquered in war as these groups were, their loyalty was secured by a combination of carrot and stick. In return for administering the imperial "peace" on the ground, such local elites were allowed to benefit from the collection of tribute; they became partners in empire, and it is in this relationship that the keys to the secrets of imperial taxation must be sought.[36]

The paradox of aristocratic power: compulsory cooperation and imperial tax collection

There is a paradox of power hidden in the negotiations between imperial government and aristocratic groups. Few have hit the head on the nail more precisely than Ibn Khaldun: "It should be known that at the beginning of a dynasty, taxation yields a large revenue from small assessments. At the end of a dynasty, taxation yields a small revenue from large assessments."[37] Our

[35] Hall (1985). [36] This is well set out by Mann (1986: ch. 5).

[37] See Ibn Khaldûn (2004: 230 [Book 1, ch. 3, § 36]). I am very grateful to Christian Høgel, who kindly and generously checked for me the correctness of this translation against the Arabic original.

tributary empires – and we may include most pre-industrial monarchies here – always had to work on the basis of relatively small centrally controlled administrations; they had to rely on allies who were willing to employ their own resources in the service of government, often so-called *honoratiores*.[38] Two advantages followed from this: it was cheap, and it mobilized power otherwise outside the command of the state. In bargaining with their supporting political and aristocratic elites, however, imperial governments then had to make service attractive by accepting that these groups would be able to reap considerable rewards from their relationship to the state and divert some of its resources to their own benefit. Successful empire-building promoted the formation of stronger elites and thus risked, in the long run, to breed potential competitors and rivals to the state – a phenomenon emphasized by several contributions to this volume, in particular Haldon.

Various strategies existed for countering this tendency, particularly in the higher reaches of the imperial aristocracies.[39] Two avenues of power were particularly important: control of agricultural revenues, and military capacity. By keeping control of access to either one or both of these resources, in varying combinations and degrees, rulers attempted to ensure that their nobilities would retain an interest in the continuation of imperial government.[40] Roman emperors, for instance, kept control of honorary public offices and military positions while allowing the aristocracy private ownership of land – though not to the extent of enabling its transformation into inalienable family property that could safeguard the integrity of the lineage for generations irrespective of its political fortunes.[41] The Mughal emperors liaised with an aristocracy that constituted the backbone of the army, so instead they attempted to keep a firm grip on agricultural revenues. These were rewarded to the military elites as prebendal – that is, periodically recycled holdings, in principle remaining in the hands of

[38] Weber (1972 [1922]: 580–624) remains both classic and illuminating; Bang (2011a) analyzes imperial patrimonialism; see Bang and Turner (2015) for a comparative discussion of elite formation in Rome and Han China as *honoratiores*.

[39] Gellner (1983: 14–18) neatly models "the varieties of agrarian rulers"; see also the discussion by Hall (2012).

[40] See Bang (2008: ch. 2) for a basic comparison of taxation and elite formation during the Roman Principate and in the Mughal Empire.

[41] Fundamental analyses of elite formation in the Roman Empire include those by Hopkins and Burton (1983) and Garnsey and Saller (1987: ch. 2). In this connection, the notion of the domestication by courts of their aristocracies, developed by Norbert Elias (see Elias 1969), is also relevant. For Roman history, analyses are provided by Winterling (2003), Paterson (2007), Wallace-Hadrill (2011), and Bang (2011b).

the emperor to bestow on whosoever he wished.[42] In practice, though, there were limits to these policies. Access to office remained an important tool for accumulating landed wealth in the Roman world, while Mughal elites often managed to secure a base of agricultural wealth. "Divide and rule," therefore, was always a necessary strategy, whereby competing aristocratic factions would occasionally be enabled to cannibalize each other, and the emperor put over-mighty "allies" out of action.

In these circumstances, it is an open question as to how to delimit the state. Illustrative is an interesting debate that has unfolded among late Roman and Byzantine historians in recent decades. Discussions have focused on how to interpret the large estates that we know in some detail from Roman fifth- and sixth-century Egypt, especially the properties around the city of Oxyrhynchus owned by the senatorial Apiones. This powerful aristocratic family produced several members who reached the very highest offices in imperial service at the court in Constantinople; its shadow also loomed large over the provincial Egyptian city, which constituted its home base. On its estate were housed military troops, and its household also played a key role in collecting taxes and much more. The French papyrologist Jean Gascou has responded to this arrogation of "public" functions by advancing an interpretation that expanded the state to cover such large aristocratic houses. He imagines a formally institutionalized structure that saw government take place across the provinces through such "public" houses.[43] But this theory has turned out to be both over-systematic and too formalistic. The reality was much more varied and muddled. What happened, therefore, was not that the great estate was "becoming a 'semi-public' institution, but, rather. . .the state was becoming a 'semi-private' one," a recent analysis concludes.[44] That is precisely the question, however, and not only in late Roman Egypt, but generally. Far away from the court, this public–private distinction would not have been easy to make. There, the estate would often have been the most obvious representative of state power, yet also not easily controlled by the monarchical government. Stein, the late historian of India, attempted to tackle

[42] There are a number of basic treatments of the Mughal elite of *mansabdars* and the system of revenue assignment: e.g., Richards (1993: 19–25, 59–68), Ali (1997), Hintze (1997: 58–86), and Habib (1999: ch. 8); see also Alam (1986: 122–33) and Bayly (1988: 20–1, 49) on the increased ability of nobles to convert revenue grants into more permanent holdings during the late Mughal period.

[43] Gascou (1985).

[44] Sarris (2006: 176); so also Liebeschuetz (2001: 181–201) and Banaji (2001: 93–100), countered again by Hickey (2011). For a fuller discussion of the Apiones and their implications for the history of Roman taxation, see my forthcoming contribution to the *Oxford Handbook of Economies in the Classical World.*

this problem with a notion of state power as segmented. By this he meant that, in local societies, government was not simply indirect and delegated. Rather, the power of these local aristocratic landowning groups was partly independent of the central government, whose influence and prestige they got symbolically to share in.[45]

At all times tributary empires depended on the collaboration of such locally entrenched groups, mostly of landowners, for the crucial process of tax collection. In the ensuing negotiations these had considerable leeway, and significant wastage was intrinsic to the way the system operated. In this volume, Brown (Chapter 14) and Deng (Chapter 10) both point to the strategic strength of provincial landowners and their control of the revenue of agricultural production, while Scheidel (Chapter 7) emphasizes their abilty to siphon off a substantial proportion of collected taxes. Perhaps one of the most thorough and instructive expositions of such provincial processes of taxation and "corruption" was offered by Zelin in her magisterial study of the attempts to reform the tax system under the Qing dynasty. Traditionally provincial administration had been chronically underfunded in the vast empire. Instead, local officials would customarily resort to various forms of tacitly accepted and illicit surcharges and gifts to make ends meet – and to profit. But during the reign of the Yōngzhèng emperor (r. 1723–35) a set of reforms were introduced that attempted to bring these clandestine and irregular fees out into the open by converting them into a regular tax allocated to fund local government. After some initial successes, however, the effects of these modest reforms were gradually eroded during the eighteenth century. Officials and bureaus higher up in the administrative hierarchy would attempt to encroach on the taxes set aside for local government, and thus throw its members back on the old pre-reform practices. At a more fundamental level still, though, effective control of local societies at collection point escaped even the (in comparative terms) substantial Chinese mandarin bureaucracy. This enabled local elites to manipulate the tax collection process considerably to their own advantage. Sampled from across Zelin's study before and after the reforms, a motley collection of the methods employed by the local elites to manage their relationship with central government would include operating with one set of records for their own use and one for the state, registering fertile fields as flooded, failing to measure all the agricultural lands in the district, avoiding paying their own dues while collecting those of the peasantry, and allowing

[45] Stein (1985). See Goldstone and Haldon (2009: 17–18) for a brief discussion of the segmented character of premodern statehood.

arrears to accumulate for years before the government gave up and remitted taxes or redistributed the outstanding amount on all the households in the district. Either way, the elites would benefit disproportionally from such imperial largess; they were the main debtors, while the peasants might find themselves having to pay again toward a tax they had already once defrayed.[46]

The catalogue of methods can be made even longer, and sounds uncannily familiar to the student of Roman history.[47] So allow me to complement the image of late imperial China by briefly relating a fascinating case hailing from Roman Egypt at the turn of the first century CE. In the Arsinoite nome or district, the archive and contents needed repair.[48] The function of public record-keeper circulated among the city *honoratiores*, however, none of whom were too fond of having to pay for the repair of the damaged papyrus scrolls and building. When one Roman governor, with a particularly keen interest in maintaining the quality of public records, intervened in the 90s CE, the transfer of the damaged records between the alternating office-holders became a problem. This generated a fascinating and meandering game of cat and mouse about who would be responsible for mending the archive, lasting across generations and prompting the intervention of more than five Roman provincial governors (prefects, as they were titled in Egypt) before the case with roots in the 70s finally found a resolution of sorts in the 120s CE with the confiscation of some property. This is a strong illustration of the resilience and the ability of local elites to frustrate, outwit, and manipulate the representatives of imperial government. As a consequence, local elites normally possessed considerable negotiating power in their dealings with the royal court and its officials. There were generally very clear limits to how much could be extracted, and, as Coşgel points out in his contribution, moderation was often the

46 See Zelin (1984: ch. 6) in particular on the obstacles limiting the effect of the reforms attempted by the court. In chapter 7 she describes how the initial successes of the tax reforms were undermined during the remainder of the eighteenth century.

47 I am grateful to the late Keith Hopkins for long ago having drawn my attention to Zelin's study, as well as to the set of papyri discussion of which now follows.

48 See van Groningen (1950: nos. 15, 24), including the extensive summary of the case by the editor (ibid.: 97–108). A brief, but more recent discussion is offered by Monson (2012: 242–3), though I differ a little as to where to put the emphasis. The duty to maintain the archive was part of a set of state compulsory services. Even so, it is remarkable just how long the members of the local elite manage to stall and frustrate the implementation of the decisions of the Roman authorities before the latter, after decades of bug-passing, finally managed to seize on someone to bear the costs. As van Groningen concludes: "[T]he whole administration produces an. . .impression of inefficacity. . . [I]t is too easy to offer passive resistance" (van Groningen 1950: 108). See, in general, Kelly (2011: ch. 3) on the manifold opportunities for "strategic delay, obfuscation and evasion" (ibid.: 120) available to the parties within the juridical (/administrative) system of Roman Egypt.

preferred strategy to avoid alienating this powerful segment of landowners and local dignitaries. Many taxes would have been taken over from previous generations as sanctified by custom, and – an observation also made by Scheidel and Smith – locally the implementation of the tax demands of central government would have been articulated in a large variety of arrangements. The great diversity of forms under which taxes were being defrayed, in kind, money, or labor, did in itself hamper the ability of central government to impose a standardized form of measurement on subject communities, and thus reinforced their bargaining power by putting a premium on local knowledge.

This brings me to two methodological observations with which to conclude this chapter. As students of premodern societies and systems of taxation in particular, we must take constant care not to work on an implicit assumption of uniformity and coherence in reconstructing the taxation systems of past societies. Often our evidence is so fragmentary that it may convey a false impression of homogeneity. Over-systematization is an omnipresent analytical temptation. But a set of multifarious and historically accumulated arrangements is likely to be the norm, and the more so, the bigger the political entity. Caution here, too, is required in assessing the level of taxation. Proper statistics are generally lacking from most of our premodern societies. A reader of this book will not find it easy to make a precise comparison of the size of revenues across the chosen examples. Were they high or low? Among students of premodern taxation, one can find proponents of both views, also in this volume. But, given the scarcity of statistics, it is wiser to err on the side of caution. That we are dealing with relatively low-taxation societies seems the most plausible working hypothesis. It may not be possible to document the exact size of government income; but we are better placed to assess the kinds of activities undertaken by states and the administrative apparatus they had available. Neither would lead us to expect a different scenario. After all, if not even the Chinese imperial government, with one of the most elaborate administrative organizations of the premodern world, was able to ratchet up the level of taxation, why would we impute to other, smaller, governmental establishments greater extractive strength?[49]

[49] See O'Brien (2012), identifying a clear contrast between the heightened level of taxation achieved during the early modern period by states in Europe, with England as the trailblazer, and the great agrarian empires such as the Ming and Qing in China, the Ottomans, and the Mughals. The latter might be thought of as an exception to this pattern; but this view rests on a set of normative claims that, as O'Brien observes, are unlikely to reflect reality. See especially Alam and Subrahmanyam (1998: 12–16) for a critical discussion of the high interpretation of Mughal revenue extraction, showing that the government did not have the means to impose a system sufficiently uniform to that end.

References

Ágoston, G. (2007) "Information, ideology, and the limits of imperial policy: Ottoman grand strategy in the context of Ottoman–Habsburg rivalry," in *The Early Modern Ottomans: Remapping the Empire*, ed. D. Goffman and V. Aksan. Cambridge: 75–103.

Alam, M. (1986) *The Crisis of Empire in Mughal North India*. New Delhi.

Alam, M., and Subrahmanyam, S. (eds.) (1998) *The Mughal State 1526–1750*. New Delhi.

Ali, M. A. (1997) *The Mughal Nobility under Aurangzeb*, rev. edn. New Delhi.

Ando, C. (2000) *Imperial Ideology and Provincial Loyalty in the Roman Empire*. Berkeley, CA.

Banaji, J. (2001) *Agrarian Change in Late Antiquity*. Oxford.

Bang, P. F. (2007) "Trade and empire: in search of organizing concepts for the Roman economy," *Past and Present* 195: 3–54.

(2008) *The Roman Bazaar: A Comparative Study of Trade and Markets in a Tributary Empire*. Cambridge.

(2011a) "Lord of all the world: the state, heterogeneous power and hegemony in the Roman and Mughal Empires," in *Tributary Empires in Global History*, ed. P. F. Bang and C. A. Bayly. Basingstoke, UK: 171–92.

(2011b) "Court and state in the Roman Empire: domestication and tradition in comparative perspective," in *Royal Courts in Dynastic States and Empires*, ed. T. Artan, J. Duindam, and M. Kunt. Leiden: 103–28.

(2012) "Predation," in *The Cambridge Companion to the Roman Economy*, ed. W. Scheidel. Cambridge: 197–217.

(2013) "The Roman Empire, II: the imperial monarchy," in *The Oxford Handbook of the State in the Ancient Near East and Mediterranean*, ed. P. F. Bang and W. Scheidel. New York: 412–72.

Bang, P. F., and Bayly, C. A. (2011) "Tributary empires: towards a global and comparative history," in *Tributary Empires in Global History*, ed. P. F. Bang and C. A. Bayly. Basingstoke, UK: 1–17.

Bang, P. F., and Turner, K. (2015) "Kingship and elite formation," in *State Power in Ancient China and Rome*, ed W. Scheidel. New York: 11–38.

Bayly, C. A. (1988) *Indian Society and the Making of the British Empire*. Cambridge.

Brewer, J. (1988) *The Sinews of Power: War, Money, and the English State, 1688–1783*. London.

Burke, E. (2000) *The Writings and Speeches of Edmund Burke*, vol. VII, *India: The Hastings Trial 1789–1794*, ed. P. J. Marshall. Oxford.

Cameron, A., Long, J., and Sherry, L. (1993) *Barbarians and Politics at the Court of Arcadius*. Berkeley, CA.

Christensen, P. (1993) *The Decline of Iranshahr: Irrigation and Environments in the History of the Middle East, 500 BC to AD 1500*. Copenhagen.

Duncan-Jones, R. (1990) *Structure and Scale in the Roman Economy*. Cambridge.

Elias, N. (1969) *Die höfische Gesellschaft: Untersuchungen zur Soziologie des Königtums und der höfischen Aristokratie, mit einer Einleitung: Soziologie und Geschichtswissenschaft*. Neuwied, Germany.

Garnsey, P., and Saller, R. (1987) *The Roman Empire: Economy, Society and Culture*. London.

Gascou, J. (1985) "Les grands domaines, la cité et l'état en Egypte byzantine," *Travaux et Mémoires* 9: 1–89.

Gellner, E. (1983) *Nations and Nationalism*. Oxford.

Glete, J. (2002) *War and the State in Early Modern Europe: Spain, the Dutch Republic, and Sweden as Fiscal-Military States, 1500–1660*. London.

Goldstone, J. A., and Haldon, F. J. (2009) "Ancient states, empires, and exploitation: problems and perspectives," in *The Dynamics of Ancient Empires: State Power from Assyria to Byzantium*, ed. I. Morris and W. Scheidel. Oxford: 3–29.

Habib, I. (1999) *The Agrarian System of Mughal India, 1556–1707*, 2nd edn. New Delhi.

Haldon, J. F. (1993) *The State and the Tributary Mode of Production*. London.

Hall, J. A. (1985) *Powers and Liberties: The Causes and Consequences of the Rise of the West*. London.

(2012) "Imperial universalism: further thoughts," in *Universal Empire: A Comparative Approach to Imperial Culture and Representation*, ed. P. F. Bang and D. Kolodziejczyk. Cambridge: 304–9.

Hickey, T. M. (2011) *Wine, Wealth, and the State in Late Antique Egypt*. Ann Arbor, MI.

Hintze, A. (1997) *The Mughal Empire and Its Decline*. Aldershot, UK.

Hopkins, K., and Burton, G. (1983) "Ambition and withdrawal: the senatorial aristocracy under the emperors," in *Death and Renewal*, ed. K. Hopkins. Cambridge: 120–200.

Ibn Khaldûn (2004) *The Muqaddimah: An Introduction to History*, trans. F. Rosenthal, abridg. N. J. Dawood. Princeton, NJ.

Kafadar, C. (2007) "Janissaries and other riffraff of Ottoman Istanbul: rebels without a cause?," in *Identity and Identity Formation in the Ottoman World: A Volume of Essays in Honor of Norman Itzkowitz*, ed. B. Tezcan and K. K. Barbir. Madison, WI: 113–34.

Karaman, K. K., and Pamuk, Ş. (2010) "Ottoman state finances in European perspective, 1500–1914," *Journal of Economic History* 70: 593–629.

Kelly, B. (2011) *Petitions, Litigation, and Social Control in Roman Egypt*. Oxford.

Kiser, E., and Sacks, A. (2009) "Improving tax administration in contemporary African states: lessons from history," in *The New Fiscal Sociology: Taxation in Comparative and Historical Perspective*, ed. I. W. Martin, A. K. Mehrotra, and M. Prasad. New York: 183–200.

Klauser, T. (1944) "Aurum Coronarium," in *Mitteilungen des Deutschen Archäologischen Instituts, Römische Abteilung*, vol. LIX. Munich: 129–53.

Landskron, A. (2006) "Repräsentantinnen des *orbis Romanus* auf dem sog. Partherdenkmal von Ephesos: Personifikationen und Bildpropaganda," in

Das Partherdenkmal von Ephesos: Akten des Kolloquiums Wien, 27. – 28. April 2003, ed. W. Seipel. Vienna: 103–27.

Lane, F. C. (1958) "Economic consequences of organized violence," *Journal of Economic History* 18: 401–17.

Lavan, M. (2013) *Slaves to Rome: Paradigms of Empire in Roman Culture.* Cambridge.

Levi, M. (1988) *Of Rule and Revenue*. Berkeley, CA.

Liebermann, V. (2009) *Strange Parallels: Southeast Asia in Global Context,* c. *800–1830,* vol. II, *Mainland Mirrors: Europe, Japan, China, South Asia and the Islands*. Cambridge.

Liebeschuetz, J. H. W. G. (2001) *The Decline and Fall of the Roman City*. Oxford.

Mann, M. (1986) *The Sources of Social Power,* vol. I, *A History of Power from the Beginning to AD 1760*. Cambridge.

Manning, J. G. (2009) *The Last Pharaohs: Egypt under the Ptolemies, 305–30 BC.* Princeton, NJ.

Martin, I. W., Mehrotra, A. K., and Prasad, M. (2009) "The thunder of history: the origins and development of the new fiscal sociology," in *The New Fiscal Sociology: Taxation in Comparative and Historical Perspective*, ed. I. W. Martin, A. K. Mehrotra, and M. Prasad. New York: 1–28.

Monson, A. (2012) *From the Ptolemies to the Romans: Political and Economic Change in Egypt*. Cambridge.

Necipoğlu, G. (1989) "Süleyman the Magnificent and the representation of power in the context of Ottoman–Hapsburg–papal rivalry," *Art Bulletin* 71: 401–27.

O'Brien, K. P. (2012) "Fiscal and financial preconditions for the formation of developmental states in the West and the East from the conquest of Ceuta (1415) to the Opium War (1839)," *Journal of World History* 23: 513–53.

Oliver, J. H. (1989) *Greek Constitutions of Early Roman Emperors.* Philadelphia.

Oppenheimer, F. (1990 [1929]) *Der Staat: eine soziologische Studie.* Berlin.

Paterson, J. (2007) "Friends in high places: the creation of the court of the Roman emperor," in *The Court and Court Society in Ancient Monarchies*, ed. T. Spawforth. Cambridge: 121–56.

Richards, J. F. (1993) *The Mughal Empire*. Cambridge.

Salmeri, G. (2011) "The emblematic province: Sicily from the Roman Empire to the Kingdom of the Two Sicilies," in *Tributary Empires in Global History*, ed. P. F. Bang and C. A. Bayly. Basingstoke, UK: 151–78.

Sarris, P. (2006) *Economy and Society in the Age of Justinian*. Cambridge.

(2011) *Empires of Faith: The Fall of Rome to the Rise of Islam*. Oxford.

Scheidel, W. (2013) "Studying the state," in *The Oxford Handbook of the State in the Ancient Near East and Mediterranean*, ed. P. F. Bang and W. Scheidel. New York: 5–57.

Stein, B. (1985) "State formation and the economy reconsidered: part 1," *Modern Asian Studies* 19: 387–413.

Tezcan, B. (2010) *The Second Ottoman Empire: Political and Social Transformation in the Early Modern World*. Cambridge.

(2011) "The new order and the fate of the old: the historiographical construction of an Ottoman ancien régime in the nineteenth century," in *Tributary Empires in Global History*, ed. P. F. Bang and C. A. Bayly. Basingstoke, UK: 74–95.

Travers, R. (2007) *Ideology and Empire in Eighteenth-Century India: The British in Bengal.* Cambridge.

Tilly, C. (1992) *Coercion, Capital, and European States: AD 990–1992*, rev edn. Malden, MA.

Van Groningen, B. A. (ed.) (1950) *A Family-Archive from Tebtunis (P. Fam. Tept.).* Leiden.

Wallace-Hadrill, A. (2011) "The Roman imperial court: seen and unseen in the performance of power," in *Royal Courts in Dynastic States and Empires*, ed. T. Artan, J. Duindam, and M. Kunt. Leiden: 91–102.

Weber, M. (1972 [1922]) *Wirtschaft und Gesellschaft.* Tübingen.

Wickham, C. (1985) "The uniqueness of the East," *Journal of Peasant Studies* 12: 166–96.

(2005) *Framing the Early Middle Ages.* Oxford.

Winterling, A. (2003) *Caligula: eine Biographie.* Munich.

Zelin, M. (1984) *The Magistrate's Tael: Rationalizing Fiscal Reform in Eighteenth-Century Ch'ing China.* Berkeley, CA.

CHAPTER 19

Interpreting the comparative history of fiscal regimes

Edgar Kiser and Margaret Levi

These rich and provocative chapters have a raised a series of questions and issues about how best to investigate fiscal developments in particular locations and eras. Their collective contribution is to provoke thinking about the necessary steps for producing a more comprehensive theoretical approach to inform cross-country and cross-time comparison, and even generalization. The contributions to this book encourage us to consider a more systematic approach to the study of taxes and tax structures. The specifics of each case are informative about the effect of contextual, structural, and contingent factors, but thinking about the cases together permits a move toward more general claims.

Avoiding Eurocentrism and presentism

A great strength of almost all these chapters is how much they avoid the two types of biases common in this literature: Eurocentrism and presentism. As a result of language barriers, data availability, and cultural biases, there is often a tendency to view the rest of the world through the lens of the European experience. European states are taken as (usually implicit) baselines, and others are analyzed as deviations.[1] The contributions in this volume consistently avoid this bias, both by using other, more appropriate baselines, and by evaluating their cases within their own historical contexts.

Presentism is equally problematic. One of the worst ways of judging the fiscal systems of premodern[2] states is to evaluate them in terms of contemporary states.[3] Large, centralized bureaucratic states that characterize the modern, developed world are seen as good, strong, and effective,

[1] Tilly (1975); North, Wallis, and Weingast (2009).

[2] We use the term "premodern" fairly loosely here, essentially to refer to pre-industrial societies.

[3] This presentist view is often coupled with a general understanding of history as leading up the present. Modernization theory is the most obvious version of this.

and the premodern states that lack these features are seen as flawed as a result, simply awaiting their eventual (usually linear) evolution toward the good, modern form.

These chapters show how silly this presentist bias is. They document nonlinear development; premodern states just as often move away from centralization and bureaucratization as toward it. They reveal the prevalence of mixed forms; bureaucratic and patrimonial elements are combined and layered in many different ways. Perhaps most importantly, in reading these cases it becomes apparent that various forms of patrimonialism were not mistakes on the road to modernization but were often the most efficient ways to collect taxes given the structural conditions faced by premodern states.

In fact, presentism does not even work for the present.[4] Like premodern states, contemporary African states have found that centralized bureaucracy is often not the most effective form of tax administration. After a period of imitating the centralized bureaucratic administrative systems that are dominant in the developed world, with very little success, African states in the last couple of decades have begun to decentralize and partially privatize their tax administrations, moving more in the direction of administrative systems used by premodern states. Agency theory suggests that these decentralized and partially privatized systems should be more efficient than centralized bureaucratic tax administration when monitoring capacity is poor because of poor communications, transportation, and record-keeping. The structural conditions and monitoring capacity of contemporary African states are more like those in premodern states than in contemporary developed states, so they might be better off looking to the former for models. Although the jury is still out, because of their short duration and the lack of detailed data, decentralization and partial privatization using semi-autonomous revenue authorities both seem to be increasing efficiency and decreasing corruption.

General questions: what determines tax rates, tax structures, and forms of tax administration?

The chapters in this volume address two very general questions: what types of fiscal systems were used in premodern states, and how well did these fiscal systems work? The first question can be further divided into assessments of the overall tax rate, the form of the tax structure (what and who

[4] This paragraph draws on material expounded by Kiser and Sacks (2009; 2011).

was taxed), and the types of administrative systems used to collect taxes. The second major question really has to do with the effectiveness, both economically and politically, of the tax policies and extractions. To answer it requires, on the one hand, an analysis of the relationships of power in a polity and, on the other hand, the extent to which taxpayers believe the system is legitimate.

One of the most interesting unifying leitmotifs across the chapters is the recurring observation that taxes often appear to be low. This was one of the main themes of the contributions on China (Deng: Chapter 10), Japan (Brown: Chapter 14), Rome (Scheidel: Chapter 7), and in the comparative analysis of empires (Bang: Chapter 18; Monson: Chapter 5). But what is the implicit counterfactual here, the baseline against which the actual taxes appear to be too low, and what theoretical or empirical factors are responsible for setting the baseline? We do not provide a complete answer to this question, but we do raise a few theoretical issues that might help us think about it.

Types of fiscal systems

Fiscal systems cannot be divorced from state expenditures; the demand for tax revenue in part determines its supply. For this reason, many of the chapters discuss the spending patterns of premodern states: on war, domestic security, education, social insurance and public welfare, religious buildings and ceremonies, disaster relief, and payoffs for political support ("bread and circuses"). War and security issues are especially important determinants of the demand for tax revenue, because the failure to fund them adequately can result in the demise of the state itself. This is why Tilly's work on war and state-making has been so important.[5] Tax rates are not simply a product of the demand for revenue, however, in part because spending can be funded by other means than taxation (borrowing, state lands or other resources, and profits from successful conquests, for example). Tax rates are also influenced by legitimacy considerations[6] and by the relative bargaining power of rulers and taxpayers,[7] as we discuss in the sections below.

With respect to tax structure, the types of fiscal systems used by premodern rulers are numerous and diverse, including tribute, booty, corvée labor, poll taxes, land taxes, customs, many types of excise taxes, and of course borrowing. Like tax rates, tax structures were determined by

[5] Tilly (1992); see also Kiser and Linton (2001). [6] Levi and Sacks (2009). [7] Levi (1988).

many factors, including economic structure (which set the upper bound of what was available to be taxed), the administrative capacities of the rulers of states, the relative power of rulers and taxpayers, and the ways rulers chose to maintain their legitimacy.[8]

Premodern rulers also used many different types of tax administration. Some were highly centralized, with rulers selecting, monitoring, and paying officials, while others were very decentralized, including collection by local notables, locally elected officials, feudalism, and prebendalism. Tax collection was often privatized in the hands of tax farmers, and this too could take many forms. Some officials purchased their positions, others were chosen by lot. The determinants of tax administration were also complex. Efficiency considerations were important (which type of administration can produce the most revenue for the lowest cost in particular circumstances), as stressed by economic versions of agency theory.[9] As with other aspects of fiscal systems, relative bargaining power, the discount rates of rulers (the extent to which they discount future gains and losses relative to present ones), and the requirements of maintaining legitimacy were important, too.[10]

How well did these fiscal systems work?

Answering the question of how well the fiscal systems worked has at least two dimensions, both represented in chapters in this volume. One criterion is efficiency, in the strictly economic sense of producing the most revenue. Another approach considers effectiveness, however, taking things such as power and legitimacy into account.

The issue of how well these fiscal systems worked is complicated. First, what do we mean by the efficiency of tax administration, in a strict economic sense? The most efficient tax administration is the one that produces the highest net revenue within the set of structural constraints present at the time, net revenue meaning gross revenue (set by the tax rate and tax structure) minus administrative costs, the costs of agent corruption, and the costs of taxpayer evasion (Coşgel's contribution, Chapter 13, is a great model of how to set an efficiency baseline in a particular historical context). Analyses of premodern states that focus

[8] We use the term "taxpayers" as a convenient shorthand here and elsewhere, knowing that this is a heterogeneous category including many different groups with different levels of bargaining power relative to rulers.

[9] See Kiser (1999) for a comparison of how agency theory is used in different disciplines.

[10] Levi (1988; 1997).

on efficiency tend to concentrate on structural constraints (on account of things such as size, geography, poor communications, transportation, and record-keeping technologies) that set limits on efficient tax collection. Economic structure is perhaps the most important ultimate cause here: the form of agriculture, the types of extractive industries, land ownership patterns, the extent and type of industrialization, the level and type of trade, and the level of development of human capital.

Power and fiscal systems

One answer to why taxes were so low is power: the power of taxpayers (or some subset of taxpayers) to either limit tax rates or evade tax payments. Taxes are low when taxpayers have the means to exercise power relative to rulers. In fact, the "new fiscal sociology" has stressed the fact that no rulers have absolute power, and that taxes are determined by negotiations between rulers and taxpayers.[11] This claim has a long-standing intellectual tradition,[12] but the new work is providing more detailed accounts of the relevant processes and institutions in a much wider set of countries.[13]

Rulers are obviously concerned with more than simple efficiency: the power of groups of taxpayers often prevent the development or use of the most efficient fiscal systems in the given conditions, and shape rulers' choices of fiscal systems. One of the major findings in *Of Rule and Revenue* is that the political transaction costs of extracting taxes often outweigh the economic transaction costs in determining what kind of tax system is viable and efficient in a particular place and time.[14] It is self-evident that the relative bargaining power of groups of taxpayers is a key causal factor; a ruler has to make concessions to those who control key resources, otherwise they could pose a threat to the ruler. What is not so obvious is that the ordinary citizen or subject also possesses power. Killing the tax collector was not uncommon in remote parts of the Roman Empire or in the walled towns the French kingdom was attempting to penetrate. Unless rulers could succeed in getting a high degree of quasi-voluntary compliance – that is, compliance that, albeit required, is given as a consequence of support or acceptance of the

[11] Martin, Mehrotra, and Prasad (2009).

[12] See, for example, Levi (1988), Bates and Lien (1985), North (1981), Barzel and Kiser (1997), and Kiser and Barzel (1991).

[13] Brautigam, Fjeldstad, and Moore (2008); Timmons (2005). [14] Levi (1988).

system – the costs of extraction become ridiculously high. This was as true for the ancient Chinese Empire as it is for the contemporary US government.

The focus of most of the literature and most of the chapters here is on formal power exercised in formal institutions. In other words, how do different political regimes, which allow different types of negotiations between rulers and taxpayers within various kinds of deliberative bodies, lead to different types of fiscal systems? The nature of the political regime and its formal institutions certainly affect tax rates (and also the tax structure and tax administration).

Negotiations via formal political institutions are far from the only way of exercising power, however. Taxpayers can also exercise power by means of individualized noncompliance, exit, and force. By "individualized noncompliance" we are referring to what Scott has labeled the "weapons of the weak": shirking, vandalism, and other forms of individual actions to hurt the powerful.[15] Collective action is not required for this exercise of power. When desertion from the military or tax evasion becomes widespread, it can have profound effects on political outcomes, including limiting the taxes that states are able to collect or the wars that they can fight.[16] The power of the exit option is outlined in Hirschman's important work; actors can exercise power simply by leaving.[17] More precisely, actors who are able to make a credible threat to leave are often able to bargain for lower tax rates than actors for whom the costs of exit are higher. For example, capitalists and those living close to borders have more exit power than landed aristocrats or those living near the capital, so, all else equal, they should pay lower tax rates. But, of course, all else is not equal. Why did landed aristocrats often pay no tax in many premodern states if they had little exit power? They had a lot of the most basic form of power: the ability to use force. To the extent that rulers lacked a monopoly on the means of violence, they were forced to compromise with those who could credibly threaten violence against them, and part of this compromise was an exemption from taxes.

As the examples above illustrate, power, formal and informal alike, is very unevenly dispersed throughout a society. Those with no votes or representation clearly have less than those who are fully enfranchised. But the power-disadvantaged also include those who lack the resources to exercise sustained harm on the rulers' ability to collect revenues, or, for that matter, on the person who is ruling. In most premodern societies

[15] Scott (1985). [16] Levi (1997). [17] Hirschman (1970).

the "selectorate"[18] – the actors who choose the ruler and the government – was very narrow, usually consisting of landed aristocrats plus, in some cases, rich merchants. The tax system tended to serve them and not the population as a whole.

Power also affects tax administration. For example, tax collectors, like other state officials, were often chosen not on the basis of their skills but because of their power relative to rulers. This not only decreased efficiency in the short term, but in the long term it made tax administration very difficult to reform. Once powerful actors had become entrenched in lucrative administrative positions it was difficult to dislodge them, even when changes in conditions made other administrative arrangements (such as bureaucracies that hired on the basis of merit) more efficient. This is why the transition to bureaucratic administrations is often caused not just by changes in economic conditions but by events such as revolutions, which dislodge the power of entrenched officials.[19]

An effective government is one that protects the population from violence, ensures the security of property rights, and provides the infrastructure that makes possible the exchange of goods and delivery of services.[20] If it is also a trustworthy government it is, by definition, competent and credible in its commitments to provide services and benefits that enhance citizens' welfare, and motivated to implement laws and regulations fairly.[21] The more a government is effective and trustworthy, the more legitimacy that government is likely to attain, and the more it will possess the potential to elicit compliance without excessive monitoring or punitive action.[22] In other words, the government can achieve a high degree of quasi-voluntary compliance with the taxation system.

Quasi-voluntary compliance[23] involves a strategic interaction with government, but it also has an ethical element: An individual who feels it is right to cooperate with government will do so only if he or she feels government is doing its part and if others are also cooperating. Quasi-voluntary compliance is most likely among taxpayers who perceive

[18] Bueno de Mesquita *et al.* (2003).
[19] See Kiser and Kane (2001) on the effects of the English and French Revolutions.
[20] Levi (2006: 5). [21] Rothstein (2005); Cook, Hardin, and Levi (2005).
[22] Tyler (1990; 2006); Levi (1997).
[23] This term originated with Levi (1988) but has been elaborated most recently in the context of Afrobarometer data concerning the reasons citizens are willing to pay taxes. See Levi and Sacks (2009; 2012), Levi, Sacks, and Tyler (2009), and Sacks and Levi (2010).

that government is engaging in serious efforts to meet its fiscal contract with constituents by delivering infrastructure and services or quickly developing the competence to do so. In addition, an increasingly large body of evidence points to the importance of government also meeting prevailing standards of procedural fairness in its provision of goods and implementation of policies. Individuals are less likely to comply if they feel government is breaking its fiscal contract with them, is exercising favoritism or revenge through its policies, or is unacceptably corrupt. Individuals are also less likely to comply if they perceive a high incidence of evasion by others. Quasi-voluntary compliance is compliance motivated by a willingness to comply but backed up by coercion, particularly coercion that ensures that others will be obeying the law. The achievement of compliance with government extractions and regulations depends on the competent exercise of the coercive capacity of the state, including its ability to detect and punish those who illegally evade their obligations.

When taxpayers perceive that government is relatively effective, competent, and procedurally just, there is the potential for the development of a virtuous circle. The more effective and procedurally just the government, the greater the willingness of citizens to accept governmental authority, and therefore the greater the degree of quasi-voluntary compliance, which then improves government's capacity to become more effective and to evoke deference, which in turn increases quasi-voluntary compliance (see Figure 19.1).

Obtaining quasi-voluntary compliance is at issue in any relationship between a government and those from whom it is attempting to extract taxes, be they subjects or citizens. Polities vary in the percentage of the population that is subject to enslavement or other forms of direct coercion, but even the politically and economically weak can shirk and evade, as we have already noted.

Governments can easily lose the confidence of taxpayers, however, by failing to deliver promised returns for taxes or by engaging in favoritism or corruption. Once quasi-voluntary compliance breaks down, the question is how to elicit it again. Rebuilding confidence in government, rulers, and the tax system often takes a major effort and a high degree of leadership, capable of coordinating a coalition in support of reform and making credible commitments that the expected benefits and enforcement procedures will occur.

As many of the chapters in this book illustrate, the virtuous cycle depicted in Figure 19.1 is quite rare historically. At least until the advent of mass democracies, and even within many democracies, rulers do not try

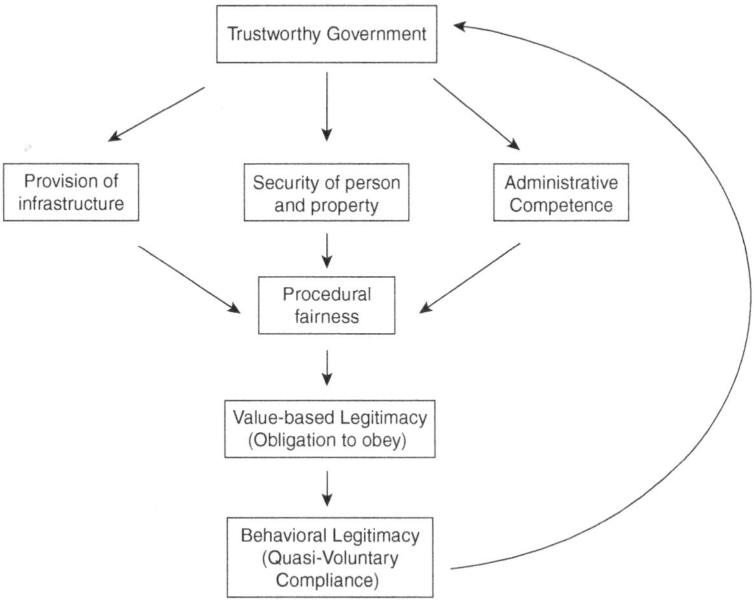

Figure 19.1 Virtuous circle of government and compliance

to appeal to all members of the society by providing public goods and ensuring that all taxpayers pay or receive their fair share. They chose a different strategy for maintaining power. They focus on building a "minimum winning coalition" of the selectorate by offering them particular benefits.[24] There are many ways to do this, but we focus here on the main ways this can be carried out using the fiscal system. First, rulers can gain the support of some either by exempting them from taxes or by allowing them to evade tax payments via intentionally lax administration. Second, rulers can spend much of their revenue not on public goods but on club goods for particular groups whose support is especially important, or even on individual goods such as state jobs with high salaries but requiring little work. Rulers can achieve the quasi-voluntary compliance of the few, often to the detriment of the many.

[24] Riker (1962).

Recognizing that rulers need only to obtain a minimum winning coalition, sometimes even within a relatively narrow selectorate, raises a set of interesting analytic questions.[25] The first is the stability of a system that benefits the few to the detriment of the many. As we know from the cases in this book and from many others, such inequity is often long-enduring. Occasionally it is the stratagem of rulers with high discount rates who care little about long-term consequences. In these cases, the tax policy will begin to shift as the discount rates become lower, as the battles are won or the natural disasters alleviated. More often, however, the durability of greatly inequitable tax systems is the consequence of powerful members of the selectorate being in a collusive bargain with the rulers.

The second analytic question has to do with the sources of change in such an equilibrium. Over time, if too many taxpayers are being disadvantaged, if there is a vicious rather than a virtuous circle, then non-compliance, exit, and rebellion responses are likely to come into play and pose a threat to the ruling coalition. Peasants could and did use non-compliance and violence; actual peasant revolts often resulted in a lowering of tax rates.[26] Rulers had a difficult choice in dealing with revolts, either using force to crush them, or bargaining about the rebels' grievances and granting concessions. Which they chose was a function not only of power but also of legitimacy considerations. According to some of the most interesting recent claims and research,[27] at various moments in history the ruling class realizes that its best chance for survival is in a bargain with the dominated groups. It is at this point that democracy emerges, and with it a commitment to ensure that taxpayers receive a share in government services and economic growth. The possibility of a truly virtuous circle arises.

25 The contemporary Greek and Italian states may prove to be especially good cases for answering some of these questions. It appears that both states over the last few decades have primarily pursued minimum winning coalition strategies within a very narrowly conceived support base. Both have been characterized by very high rates of tax evasion among certain sectors of the population (primarily small business owners and service sector workers), but was this the result of a conscious strategy to win support from those groups or simply evidence of very low state administrative capacity? Both states also provided many jobs in the public sector for which the salaries far exceeded the work required, to say the least. Was this done primarily as a means to maintain legitimacy by, essentially, buying votes? If so, the cost seems unusually high. If further research reveals that this was indeed a strategy aimed at winning the support of a small elite at the expense of the larger population, the long-run consequences seem to have been negative not just for state debt but also for the legitimacy of both states.

26 But the relationship is a complicated one; see Kiser and Linton (2002).

27 Acemoglu and Robinson (2006); Boix (2003).

The microfoundations of action and fiscal choices

The focus on power and legitimacy is an important elaboration of standard economic models that stress only efficiency, but this move raises significant and difficult issues about models of individual choice and action. Most standard economic models are based on precise and simple assumptions of rational action. Rulers, tax collectors, and taxpayers are assumed to be weighing the costs and benefits of alternative actions, and choosing the action that maximizes their wealth and, in the case of rulers, the security of their rule.[28] Although this type of rational action is also important in the realms of power and legitimacy, it is not the only relevant type of action there. As we broaden our macro-level focus to include these issues, we must also think about broadening the microfoundations to include things such as satisficing, and actions based on values (forcing us to look seriously at culture) and emotions. This necessary theoretical move raises many new questions and complications.

Unfortunately, many macro-level analyses of institutions, including many of the chapters here, are not explicit about the assumptions or empirical data they use to specify the microfoundations of action of key actors.[29] This is an important lacuna, because except in cases when either (1) structural conditions totally dictate one unique choice in each situation or (2) evolutionary selection mechanisms are so strong that all actors are forced to make the most efficient choice in order to survive, the microfoundations are a necessary and important part of any explanation. When they are left implicit, as they so often are, they cannot be evaluated, and the explanations based on them are difficult to judge. Moreover, when they are left implicit, they almost always go to the default assumption of instrumental rationality (albeit a loose version of the theory compared to the explicit version). This is a problem, because, in many cases of interest to us, microfoundations other than standard rationality are important.

So, if we are to pay more attention to microfoundations, how should we do so? First, staying within the framework of rationality, do actors maximize or, as Simon has famously labeled it, satisfice?[30] Note that satisficing

[28] We are well aware of the fact that some rational choice models use more nuanced and complicated micro-level assumptions than these. Our intent in this paragraph is not to provide a detailed critique of this work but simply to summarize the most general features of most of it.

[29] By "microfoundations" we mean assumptions regarding both the preferences of actors and the process of decision-making.

[30] Simon (1947).

on the part of rulers can provide one explanation for low tax revenue. We cannot simply assume, however, that, if tax revenue is low, rulers must be satisficing; this type of ad hoc explanation is never compelling, especially when several other explanations of low tax revenue are possible (see above). We must be able to specify the conditions under which actors are more likely to satisfice than to maximize.

Other ways of adding to standard rational choice assumptions are also important. For example, Levi shows that the discount rates of rulers are an important determinant of fiscal policies, and shows that discount rates are a function of regime type and warfare.[31] The extent to which rulers are risk-averse can also have significant effects. One explanation for the use of tax-farming, for example, is that it is chosen by risk-averse rulers who prefer the predictable revenue it provides.[32]

Actors may not rationally weigh costs and benefits at all but, instead, act on the basic of values. Gorski argues that the efficiency of Prussian tax collection was in part attributable to the use of Protestant officials who had internalized values of discipline and honesty.[33] Differences in culture and values also shape many aspects of contemporary fiscal systems. For example, anti-tax sentiment is much stronger in the United States than in Sweden, in spite of the fact that tax rates in Sweden are much higher. There are, no doubt, major differences in the values of median voters in these two countries. Values and rationality may also jointly contribute to action, which is probably the case with the effects of legitimacy on tax compliance.[34]

Some action is purely habitual, as Weber has stressed in his discussion of traditional authority.[35] Habitual action on the part of rulers should produce patterns in tax rates that look like a punctuated equilibrium model: long periods of stasis in which rulers collect "customary" revenues, interrupted by sharp break points that lead to a new customary level.[36] The same may be true about tax structure and tax administration. Habitual action may be one of the main reasons for the stickiness of fiscal structures, often attributed to increasing returns dynamics.

Emotions also play a role in fiscal systems, at least in the case of peasant revolts against taxes, in which the actors take great risks (including risking their lives) in order to avoid fairly small tax increases. How can we explain this if not as at least partially emotionally based

[31] Levi (1988). [32] Kiser (1994). [33] Gorski (2003).
[34] Levi, Sacks, and Tyler (2009); Moore (2004). [35] Weber (1968) [1922]).
[36] Barzel and Kiser (1997).

action?[37] In all these cases, the key is at least to be explicit about what we posit as the microfoundations of action, and, if possible, to be able to specify the general conditions in which different microfoundations are more or less important (granted, not an easy task).

To make matters even more complicated, different actors may be motivated by different microfoundations. For example, in Coşgel's contribution (Chapter 13), taxpayers act in part on the basis of values, but rulers and their agents collecting taxes are both seen as fairly standard rational actors. On the other hand, Deng argues (Chapter 10) that values such as the "mandate of heaven" influenced the actions of not just taxpayers but Chinese emperors as well, and Kennedy (Chapter 12) stresses the religious foundation of fiscal systems in early Islamic states.

Conclusions

The chapters in this volume represent the best work currently being done on the history of fiscal systems. They are analytically sound and amazingly detailed, especially given the dearth of data in several of the cases. The breadth of the history covered here both shows the general features of all premodern and early modern fiscal regimes and highlights the unique features of each of the cases. This volume will be equally indispensable to scholars doing comparative work involving any of these cases and to those studying other fiscal regimes.

It is an exciting time to be working on fiscal regimes. This book makes it clear that we know a great deal about the structure of fiscal systems and the causes of their transformations. Further progress on this important topic will require more systematic comparative studies (the chapters by Monson and Bang show the way here) and more systematic theoretical attention to the complex interactions between efficiency, power, and legitimacy, and the microfoundations that produce them.

[37] For excellent discussions of emotion in violent rebellions and revolutions, see Wood (2003; 2001) and Petersen (2002). Another possibility, which might in fact interact with emotions, is that decisions to revolt are based on taxpayers' perceptions that general norms of fairness have been violated by rulers' decisions to increase tax rates. This is an important claim of Levi's (1988; 1997). Studies of ultimatum games have shown that experimental subjects are often willing to pay high costs in order to punish other actors for violating norms of fairness. See, for example, Henrich *et al.* (2004) and Hoff, Kshetramade, and Fehr (2011).

References

Acemoglu, D., and Robinson, J. A. (2006) *Economic Origins of Dictatorship and Democracy*. New York.

Barzel, Y., and Kiser, E. (1997) "The development and decline of medieval voting institutions: a comparison of England and France," *Economic Inquiry* 35: 244–60.

Bates, R. H., and Lien, D.-H. D. (1985) "A note on taxation, development and representative government," *Politics and Society* 14: 53–70.

Boix, C. (2003) *Democracy and Redistribution*. New York.

Brautigam, D., Fjeldstad, O.-H., and Moore, M. (2008) *Taxation and State-Building in Developing Countries: Capacity and Consent*. Cambridge.

Bueno de Mesquita, B., Smith, A., Siverson, R. M., and Morrow, J. D. (2003) *The Logic of Political Survival*. Cambridge, MA.

Cook, K. S, Hardin, R., and Levi, M. (2005) *Cooperation without Trust?* New York.

Gorski, P. S. (2003) *The Disciplinary Revolution: Calvinism and the Rise of the State in Early Modern Europe*. Chicago.

Henrich, J., Boyd, R., Bowles, S., Camerer, C., Fehr, E., and Gintis, H. (eds.) (2004) *Foundations of Human Sociality: Economic Experiments and Ethnographic Evidence from Fifteen Small-Scale Societies*. Oxford.

Hirschman, A. (1970) *Exit, Voice, and Loyalty: Responses to Decline in Firms, Organizations, and States*. Cambridge, MA.

Hoff, K., Kshetramade, M., and Fehr, E. (2011) "Caste and punishment: the legacy of caste culture in norm enforcement," *Economic Journal* 121: 449–75.

Kiser, E. (1994) "Markets and hierarchies in early modern tax systems: a principal–agent analysis," *Politics and Society* 22: 284–315.

(1999) "Comparing varieties of agency theory in economics, political science, and sociology: an illustration from state policy implementation," *Sociological Theory* 17: 146–70.

Kiser, E., and Barzel, Y. (1991) "The origins of democracy in England," *Rationality and Society* 3: 396–422.

Kiser, E., and Kane, J. (2001) "Revolution and state structure: the bureaucratization of tax administration in early modern England and France," *American Journal of Sociology* 107: 183–223.

Kiser, E., and Linton, A. (2001) "Determinants of the growth of the state: war and taxation in early modern France and England," *Social Forces* 80: 411–48.

(2002) "The hinges of history: state-making and revolt in early modern France," *American Sociological Review* 67: 889–910.

Kiser, E., and Sacks, A. (2009) "Improving tax administration in contemporary African states: lessons from history," in *The New Fiscal Sociology: Taxation in Comparative and Historical Perspective*, ed. I. W. Martin, A. K. Mehrotra, and M. Prasad. New York: 183–200.

(2011) "Patrimonialism in premodern states and contemporary Africa," *Annals of the American Academy of Political and Social Science* 636: 129–41.

Levi, M. (1988) *Of Rule and Revenue*. Berkeley, CA.

(1997) *Consent, Dissent, and Patriotism.* New York.
(2006) "Why we need a new theory of government," *Perspectives on Politics* 4: 5–19.
Levi, M., and Sacks, A. (2009) "Legitimating beliefs: concepts and measures," *Regulation and Governance* 3: 311–33.
(2012) "Gobierno eficaz, consentimiento ciudadano y, quizá legitimidad," in *Democracia y socialdemocracia: homenaje a José María Maravall,* ed. A. Przeworski and I. Sanchez-Cuenca. Madrid: 61–89.
Levi, M., Sacks, A., and Tyler, T. R. (2009) "Conceptualizing legitimacy, measuring legitimating beliefs," *American Behavioral Scientist* 53: 354–75.
Martin, I. W., Mehrotra, A. K., and Prasad, M. (eds.) (2009) *The New Fiscal Sociology: Taxation in Comparative and Historical Perspective.* New York.
Moore, M. (2004) "Revenues, state formation, and the quality of governance in developing countries," *International Political Science Review* 25: 297–319.
North, D. C. (1981) *Structure and Change in Economic History.* New York.
North, D. C., Wallis, J. J., and Weingast, B. R. (2009) *Violence and Social Orders: A Conceptual Framework for Interpreting Recorded Human History.* New York.
Petersen, R. D. (2002) *Understanding Ethnic Violence: Fear, Hatred, and Resentment in Twentieth-Century Eastern Europe.* Cambridge.
Riker, W. (1962) *The Theory of Political Coalitions.* New Haven, CT.
Rothstein, B. (2005) *Social Traps and the Problem of Trust.* Cambridge.
Sacks, A., and Levi, M. (2010) "Measuring government effectiveness and its consequences for social welfare in African states," *Social Forces* 88: 2325–52.
Scott, J. C. (1985) *Weapons of the Weak: Everyday Forms of Peasant Resistance.* New Haven, CT.
Simon, H. A. (1947) *Administrative Behavior.* New York.
Tilly, C. (1975) *The Formation of National States in Western Europe.* Princeton, NJ.
(1992) *Capital, Coercion, and European States: AD 990–1992,* rev edn. Malden, MA.
Timmons, J. F. (2005) "The fiscal contract: states, taxes, and public services," *World Politics* 57: 530–67.
Tyler, T. R. (1990) *Why People Obey the Law.* New Haven CT.
(2006) "Psychological perspectives on legitimacy and legitimation," *Annual Review of Psychology* 57: 375–400.
Weber, M. (1968 [1922]) "Bureaucracy," in *Economy and Society: An Outline of Interpretive Sociology,* trans. E. Fischoff, ed. G. Roth and C. Wittich. New York: 1381–469.
Wood, E. J. (2001) "The emotional benefits of insurgency in El Salvador," in *Passionate Politics: Emotions and Social Movements,* ed. J. Goodwin, J. M. Jasper, and F. Polletta. Chicago: 267–81.
(2003) *Insurgent Collective Action and Civil War in El Salvador.* Cambridge.

Index